In Search of Nella Larsen

IN SEARCH OF NELLA LARSEN

A BIOGRAPHY OF THE COLOR LINE

GEORGE HUTCHINSON

The Belknap Press of
Harvard University Press
Cambridge, Massachusetts
London, England
2006

Designed by Dean Bornstein

Library of Congress Cataloging-in-Publication Data
Hutchinson, George.
In search of Nella Larsen : a biography of the color line / George Hutchinson.
p. cm.
Includes bibliographical references and index.
ISBN 0-674-02180-0 (alk. paper)
1. Larsen, Nella. 2. Novelists, American—20th century—Biography.
3. African American novelists—Biography.
4. Harlem (New York, N. Y.)—Intellectual life—20th century.
5. Harlem Renaissance. I. Title.
PS3523.A7225Z69 2006
813'.52—dc22   2005058129

To James M. and Iris B. Hutchinson

CONTENTS

ILLUSTRATIONS

Showing the best and dividing it from the worst, age vexes age.
—Walt Whitman

Introduction

BECAUSE this book looks and feels like a biography, even calls itself a biography, I must begin by warning you that it is different from most biographies. It is the kind of biography one writes about a person who has been "invisible"—the so-called mystery woman of the Harlem Renaissance—and about *why* she has been invisible. It is also about the suppressions demanded by the constant work of maintaining the color line in American society from Nella Larsen's day to our own—the myriad stories, customs, expectations, unconscious habits, laws, intellectual positions, political strategies, cultural presuppositions, threats, and preferences by which distinctions between black and white identities are reproduced and important aspects of American experience repressed. These processes and Larsen's lifelong resistance to them lie at the existential core of her life, a life that cannot be understood apart from them. The difficulty inherent in the search for evidence and the liminality of the subject are at the heart of the story.

Larsen herself no doubt felt like a shadow through much of her life. She did not long inhabit the sort of place in which she could feel at home. For me, the greatest interest of this tale lies precisely in such difficulties. Nella Larsen did not write a string of significant novels, or found an institution, or lead a movement. She is not the peer of someone like Thomas Mann—as a novelist, that is. She seems to have had little interest in leaving a legacy. She lived a life that should never have been, one that many seem to think *could not* have been. Briefly, she wrote about that life, and revealed part of what she perceived about the world and people of her time. Her two novels brought her fame if not fortune; many regarded her as one of the chief talents of the Harlem Renaissance, and the best black novelist of her generation. Yet within a few years she "disappeared," from a literary historian's point of view—which is to say, she left literature behind, moved into an apartment where her friends could not find her, and forged a career as a nursing supervisor in lower Manhattan. Soon she was all but forgotten.

In 1980, Mary Helen Washington published a brief article in *Ms.* magazine dubbing Larsen the renaissance's "mystery woman" and pointing out that five decades after her novels had appeared, Larsen was "for the most part unknown, unread, and dismissed—both by black critics and their white counterparts."[1] Although many had considered her the most accomplished black novelist of her generation, Larsen had practically disappeared from historical treatments of the renaissance, and little was known about her. Washington recounted the story of her life as Larsen had once recorded it for her publisher.

A few years later, two decades after Larsen's death, the scholar Charles R. Larson asked, "Whatever happened to Nella Larsen?" and presented some of his findings. After the dramatic retrieval of Zora Neale Hurston from obscurity, black feminist critics began turning to Larsen's work as an alternative form of black women's fiction. Since then, first slowly and then rapidly, interest in her work has spread. By the late 1990s, her enigmatic novels, dismissed at the time of her death in the mid-1960s as trivial, misguided, and poorly written, had become canonical and were being taught in classrooms around the world. Editions multiplied at the turn of the twenty-first century; advanced scholars in several fields came to see her as one of the truly important modernists, and students responded to her work enthusiastically in the classroom. The work of reconstructing her long-hidden life had also begun.

Charles R. Larson's *Invisible Darkness: Jean Toomer and Nella Larsen* appeared in 1993 and Thadious M. Davis' *Nella Larsen, Novelist of the Harlem Renaissance: A Woman's Life Unveiled* in 1994, the latter to considerable scholarly acclaim. Since both of these studies conclude that Larsen concocted elaborate lies about her early life, particularly about its interracial aspects, we would do well to review the story of her formative years as she presented it. Her mother, she said, was a Danish immigrant to the United States who married a Negro from the Danish West Indies. Before Nella was old enough to know anything about him, her father died and her mother married a white Danish immigrant, subsequently giving birth to a second daughter. Nella was unwanted by the stepfather and half-sister, her connection to them creating difficulties for the family. She spent some time in Denmark as a child, an experience that formed the basis of her first two publications—translations of Danish children's riddles and games for a black children's magazine. Around the age of sixteen, Nella spent a year attending the Normal School at Fisk University, in Nashville, Tennessee, then visited Denmark for three years, staying with her mother's people. Eventually, however, she returned to the United States and studied nursing in New York City, then worked as a nurse supervisor at Tuskegee University, in Tuskegee, Alabama. She and Tuskegee parted ways "in mutual disgust and relief" and she returned to New York. She worked as a public health nurse with the New York Department of Health before marrying a rising black physicist, Elmer S. Imes. Shortly afterward she became a librarian with the New York Public Library, and through that work eventually moved into the literary field just as the Harlem Renaissance picked up steam. Her contact with her family had effectively ceased by this time because of the difficulties it might cause them, particularly her mother and half-sister.

The new biographies, though not agreeing with each other on all points, claimed that much of this story was false. They charged that Larsen never visited Denmark and that she played up her Danish roots to gain status. Davis hypothesized that her natural father, Peter Walker, decided to "pass" and thus became the "white" Peter Larsen; the second child, Anna, was light enough to pass but Nella was not. The mother, Marie, emotionally abandoned Nella early on because of her blackness and Peter took primary responsibility for her; Nella hardly knew her mother, according to Professor Davis. Peter Larsen, probably Nella's "passing" colored father, served as her main support. Marie's racism and abandonment resulted in Nella's purported ambivalence toward black identity, her "confusion" about race, her competitiveness toward other women, and an inability to find her true place among other African Americans. Out of all this pain and trauma, Larsen invented compensatory fictions of a loving mother, a trip to Denmark in her teens or possibly earlier, and an exotic story of her family background that was intended to win status among the black elite. Internalizing white racist attitudes (the biographies argued), she became a snob and a social climber, valuing her connections with powerful whites above those with the community of black women, and eventually—particularly after her husband betrayed her for a white woman, putting her claims to "whiteness" in crisis—she paid the price of psychological disintegration and failure as an artist.

As I read these books, I recognized a pattern not atypical of the way children from interracial families had often been misunderstood and—there is no other word for it—pathologized. At crucial junctures the evidence seemed lacking and the conclusions unwarranted, despite the extremely enthusiastic reception that Davis' book, particularly, enjoyed among scholars. Red flags kept going up as I saw potentially productive features of Larsen's Danish and interracial background dismissed, her relationship with her white mother negated or minimized, and her ambivalence toward the black bourgeoisie and the rhetoric of race pride attributed to internalized racism. Her novels supposedly allowed Larsen to discharge her feelings of violence against her mother and to achieve a precarious stability through identification with her black father. A black child's psychological identification with a white parent, after all, can only be debilitating, we have been led to believe. Psychic health, as many would have it, requires the child to develop a normative black racial identity, assimilating "realistically" to the law of the color line.

The pattern of rationalization for Larsen's unusual self-positioning and per-spective on race resonates with tendencies in the interpretation of her novels and effectively neutralizes her nervy assault on the institution of race as such. This was the institution that had divided her from her mother, the institution that she presented as founded on the oppression of women and the control of their sexuality. It felt to me as if Larsen scholarship was sustaining a popular consensus about race and identity in the United States at the expense of her rep-utation—although, to be sure, this was sincerely intended as a compassionate gesture.

Long before I had any notion of writing a book on Larsen, I decided to check on a few assertions that bothered me. Both Professor Davis and Professor Larson suggested that Larsen had lied about visiting Denmark in her youth because they could find no evidence of this visit; moreover, as Larson astutely pointed out, she had never applied for a passport before 1930, when she was about to visit Spain and France. I wondered: Would the teenage daughter of a Danish immigrant, being picked up at the dock in Copenhagen by Danish relatives, necessarily have needed a passport?

I went to the University of Tennessee library one afternoon and pulled from the stacks a 1912 Baedeker guide to Scandinavia. On the first page it stated that for Americans entering Denmark, passports were unnecessary. I next looked up the standard reference on Danish emigration to America, Kristian Hvidt's *Flight to America*. The preface to this book indicated that records of all travel from Denmark to the United States during the high tide of Danish emigration were available in several archives. After writing two or three letters to offices in Den-mark, I tracked down the proper archive and asked them if they had any records showing that a Nelly Larsen from the United States, born in April 1891, had vis-ited Denmark between about 1908 and 1912 (dates corresponding to those in Larsen's brief autobiography). Sure enough, they had a record for such a person, a native of the United States. I ordered from the U.S. National Archives a mi-crofilm copy of the passenger manifests for the ship she took back to New York. The manifests gave her correct age, address in Chicago, relatives' names, and so forth.

Then it occurred to me that perhaps Larsen, like the protagonist in her partly autobiographical first novel, had also visited Denmark with her mother at the age of seven or eight. Her first publications, after all, were translations of chil-dren's games and riddles that she implied she had learned in Denmark as a child (a claim the biographers attributed to her pathetic attempt to play up her "whiteness"). I wrote to the archive again. Yes, in 1898, a Nelly Larsen had re-turned from Denmark to the United States with her mother Mary and her half-sister Anny on board the *C. F. Tietgen*. The passenger list compiled on disembarkation in New York gave all the right ages and their Chicago address, mentioning that Mary was going back to her husband. This proved much of what Larsen had said about her early connections with Denmark, and contradicted the notion that Nella's mother had abandoned her in very early childhood, possibly even placing her in a Chicago orphanage. My interest piqued, I decided to pull on another thread.

The suggestion in Davis' biography that Larsen's mother had put her in an orphanage was thrown into question when I looked up the very census records (of 1900) cited by Davis to support this claim and discovered that the "Nelly Larson" listed in the census as living in Chicago's Erring Woman's Refuge was two years too young, born in July rather than April, and listed as "white." This information conflicted with the notion that Larsen had been abandoned because she was "too dark to pass." The assertion that the mother had denied giving birth to her black daughter—a statement made by both biographers on the basis of a 1910 census form—seemed unsubstantiated, since the respondent to the census officer was not named on the form. Several people lived in the home, including Anna, who was unemployed and not in school. Why should we assume that Mary Larsen told the census worker she had only one daughter, the white Anna? I discovered that in 1910 the Census Bureau required the "head" of each household in Chicago to fill out the forms in advance of collection. It was therefore probable that Larsen's white stepfather, whom Nella had represented as resentful of her existence, had lied on the form and erased Nella from his wife's past.

Similar errors—some major, others minor—kept cropping up for every period of Larsen's life with a cumulative effect that was startling, and in which I detected a definite pattern. In some cases the problems derived from the great difficulty of finding source material, in others from a tendency to avoid looking in certain places, in others from a simple misreading of sources that could be difficult to decode, and in yet others from a not unreasonable urge to make speculations and assertions based on unsupported hunches or fragments of seemingly related evidence, all driving toward a certain narrative expectation. The interplay among these various factors magnified the effects of each. For example, convinced that Mary Larsen would deny giving birth to Nella in 1910, and that Larsen had lied about her childhood in Denmark, Davis understandably surmised that Larsen's family forced her to leave Fisk after only a year, being unwilling to support her. Or perhaps, since scholars could find no record of Larsen for the next three years and suspected that her story of living in Denmark was a fabrication, she had gotten pregnant or married a black man and settled in the South for several years. I went to Fisk in hopes of discovering what had happened, despite assurances that nothing there was likely to be of help. Eventually, in the long-undisturbed minutes of faculty meetings, I discovered that Larsen had been told not to return after she was involved in a student rebellion against dress codes and social restrictions on girls. Her family had not pulled the plug on her education, after all. In fact, it became clear that Mary Larsen had been very concerned for her child, and remained so. After this expulsion, Larsen went to live in Denmark with her mother's family—the trip that supposedly had never happened.

When she returned to the United States in 1912, Larsen entered a black nursing school at Lincoln Hospital and Home in the Bronx. Since this was a "black" institution, originally founded as a nursing home for destitute African Americans in Manhattan, Professor Davis naturally assumed that its patient base was black and poor. Davis surmised that working for poor and infirm black patients had bred in Larsen a disdain for poor black people. Yet when I dug a little deeper into the history of the institution and into the census records of the Bronx, it became clear that the hospital patients at Lincoln were overwhelmingly white; only the nursing home inmates were black, and students worked with them only in their first year. Larsen's early advancement in the nursing profession has been attributed to the activism and nurse registry of the National Association of Colored Graduate Nurses, to which Larsen was said to have belonged. But I found that Larsen, like the overwhelming majority of black nurses at the time, never joined the NACGN and that the nurse registry had nothing to do with her employment. Nor had the NACGN, as admirable as that organization may have been, engaged in any activism that remotely influenced Larsen's professional career. The truth of this part of her life had been buried under a narrative of organized racial self-help and uplift.

Concerning the nature of Larsen's experiences at Tuskegee, it seemed that almost no evidence remained. A few letters in the Booker T. Washington Papers at the Library of Congress made some mention of the circumstances of her hiring and her first few weeks of work, but Washington had died just after her arrival. I called the archives at Tuskegee and was assured that they had nothing on Nella Larsen. Indeed, it was difficult to know where to look in the uncatalogued boxes of old files, and certainly Nella Larsen's name did not appear on any of the folders. But in an afternoon of fishing among old treasurer's reports and administrative files from the period after Washington's death, I came upon a series of yellowing papers detailing Larsen's experiences at the school, including memoranda to, from, and about her. These made it clear that Larsen's satirical attitude toward some elements of the black elite and toward racial "uplift" had less to do with her white mother's treatment of her than her own repeated bruising experiences with highly regarded hypocrites.

After returning to work at Lincoln Hospital and Home for two years, Larsen got a job with the New York City Department of Health on the recommendation, supposedly, of her black supervisor at Lincoln Hospital, and was allegedly assigned to all-black neighborhoods such as Columbus Hill and Harlem, in keeping with the segregationist practices of the Health Department. Yet the periodical of record for the New York Civil Service system and the dust-coated minutes of the Health Department reveal that Larsen got her job with the Bureau of Preventable Diseases because she had earned the second-highest score on the Civil Service examination, and she was assigned to the "white" Bronx. In her nursing career, except for the year at Tuskegee, Larsen never worked in predominantly black neighborhoods. The Health Department, as much as it may have wanted to, did not at the time make black nurses' assignments based on race.

Neither did it turn out to be true that Larsen joined the public health service after the "Spanish flu" pandemic of 1918 had increased the need for public health nurses, thus making the city willing to accept black nurses as a last resort. She entered service in June 1918; the pandemic reached the United States in September, and Larsen worked all through it, in mostly white neighborhoods alongside mostly white colleagues. The nurses of her bureau were regarded as the heroes of the crisis in New York.

We have been told that Larsen became disillusioned with the long hours and hard work of public health nursing in impoverished black tenements, and with her discriminatory treatment by the Health Department, so she began stopping in at the "colored" YWCA job placement office in Harlem, until she found a job with the 135th Street Branch of the New York Public Library (NYPL). Yet municipal records and minutes show that Larsen's pay and status in the Health Department were completely consistent with her seniority, and her salary grew 60 percent in just three years. Her white colleagues by no means earned more or advanced more quickly than she did. She became interested in a library career while working evenings and weekends as a volunteer to help organize the first exhibit of "Negro art" in New York in 1921, the records of which, including letters to and from Larsen, have languished unread at the 135th Street Branch of the New York Public Library ever since. This show, conceived and organized by librarian Ernestine Rose, marked the beginning of the Harlem Renaissance in the visual arts; Larsen was the secretary of the executive committee, even as she worked full time in the Bronx Health Department. Rose, along with E. C. Williams of Howard University Library, urged Larsen to go into librarianship and to enter library school at the NYPL.

Larsen was the first black woman ever to graduate from library school—hand picked by Rose to break the barrier—but this fact has been buried by misinformation about other black employees of the New York Public Library at the time who had stronger connections to the Harlem elite, and by the fact that Larsen did not stay in the profession for very long. Trying to find the documentation of Larsen's library education proves a challenge, since historians have so far shown little interest in the history of this "women's" field. The NYPL Library School folded in 1926, and no one at the library whom I could track down knew what had happened to the old files. On a job application of 1961, Larsen stated that she had attended the NYPL Library School connected with Columbia University. Suspecting that the records had been transferred to Columbia, I called Columbia's Butler Library. Sure enough, the rare book and manuscript collection had the old records. Consulting the old catalogue of these records, I ordered the box of student files in which I expected to find those of "Nella Imes." Alas, there was no Nella Imes. My heart sank. But then I noticed that the contents of the box in other respects did not match the listings in the catalogue. I asked the librarian at the desk to check how many boxes were in the collection, and we discovered that the collection was miscatalogued. Several "lost" boxes were brought to me and there, indeed, I found the files on Nella Imes, including her application, letters of recommendation, grades, reports on fieldwork, and the like. These records proceeded to unravel yet more assertions about Larsen's professional experience.

According to prevailing historical wisdom, black librarians in New York were "pigeonholed" at the 135th Street Branch of the NYPL during the 1920s and hindered from professional advancement because their white supervisors would not let them move between branches as white women did. Moreover, Ernestine Rose allegedly would not leave the Harlem branch and allow a black woman to take over, because she faced her own glass ceiling, being Jewish. But Ernestine Rose was not Jewish. Furthermore, Larsen's library school file clearly showed that Larsen had strong support from her white supervisors at three different branches, only one of which was in a "black" neighborhood. All of the supervisors said that, despite their concern that some colleagues might object, they would be happy to have her in their branch. The reason other black librarians had not progressed in the system was that they had not gone to library school. To be sure, most library schools at the time excluded black people. Part of the significance of Larsen's library career is that she opened the way for the integration of the system, specifically with the collaboration of her white supervisors, Ernestine Rose in Harlem and Alice Keats O'Connor at Seward Park. Larsen spent her first year after library school not in the Harlem library, but at the Seward Park Branch, in the heart of the Jewish Lower East Side. In Davis' biography this period shrank to two months.

As I became increasingly drawn to the mystery of Larsen's life, I grew interested not simply in how wrong the current story of Larsen's life turned out to be, but in how much of the actual life one could reconstruct, and how, in the process of doing so, one kept happening upon aspects of the past hidden by common assumptions or mere lack of curiosity. This is partly because Larsen was a black woman professional, but also because, like her most important fictional characters, she nearly always inhabited the space between black and white, by necessity and by choice. (Now as then, her choices have opened her up to severe criticism, not all of it unfair.) That space, her fiction itself testifies, is hidden. I kept stumbling upon troves of overlooked documentary evidence concerning Larsen's youth and adulthood. In large part, it had been missed because of the neglect that has long characterized black, women's, and working-class history—and many of the archives that might support work in these areas. While historians have made mighty strides in these fields over the past three decades, much remains to be learned.

Yet even for the fairly well-documented and intensely scrutinized renaissance period, scholars have almost totally ignored key resources, such as the records of the New York Public Library and the daybooks of Carl Van Vechten, one of Larsen's most intimate friends. These daybooks (in which Larsen often appears several times a week) and the society notes of Harlem newspapers, also previously ignored, disclose a fairly exact record of Larsen's social life during the glamorous Twenties, which contradicts many current understandings of the social networks and divisions of Manhattan modernism. The newspapers of the time, too, provide a wealth of revelations about unknown or misunderstood aspects of the Harlem Renaissance, but up to now scholars have generally been content to look only at clippings files and scrapbooks, putting themselves at the mercy of the prejudices of the original collectors. We are in the habit, as well, of projecting back onto black intellectuals of the 1920s our own judgments about events, persons, and cultural phenomena of the time. Much that we now perceive as simply continuous with a racist history of white coercion or cooptation looked very different to Nella Larsen's contemporaries; and it was much more ambiguous, not to mention ironic, in its historical meaning and effect than we seem willing to allow. While most biographical and critical work fits Larsen within existing historical understandings of the Harlem Renaissance—not co-incidently resulting in major misconceptions about Larsen—I found myself discovering, by way of Larsen, much that has been passed over or demonstrably misrepresented in prior accounts of the movement, including my own. Following Larsen's life, and forced in doing so to open doors I did not know existed, I came repeatedly upon unexpected sidelights revealing aspects of the renaissance that had long been lost to view.

What began to emerge, as in an archaeological dig at a site with mythical associations, was a marked correlation between the pattern of erasures and fabrications in the prior biographies and histories, on the one hand, and the patterns of racial subjection in Larsen's life experience on the other. In both, a stark color line eliminated "gray areas" and ambiguities, buttressed the division between black and white, and supported diagnoses of Larsen's audacious social consciousness as pathological. This phenomenon has significance extending well beyond the understanding of Nella Larsen alone.

Just as Larsen was traumatized in childhood by the particular ways in which the color line affected interracial families, attempting (very successfully for the most part) to make such families disappear, so has the understanding of her life and work been determined by the later intellectual and institutional effects of that very phenomenon. Related patterns can be found in the interpretation of Larsen's fiction and its place in literary history. Her "invisibility," or mysteriousness, is a precise marker of unresolved contradictions, of moral, political, and imaginative failures endemic to American society. And there is no better way to observe their workings than by reconstructing her life and reputation. To write the life of Nella Larsen is to write a biography of color line culture by way of what that culture hides.

The problems I have outlined are not the results of poor scholarship or bad faith but rather symptoms of how we normally think about race, identity, and literary tradition—products of a long history that is the heritage of the West. The study of Larsen's life and of her fiction exposes a diverse, transatlantic ideological investment in the color line that formally depends upon the invisibility and silence of persons like Larsen—that attempted to make the existence of people such as Nella Larsen literally impossible. The work of telling the life of an author who spoke from that position and made herself a public figure, however briefly, thus becomes a uniquely difficult yet compelling task.

But we are left to ponder: Why did she herself not make the job easier? She seems almost to have preferred to be forgotten. In her late years, her once-intimate friends Carl Van Vechten and Dorothy Peterson repeatedly tried to get her to turn over her papers to the James Weldon Johnson Memorial Collection (named for one of her most esteemed friends) at Yale University. As a librarian present at the founding of what would become the Schomburg Center for Research in Black Culture, Larsen fully appreciated the importance of such archives. She did, in fact, promise at one point to donate her papers and correspondence, but she never followed through. This reticence seems connected to the fact that she kept much of her early life a secret—another reason it is so difficult to reconstruct today. Had she spoken more of herself, more details might have come down to us. Instead, most of her feelings about her youth must be gleaned from her fiction and read between the lines of "objective" historical facts, census forms, school applications, and the like.

The evidence is overwhelming that her reticence derived from her childhood, attributable to the racial pressures under which she and her family—particularly she and her mother—lived. Her fiction dwells obsessively on the sources and effects of such reticence, even when the fiction is "nonracial." Like her most captivating characters, she grew to prefer a certain invisibility and mysteriousness as a form of self-protection. She did not want people to know much about her. She said little of her past life because she did not wish to revisit it. She could write of it only obliquely, and some of her best potential subject matter remained off-limits. Partly for this reason, it is important to specify, to whatever extent possible, the precise nature of the pressures under which Larsen grew up and their relation to her "invisibility." The fragility of Larsen's connection with her mother, which is directly attributable to the color line, also accounts for the attachment problems that afflicted her throughout her life. Larsen did not cut off her friends because of a warped value system and internalized racism, as previously believed; she cut them off because she feared that, white or black, they would leave her. This is the reason that so few of her papers remain.

When Larsen died, many of her books and papers were in her apartment, but by then she had ended nearly all of her old friendships for reasons that hark back to her early life: a history of triangulated relationships in which she felt she was losing out, intuitions of loss. Had it not been for these patterns of feeling and behavior, we would have much more to go on today. Nonetheless, it became clear to me over time that not only *should* a new biography of Larsen be written; such a work actually *could* be written, although not like most biographies. The justification for the task grew as I learned more about the amazing breadth and depth of Larsen's experience of "the modern"—in labor history, in the medical professions and the rise of public health, in librarianship and children's publishing, in transformations of urban geography (both Chicago's and New York's), in transformations of women's "place" and sexuality, in the emergence and blossoming of the Harlem Renaissance. Larsen was always on the cusp of the modernist transformation in these fields, just as she always was positioned or deliberately positioned herself on the precarious racial boundary that recent studies suggest was crucial to literary modernism. But much of the story of her engagement in these historic developments has played little part in our understanding of Larsen because it has been difficult to recover, and because it seems a distraction: it is not black history or literary history, as commonly understood. Similarly, the development of Larsen's particular form of racially conscious feminism requires an adjustment of assumptions about traditions of black feminist/womanist thought and their origins. Larsen's feminism derived not from a black line of descent but from her first-hand observations of the way female sexuality was implicated in the reproduction of race, from her experiences in Denmark and from Scandinavian modernism, from her nursing experience and her teaching of nursing history, and from her friendships with remarkable women, both black and white, in the high interracial bohemia of the 1920s.

Larsen is a challenging figure for the biographer because her surviving correspondence pertains to a relatively brief period of her life. We have none of the correspondence she received from or wrote to her family, including her husband, and none that she received from her friends. We do not have her literary manuscripts. We have no lengthy memoir or autobiography. She dropped out of the literary limelight long ago, and nearly everyone that knew her is dead. She grew up poor in some of the most squalid neighborhoods of Chicago—and, for a while, somewhere in Denmark—with people whose individual lives rarely find their way into public records. No family mementos are to be found; there are no descendants to be interviewed.

In modern biography, one chooses a subject about whom much can be known—someone who has left behind an extensive correspondence, diaries, well-informed acquaintances, and the like. Normally this will be a person of great note, or at least from a noted family; for who else would leave enough behind to support the biographical project, and why would anyone care about her? One assembles the materials meticulously in chronological order and sits down to write. In the writing, the process of the search is outside the frame as one creates a dynamic portrait of the individual against the background of her times. This will be an individual of strong identity, someone in a certain relation to the age in which she lived, someone often identified with a powerful group presence, for it is these conditions that ensure the preservation of materials as well as the gathering of an audience. In the foreground, the vivid portrait with its sharp and revealing highlights, the leitmotifs of a personality; in the background, everything else. And no scaffolding, no sign of the conditions of the work.

Here the method will be different. The unitary subject of traditional biography, who makes her choices, makes her mark, and leaves behind much personal testimony, is shown the door as we invite onto the stage a person often invisible and silent, a kind of shadow. One turns of necessity to a different type of story, in which the individual ego is not always as central as the forces acting upon it. One can only, at times, reconstruct the settings in which the subject lived and summon her from their midst. Peering into the interstices, one must reverse the processes by which the subject was overshadowed, hoping at the same time to expose those very processes. Nella Larsen must be, as T. S. Eliot noted of Flaubert's Frédéric Moreau, constructed "partly by negative definition, built up by a great number of observations. We cannot isolate [her] from the environment in which we find [her]; . . . it, and the figure in it, consist of very many observed particular facts, the actual world. Without the world the figure dissolves."[2] The story begins in Chicago.

ONE

Nellie Walker

THE Chicago of Nella Larsen's early childhood was a sprawling chaos sprung from the ashes of the great fire of 1871 and already surpassing in population every American city but New York. "Think of all hell turned loose," wrote the newcomer John Dewey to his sister in 1894, "& yet not hell any longer, but simply material for a new creation."[1] "The Cloaca Maxima of modern civilization," in Henry Blake Fuller's ripe phrase, Chicago of the 1890s was an unlikely birthplace of American modernism.[2] Prowling the neighborhood bordering Nella's to the north, the young journalist Theodore Dreiser left a vivid report in his first feature story for a newspaper: "Entering the district at midnight and wandering along the broken wooden pavements, ill-lighted by lamps and avoided by the police, the nerves tremble at the threatening appearance of the whole neighborhood. From out of windows where glow spluttering lamps the faint cries of infants are heard. Women lie with their heads on their arms and almost nude, panting for a cooling breath as a relief from the stifling air. On the sidewalks men lay face upward with arms outspread muttering and going over some quarrel of daylight hours." Dreiser could see only filth, misery, and vice in the area—drunken men and despondent women, children with "wan, peevish faces."[3]

Here were not the large brick tenements of Manhattan, but block on block of mostly wood-frame buildings one or two stories high, bursting with families recently arrived, generally from the rural Midwest and Europe. Narrow alleys threading behind the buildings that faced the street led to "rear" apartments thrown up in what had once been back yards. A thick layer of soft-coal smoke blanketed the city and begrimed the buildings. Raised wooden sidewalks kept pedestrians out of the mud. The poorest families inhabited perpetually damp and occasionally flooded basement apartments beneath the level of the sidewalks. In the winter, people bundled up and shivered in freezing rooms, trying to save on coal. On sweltering summer nights they spilled out of the suffocating apartments to sleep half-dressed on the roofs, porches, and sidewalks. There were several saloons to every block, often with an upstairs or back room for gambling and prostitution.

Along with flat Midwestern accents and Southern-inflected African American speech patterns, imagine the languages of all of Europe and Scandinavia, or, as in the case of Larsen's family, an English thickly accented and punctuated with foreign expressions. More than three-quarters of the million inhabitants were foreign-born or children of foreign-born parents.[4] Chicago was one of the fastest-growing cities in the world, the population tripling between 1880 and 1900, quadrupling between 1880 and 1910.

Residential racial segregation was already an issue but there was no true "ghetto," because African Americans were still so few. As of 1890, only 1.3 percent of the Chicago population was black. By 1910 Chicago was still only 2 percent black, but a distinct "black belt" had taken form, always shadowed by the well-known vice district that politicians tolerated on the near South Side. The basic outlines of the city's notoriously segregationist housing patterns developed in Nella Larsen's childhood. Along the edges of the moving "black belt" that spread south, mostly between State Street and the railroad tracks beyond Clark Street in the 1890s and early 1900s, one finds "mixed areas" turning "black" and then degenerating into crime-ridden slums. These were the border areas in which Nella Larsen grew up.

Her birth certificate, filled out in an uncertain hand with several slips in spelling and penmanship, gives the name as "Nellie Walker," a girl, colored. She was born April 13, 1891, though the form was not filled out until nearly a month later, on May 10, by Elijah A. Lyon, a druggist who lived at 2506 Wabash Avenue and ran his business at 2141 State Street. The parents are listed as Mary and Peter "Waker," the mother's maiden name as Hanson, possibly Hansen. The father, "Colored," worked as a cook—one of the better jobs for a black man in Chicago at the time—and the couple lived, presumably, at the address given as "place of birth," 2124 Armour Street, in the second ward—two blocks west of Lyon's drugstore. Mary, the mother, was twenty-two according to the form, born in Denmark and of Danish nationality.[5]

2124 Armour Street (Federal Street today) composed part of a three-story brick building that took up about half of the block on the west side of the street between Twenty-First and Twenty-Second, in the midst of what was fast becoming the Western Hemisphere's most infamous red-light district, the so-called Levee.[6] Most of the block was filled with boardinghouses, rooming houses, and saloons—not a few bearing the trademark red glass in the transom over their front entrance. Across the street and down the way at the corner of Twenty-Second was a recently built varnish factory.[7]

Since the late 1880s, the police had been driving prostitutes into this area and allowing a red-light district to develop around South Dearborn and Twenty-Second (a block from Nella's birthplace), on the fringes of the chief "Negro"

1. *The 2100 block of Armour Street (today Federal Street) in Chicago, circa 1914, looking across the street from the address at which Nella Larsen was born. The street and sidewalks have been paved and electric lights installed. Negative DN-0063323, Chicago Daily News Negatives Collection, courtesy of the Chicago Historical Society.*

section of the city.[8] In the 1890s, "Satan's Mile" ran down State from Van Buren to Twenty-Second Street. According to Herbert Asbury, the section south of Taylor Street was known as "Coon Hollow" and was populated mostly by blacks, with "a scattering of whites, and several bawdy houses where white women were kept for the pleasure of Negro men."[9]

Brothels, peep shows, and burlesque houses were ubiquitous in the area. Mary Hastings, a Belgian-born madam, held court at 2004 Dearborn in 1891. In 1892 she built a whorehouse on South Dearborn near Twenty-Second Street, one street east of where Nella was born.[10] On Armour near Nineteenth, a saloon called the Bucket of Blood faced a string of flophouses known as Bed Bug Row.[11] Between Twentieth (now Cullerton) and Twenty-First, Black May's "provided light-skinned Negro girls for white men" and "the most bestial circuses ever seen in the United States."[12] Also on this stretch of Armour were the Silver Dollar, the House of All Nations, and the classically named "Why Not?" In 1890 Lizzie Allen and her lover Christopher Columbus Crabb had built a big double house for prostitution one block over from Nella's birthplace, at 2131–33 South

Dearborn (behind the varnish factory). It was later bought by the "Everleigh Sisters" and became perhaps the most famous "high-class" whorehouse in the world. At the Lone Star Saloon, Mickey Finn served knockout drinks to out-of-town visitors so his accomplices could empty their pockets before they woke up. At 2017 South Clark, the Clark Street Mission tried to extend a civilizing influence over the neighborhood, evidently to little effect.[13]

A guide to the city published in 1892 claimed that "the very scum of the population" lived in the area of Nella's birth. "The entire district from Van Buren street south to Twenty-second street, and from the railroad tracks (two blocks west of Armour) to and including the east line of State Street, was in the hands of thugs, thieves, murderers and prostitutes."[14] Walking south from Van Buren along streets like Clark and Armour, toward Twenty-Second, one came to the brothels and bagnios, "where depraved women, white and black, pursue their avocations and carry on, in company with males of their class, nightly orgies that are either unseen or unnoticed by the police."[15] Like other scandalized reporters, the author of the guide uses phrases denoting interracial prostitution as a code for vice of the very "lowest" sort. "The most disreputable streets of the city" are occupied by "the most depraved of men and women, black, white, and mixed."[16] One finds this particular series of terms only in descriptions of areas associated with sexual perversity: "black, white, and mixed"—to these writers—signifies a zone of abjection, unpoliced, bottomless in depravity. Comprising black, white, and Chinese, it is where order gives way, where categories break down. If the color line tried to order relations of race, this was the area where it wavered and grew dim.

Information about Nella Larsen's mother is hard to come by and contradictory on certain details. What is not in question is that her maiden name was Hansen, and that she immigrated to the United States from Denmark in the late 1880s. The preponderance of the evidence suggests that she was born September 24, 1868, and that she immigrated as a teenager, alone, in 1886.[17]

There is reason to believe that Mary was born in the borderland between Denmark and Prussia, over which Danes and Germans fought for many years. Frankie Lea Houchins, an acquaintance of Nella's in the early 1930s, and Alice Carper, a friend of Nella's in her later years, both told biographer Thadious Davis that Larsen had said "her mother was German, though born in Denmark." To Charles R. Larson, Carper said Nella "spoke of her mother quite a bit" and said she was German; then Carper corrected herself: "Now, thinking about it, it could be Denmark."[18] Ethnically, Mary Hansen clearly was not German, to judge not only from Larsen's other statements about her but also from her maiden name, along with all known written records. It seems likely, instead, that her people came from the land taken over in 1864 by Prussia after the Dano-Prussian war in which Denmark was humiliated and lost control of Schleswig-Holstein, one of the defining catastrophes of modern Danish history.[19] The takeover of Schleswig and Holstein by Germany provoked massive emigration to the United States by Danes whose homes were now in Germany.[20] Some 40 percent of Danes from South Jutland emigrated in the years following the German takeover (the figure for Denmark as a whole was roughly 10 percent), and contemporary observers commented on how many "Schleswigers" were living in places like Chicago.[21] Many of them were listed as "German" by U.S. immigration authorities, though they were Danish in language and culture. And many were single female servants.[22] It seems clear that Marie Hansen emigrated about 1886, as a teenager, and probably alone.[23] Unfortunately for the genealogist, both "Marie" and "Hansen" are extremely common names (more common than "Smith" in English), and dozens of Danish Marie Hansens immigrated to the United States by way of Copenhagen, Hamburg, or Bremen in the 1880s. The records from Bremen were destroyed in World War II, but in the emigration lists from Hamburg and Copenhagen the Marie Hansens between the ages of fifteen and twenty were invariably single and traveling alone. Nella's mother might have been one of several who appear in the lists between 1886 and 1889.[24]

After disembarking from the passenger ships at Castle Garden (the immigrant receiving center in Lower Manhattan), Scandinavians typically headed for the trains bound for Chicago. Once there, they either settled in the city, fast becoming one of the greatest concentrations of Scandinavians in the world, or fanned out across the upper Midwest. If Nella's mother was not the "dressmaker" who first appears in the directory of 1885, "Mary Hanson" (as her name was most often spelled after she reached America) most likely made her start as a servant. Scandinavian women had a reputation for exceptional cleanliness and orderliness, and were much in demand.[25] Mildred Phillips, a close friend of the Larsen family over several decades, told biographer Charles Larson in 1986 that her mother, Mary's close friend, had told her that Mary's first daughter had been born of her union with the black chauffeur of a family for whom she worked.[26] But Mary Hansen knew how to make a dress, dressmaking being the "queen of all trades" for single women in Chicago, and one largely in the hands of Scandinavians.[27] We know for certain that Mary Larsen worked as a dressmaker in Nella's youth, so she may well have taken up such work soon after arrival.

At a time when working women's wages generally fell below the level of subsistence, Mary Hansen had to make her own way in the world. Even employers admitted they did not pay women enough to live on, assuming that they lived in families supported mainly by men.[28] "Women adrift," as they came to be known, formed liaisons with men out of sheer necessity.

About Nellie Walker's father we know painfully little beyond what the birth certificate tells us and what the adult Nella Larsen said about him. In both 1890 and 1891, only two Peter Walkers appear in the Chicago city directory: one who worked at a firm, Bigelow Brothers, and boarded at the Southern Hotel; another listed as a "laborer" living at 2034 Armour Street, a boardinghouse for single men that was located above a saloon. Clearly, the latter is the man who would be Nella's father. After 1891 he disappears from the directory and only the man working for Bigelow Brothers remains.[29] Larsen always said that her father had died before she was old enough to know much about him except that he was a Negro from the Danish West Indies (now the U.S. Virgin Islands).[30]

Whether Peter's surname derived from his mother or his father, he was most likely a near descendant of either Henry A. or George Walker, white natives of Albany, New York, who settled in St. Croix by 1840 and became important businessmen and planters, based in the port of Frederiksted. Very few people named Walker lived in the Danish West Indies, and when one eliminates those who could not possibly have been Peter's parents, one is left with five men and four women. Records suggest that the five women were all childless as of 1870. Unfortunately, no Peter Walker appears in the church records of baptisms and confirmations, nor in the 1870 census, where one would expect to find him. But Peter's nonappearance in the census could be due to his being off the island at the time it was taken—as were Henry A. and George Walker, and Henry's mulatto son Robert Walker, who helped people the island with Walkers in the 1860s. Lacking solid evidence, one can only assert that Peter was a likely son of Henry, George, or Robert Walker and one of their "colored" mistresses. The records show that each of these men, who were unmarried, acknowledged their illegitimate children and helped provide for them.[31]

If Nella's mother had arrived only recently in the United States when she took up with Peter, it is easy to believe their relationship owed something to his familiarity with the Danish tongue. That he was "colored" and she "white" would not have seemed the obstacle most "native" Americans considered it. In the Danish West Indies—St. Thomas, St. John, and St. Croix—which would not be sold to the United States until 1917, racial classifications differed dramatically from those in the United States. It was illegal in the Danish West Indies to designate a person's race on official forms such as census and church records. In the informal realm of everyday life, the "Negro" designation applied only to lower-class and so-called "full-blooded Negroes." Even those whom Americans would consider dark-complexioned black men could be designated "white" on the basis of social position and reputation, and Virgin Islanders had a whole series of intermediate designations for those between "Negro" and "white."[32] Unlike his daughter, Peter Walker may never have considered himself a Negro. Had Nella's parents thoroughly assimilated American concepts of race and nationality, she might never have been born. Census forms of the early twentieth century (those of 1890 were destroyed in a fire), show that most racially "mixed" families in Chicago involved blacks and recent white immigrants from Northern Europe and Scandinavia. Native-born whites were all too aware of the costs of "crossing the line."

There is no firm evidence that Nella's mother and father were officially married, but they were issued a license on July 1, 1890, when Mary was twenty-one and Peter twenty-eight, nine and a half months before Nellie's birth.[33] In the late nineteenth century people often held onto their marriage licenses without filing them; moreover, records of marriages performed by a justice of the peace often remained in that official's possession rather than being filed with a central office, so that often no marriage record exists for couples who married without the blessings of the church.[34] Notably, no record can be found of Mary Hansen's second marriage, either.[35] Nella's white half-sister, Anna Larsen, had her marriage performed by a justice of the peace. However, one must also take into account the fact that the intense animosity against interracial marriages often prevented them from officially taking place, even where they were legal. In states like Illinois, Wisconsin, and Michigan, it was difficult to find a minister or justice of the peace willing to perform the ceremony.[36]

Understandably, in adulthood Nella Larsen would be less than forthcoming about her early life. Being born to a white woman was in itself enough to cast suspicion upon her "legitimacy." Knowing little about her father made the situation far worse. As one early Danish immigrant to Chicago would write for a readership back home: "In Illinois . . . one finds no law forbidding a Negro to marry a girl of the Caucasian race. Naturally, here as everywhere in this country one finds a strong animosity to this sort of marriage; but one can maintain without exaggeration that the Negroes in such cases draw the shortest straw, the rule being that the white girl, in almost every case, has climbed on Prostitution's lowest rung."[37]

If queried on the issue of her parentage, Larsen had little defense at a time when being thought an illegitimate mulatto daughter of a white woman would have devastating consequences for any attempt to "make it" in respectable society. Children of interracial couples often did not suffer if their father held a high position in the African American community and the family remained intact with him firmly at the head of it, but for mulatto children of the working class and questionable origins, the situation throughout the late nineteenth century and most of the twentieth was different, especially if the black father was not present. In black communities, rumors of "bad mixed blood" circulated in streets, alleys, kitchens, and hallways. Lower-class white women with "mixed" children were routinely assumed to be prostitutes. A white mother in this position could expect vicious calumny from whites, and little better treatment from most blacks, if they would have anything to do with her at all. In most cases they would not.[38] Such matches, perceived as usually involving black men and desperate white women with "nothing to lose," contradicted "group loyalty and race pride."[39] Moreover, further race mixing threatened "race suicide and moral degeneration."[40] Black men who "married white," as one woman wrote, "entail upon themselves and their children the deadly association of a nature vile, miasmatic and filthy, dealing death to all hope of moral cleanliness."[41]

Many who knew Larsen later in her life were fully aware of the reputation of her birthplace, which became notorious on an international scale in the years after she was born. Larsen's acquaintances in New York who had known her as a girl—and those, like Carl Van Vechten and Nora Holt, Charles S. Johnson and Jean Toomer, who had not previously known her but had lived in Chicago—knew exactly what addresses on Armour, Clark, and State Street signified near the turn of the century.

The neighborhood in which the Walkers lived was not far from more respectable areas that included prestigious African American institutions. Quinn Chapel—with one of the largest and most prosperous black congregations in the country—was at Twenty-Second and Wabash, east of State Street and thus buffered from the vice district in what was basically an all-white neighborhood as late as 1900. The Bethel African Methodist Episcopal Church stood at Thirtieth and Dearborn. At the corner of Dearborn and Twenty-Ninth streets, Provident Hospital—the first hospital in history to be run by African Americans, with an integrated staff and patient population—opened its doors on May 4, 1891, just three weeks after the birth of the future nurse. In fact, the number one issue in black Chicago in the spring of 1891 was the controversy over the founding of this institution.

Today one thinks of the founding of Provident as a triumph of black pride and self-determination, but at the moment of Nellie Walker's birth, black Chicagoans were not so sure. Throughout April and May they were in an uproar, many suspecting the new hospital to be a ruse for initiating segregated health care in the city by creating a "Negro hospital." Protest meetings in local black churches condemned the organizers as race traitors, and rumors circulated that those behind the venture had asked Chicago hospitals to refuse black patients in order to force them into the new institution. On Tuesday, April 14, during Nellie Walker's first full day in the world, resolutions were adopted "by the colored citizens of Chicago, in mass meeting assembled," at the A.M.E. Zion Church on Dearborn near Twenty-Ninth Street, branding the "originators and promoters" of Provident Hospital "arch traitors and enemies to our race" who "ought to be ordered to leave the state."[42] If one considers the rapid spread of Jim Crow laws and customs throughout the United States, the fears are understandable, although the object was inappropriate since the founders of Provident were actually avid integrationists who planned on an interracial staff and clientele. They had no intention of founding a "Negro hospital," although they saw a practical need for an institution that would be welcoming to African American interns and nurse trainees. Opponents called on any "respectable" Negro who had been turned away from the city's nursing schools or hospitals to identify themselves and prove the need for such a facility.[43]

The episode epitomizes the tactical dilemma African Americans faced during a watershed period in the racial history of Chicago. Should one push for total integration of civic institutions or, recognizing the existence of de facto segregation, opt for development of separate institutions in order to provide opportunities otherwise denied the city's black citizens? To many, the latter course threatened to play into the hands of the Jim Crow movement that was rapidly engulfing the nation. At the political heart of that movement was the attempt to maintain white supremacy; at its socio-psychological core was a need to control women's sexuality in the interests of "race," and thus to make such persons as Nellie Walker impossible, to institute an absolute chasm between black and white "identity." That chasm, which had a long history already, helped to define twentieth-century America. It nurtured separate institutions, separate neighborhoods, separate mentalities, loyalties to separate "races" thought of as extended families—all of which, in their complicated interrelations, could only be "mixed" even while antagonistic to one another in fierce struggles for power and survival.

What was it like to be born into this developing world as the "colored" daughter of a white immigrant mother? What accommodations would have to be made to a society that would wish one into nonexistence or, barring that, into patterns of selfhood that felt too often like forms of self-betrayal? The force of the racial order so opposed to Larsen's conception, and denying her emotional security, makes the recovery of her experience unusually difficult—and also fascinating, a work of detection at cross-purposes with racial expectation.

TWO

Inheriting the Color Line:
1892–1898

JUST after Easter 1964, when told that she was in a position to inherit $35,000 from Nella Larsen Imes, Anna Elizabeth Larsen Gardner exclaimed, "Why, I didn't know I had a half-sister!" But she did know, and there was no need for the ruse. Even the friend she said this to, Mildred Phillips, knew about Anna's dark half-sister "Nellie." Mary Larsen had spoken of her to Mildred's mother years before. But Mildred had never asked Anna or Mary about the "other" Larsen daughter, and never heard her mentioned in the Larsen or Gardner homes.[1]

Life had not been easy for Anna Gardner. Her marriage of 1913 had dissolved about 1946 and her husband had remarried someone she knew. Having lost the use of her hands and feet, she had been confined to a wheelchair much of her adult life by the multiple sclerosis that was slowly killing her. She had spent the previous half-century or so pretending that she was an only child, and now she needed a lawyer to legally prove that she was Nella Larsen Imes's half-sister.

Her birth certificate, dated June 21, 1892, gave her name as "Lizzie Larson" and the place of birth as 1901 South Clark in Chicago.[2] Some details of the record are so anomalous as to make one wonder if this is really Anna's birth certificate, despite the fact that it is the document her lawyer would use seventy-two years later to help prove her claim to her half-sister's estate. Both parents are listed as "Swedish," and the twenty-four-year-old mother's maiden name is given as "Peteralina Mary Hanson." The father, twenty-five-year-old Peter "Larson," was termed a "Teamster." Jno (Jonathon) Leeming of 3400 Indiana Avenue, a physician, returned the official form to the county clerk; a "Mrs. Rea" had also attended the birth. "Lizzie," like her mother and her "Swedish" immigrant father, was white.

This is the only document in which Mary/Marie's first name is given as Peteralina, and the only one in which Peter and Mary are listed as Swedish. But Danes were routinely called "Swedes" in turn-of-the-century Chicago, and Danish names ending in "-en" frequently ended in the Swedish form "-on" when written down by Americans.[3] More problematically, "Peteralina" is not a name in Scandinavia (or Europe); "Petronella," however, is a relatively common Danish name, which may have some bearing on the name "Nella" which Larsen used beginning at the same time she started formally using the name "Marie" as a middle name. What finally convinces a researcher that the certificate is that of Nellie's half-sister is the fact that the birthdate matches the one given for Anna on other documents, which also list Anna's middle name as "Elizabeth." "Lizzie" is also identified as her mother's second child. And the place of birth, at the corner of Nineteenth and South Clark, was less than three blocks from where Nellie Walker had been born.[4]

As in the case of Mary's marriage to Peter Walker, no marriage license can be found, although the fact that the former Mary Hansen bears Peter Larson's/ Larsen's surname and that they both lived at 1901 South Clark Street indicates that they considered themselves married. Later census records suggest they married sometime in 1891, about the time Mary became pregnant with Anna.[5]

It seems appropriate here to mention a broadly credited hypothesis that Peter Larsen was actually the same man as Peter Walker, and that he was "passing." Most of the rationale for this hypothesis—based on faulty analyses of two census listings, a school record, a marriage license, and peripatetic spellings of "Larsen" as "Larson"—disintegrates on close inspection, as I will demonstrate in due course. Larsen always said that her father was black and her stepfather white, and in 1928, when Peter Larsen was still alive, she said her only relatives in the United States were Anna and Mary. Again in 1929 she told an interviewer that her stepfather and half-sister were white, adding that she no longer saw much of her family, because "it might make it awkward for them, particularly my half-sister."[6] Confirming her reports is Anna Gardner's will, in which she stated that "Peter Larsen had only one child during his lifetime, namely, myself, and my mother had two children during her lifetime, namely, my half-sister, Nellie Imes, and myself."[7] Peter Walker was five years older than Peter Larsen. He would have had no reason to change his age by five years, or even to change his surname, in order to "pass." More important would be to change neighborhoods. Yet Peter Larsen, a teamster in 1892, settled with his "mixed" family less than three blocks from the birthplace of Nellie Walker and would become a streetcar conductor by 1903, working on a trolley line that served the very area in which, had he been passing, people would have remembered him as the "colored" cook Peter Walker.

Also confounding the possibility that Peter Larsen was passing is the fact that if he could have passed, then Nellie Walker almost certainly could have done so more readily than he.[8] Nellie could have been more "Negro" in appearance than Peter only if Mary Larsen was also "colored." But if advanced scholars in 2005 can believe that Peter and Anna Larsen were "passing," it only goes to show that

Peter and Anna had reason to believe that working-class neighbors and classmates in the 1890s might suspect the same. Peter and Anna never "passed" as white, but after "Nellie" was grown up, the family would pass as one that was not "mixed." Conversely no one in later years would have imagined that Nella Larsen had a white mother unless she explicitly told them so. This was the default situation of all Americans with close relatives on the "other side." In a society that placed such importance on racial definition, it endowed one with a sense of partial invisibility which could be simultaneously an affliction and a source of insight.

Born in 1867, Peter Larsen had immigrated to the United States in the late 1880s.[9] His decision to marry Mary Hansen/Walker was a godsend for her. Husbandless, with a mulatto child, thrown on her own resources in a squalid tenement district, Nella's mother faced a future of abject misery and shame. Remarriage was the only way out, and the only way of keeping her daughter out of the orphanage. As Nella Larsen herself would write in her first, semi-autobiographical novel, "That second marriage, to a man of her own race, but not of her own kind—so passionately, so instinctively resented by Helga even at the trivial age of six—she now understood as a grievous necessity. Even foolish, despised women must have food and clothing; even unloved little Negro girls must be somehow provided for."[10]

If Mary's second marriage saved Nellie Walker from a miserable destiny, it was also a defining event in her emotional life. As she grew older, she would come to recognize that she was a burden to her mother and a blot on her existence, as well as a cause of constant tension in her home. At a time of widespread belief that white women could give birth to brown or "coal-black" babies if they were married to "invisible"/passing Negroes, Nellie's obvious "African" features would have raised suspicions about the racial identity of Peter and/or Mary, not to mention her sister. The clarification that Mary Larsen had previously been married to a "colored" man, and that Nellie was his daughter, would hardly assuage concerns of those with the temerity to ask. We will find repeatedly that, within her limited means, Mary went to remarkable lengths to find potential paths for her "colored" daughter into a fulfilling life, one of a higher class status than both her own and her white daughter's. But it gradually became clear that Nellie would have to live a life apart. Tangled feelings of love and abandonment, anger and self-loathing, empathy, shame, and powerlessness stamped Larsen's emotional development in childhood and shaped the attachment problems that would afflict her until she died.

The early 1890s were momentous years for both Chicago and African Americans. The big story of the time was the competition to host the World Columbian Exposition of 1893, the argument about where to build it, and the planning of its components. The fair was to represent, as a recent historian writes, "an antidote to social disorder"—the antithesis of the Levee.[11] Public pronouncements about a coming "millennium of universal liberty and of the brotherhood of man" were baldly contradicted by the racial exclusions of the exposition, which nearly everyone in town attended.[12] Frederick Douglass participated as the official representative for Haiti. Scott Joplin showcased a new form of syncopated music, not yet called ragtime, on the Midway. Otherwise, the only black exhibit was a "Dahomeyan" village of grass huts with African Americans in "native" attire, included in the Midway as an ethnographic display. Visitors would pass this exhibit and others from "backward" regions before crossing a bridge into the featured city of gleaming white Italian-Renaissance–style palaces skirting the central lagoon.[13]

Working-class visitors were most drawn to the excitement of the commercially run Midway Plaisance, where the landmark of the fair, the huge wheel invented for the occasion by George Washington Gale Ferris, spun its great cabins, packed with passengers, in a two-hundred-fifty-foot vertical orbit, higher than the Statue of Liberty's crown. "The forerunner of all entertainment wheels," historian Donald L. Miller writes, "it helped usher in the age of the amusement park."[14] In the Midwest such parks were off-limits to blacks except on special days marked out for them.

This practice was foreshadowed by "Colored People's Day," on which the fair gave out 2,500 watermelons, as if ridiculing the African Americans who showed up in spite of Ida B. Wells-Barnett's call for a boycott. Douglass used the occasion to assail the American betrayal of its black citizens since the Civil War: "Men talk of the Negro problem. There is no Negro problem. The problem is whether the American people have . . . honor enough, patriotism enough, to live up to their own Constitution. . . . We Negroes love our country. We fought for it. We ask only that we be treated as well as those who fought against it."[15] Wells-Barnett and Douglass felt they were witnessing the reconciliation of Northern and Southern whites at black people's expense—and they were right.[16]

By the summer of 1894, when Nellie was three, the Larsen family tried to escape the Levee by moving several blocks west to 325 Twenty-Second Street, just beyond Wentworth. Peter worked as a "driver," very likely of a horse-drawn streetcar on the Twenty-Second Street line that passed in front of the family home, connecting the working-class neighborhoods of the West Side with the central business district. Peter disappears from the city directory in 1895 and 1896, but reappears at this address in 1897, still as a "driver."[17] The location was buffered from the developing "black belt" by the Chicago, Rock Island, and

Pacific Railroad, and located practically across the street from the furiously active Third Precinct police station. The Larsen home directly faced the neighborhood fire department, home of Chicago's Hook and Ladder Company 4. German Americans predominated, joined by Scandinavians and a few Dutch, Irish, and Italian families. This ethnic composition may have given the Larsens hope of acceptance, but they soon learned differently, for the neighborhood was literally on the wrong side of the tracks for a "mixed" family.[18]

The intensifying residential segregation in Chicago between 1890 and 1900 correlated with a number of landmark events in the history of American racial culture. With slavery over and a black professional class coming into existence, whites sought by myriad ingenious measures to preserve racial division and white supremacy. African Americans debated whether to confront the rise of segregation head-on or to accept a certain level of separation and concentrate on building up the race from within, with aid from white philanthropy. The term "social equality" came to define the essential difference between positions.

"Social equality" meant different things to different people, but it was associated with a full-scale assault on all measures that instituted or implicitly tolerated social divisions based on race. To its opponents, social equality meant, ultimately, interracial marriage. Although proponents of social equality often objected to this equation and were not particularly interested in seeing a lot of interracial marriages, in a sense the racist opposition was absolutely right. The logic of the push for social equality could not but allow, on some level, that with the end of all "artificial" social barriers based on race, lifelong interracial unions would multiply, and "whiteness" itself could hardly survive in the long run. The earliest laws instituting racial divisions and definitions in many states, after all, had been written to control the spread of such unions. The necessary precondition of racial supremacy was the institution of race, and that institution, in a society as mixed as that of the United States, could not survive frequent marriage across racial lines.

In the mid-1890s, Booker T. Washington rose to prominence as a "race leader" through his infamous compromise with whites on the issue of social equality. At the Cotton States International Exposition in Atlanta in 1895, he urged economic cooperation of blacks and whites on a basis of social segregation, appealing simultaneously to nativist resentment of "foreign" labor unionists and fear of miscegenation. Washington opposed a vision of organized immigrant labor, epitomized by the great strikes in Chicago, to that of native, loyal black labor: "To those of the white race who look to the incoming of those of foreign birth and strange tongue and habits for the prosperity of the South, . . . I would repeat what I say to my own race, 'Cast down your bucket where you are.'

. . . Cast down your bucket among those people who have without strikes and labor wars tilled your fields, cleared your forests, builded your railroads and cities. . . . As we have proved our loyalty to you in the past . . . so in the future, in our humble way, we shall stand by you with a devotion that no foreigner can approach." Next, lifting his hand with fingers spread and then closing it in a raised fist, Washington uttered his electrifying statement: "In all things that are purely social we can be as separate as the fingers, yet one as the hand in all things essential to mutual progress."[19]

As David Levering Lewis has written, Washington's speech "turned out to be one of the most consequential pronouncements in American history. Neither black people nor white people were ever quite the same again."[20] He was immediately anointed the national spokesman of the Negro race, and Tuskegee Institute was held up as a beacon of black pride. Frederick Douglass, the champion of absolute social equality, whose second, white wife had never found acceptance in either the black or the white world, was dead.

The "wisest among my race," said Washington, "understand that the agitation of questions of social equality is the extremest folly," that "the opportunity to earn a dollar in a factory just now is worth infinitely more than the opportunity to spend a dollar in an opera-house."[21] Implicit in this view is a notion of separate "peoples," races, in social isolation, belonging to separate families and institutions. Even most of Washington's critics would not think to question the essential terms of this argument, for they too were committed to "race" as extended "family" and the focal point of personal identity. Such beliefs were simply part of the basic equipment for living throughout the Western world at the turn of the twentieth century. W. E. B. Du Bois, later Washington's harshest critic, wrote to him from Wilberforce University: "Let me heartily congratulate you upon your phenomenal success at Atlanta—it was a word fitly spoken."[22]

In "The Conservation of Races," presented before the anti-Tuskegee American Negro Academy, Du Bois posited: "The history of the world is the history, not of individuals, but of groups, not of nations, but of races, and he who ignores or seeks to override the race idea in human history ignores and overrides the central thought of all history."[23] Although some "race men" and "race women" would argue vehemently with Washington over the means and ends of racial uplift, the centrality of racial integrity to black progress—and the alignment of "race" with "family"—was never even remotely in question.

While Larsen suffered acutely from antiblack racism throughout her life and considered herself a Negro, on a more intimate plane her relationship to the rhetoric of race pride that grew to main strength while she was still a girl living with her mother was oblique and inherently vexed. The mere fact of having bio-logically "mixed" ancestry was insignificant. (Booker T. Washington himself, af-ter all, was the son of a white man he never knew, and Du Bois freely acknowl-edged his Dutch and French Huguenot ancestry.) At issue was the problem that "race" posed to the security of Larsen's primary attachments.

For young Nellie Larsen, social equality meant the freedom to be a member of her own family, to sleep in her family's apartment, to eat with them at the same table, to be identified with her mother, to be carried on her mother's hip in the butcher shop, to toddle down the sidewalk at her sister's side. Larsen's whole private relation to the public discourse of race, manhood, womanhood, and nationality could scarcely be acknowledged or comprehended in the world into which she had been born. The only place for her in contemporary formula-tions was as a "type" destined to vanish.

The regime of race in the United States was set up precisely to ensure a "nat-ural" correlation between race and family identity—which, in turn, would help secure for the future the powerlessness and exploitation of the racial minority. The family was the basic unit in the reproduction of race. So-called mixed fami-lies thus became "unnatural," as new theories promulgated by the most presti-gious natural and social scientists in the United States and Europe seemed to prove on objective scientific grounds. These theories, in turn, became the intel-lectual bulwark for judicial opinions—most crucially *Plessy v. Ferguson*—af-firming racial segregation on the basis that "legislation is powerless to eradicate racial instincts," and thus, in a sort of circular effect, reinforced the social, cul-tural, and political practices that sustained the "naturalness" of racial separation in the making of Americans throughout the twentieth century.[24]

In 1892, two weeks before Nellie's white half-sister was born, a thirty-year-old French-speaking "colored" man who looked white boarded a "white" passenger train car in Louisiana with the purpose of getting himself arrested. The arrest had been carefully arranged by a committee composed primarily of "colored" Creoles in New Orleans and their white pro bono lawyer, the novelist Albion Tourgee, who believed that assorting people by race perpetuated the features of slavery. Aiming to have all racial distinctions in law declared unconstitutional, Tourgee's strategy was to have someone of "mixed blood" violate the law in or-der to highlight the arbitrary nature of racial classification and thereby bring the whole "equal-but-separate" system into crisis. Homer Plessy had agreed to be the guinea pig, and a railroad conductor and a private detective arranged the arrest. Over the next four years, the case worked its way to the Supreme Court of the United States.

In the 1896 decision that would profoundly shape American society for the next half-century and more, the majority of judges famously concluded that the Fourteenth Amendment "could not have been intended to abolish distinctions based upon color, or to enforce social, as distinguished from political equality, or a commingling of the two races upon terms unsatisfactory to either." Social mingling of the races was against nature; it was primarily the unnatural mulattos, according to scientists of the day, who were always trying to "force" themselves into white company. Moreover, antimiscegenation laws proved the "'universally recognized' power of states to enact ordinances separating the races."[25] In dissent, Justice John Harlan declared the Constitution "color blind" and argued that the ruling would only promote "race hate" and distrust. Though a defeat, *Plessy* granted one crucial legal point to blacks: Jim Crow laws must guarantee equal facilities. Not until the 1950s did the NAACP legally challenge the "separate" concept, because doing so earlier would have surely failed.[26]

Those whose family identity conflicted with their racial designation bore the psychological brunt of the law of the color line—Race Trumps Family—in ways no other persons did. The whole discourse of race as it developed in the years surrounding Larsen's birth was at war with her emotional security. In adulthood, Larsen could come to understand the need for race loyalty and political commitment to the cause; but at a more private level, revealed in her fiction and in her correspondence with intimate friends, she remained a nonbeliever utterly opposed to race's defining force. Always liable to be misunderstood, she grew guarded and keenly observant, perceiving the presumptions, idealizations, and self-deceptions common to color line culture as well as the inordinate cost of resisting it.

Racially mulatto and then Negro, according to official designations, Nella Larsen was Danish American as well. In a period when the vast majority of African Americans came from generations of people born in North America and traced their most personally meaningful line of descent to slaves in the South, Larsen had no Southern ancestors, black or white. Her extended family was Scandinavian, a fact that was and is difficult to integrate with American assumptions about race, ethnicity, and culture. She never knew a black grandmother, or any black relative, for that matter, except the father she lost in infancy.

Larsen's difference lay not only in the fact that she had a white mother and lived in a white family with no knowledge of her black relatives; it lay also in the fact that she was the daughter of recent immigrants. Mary had been in the United States for only three to five years when Nellie was born. She probably still spoke at least some Danish in the home. In adulthood, without having studied the language formally in school, Nella could both speak and read Danish without the help of a dictionary.

Many African Americans looked down on immigrants and took pride in their "native" American status in the early twentieth century. This was a status Nella Larsen was never able or (apparently) willing to claim in quite the same way. She did not feel much loyalty to any national identity, and as an author she criticized the patriotism of African Americans. Moreover, the great influx of Afro-Caribbeans had not yet begun when she was a child, and by the time it did —in the New York of her adulthood—she had no real connection to Afro-Caribbean identity, for she had grown up completely cut off from it. Peter Walker, as a Caribbean immigrant, was very unusual in the Chicago of the 1890s.

A common experience for Danish Americans, an extended visit to "det Gammel Land" (the Old Country) both enhanced Larsen's sense of connectedness to Danish culture and exacerbated her sense of racial difference. We will probably never know exactly when Mary took her girls to Denmark. Only the passenger lists for ships coming to the United States in those years have been saved, not the lists for those departing. But at age seven, on her return to New York in 1898, Nelly Larsen could neither read nor write. Clearly, she had not entered school the previous fall in Chicago, as was required. In her autobiographical statement for Knopf in 1926, she noted that she'd started school late by American standards. In 1929, she told an interviewer that "for a considerable part" of her life she had been "brought up" in Denmark, first as a very small child and then when she was seventeen to twenty-one.[27] In a library school application of 1922, the only document in which she dates her first trip to Denmark, Larsen wrote that she was there for three years.[28] These years had to be 1895–1898, from shortly after Peter Larsen moved to 325 Twenty-Second Street until shortly before he (and they) moved out of that address to 201 Twenty-Second Street. This would comport with the fact that 325 Twenty-Second Street was no place for a "mixed" family to live.

The Thingvalla Steamship Line offered the only direct route from New York to Denmark, and a dock on the Hudson where the Chicago and Erie Express train terminated. It had an agency on East Kinzie Street in Chicago, where the Larsens bought their tickets, perhaps for one of the popular fall excursions often advertised in the Danish-language papers. The family had been saving for months, at least. The cheapest tickets for Mary and the two girls cost roughly two months' wages for a streetcar driver or skilled dressmaker at the time.[29]

The Chicago and Erie Express departed from Dearborn Station, a short streetcar ride from home. As they settled self-consciously into their seats amid curious stares, the train made the slow grade to Sixteenth Street, then followed the dark river south into the charnel-house stench of the stockyards, where oily black smoke of burnt offal rose from huge chimneys to blot out the sky. Finally Chicago receded behind great hills of coal and the train turned east to traverse Indiana, where interracial families were illegal.

A day and a half later, the train emerged from underground Manhattan into the roar, screech, and bang of downtown New York, facing the wharves. Mary and the girls almost certainly had third-class tickets for the steamer, but women traveling third class with children could get a separate room with four bunk beds and a sink for 30 percent off the usual second-class fare, and they had the dining room and salon for stretching out, not to mention the decks.[30] The social atmosphere in the dining hall was something new to Mary Larsen's girls. Here they could sit and eat together cheerfully. In *Quicksand,* Larsen would sketch into a shipboard scene a friendly purser who remembers Helga Crane from her childhood journey with her mother and invites her to dine with him—in pointed contrast to American mores and the usual awkwardness or secrecy surrounding Helga's relationship with her mother.

The meals themselves tasted of Denmark—breakfasts of sweet barley or wheat porridge, with rye bread and smoked herring or sausage; lunches featuring beef, pea, or cabbage soups, salt pork or beef and potatoes; dinners of cheese and sausage with buttered wheat or rye bread—the ubiquitous Danish smørrebrod—freshly made every day in the ship's bakery.[31]

On the second day the ship reached the Outer Banks near Newfoundland, with plenty of seasick passengers, and then crossed the open sea, finally catching the warm Gulf Stream, in which the ship would rock for a week. The passengers streamed on deck when the weather was good, sounds of laughter and harmonica music drifting about while children played together and made friends.[32] Schools of fifty to a hundred porpoises commonly appeared alongside the ships on this route, and spouting whales could often be seen in the distance.

On the thirteenth day out of New York, the ship skirted the north coast of Scotland—the passengers could see green slopes visibly speckled with sheep when the sky was clear—and curved across to Norway, out of the Gulf Stream, to stop at Christiansand. After pausing in Christiania (now Oslo), they finally entered the long and stately harbor of Copenhagen from the north, passed the old castle fortifications and moat, and coasted within sight of Hans Christian Andersen's Little Mermaid—her bronze replica, that is—who gazed out serenely on the incoming ships from her rocky perch by the shore while passengers lining the rails pointed her out to their children. Home.

They were towed to a berth at Larsensplads (Larsen Square), with a direct view up a broad, short boulevard to the quadrangular Amalienborg Palace and the stately dome of the Marble Church beyond, framed by the palace gates. A big brass band, with bass drum booming and snares rattling amid a chorus of horns, often greeted the returning emigrants with national anthems and traditional airs, and American and Danish flags flew over the warehouses just to the right of the plaza that gave a full and impressively symmetrical view of the palace. Hundreds of Danes crowded the quay, yearning for the first appearance at the ship's rails of siblings, sons, and daughters gone long years, nieces and granddaughters never seen before.[33] It was Mary's first return home since her emigration a decade earlier, and Nelly and Anna's first experience of grandparents—who, no doubt, could communicate with the girls only in Danish. It was a new life.

Just where Mary's family lived in Denmark at the time remains a puzzle.[34] In 1922, on her application for admission to the New York Public Library's library school, Nella claimed to have once lived in "Askov J" (the "J" referring to Jutland, or Jylland). To Danes, Askov had, and still has, an immediate resonance as the home of N. F. S. Grundtvig's most famous folk high school, an icon of Danish romantic nationalism in the wake of the Dano-Prussian war. Many "Schleswigers" settled in the area following their defeat and abandonment of the lands to the south. Askov was a hamlet set in gently rolling hills near the larger village of Vejen, with a few stone Viking mementos scattered across the countryside in the middle of carefully tended grain and vegetable fields, thatched-roof barns and houses punctuating a green-and-gold landscape.

In the mid-1930s, Larsen would tell Bryher about a period of her childhood spent in small-town Denmark: "Alas, she has the Danish intensity," Bryher wrote her intimate friend, the poet H.D. (Hilda Doolittle), "lived there, as tiny pup, with very dark skin, and it must be intensely difficult for her."[35] A few nights later, after another meeting with Larsen ("my dear 'Miss Nelly'"), Bryher added: "She tells me she was brought up in Denmark, the only dark child in the family and town, [and she] loathes music, because people always insisted that [as] a negro she must sing."[36] The particular version of one of the Danish games Larsen later described in her first publication was played specifically on the rural Jutland peninsula in the 1890s.[37] Such details place Larsen's childhood experiences not in the great capital city, the Scandinavian gateway to Europe and to Denmark's Caribbean colonies, but in a provincial town setting where she would have felt her "difference" even more keenly.

Living in such a town, Nellie would have been quite a sensation.[38] Many villagers in such provinces lived and died without ever seeing a person of other than German or Scandinavian complexion and physiognomy. Yet they were not, of course, ignorant of the existence of the "darker races." The Danish colonies in the Caribbean were part of what made Denmark an empire in spite of its recent humiliations, and traveling black entertainers from the United States were already the hit of Copenhagen in the field of popular culture. The cakewalk was taking the "Klunker" (haut bourgeois) aristocracy by storm. In 1880, Tivoli had hosted a "Nubian Caravan" from Africa, and an entire village of Ashanti people from Ghana would be brought in for the summer of 1898 to be gawked at by visitors, entertained by diplomats, and caricatured alongside those diplomats in the popular press.[39] During the winter season, the Cirkus building in Copenhagen put on variety shows each year, the most popular of which in the 1890s was the "black opera" with fifty Negro performers. The musical comedian George Jackson taught Danes the latest American dance melodies.[40] Many country people in Denmark who had never seen a "colored person" before certainly had notions about them. If Nellie had been hoping to find acceptance among her mother's people, not as an exotic but as one of themselves, this would have been very disappointing.

It could not have been all bad, however, since Larsen would later return to Denmark for an extended stay. She did, in short, "have fun." Denmark prided itself on its children's culture. The national hero was not a politician, playwright, or general, but Hans Christian Andersen. Years later, in the introduction to her first known publication, Larsen wrote, "These are some games which I learned long ago in Denmark, from the little Danish children. I hope that you will play them and like them as I did."[41] Among them were "Hawk and Pigeons," an outdoor game with a song that Larsen carefully transcribed with musical notation; and "Travelers," like the others a game for very young children. Larsen's second publication, "Danish Fun," began, "Dear Children: These are pleasant memories of my childish days in Denmark." For "The Fox Game," she specifies that if the game is played outdoors in warm months, the "fox" sits on a stone; if indoors during the cold months, on a stool or box. Other games included "Hide the Shoe" and "The King Is Here," a Danish cousin of "musical chairs":

> All sit in a circle except one, who stands and is called the jester. He is supposed to begin a story, inventing it as he goes along. Frequently without warning he uses the words *"Change places."* The players however pay no attention at all to this, but when the jester adds the information *"The King is here!"* all jump up and change places and the jester endeavors to get a seat. If he succeeds the one without a seat becomes the jester. No change is to be made unless the jester says plainly *"The King is here!"* If, for instance, he says *"The King is coming!"* the players are not to change. This uncertainty adds to the excitement and fun.[42]

To play this game, young Nelly Larsen had to be proficient in spoken Danish. What is even more remarkable is that she would be able to remember it in such detail, along with the other games and riddles, twenty-two years later.

One wonders if Mary ever thought of leaving Nelly in Denmark, or of staying there with both girls—an unanswerable question but one that brings attention to the fact that Mary Larsen kept her black daughter with her until Nelly was a young adult; until, in fact, she was the same age that Mary had been when she set off for America. While we may never know more of Larsen's Danish relatives than that she lived with them before the age of seven and again in her late teens, we do know that in the late 1890s the situation for interracial families was quickly deteriorating in Chicago. In Denmark, Nelly would perhaps always be a curiosity, but this was not nearly as threatening as the situation she, her mother, and her half-sister faced in turn-of-the-century America.

They boarded the *S.S. Norge* at Larsensplads on April 19, 1898—just after Nelly's seventh birthday. This was well past the usual time for Christmas visitors to return home, and most of the passengers were emigrants. They stopped the first day in Christiania to take on forty more people, mostly emigrants from Sweden and Norway, and then continued to Christiansand to pick up another thirty-eight passengers before casting off for the Atlantic crossing.[43]

Nearly two weeks later, they got their first sight of America—the Nantucket lighthouse—off the starboard bow. Reaching Fire Island, the ship sent up rockets to announce its arrival, passed Sandy Hook, and finally, on May 6, entered the great harbor in view of the Statue of Liberty. Beneath her shadow, dampened by light rain and temperatures in the low fifties, a health official and a customs inspector pulled alongside in launches and boarded to fulfill their duties.[44] The health official went over the passenger manifests filled out in the Scandinavian ports two weeks earlier. Those sheets, now in the National Archives, show "Mary Larsen" as age twenty-nine, married, able to read and write, and daughters "Nelly" and "Any" as seven and five. Since Mary was considered a U.S. citizen, most of the columns on the form (which was intended mainly for aliens) were ignored. Across the page, starting in the space for "nationality," is written in a Scandinavian hand: "returning from a visit in Denmarc; 12 years stay in U.S.A.; going back to my häusband." Mother and daughters were all in good health. The official asked Mary for her address in Chicago and scrawled "325 27th Str." over the line giving that city as her destination. Either he had misheard Mary's "twenty-second" as "twenty-seventh," or his hand had slipped while writing; for they were on their way to 325 Twenty-Second Street, where Peter awaited them.[45]

THREE

State Street Years:
1899–1907

A LONG period of unhappiness followed the return from Denmark. Almost thirty years later, Larsen would draw on searing memories of that decade in imagining Helga Crane: "Before her rose the pictures of her mother's careful management to avoid those ugly scarifying quarrels which even at this far-off time caused an uncontrollable shudder, her own childish self-effacement, the savage unkindness of her step-brothers and sisters, and the jealous, malicious hatred of her mother's husband. Summers, winters, years, passing in one long, changeless stretch of aching misery of soul."[1] This is not a memoir, yet it draws from the aquifer of buried feeling that nourishes many a debut novel. In *Quicksand* Helga Crane's mother remarries when her daughter is six, takes her to Denmark to visit family, and brings her back to Chicago, where they settle in with the new husband and his children. Helga suffers as the dark step-daughter until the age of fifteen, when her mother dies and an uncle sends her to a Negro boarding school. Her purgatory reflects the period between Mary, Nellie, and Anna's return from Denmark and Nellie's matriculation at Fisk University's Normal School at age sixteen.

This was exactly the period in which Chicago developed into an overwhelmingly segregated city, establishing the basic pattern that would characterize it for the rest of the twentieth century. The areas within a twenty-block radius of Larsen's family home led the way in the racial segregation of American urban life that continuously accelerated from the 1890s to 1970 and fundamentally shaped American society as we know it—shaped the racial awareness of most Americans alive today and served as a basic instrument of white supremacy.[2] By the time Larsen reached age sixteen, she could no longer live with her family, so they sent her away to school in the South.

In 1926, Larsen said in a handwritten autobiographical statement for her publisher: "Her formal education began at the age of eight," when "she and her half-sister—child of the second marriage—attended a small private school, whose pupils were mostly the children of German and Scandinavian parents."[3] Today this conveys the impression of a higher-class background than

Larsen had, but in her childhood one-fourth of Chicago's school-age children—most of them from immigrant families—attended private schools, and there is no reason to doubt Larsen's word. On a corner less than a block from the Larsens' home was Herford Kindergarten, a private school, at 406 Twenty-Second Street.[4]

Chicago kindergartens at the time were all private and commonly associated with German and Scandinavian immigrants, since this type of schooling had originated in Germany. Many of them were "free" and located in working-class immigrant areas. Maintaining close ties with home and family life, kindergartens softened culture shock and helped children adjust to "American conditions." Believing that children under eight were not ready for the abstract learning required in book-oriented elementary schools, the educators used carefully supervised play to develop the children's mental and physical capacities and claimed that those who attended kindergarten, even though they started school late by American standards, ended up surpassing pupils who started elementary school at earlier ages.[5] All of this leads one to suspect that Larsen began her education, with her sister, at the kindergarten just down the street from where she lived.

The family could not, however, stay in the neighborhood for long with a "mulatto" girl in their midst, and by the summer of 1899 the Larsens moved several blocks east on Twenty-Second Street to number 201, back in the heart of the Levee.[6] Their three-story brick apartment building stood in a racial border area on the southeast corner of Twenty-Second and State, facing the shop of the very druggist who had filled out Nella's birth certificate in 1891.[7] Just around the corner was the Chicago Orphan Asylum. The eight-year-old could not have been unaware of the reason for the move, and likely blamed herself for it. By now she could begin to understand the stigma her mere existence brought on her family, and her growing comprehension of the situation, not to mention Anna's, could only add to her misery and self-effacement.

Larsen began her public education at Moseley School, two blocks south and two blocks east of her home. It was a large school in an aging building with more than 1,300 pupils, nearly one-third of them missing on an average school-day and about as many failing to be promoted from one year to the next (on this measure, Moseley was one of the least successful schools in the system). Still, each classroom had more than fifty students on an average day, the vast majority being natives of Europe or children of immigrants.[8] In these years before 1905, by most accounts white and black pupils got along tolerably well in schools like Moseley, playing together and forming friendships in the early grades. One can assume this was so with Larsen, who always had white friends in later life and was never as inclined as most African Americans to hold white people at arm's length.

The Larsens had four roomers, the only ones in the building, to help pay the rent: a thirty-three-year-old Englishwoman named Edith Thonsing; twenty-seven-year-old Ida Sonneman, born to German parents in Ohio; a thirty-three-year-old Danish freight-handler who had immigrated in 1897; and thirty-year-old Daniel Bonner of Illinois, a common laborer. In total, the building housed twelve working-class families—an ethnically mixed (but all white except for Nellie) assortment of people from the Midwest, Ireland, Denmark, and Switzerland. An Irish widow and her three grown children lived in the neighboring apartment.[9]

Although the immediate neighbors were white, many black people lived nearby. Twenty-Second Street from the east side of State to the shore of Lake Michigan was all white, while it was practically all black between the west side of State and the Chicago Rock Island and Pacific tracks (encompassing Dearborn, Armour, and Clark). A fair number of black actors and actresses, as well as saloon keepers, inhabited Twenty-Second Street boardinghouses on the west side of State and staffed the local entertainment establishments. Some black families, however, lived on the east side of State in this area. Wabash, a block east of State, was all white, and east of that street all the way to the lake, African Americans were rare as hen's teeth except where they were live-in servants. The El (elevated train), running north and south right next to the Larsens' building, defined the eastern racial boundary of the near South Side.

As the intersection between black and white, Twenty-Second and State was also, like the nearby blocks in which Nellie and her sister had been born, well known as "the largest, the most notorious, and the most vicious of all Chicago's concentrations of vice."[10] Ever since Mayor Carter Harrison had ordered Clark Street north of Twelfth "cleaned up" in 1897, the area between Eighteenth and Twenty-Second, from Wabash to Clark, had monopolized gambling and the sex trades on the South Side, with the cooperation of City Hall.[11]

There were four saloons on the Larsens' block of Twenty-Second Street. Across the street at the east end, Freiberg's dance hall, under the management of Ike Bloom ("King of the Brothels"), was a well-known rendezvous for prostitutes and their clients, hosting a multiethnic crowd of "bohemians" and the "sporting set." Here gamblers, politicians, gangsters, pimps, vaudeville performers, and out-of-town thrill-seekers of the professional and business classes drank and danced with the female staff of "dance instructors."[12] Pony Moore, a black gambler and crook from Texas who considered himself the "Mayor of the Tenderloin," owned the Turf Exchange on Twenty-First Street between State and

2. East 22nd Street, Chicago, circa 1906. Looking east from the El station adjacent to the building in which the Larsens lived in 1900. Negative DN-0051398, Chicago Daily News Negatives Collection, courtesy of the Chicago Historical Society.

Dearborn.[13] The fire-trap hotels on State Street in this section served as well-known brothels for both black and white clients.

The neighborhood also incubated new forms of black popular music and performance that radiated from Chicago to New York, then to London, Paris, Berlin, and Copenhagen. Five blocks south, Robert Mott's saloon, the Pekin Inn, was becoming a launching pad for many black vaudeville shows and musical successes (including the new ragtime), a major site of the developing black entertainment industry, and a cause of complaint from nearby black churches because of the upstairs gambling dens.[14]

Ada Smith, later known as "Bricktop," a celebrated nightclub hostess in Paris during the heyday of the "jazz age," grew up on State Street not far from the Larsen apartment: "Crime was no stranger to State Street, or to anyone who lived on it," she would remember. "People got into knife fights there. The police would come and haul them off to jail, if they didn't have to go to the hospital."[15] "Everyone knew everybody else's business," she added, "and that wasn't as bad as it sounds. We helped each other out."[16] In the evening the men headed for the saloons and women gathered outside the tenement buildings to chat while the children played; sometimes a child would be sent to a saloon's back door for a pail of beer. But the apartment houses were segregated, even where "black" and "white" buildings stood side by side.

Prostitutes were easy to spot on the street because of their dress, and so were the pimps: "You couldn't grow up on State Street in Chicago and not learn to recognize them" in their close-fitting suits, with "diamond rings [and] matching stickpins."[17] The men of the neighborhood stopped at the saloons after work, not only for beer but for the free food. Behind the swinging front doors, "the floors were covered with sawdust, but the bar was always polished and smooth and piled high with food"—"plates with mounds of cold cuts, salads, pickles, olives, relishes, . . . loaves of bread [and] chunks of butter."[18] As men walked past the shadier "resorts," women in low-cut blouses and above-the-knee skirts would open a curtain and tap rapidly on the glass to catch their eye. These were sights Larsen glimpsed often as a girl, living as she did on one of the beeriest intersections in Chicago. She couldn't walk out the front door of her building without seeing the entrance to Cahill and Vancleave's Saloon right across the street, and she couldn't get to school without passing at least a half dozen others.[19] Freiberg's Hall was only steps away on the other side of Twenty-Second, in the afternoon shadow of the El.

Peter's job with the street railways always partly determined where the Larsens lived, and their new home was right on a corner where two major streetcar routes crossed: the Twenty-Second Street horse-car route and the State Street cable-car line. The company he worked for, Chicago City Railway (CCR), had its headquarters and a horse-car depot at the corner of Twenty-First and State, where drivers and conductors gathered and reported for work.[20] They gained seniority within the particular car-barn to which they were assigned, so Peter had reason to stick to lines running through the one where he had started out—a key to the family's various addresses.

At some point in Nella's youth or earlier, Mary Larsen went into business as a dressmaker, working at home.[21] Dominated by Scandinavians, dressmaking was the "queen" of all women's trades. The most skillful women could depend on steady work and up to $40 a week, along with considerable autonomy. They would put signs on their homes and often employ girl apprentices, unless they had daughters who could learn the trade and help out.[22]

When customers came to the Larsen home, they probably assumed that the "colored girl" was a servant or apprentice rather than the white dressmaker's daughter, and it seems likely that for the sake of business Nellie and Anna did not disabuse them of this notion. Whites routinely lost work in Chicago if they were discovered to have black spouses or children. For most members of black-white interracial families, a type of invisibility or "passing" was (and is) a normal aspect of daily life, since they were presumed to be unrelated. And in some situations, it was just as well.

Nella Larsen was an expert at "making over" dresses as an adult, though her formal schooling never included instruction in sewing. She had an unusual appreciation for textiles and fashion, and she enjoyed exchanging clothes with friends or giving them away. In old age, living alone on a nurse's salary, she always had "beautiful things," but she got them cheaply in used-clothing stores, and she knew how to alter them and fix them up.[23] Larsen's novels not only lavish attention on the details of women's dress and other fabrics, but even describe features of landscape in terms of fabric textures. In *Quicksand*, for example, the surface of the Atlantic on a serene September day is "smooth, like a length of watered silk."[24] Only someone intimate with fine evening-dress fabrics would have used that simile. Clare Kendry in *Passing* works as an assistant to a dressmaker when she is young, and begins sewing her own dresses in her early teens.

A woman's ability to dress herself in garments of her own choosing would always signify, in Larsen's fiction, her freedom and personal agency. Larsen's love of fabric and what could be done with it, the comforts it afforded, derived from her youth, when her mother, from whom she would be separated by the color line for most of her life, taught her to cut, fit, and sew.

Moving up the economic scale on the combined incomes of Peter and Mary, in 1903 the Larsen family moved south to 4538 State Street, settling in an apartment above a store in a three-story brick building, and Nellie entered seventh grade at the nearby Colman School in September. A bright child, she had skipped at least one grade, probably two, since 1898. Significantly, Anna did not attend Colman in 1903–1904, though this was the school for which both girls were zoned.[25] It would seem that they attended different schools as a protective measure. Increasingly, the family conspired to hide, insofar as they could, the relationship between the half-sisters.

As a "mixed" family, the Larsens were not entirely alone, however. A surprising number of such families lived in the new neighborhood—far more than anywhere else in the city—along with a number of white families, but in general the whites, who had been here earlier, were moving out.[26] The Larsens found themselves in the same situation as black families of their class, who often moved into newly opened areas to escape the deteriorating conditions of their old neighborhoods, only to find the same cycle of overcrowding and decline quickly following them. All around the Larsen household the South Side "black belt," later the setting of Richard Wright's *Native Son,* was in its early stages of development.[27]

While the section of State Street on which the Larsens lived was all white in 1900, a block west on Dearborn African Americans of the middle and lower-middle class were moving in. Colman School was right in the middle of this neighborhood. One "mixed" family, with the wife from Sweden and two children, lived at 4412 Dearborn. There were also two "mixed" families with children Nellie's age at 4413 Armour and 4536 Dearborn; in both cases, the wife was German. In 1900, all down Armour and Dearborn on the 4500 and 4600 blocks, one finds an alternation of "black" and "white" apartment buildings, with an occasional "mixed-race" family.[28] A fair number of the whites were Scandinavian. A Danish family lived at 4600 Armour, with a daughter named Helga; and at 4624 was a Swedish family with a girl just Nella's age, named Helga Anderson, who most likely was one of Nella's schoolmates. Both "Helga" and "Anderson" are significant names in Larsen's first novel.

As Thadious Davis has pointed out, Larsen made a long-term friendship in this neighborhood with the Mayo family, African Americans (termed "mulattos" in the 1910 census) who lived at 4811 State Street. Pearl Mayo, born in Louisiana and almost a year younger than Nellie, apparently became a close friend, for the adult Nella Larsen Imes stayed with the family for several days after her divorce in 1933. John Mayo, Pearl's father, worked as a Pullman porter, which conferred fairly high status in the African American community. The Mayos may well have given Nellie her first close and extended positive contact with the black middle class, during the four years before she departed for normal school.[29] They are not unlikely models for the family of Irene Redfield in *Passing,* Irene's father being unusually sympathetic to the lower-class Clare Kendry, who was partly raised by white aunts on the West Side.

Nellie's new school was much smaller than Moseley, much newer, and much less crowded.[30] Nonetheless, racial tensions in schools like Colman grew relentlessly. A black schoolteacher described the changes in her South Side school over a period that began in Larsen's childhood: "When I began teaching at the Farren School there were no colored children there, but very well-to-do white people who lived in the neighborhood. Later, children of the better class [African American] families who were moving in the district began coming to the school. There were no problems, for they acted just like the white children. They played with them and chummed with them. There were no difficulties. But later the lower-class Negroes began moving into the district. Then the trouble began." Some of these children "were altogether different from the white or colored students in our school."[31] In 1906 Fannie Barrier Williams, an influential "clubwoman" of Chicago's black elite, contrasted "the city-born Afro-American children," whom she considered "neither afraid nor proud of being noticed by the white pupils," with "those who have recently come from the South . . . [who] segregate themselves," showing "little or no spirit of self-assertion."[32] The migration from the South, she felt, was altering the black community at the same time that some white Chicagoans (many of them also Southern migrants) were agitating for racial separation.

If white parents learned their child had been assigned a seat next to a "colored" pupil, they frequently demanded that the teacher change the seating. Between 1900 and 1905, rumors increasingly circulated of racially motivated fights or "near-riots" by white pupils in the schools of the South Side that had black students. Some black leaders predicted that within five years Chicago's public schools would be segregated.[33]

The move to 4538 State followed the closing of the Twenty-Second Street horse-car line as horsepower was phased out; Peter Larsen became a conductor on a cable-car, probably on the State Street line, since he would have kept his seniority at the Thirty-Ninth Street car-barn on State.[34] At about the same time the CCR workingmen formed one of Chicago's most important unions, Local 260 of the Amalgamated Association of Street Railway Employees, headquartered at Thirty-Ninth and State. During the fall that Nellie started school at Colman, Peter's year-old union called a strike that led to running battles in the streets and briefly threatened to bring all business in Chicago to a halt. The Larsens' neighborhood was at the very heart of the unrest.

In those days, streetcars provided most people's transportation, and the uniformed conductors were much admired by the neighborhood boys. Physically imposing men who often had to face down street-toughs and drunks, besides taking fares and ringing the bell to signal stops and starts, they walked along running boards on the outside of the car and kept an eye on unpredictable traffic in the streets.[35] In winter they stood on an open platform at the rear of the car, bare-handed and shivering in their sheepskin coats. They worked long hours and could easily be replaced, until the unions grew in power during Nella Larsen's State Street years.[36] In 1903, CCR conductors like Peter made $2.49 per day, for a "ten-hour" day, six days a week, but the ten hours actually lasted anywhere from eleven to nineteen, because only the time actually spent on a run counted, and men had to wait in the car-barns between runs.[37] Peter's union wanted to change these conditions and raise the wages of lower-paid electric trolley workers. The company tried to dissuade new men from joining the young union, enraging the rank and file. Finally, in October 1903, after an earlier strike threat, the union submitted a list of demands to the company, which refused all of them on the spot and drove the workers into a fury. They voted overwhelmingly to strike beginning November 12, and the men prepared to block the tracks and attack any cars trying to leave the barns. The firemen, teamsters, electricians, and machinists working for CCR had agreed to strike in sympathy, so that the entire South Side public transportation system would come to a standstill. In response the company hired an infamous strikebreaker, James "Boss" Farley, to recruit and organize a strikebreaking force.[38]

As day dawned on the twelfth, crowds filled the streets in sympathy with the streetcar men while tens of thousands of people walked to work. Strikers rolled boulders onto the tracks and clogged cable slots. Sympathetic teamsters blockaded the roads with coal wagons, and the police dragged many to jail. When the streetcars stopped at blockades, they were met with fusillades of bricks and stones; then crowds descended on them, smashing the windows and woodwork and beating anyone on board. There was rioting along Wentworth and Clark, including battles with police. The CCR did not even attempt to run cars along State Street for about a week; it would have been not only impossible but incendiary, especially in the 3900 to 4700 blocks of State Street, the Larsens' neighborhood.

The strike grew quickly into a working-class cause célèbre. On the nineteenth, the teamsters threatened to strike throughout the city, bringing virtually all business to a halt, if the corporation did not settle. On the twenty-second, fifteen thousand men and women from many unions—an "army of labor"—showed up for a mass meeting supporting the streetcar union and heard their attorney, Clarence Darrow, one of the great orators of the age, call for mass organizing to win the aldermanic elections for labor and municipal ownership the following spring.[39]

The next day, for the first time the CCR tried to open the State Street cable line, setting off a furious rebellion in the 4700 block. When the cars, after numerous skirmishes, reached the Larsens' neighborhood they faced a blockade of giant boulders and iron rails. A pitched battle broke out with the police until a volley of bullets sent the strikers into retreat. After four hours the smashed cars made it to the city center, but the police abandoned any further attempts to open the State Street line. Returning south on State, they encountered a large crowd in front of the union headquarters and attacked with drawn clubs. The rioters took refuge in a saloon at 3900 State, and when the "bulls" entered to make arrests, the owner met them with a drawn gun; the police carefully backed out.[40]

On the same day, the Teamsters Union refused to deliver any goods that might aid the railway company, pledging a strike if their employers tried to force them. At this point, both the city administration and the corporation decided they had had enough. The owners agreed to meet with the leaders of Peter's union the next day under the mayor's auspices. Within twenty-four hours the war was over.[41]

Besides accomplishing some of the union's aims, the strike galvanized the movement for city ownership of the streetcar system. A new labor-led coalition, including teachers and civic reformers, whites and blacks, elected Democrat Edward Dunne mayor on a platform of "immediate municipal ownership."[42] A labor-friendly judge with strong links to progressive educational reformers, Dunne was staunchly antisegregationist and regarded as an ally of African Americans. Black Chicagoans, despite strong ties to the Republican Party, backed municipal ownership because they felt it would put the streetcar system under civil service and thus open up new lines of employment. White workers backed it because they felt it would strengthen the unions and control the streetcar fares. And the unions, fearing that the new emphasis on "industrial" education for the working class would limit their access to power and mobility, joined the teachers in demanding school reform.[43]

The municipal ownership movement failed, however. The main effect of Dunne's election—and a very positive one for Nellie Larsen—was to institute educational reform, beginning just as Larsen graduated eighth grade and prepared to enter high school.[44] The new educational administration instituted policies and pedagogical practices that shocked the city "establishment," and that would be in force during Larsen's two years of high school, though they were rolled back soon after, when Dunne failed to be reelected.

The victory of the Dunne campaign under the banner of municipal ownership briefly united the interests of Chicago's white working class, African Americans, and middle-class reformers (including the public school teachers), but powerful forces worked against the maintenance of such a progressive coalition, and it soon fell apart. The neighborhood where Nellie Larsen lived between 1902 and 1907 shows better than any other the wedge that was driven between the organized labor movement and the black freedom movement in America. Practically speaking, blacks were being shut out of the union movement in Chicago.[45] As immigrant workers—who helped build the labor movement in crucial ways, bringing European notions of class conflict with them to the industrial Midwest—assimilated to "white" America, they adopted American notions

45

of racial difference. Blacks, in turn, felt all the more bitterly their subordinated yet "native" status, as white immigrants stepped on and over them on their way up the ladder of opportunity.

An important factor was the use of African Americans as strikebreakers in South Side labor disputes, beginning in the 1890s.[46] Gradually an automatic association of "Negro" with "scab" developed in white workers' minds, especially after a failed stockyard strike in 1904. In the aftermath of the conflict, U.S. Senator Ben Tillman (a Democrat from South Carolina) came up to Chicago to address the defeated strikers, telling them the black workers were the source of their problem. Supported by a city alderman, he harped on the threats of "miscegenation" and "amalgamation." Finally he announced, "It was the niggers that whipped you into line. They were the club with which your brains were beaten out, if you ever had any!"[47]

As Nella Larsen approached graduation from the eighth grade in May 1905 and began thinking about high school, a teamsters strike—with its storm center just west of her home—"brought Chicago to the brink of a race riot."[48] The conflict began when the largely Scandinavian and female Special Order Garment Workers' Union went on strike against the large department stores for failing to honor promises against "section work" (subdividing pieces of clothing among different seamstresses), which they perceived as a step toward sweatshop conditions. Reformers attributed the tenacity of the Scandinavian women to inherited racial and cultural characteristics, including a democratic "spirit," high levels of education, and reverence for the dignity and value of skilled labor.[49]

Their cause was so appealing that the Teamsters Union joined in with a sympathy strike, and businesses came to a standstill. On May Day, merchants brought in African American "scabs" from Mississippi "levee" districts, provoking violent attacks on black drivers. Even the Chicago *Tribune* viewed this as a cynical attempt to destroy the Teamsters Union by sparking racial warfare.[50]

Hostility to blacks predictably centered just northwest of the Larsens' neighborhood. In the week after May 16 came a reign of terror. "Negroes were dragged from streetcars and beaten," writes historian Allan H. Spear, "and even heavy police guards, posted throughout the area, could not protect Negroes from white attacks."[51] Painted signs hung on either side of a rope stretched across the intersection of Wentworth and Twenty-Seventh: "Negroes not allowed to cross this Dead Line."[52] "Since the beginning of the teamsters' strike," the *Broad Ax* (a black newspaper) reported, "it has been impossible for any respectable colored man, woman or child to ride or walk in any section of the city without being grossly insulted and many times assaulted."[53]

When the conflict ended in June 1905, the Special Order Garment Workers'

Union was doomed. Manufacturers established open shops or took the United Garment Workers label. Many of the Scandinavian seamstresses, refusing to continue in what they considered demeaning conditions, turned to specialty dressmaking in their homes—Mary Larsen's own trade by at least 1910. The entire union movement declined for women garment workers in the aftermath. Similarly, the Teamsters admitted defeat, a devastating blow to local trade unions.[54]

The position of Nellie Larsen in the midst of all this could hardly have been worse. Not only was her mother a Scandinavian seamstress; her stepfather, a former teamster himself, belonged to a pugnacious union that was sympathetic to teamsters' concerns. Just two years earlier the Teamsters Union had struck in sympathy with the streetcar workers' union and helped them win one of Chicago's great labor battles. Now, for striking in sympathy with the "Swedish" seamstresses, they had been beaten, as many white union members saw it, by a demonic combination of "nigger scabs" and the police. After 1905, hostility toward black strikebreakers "generalized into hatred for the black race as a whole; any black man was a potential target."[55] Conversely, African Americans lost sympathy for a labor movement that, by and large, would have nothing to do with them.[56]

The strike dramatically affected the racial situation in the schools, and in June 1905 the school board redrew the school zones for Wendell Phillips High (which Nellie was about to enter) and Lake High School, immediately to the west, exactly following the Dead Line defined by the white rioters of the West Side. When classes resumed in September, whites in integrated districts began transferring their children to other schools. By December, such transfers had seriously cut attendance at five "mixed" schools, while "white" schools became badly overcrowded, creating a dilemma for the Board of Education, which feared that denying further transfers would provoke widespread anger in the South Side populace and racial conflict among the pupils. By 1908, Moseley School was about 50 percent black and plagued by constant fights.[57] In retrospect, the entire scenario scripted and rehearsed patterns that would characterize Northern urban life for the rest of the twentieth century.

The pressures for racial segregation, though resisted by the school board under Mayor Dunne, seemed relentless. In 1907 Dunne was defeated for reelection largely because of objections to the "radicals" running the school system, and because his base of support among union workers had eroded over his handling of the teamsters' strike. African Americans, on the other hand, felt he had not protected them from the white rioters.[58]

Though surely distressed by all the turmoil, Larsen kept up with her school-

47

work. In June 1905 she was one of only forty-six eighth graders from Colman recommended for promotion to Wendell Phillips High School. The school had been open only a year when Larsen entered as a freshman in the fall of 1905.[59] It was the most integrated high school in the city by far, but if, as Fannie Barrier Williams asserted, Phillips had "as many as two hundred Afro-American students," they made up less than one-eighth of the student body.[60] A three-and-a-half-story brick structure on Thirty-Ninth Street between Prairie and Forest Avenue (today South Giles)—then close to but outside the "black belt"—Phillips was also the biggest high school in the city but, with just thirty-four students per teacher and more than four hundred seats to spare, not nearly the most crowded—undoubtedly because it was integrated. Most high schools were overflowing.[61]

Freshmen took a core curriculum of English, German, Algebra, and Science.[62] Sophomores took Ancient History as well, which covered not only Greek and Roman history but that of the "Orient"—Babylon, Egypt, Assyria, the empires of Persia and Chaldea, and other ancient Asian civilizations in which Larsen maintained a strong interest into adulthood.[63] Larsen's English classes, in which she got her best grades, used methods developed by the pragmatist educational reformers who had taken control of the school board under Mayor Dunne and who had, since the 1890s, helped to make Chicago the storm center of educational reform in the United States. Jane Addams, John Dewey's friend and ally, chaired the school board's Committee on School Management, which set curricular policies, chose textbooks, and defined the aims and methods for all courses in the system. And Ella Flagg Young, another Dewey ally, headed the city's Normal School, which trained most of the city's teachers. They emphasized the need to integrate schoolwork with each child's experience as a member of a community and to build upon the child's inherent creativity instead of forcing the mind into predetermined patterns.

"The principal aim of the [English] teacher," the Committee on School Management stated, "is to know the attitude of the pupil's mind and to develop his individuality. Results should be measured in terms of the pupil's love of good literature and his ability to speak and write the mother tongue."[64] In the freshman year, the list of "classics" included works by Robert Browning, Edward Eggleston, Washington Irving, Charles Lamb, James Russell Lowell, Thomas Macaulay, Charles Dudley Warner, John Greenleaf Whittier, assorted short stories by a range of nineteenth-century British and American authors, the Arabian Nights, Cooper, Dickens, Scott, Shakespeare, and Robert Louis Stevenson. It was a distinctly modern reading list, supplemented by "outside" books each student chose for herself. Sophomore-year readings moved to literary works that stressed characterization, setting, and ethical intention over plot. Weighted toward Dickens, Homer, Scott, and Shakespeare, the reading list also included Matthew Arnold's *Sohrab and Rustum*, R. D. Blackmore's *Lorna Doone*, Byron's *Prisoner of Chillon* and *Mazeppa*, George Washington Cable's *Creole Days*, Plutarch's *Lives*, and Tennyson's *Idylls of the King*.

But the very heart of the English course, in tune with the pragmatist pedagogy, was creative writing—chiefly fiction and autobiography. As a freshman, Larsen learned the essentials of plot structure and how to select incidents based on probability, interest, and narrative unity. She was taught to describe landscape, interiors, and personal appearance; how to gather material, determine point of view, and create "order in space"—excellent preparation for fiction writing. Her sophomore course, again emphasizing creative writing, moved to more complex narrative and descriptive strategies, "to present character and mood in themselves and as influencing situation." Authorial intrusion was "out"; pupils learned the dramatic method in fiction-writing, allowing the speech and action of characters in their relations with each other to create the meaning and emotional timbre of the story.[65] Although Larsen also practiced "elementary exposition" in her sophomore year, the emphasis fell on fiction and autobiography. The teachers at Phillips gave her the only formal training she probably ever received in the kind of writing for which we know her today. As a sophomore, she got her best grades in English (89.5) and history (87.5)—strong grades indeed for 1906–1907, but she got an F in second-year German. She also took free-hand drawing but did not receive a grade in that subject.[66]

The social life at Phillips was marked by secret fraternities and sororities, and —since there was a fairly large black student body—various cliques among the black students; but if Larsen sought inclusion in these, she would probably have found her way impeded by her family circumstances. Given her questionable paternity and white immigrant working-class family background, Larsen's relationship to the black "society" girls at Phillips, regardless of her academic success, could not have been simple. After all, the black children who went on to high school were usually of the Negro upper crust—people who looked down on working-class immigrants even if they themselves were not much better off financially. A number of Phillips students later ended up in Harlem when Larsen was there; some of them knew her from their schooldays, but she did not socialize with them, and she would never be listed among those attending functions of the rather large "Chicago club" in Harlem, which often entertained visitors from the Windy City.

The social mingling of black and white was, of course, always on people's minds, another constant reminder of Nella's marginal status. In December 1904, residents and property owners in the vicinity of Phillips had even petitioned the school board to "discontinue" the newly opened, integrated student lunch room there. (The board refused the request.)[67] Fearing black "immorality," some white parents insisted on segregating the social events, arguing, in one parent's words, "Unless this separation is made you will ruin the future generation and debauch your home."[68] On the other hand, blacks in the district were not about to go to the wall for such frivolous things as interracial dancing in social rooms or integrated "social hours" at the school. Fearing that a conflagration over social mixing would shut them out of white schools and institutions, they did not openly object to the lines drawn against interracial intimacy.[69] After all, they had their own society and did not, for the most part, want white company, with its usual range of condescension, pity, and scorn.

While a wedge was driven between white and black labor, members of the black poor and working class naturally identified their interests with those of black professionals, who, on the one hand, maintained a strong sense of social and class distinction—what Larsen later called snobbishness—and, on the other, depended on the black masses as clients and as a political constituency. Larsen's own fiction would depict the black elite's sense of identity as dependent both on the absolute division between black and white and on social stratification within the "black community." Such dynamics, coupled with the class and racial dynamics of the immigrant working class, left persons such as Nella Larsen in an alienated and abject position—one that might well nourish a carefully veiled yet fiercely independent intelligence. In Larsen, they bred an attitude of sardonic skepticism toward all collective notions of identity, with their attendant idealizations of the "group"; a strongly developed sense of irony; and a private unwillingness or inability to fully identify with either the class from which she came or that to which her own future was ineluctably tied. This new class is pointedly represented in *Quicksand* through the character of Mrs. Hayes-Rore, widow of a South Side politician who at the time of the story is a nationally renowned clubwoman and orator. As Helga Crane tells her a story much like the one Larsen told of her own life, Hayes-Rore turns her face away, feeling that "the story, dealing as it did with race intermingling and possibly adultery, was beyond definite discussion. For among black people, as among white people, it is tacitly understood that these things are not mentioned—and therefore they do not exist."[70] She then advises Helga not to tell anyone in Harlem about her background: "Negroes," she says, "won't understand it." Excluded from white society, Larsen had reason to feel alienated from black society as well; but it was a society into which she had to integrate, or else.

In stark contrast to "Nellie," Anna Larsen never went to high school.[71] Indeed, she would always be of the working class and live in close proximity to her mother, especially after developing multiple sclerosis in adulthood. The two girls had to be cared for differently. Mary Larsen was especially concerned that her first child receive good schooling—an education far better than the average. Nella was one of only 12,400 Chicagoans enrolled in secondary school in 1905, when the city's population totaled nearly two million. In 1906, only 1,169 students graduated in all of Chicago.[72] To most working-class people, high school seemed unnecessary.

The extreme dearth of employment options for black women in Chicago, and elsewhere, demanded special efforts to keep Nellie out of a life of misery and despair. Even single women who were white, without advanced education, could face a bleak future if they did not find a husband who was a steady provider, as Mary Larsen herself well knew. Her mulatto daughter, because of her family background and suspect origins, could not count on a "good" marriage to a rising young man, black or white; nor could she get the sort of clerical and shopkeeping jobs many white women of her class took up. She would have to be prepared for one of the few professions open to Negro women—mainly teaching, nursing, or librarianship. Teaching was most attractive; black teachers in Chicago denied experiencing any racial prejudice in their hiring or placement at this time, while virtually all other occupations were either closed to black women or rigidly segregated.[73] Offering both job security and prestige, teaching required a certificate from a "normal school," and it was on this that Larsen set her sights.

In early August 1907 Mary and Peter Larsen bought a house on West Seventieth Place, only a few blocks away from the Chicago Normal School, which was the usual route to a teaching position in the Chicago public schools for both black and white teachers-to-be. As part of the public school system, Chicago Normal would have cost nothing but book fees. Its principal, Ella Flagg Young, had consistently stood up against racial discrimination. One of the great educators of the era (the first woman president of the National Education Association), she had made the Chicago teaching force among the most progressive in the nation.[74]

Why, then, did the Larsens send Nellie to Fisk University for teacher preparation? Possibly Larsen applied to Chicago Normal and was rejected or did not get a high enough score on the entrance examination. More likely, the family had decided Chicago was not the place for her. Their new neighborhood, Englewood, was all white and hostile to blacks, and Anna was fifteen, old enough for a working-class girl in those days to begin worrying about marriage prospects. Besides, Nellie had nothing to gain by staying with them. It was time for her to find her place in the Negro world to which they would never belong.

One of the most respected institutions of the race, Fisk could prepare Larsen admirably for entry into the higher echelons of that world. Fisk graduates could be found in prestigious posts all over the country. Moreover, many marriages came out of relationships formed at the school, where men far outnumbered women.[75] But Fisk required a stiff sacrifice on the part of the Larsen family. Tuition and board, including laundry, cost $12 per month, plus a $4 annual fee and incidental expenses, at a time when Peter was making about $60 per month and he and Mary had taken on a new mortgage. Minimum annual living expenses for a working-class family of four were estimated to average $66 per month in Chicago at the time.[76] It is safe to assume that Mary Larsen sent Nella to Fisk on her profits from dressmaking.

When Nella left for Nashville in the fall of 1907, her Chicago years were over, but they left an enduring imprint on her personality. The relentless pressures on her most intimate relationships bred a chronic fear of abandonment she would never be able to shake. Keenly sensitive to the stigma of blackness, on the one hand, and that of presumed illegitimacy on the other, she adopted a protective mask of diffidence and intense self-restraint. As much as she longed for intimacy, she would always be ready to break off with people before they could break off with her. She was used to being on the outside, attentive to hypocrisy and accustomed to slights. She approached group identity cautiously. To what "group," after all, had Nellie Larsen ever really belonged? Hadn't groups always spelled trouble for her, inhabiting as she did the bristling borders along which they faced off? But maybe Fisk would be different. There, sheltered by Jubilee Hall and surrounded by African Americans—her "people," as fate would have it —perhaps the dark daughter would come into her own.

[FOUR]

Turning South: Nashville and Fisk, 1907–1908

TRAILING a long plume of black smoke and white vapor, the train clicked past Jackson Park and Oakwoods Cemetery, crossing street and cable line where wagons, streetcars, and pedestrians stood watching. The bells clanged and clanged. Across Seventy-First Street, Seventy-Third, came the new suburbs, high grass, and then the wide hush of the prairie. Rolling south on the Illinois Central, gazing now and then over the neat rows of high-tasseled corn that stretched to the horizon on every side, Larsen prepared herself for new experiences. A few hours, and the plains began wrinkling into low ridges and tree-covered hills. After crossing the Ohio River, the train stopped at Hopkinsville, Kentucky, where the passengers got up to stretch their legs and grab their bags. There was a general shift of seating, and Larsen was introduced to the Jim Crow car.[1]

If her mother was with her—one suspects she was not—they were separated at this point. Nellie could not have sat with her mother, could not enter the dining car, probably could not use a "ladies'" lavatory or restroom on the train.[2] Upon arrival at Nashville's Union Station, the city's pride, she was not allowed into the lofty magnificence of the lobby, or into the dining room, the lunch room, or the ladies' waiting room. One "colored" waiting room accommodated men and women of her race together.[3]

From the station she boarded the Jefferson Street trolley, and here, too, she could not have sat with anyone in her family. Just two years earlier, on the day after the Fourth of July, the state legislature had passed a law segregating the streetcars.[4] Another Chicagoan raised by his white mother in the absence of his black father described the shock of moving to a black college in the South at this time and encountering a "wide and bridgeless gulf between the races. . . . In the North, an ambitious Negro bumps into the colour line unexpectedly, on the street cars, in hotels, theatres, parks, public buildings and schools, on trains, in pleasure resorts, or at the polls, and even in the church of Christ. Yet he may go a week or a year, sometimes, without meeting with any *unusually* humiliating experience. In the South he is given immediately and unmistakably to understand that he must get definitely on his side of the colour line, and *stay* there."[5] All this was epitomized in the uniquely Southern signs one found nearly everywhere: "For COLORED People" / "For WHITE People."[6]

When Larsen stepped off the streetcar onto Jefferson Street at the campus entrance, she saw a broad open lawn with several large, relatively new buildings arranged in a quadrangle, Jubilee Hall rising regally above them all, a symbol of the race's progress. A bust of Abraham Lincoln presided over the entrance on the south façade, and the area in front of it was known as Victoria Square, in honor of the queen's kindness to the Jubilee Singers during their triumphant European tour.[7] The building itself, which served as the women's dormitory, fairly breathed Victorian splendor. The city of Nashville had few structures to rival it. One later star of the Harlem Renaissance, Roland Hayes, recently arrived when Larsen matriculated, remembered his own first impressions of "lawns and lanes . . . dominated by the cupolas and dormers of a shining palace. . . . I had not thought that so splendid a structure existed this side of the moon."[8] Larsen, who knew the Masonic Temple of Chicago and other great buildings fronting Lake Michigan, might not have been as awed as Hayes was, but the campus would have been impressive nonetheless for a girl raised in working-class tenements. And she was to live in its palace, with formal parlors flanking the entryway and a queenly staircase rising in a broad sweep to the dormitory above.

The girls' and women's housing in Jubilee Hall, the architectural symbol of the university, expressed the sense of their sacred role in the race's progress. According to the university catalogue, the "elevation and advancement of the race" depended on "the *right education* of the girls and young women of the race. . . . The highest interest of every race and community depends largely upon the intelligence, frugality, virtue, and noble aspirations of its women."[9]

Soon after arrival, Larsen bought a navy blue uniform, one of the two outfits required—the other being a plain white shirtwaist suit she probably brought from home. "As these serve for all public occasions," the catalogue stiffly informed, "there will be no use for other than everyday dresses."[10] A hat to match was "furnished at Jubilee Hall at the lowest wholesale prices."[11] Silk, satin, and expensive trimmings were forbidden and jewelry was discouraged.[12] Notably, in the one known photograph of Larsen from about the time she attended Fisk, she is wearing an attractive necklace with a jeweled pendant, and a delicate white blouse with a plunging neckline, trimmed in fine lace. She stares directly into the camera with large, slightly prominent eyes under thick black eyebrows, her long, dark brown hair drawn up into a bun.

She registered as "Nellie Marie Larsen," a third-year student in the Normal Preparatory course.[13] We have no way of knowing at what point she had ac-

3. Nella Larsen, circa 1907. Photographer unknown. Moorland-Spingarn Research Center, Howard University.

quired her mother's Christian name as a middle name, but for the rest of her life she would continue to use variations of it in formal situations—professional correspondence, official forms, and the like. (She may have had the name since birth. Her sister's full name was "Anna Elizabeth Larsen," though her birth certificate reads "Lizzie Larson.") It clearly marked a bond she felt with her mother at this stage of her life, when they were first separated and beginning to move in different spheres.

For Nellie Larsen this was, to say the least, a new world. Practically one-third of Nashville's population was Negro, compared to one-fiftieth of Chicago's. The city was bidding fair to become the Negro capital of the "New South." Having grown up on one of Chicago's major thoroughfares, Larsen found herself on a green campus of thirty-five acres on Nashville's outskirts where, a decade earlier, razorback hogs had grazed. Students rarely left campus, where racial insults of the immediate, personal sort hardly existed.

Larsen was accustomed to being one of the few "colored" students in a sea of whites. Here there were no white students. Fisk's total enrollment of 364 for its Normal and College divisions was not even one-fourth of her Chicago high school's enrollment. Larsen had always lived in a racially mixed and working-class immigrant world, as well as a union household. Here the community generally frowned on both immigrants and unions. "Union men," the student newspaper complained in a feature editorial that fall, "never seem to be satisfied. The ranks are being crowded with foreigners who come to this country to stay long enough to acquire a little wealth. They are mainly the ones who continually create disturbances. . . . Now unions are becoming obnoxious and a menace to the world's progress. They endanger life and property through strikes; they harass employers; they are disastrous to industry; they cause an increase in prices making those not concerned suffer." And of course they were generally closed to black men: "The colored man with a trade stands little show where unions exist."[14]

Whereas Larsen had probably never been religious, here African American Protestantism was especially strong. "The religious atmosphere of Fisk University has always been of the best," boasted the *Fisk Herald* shortly after she arrived. "The students come largely from the best churches among the Negroes in the South. Usually the persons who come to Fisk are among the most earnest young people in the communities from which they come."[15] Yet there was one comfort, the sweetest compensation of a segregated world. Fisk was a place where, as Larsen would later write apropos of a fictional school called Devon, "for the first time she could breathe freely, where she discovered that because one was dark, one was not necessarily loathsome, and could, therefore, consider oneself without repulsion."[16] The students were all black together, cocooned within colored Nashville.

The area around Fisk was a black residential district, and not far away were Greenwood Cemetery and Greenwood Park, for blacks only. The black community had its own medical facility and nursing school, Mercy Hospital; and next to Fisk was Walden University, with its Meharry Medical College. The National Baptist Publishing House and A.M.E. Sunday School Union were based in Nashville, the headquarters of the religious and business concerns of the dominant African American churches of the day.[17] Nashville was the communications capital of black Christianity in the United States. A white-authored guide to Nashville of 1912 expressed pride in the city's black institutions, which were careful not to challenge the doctrine of "separate development."[18]

The school, established in 1866, still sounded a strong missionary note, with nearly all of its board members living in Boston and New York, and most of them holding doctorates in Divinity.[19] In contrast, the student population came overwhelmingly from the South. Of 119 students in the Normal Department when Larsen was there, only ten were from the North, four of them being Chicagoans.[20] The only other Northerner in her class of twenty was Grace Virginia Frank of Dundee, New York. Many long-time professors (nearly all white) had sacrificed opportunities for more lucrative and prestigious appointments in their zeal to further the cause of Negro "progress," and had moved far from their New England homes to a city in which they were social pariahs. Their salaries, mainly paid by the American Missionary Association, in most cases fell below the wages of Chicago streetcar conductors.[21] Not surprisingly, they tended to be religious zealots. The school's rule of faith was patterned after that of Oberlin College, which preached the "voluntary total depravity of the unregenerate and the unalterable necessity of a radical change of heart by the Holy Ghost."[22]

The president, Reverend James G. Merrill, a (white) native of Massachusetts educated at Amherst College and Princeton Theological Seminary before the Civil War, had been editor of the *Christian Mirror* prior to joining the Fisk faculty in 1898. His motto for Fisk: "The development of Christian manhood in an education for service."[23] Roland Hayes, trying to gain admission to the school in 1905, found him terrifying, with a stern bespectacled gaze peering out between a "big Roman nose and heavy, overhanging eyebrows": "'The man is an eagle,' I said to myself. 'He is the American eagle himself.'"[24]

At the turn of the century, the popularity of "industrial education" for African Americans had crippled fundraising efforts for classical liberal arts colleges like Fisk. In 1907–1908, the General Education Board, an important university benefactor that supported black education in the South, had given Fisk nothing while allocating $80,000 to promote good farming techniques.[25] In contrast, Fisk, in the words of its president, did "not expect to make farmers, carpenters, masons, laundrywomen, dressmakers."[26] It intended to make race leaders, through rigid discipline in academics and conduct. For the college students, this meant a challenging course of study in Greek, Latin, and Mathematics, as well as constant emphasis on the Bible in and out of class.

The new principal of the Normal Department—also its first, since previously the department had functioned without a principal as such—Mrs. Minnie L. Crosthwait, was herself African American, and a graduate of both the Normal Department and the College at Fisk.[27] Her appointment presaged the gradual shift from white to black leadership of the institution over the next three decades, as new generations of college-educated African Americans took over formerly white-missionary-directed institutions and the whites, increasingly unwanted in positions that were black professionals' only opportunities for advancement, withdrew or were cast out.

All the new students took an examination at the end of September, in English and any other subjects they wished to count as equivalents for courses at Fisk. They also had to bring a statement about the nature of their prior work in each branch of study.[28] Nella's "F" in German was of no particular consequence, since Fisk required Latin rather than a modern language, but she did have to make up for weaknesses in Geography, Advanced Algebra, and Mythology (an English course), in addition to starting Latin two years behind others in her class.[29]

The curriculum differed dramatically from what Larsen had known in Chicago. Students had no choice in classes, and within the literature classes they had no choice in what they read. Variations occurred only when, as in Larsen's case, a student transferring to the school had to make up required work. Larsen's five-hour-per-week courses for the year consisted of thirty-six weeks of first-year Latin and Plane Geometry, eighteen weeks of Advanced Algebra, twelve weeks of Mythology, twelve weeks of Rhetoric, six weeks of Grammar Review, and six weeks of Geography Review. Third-year students also took one-hour classes in Vocal Music, Elocution, Writing, and Drawing.[30] All boarding students also had to attend two periods of Physical Education each week, which for girls consisted of such "hygienic" exercises as marching, lifting weights, roller skating, basketball, tennis, indoor baseball, and "fancy steps."[31]

The Mythology class consisted of the study of Greek, Teutonic, and Celtic myths in Margaret Mooney's *Foundation Studies in Literature,* with Webster's *Composition and Literature* as a supplementary text. The Formal Rhetoric course went through the whole of Webster's *Composition and Literature,* covering word usage, sentence and paragraph structure, outlining, and "the five forms of discourse."[32] A far cry from the creative-writing emphasis in Chicago. The study of Mythology, in which Larsen got her best grades, stuck with her, and her interest in the topic would find expression in her own fiction, notably *Quicksand*, which makes extensive and ingenious use of Greek mythology in particular. All Normal School students took music through the third year; Larsen was placed in the first level of the Music Department, beginning piano, along with Booker T. Washington, Jr.[33]

The academic schedule was highly ritualized, almost monastic, punctuated by ringing bells from 5:45 A.M. until "lights out" at 9:45 P.M. Classes ran from 8:35 until 3:35, and an enforced two-hour study period began at 7:00 P.M. Students ate together in the dining hall for each meal, following a prayer. Slight variations occurred for Wednesday evening chapel meetings and Saturday nights, when students could socialize between 8:30 and 10:00 P.M. On Sundays, everyone met at church service in the morning and vespers in the late afternoon.[34]

Extracurricular activities for girls included three literary and artistic societies, which were said to provide "admirable drill in writing and speaking, also discipline in parliamentary usage."[35] But we have no way of knowing if Larsen belonged to any of these. The main extracurricular activity, by far, was worship. The fall that Larsen arrived, a religious awakening took hold on campus, inspiring many conversions. President Merrill noted that the "week of prayer" at the beginning of the academic year had been "phenomenal in its results."[36] And the Young Ladies Society of Christian Endeavor, the campus newspaper noted, attracted an unusually large pledge class among the new students.[37]

In the fall everyone came out for the weekend football games between the "Blue and Gold" and other black colleges, on Bennett Field, in the middle of campus. Every other Friday evening, the chapel was the scene of compulsory "Public Exercises" consisting of lectures, recitals, and elocutionary readings brimming with puritan earnestness and Victorian idealism. A good example is the program of November 8, 1907, which began with a piano solo, followed by the invocation by President Merrill. There followed a voice solo, "Anchored," by Michael Watson; then a student reading of W. E. B. Du Bois's essay "Garrison and the Negro." Next two girls read their essays, "A Wonderful City" and "A Summer Lesson in Temperance." Then came readings of "Brave Kate Shelly" and Longfellow's "The Legend Beautiful," another piano solo, a student oration entitled "True Manhood," a declamation of Homer's "Hector and Achilles," an essay entitled "A Critique of the Sky Pilot," another entitled "The Inhabitability of Other Worlds," a voice solo ("Goodnight, Dennee"), a reading of "The Story the Doctor Told," a declamation of Cushing's "New England," an oration called "The Star of the Unconquered Will," an essay entitled "The Need of Missionaries in Africa," and finally the Fisk Glee Club singing "Sailor's Chorus."[38]

As fall passed into winter and the days grew shorter, visitors and professors gave special lectures during the evening exercises, often on "race" subjects. In December the Jubilee Club performed an original cantata, "From Out of the Depths," by Professor J. W. Work.[39] Inspired by the stories of former slaves and built around the spirituals, Work's composition contributed to the canonization of black folk song and its integration with European traditions of "art music" years before the "Negro Renaissance" brought such efforts (in the person of Roland Hayes himself, who sang in the cantata that winter) to the great performance halls of New York, Paris, and London. The program drew Nashville's most "cultured" white citizens to Jim Crow seating on the Friday and Saturday after Christmas—one reason for the students' growing dissatisfaction with school policies about concerts.[40] It managed to celebrate African American culture without upsetting the white elite, by portraying a Tennessee plantation with many slaves and plenty of religious services—in which, according to the local black newspaper, all delighted.[41]

Larsen got to know some of the male students—including, almost certainly, Roland Hayes—but at sixteen she was too young to go on dates. Even after she turned seventeen, in April 1908, she still could not venture off campus without a chaperon, according to university rules.[42] At a time when white Nashville expressed its contempt for blacks in its refusal to acknowledge them in public accommodations as "Ladies" and "Gentlemen," the administration and faculty of Fisk zealously enforced Victorian gender mores. As Hayes would recall, "It was . . . a rule at Fisk that students should be under constant surveillance." Boys had to ask permission to meet with girls, and when they arrived at the dormitory, they were "met by a chaperon who sat in plain sight throughout the evening. Girls were only rarely permitted to go out after dark, and then they went in squads, led by lady sergeant-majors."[43] On a typical date, a boy would present himself to the preceptress at Jubilee Hall, make a polite bow to the girl he was to take out, and then accompany her, in procession, to the chapel for a rhetorical program. At the end of the program, they would return in the same fashion to Jubilee Hall, and there the boy would take his leave. "That was about as much of each other's society as Fisk boys and girls were allowed to have."[44] They could not stop and pass the time of day on campus together, nor could they ever see each other alone. And if a boy took the same girl to chapel two weeks in a row, he had to take a different girl the next time.

The school did provide opportunities for the sexes to mingle. At the "George Washington Social" in Jubilee Hall on the eve of Washington's birthday, each student, upon entering, received a souvenir card in the shape of a hatchet, inscribed with five topics of conversation and blank spaces, as on a dance card, "for the names of five persons whom the bearer could select at will, to discuss the subjects with." Two cherry trees were placed in the parlors, and the students, wearing blindfolds, attached their hatchets as close as possible to a slash-mark near the base of each tree, much as in "Pin the Tail on the Donkey." Music and marching in the dining room followed. The whole evening concluded with a singing of the national hymn, "America," and a prayer by President Merrill.[45]

In the late winter of 1907–1908, a tantalizing notice in the campus newspaper reported: "Mrs. Larsen, of Chicago, spent a few days with her daughter."[46] We have no way of knowing what they talked about, but the sixteen-year-old girl must have been longing for her mother after several months away from home. Nella probably didn't yet feel as if she really belonged at Fisk. On holidays such as Christmas, the other students had "people" to visit or receive, whereas she seemed not to have any "people." In the informal intervals of daily life, other students were accustomed to the rituals, expression, faith, and customs of the Black South. They could fall in with each other's ways freely and unselfconsciously, whereas for Larsen attempts to fit in felt staged, a little awkward. And these alternated with the frequently staged formal occasions in which behavior followed the highly mannered choreography of Jim Crow. The behavior, the very shape of feeling, in each realm was conditioned by the rituals of the other.

On May 22, a Friday, the entire Fisk community came together at a ceremony in which Secretary of War William Howard Taft, then running for president on the Republican ticket, laid the cornerstone of the new library funded by Andrew Carnegie. A bad thunderstorm had hit the area at noon, but by 2:00 the sky had cleared and a crowd gathered on Bennett Field. The students entered in a procession from the college gate, led by the Glee Club and singing the college songs. Taft gave a short, patronizing speech on the progress of the race and the need for institutions such as Fisk to educate professionals and race leaders, at the same time expressing his belief in the "Booker T. Washington doctrine" of making others see how indispensable the Negro could be to the nation: as Negroes became more valuable members of society, he averred, race problems would disappear. "The speech was received with great enthusiasm and applause," the *Nashville Globe* reported, "for it seemed sincerely meant."[47] The dean of the university then placed fifty articles of historical importance in a box and Taft laid the cornerstone, the crowd laughing as he called jestingly for extra mortar.

Taft's appearance at Fisk was part of a frantic effort on the government's part to win back the faith of African American voters in the wake of the "Brownsville Affair" of 1906. President Theodore Roosevelt had dismissed three companies of black soldiers "without honor" and without trial for allegedly "shooting up the town" of Brownsville, Texas—a completely unsubstantiated charge that infuriated African Americans throughout the country. Moreover, white Republicans in Southern states had started excluding blacks from party conventions, shaking African American allegiance to the party of Lincoln. Although Taft had briefly suspended Roosevelt's dismissal of the soldiers on his own authority, some of his own statements on the "Negro problem" seemed to countenance segregation. The question of whether Negroes should, or would, vote for him was getting widespread coverage in black periodicals in the spring and summer of 1908.[48] A lengthy political analysis in the *New York Times* that May concluded, "It must be admitted that Brownsville has created a new phase in American politics."[49] At issue was a growing division between black and white Republicans, the sense of a separate political identity that comported with the general chasm opening between whites and blacks in every phase of life across the republic.

The chasm was opening at Fisk itself. A shift in generational and racial sensibilities first became evident to school administrators during Larsen's year there, as a growing number of students, including Roland Hayes, interpreted the strictures on their social and sexual lives as not only outmoded but racially motivated. The largely white faculty, some believed, acted on stereotypical notions of Negro "immorality." Such suspicions may well have been merited, but part of the problem was that, isolated and aging as they were, the faculty were out of touch with the world beyond the campus gates. In fact, the administration grew even more rigid in its approach to "morality" as it felt the threat of change on the horizon.[50]

During the latter part of the school year, submitting his resignation to the Board of Trustees (mainly in frustration over his inability to raise adequate funds), President Merrill stated: "The last part of the year has had some serious cases of discipline and there has been a spirit of unrest, possibly due to the general attitude of the Negro, as seen especially in their relation to President Roosevelt and the Brownsville affair."[51] A letter from the junior and senior classes to Fisk's president and Prudential Committee complained that just one chaperon went to town only once a week, so that "young ladies" were stuck on campus virtually every day. And because of the conduct of one "young lady," women were no longer allowed "to take walks after supper with a chaperon." More insultingly, a new rule had been passed "restricting the wearing of jewelry by young ladies to one ring, and requiring them to wear uniform on all social occasions, because a few have dressed in a manner contrary to the wishes of several of the faculty."[52] The latter complaint has the marks of Nella Larsen all over it.

The faculty responded on June 10 by reaffirming the "rules regarding extravagant and expensive dress and jewelry." On June 13 they "voted that the following students be not allowed to return to the university next year: Misses Lexie Cope, Edna Cameron, Alma Delavallade, Lenora Cowan, Nellie Larsen, Madeline Duncan, Octavia Weakley, Maggie Cheatham, and Messrs. Earl Deis, Purnell Deis, and Holland Register."[53]

For Larsen the announcement was devastating. Admittedly, her grades were mediocre: her lowest mark was in Latin, a 63; she'd gotten a 76 in Plane Geometry, a 77 in Grammar Review, a 78 in Rhetoric, a 79 in Geography Review, an 81 in Algebra, and an 87 in Mythology.[54] But by the standards of the day these marks would not merit expulsion, and one suspects that she had broken some regulation of dress or conduct.[55] This suspicion is strengthened by the disproportionate number of girls who were expelled with her. Her attack on dress codes in black educational institutions in her first novel, coupled with the problems she said she had over this issue at Tuskegee in 1916–1917, strongly suggests that this problem first arose at Fisk. But the problem went way beyond Fisk, or "Negro" institutions. As Larsen grew up, she would discover that very few opportunities for a black woman were free of this constraint: the insistence that she allow herself to be dressed by others.

Larsen's feelings on leaving Fisk seem to have inspired her description of Helga Crane's feelings upon leaving a black boarding school at about the same age: "She had been happy there, as happy as a child unused to happiness dared be. There had always been a feeling of strangeness, of outsideness, and one of holding her breath for fear that it wouldn't last. It hadn't. It had dwindled gradually into eclipse of painful isolation. As she grew older, she became gradually aware of a difference between herself and the girls about her. They had mothers, fathers, brothers, and sisters of whom they spoke frequently, and who sometimes visited them. They went home for the vacations which Helga spent in the city where the school was located. They visited each other and knew many of the same people. Discontent for which there was no remedy crept upon her, and she was glad almost when these most peaceful years which she had yet known came to their end. She had been happier, but still horribly lonely."[56] All the key elements of the description match the situation of Nellie Larsen in the spring of 1908, except for the fact that her mother had visited her once, at least. Helga Crane's mother was dead.

Yet however lonely Larsen may have been at Fisk, her expulsion was a terrible blow. What was to become of her? Where could she turn now?

FIVE

Coming of Age in Copenhagen:
1908–1912

SHE turned to her mother's people in Denmark. Leaving behind the color line, she would begin a new life. She had not seen her relatives since the age of seven and her Danish was rusty, but childhood memories and the bonds of family remained—thicker than the waters of the Hudson as passengers lined the rails of the steamer and the crew flew into frantic motion, casting off lines, battening down. Larsen later described something like it in *Quicksand:* a scene of wet cheeks, soft crying, drawn handkerchiefs, names called out, a girl on her own. The slate-colored waters churned below while oscillating gulls hovered within arm's length. As the ship reached the outer bay, ripples became waves, the gulls wheeled off toward the receding skyscrapers astern, and passengers returned to their cabins to unpack. Soon it came time for the first meal. How would she be received in the second-class dining salon? With whom could she sit? What would it be like in Denmark, to be speaking Danish again, without her mother as a bridge?

There is good reason to believe that she and her family considered this a possibly permanent move. From the time she left Fisk in June 1908 until May 1912, when she entered Lincoln Hospital and Home Training School for Nurses in the Bronx, the only contemporary documentation of her whereabouts is a ship's manifest of January 1909 marking her return from a trip to Denmark and giving her address in Chicago. Larsen consistently maintained that she had lived in Denmark with her mother's relatives during the years between her departure from Fisk and her entry into nursing school, and she seems to have been telling the truth.

In her handwritten biography for Knopf's publicity department in 1926, which gave her birth year as 1893 (rather than 1891), Larsen wrote: "When she was sixteen she went alone to Denmark to visit relatives of her mother's in Copenhagen where she remained for three years. On her return to America she entered a training school for nurses in New York City."[1] She used the same statement in her application for a Harmon Foundation award in 1928–1929. Her Guggenheim Fellowship application of 1929 says that she was an "auditor" at the

University of Copenhagen from 1910 to 1912 but received no degree, diploma, or certificate. That application also says she had a "fairly fluent" speaking knowledge of Danish, as well as "good" reading ability and "fair" writing ability in the language—which is about what one would expect if she had lived there for some time as a young child and then again for three years in her late teens, nearly twenty years before she filled out the application.[2] In a 1929 interview Larsen said she lived in Denmark from age seventeen to age twenty-one, a stretch of time perfectly corresponding to the period between her expulsion from Fisk and her matriculation at nursing school.[3] But in the midst of this period she came home for a visit, which explains why she said she lived in Denmark for three years rather than four.

The most detailed record of Larsen's whereabouts, and the one nearest in time to her trip as a teenager, appears in her 1922 application for admission to the Library School of the New York Public Library, a document previously unknown to scholars. Here, one must make allowances for the fact that to have any chance of admission Larsen had to claim she had considerably more formal education than she could prove, for she had no high school diploma or proof of college enrollment, at a time when the school normally required a diploma and preferred a college degree. Larsen changed her birth year from 1891 to 1892 and, to accord with this, moved a number of other dates forward one year, including those for her attendance at Fisk and her trip to Denmark. She wrote that she had attended middle school in Askov, Jutland, from 1909 to 1910, and then had moved to Copenhagen and taken an "open course" at the University of Copenhagen from 1910 to 1912. This suggests that she may have stayed in the Askov area from 1908 to 1909, returned home for a visit (the independently verifiable trip), and then gone back to live in Copenhagen for two or three years. In response to a question about travel and other relevant experience, she wrote that she had traveled in Denmark from 1900 to 1903, and in Denmark, Norway, and Sweden from 1909 to 1912.[4] The first of these trips obviously refers to her journey of the late 1890s with her mother and half-sister. From Copenhagen Larsen could well have visited Norway and Sweden, both of which were an easy ferry ride from the harbor. We know that all of her claims from the point of her entry into nursing school are accurate. There is, then, scant reason to doubt that Larsen spent all or most of her time in Copenhagen between leaving Fisk and entering Lincoln.

She first returned to the United States, alone, on the steamer *C. F. Tietgen,* which left Copenhagen on January 14, 1909. At Larsensplads, "Nelly" Larsen was one of fifty second-class passengers who ascended the gangplank; 114 boarded for steerage berths. This was the first departure of one of the "Amerikabaadene"

(America-ships) of the year, and the newspaper *Politiken* had a reporter at the scene. Despite inclement weather, "a great many people flocked around the ship to bid farewell to the many travelers, . . . the greater part of them Christmas visitors returning home."[5] The ship crossed over to Norway and stopped for a day at Christiania (now Oslo), then continued to Christiansand, from which it sailed January 17 for a twelve-day voyage.[6] Twenty-one of the second-class passengers, including Larsen, were U.S. citizens. Nelly's nationality was listed as American, of course, but the ship's surgeon, Dr. C. A. Larsen, identified her "race or people" as "Scandinavian," despite explicit instructions that anyone with a visible "admixture of Negro blood" was to be listed as "African (black)." It may be that the surgeon was not required to examine U.S. citizens, or perhaps he simply felt that identifying Larsen as African was absurd. She had no occupation, being listed simply as "Miss," as were most young single women, and she was returning to her "parents" at the home of Mr. Peter Larsen, "143–W–70 Str.," Chicago. Her age had been listed initially as seventeen, but this was crossed out, apparently on arrival in New York, and "18" was written over it. In truth, she would turn eighteen in April.[7]

This trip, notably, does not match the one in *Quicksand:* Helga Crane leaves for New York on a clear spring day after two years in Denmark, planning to return in the fall. It is puzzling that Larsen has her protagonist intending to return to Denmark even though she has already made up her mind not to marry a Danish man and is disillusioned with her host-relatives. Larsen realized that having Crane return to Denmark would have marred the plot of *Quicksand,* needlessly stringing it out. Helga never does return, but ends up being "born again" and marrying a Southern preacher. The return trip in *Quicksand* would seem to be a composite of the two return trips Larsen herself had probably made, the first in January 1909 and the second in the spring of 1912.

That no other passenger list identifies Larsen after the 1909 return to Chicago does not mean she remained in the United States between then and 1912, for some lists have been lost. Specifically, the passenger manifests of the steamship *Hellig Olav,* which arrived in New York on April 17, 1912, are missing (probably because of the turmoil that followed the *Titanic's* sinking on the fifteenth), and these are the very records in which Larsen's name would most likely appear.[8] Two weeks after the ship's landing, Larsen began nursing school in New York. Moreover, the mid-April date of return corresponds with the description of Helga Crane's return in *Quicksand.* Larsen was not living in Chicago in 1910. It is conceivable that she was traveling or in some other place in the United States, but considering the consistency of her own accounts of the period, and her lack of American connections outside Chicago, one can only conclude that she was living in Denmark and expected to stay there.

She could not have stayed in Chicago for long after January 1909. The family home on West Seventieth Place was not a safe harbor. Englewood was a particularly unfriendly place for a black teenager, since residents feared the southward movement of black citizens. In the fall of 1908 a wave of antiblack violence had hit the South Side in the wake of the race riot in Springfield, Illinois. The *Chicago Tribune* had expressed a common sentiment concerning that event in reporting that "one good thing has been accomplished": the wiping out of neighborhoods in which "whites and blacks lived together" and children roamed the streets with hair texture indicating one race "and their fair skin another."[9] According to the census taken in the Larsens' neighborhood in the spring of 1910, not only was Nella not living with her family, but her mother had borne only one daughter—clearly Anna, who still lived at home. Although one might reasonably surmise that the mother herself had provided information on the family, nothing on the census form indicates who in the household had spoken with the census officer. We know, thanks to Charles Larson, that Mary spoke several times about Nella to a white friend after 1910, identifying her father as a Negro.[10] Why would she identify her older daughter as black to a white neighbor but then tell a census worker, who was not asking about the race of any nonresident children, that she had only one daughter?

It turns out that Mary Larsen was not responsible for this lapse. In 1910 the census bureau in Chicago mailed out an "advance population schedule" to each household, to be collected by enumerators on their rounds. A letter from the Census Director to the "Head of the Family" was printed on the back of each form, instructing that individual alone to fill it out in advance.[11] Peter Larsen had erased Nella from the family, an act of denial indicating both shame about his "colored" stepdaughter and the expectation that she would never return.

If she came home for a visit in the winter of 1909 and then returned for at least two more years, which seems likely, then she spent a crucial period of her life in Scandinavia, a period in which society would have expected her to seek a husband. That she had affectionate contact with relatives in those years is suggested by the fact that her grandmother gave her a pair of silver candlesticks as a keepsake.[12] Larsen was never officially enrolled in the University of Copenhagen, but she could easily have followed lecture series there or attended the affiliated "Folk University," which offered free courses in the liberal arts, taught chiefly by the faculty of the University of Copenhagen. The Folk University was equivalent to what the Library School of the New York Public Library called its

"open course"—free and open to the public, conducted by esteemed intellectuals under the auspices of the school itself. It offered adults a way to continue
their education free of charge and without having to pass entrance exams.[13]

Lacking correspondence, memoirs, or diaries, we have only the episodes in
Quicksand to go by in imagining Larsen's experience, an inherently hazardous
enterprise. How much is based on experience and how much is made up?
Leaving New York on a liner bound for Copenhagen, full of hope that Denmark
will provide a true home, Helga Crane observes the "churning slate-colored waters of the river" giving way to ripples and then small waves on the open sea as
the sky fades to dusk.

> Almost at once it was time for dinner. Somewhere a bell sounded. She turned
> and with buoyant steps went down. Already she had begun to feel happier.
> Just for a moment, outside the dining-salon, she hesitated, assailed with a tiny
> uneasiness which passed as quickly as it had come. She entered softly, unob-
> trusively. And, after all, she had had her little fear for nothing. The purser, a
> man grown old in the service of the Scandinavian-American Line, remem-
> bered her as the little dark girl who had crossed with her mother years ago,
> and so she must sit at his table. Helga liked that. It put her at ease and made
> her feel important.[14]

Newly arrived in Denmark, waking in her aunt's home, Helga hears "a discreet
knocking on the tall paneled door. . . . [A] respectful rosy-faced maid entered
and Helga lay for a long minute watching her adjust the shutters. She was conscious, too, of the girl's sly curious glances at her, although her general attitude
was quite correct, willing and disinterested. In New York, America, Helga would
have resented this sly watching. Now, here, she was only amused. Marie, she reflected, had probably never seen a Negro outside the pictured pages of her geography book."[15] The images, the subtleties of the interaction, derive from first-
hand experience, independent of plot.

It is unlikely that Larsen's relatives were as well-off as Helga Crane's, although they could have inhabited the same building. But she knew exactly what
it was like to be a Negro curiosity in Copenhagen—this is beyond question. And
some passages in *Quicksand* are as vivid as any documentary history could be:

> Her dark, alien appearance was to most people an astonishment. Some stared
> surreptitiously, some openly, and some stopped dead in front of her in order
> more fully to profit by their stares. *"Den Sorte"* dropped freely, audibly, from
> many lips.
>   The time came when she grew used to the stares of the population. And

the time came when the population of Copenhagen grew used to her outlandish presence and ceased to stare. But at the end of that first day it was with thankfulness that she returned to the sheltering walls of the house on Maria Kirkplads.[16]

Maria "Kirkeplads," as it is and was actually spelled, was a small row of bourgeois apartment buildings facing a small church off Istedgade near the train station—so small, in fact, that it appears only on detailed maps of the city. The complex had three apartment buildings, numbered 2, 4, and 6. In *Quicksand,* Helga lives in Number 2. The real-life model for the building had four floors plus a garret and a cellar, with a main stairway, and a back stairway for servants. Tall tripartite casement windows, shuttered inside, looked out over the square to the church opposite. In 1908 each of the four main floors held two five-room flats, housing families headed for the most part by professionals and small businessmen—an editor, a clockmaker, an architect, a music teacher, a tobacconist, a grocer, and the owner of a laundry business, for example.

Architecturally, Number 2 Maria Kirkeplads matches Larsen's description, and Helga Crane's relatives are *almost* credible inhabitants: a middle-class couple hoping to advance their status by marrying their exotic niece to a man of higher social standing—the chief candidates being a well-known artist, an officer of the Landsmansbank (which was an actual bank) who owns shares in an Aalborg cement factory (which was, in fact, the cement capital of Denmark), and the owner of a new theater.[17] In 1908 an important new theater was in fact opened in Copenhagen, called Det Nye Teater. Thus, Larsen drew upon a fairly wide experience and intimate knowledge of the city at a particular moment—but she was not simply trying to reproduce what she had known. Though her uses of Copenhagen draw heavily upon personal observations embedded in her memory, they serve the fiction she was writing.

Many of the observations about Copenhagen in *Quicksand* could only derive from extended residence there. Moreover, although the novel seems to be set in the 1920s, Larsen's physical descriptions of the city pertain to an earlier decade. These descriptions give reliable clues to Larsen's activities, for she could have derived many of them only from memory—and fairly extensive experience, over several seasons at least—during the period between the turn of the century and World War I. Indeed, the precision of Larsen's rendering of Copenhagen is remarkable, considering that the author had not been there for at least fourteen years at the time of writing. On the other hand, the minor irregularities of spelling support the argument that she was working from memory.

The walks that Helga Crane takes in Copenhagen follow common pedestrian routes to picturesque spots in and around the city, and the descriptions are accurate for the period of 1908 to 1912:

> When she had learned to cross the streets in safety, dodging successfully the innumerable bicycles like a true Copenhagener, she went often alone, loitering on the long bridge [now called Dronning Louises Bro] which spanned the placid lakes, or watching the pageant of the blue-clad, sprucely tailored soldiers in the daily parade at Amalienborg Palace, or in the historic vicinity of the long, low-lying Exchange, a picturesque structure in picturesque surroundings, skirting as it did the great canal, which always was alive with many small boats, flying broad white sails and pressing close on the huge ruined pile of the Palace of Christiansborg.[18]

Christiansborg Palace had burnt down in October 1884 and was rebuilt between 1907 and 1928. A painting by Paul Fischer done in 1914 shows it in the background of a scene near the Gammelstrand in the process of reconstruction, tall scaffolds surrounding it. Thus, Larsen's description fits the appearance of the ruin before that time.[19]

Larsen also describes the scene on the Gammelstrand, the canal that served as a sort of inner harbor. Along its west bank the fishwives gathered every day to sell the latest catch: "There was also the Gammelstrand, the congregating-place of the venders of fish, where daily was enacted a spirited and interesting scene between sellers and buyers, and where Helga's appearance always roused lively and audible, but friendly, interest, long after she became in other parts of the city an accepted curiosity. Here it was that one day an old countrywoman asked her to what manner of mankind she belonged and at Helga's replying: 'I'm a Negro,' had become indignant, retorting angrily that, just because she was old and a countrywoman she could not be so easily fooled, for she knew as well as everyone else that Negroes were black and had woolly hair."[20] This is one of many instances in which Larsen dramatizes the differences between Danish and American perceptions of racial identity, based on her personal experiences of being an exotic "mulatto" of marriageable age in old Copenhagen.

Axel Olsen, the artist who shows interest in Helga Crane and paints her portrait, has an "eccentric studio opposite the Folkemuseum," another sign of Larsen's intimate knowledge of the city. The buildings opposite the Folkemuseum (the "people's museum," focusing on labor history, crafts, clothing, and daily life), then located near Tivoli Gardens along Vesterbrogade, housed an eclectic mix of artists, working people, entertainers, musicians, university students, and even an art dealer.[21] Helga attends art shows with Olsen at the impor-

4. *Fishwives on the Gammelstrand, Copenhagen, circa 1905. Photographer unknown. Københavns Bymuseum, Copenhagen.*

tant exhibition spaces of the time—the Royal Academy and Charlottenborg Palace, on Kongens Nytorv, the heart of Danish "high culture."

One might well suspect that Axel Olsen is based partly on a person Larsen knew, but the candidates are few, and very few paintings of blacks or "mulattos" are to be found in the collections, studies, catalogues, archives, and indexes of Danish art at the time. The most likely model would be the expressionist Emil Nolde, born Emil Hansen in the North Schleswig border town whose name he later took. A sort of pagan-Christian mystic with authentically primitivist tendencies (being of peasant origins and initially self-taught), Nolde was fascinated by "exotic" races and most forms of dance, which he felt exemplified a primitive vitality and participation in the divinity of nature. Between 1910 and 1912, he had a new burst of creativity inspired by cabaret and café culture on one hand and primitive art on the other; in fact, in 1912 he was planning a book on primitive art. His wife lived in Copenhagen while Larsen was there, and although he mostly shuttled between Berlin (winters) and rural Alsen in Schleswig (summers), he could have encountered Larsen. He would certainly have been interested in meeting, and painting, a young, intelligent "mulatto" in Copenhagen at a time when such "types" were rare in Scandinavia. He painted a number of portraits and other works featuring people of color in the early teens, including *Mulattin* of 1913. Yet he was by all accounts very happily married, and I have found no evidence that he and Larsen met.[22]

Helga Crane goes with a number of friends, including Axel Olsen, to a vaudeville show in the winter at the Circus, and after being bored by the first several acts, is embarrassed by the sudden appearance of an African American duo who perform out-of-date ragtime songs and dances: "More songs, old, all of them old, but new and strange to that audience. And how the singers danced, pounding their thighs, slapping their hands together, twisting their legs, waving their abnormally long arms, throwing their bodies about with a loose ease! And how the enchanted spectators clapped and howled and shouted for more! Helga Crane was not amused. Instead she was filled with a fierce hatred for the cavorting Negroes on the stage. She felt shamed, betrayed, as if these pale pink and white people among whom she lived had suddenly been invited to look upon something in her which she had hidden away and wanted to forget. And she was shocked at the avidity at which Olsen beside her drank it in."[23]

The cylinder-shaped "Cirkus" building in Copenhagen held vaudeville and variety shows in the winter months, the "off-season" for circuses, occasionally featuring African American entertainers in song-and-dance routines.[24] The team of Johnson and Dean, for example, appeared there during their seven-year tour of European cities, from which they returned to the United States in September 1909. A review in *Variety* in October of that year, consonant with Helga Crane's critique, complained that they had fallen off in quality while abroad and been spoiled by European adulation; and though "high class," they were still doing "coon songs." Out of date by American standards—those of State Street in Chicago, especially—they were the most acclaimed "colored" act in Europe at the time.[25] Larsen may well have seen Johnson and Dean, or some other African American performers, in the Cirkus during her time in Copenhagen. After 1911, black vaudeville of the sort described in her novel declined in popularity among whites and the European tours largely ceased. Only in the 1920s, during the "renaissance," did such tours revive, but the shows were substantially different.

Helga Crane's aunt takes her to the Hotel Vivili for coffee, where a live band performs. Larsen apparently bases this restaurant on that of the Hotel Wivel (pronounced "*viv*-el") which was located at the entrance to Tivoli and was a fashionable place to go for tea and coffee between 1908 and 1912, featuring a live band.[26] Today the same building houses Copenhagen's Hard Rock Café.

Larsen apparently kept up with news by way of Copenhagen's most highbrow and liberal newspaper. After Helga Crane declines Axel Olsen's offer of marriage, she reads in the columns of *Politikken* that he has gone to the Balkans to rest. In fact, *Politiken* (as it is actually spelled) was one of the chief Copenhagen newspapers, and it ran a unique feature on the front page: "Dag til dag" (Day to Day), which kept track of the doings of artists, writers, distinguished professors, and other cultural figures—exactly the kind of notes Larsen describes in her novel.[27] A major force in the development of modern Danish literature, the newspaper avidly followed general artistic and intellectual developments, offering front-page, illustrated coverage of important lectures at the university as well as of art exhibits and plays, and feature articles by the most renowned scholars and intellectuals of the country. An original feature of *Politiken* beginning in 1905 (and continuing to this day) was the "Kronik," in which intellectual celebrities would comment on modern social problems, science, literature, and art. One could get a fair education in early Scandinavian literary modernism—and the preceding Modern Breakthrough (1870–1910), starring Ibsen, Strindberg, Jens Peter Jacobsen, and others whom Larsen later cited—merely from following this newspaper. Georg Brandes, one of Europe's greatest critics —arguably the first modernist critic—and an early champion of Ibsen, wrote regularly for it. He was strongly identified with Scandinavian feminism as translator of John Stuart Mill's *The Subjection of Women*.

By 1910, the great Nordic "war" over sexual morality, dating to the 1880s, had not yet spent itself but was permeating Danish culture (and affecting the young Isak Dinesen), still led by Brandes' insistence on acknowledging women's desires. Tales written in the "new manner" had become "household reading matter."[28] The naturalist problem plays and novels concerning marriage, sexuality, and women's subjection may well have made their first impression on Larsen at this time. The interest in literature and drama was not confined to the bourgeoisie. Visitors from abroad marveled at the way working-class Copenhageners flocked to the theater for Ibsen's plays, how railroad conductors could be heard debating Brandes' latest piece in *Politiken*. Trade unions would lease the Kongelige Teater (King's Theater) to stage productions of Ibsen and Strindberg for their members' families and friends.[29]

Larsen's experiences in Denmark, as best as one can tell, were both profoundly enriching and emotionally discouraging. Whether she studied formally in Copenhagen or not, her later knowledge of Scandinavian high culture and literature indicates that she advanced her education in the broad sense and developed a richly cosmopolitan perspective on the shifting contours of modern life. Yet if Larsen had hoped to find her true home and future in Denmark, she must have been sadly disappointed. Though free of the countless daily humiliations of being a Negro in the United States, as she approached the age of twenty she faced the question of marriage. Only marriage could provide her security in adulthood; if she could not attract a husband in this land of arranged marriages, or would not marry a white man, she would remain not only an outsider to Danish society but a permanent dependent of her relatives.

Like Larsen's *Quicksand,* Scandinavian American immigrant novels with American-born protagonists regularly dwell on their heroines' feelings of being "betwixt and between"—going to Scandinavia in hopes of finding a sense of belonging that they lack in America, only to discover that they do not, after all, fit in.[30] As a biracial woman, of course, Larsen experienced such difficulties in unique ways, and the sense of racial difference attracts much of the attention in her novel. One cannot help thinking that Larsen's hopes for a life in Denmark were defeated by a combination of racial alienation, cultural difference, and gender entrapment. The pattern of emotional abandonment/detachment was further embedded in the history of her spirit. She decided at last to make her way in the Negro world of the United States. Even if she found comfort among Negroes, as she clearly did, this was a daunting prospect, and she would have to meet it on her own.

SIX

A Black Woman in White:
New York, 1912–1915

NELLA Larsen turned twenty-one in April 1912, shortly after returning from Copenhagen; yet she had insufficient training to find work adequate for her own support, and living with her family was not an option. In Englewood and other nearby neighborhoods, white residents had banded together against black and "mixed" families seeking to move in, and were driving out those African Americans who already lived nearby.[1] Larsen faced the problem of supporting herself, and her situation was dire. The jobs that single white women could get without high school diplomas—as saleswomen, clerks, stenographers, and the like—were almost entirely closed to black women.[2] Employment agencies assumed they would work as domestics in seedy hotels and brothels. They were commonly insulted and sexually harassed even in those few bookkeeping or stenography positions they might manage to pick up.[3] Black women with a secondary education, presumed unfit for domestic work, faced the greatest barriers of all. "High school girls of refined appearance," as a white reformer pointed out, "after looking for weeks, will find nothing open to them" in the respectable establishments, except as maids in women's waiting rooms.[4] Larsen's first novel dramatizes the situation precisely: Helga Crane returns to Chicago to discover that she is considered too educated for domestic work and that few other options exist. To make matters worse, having been out of the country for several years, Larsen was unable to provide references.

A 1909 guide to employment for young women mentions the position of "companion" or private secretary for a clubwoman, a "trained or semi-trained attendant"—precisely the position that Helga Crane acquires through the YWCA employment bureau and that becomes her vehicle into the black community of New York. *Quicksand* describes the relationship between Helga and her "lecturing female," Mrs. Hayes-Rore, with great credibility and subtlety, and makes their brief acquaintance pivotal to the young Chicagoan's career. Such positions required (according to the author of the 1909 guide) a very neat appearance, intelligence, and great tact.[5] Larsen had all of these qualities and may well have found her way out of Chicago via such a position.

This possibility aside, she needed a dependable career of some sort. In those days, black women in Chicago considered teaching, librarianship, and nursing the best professions open to them. Teaching and librarianship came under the civil service system, which could not legally discriminate, but Larsen lacked qualifications, including a diploma. Nursing school did not require a diploma, and it would provide room and board. Although beginning nurses worked killing hours and had lower social status than novice teachers, librarians, and social workers of the time, they made better money, and there were never enough of them.

Larsen's position exemplifies the relationship between the rise of Chicago's "New Negro" professional class and de facto segregation. Blacks in the professions far outnumbered those in proprietary, clerical, and skilled craft groups because they could make a living from a black clientele; they did not need whites to employ them. As whites intensified racial barriers in all phases of life, the "black belt" grew, and black demand concentrated spatially while political power shifted, sidelining the old integrationist leadership. In this respect, Chicago was ahead of New York and most other Northern cities. The city developed a new elite that derived its power and wealth from the black community itself: "With their ascendancy, the ideal of an integrated society and the fight against racial segregation went into a long remission."[6] The more ambitious and better educated turned to the formation of separate institutions and to taking over the leadership of "black" institutions previously run by whites or racially integrated groups. By the same token, close connections to whites or white institutions invited charges of disloyalty, boot-licking, lack of race pride.

Such charges affected the career of the renowned Daniel Hale Williams, founder and chief surgeon of Chicago's Provident Hospital, at the very time Larsen entered nursing school. Insisting on an integrated staff and admission of patients regardless of race, he kept his admitting privileges at "white" hospitals and served whites as well as blacks. A new group of Tuskegee-linked business leaders gained power, however, and accused him of lacking race loyalty. In 1912 Williams quit the institution as it came under the control of those who wanted to consolidate black business and turn Provident into the "black" hospital of Chicago. They forbade Provident doctors from sending patients to "white" hospitals, so Williams packed up and left. According to the historian Allan Spear, Williams spent the rest of his career "divorced from the Negro community."[7]

The pool of trained professionals constantly expanded and provided community leadership. If they could not have equal access to mainstream organizations, then they would insist on at least controlling their race's own. After all, in such a racist environment how could whites be expected to serve blacks as effectively as blacks themselves could? Yet as black institutions proliferated, they also became an excuse for denying blacks access to "white" institutions, despite civil rights laws. Larsen, like Williams, was always on the "integrationist" side of the African American political spectrum. Yet despite her integrationist priorities, Larsen at times had to depend on institutions specifically created for African Americans. She had noplace else to go.

Significantly, Larsen got into the profession not by way of Provident Hospital in Chicago but through Lincoln Hospital in the Bronx. It was an excellent choice. Provident was "always on the brink of financial collapse," according to Darlene Clark Hine (from whom I borrow the title for this chapter), and "the student nurses endured unending hardships."[8] Yet it is likely that one reason Larsen did not go to Provident, just as she had not gone to the Chicago Normal School, was the wrenching pain of residing in the same city as her mother and half-sister while being estranged from them. Far better to start anew somewhere else, preferably in a big city with a complex and decentered black social world, where questions of her family background need not be a hindrance to her prospects for social advancement or marriage. Her mother and stepfather probably had no knowledge of black nursing schools around the country, but any number of black clubwomen in Chicago may well have become acquainted with Larsen and suggested nursing school in New York.

In the spring of 1912, one in seven Americans lived in the Greater New York area. The rivers teemed with tugboats, fishing boats, and great steamers, smoke rising from stacks at piers hemming the shorelines of Manhattan and Brooklyn. As the newcomer emerged from underground into the cavernous train station, she felt utterly insignificant amid the swirling crowds; a frightening impersonality pervaded New York, "more appalling, more scornful," Larsen would later write, "in some inexplicable way even more terrible and uncaring than Chicago."[9] Here, in what Larsen termed a "shining city," was the urban sublime: the towers of downtown, the great hotels and department store windows of Fifth Avenue putting those of Chicago's Michigan Avenue to shame, the huge green lung of Central Park. The city's five boroughs spread out across islands and peninsulas, strung together by stupendous bridges, busy ferries, and subways. The tenements of lower Manhattan were crowded with immigrants speaking all at once in myriad tongues.

Black people from the Caribbean, South America, and even Africa, speaking Spanish, French, Portuguese, Creole, and the King's English, had settled (at times uneasily) alongside the native-born New Yorkers and new migrants from the South in old haunts like Columbus Hill, on Manhattan's West Side, and now began taking a foothold in airy Harlem north of Central Park, where beer gardens still hummed with accordions. Although blacks concentrated in a handful of neighborhoods and braved dirty looks elsewhere, New York was not like Chicago; they could be found in many sectors of the city, even Staten Island, and certainly Brooklyn, where some of the most comfortable lived. At first frightening, perhaps, New York was the right place for Nella Larsen. No single group could dominate the black social world, and blacks were not crammed together in one narrow belt between iron rails. One could dream of mobility—within limits.

Nursing schools in New York could not legally discriminate against African American applicants, but in practice black women were no longer admitted, and rarely applied, to "white" training schools. Even the most liberal white nursing leaders—including Lillian Wald, a board member of the NAACP whose own nurse service hired black nurses—feared the effects of integrating nursing education in the city on the grounds that many white women would refuse to live and work with black women on the intimate terms common to nurse training, and white patients would object. Wald's antiracist activism came head to head with the Hippocratic Oath. Even if a black woman pressed her rights, at the end of her probationary term she would be helpless if the white supervisors wished to fire her. But Wald rationalized that black women did not need "white" schools of nursing, for "there are good training schools for colored women, and their graduates rank well." She doubtless had Lincoln Hospital's nursing school in mind.[10]

Lincoln Hospital and Home, as it was known by the time Nella Larsen arrived on May 2, 1912,[11] was utterly unique from a racial standpoint: it had a nearly all-white hospital patient base, an all-black nursing home, an all-white (and male) staff of physicians, and an all-black (and female) nursing school. The history behind this setup is worth sketching. The institution dated back to an 1839 meeting of white women in New York who formed a "Society for the Relief of Worthy, Aged, Indigent, Colored Persons." In 1840, the year that several of them were barred, because they were women, from taking seats at the World Anti-Slavery Congress in London, they opened a "home" for the elderly black poor.[12] Over the years, it moved several times around what is now midtown Manhattan and became incorporated as the "Colored Home," finally settling on Avenue A between Sixty-Fourth and Sixty-Fifth Streets. By this time it had added a hospital, which soon grew more important than the nursing home, and so the name changed to the "Colored Home and Hospital."

By the turn of the century, needing more space and able to take advantage of the increased value of their Manhattan property to purchase a larger physical plant, the directors decided to sell the facility and erect a new one in the Bronx, where land was cheap. Partly as the fruit of this business decision, the dream of establishing a training school for black nurses was realized in 1899 and the first class graduated in 1900. But since the facility was now located far from the "colored section" of Manhattan (the Bronx being overwhelmingly white), the hospital remained nearly vacant for several years. In 1902 the name of the institution was changed to "Lincoln Hospital and Home" and the hospital portion became a general hospital, "open to the public without regard to race, creed, or color."[13] The residents of the nursing home remained all black, as did all of the nurses except for the superintendent of nursing, while the hospital, which became by far the largest part of the operation, filled with white patients from the surrounding area. Florence Jacobs Edmonds, a nursing student of 1917–1920, remembered the patient population at Lincoln as practically all white and predominantly Jewish: "We got very few colored patients."[14]

In 1907, the city gave Lincoln $62,000 to subsidize the care of indigent patients, and from that time it became one of the chief hospitals for "city" patients in the Bronx—that is, nonpaying patients, who made up the vast majority of the cases. Lincoln Hospital and Home quickly became a treasured institution of the borough, one of its first and most important general hospitals. Continuing to expand through the early decades of the century as the Bronx boomed, it attracted the services of well-known physicians in surgical, gynecological, and obstetrical specialties, and provided ambulance service for the Thirty-Fifth Police Precinct. Many medical leaders of New York served on the staff when Larsen was there, and Lincoln graduates were among the most influential black R.N.'s in the United States.[15] The nursing school therefore offered training opportunities at the highest level available to black women of the time—equal (as Lillian Wald had pointed out) to those of the best white schools.

The Lincoln nursing school was unique as a "black institution," for other African American nursing schools had been developed in conjunction with black hospitals—hospitals created and staffed by black physicians for a black clientele; those hospitals had been founded above all to give black doctors access to hospital facilities as such facilities became central to the new scientific medicine.[16] But the opportunity for nurse training in these hospitals was only one reason for the establishment of schools; just as important was the use of nurse trainees as inexpensive hospital staff, and the farming out of nursing students to treat private patients in return for fees paid to the hospital. (These practices were common at white as well as black nursing schools.) With no independent financial base, nursing education was perpetually subordinated to staffing and funding considerations of hospitals. At Lincoln, in contrast, because of the different relationship of the school to the hospital, rooted in the original "Society" founded by abolitionists, the school had an independent budget, which helped protect against the most exploitative practices.[17] The remnant of that separate budget still exists, long after the demise of the hospital, in the form of a foundation named the "Lincoln Fund" with an office on Madison Avenue.

The ratio of classroom instruction to practical labor at Lincoln was much greater than usual, and the curriculum included the newest subjects in the field, because the school's leaders had brought it under the Board of Regents system of the University of the State of New York. Moreover, starting in 1907, the first professional Nurses Director hired orderlies and maids in connection with her reorganization of the school, so students could spend more time nursing—a very rare, possibly unique, condition in black nursing schools of the time, and unusual even for white schools. During her two-month probationary period, Larsen would have to scrub the floors and clean the bathrooms of the nursing home, but once past the hurdle of probation, never again.[18] Whoever gave Larsen the tip about Lincoln had done her a grand favor indeed.

As she approached it from the trolley stop on Southern Boulevard, she could see that the Lincoln complex filled an entire block between Concord and Wales avenues, dominated by the main building, an imposing brick structure four stories high with plenty of windows on the four wings extending east and west from the central block. Down the street, a large bakery filled the neighborhood with the sweet scent of fresh bread. But with the New York and Harlem Railroad rumbling diagonally across the two blocks to the northeast, and some light industry nearby, the neighborhood was hardly quiet.[19]

In the superintendent's office she gave her name as Nella Marian (or Marion) Larsen, adopting the middle name that she would use for the rest of her life.[20] This was obviously a variation on "Marie," which she used as her middle name at Fisk. She impressed the Superintendent enough to be admitted when a vacancy opened up in May, and by the end of July she had passed probation.[21] She had a new home for the coming three years, in a large dormitory on the third floor of the hospital.

She was assigned a bed in one of the two rooms, and a metal locker for storing her clothing and belongings, including any luggage she may have saved. She and her two dozen roommates shared a single bathroom, furnished with two toilets, three sinks, a bathtub, and a shower. According to a later report, the women all used a single "make-shift desk" they put together themselves.[22] Life was awkward. One painfully imagines the lines for the bathroom each morning, when everyone had to wash, dress, and use the toilets in time to make the seven o'clock religious service—the rushed bathing and showering, the hurried donning of starched white uniforms and caps.[23]

After prayers and breakfast the trainees headed for their duties in the various wards, weaving through the high-ceilinged corridors with scrubwomen forever on their knees, brush in hand and pail beside them. Soapsuds and carbolic acid constituted the "hospital smell" of 1912. There were strange customs to mind. Rules of seniority dictated that a nurse couldn't go through a door or an elevator before anyone who had enrolled in the school ahead of her, even an hour ahead of her. That each was admitted as a vacancy occurred made keeping track of everyone's position a matter of some moment. The young women knew exactly where they stood in the pecking order and would physically snatch each other out of doorways and elevators.[24]

Through a tall door they entered the light-filled ward, lined with fifteen to twenty mostly occupied iron-frame beds along either wall, with a large space in the middle for moving about and carting things back and forth. Tall windows let in plenty of sunlight and air. A doctor might appear occasionally on his rounds, and more often an intern or two, but for the most part the nurses had the patients to themselves.

All first-year students started out in the "old folks' wards"—the "colored home," comprising three wards for women and two for men, with thirty to forty residents in each ward, mostly bedridden and chronically ill.[25] During her two-month probationary period, Larsen had to help scrub the floors and clean the bathrooms, but after that she helped care for the residents.[26] Some were relatively well and able to move around on their own, but others suffered unbearably and longed to die. In one of the wards Larsen came under the wing of the head nurse, who first showed her how to keep the room clean and ventilated, and then taught her to make a bed without disturbing the person who lay in it— how to brace, lift, and turn.

From the beginning, nurse trainees learned the arts of perception. According to the adages of Florence Nightingale, axioms of the profession, the distinguishing qualities of the nurse were her nearly instinctive habits of observation, her finely tuned awareness of the conditions in a ward, and her ability to read each patient's mental and physical state. A nurse had to be able to see beyond the immediate appearance, to note subtle changes, and to perceive the hidden needs of those too proud, shy, or embarrassed to ask for help. A common exercise was to practice observing in detail the appearance and actions of all the patients in the course of a day and then write them down later from memory. The distance from nurse to writer, after all, may not have been so great.

Gradually Larsen was introduced to the nurse's offices in all of the intimate, embarrassing, ungainly exercises of the ward—performing the morning toilet; feeding, brushing teeth, washing out a mouth, placing a bedpan and reporting the appearance and odor of a stool; giving an enema. Such was the elementary coursework, joined with disciplines of sympathy and patience, and a rigorous education in tact.[27]

There was no special place to take the patients for privacy as they neared the end. They died in the ward. When the head nurse felt the time was near, she would have her aides draw a screen around the bed and call in relatives. The prayers, weeping, gasps, cries of the bereaved could be heard by all, while other bedridden inmates lay passively and the students went quietly about their duties. Most often, only a nurse and the family would be present at the moment of death—the nurse to give what comfort she could, to note the moment of the last breath, and to summon the doctor for the official pronouncement.

Only after some time would Larsen take part in what came next. Behind the screen, with an experienced nurse leading, she would quickly and quietly help straighten the body, close the mouth, bathe the face, set the jaw with a bandage, prop up the head to keep blood from coagulating in the face, strip the body, remove any jewelry and make a list of it, change the linens, prepare an oakum pad and muslin diaper to catch feces from the relaxed anus, and then bathe the body quickly and thoroughly. The nurses would then put the mortuary gown on, tie the ankles and knees together, fasten the wrists together with a name tag, and wrap the body in a shroud. After lifting the body onto a stretcher they bore it solemnly from the room as other students came to put fresh linens on the bed and remove the screens.[28]

As she acquired seniority, Larsen moved to the other wards of the hospital—surgical, medical, emergency, gynecological, maternity, and pediatric—where she would spend several months in each. Here the patients were almost all white.[29] As in the nursing home wards, all of the nursing care, personal hygiene, groans, cries, and arguments occurred in plain hearing, if not in plain sight, of everyone on the ward. The ward supervisor, a registered nurse (R.N.), was the chief authority, with her several student aides doing most of the nursing itself. There was little traffic in and out. The sickest patients lay nearest to the nurses' station, essentially a large desk and a cabinet near the door. The healthier patients, who could take care of themselves, slept at the far end and spent most of the day out of bed. Doctors were rarely present.

In each ward, Larsen learned new nursing techniques. She prepared patients for surgery and learned all of the methods for dressing wounds and incisions and for bandaging each joint and appendage. Since antibiotics were still unknown, careful cleansing and hygiene were the only defenses against ravaging infections. In the medical wards, new testing techniques had brought diagnostic advances, but for most diseases medical science had yet to produce cures, so nursing was the key—making patients comfortable and hopeful. Many were given nothing but cod liver oil and doses of brandy, calomel, whiskey, or mustard paste. To combat boredom, nurses would read stories to children on the pediatric wards or show them pictures and take them outdoors. Two open-air wards on the roof provided some relief during the sweltering summer months.

Separate buildings held tuberculosis and maternity patients, and infectious diseases were treated in a special pavilion.[30] Pneumonia, polio, rheumatic fever, meningitis, and typhoid fever were nearly incurable and highly contagious, threatening the nurse herself. Just about all she could do was help Nature win out over death through various baths, poultices, cold compresses, exposures to fresh air, and attempts at good cheer.[31] Of her own difficulties and exhaustion she must speak not a word.

The nurses had a large room on the first floor of the hospital for recreation, but there was not much time for that. Even as the eight-hour day became an achievable standard for unionized laborers in the New York area, Larsen worked twelve-hour shifts Monday through Saturday, with a half-day off at some point during the week, and a four-hour shift on Sunday. Unable to go home to her family, she must have been at a loss when it came to her two weeks of annual vacation. All the students had several months of night duty—lighter work than normal, but hard on their sleep schedule. It was not unusual for them to put in a twelve-hour night shift and then have to attend class at seven in the morning.[32] On top of the free room, board, laundry, and tuition, they were paid six dollars a month—a bit more than enough to cover the inevitable equipment breakage, along with uniforms and textbooks.[33]

Most patients were long-term, temporarily unable to earn a living because of illness or injury. Only one-tenth of the patients paid for their care. They were generally working-class, neither paupers nor comfortably well-off. The wealthy stayed in proprietary hospitals with private rooms. Middle-class people, who could not afford such care, did not like being lumped in with the lower-class charity patients on the wards of city hospitals and therefore stayed at home.[34]

Despite the pervasive racism of the period, and the intense resistance black nurses faced from white patients in other northern cities, at Lincoln the white clientele did not mind being cared for by black nurses, according to all reports. The nursing staff and students enjoyed a high reputation in the Bronx. According to some of the white supervisors, however, were the nurses to be put under "colored supervision . . . they would not be accepted at all and a valuable nursing experience would thus be lost to them."[35] In August 1912, when the white superintendent who had hired Larsen resigned because of her impending marriage, she was briefly replaced by her black assistant, Adah B. Samuels, but by

October a new superintendent named Alice Thayer took over and Samuels was relegated again to the Assistant position. She resigned soon after to join a new husband in the South. (She returned a year or so later, probably divorced, as Adah B. Thoms.)[36] Just as the all-white, all-female, and all-volunteer Board of Managers believed their patients would rebel if the Superintendent were black, they were convinced that white patients would not abide black physicians. All the interns were white. Thus, the color line ran its jagged path through this unique hospital, regardless of civil rights statutes.

The line was less jagged back in Illinois, where Anna Larsen married a clerk named George Gardner before a justice of the peace on November 8, 1913.[37] The Gardners would move into a "double" next to Peter and Mary in Chicago and live near them until the early 1920s, thus making Nella's connection to her nearest relations even more problematic emotionally, since her sister's continued intimacy with their mother starkly contrasted with Nella's enforced isolation.

At least one of Larsen's peers found her, in Adelaide Cromwell Hill's words, "different, even a bit strange, not at all at home with those around her," and attributed this quality to her difficult upbringing.[38] In addition to the acute sensitivity deriving from her childhood trauma, Larsen almost certainly felt culture shock. It would take some time for her to feel as if she "belonged." Older than most entering students, though small in stature and young in appearance, she was awkward in company and painfully self-conscious. Her aloof manner, however, may have helped in one respect. Leadership required the maintenance of personal distance, a constant difficulty for African American nurses in supervisory roles, for in the eyes of many black nursing students, staff nurses, and other employees, such distance marked one's manner as "white." Black co-workers often expected a more casual camaraderie. In the eyes of white authorities, on the other hand, such familiarity looked like lax discipline.[39]

The more serious discipline problems, however, involved interns who took "liberties." They provided most of the medical care, and they were a rambunctious lot in all the hospitals of those days, given to bouts of drinking, carousing, and coming to work hung over. Judging from various hospital reports of the time, including those on Lincoln, they could be undependable, disrespectful, and sexually aggressive. The nursing superintendent at Lincoln told an interviewer in 1925 that when she had first arrived, "the attitude of the interns to the colored nurses was arrogant and lacking in professional respect. Moral lapses were of too frequent occurrence." Often, when such lapses occurred, only the nurse was disciplined.[40] Larsen's reserve may have helped to hold the rogues at bay. She learned in time how to put a "masher" in his place with a scathing reply or an appraising stare.[41]

With seniority, Larsen gained practice supervising the work in each of the wards, which brought her into closer collaboration with the doctors and administrators and provided valuable leadership experience. She was singled out for her executive ability, developing a confident manner, discretion, diplomacy, organizational skills, and an ability to tell people what to do while keeping their friendship and respect. These were the most sought-after qualities in nursing graduates of the day, the qualities identified with the future of the profession.

Irreligious though she was, Larsen had to attend chapel every morning at six and every Sunday evening. Since seniors from Union Theological Seminary regularly led the religious instruction and Sunday evening services, she almost certainly crossed paths with her future brother-in-law, William Lloyd Imes, whose senior year at Union Theological Seminary exactly coincided with hers at Lincoln. That year he also married Larsen's old Fisk classmate, Grace Virginia Frank. Himself a 1910 graduate of Fisk, Imes would surely have remembered Larsen.[42]

Lincoln's three-year program was very progressive for its day, with more academic preparation and general education than most schools, black or white. Outside the regular training, a reading group met in the first-floor recreation room once or twice a month. The students also took field trips to museums and libraries, and attended concerts and plays. These programs followed new ideas about connecting nurses' duties with community development, civic institutions, and "liberal" education. They exemplified the move in top schools away from preparing students for private-duty nursing and toward more independent and administrative functions. When Larsen enrolled, almost all of the school's practicing alumni were engaged in private duty, whereas a number of the students, including Larsen herself, would move into hospital supervisory roles, nursing education, or public health work. By 1923, Lincoln graduates in public health, school nursing, and social service outnumbered those in private duty.[43]

Presiding over the Board of Managers of Lincoln was Mary Wainwright Booth, who had begun working with the home in the midst of the Civil War and remained deeply involved until she died in 1920.[44] Booth took a personal interest in the students, visiting the hospital every Monday and Thursday. According to Adah Thoms, who described her glowingly in an early history of black nursing, she knew each of the nurses by name "and always wanted to talk with them; their problems were hers and she was always interested and anxious about their health and happiness, their religious life and recreation." She bought them Christmas presents every year, personally wrapped and signed.[45] Yet the nurses increasingly resented the implication in the makeup of the hospital hierarchy that Negroes were unsuited to supervisory positions—an idea that the superintendent of the nursing school in the mid-Twenties stated clearly and unequivocally to the British investigator Ethel Johns.[46] Nella Larsen herself later reported that "all infractions of rules and instances of neglect of duty were reported to and dealt with by the superintendent of nurses, who was white. It used to distress the old folks . . . that we Negroes had to tell things about each other to the white people." One Mrs. Christopher, in particular, used to say over and over that "if the Negro race would only stick together, we might get somewhere someday, and that what the white folks didn't know about us wouldn't hurt us."[47] "All this used to amuse me," Larsen added—possibly playing to her predominantly white audience, and possibly not. She was never much for holding the barrier between races, let alone shoring it up.

Although black nurses had immediate supervision over the individual wards, "All the doctors and executives were white," Larsen reported.[48] The hospital had many staff, attending and consulting M.D.'s in a wide range of specialties, in addition to the sixteen who served on the "Medical Board." Nine doctors composed the house staff, including three gynecologists and three surgeons. The staff physicians in 1915 were a very international group—including two from Australia, one from Italy, and one from France. Many were Jewish, due less to the local Jewish population than to the pervasive discrimination against them in the proprietary hospitals. The orderlies were also white, but the waiters, chefs, and domestic workers were all black, including several from Africa, and many from the Caribbean and South America. Several of the nurses came from the Caribbean, Canada, and Mexico.[49]

The leadership of the nurse training school changed several times in Larsen's three years as a student, but Adah Thoms, after her return as Assistant Superintendent in Larsen's senior year, formed a special relationship with her. A native of Virginia, Thoms had entered nursing through the Women's Infirmary on Manhattan's East Side, a remarkable institution staffed entirely by women and founded by the first female M.D. in New York. She had also been Head Nurse at a black hospital in Raleigh, North Carolina, for three years before matriculating at Lincoln's new nursing school in 1902–1903 and graduating in 1905. She stayed on at Lincoln to supervise the nurses in the surgery department before being named Assistant Superintendent of Nurses, and she served off and on as "Acting Superintendent," apparently always being passed over for the official designation since she was not white.[50] A portrait published in the *New York Age* in 1928 shows a broad-featured, brown-skinned woman with wide-set eyes and with the determined yet reposed look typical of such portraits of the time.

Thoms was the most consistent black authority figure Larsen knew at the school—possibly the first black supervisor she had ever encountered. She became, in fact, one of the key figures in Larsen's life between her return from Denmark and her marriage, helping to guide her into the black world of greater New York. Their relationship no doubt began as a typical student-teacher encounter and deepened as Thoms gained a sense of the potential in the neat, sophisticated, well-traveled, restrained young Northerner.[51]

In the first book-length history of black nursing, Thoms wrote a short and glowing account of Larsen's early career, outlining Larsen's supervisory work and adding, "This administrative experience was enriched by close association with many well-known physicians and surgeons on the staffs of the above named nursing schools."[52] Thoms stressed Larsen's "executive" ability because black nurses were presumed to have none and were discriminated against on that basis. As Thoms wrote in her 1917 Annual Report, when she was Acting Superintendent and Larsen her assistant, "We are making special effort to train the present Senior Class for executive work in order to fill the demand for Head Nurses in institutions."[53]

Idealistic, shrewd, and devoted to the advancement of black nurses, Thoms was also well connected to the middle ranks of New York's black elite. Ethel Johns, a British investigator who interviewed her about 1925, was much impressed, noting that Thoms was respected by all, "a woman in middle life of a distinctly negroid type but with native dignity and refinement."[54] She had helped to found the National Association of Colored Graduate Nurses (NACGN) and became its president in 1915. By the 1920s, when she had remarried and was using the name Thoms-Smith, she showed up with some regularity in society columns of New York's black newspapers for her entertainments, including bridge parties (which Larsen did not attend at that time), as well as for her nursing work and volunteer work with the Colored Women's Branch of the New York YWCA.

Although Adah Thoms was elected president of the NACGN in 1915, and doubtless urged Larsen to join that organization, Larsen does not show up on any of the membership lists of the group, nor did she attend its conferences. In this, however, she was not at all unusual. The NACGN had a very small membership base, as did the American Nurses Association at the time.[55] Although the Lincoln School for Nurses Alumnae Association had been instrumental in founding the NACGN in 1908, few of its graduates joined. Neither did Larsen need the NACGN for aid in finding employment. In short, Larsen—who was never much of a "joiner"—apparently judged that there was really no benefit to joining the NACGN. Most of her peers, to Thoms's intense dismay, agreed.[56]

As Larsen approached graduation from Lincoln, she of course faced the

5. *Lincoln Hospital and Home Training School for Nurses, class of 1915. Nella Larsen is second from the left in the front row. Photographer unknown. Photographs and Prints Division, Schomburg Center for Research in Black Culture, The New York Public Library, Astor, Lenox and Tilden Foundations.*

question of what to do next. In January 1915, she sat for a battery of examinations for the R.N. license and excelled, earning the extremely rare distinction of passing with "honor."[57] Officially, the license took effect on May 1, 1915. Larsen graduated on May 13, 1915, with the nursing school director's statement that her executive abilities were "above the average."[58] As one of the school's top students, she took a job as head nurse in one of the wards and by October was serving as Assistant Superintendent of the nurse training school.[59] Larsen thus stayed on at Lincoln for some five months, in a prestigious role for a new graduate. But this did not resolve the question of a permanent career move.

The top Lincoln graduates of her time looked forward to careers in public health nursing and supervisory roles in black hospitals or nursing schools. Those who went into private-duty nursing often found positions through nurse registries, such as those run by the Lincoln alumnae or the NACGN. The New York Health Department was legally barred from discriminating against black nurses, and several Lincoln graduates joined that department in the mid to late

1910s. Others stayed on at Lincoln to supervise the wards and to help train students. Yet others took jobs with the Henry Street Settlement, which placed them exclusively in African American neighborhoods of New York. Lincoln graduates were also in demand for supervisory positions in black hospitals down South. Over the years, several of them would head up the nurse training school at John A. Andrews Memorial Hospital at Tuskegee Institute, in Alabama.[60] As the first of this group, Nella M. Larsen was in for a series of big shocks.

SEVEN

Rebel with a Cause:
Tuskegee, 1915–1916

USED to living in big gray cities criss-crossed by streetcars, Larsen must have felt the difference even more starkly than expected as she looked out over the fields of brown-stemmed cotton, passed through a rolling, still-green landscape, and finally alighted from the "colored" car onto the platform of Chehaw Station, where she would change to the Tuskegee Railway for the last five miles of her journey. One imagines her relief, as she looked for those waiting to bear her to campus about a mile away, at being able to bathe and rest after spending two days and a night in Jim Crow cars.

Neat and orderly, laid out amid pastures and gentle tree-covered hills, Tuskegee Institute was an oasis in the near-squalor of the surrounding counties, to the pride of African Americans in the area and the envy of many whites. Relations between the white citizens of Tuskegee, Alabama, and the inhabitants of the institute were delicate, despite all of Booker T. Washington's famous ability to accommodate whites' concerns. White visitors ate, slept, and used the bathroom in separate facilities at Dorothy Hall; they sat in a special section of the chapel, and entered it by a "white" entrance. One had to worry about the local Ku Klux Klan. Yet white doctors clamored for access to the institute's hospital, by far the best in the region outside Montgomery, and shortly before Nella Larsen arrived Booker T. Washington was urging Dr. John A. Kenney, Tuskegee's medical director and chief surgeon, to let them in.

On a height overlooking the campus, the three-year-old John A. Andrew Memorial Hospital was an impressive colonial structure in red brick, with a broad two-story portico framed by white columns. Larsen's quarters on the second floor, reached by a wide staircase, included a private bedroom and a sitting-room shared with Janie Armstead, the Assistant Head Nurse. Peering out of the second-story windows from the front of the hospital, one could see the neat brick buildings arranged below: the two-story colonial Carnegie Library and twelve dormitories, laid out in quadrangles and nearly all funded by white Northerners in honor of their relatives. The largest structure on campus, Tompkins Hall, held a dining room that could seat all 180 boarding teachers and 1,600 students at once. Then there was the academic center, Huntington Hall, and the Trades Buildings—and, of course, the chapel. But hard by the hospital were the horse and cattle barns, sources of stench and insect-borne bacteria that compromised Dr. John A. Kenney's perpetual battle for modern sanitation and hygiene.[1] Her first evening on campus, Larsen also no doubt learned that the water was turned off in the hospital at sundown.

One might well wonder what motivated a Northern "city girl" like Larsen to accept a position at rural, segregated Tuskegee—in one of the most unabashedly racist regions of the country. Apparently idealism had much to do with it. Despite growing dissatisfaction with Booker T. Washington's political power, the institute retained a strong profile on the national scene. From a distance, it resembled Askov, the great Grundtvigian "folk high school" of Denmark that Larsen would later indicate she had attended. On paper their philosophies were much the same, and their histories in certain respects were parallel. The defining feature of both was an emphasis on the marriage of practical work and book-learning. Like Askov, Tuskegee derived the subject matter of education from the life of the people it meant to serve and related educational outcomes to the activities and occupations of the pupils in their wider community. From a distance, it seemed to some progressive educators the very embodiment of contemporary educational theory.

The method of the institute had always been to develop departments based on locally discovered needs. The school started by teaching farmers to diversify their crops, so that they could gain independence from tenancy and unforeseen calamities. When the school needed new and larger buildings, they developed a brickyard and built the halls. To transport bricks, they needed wagons, so they developed a course in wagon-building and a wheelwright shop. The same process led to programs in printing (1885), mattress- and cabinet-making (1887), tin-smithing, harness-making, and shoe-making (1889); and, in 1892, the creation of a hospital and nurse training school. By 1895, Washington had created an institution with an all-black faculty, dormitories, numerous departments, and an ever-expanding budget. "The development had been unspectacular," a biographer would write, "but the achievement, viewed from the angle of the Institute's origins, was staggering."[2]

Booker T. Washington and Tuskegee Institute were still internationally renowned in the fall of 1915, and the school had some of the most powerful men in the country behind it—including trustees like Theodore Roosevelt and Seth Low (social activist, mayor of New York, and longtime president of Columbia University). Margaret Murray Washington, the founder's wife, was president of the National Association of Colored Women and one of the nation's leading "race women." Only three years before Larsen's arrival, young Claude McKay—future literary light of the Harlem Renaissance, already radicalized by his experiences as a constable in Kingston—had been drawn to Tuskegee from Jamaica, thinking the institute a beacon of black self-determination and progress. He did not stay long, but he remained impressed enough after leaving to write a poem in honor of the founder after Washington's death in 1915. The hospital was arguably the best in the black South, and the nursing school one of the best in the region for African Americans.

Tuskegee differed from all of the other prestigious "Negro" colleges and institutes of the time in being run entirely by African Americans. Pride in this fact created an esprit de corps that helped to define Tuskegee. "Race consciousness" was one of the institute's mantras. By the time Larsen arrived, more and more African Americans had their doubts, particularly because of the immense power Washington had come to wield, his accommodations to white supremacy, and his attempts to control the black press and to squelch dissent. But on the campus itself, nearly all were under the spell of their leader and full of pride in what they were accomplishing.

There was no room for ambiguity or ambivalence at Tuskegee. One either got with the program and entered wholeheartedly into the mission, or one resigned or got kicked out. The demand for loyalty and unity was overt and constant, never more so than in the year of Larsen's residence. In a Sunday address shortly before Larsen's arrival, Washington spoke on the importance of teamwork: "We want to have team-work, not only in the direction to which I have referred, but most of all . . . we want to have team-work in our spiritual life, in our religious life, everywhere, in the prayer meetings, . . . in every devotional exercise . . . everywhere, we want to have team-work, all working together in the direction which shall bring about the highest spiritual usefulness in this institution."[3] For nurses and nursing students at Tuskegee, such "team-work" entailed silent acquiescence to intense institutional abuse and exploitation.

In the South generally, nursing was classed with personal service and associated with the traditional role of the black "mammy." In fact, whereas white Northerners generally objected to being treated by black nurses, in the South nursing was widely regarded as a "natural" occupation for black women of minimal education, and many white doctors, especially in the countryside, preferred black nurses. As a result, ambitious African American women associated nursing with precisely the sort of roles from which they were trying to extricate themselves. They regarded teaching and social work as vastly superior occupations.[4] To make matters worse, Larsen and her students had to fight pervasive Southern stereotypes of nurses as "immoral and sexually promiscuous," one reason that every nursing school candidate at Tuskegee had to produce a refer-ence from a minister testifying to her moral character.[5] At Hampton Institute (Washington's alma mater, in Virginia) and Tuskegee, faculty and administra-tors regarded nursing as a "convenient exit for the less intelligent," certainly not a suitable career for the "superior black woman."[6] And they tended to regard pupil nurses as a workforce rather than a student body.[7] By extension, the Head Nurse's "faculty" status was quite ambiguous.

Washington himself considered nursing to be not a profession but rather a form of "domestic and personal service."[8] He categorized nurses with house-keepers and stewards, unskilled laborers, servants, and laundresses. They occu-pied the very bottom of the totem pole. In fact, a year before Larsen arrived, Washington had urged Dr. Kenney to make the hospital partly a summer vaca-tion resort for wealthy blacks, with nurses doing the domestic work. Not sur-prisingly, student nurses did all the basic housekeeping, laundry, and cleaning work of the hospital. Concern about their "morals" dictated that their where-abouts were to be constantly monitored, and if they left the hospital for any rea-son, the Head Nurse was to report it in writing to the Dean of Women. None-theless, Washington wanted as many nursing students as possible going out to serve private patients in the community—meaning, in most cases, white pa-tients of white doctors.[9] For such service, which was regarded as one of the most exploitative practices in nurse training at the time, the school received between one and four dollars per day for each student employed.

Dr. Kenney's view of nurses was little more enlightened than Washington's. When he arrived at Tuskegee in 1905, his response to nurses' complaints about their interminable hours and poor work conditions was to suspend the com-plainants, and he continued to attribute nurses' protests to lack of professional seriousness. Addressing the 1920 annual meeting of the NACGN, he complained that nurses charged too much for their services.[10] The opening for Larsen had come up because both the Head Nurse and Assistant Head Nurse had quit—the Head Nurse because Washington insisted she live in the hospital to save the in-stitute money on her salary, despite the fact that she was married. A 1914 gradu-ate of the nursing school, Janie Armstead, had temporarily taken over their du-ties. Kenney first offered the Head Nurse position to a superintendent of nurses in the "colored" department of a hospital in Atlanta, "an excellent disciplinar-ian" and "respectable in every way," as he assured Washington, but she had de-clined his offer of $63 per month plus board.[11]

Conditions for the nurses depended on the finances of the institute, and Tuskegee was in desperate straits in the fall of 1915. The war in Europe had dried up donations in the midst of a building spree. By mid-August the institute had not paid its coal supplier in six months. Warren Logan, the treasurer, had no funds to pay either outside creditors or students for the allowances they were supposed to get out of their July earnings. In October, Washington ordered Logan to put austerity measures into effect, reducing every division's funding. A week later, he wrote again to tell Logan not to employ any new teachers, "or teachers to fill even positions that have been vacated, without my personal knowledge."[12] That week Logan made a special effort to settle teachers' overdue salaries, after which he informed Washington that the institute now had an overdraft at the bank.[13]

On October 21, two days after Logan's letter about the overdraft, Kenney wrote Washington that he had "engaged the services of Miss Nella M. Larsen," to begin "on or about November 2d as Head Nurse," at a monthly salary of $40 plus room and board. Scrawled in the top left corner of this missive is the word "Council"—indicating that Washington wanted the Executive Council to reconsider the action—and at the bottom, in the founder's own hand, "Mistake— / to displace Miss Armstead."[14] The next day, October 22, the Executive Council voted to allow Kenney to make the appointment he had already offered Larsen.[15]

On October 25, Logan informed Washington that the institute had overspent its general budget by $19,000 as of October 1.[16] Meanwhile, Washington was getting complaints of serious understaffing from virtually every department—not least the hospital, where Kenney was desperate for professional assistance. He wanted an Assistant Physician and two interns, but Washington would allow only the assistant and one intern. The first intern Kenney hired that fall never showed up for work. In fact, Kenney had constant problems with his male assistants and interns. Prior to the opening of school, a Dr. Strawbridge had been fired in July for "ruining" one of the student nurses, who was likewise expelled.[17]

Larsen was hired and arrived on campus at the same time as Dr. A. M. Curtis, Kenney's new assistant. Kenney did not consider Larsen's arrival important enough to mention in his memorandum to the editor of the school newspaper about staff additions at the hospital, but the *Tuskegee Student* duly reported that "Miss Nellie M. Larsen, of Chicago, Illinois, who has gained wide experience at the Lincoln Hospital in New York City, has been appointed Head Nurse."[18] None of Larsen's correspondence would have suggested the name "Nellie" to the person writing the copy. Regarding Dr. Curtis' appointment, the paper copied Kenney's words exactly: "The son of the well-known surgeon and physician of the same name who has such a distinguished record of achievement in the practice of medicine and surgery," Curtis had finished a year as an intern "in the celebrated Freedmen's Hospital, of Washington." His brother, moreover, was a graduate of Howard Medical School practicing in the national capital.[19]

The hospital also had a male intern, Dr. Rupert O. Roett, of Port of Spain, Trinidad. Other faculty members in the hospital, besides Janie Armstead, Larsen's assistant, included the pharmacist, Evelyn G. Houston of Atlanta; Mrs. C. E. "Mother" Watkins of Montgomery, the matron (in charge of daily discipline and housekeeping); and Chicagoan Edna M. Clanton, a stenographer. Watkins, thirteen years older than Larsen, was a Tuskegee institution in her own right, re- membered by reputation even today for her devotion to school discipline. Of spare figure and severe mien, she may have been a partial model for Miss MacGooden, the matron of the girls' dormitory created by Larsen for *Quicksand.*

The dominant figure was Dr. John A. Kenney, who had arrived in 1902 as sur- geon and resident physician, and who was now head of the nursing school. Larsen took her orders directly from him when he was around, and when he was away she was in charge of the hospital as well as the nurses. Straight-backed, slim, brown-skinned, serious, with a carefully clipped mustache and military bearing, he was one of the top black surgeons in the country. In 1915, when Larsen arrived, he presided over the National Medical Association (the national organization for African American doctors) and served as the managing editor of its journal. He had graduated from Hampton in 1897 and from Leonard Medical School of Shaw University in 1901, then had come to Tuskegee and de- veloped the medical department into one of the most respected in the South for African Americans. Largely because of his work, Tuskegee had secured funding for the $55,000 hospital, billed as "one of the finest Negro hospitals in the South and the third largest in the world."[20]

Larsen's daily routine began with prayers and breakfast at Tompkins Hall. On her way to breakfast, she would have witnessed the morning military drills for the boys of the institute, known as "cadets," finishing up on the large green— dark phalanxes in navy blue uniforms brandishing wooden "guns."[21] After break- fast, at the ringing of a bell, the locked doors came open and the hundreds of students and faculty members made their way to the day's duties.

Larsen worked much longer hours than other teachers at the school, al- though she was also paid more than many of the women teachers. Her duties involved both heavy nursing responsibilities and supervision of the pupils. The school *Bulletin* claimed that the nursing school held regular classes in anatomy, physiology, materia medica, and the theory and practice of nursing, though a later investigator questioned how often the one classroom was actually used.

Certainly, it is hard to imagine how regular classes could have been kept up through the series of crises affecting the hospital while Larsen was in residence. Most of the instruction took place at bedside. Practical nursing probably fell under Larsen's auspices, along with fever and surgical nursing, massage and hydrotherapy, and urinalysis. Most of her time was spent in simply supervising the general work of the hospital, for she and Armstead were the only experienced nurses there, and soon Larsen decided that her assistant should take the days off in order to do night duty. She also alternated with the Dean of Women and the kindergarten teacher in giving all the women students of the institute lessons in household hygiene and child health.[22]

The fifty-three-bed hospital averaged more than a hundred patients per month, and with only two (or, briefly, three) experienced nurses, as well as the three doctors, the hospital staff had their hands full day in and day out. Larsen's name never shows up in the lists of women attending social affairs and literary evenings during the year. Much of the year, in fact, she had to work both day and night. Nonetheless, teachers were expected at evening devotional exercises Monday through Thursday in Tompkins Hall, and Sunday evenings in the chapel, beginning at 6:30 P.M. Larsen, however, had no time even to settle into the routine before the school received the greatest shock in its history.

Immediately after she arrived, Dr. Kenney left for New York to attend to the failing health of Booker T. Washington. Larsen was left in charge of the hospital and of students she had barely come to know. Determined to die at Tuskegee, Washington left New York on November 12 with his wife and Dr. Kenney; doctors did not expect him to survive the trip. He made it, barely. An ambulance picked him up at the train station and took him to his home, the Oaks. On Sunday the fourteenth at 4:45 A.M. Washington died in bed, surrounded by family. The campus awoke that morning in a solemn hush, bereft of its leader.[23]

Students placed the body in a hearse at noon on Tuesday, November 16, and drove it to the chapel, where it lay in state, to be buried the next day.[24] The Montgomery *Advertiser* reported that the funeral was "simple and impressive"; "the humble and unlettered colored people of the cotton fields" filled the school grounds. At 10:20 on Wednesday morning, a procession of teachers, trustees, alumni, students, and visitors proceeded from the Oaks to the chapel to the sound of muffled drums. "Inside, the building was packed to suffocation." Black leaders from all over the country attended, along with "the hosts of whites, [and] the multitudes of the simple country folk whom Dr. Washington loved so well."[25] Every few minutes the student honor-guard changed, keeping watch over the casket. Following the benediction, the casket and audience moved to a vault just outside the chapel, the last words of the burial service were read, taps sounded, "and a heavy-hearted crowd turned slowly and sadly away from the tomb of their prophet."[26]

In the wake of this catastrophic loss, which cast a pall over the campus for the rest of the academic year, school leaders more than ever called for unity of purpose, loyalty, and absolute devotion to the cause. As trustee William G. Willcox urged in his remarks the day of the funeral, "In the work before us, the cause is everything, the individual is nothing. There is no room for personal ambition, jealousy or fractional difference. The crisis demands as never before unselfish, disinterested and loyal co-operation."[27] Of course, the question of Washington's successor came up immediately; Emmett Scott, the school secretary, had many friends and partisans, as did the treasurer, Warren Logan. But it was generally agreed from the moment of the founder's passing that R. R. Moton would succeed him.[28] Moton was commandant of the cadets at the Hampton Institute, and the only black person on its faculty, the right-hand man of N. B. Frissell, Hampton's white director. Moton had been a close friend and frequent fellow-traveler of the Tuskegee founder, had often spoken from the same platform, and was regarded by black Southerners as the foremost leader of the race after Washington's death. The trustees seem to have quickly made up their minds that Moton would take over, but Moton would not be available until the end of the school year, so they turned to Warren Logan to take over as Acting Principal until May 1916.

Logan was having his own problems. Throughout the autumn his wife, the feminist Adella Hunt Logan, had been "a good deal run down nervously," according to Booker T. Washington in a letter to trustee H. J. Kellogg, who ran a famous sanitarium in Battle Creek, Michigan. In early October, Washington had arranged for her admission to the sanitarium, where the fact that she was not white could be kept secret, and she had spent a month taking the "rest cure" — the treatment for "female hysteria" that Charlotte Perkins Gilman indicted so chillingly in "The Yellow Wallpaper." The patient got back to Tuskegee in early November, hours before Booker T. Washington's death. Between then and the official memorial service scheduled for December 12, rumors began circulating that her husband was involved in an affair, and the rumors may have reached her ears. She became increasingly unstable. On Friday, December 10, while the famous trustees were gathering on campus, she walked to a fourth-floor window of the academic building, in which her sister and daughter were teaching, and jumped, breaking her body on the pavement below. Her horrified daughter took her to the hospital, where Larsen had charge of the nurses and patient admissions. Logan lay unconscious until a little after 6:00 P.M., woke briefly to look around and say, "Oh, where am I?" and then died.[29]

It was a terrific scandal. Adella Hunt Logan had been a teacher since the earliest years of the school, as had her husband; people would not even mention the cause of death. She was buried quietly during the regular Sunday morning service on December 12.[30] That same evening the school held the memorial services for the founder, attended by the trustees and a crowd of about three thousand, black and white, who heard Theodore Roosevelt speak feelingly of his former adviser.[31]

Through all this uproar, the hospital was crowded with patients, and Larsen kept at her daily tasks, putting in fourteen-hour days. On Saturdays between 2:00 and 3:00 P.M. she aided Dr. Kenney in his weekly "Health Hour" demonstrations for anyone wishing to attend.[32] What Kenney called an "epidemic of grippe" hit the school in mid-December, taxing the staff to its utmost; to the Executive Council he proudly commended Larsen and the others for their work, which included feeding nearly one hundred people on less than five dollars per day.[33] There was need to be frugal. The institute still staggered under the debts with which Washington had been struggling to the moment of his death.

The epidemic kept up into February, at least, when Kenney decided to postpone the annual "Tuskegee Clinic," in part because, as he informed the Executive Council, "we have had such a hard time over here [in the hospital] this winter with so much sickness, working our people so hard, and not knowing whether the epidemic would be abated."[34] In the month of January they had treated five times their usual patient load. As Larsen worked on to the limit of her endurance, some of the staff members could not bear the stress. Around the beginning of February she had to recommend that two student nurses be let go.[35] In mid-February, Kenney's assistant Dr. Curtis, he of the illustrious family, abandoned ship. "From the best information available it seems Dr. Curtis left the School last night," Kenney reported. "He gave me no word of his intention and left no message for me. . . . His whereabouts I do not know." Kenney assumed, rightly, that "in the light of developments," he had gone home.[36] This, of course, only threw more responsibility onto Larsen. The hospital carried on for more than two months with no replacement for Curtis.

Larsen had plenty of other problems with her job. The organization and conduct of the nursing school violated all sorts of modern standards for nursing education, including the registration and accreditation rules of the State of Alabama. By late February, the violations had come to the attention of the state medical authorities, as Kenney informed Emmett Scott, who hurriedly appointed a committee to advise on changes in the nursing program. No one thought to appoint an experienced nurse to this committee, which included Kenney and two other men unconnected to the hospital.[37] The committee quickly discovered that Alabama law required a three-year course of study, as opposed to the two-year course at Tuskegee (the third year at Tuskegee involved no classroom instruction but only practical work off campus); that a nurse must hold the position of Superintendent of the nursing school; that pupil nurses must not be farmed out for private duty in the community; and that pupils who had not completed at least one year of high school before starting their training could not expect to pass the state examination for registered nurses. All of these requirements contradicted the reigning institutional culture of Tuskegee, and the administration proceeded to find ways to effectively evade each of them, except the hard and fast rule of a three-year course.

The committee headed by Kenney recommended that girls who had passed the middle school course be considered to have the equivalent of a year of high school. The Executive Council approved both this alteration and an extension of the coursework to three years, but did nothing at first about the other requirements.[38] A month later, Kenney tersely informed the council that "it is not only necessary for nurses but for Training Schools to comply with the requirements of the law," pointing out that "the superintendent should be a registered nurse" and that pupils were to be trained in the hospital and not sent out to work. To cope with the first difficulty, he recommended that Larsen's position be retitled Superintendent of Nurses, "in keeping with the law and all other large training schools." Knowing that the administration would not want a lowly nurse and outsider like Larsen to hold such an august title, Kenney insisted that it was a change in name only, not in authority or substance. The prohibition on hiring out student nurses was much more daunting. "We must find means of getting around that," Kenney concluded.[39] He then urged a white doctor in town, L. S. Johnston, to exert influence on the accreditation officials so that Tuskegee students could continue to "serve the community." Glossing over the fact that the hospital partly depended on the fees paid for such service, Kenney emphasized the late founder's desire that the nurses be of the greatest possible help to the people of the region.[40] Johnston apparently sympathized, and the state waived the requirement for Tuskegee pupils, to Nella Larsen's disgust. She registered her feelings about such abuses years later in *Quicksand*, in which Helga Crane, explaining why she hates Naxos and wants to leave, tells its new director, "I hate hypocrisy. I hate cruelty to students, and to teachers who can't fight back."[41]

The final hurdle in the accreditation process was the fact that Tuskegee granted only certificates, not diplomas, to nursing graduates. Repeated requests to the Executive Council that they grant diplomas to nursing graduates fell on deaf ears, no doubt in part because nursing students could matriculate and graduate with no high school education whatever. In the spring of 1916, after receiving the "encouraging news" from the state board of examination and registration of nurses that "they have registered us; that is, our Training School and that they are accepting our *certificates* in Nurse Training, but that hereafter it will be necessary to give *diplomas*," Kenney urged the administration once again to change its policy. "Please understand," he added, "that I am not asking for your Academic diploma."[42] Kenney was actually responding to fervent pleas and complaints from his own nurses and nurse graduates, who found that after all their training and work for Tuskegee they could not gain Registered Nurse status even in the rural South.[43] The Executive Council continued to stonewall through the month of April while Kenney kept pleading with them.

Larsen's status among the women's faculty at Tuskegee was little better than that of her students among the entire student body. The chief extracurricular institution for female teachers was the Tuskegee Woman's Club, founded by Margaret Murray Washington (Booker T.'s wife) in 1895. Though dedicating itself to promoting the "general intellectual development of women," it prided itself on its exclusivity. Meeting twice a month, it did encourage new women faculty to join; but even if they accepted Larsen, she could hardly have participated, because she was working fourteen hours a day, every day (or nearly so), in the hospital.[44] It is, in any case, questionable whether they considered her "faculty." The many reports of their activities in the campus newspaper, which often list attendees and active members, never mention Larsen.[45] Throughout the winter and early spring of 1915–1916, the club's chief project other than the Shakespeare Tercentenary was "a series of programs presenting the various European countries engaged in war—their standing with regard to the original issue, their history, development, customs, etc., with especial attention to the interests and activities of the woman and their attitude toward the present struggle."[46] Over the course of several months, they offered programs on Austria, Russia, Germany, Serbia, France, England, Japan, Italy, and "the Land of the Turk." A long list of the club's members in association with these activities includes the names of many faculty wives and teachers in the academic department, but no Nella Larsen. Although she may have made it, somehow, to some of these affairs, one wonders how she would have responded, for example, to the program on England organized by Emmett Scott's wife, one of the leading ladies of the institute. Part one, on "Merrie England before the war," featured Britannia (played by Mrs. Scott) on her throne, entertained by her colonies and provinces with songs, dances (e.g., an Irish jig), and humorous sketches. Then a herald announced that Germany had declared war: "Britannia swoons, the colonies rush to her support offering their ships, men, nurses, food, money. The audience could not but feel the tragedy of the scene, so realistic was the despair of Britannia, so earnest the colonies in their offers of aid."[47]

Margaret Murray Washington presided over the women's club and everything else pertaining to women at Tuskegee. She was one of the leading "race women" in the country and at the peak of her influence. For a number of years she served as president of the National Association of Colored Women, for which she spoke all over the country. When she stepped down from the presidency in the fall of 1916, she was named honorary vice president and a life member of the Executive Board. As "lady Principal" of Tuskegee, she had charge of all the girls' training programs.[48] Tall, light-skinned, of full figure and commanding appearance, she was a strict disciplinarian and completely devoted to the Tuskegee program.

Margaret Murray Washington personally authorized the style of uniforms for female students while Larsen was at the institute, and she was the person Larsen had to inform whenever a nurse left the hospital. She was ultimately responsible for the strict regulations on women's behavior, including official reprimands of women teachers for setting a bad example by spending too much time with young men.[49] (There is no indication that Larsen got in trouble for such infractions, but she would later attest that the school authorities disapproved of her "manner and appearance.") When the Dean of the Women's Department, who had always confided in her, resigned due to ill health sometime in February, Mrs. Washington took over her duties, immediately ordering that the catalogue for the next year specify a uniform outer wrap of three-quarter length for the girls: a heavy dark-blue "goods coat" ordered upon arrival at the institute.[50]

Larsen's memories of similar policies at Tuskegee would later provide material for the early chapters of *Quicksand:*

> Turning from the window, [Helga Crane's] gaze wandered contemptuously over the dull attire of the women workers. Drab colors, mostly navy blue, black, brown, unrelieved, save for a scrap of white or tan about the hands and necks. Fragments of a speech made by the dean of women floated through her thoughts—"Bright colors are vulgar"—"Black, gray, brown, and navy blue are the most becoming colors for colored people"—"Dark-complected people shouldn't wear yellow, or green or red."—The dean was a woman from one of the "first families"—a great "race" woman; she, Helga Crane, a despised mulatto, but something intuitive, some unanalyzed driving spirit of loyalty to the inherent racial need for gorgeousness, told her that bright colors *were* fitting

and that dark-complexioned people *should* wear yellow, green, and red. Black, brown, and gray were ruinous to them, actually destroyed the luminous tones lurking in their dusky skins.[51]

Larsen had a dress designer's eye for color and texture, and a feminist resentment of social restrictions on women's clothing. But in a larger sense, what she resented about Tuskegee's policies in such areas was the general culture of moral suspicion pervading the campus. And Margaret Murray Washington bore a large part of the responsibility for that culture when it came to the lives of women. Throughout the spring, summer, and fall of 1916, the Executive Council files reveal her steady surveillance of female behavior, which nourished a culture of petty backbiting, gossip, and subtle intimidation. In each division of the work, the matrons served as her eyes and ears, but all women faculty were supposed to report any lapse in "discipline."

Such disciplinary issues were not Larsen's only problems with the "lady Principal." Mrs. Washington had been clamoring since at least December for completion of a new laundry, one aspect of women's industrial training being the laundering of all the clothes and linens worn and used at the institute.[52] Finally, in mid-March, the new campus laundry was completed, and Larsen promptly discovered that the hospital laundry had been emptied of appliances to equip it. She wrote Dr. Kenney a carefully typed and signed letter: "We have recently investigated the condition of the laundry belonging to the hospital and found that all appliances have been removed, rendering it impossible for us to use the laundry, when necessary." Noting that the hospital frequently had patients with infectious diseases, she wrote: "It is imperative that the bed linen and night clothing of the patient be disinfected and boiled before being sent to the general laundry for washing. Without the Hospital laundry, we are reduced to a crude and inadequate method of disinfecting these things; namely, an old pot in the woods." The nurses, moreover, were reduced to using the kitchen to wash and iron towels and disinfect sponges for the operating and wound-dressing rooms. She closed tersely, with a hint of sarcasm: "Can the school see its way to having the stove, tubs and ironing boards returned to the laundry built for the hospital, so that it may be put into use. / N. M. Larsen / Head Nurse."[53] Kenney forwarded a less explicit and more diplomatic letter about the same problem, written by the matron, C. E. Watkins, to the Executive Council along with Larsen's. Scrawled at the bottom of Watkins' letter by the clerk of the council, E. Davidson Washington (Margaret's stepson), are the words: "Cannot afford this."

Larsen had yet other reasons for rebellion. With only one Assistant Head Nurse and a nursing staff otherwise composed entirely of students, she worked to exhaustion every day. Finally, in preparing his budget for the 1916–1917 school year, Kenney petitioned the hospital for funds to hire a Night Supervisor: "We need two head nurses for the day work; one cannot do it satisfactorily and the night work certainly does require the services of a trained nurse in charge. Much of this year our head nurse has worked fourteen hours a day, day after day, in order to relieve the situation and that the assistant might do night duty."[54] The night shift was easier than day shift, of course, since most of the patients were asleep. Kenney asked if he could appoint a graduate nurse each year to take over night supervision for $25 a month plus board. The Executive Council approved the request, but this did not help Larsen, for it would not take effect until the fall.

Also in mid-March the one M.D. remaining other than Kenney, Dr. Roett, threatened to leave. The school had little choice but to promote him from intern to Assistant Physician and raise his salary, which was actually lower than Nella Larsen's.[55] In granting this promotion, Kenney made no changes in the relative authority that Roett and Larsen had over the hospital; thus, Larsen remained in charge when Kenney was gone.

The hospital now had an Assistant Physician but no intern, and Kenney could not find anyone willing to hire on.[56] When various health-related meetings took place on campus, Larsen held down the hospital while Kenney and others oversaw those activities—such as Better Baby Week, first observed in March 1916. Kenney and other black health leaders had turned their attention to public hygiene and infant mortality, out of concern for "survival of the race." Formerly, believing that infant mortality carried off the weak and "unfit," leaving the race stronger as a whole, they had not been overly concerned with it. Modern science, however, had decided that the strength of every race or nation depended on low infant mortality—and that low infant mortality depended on good motherhood combined with strict sanitation standards.[57]

Black doctors also feared racial extinction by tuberculosis. Dr. Kenney kept two copies, and was sent a third by Emmett Scott, of a widely distributed 1914 pamphlet arguing that the disease might "seal the fate of our race." "The logic of the Negro's present status is progressive, cumulative lowered vitality and ultimate extinction. If he does not stop short and rebuild his shattered vitality his grave will take its place along side the Maori, the Hawaii[a]n, and the North American Indian; among the races of men who have perished from the earth. . . . The duty of the present generation is to stem the tide."[58] Negroes had to avoid the cities and stay in the healthy countryside, adhering rigidly to "primitive, Puritan virtues," or in two to three centuries they would vanish from the earth. Moreover, "marriage of the unfit or those who cannot comply with the eugenic test transmits a hereditary predisposition or susceptibility to consumption."[59] Black doctors should call for a return to country living and to eugenic mating. Larsen would attribute precisely such beliefs to Helga Crane's fiancé at Naxos. "Superior" Negroes, he believes, have a duty to propagate or else see the race overwhelmed by the unfit.

Worry about racial survival had inspired Moton's call for the first Negro "clean-up week" in March of 1913. Booker T. Washington chimed in, asking blacks throughout the South to join the campaign. Especially aimed at combating flies and mosquitoes, it responded to discoveries of the relationship between bad drainage, insect-borne bacteria, and infectious disease. As editorials in the *Southern Workman* pointed out, death from preventable diseases impeded the "progress of the race," costing money, depleting savings, destroying families, and carrying off potential race leaders.[60] Thus, National Negro Health Week was born, more than a decade before Negro History Week (now Black History Month). As Principal-elect of Tuskegee, Moton demanded constant attention to the "sanitation drive," making Tuskegee, that spring of 1916, the leader of the effort throughout the black South.[61]

National Negro Health Week was barely over, however, when the flies began breeding on campus, and soon they had besieged the hospital. The afternoon of April 18, they were "swarming . . . through the front door" because of ill-fitting screens. Larsen had stationed a nurse there with a fly swatter, but Kenney was afraid to open the door to leave until Dr. Roett fanned the flies away from outside and other staff members banded together on the inside to kill any coming in. A newly dubbed "Sanitary Nurse" spent all her time swatting, putting down flypaper, and looking after trays of fly poison. It was not only embarrassing, wrote Kenney to the Executive Council, but "really criminal for the hospital to have such an alarming number of flies."[62] The nearby horse and cattle barns, which they had refused to move, did not help matters.

Toward the end of the school year, work in the hospital fell off its frenetic pace and a momentous Commencement approached, with Robert Russa Moton's inauguration as Principal. Special trains and cars brought people from north, south, east, and west, from black churches, schools, and colleges. On May 25, thousands of farmers and field hands with their families began gathering on campus as early as 3:00 A.M. They toured the facilities and fields while students on raised platforms demonstrated skills and gave orations.[63] As the inaugural moment neared, the chapel crowded to overflowing with those anxious to hear the new race leader chosen by the white trustees.

"There must be no cantankerousness here—we must all work absolutely together," Moton intoned. "If team-work, my friends, was necessary in this school under the leadership of Doctor Washington, how much more imperative the necessity is now."[64] It was a deliberate reiteration of the last speech Washington had given on campus before he died, which had been printed in the campus newspaper immediately after Larsen's arrival. Moton closed with a quotation from that Sunday evening talk: "We want to have team-work, not only in the direction to which I have referred, but most of all . . . in our spiritual life, in our religious life, everywhere, in the prayer meetings, . . . in every devotional exercise . . . everywhere, we want to have team-work, all working together in the direction which shall bring about the highest spiritual usefulness in this institution."[65] According to a sympathetic faculty witness, the address was a "triumph."[66]

But for Nella Larsen, Tuskegee's "teamwork," like its "race consciousness," was a cruel hoax, crushing individuality and spontaneous joy, suppressing independent thought and feeling, exploiting the powerless. She would draw from her dressmaker's lexicon for the right metaphor, describing her fictional Naxos as a large knife "ruthlessly cutting all to a pattern, the white man's pattern."[67] "There has been no friction during the year," reported the *Tuskegee Student* in June. "As an expression of their sincerity both teachers and students put aside practically all forms of even the few diversions they were accustomed to having."[68] It was enough to disillusion Larsen forever about "uplift" and the notion of collective identity as preached from on high.

Warren Logan continued as Acting Principal, and Larsen had little contact with Dr. Moton because even after he officially took over in late May he started on a cross-country speaking tour to raise a memorial fund in Washington's name.[69] Two brief notes do survive in which Larsen asks Moton, in early September and then again in October, to sign diplomas for graduating students—the first signed "Nella M. Larsen R.N.," the other merely "N. M. Larsen."[70]

By the end of the summer of 1916, Larsen had had quite enough of what teamwork meant at the institute. For one thing, she and the new pharmacist were not getting along with Dr. Roett, the Assistant Physician. Already the pharmacist, Miss Richie B. Kyles, had offered her resignation in protest against disrespectful treatment. In late August, Dr. Kenney left for the National Medical Association conference: "During my absence, Miss Larsen, the Head Nurse, will be in charge as usual. Dr. Roett will be in charge of the Medical Work with the assistance of Dr. Norris, and with the usual instruction during my absence if there are any serious cases to call in Dr. Johnston"—Johnston being the local white physician.[71] While Kenney was gone, Larsen called in Johnston four times, twice without Roett's prior knowledge and once against his wishes. In an awkward letter to Kenney, the aggrieved Roett demanded Executive Council action to affirm that Larsen must submit "things in a purely professional line . . . to the resident or visiting physician." He went on:

> I do think it is professional discourtesy when a nurse is set over a young medical doctor, or is told that her decision overrules him when she thinks another doctor should be called in to a case in his charge. In submitting this to you and the Executive Council, I beg to state as can be plainly seen
>
> That it is first discourteous to me professionally. It shows me up to be unconfidential and puts me in a place of mistrust.
>
> It casts around me bad reflexion, as some hearing, who are not acquainted with the circumstances and ruling will think differently.

If the council had found him incompetent to take charge of cases in the absence of Dr. Kenney, or even decide when to call in outside help, he should have been asked to resign. "As that is not the case, and the head Nurse has authority to overrule my professional opinion I am embarrassed and hurt, and will not be able to demand in cases medical the respect of the head Nurse and probably her staff, and others outside of the Hospital. I beg therefore that if the ruling is still to be carried all the time, in the absence of the Medical Director to offer now my resignation to go into effect on October 15, 1916."[72] Kenney forwarded the letter to Moton without any response by Larsen or representation of her point of view. On September 12, Kenney wrote Moton a letter signed by Roett and himself confirming Roett's point and asking for Moton's approval.[73] Moton approved.

Less than a month later, on October 7, Kenney had to write Moton again on personnel matters, this time in regard to Richie Kyles, the pharmacist. She had recently refused to fill a prescription for a private-room patient when asked by Roett to do so, saying she had filled it already and if it had got lost upstairs it was not her fault. "Miss Kyles' attitude in the matter was very unsatisfactory." She no longer seemed to care about her position: "Her attitude is that of indifference, as can be seen by the note which she writes."[74] Kenney asked for permission to fire her, enclosing as incriminating evidence a letter she had written him stating that she felt grossly insulted by the manner in which he spoke to her and by having to clean and mop floors, working unpaid overtime while he offered only insult in return. Across the top of Kenney's letter asking to fire Kyles, Moton scrawled "Approved."

Three days after Kenney penned that letter, Nella Marian Larsen decided to quit: "Dr. Kenney:—I am writing to ask, if you will obtain a release from, the work here, for me. I would of course be willing to remain until the work at the hospital is regularly adjusted, unless an earlier date is agreeable." The diplomatic closing reads, "Thanking you, for all considerations shown, during my period of service here / Very Truly / Nella Marian Larsen."[75]

In her frustration, Larsen had not thought to plan her exit carefully. Kenney held on to the note for three or four days. On the fourteenth, he wrote Moton: "Miss Nella M. Larsen, our Head Nurse, asks to be relieved of her duties. Under the existing circumstances, I recommend that her request be granted. That it go into effect at once and that I be empowered to arrange for the filling of her place."[76] The Executive Council approved the recommendation the same day. On the sixteenth, Kenney surprised Larsen with a letter (a copy was sent to Moton). "Miss Larsen: Agreeable to your request of a release from the work here in our hospital, this advises that it is granted to take effect from the present date. Thanking you for the services which you have rendered since being with us and regretting that conditions make it necessary for such an early termination of your connection with our Institution. A copy of this is forwarded to the Principal."[77] At the same time, he wrote to the Executive Council recommending that Janie Armstead take over immediately as Acting Head Nurse and receive the full salary currently paid to Larsen.[78]

In a panic, Larsen immediately dashed off two nearly identical, very brief letters to Moton and the Executive Council, asking for her resignation "to take effect in thirty (30) days from date."[79] She was too late, for the same day she received a perfunctory note from the Principal addressed to "Miss Nella N. Larsen." Acknowledging her original note of October 10 offering Dr. Kenney her resignation, it stated, "Your resignation is hereby accepted in accordance with your request."[80]

Larsen made directly for Moton's office. A small handwritten note can be found in Moton's office papers dated October 16 and reading, "Dr. Moton: — May I see you at once? / Very Truly. / Nella M. Larsen R.N." If Moton met with Larsen, he told her she no longer had a job. The next day, he wrote Janie Armstead, Larsen's assistant, that the council was appointing her Acting Head Nurse with Larsen's salary, $57, until a permanent replacement could be found; and he sent Richie Kyles a letter officially accepting her resignation as pharmacist.[81]

The *Tuskegee Student* made no mention of Larsen's departure. Practically the only direct records of her outraged existence at the institute have lain buried in obscure office correspondence for more than eighty years, in folders marked "Kenney, John A.," and "Executive Council."

"Naxos? It's hardly a place at all. It's more like some loathsome, venomous disease."[82] When her first novel appeared with this description of a school transparently based on Tuskegee, Larsen lived in the same apartment complex as some of her well-connected Tuskegee acquaintances, people she saw all the time in Harlem and who formed part of its high society, just as they had formed the high society of Tuskegee when she was a displaced and overworked "nobody" there.[83] She well knew that they would recognize her attack on the institution with which their families remained intimately identified. But Larsen was not one to look back. She let the bridges burn.

EIGHT

A Nurse in the Bronx:
1916–1919

LARSEN may have returned briefly to Chicago after her sudden release from Tuskegee; and if so, she may well have been turned away. In late June and early July her mother and stepfather had bought a new home at 6418 Maryland Avenue, deeding their old house to the owner and borrowing money to make up the difference. They owned the new house "jointly" rather than "in common," a very rare arrangement indicating that Mary was keeping her finances separate from Peter's. Anna and her husband, with Nella's two-year-old nephew, George Larsen Gardner, moved into the other half of the same building, 6420.[1] The new neighborhood, Woodlawn, was one of those east of State Street that had been bitterly, and successfully, fighting the "invasion" of Negroes since the turn of the century.[2] It is not certain how aware George was of Anna's black half-sister, and in this may rest a basis for the scene in *Quicksand* when Helga Crane visits her uncle's Chicago home after leaving Naxos, only to be turned away from the door by her uncle's new wife.

Whether Larsen stopped in Chicago or not, she was soon back in New York and working under Adah Thoms as Assistant Superintendent of Nurses at Lincoln. Taking up residence once again in the hospital, Larsen helped to supervise the nurses and taught Materia Medica (precursor to Pharmacology) and History of Nursing—two of the most "academic" courses. History of Nursing, a new subject not offered at most schools, was a key component of the attempt to prepare nurses for expanding supervisory and public health roles by incorporating more liberal arts into their training. It sought, above all, to inspire students with a sense of nursing's dignity and importance while teaching its ethical principles and traditions.[3] An outline of the general history of the world, introduced early in the semester, provided the skeleton on which the development of nursing as an activity essential to all civilization was fleshed out, from the period of human emergence to the present.

We can be reasonably certain of what Larsen studied in preparation and lectured about, because the only full-length book on the subject then in use in the United States was Adelaide Nutting and Lavinia Dock's monumental *History of*

Nursing, virtually a primer in women's history. *History of Nursing* emphasized over and over, across a comprehensive historical span, the ways in which women had used nursing and the institutions connected with it to assert their independence, to develop intellectually, and to acquire social authority. Progress and regress in the ethical treatment of the sick, and the general level of public health, correlated with the cultural and social status of women. These lessons contradicted the common assumption that nursing was a lowly occupation for nonintellectual women who had to support themselves.[4]

Beginning with animal behavior and early human health and grooming practices, the text covered ancient forms of nursing in India, Ceylon, Egypt, Babylon, Assyria, and Israel before coming to ancient Greece, with emphasis on the ethical ideals embodied in the Hippocratic Oath. Lectures and reading assignments in courses like Larsen's would then cover the development of nursing in association with the early church and introduce heroines: Paula, Marcella, and Fabiola of Rome; Hildegard and Radegunde of Northern Europe and Scandinavia. These women had been intellectuals and founders of institutions, including the first public hospital in Rome. They had given up aristocratic privileges, lived without the protection of men or the aid of servants, and taken on the most basic tasks of nursing alongside administration, showing how "men and women might find self-expression outside of family ties," a development to be vastly expanded in the Middle Ages.[5]

The monastery, or the "religious settlement," as Dock and Nutting called it, "was for centuries the only place where women at least could find freedom from social fetters or distasteful matrimony, and have liberty to conduct satisfying work in their own way, with opportunity to develop and cultivate intellectual tastes."[6]

Nursing history amounted to a correction of male-oriented histories of Western culture. Recent historical research—much of it by women—had revealed that monastic nurses could dress as they pleased and move freely about the towns and countryside. They often commanded both men and women. A line of thirty-two abbesses ruled the Benedictine settlement at Fontevrault for six hundred years, maintaining their hold only through constant vigilance against the onslaughts of men seeking to subordinate them. Wherever women's orders were ruled by an abbot, they failed. Modern scholars had found that "it is a fact capable of daily proof that a woman is a more successful leader of men and women than a man."[7]

While the so-called Dark Ages and medieval period were a Golden Age of nursing, the period from the Enlightenment to the mid-nineteenth century constituted the "Dark Period of Nursing" and of European medicine, which sank, along with the status of nurses, to "an indescribable level of degradation."[8] Nursing history showed that any assault on women's equality was an assault on the progress and well-being of the human race. "Even where a woman still apparently stood at the head of a nursing body," in the Enlightenment and after, "she was only a figure-head, with no power to alter conditions, no province that she could call her own. The state of degeneration to which men reduced the art of nursing during this time of their unrestricted rule, the general contempt to which they brought the nurse, the misery which the patient thereby suffered, bring a scathing indictment against the ofttime reiterated assertion of man's superior effectiveness."[9] After her experiences at Tuskegee, Larsen could teach this lesson from the heart. In her knowledge of women's history, Larsen was far ahead of most college-educated women of the time.

The chief figure of modern nursing, of course, was Florence Nightingale, the Englishwoman famous for her service during the Crimean War, who founded a nurse training school in London in 1860. Nursing history emphasized her "new conception of nursing as an economically independent secular vocation or art demanding intelligence, knowledge and skill," not madonna-like devotion.[10] Nightingale's organizational and political acumen, and her ability to assert her authority despite the perpetual hurdles thrown up by male officials, demonstrated that nurses were not to be ministering angels or helpmates to doctors but modern, self-directed professionals and administrators.

The later stages of the nursing history course stressed the growing intersection between advanced nursing and social work and demonstrated how bad housing, low wages, child labor, industrial exploitation, lack of education for women, and lack of recreation undermined public health. Larsen's background in nursing history helps to explain why her writing would be more advanced from a feminist standpoint than that of other authors of the Harlem Renaissance.

About a year after Larsen's return to Lincoln, the United States entered World War I. By the spring of 1918, an acute nursing shortage had developed, particularly in New York. In early May, calls went out for massive recruitment of nurses for the Red Cross.[11] Black leaders in the field of nursing saw an opportunity to break down a racial barrier of utmost symbolic as well as professional importance, and spearheading their drive to enroll black nurses was Larsen's mentor, Adah B. Thoms.

On May 18, a radiant, cloudless afternoon, one of the largest parades in the history of the Bronx marched down the Grand Concourse in honor of the Red Cross War Fund. At the front marched a phalanx of women—sixteen abreast— who had husbands and sons in the military. These were followed by mounted policemen, city officials, regiments of the U.S. Army, members of the Coast Guard artillery, and sailors from the Pelham Bay Park Naval Group. Then came the nurses. Thoms and Larsen had their people out in force. They marched between groups of white Red Cross nurses, along with nurses from Lebanon and Fordham hospitals, followed by the Bronx Red Cross chapters and women's auxiliaries. "The nurses from Fordham, Lebanon and Lincoln Hospitals were greeted with cheers at various points along the line," reported the *Bronx Home News*. "Behind the graduate nurses came a group of student nurses. Before them marched a sailor carrying a placard on which was printed, 'The Future Red Cross Nurses.'"[12] Despite the placard, no black nurses had yet been allowed into the Red Cross. Adah Thoms was determined to change that.

In July black nurses met with local representatives of the Red Cross at Lafayette Hall in Harlem, and Thoms spoke on behalf of "colored nurses." Her speech could have been scripted at Tuskegee:

> It is far from our desire to become members of this or any other organization for the sake of "social equality." We are, as you know, a very happy race. Wherever we are and under all circumstances. Besides, there are so many social standards in our own race that we can very easily find our social center. What we are earnestly seeking is an opportunity to serve. As nurses we have only one desire in our hearts. That is to enter into this great struggle for democracy, to work side by side with our more fortunate sisters if needed, or to be assigned to our own troops that we have so willingly given to fight and shed their blood in order to make the world a better and happier place to live in.[13]

All felt the justice of her appeal, according to the *New York Age,* the influential African American weekly newspaper, and local Red Cross leaders pledged their support.

A second, mass meeting at Harlem's Palace Casino drew a distinguished, capacity crowd to hear representatives of the Red Cross speak to the issue, followed by a musical program of patriotic songs led by J. Rosamond Johnson. About a hundred black nurses in uniform, gathered from all over New York City, filled the front seats. James Weldon Johnson reported that they were one of the event's most striking features and "attracted a great deal of attention." In part because black nurses were not exclusively concentrated in black neighborhoods, few black New Yorkers had suspected that "there were that many trained nurses of the race in the city."[14]

Within a week of the rally, Frances R. Elliott of Jackson, Tennessee, then Head Nurse at the Tuskegee Institute, received word that she would be the first black nurse to wear the red cross.[15] Emmett J. Scott, Tuskegee's former secretary, was now special assistant to the U.S. Secretary of War and no doubt had much to do with Elliott's selection. He issued a statement that the U.S. Surgeon General would be seeking colored nurses to "render service for their own race in the army." Instantly, the Red Cross asked Adah Thoms for the names of twenty-five Lincoln Hospital nurses for "immediate service," and she inaugurated a drive to get "all colored registered nurses in and out of New York to enroll in the Red Cross."[16] Unmarried, highly skilled, independent, tactful yet firm and even courageous, Larsen would have made a perfect Red Cross recruit. Unlike her mentor, however, she was unpatriotic and detested segregation. She never answered the call, although several of her Lincoln colleagues did and joined the first wave of black nurses to engage in war service.

Instead, Larsen decided to follow the lead of some of her recent colleagues and join the Health Department of New York City. Others had gone to work for the Henry Street Visiting Nurse Service, led by Lillian Wald. But the municipal Health Department was more attractive from Larsen's standpoint. The city's public health nurses did no bedside nursing—their functions were educational and investigative. Henry Street's visiting nurses did a great deal of bedside nursing, and its black nurses served black neighborhoods exclusively, for the leaders at Henry Street found that they could serve the black population better than white nurses could, and that black nurses faced too much resistance among whites to be at their best in nonblack settings. In contrast, under civil service regulations black nurses in the Health Department could not be assigned to districts based on race, and white nurses in public health were considered the most fair of all in their dealings with black colleagues.[17] This made the department very attractive to Larsen. Moreover, public health nurses had suddenly come into high demand in the Bureau of Preventable Diseases.

Coincident with Thoms's Red Cross campaign, a huge public health controversy erupted over the policies of the new mayor of New York, John F. Hylan, and this crisis gave Larsen her opportunity. In 1917–1918, the United States had only 98,000 registered nurses (20,000 of whom were in the military service) and only 6,000 public health nurses (1,000 of these being in New York), at a time when the demand for them was increasing exponentially in the battle against infant mortality, tuberculosis, and infectious disease.[18] With little foresight, Hylan proposed eliminating both the Bureau of Child Hygiene and the Bureau of Preventable Diseases as a savings measure. This sparked a public outcry of national proportions, for New York was the major point of embarkation for soldiers going abroad, as well as their chief place of recreation. The Health Commissioner resigned in protest. National magazines suggested that, as a war measure, the federal government might have to take charge of the city administration. After the Surgeon General and the War Department began breathing down his neck, Hylan made an about-face. The new Health Commissioner immediately announced a "Health Drive," and in mid-May the Health Department asked for forty new nursing positions to be filled from the civil service list. Nella M. Larsen was one of sixty-four women who sat for the examination in late May. She earned the second-highest score, 89.20.[19]

Along with a friend from Lincoln who had supervised the Children's Medical Ward, she entered the Health Department in the Bureau of Preventable Diseases on June 17 at a standard beginning salary of $960 per year. Her friend Ruth Ina Strickland was assigned to Manhattan, but Larsen took a post in the Bronx, possibly at her own request since she was one of the top performers on the examination. The two women moved in together at 280 East 161st Street.[20]

The population of the Bronx at the time was less than 1 percent black, and Larsen's new home was in a three-story house on a good-sized lot in a "German" area. Not too far away, on Morris Avenue near 164th Street, a very few middle-class black and "mulatto" families lived in a couple of neat row houses. With the railroad half a block away, Larsen and Strickland could hear trains all day and night. On Sunday mornings, hymns and organ music emanated from the Baptist church kitty-corner to their back yard. They could easily catch a train to Manhattan from the Melrose station or take the Third Avenue El from 161st Street.[21] At the Melrose Branch of the public library, just a block away, Larsen could check out books or attend lectures and readings, while Melrose Park was considered a good place to read.[22]

In her new position, Larsen worked six days a week from nine to five—nine to four in July and August—with an hour for lunch. The benefits included fourteen paid sick days and three weeks of vacation every year. And there was no chapel, no requirement to be up early for grace and breakfast in a dining hall, no after-hours supervision of several dozen young women. Best of all, by the nature of the work she had considerable autonomy in her daily routine.[23] And at the age of twenty-seven, this woman who had grown up amid saloons and dance halls could finally look forward to a social life. When she was off-duty, her time was her own. The salary was not bad from Larsen's perspective, and would grow rapidly.

Public health was a new field, at the cutting edge of the nursing profession, and in 1918 the New York Health Department was at the cutting edge of public health. Perhaps more than any other field in health care at the time, public health nursing epitomized "modernism," with its emphasis on wellness, prevention, hygiene, and education for the entire population. Furthermore, public health nursing offered unusual opportunities, among "women's" professions generally, for autonomy and authority.[24]

The low infant mortality rates and sanitary conditions we now take for granted are in no small part results of the spread of public health nursing in the early twentieth century, particularly between 1915 and 1920, when nurses like Larsen demonstrated the effectiveness of this branch of the profession.[25] The nurses' charge was to spread "good habits of living" and modern notions of hygiene and sanitation. They needed a strong general education and exceptional communication skills in order to mediate between poverty-stricken tenement dwellers, new immigrants who could not speak English, doctors, social agencies, and city officials. Most crucially, they had to win the trust of the communities in which they worked. Rather than providing direct bedside care, they mainly gave advice, secured medical aid, taught about sanitation and health hazards, discovered cases of infectious disease, contacted social agencies to help people in need, and canvassed neighborhoods to collect information.[26]

Though dating back to late nineteenth-century Liverpool, public health nursing (first known as "district nursing" or "visiting nursing") really started coming into its own only after 1910, and in New York City. In 1893 Lillian Wald had started the first "nurses' settlement" (Henry Street Visiting Nurse Service) on Manhattan's Lower East Side, and in 1912 she became the first president of the National Organization of Public Health Nursing. Three years earlier, she had been involved in founding the National Association for the Advancement of Colored People (NAACP) and hosted its first reception in her nurses' settlement; and black playwright Angelina Weld Grimké's play *Rachel,* a harbinger of the Negro Renaissance, took place in the settlement's Neighborhood Playhouse in 1917. Largely through Wald's leadership, public health nursing in New York became associated with "liberal" ideas about race and opportunities for black professionals. By 1925, almost a fifth of Henry Street's visiting nurses were "colored."[27] The example of Henry Street had a leavening effect on public health nursing in New York generally. Other institutions, such as hospitals, were far less open. Nonetheless, Larsen faced daunting challenges as a black nurse in the white Bronx.

Among the nurses themselves, an unusual degree of cordiality existed in Larsen's bureau, according to British investigator Ethel Johns, who interviewed a number of nursing leaders, both black and white. At a time when most social functions in New York were segregated despite civil rights statutes and when an interracial dinner could provoke vituperative correspondence in the mainstream press, black nurses in the Bureau of Preventable Diseases not only engaged in conferences on equal terms but "share[d] the official social activities of the group and even attended the official luncheon at the Biltmore Hotel. No objection whatever was raised to their presence there."[28] The nursing supervisor of the bureau saw "no good reason why a black nurse who passes the exam shouldn't be promoted," although she believed that when a black nurse gained authority over white ones, some of the whites would "actively rebel."[29] So far, no black nurses had taken and passed the necessary civil service exam; but this started happening in the mid-1920s, when black nurses for the first time began achieving supervisory positions. Had Larsen stuck with the service, she might very well have become one of the first black supervisors; but most supervisors worked in the bureau for at least eleven years before attaining their positions.

Larsen surely encountered hostility; the director of her department later admitted to having difficulty getting recognition for black nurses.[30] In the special area of tuberculosis control, black nurses had a good record in New York; but, wrote Ethel Johns, their attempts to serve "both races" met resistance and compromised their effectiveness. "For this reason the department concerned would prefer not to employ them."[31] Even the most "sympathetic" white leaders felt an underlying anxiety that if too many black nurses joined the Health Department because of its "liberal" policies, white applications would decline and the quality of the labor pool would eventually suffer.[32] Black nurses also struggled constantly against white colleagues' suspicions that their training and "executive ability" were inferior.[33]

Larsen probably worked out of the Mott Haven clinic at 493 East 139th Street, in the Melrose telephone exchange, for her home on 161st Street was within this district, as was Lincoln Hospital. If she worked in the area surrounding her own address, she would have had some African American homes to visit—more than in most districts of the Bronx—but very few. Those African Americans she did serve were better off than most in New York at the time; the Bronx was a step up from the poorer districts of Manhattan, and the black families near Larsen's home tended to be headed by skilled laborers—porters, especially—and professionals or municipal officers.[34]

Larsen reported to the office each morning at nine to receive and write out her assignments for the day, then wrote a description of her work the day before. While at the office, she also met with patients about their various ailments or other troubles, including marital difficulties, unwanted pregnancies, or unemployment. In the attached tuberculosis clinic, she spent some time each week preparing people for physicals and teaching sanitary precautions.[35] When not doing this work or organizing her field notes and writing formal reports, she was expected to read in the office files and library to keep up with developments in her field. Each week, she also met with workers in all the related agencies of the district to confer about local problems, and in this way she made valuable contacts.

The heart of her work, however, was walking through her district, observing, questioning, listening, teaching, cajoling, and taking notes. She had to convert people to new sanitary or hygienic habits that they found strange and inconvenient. Wearing the badge of the Health Department on her blue blouse or overcoat, she represented the law when businesses broke sanitary codes and when patients violated quarantine. A lot of the job had to do with simply getting people to clean their homes regularly, cover their garbage, protect their food against flies, put up screens—and brush their teeth.

The conspicuous bag she lugged wherever she walked contained no bandages, scissors, or syringes. It held mostly written material: history cards, patient referral cards, circulars and hanging cards with information on infectious and contagious diseases, a thermometer, a watch with a second hand, sputum bags and paper napkins, certificates of infectious disease, school exclusion and readmission cards, postcards for reporting new cases to headquarters, and one copy of the Rules for Employees of the Bureau of Preventable Diseases.[36]

Entering a building for the first time, she would seek out a janitor or supervisor and ask if anyone was ill. If so, she investigated immediately.[37] She stopped people on the sidewalks and in hallways to talk, which required a lot of tact, for people feared quarantine or the hospital, and building managers did not want their premises placarded. She had to win over housewives on questions of diet and general hygiene and connect destitute families with social service agencies. One can imagine the difficulties for a black nurse in white neighborhoods. But judging from her salary increases, which kept pace with or exceeded those of all who started with her, Larsen had little problem with the "efficiency ratings" her supervisor periodically gave. By the time she resigned in 1921, Larsen was making $1,537 annually—a 60 percent increase in only three years.[38]

Larsen's gravest concerns were typhoid, scarlet fever, measles, cerebrospinal meningitis, diphtheria, and infantile paralysis. For active cases, she had to decide on the best measures for preventing further spread of the disease—from keeping children home from school, hospitalization, or various levels of quarantine, down to nailing bright quarantine placards to the entrances of apartments or entire buildings. She had to order family members who worked in food handling or who did tailoring or dressmaking on the premises to either quit working or move out. She wrote detailed histories of typhoid fever cases to help identify carriers and sources of the disease, tracking the milk and food supply to local shops. She took nose and throat cultures for diphtheria and reported on new scarlet fever cases, then returned after a month to look for runny noses, eyes, or ears and ensure the cleaning of the premises. Cases of overcrowding and extreme duress she reported to various relief agencies.[39]

Often the most difficult part of the job was simply convincing a mother to reserve special cutlery and dishes for the sick family member.[40] If caretakers failed to follow her sanitary instructions, she could order patients taken to the much-dreaded hospital. In cases of death from infectious disease, she wrote a "history" and made sure that the remains were placed in a proper casket, closed and marked with the official seal of the Department of Health—and that the funeral was private.[41]

Just as Larsen entered the service, with masses of military men passing through New York, her department took on the battle against venereal disease. Nurses went into the community and met with families to speak frankly about sex and about syphilis and gonorrhea as "diseases common to adult life." They taught women and girls, especially, about sexual anatomy so they could "discuss sex problems more freely," as the New York nurses' manual put it.[42] It was a startling role for women at that time. Only two years earlier, the New York public health nurse Margaret Sanger had stood trial for writing and speaking frankly about "sex problems" and advocating birth control.

Yet in 1918 the naval bases of New York, including Pelham Bay in the Bronx, brought a scourge more deadly than syphilis. Just as her probationary period ended, Larsen found herself on the front line of the war against the most murderous epidemic the world had yet experienced: the "Spanish flu" pandemic of 1918–1919, spread by the transportation networks of World War I. By the end of the summer, virtually every country outside North America had been hit. By early October the U.S. Surgeon General had declared the epidemic unchecked throughout most of the nation, and it was sweeping through the military camps around New York. By Columbus Day more than 2,000 New Yorkers had died of flu or pneumonia; a week later more than 4,000; and the numbers kept climbing.[43]

The disease was mysterious, different from any flu previously known. Usually influenza struck in the winter and early spring, killing mainly children and old people. But this strain was by far most deadly to those between fifteen and forty-five. It hit poor and rich alike. It carried away family heads and pregnant women and left thousands of orphaned children in its wake. Nurses and doctors scrambled to learn more about the symptoms and duration of the disease. The sick usually got better within a week, but too often they caught pneumonia just as they were getting over the flu, and died within hours.[44]

Since the flu had no cure, nurses were the critical agents for dealing with the crisis, and there weren't nearly enough of them. The leading nurses of the city organized an emergency council, chaired by Lillian Wald, and appealed to all families and organizations employing nurses to release them for service against the epidemic, while calling for volunteers to serve as nurses' aides and orderlies. They placarded theaters, showed slides in movie houses, appealed in churches, distributed handbills by the thousands on street corners. Nursing schools suspended classes so that staff and students could serve the effort. The Red Cross and police began a house-to-house canvass for women to serve as salaried aides.[45] But most important was the release of the nurses in Larsen's bureau to fight the flu.

To the Bureau of Preventable Diseases fell the largest burden in planning, organizing, and executing the campaign. On Sunday, October 13, Larsen met with colleagues to map out the city effort and organize tasks. They suspended their routine work and went into bedside nursing, long unfamiliar to most of them.[46] Larsen's superintendent wrote that, "wholly unprepared for the duties that confronted them," they "bravely gathered together the remnants of their hospital and private nursing outfits to equip themselves for the work."[47] With Tuskegee and Lincoln not so far behind her, Larsen was better prepared than most.

The nurses of the Bronx started on Wednesday the sixteenth, many working through the night. For at least the next month Larsen worked seven days a week, with little sleep.[48] The work was harrowing. A nurse might enter a stinking apartment to find both parents dead, or children dead and parents too sick to know it. Many families desperately needed food, clean linen, and warm covering —not necessarily because of poverty but because everyone was too sick to cook or wash. Desperate families resorted to kidnapping nurses or locking them into their homes.[49] And no one was sure that their gauze masks would protect the nurses themselves.

Nurses ordered whole apartment buildings turned into impromptu hospitals. Police were authorized to imprison any landlords who didn't provide adequate heat to their tenants, yet so many collieries had been shut down because of the epidemic that the East Coast was short of coal. By mid-October it was illegal to spit in public. Coughing or sneezing became a misdemeanor soon after. On the fourteenth, movie releases were suspended across the country. On the fifteenth the head of the New York Health Department announced nearly 5,000 new cases in the previous twenty-four hours and begged wealthy families to assign servants to the Health Department as nursing aides.[50]

No one knew how long the epidemic might last. Each week, the head of the Health Department made optimistic projections, and each week those projections were proven wrong. On October 10, the chiefs of the Bronx and New

York health departments expressed confidence that they had the flu under control, but then the local newspaper printed the largest death list ever issued by the Health Department for the Bronx. In fact, the epidemic at that point had barely begun. On October 17, the Bronx *Home News* reported that despite glowing reports from the head of the Health Department, the epidemic was still raging. Undertakers could not keep up with the need for coffins and hearses. At Lincoln Hospital so many people had died that the crowds of grieving relatives made it impossible to release bodies for burial.[51]

By October 20, more than 5,000 cases had been reported in the Bronx, but the borough's district sanitary superintendent, Dr. Arthur O'Leary, said the disease was "on the wane"; if the cool weather would just continue, it would be quickly "stamped out." He was wrong. On the twenty-third, O'Leary announced a drop in the number of cases and deaths, yet the *Home News* reported: "So many persons have died in the Bronx within the past few days that it has been utterly impossible to bury them."[52] The cemeteries could not muster the manpower. Soon the local casket companies found they could not get enough wood to fill the orders for coffins.[53] O'Leary's drop in numbers turned out to be a result of late reporting by overtaxed doctors.

Today, it feels eerie to go through the newspapers filled with page after page on the battles in Europe, and at most one or two short reports of statistics or rosy statements by bureau chiefs on the epidemic that was ravaging American cities, killing far more people than the war. Worried about public panic, the Health Department continually underplayed the extent of the epidemic while newspaper death lists grew to amazing lengths.

As Larsen picked her way around the piles of uncollected garbage on sidewalks and entryways, she hoped for any sign that the plague had crested, which it finally did at the end of October, after more than half a million people in the city had been stricken. After November 6, Larsen was able to go back to her normal routine, and all bedside work reverted to the visiting nurses of the Henry Street service.[54]

The epidemic eased up just in time for the Armistice, and on Monday morning, November 11, the Bronx erupted in celebration. A week before, large public gatherings had been prohibited and people had been afraid to talk to one another. Now they poured out of their homes in pajamas, shouting at the top of their lungs. Spontaneous parades marched up and down the streets all day and into the night, while Larsen pursued her work.[55] Even in the week of the Armistice, more than 1,000 New Yorkers died of flu and pneumonia, and calls kept coming in to the clinic for food for orphaned children still fending for themselves. On the seventeenth, newspapers announced that the epidemic was "officially" over. Now worries arose that an epidemic of tuberculosis would fol-low.[56]

Instead, the flu came back. It resumed again and again into the early months of 1919, and the nurses of the Health Department went back to bedside nursing. The epidemic cost more American lives in four months than all the wars the United States has fought to this day. It produced armies of orphans. It scarred many thousands of Americans more deeply than the war that supposedly pro-duced the "lost generation"; and then, like a trauma too difficult to absorb, it nearly vanished from national memory.

Amazingly, the nurses held up against the disease. Larsen herself—who in later years would be peculiarly susceptible to the flu, colds, and pneumonia—did take four days off, probably for illness, in mid-January 1919.[57] But in her bu-reau, as of December at least, none died. In the most devastating, early months of the crisis, only two nurses came down with pneumonia and four with flu.[58] Their techniques and gauze masks had proven their worth. The nurses of the Bureau of Preventable Diseases were regarded as the heroes of the crisis in New York, which had more casualties than any other city in the United States but half the death rate of most—mainly because of the effectiveness of the nurses. Along with the Red Cross work in the war, the work of the nurses during the pandemic established the importance of public health nurses and raised their status.[59]

It also helped to raise their pay. The Health Department nurses had enjoyed a raise of only $60 in the previous sixteen years. In January 1919, they each received a $100 raise (promised before the epidemic); in 1920, $200; and the increases kept coming. In late February the Surgeon General announced a na-tionwide drive to raise the number of public health nurses.[60] Nursing—espe-cially public health nursing—began looking like a very "decent" profession, and better paid than teaching.

Things were looking up for Larsen in other respects as well. She had met the proverbial promising young man, probably in the summer or fall of 1918, and had him well on the hook. Actually, Dr. Elmer S. Imes (pronounced *eye*-mz) was beyond promising. Of medium height and slender build, about half a foot taller than Larsen and eight years older (ten, he thought), he was good looking if not classically handsome. A calm demeanor and high forehead, accentuated by a slightly receding hairline and thoughtful, bespectacled brown eyes, gave him a professorial air, particularly when he had his pipe in hand, as he often did. His complexion was much like Larsen's, light brown. Neat and well groomed, a natty dresser, he seemed mature and sophisticated, confident and sensitive to women, flirtatious within accepted bounds.[61] He was attracted and attractive to strong, independent women, both black and white.

His attraction to Larsen may have owed something to her being a "mulatto" but not necessarily to "light skin." Though having long hair, softly curled by nature and always worn in a thick bun, Larsen was darker in complexion than Elmer's mother and sister-in-law and other women he might have pursued. Like most men of his background and generation, he may not have been attracted to very dark women; but in the circles he was used to moving in, Larsen was not so "white" in appearance. On the other hand she was remarkably self-sufficient, smart, interesting, well traveled, undeniably "different"—in short, exotic—and she shared both his charming ironic wit and his interest in books.[62] Like Larsen, he liked to challenge boundaries. Certainly, his engagement to her suggested a renegade side to his personality, for he was a man of "background" and she had none to offer. Moreover, her temperament and irreligion contradicted his family traditions.

Imes had earned a Ph.D. in physics at the University of Michigan in 1918 and moved to New York to take a job on Staten Island the same year.[63] He may have met Larsen at a function associated with social work in the city—Elmer was invited to such events, being of some note for his learning, Fisk associations, and family background, and Nella would have been invited in connection with her work.[64] Perhaps Elmer's brother, the Reverend William Lloyd Imes, and his wife Grace introduced them. William likely knew Larsen from Lincoln as well as Fisk, and Grace had been the one other Northerner in her class at Fisk.

Elmer's father, Benjamin A. Imes, was a graduate of Oberlin College and Theological Seminary, in Ohio, and a pioneer in "the southern field of the American Missionary Association"[65]—which supported Fisk and many other black colleges in the South. Elmer came up through, and made his start teaching in, AMA schools, but he was not exactly a Southerner. Benjamin (who had died in 1908) came from a south-central Pennsylvania family that had been free for several generations and owned their own farm. Elmer's younger brother termed Benjamin a "pietiest" in a warm filial tribute. "Never could anyone live in the home and daily life of Benjamin Imes and gainsay his sincere and thoroughgoing piety."[66] He was also a passable poet, judging from the neat quatrains of his "Lines to Mother" (1870), written at Oberlin. After graduation, he worked for Berea College in Kentucky—like Oberlin, one of the first "integrated" colleges, and one of the first to accept women. He returned to Oberlin for seminary and there met Elizabeth Rachel Wallace, Elmer's mother. Rachel, once a "contraband of war," had been sent to Oberlin by a missionary who met her on the streets of Natchez, Mississippi, selling pies to Union soldiers. Together Rachel and Benjamin went south to take over a tiny mission church in Memphis, which they nurtured to self-sufficiency in a dozen years.[67] An integrationist,

6. Elmer S. Imes, passport photo, 1930.
U.S. Department of State.
Courtesy of Charles R. Larson.

Benjamin had the courage to assail racism and the color line within the home mission movement itself.

Elmer had been born in Memphis on Columbus Day, 1883, but he had attended grammar school in Oberlin, high school at Alabama A&M (Agricultural and Mechanical), and college at Fisk, where he graduated in 1903. For eleven of the next thirteen years he taught at various AMA schools (mostly Albany Normal in Georgia) and at Fisk, where he served as an instructor between 1913 and 1916. The summer before Nella matriculated at the school, he had organized Fisk's highly acclaimed booth in the segregated "Negro Exhibit" at the Jamestown Tercentenary in Norfolk, Virginia, a sign of his close ties to the institution and its president's faith in him. The year after Nella left Fisk, 1908–1909, Elmer returned to study for a Master of Science degree, which he received in 1910—the same year his brother William, six years younger, received his Bachelor's degree there. One of their aunts by marriage, Mabel Imes, had been an original member of the Fisk Jubilee Singers.[68] Imes had deep connections to the school from which Larsen had been thrown out.

He was, by the same token, well connected to the national black elite. He belonged to the graduate fraternity Theta Sigma and, more important, the New York chapter of Sigma Pi Phi—known as Boulé, the most aristocratic and exclusive of black fraternities. He was well enough known in New York that when the (black) Social Workers' Club held a special meeting in May 1919, he was asked to speak briefly as one of the specially invited guests. He probably belonged already to St. Philip's Protestant Episcopal Church in New York—a bulwark of the colored aristocracy that Wallace Thurman would describe as "the religious sanctum of the socially elect and wealthy Negroes of Harlem," reportedly the wealthiest black church in the world.[69] With more than a million dollars' worth of real estate on 135th Street as early as 1910, it spurred the black colonization of Harlem, and its parish house was one of the elite social centers of the district.[70]

At the time Nella met Elmer, his work on infrared absorption of diatomic gases was helping to demonstrate that quantum theory applied to all electromagnetic radiation, and was therefore potentially of broad practical use.[71] Hence his hiring straight from graduate school as a research physicist—a remarkable job for a black man in those days. (He was the second black Ph.D. in physics in U.S. history.) At the same time, there was a strong strain of the aesthete and cultural aristocrat about him, tempered by an awareness of what it took for a man in his precarious position—that is, a black research physicist—to make a good living. One of his white Michigan colleagues fondly recalled that "his research laboratory was a mecca for those who sought an atmosphere of calm and contentment. Peacefully smoking his pipe, Imes could always be relied upon to bring to any discussion an atmosphere of philosophic soundness and levelheaded practicalness. Gifted, moreover, with a poetic disposition, he was widely read in literature, and a discriminating and ardent appreciator of music. He had a delightful sense of humor and a skill in repartee, which he always used, however, with the kindliness and consideration so characteristic of his sensitive nature."[72]

Through Elmer, the world of the black New York elite opened up before Larsen like a place in which she might finally belong. Some of the most up-and-coming men of the race were his fraternity brothers and acquaintances, and he was welcome in the homes of the most elegant and articulate young women of the race, people who lived in the prime black precincts of Brooklyn, the Jersey suburbs, and Harlem. He was even on friendly terms with famous men like W. E. B. Du Bois.

Larsen's twenty-eighth birthday, or twenty-sixth to Elmer, fell on a Sunday in 1919. The day before, the handsome couple went to obtain a marriage license at the borough hall in the Bronx. Larsen signed the application "Nella Marian Larsen" and gave her mother's maiden name as Marian Hansen.[73] At the time, Elmer was living at 115 Belmont Place, Staten Island, and she had moved, apparently between January and April 1919, to 984 Morris Avenue, only a few blocks from the place she had shared with Ruth Strickland.[74] (Strickland, meanwhile, moved up to 230th Street.) Larsen may have taken over the apartment from an acquaintance in the Health Department: Alice S. Thomas, also a nurse for the Bureau of Preventable Diseases, lived at 984 Morris in 1918, moving out just as Larsen moved in.[75]

Larsen may have taken the apartment in anticipation of the marriage, for Elmer moved in with her at first.[76] They married on May 3, 1919, in the chapel of Union Theological Seminary, with Elmer's brother William presiding over the ceremony and Adah Thoms serving as Nella's witness. It is very unlikely that anyone from Larsen's family attended. Some of her Lincoln associates were there, however, along with friends of Elmer and his family.[77] The newlyweds had no traditional honeymoon, evidently, for Larsen asked for no leave time during the month of May, and she worked six days a week. It took her more than six months to get around to having her name changed on the Health Department rolls, and when she did so, unlike the vast majority of nurses, she kept her maiden name in full as a middle name. She even, for a time, kept her earlier middle initial, *M.*, for "Marian."[78]

Still standing, Larsen's first nuptial home was a handsome five-story building with a brick and brownstone façade and attractive ironwork balconies, located in a peaceful, comfortable neighborhood with broad sidewalks for strolling. It was part of a series of three matching row-house apartment buildings. Two blocks west was the public library.[79] By the time of the 1920 census, Nella and Elmer had already moved out, but the residents at that time give a good sense of the neighborhood during the earliest months of marriage. Fifteen black and "mulatto" families inhabited 984, most of them headed by skilled tradespersons —a teamster, a chauffeur, a chef, a stenographer, several railroad waiters and porters, and an art gallery salesman. All of the even-numbered addresses on this block of Morris Avenue (signifying the east side of the street) had black residents exclusively, although the surrounding area was all white.[80] Only the three connected buildings—984, 986, and 988 Morris Avenue—had black residents.

That summer, Larsen surely read in the papers about the disaster in her hometown of Chicago: the deadly race riot that had erupted in the midst of a streetcar strike, when a boy who was swimming off the Twenty-Seventh Street beach strayed into a "white" section, was stoned, and drowned. The *Home News* reported to Bronx residents that, as of July 28, after twenty-four hours of rioting, casualties continued to rise. In the heart of Chicago's "black belt," around Thirty-Fifth and State, more than 2,500 blacks had congregated, threatening to "move against the whites," while two blocks away a mob of 2,000 white men prepared to launch an assault of its own.[81] Larsen took a leave of absence for illness on July 29, the day this news was reported in New York.[82]

Since the fading of the flu epidemic in February, attention among New York's nurses had shifted to infant mortality, particularly resulting from diphtheria—ten times more deadly than scarlet fever and a torturous way to die. Its incidence had tripled from the previous year, and the Bronx was hardest hit because it had the highest concentration of young families. But a new procedure for detecting susceptibility had been developed and put into effect in May 1919. The nurses made a house-to-house canvass of the city to distribute literature about the test, take throat cultures, and preach the virtues of immunization—"pioneer work hitherto unknown to the citizens of New York," according to the director of Larsen's bureau.[83]

But the flu remained their chief concern. Health officials were terrified at the possibility of a return of Spanish influenza, for flu epidemics typically returned after a year; and indeed a new epidemic broke out in the fall and winter of 1919–1920. Larsen's cohort in the Bronx were reported as busy to "exhaustion." They cursed the new laws against alcohol (precursors to Prohibition), as whiskey was their favorite palliative against flu symptoms.[84] For several weeks they worked twelve hours a day, seven days a week. Merely getting from house to house became an exercise in endurance, as garbage and trash piled up all over the borough, along with snow and slush, for lack of workers to remove them. Rats from the New York Central Railroad tracks had invaded the neighborhoods around Larsen's home, fattening on the garbage piled high on the sidewalks.[85]

The flu and tuberculosis problems had been exacerbated by a housing crunch in the Bronx. Rents rose sharply in March 1919, and by the end of the year had trebled in many sections. Multiple families crowded into single flats to share expenses, causing a steep rise in tuberculosis and threatening to spread other contagious diseases. It was a problem in Nella's own neighborhood, where tenants showed up en masse for a meeting on rent profiteering.[86] At about this time—the late fall of 1919, before the secondary epidemic—Nella and Elmer decided to move out of the Bronx and closer to Elmer's workplace.

They took a two-and-a-half-story woodframe house at 785 Fingerboard Road in Grasmere, Staten Island. One of only five homes in the immediate area—a sparsely settled border of the village between Brady's Pond and Cameron's Pond—it had apparently once been a farmhouse. A realty company already owned most of the land in the area and was plotting it out for development.[87] Grasmere was a community of single-family houses inhabited by solidly bourgeois, mostly native-born whites, including several stockbrokers, the manager of an insurance company, a banker, and the manager of a wholesale house. About half of the families owned their homes. None of the wives worked, and no African Americans lived nearby. With a 1.3 percent Negro population, Staten Island had a few old black settlements, as in New Brighton, where Elmer had lived before, but the newlyweds were not especially near any of these. It could not have been a very friendly place, with a social life (such as it was) centering around church, bridge, and bingo.[88]

Grasmere was just beginning to develop into a pleasant, somewhat upscale residential suburb in the interior of Staten Island, made convenient to Manhattan by the Staten Island Railroad, which stopped (and stops) just about four blocks from 785 Fingerboard Road. But while the location was convenient for Elmer to get to his job on the island, it meant a long commute for Nella—well over an hour each way. She was four train stops from the ferry, and once in Manhattan had yet a long way to go, with at least one transfer to catch the Third Avenue El out to the Bronx. When the second flu epidemic hit and Larsen was put on twelve-hour shifts seven days a week, this made for a punishing schedule. Once the crisis was over, she could have requested a transfer from her station in the Bronx, but she never did. Within a year, however, she and Elmer would move to Harlem—just in time for the "renaissance."

[NINE]

Sojourner in Harlem:
The Dawn of the "Renaissance," 1919–1923

WHILE the Imeses were living on Staten Island in the fall of 1919, the NAACP magazine, *The Crisis*, announced the creation of a new monthly magazine for "the children of the sun." Founded by W. E. B. Du Bois and Augustus Granville Dill, *The Brownies' Book* was the world's first monthly magazine for black children, the first even to think of black children as an audience—and the first publication for which Nella Larsen wrote.[1] It aimed "to make colored children realize that being 'colored' is a normal beautiful thing" and to convey the history of black achievement while teaching "colored children . . . a code of honor and action in their relations with white children."[2] The editors also wished "to teach Universal Love and Brotherhood for all little folks," asking adults "what foreign countries you would like described, briefly what dark children—and white, too, for that matter, for we colored people must set the example of broadness—are doing all over the world."[3]

Larsen ventured into print by writing about games, riddles, and rhymes she had learned in Denmark. It was the sort of contribution she was uniquely qualified to make, and although unusual for a magazine focused on issues of black identity, it implicitly modeled the cosmopolitan sensibility that W. E. B. Du Bois encouraged. "Dear Children," she began in the June 1920 issue, "These are some games which I learned long ago in Denmark, from the little Danish children. I hope that you will play them and like them as I did."[4] "Cat and Rat," "Hawk and Pigeons," and "Travelers"—the latter two brightened by songs Larsen translated, with musical notation to match—had no true counterparts in English. The next month she followed up with another group of games and riddles under the title "Danish Fun."[5] By suggesting that these were games African American children would enjoy, was she attempting to profit socially—stressing her "exoticism" and connection to whites, as once charged—or nonchalantly countering racial patterns of expectation that begin taking hold in childhood, the very patterns that have led to so many misunderstandings of her own life and work? She had not, after all, been raised on African American folklore, with which her audience would already have been familiar.

The appearance of the games and riddles, under the name "Nella Larsen Imes," marks the author's growing involvement in New York's black bourgeoisie, thanks in part to her husband's background and professional status. At functions of the Fisk Club, to which the likes of W. E. B. Du Bois belonged and in which Elmer and Nella were listed as "active members," they would rub elbows with the black elite of New York, and Elmer's fraternity functions broadened their circle of friends in the area. Their house on Staten Island was rather remote, however, and in the latter half of 1920 they decided to move to Harlem.

By January 1921 they had settled on the southern boundary of the new black mecca, in apartment number 17 at 34 West 129th Street.[6] Midway between Lenox and Fifth Avenue on the south side of the street, they were on the fifth floor of an elegant Art Nouveau apartment house that had white marble molding and wainscoting in the halls and stairways.[7] This was by no means the low-rent district, but neither was it at the top of the scale. As recently as January 1920 the residents had been all white, mostly native-born New Yorkers in the arts or skilled craftsmen.[8] But by 1921 the block on which the Imeses lived was turning over to black residents, and a number of fairly well-known Harlem matrons were near neighbors.

A 22 percent raise from the Health Department may have helped to finance the move, which put Larsen much closer to work but also to other interests that would soon displace nursing as the center of her professional life. One of the other tenants in her building, Lillian Alexander, hosted frequent literary discussions on weekend afternoons. Light brown, large-eyed, and broad-minded like "Mrs. Imes," always on the more progressive wing of the NAACP, Alexander was also a Midwesterner, a Phi Beta Kappa graduate of the University of Minnesota. Married to a well-known dermatologist, she was a prominent clubwoman, particularly active in the YWCA, the NAACP, and the Columbus Hill Day Nursery. Larsen may have known her before the move to Harlem through her Lincoln Hospital and public health connections. Adah Thoms and Alexander both held major posts in the "colored" YWCA. Alexander had also founded Club Caroline, a cooperative housing project for working girls. Distinguished "older" people like W. E. B. Du Bois, as well as younger intellectuals, attended her gatherings.[9]

By the early 1920s Larsen was friendly with a widening circle of black doctors and other professionals through whom she made contacts in developing literary circles. She may have become involved in the Circle for Negro War Relief, an organization founded by Etnah Boutté during the war to aid the families of black soldiers, and redirected afterward to promote public health work in black communities throughout the country. Many black nurses in New York and Boston had affiliated with the group, which put them in contact with some of the cities' black movers and shakers, as well as with white literary figures serving on its board of directors, including Edward Sheldon and Emilie Hapgood.

Grace Nail Johnson, a prominent Harlemite deeply interested in modern literature and the arts, served on the circle's executive council, which organized high-profile benefit functions not only in Harlem but at places like Carnegie Hall.[10] Johnson's closest lifetime friend, Lucile Miller, had graduated with Nella from nursing school and worked, like Larsen, for the Health Department (also in a mostly "white" district); the fact that Grace always referred to Larsen as "Nellie" suggests they had met early on. Very light-skinned with naturally straight hair, tall, well-read, and intelligent, Johnson came from one of Harlem's wealthiest and most distinguished families and was married to one of the great "race men" of that or any age.

James Weldon Johnson, brown and lanky, with shrewd eyes, a nimble intelligence, a diplomat's discretion, and extraordinarily diverse talents, was also one of the chief architects of the integrationist civil rights movement of the interwar period. Prior to the 1920s he had been a public school principal in Florida, a diplomat in Venezuela and Nicaragua, a hit lyricist for the celebrated entertainment team of Cole and Johnson (for which his brother John Rosamond Johnson was composer and pianist), and an editorialist for the *New York Age*, and he was one of the race's most esteemed novelists and poets. His *Autobiography of an Ex-Colored Man* was easily the most significant novel of black life since the turn of the century. His poem "The Creation," first published in 1920, marked a turning point in the history of black poetry for its unique free-verse experimentation with the rhythms, imagery, and phraseology of the African American oral sermon, breaking away from decades of conventional "dialect" poetry. Just as important, Johnson was one of the most effective "integrationist" black leaders since Frederick Douglass.

If W. E. B. Du Bois was the intellectual spearhead and most eloquent voice of the black freedom movement, Johnson was the field marshal, the man who built the NAACP into a truly national organization. He proposed and plotted the historic silent protest parade of 1917 against lynching; he traveled the country as field secretary of the NAACP, organizing local branches, often in hostile territory of the Deep South. Simultaneously, he was a key advocate—perhaps *the* key advocate—for a black literary awakening and cultural cooperation across the color line before 1924. It was at the Johnsons' that "the first of the bohemian-elite inter-racial parties in Harlem" took place in 1922, in honor of Claude McKay just before he sailed to Russia.[11] Larsen may well have met McKay at that time, since he would remain abroad throughout the 1920s; in correspondence she would speak as if she knew him ("Mr. McKay") personally, though not closely.

Larsen also socialized regularly with Louis T. and Corinne Wright (Louis being a prominent Harvard-trained physician), whom she may have met through work, since he served on the venereal disease unit of the Health Department beginning in 1919.[12] Corinne was a longtime member of Elmer's church, St. Philip's Episcopal. A veteran of World War I and a brilliant surgeon, Louis originated the intradermal vaccination for smallpox during the war. He was also the first black surgeon for the New York Police Department and the first black physician appointed to a New York hospital staff, and in a few years he would become the first black clinic director at Harlem Hospital. An ardent integrationist like Daniel Hale Williams, Wright did not believe in "Negro hospitals"; all medical facilities and organizations, he insisted, should be open to everyone. As soon as a "Negro hospital" was set up, other hospitals would stop admitting Negroes and hiring black staff, referring them to their "own" hospitals. The end result, Wright observed, would always be poorer facilities for patients and limited opportunities for the development of black doctors and nurses. Tagged the "stormy petrel of Harlem Hospital," he fought against making that institution a "black hospital," just as he fought against racial discrimination in mostly "white" institutions. Years later he would become chairman of the board of the NAACP. Nella Larsen's own nursing career suggests that she agreed with him completely. Corinne Wright, about whom little information survives, was apparently one of Larsen's best friends in the early 1920s and someone she kept up with for years afterward.

Probably through the Wrights or the Johnsons, Elmer and Nella met Walter White, one of Louis Wright's closest friends from their youthful days in Georgia. (Wright would be one of the models for the hero in White's first novel, *The Fire in the Flint*.) In 1918 White gave up an insurance job in Atlanta to work for the NAACP in New York, and he quickly became James Weldon Johnson's right-hand man in the field secretary's office of the NAACP. Looking like a "little Irishman," according to Langston Hughes, his gray-blue eyes and "corn-silk hair" combined with keen features and white skin to make him possibly the "whitest" Negro in New York—so white that when he entered certain black neighborhoods he had to bring along a brown-skinned friend as protection. A "voluntary Negro," White would have been considered legally white in most states at the time.[13] "Small, dapper, exceedingly high strung," White was passionate about race matters, always optimistic, and always on the make.[14] He was generous yet businesslike, extremely ambitious, and incurably vain—but a loyal friend. A dyed-in-the-wool integrationist, he eventually became the first black president of the NAACP and served in that role when NAACP lawyers won the famous *Brown versus Board of Education* case in the Supreme Court. Larsen was one of many who benefited from his interest: he put her in touch with important people and encouraged her literary career.

James Weldon Johnson introduced White to the world of literature and served as his literary mentor. They would eat lunch at an automat, partly so they could browse afterward in Brentano's bookstore, where Johnson was known to all and widely admired: "Thus began for me," White wrote in his autobiography, "a liberal education in contemporary literature."[15] "Jim" bought him books, recommended others, and introduced White to celebrities from the progressive wing of the New York publishing world—people such as H. L. Mencken and Carl and Irita Van Doren.

When Mencken, editor of the magazine *The Smart Set,* met White in 1922, he asked what he thought of T. S. Stribling's recent novel *Birthright,* a sympathetic treatment of the situation of blacks in the South. White wrote a lengthy critique in response, praising the author's courage "in depicting negroes as human beings" and saying that its treatment of Negro servants was fairly good, but that Stribling "fell down badly in his portrayal of what educated Negroes feel and think."[16] Mencken suggested that White write a novel himself. This, undoubtedly, is when a conversation took place between White, Jessie Fauset, and Larsen to which Fauset would refer in a 1932 interview: "We reasoned, 'Here is an audience waiting to hear the truth about us. Let us who are better qualified to present that truth than any white writer, try to do so.'"[17] Fauset then began writing *There Is Confusion* (1924). White was already hard at work on his first novel, which would come out from Alfred A. Knopf in early 1924. It was one of the first novels of the Harlem Renaissance proper.

Larsen probably met White while he was dating NAACP staff member Leah Gladys Powell (always called "Gladys"), the "most beautiful brown woman in New York," according to Langston Hughes, and a talented singer.[18] After Powell and White married in 1922, he embarked on an ambitious social itinerary that connected with his literary aspirations even as he worked indefatigably on behalf of the NAACP to stamp out the crime of lynching. Self-effacing Gladys was well-connected in black New York and perfectly chosen to advance White's career; she immersed herself in the role of wife to the rising race man, standing quietly behind him, hosting, raising their children, maintaining a succession of increasingly expensive apartments, and stifling her own ambitions. Between Gladys and Walter, it was Walter with whom Larsen apparently had the closer relationship.

Soon after moving to Harlem, Larsen became active at the 135th Street

Branch of the New York Public Library—a branch that served a multiracial, multiethnic population under the direction of its visionary chief librarian, Ernestine Rose. Rose had recognized the demographic trends of the neighborhood and decided to make the branch at 135th and Lenox Avenue a center for black cultural self-awareness. By the early 1920s, the most progressive librarians had begun turning their Manhattan branches into general cultural centers, organizing lecture series and public programs related to the needs of their immediate neighborhoods, using the public rooms of each library as art exhibition space, and encouraging local talent. In New York, this kind of thinking came hand in hand with the spread of the concept of cultural pluralism. Ernestine Rose was one of the country's most important proponents of this ethos in librarianship years before she began working in Harlem.

Named after Ernestine Potowski Rose, a well-known nineteenth-century feminist (possibly a near relative) and friend of Walt Whitman, Rose had been born in Bridgehampton on Long Island in 1880, one of a long line of Chatfields and Roses who had settled the area in the seventeenth century. She attended Wesleyan University before entering the New York State Library School in Albany, from which she graduated in 1904. In her student years, she worked as a summer substitute on the Lower East Side among chiefly Russian Jewish immigrants. After graduation and one year in the Wesleyan library, she returned to New York to work in branches in various immigrant communities, becoming head librarian from 1915 to 1917 at the Seward Park Branch, located in the heart of the Jewish "ghetto."[19] Her leadership had more than a little to do with the legendary status this library attained in Jewish cultural memory.

Much of the vision and pragmatic approach Rose applied at the 135th Street Branch can be found in her 1917 pamphlet *Bridging the Gulf*, in which she championed the "localization of national life." The library's greatest opportunities, she believed, lay in true "communities," often ethnically or racially defined. The Webster Branch, for example, had become a social center of the Bohemian community, with a major department—occupying an entire floor—devoted to Bohemian publications, overseen by a Bohemian woman, and exhibiting creative work from the neighborhood. This department had "become, in a fashion, the national center, not only of this neighborhood, but of all devoted and cultivated Bohemians in the city," while also carrying "the message and ideals of America to New York's Bohemia."[20] Such libraries served not only as centers of intellectual exchange but as refuges for those who needed help negotiating the bewildering rules of an alien society and who, because of past experience, associated state and civic institutions with repressive force. In the library they could get friendly aid without fear of being turned over to the civil authorities. Rose also encouraged proactive efforts, especially visits to the homes of children who had applied for library cards—visits that led to fruitful contacts in the tenements surrounding Seward Park and increased the library's usefulness.

Ethnic self-expression advanced democracy and promoted civic solidarity across traditional social divides, according to Rose. "Old home" exhibits featuring arts and crafts of the old country also taught immigrant children the beauty of the traditional culture of their elders, bridging the gulf between generations. Rose also invited local community organizations to use the library for meetings. Clubs, political forums, and discussion groups rapidly blossomed during her tenure.

Rose recruited ethnic "insiders" for responsible positions but believed that the majority of assistants should be "Americans" specially trained for the work; the immigrants needed human bridges to the dominant society as they learned to negotiate its strange customs. Educating the "native" librarians was also crucial to the plan, requiring "an intimate acquaintance on the part of every member of the library staff with the history, traditions and literature of each nationality that the library expects to serve." Gentile assistants at Seward Park not only grew familiar with Jewish holidays and customs but studied Yiddish and Russian literature under Jewish colleagues and visitors.[21] Rose held a seminar-like staff meeting at the Seward Park Branch every week for book discussions and collective study, lectures from rabbis and educators, and discussions with Jewish journalists and neighborhood workers. All of this "sensitivity training" (as it would be called today) screened out assistants harboring ethnic or religious prejudices and targeted behavior that might inadvertently have aroused resentment or distrust.

Rose went on to enter national service in World War I as director of hospital libraries. She later served a stint with the U.S. Army in Paris and then in occupied Koblenz, Germany, where she worked with many black soldiers.[22] Finally returning to New York in 1920, she was immediately assigned to replace the outgoing librarian at the 135th Street Branch. Applying the techniques and philosophy she had formulated in her two years at Seward Park, she quickly laid the groundwork on which the branch developed into a major community institution. Larsen would have a special role to play in her plans.

In March 1921, Rose published an article for *Library Journal* setting out her vision for the library. She began by describing the "black city" which at that time extended from 130th to 150th Street and from Eighth Avenue to the Harlem River. She noted the ethnic divisions within the race: blacks from the Caribbean, from South America, and from the United States displayed significant cultural

7. Ernestine Rose at her desk in the reference room, 135th Street Branch of the New York Public Library. New York Public Library Archives, The New York Public Library, Astor, Lenox and Tilden Foundations.

and linguistic differences. When Rose arrived, there had been no "colored" assistants in the library; by the time of her writing she had hired three.[23] Soon she would hire a Puerto Rican woman, Pura Belpre (later White), to help serve the Spanish speakers in the area. She would also hire Nella Larsen Imes.

Rose admired the community's penchant for self-reliance—a trait that, she felt, marked the "awakening of a great people." Despite ethnic differences, "the negroes are standing together in a steadfast belief in their own destiny to be worked out within and by themselves."[24] She hoped the library could aid in the development of race consciousness and cultural independence, though always according to an idealistic belief in the possibilities of American democracy and an ultimately integrationist ethic. "It seems that the whole process of growing apart must be complete before growing together may begin," she wrote. "On the one hand, race pride and race knowledge must be stimulated and guided. . . . But the library aims not only to be an intellectual center for Negroes; its further purpose is to fulfil its function as an American democratic institution and to furnish a common ground where diverse paths may meet and clashing interests find union. To this end colored and white workers stand side-by-side against segregation in work and thought."[25]

During the period that Larsen worked for the library, the professional staff was half black and half white. Rose resisted pressures from both black and white parties to make the 135th Street Branch a "colored library" with an all-black staff and clientele (like the "colored" YMCA and YWCA nearby). To skeptics who questioned the viability of an interracial staff, Rose asserted, "I have never known a group of people who worked together with greater personal and professional harmony"; but she added that it was crucial not to hire people with racial prejudices.[26] This may have been puffery, but racial tensions between staff members do not show up in later interviews or other extant documents. Rose did not oppose "Negro" institutions as such, but she feared their ultimate use to limit the options of black workers and students.[27]

After a long and distinguished career in the field, Pura Belpre White—who had never even thought of librarianship until Rose recruited her—remembered the inspirational quality of Rose's leadership. "It was her vision which opened doors. I mean, I remember her staff meetings. . . . She would say, 'You must do this,' or 'We must do this, because the time will come—' And that time to come was a great deal of vision, and I've lived long enough to know that everything she spoke of had become a reality, especially for the blacks, for whom she was then opening doors."[28] Rose's staff meetings included book discussions and visits from well-known authors, including Larsen after her novels appeared in the late 1920s. "She had a great deal of vision and faith in the future for her young assistants who were part of her staff."[29]

The 135th Street Branch not only served as common ground between whites and blacks, English-speakers and Hispanics; it also functioned as a neutral space between diverse black social and political groups, whether radical socialists, Tuskegeeans, NAACP integrationists, or supporters of Marcus Garvey's back-to-Africa movement. Because no one group could dominate the library, it could serve as the intellectual crossroads of the community, as well as a meeting point with white "downtown." The barriers were relatively porous—just right for Nella Larsen Imes.

The 135th Street Branch struggled with the fact that many neighbors, especially from the South, regarded the library as an alien institution. Rose also knew she faced distrust as a white librarian in black Harlem. She therefore sought out the respected black leaders of various groups and asked them to help devise programs for the library, while rapidly integrating the library staff and highlighting black history and culture. Many of the special guests and speakers at library events in the early 1920s, both black and white, would later turn up as contributors to the key magazines of the renaissance—*The Crisis, Opportunity, Negro World, The Messenger*—and to the famous special issue of *Survey Graphic*, "Harlem: Mecca of the New Negro." Rose never took credit for what she orchestrated, but kept the spotlight on well-known African Americans whom she recruited, often for "honorary" positions, while her staff did the bulk of the actual work. One result is that her work and that of her staff have consistently been discounted.

The long-ignored records of the branch library contain key pieces to the puzzle of Larsen's early entry into the Harlem Renaissance, and new insight into the movement itself. By May, though still busy with diphtheria and measles work in the Bronx, Larsen had joined the organizing committee of the library's first bold experiment in the fulfillment of Rose's vision: an art exhibition. This was to mark the beginning of a new phase of Larsen's life, and the first "happening" of the Harlem Renaissance in the visual arts.

Larsen signed on as assistant to the executive secretary, the librarian Edward C. Williams of Howard University. He was a graduate and valedictorian (1892) of Cleveland's Western Reserve University, where he had also directed the library and served on the faculty before moving to Washington, D.C., to become principal of the famous Dunbar High School. Like Larsen, he was a native Midwesterner with a white mother, an Irish immigrant who had married a distinguished African American in Cleveland. A gentle man of exceptional talents and extraordinary tact, married to a daughter of author Charles Chesnutt, Williams was widely admired, and not only by African Americans.[30] Initially, Larsen's role was chiefly to inform people of the evening meetings of the executive committee, and probably to take minutes. In the course of the summer, she sent cards advertising the exhibition or soliciting aid in spreading the word. She also helped to work up a list of "hostesses" to greet people and guide them through the exhibition. In mid-July, anticipating the opening, she sent letters drafted by Williams to preachers and pastors asking for their help in promoting the event, in soliciting hostesses from their congregations, and in encouraging parishioners to exhibit their work. She also contacted ministers of the Congregational Church and the Seventh-Day Adventists in Harlem to drum up interest, while better-known, churchgoing women contacted the more prestigious congregations to which they belonged.[31]

Worried about attendance and the quality of work by local amateur artists, the organizing committee borrowed Henry O. Tanner's *Christ Washing the Feet of His Disciples* from millionaire Robert Wanamaker to serve as an anchor for the exhibition. Sculpture by Meta Warrick Fuller—a student of Auguste Rodin's

—and by May Howard Jackson was featured, along with work by William Russell, a cartoonist for the *New York Age,* and other paintings and drawings by locals, notably Reverend J. H. White's painted copies of famous classical works. One section featured the music manuscripts of Harry T. Burleigh, a celebrated singer in Manhattan churches and synagogues, and a composer of art songs. He was known especially for his setting of Whitman's poem "Ethiopia Saluting the Colors" and James Weldon Johnson's "The Young Warrior," and more recently had turned his hand to solo adaptations of black spirituals.[32]

Few of the artworks on display dealt with "racial" subject matter, but as if to encourage new directions the show included a large collection of African pottery, basketry, cloth, blankets, and metalwork in brass, iron, silver, and gold.[33] The *New York Age* termed it "probably the most comprehensive collection of Negro art work and handicraft ever assembled at one time."[34] Years later, African American art historian James A. Porter honored it as "the first worthy chronological display of modern Negro artists."[35]

Larsen took a three-day paid leave from her job to help with the formal, music-filled opening on Friday, the fifth of August.[36] On the twentieth the *Age* puffed that the show, open daily from 2:30 to 9:00 P.M. through the month of August, was "being viewed by hundreds of people of the community, as well as by visitors from all parts of the country"—the out-of-town visitors being mainly teachers attending summer school at nearby Columbia University.[37] Prominent black Harlemites and even well-known whites from downtown showed up and signed the guestbook, prompting more local residents to visit. Tanner's painting and Reverend White's copies of classics drew the most attention. Bibliophiles hovered around the display of Arthur A. Schomburg's treasures, including rare editions of Phillis Wheatley's poems, a Paul Laurence Dunbar collection, and prints and engravings of international black political and literary heroes.[38] An evening literary program, two musicales, and various special evenings for the artists and their friends and for interested groups (such as church congregations) boosted interest.

On the first of September, Larsen received instructions from Augustus Granville Dill (business manager of *The Crisis* and an associate of Du Bois's) "to see that the Negro ministers have in their hands *not later than Saturday, September 3* notices of the extension of the time for the Exhibit. She will please stress the fact that all our citizens are earnestly urged to attend and that the admission is free."[39] Nella Larsen Imes, as she signed herself in the registration book, served as hostess several times in September. She probably turned in her notice to the Health Department that month, for her resignation officially took effect on October 4, a week before the Negro Arts Exhibit closed on Columbus Day.[40] As of

September 15, although still working full time for the Health Department in the Bronx, she was named a "substitute assistant" on the library staff, at the standard biweekly salary of $37.34. She would remain in that capacity through December, when she passed an exam and earned a "Grade 1" appointment to begin New Year's Day of 1922 at the standard beginning salary of $992 per year.[41]

A Grade 1 appointment ("Junior Library Assistant") in the NYPL required a certificate of graduation from a high school "or evidence of other education recognized by the Examining Board as the equivalent."[42] As a result, Larsen began fudging about her formal education whenever she filled out official forms. But what is especially striking about her career move is the dramatic drop in her pay, and the fact that, for the first time in her life except for the year at Tuskegee, she would serve a predominantly black community.[43] Nursing paid well, but it could be downright grueling, prone to unpredictable crises that suddenly took over one's existence. Librarianship may have been perceived as a more genteel profession for a married woman at the time, but more important to Larsen was the fact that it would allow her to spend more time with books; she may well have already been harboring ambitions of becoming an author.

Furthermore, there was "the cause." E. C. Williams had been urging her to go into library work full time and help open up the field to others. Ernestine Rose, too, saw in Larsen a perfect candidate to break down racial barriers in the profession, feeling she had not only great critical skills but executive ability and personal qualities—charm, diplomacy, intelligence, articulateness—that could propel her to supervisory positions despite the hurdles. By January Larsen already had plans for attending library school, the first step to climbing the career ladder, and one that in Larsen's case, Williams and Rose believed, could be historic.

Before Larsen, Williams was probably the only formally trained African American librarian in the country, and the school of the NYPL was one of the most prestigious in the world. Yet even directors of branch libraries, with many years of experience in positions of administrative leadership, made only $1,400 to $1,800, and there had been no money for raises in several years.[44] Moreover, since the library was not technically a city institution—being run under the auspices of the Astor, Lenox and Tilden Foundations—it had no pension plan. For the same reason, it could evade some of the rules against racial discrimination that bound the Health Department. Rose was determined to see black librarians allowed into library service on equal terms, and the first step to achieving this, beyond hiring black assistants, was getting those black assistants into library school. She handpicked Larsen to open the way.[45] Anticipating trouble, Rose apparently sent word to the school in advance. The first item on a faculty meeting agenda of January 26, 1922, headed "Colored Students," states: "Mrs. Imes, assistant at the 135th St. Branch may apply for admission to the School. Should we accept her?"[46]

As a Junior Assistant, working chiefly in the Children's Department, Larsen helped with some of the library's most important outreach work, going to Sunday schools and homes, addressing clubs, and holding book meetings in the library for students and parents.[47] Public health nursing had prepared her admirably. "Visiting the homes," Rose found, "is a most effective means of advertising, for the mothers are particularly interested in what the library is offering their children, and such interest will often prompt a first visit on their part."[48] A large public school across the street held morning classes at the branch that were focused on "cultural reading," and these led scores of children to register for borrowing privileges.[49] Parents then discovered that the library even had books for adults.

The Children's Room also held "story hours" for youngsters of various ages, and librarian exchanges with other branches, as well as monthly reports, soon spread word that it had a special quality: the children were "not silent and absorbed as a Jewish group would be, but eagerly responsive, on tip-toe with expectation."[50] "The work with colored children at the 135th Street Branch," the NYPL director wrote in his annual report, had become a model for other libraries "seeking to strengthen the relation between their reading rooms and the circulation of books. As in no other community, grown people come with their children to listen to stories, to look at pictures, and to enjoy the room. Far from being a children's room set apart from the others, it is as fresh to each of them, as a new and interesting child acquaintance is to the person who cares about children."[51]

The 135th Street Branch was unique in experimenting with a "mixed" staff to serve a mainly black population. According to a survey that Rose commissioned in 1921–1922, many Southern cities barred African Americans from using the library; only two Southern cities allowed free access, and sixteen had "colored branches"—these were the only ones African Americans could enter except as janitors. In Northern and Western states, blacks generally had free access to public libraries, and Cincinnati and Cleveland had branches specially serving blacks; but all of the "colored" branches outside New York had all-black staffs (not supervisors). Although black assistants served in the "mainstream" libraries of several Northern cities, they were prohibited from advancing beyond low-level jobs because none had gone to library school. But someone was on the case: "The New York Public Library expects to have one of its colored assistants in its library school next year," Ernestine Rose reported.[52]

Larsen filled out the application in late April. School policies allowed candidates without a high school diploma to take the admission examinations only "if special courses had been taken which could be regarded as making up the high school equivalent. They would not be accepted unless they could give evidence of wide reading and unusual ability."[53] The head of the school was pushing hard, in fact, for the bar to be raised to a college degree, in keeping with the nationwide attempt to have librarians' work recognized as "professional." Larsen therefore exaggerated her formal education, claiming she had attended Wendell Phillips High School for three years (1905–1908) and Fisk University Preparatory School for one year (1908–1909). This made her year at Fisk look like a senior year of high school. The library authorities would not ask for a transcript from Phillips but would request only the grades for the year at Fisk. She gave the correct dates for her nursing education, 1912–1915. The form had a space to list "Foreign School," and for the years between Fisk and nursing school Larsen wrote that she had attended *mellemskole* (middle school) in Askov, Denmark, from 1909–1910; in the space for "College or University" she claimed she had taken an "Open Course" at the University of Copenhagen from 1910 to 1912. This made her formal education look quite respectable. Moreover, she knew three languages: she could speak a Scandinavian language and read it without a dictionary; she claimed three years of high school training in German, which she could speak and read without a dictionary; and she could read French with the help of a dictionary. On this form, Larsen claimed she had been born in 1892. Since she had claimed an 1893 birthdate on her marriage license application, one assumes she chose the earlier date so she could plausibly fit all the secondary schooling within the given time frame.

The application asked for a list of ten books the candidate had read in the previous two years, to which Larsen gave an eclectic response: Knut Hamsun's Scandinavian classic, *Growth of the Soil;* Max Beerbohm's *And Even Now;* Lothrop Stoddard's *New World of Islam;* Julian Street's *Abroad at Home;* B. L. Putnam Weale's *Fight for the Republic in China;* Lytton Strachey's controversial modernist psycho-biography *Queen Victoria;* H. L. Mencken's *Prejudices* (1 and 2); Hendrik Van Loon's *Story of Mankind* (a bestselling, often satirical history of the world, written for children but immensely popular even with "highbrow" adults); Hamlin Garland's Midwestern realist classic *A Daughter of the Middle Border;* and W. E. B. Du Bois's scathing modernist hybrid memoir and indictment of white America, *Darkwater.* For periodicals that she read regularly, Larsen listed the highbrow *Bookman,* the middle-brow *Literary Digest,* the handsome highbrow orientalist magazine *Asia;* the leftish weekly *The Nation* (owned by the early NAACP leader Oswald Garrison Villard), and two of New

York's most liberal daily newspapers, the *Tribune* and Villard's *Evening Post.* She had also begun reading *Library Journal.* Her listing of *Asia* in this group reveals her "orientalist" interests, which endured throughout the Twenties. To the question of why she thought she would be successful in library work, Larsen responded that she was interested in books, in children, and in hospital libraries—indicating that she was thinking of hospital and children's librarianship as potential career tracks. For references, she listed Ernestine Rose, E. C. Williams, and Adah B. Thoms.[54]

Thoms gave her the most perfunctory recommendation of the three. The form asked for evaluations of such attributes as "Spirit," "Disposition," "Tact," "Alertness," "Initiative," "Judgment," "Executive Ability," "Neatness," "Accuracy," "Powers of Observation," "Speed of Working," "Knowledge of Books," "Personal Appearance," and "Possible Drawbacks." It then asked for a rating of the candidate's overall ability—"unusual," "average," or "below average." With no elaborations, Thoms rated her former student and assistant excellent in all categories but of only "average" ability. Asked how long and in what capacity she had known the candidate, Thoms wrote: "Three years as a pupil nurse and have kept in touch with her since completing her training"—a puzzling response, since Larsen had accurately written on her application that she had served as Assistant Superintendent of Nurses and taught Materia Medica and History of Nursing under Thoms from 1916 to 1918.

E. C. Williams of Howard University wrote a more detailed and explicit recommendation. He did not feel qualified to rate Larsen on "Tact," "Judgment," "Executive Ability," "Neatness," "Accuracy," or "Powers of Observation," but rated her "excellent" in "Spirit," "Disposition," "Alertness," and "Speed of Working." Her overall ability, initiative, knowledge of books, and personal appearance he considered "above average" for library school candidates. He was most effusive in his concluding comment on how he had known the applicant: "Two years' friendly acquaintance in her home. I urged her to go into library work. Have never worked with her. . . . But it is a pleasure to be able to say that I recommend her *most strongly,* and feel she would be a *splendid* student." Williams' opinion carried special weight, for he had mentored the director of the library school, Ernest J. Reece, at Western Reserve University years before. In fact, Williams was Reece's favorite teacher, "among those rare men with whom once known, one wished never to lose contact"—and with whom Reece never did, up to Williams' death in 1929.[55]

The most important and detailed recommendation came from Ernestine Rose, who rated Larsen highly on all counts but especially for "Judgment" and "Spirit." Rose was impressed by Larsen's knowledge of books and singled out her "excellent critical ability." Rating her employee "Very alert," "Very neat," and accurate in her work, with a "pleasing" appearance, Rose stressed Larsen's potential for leadership. Clearly, she wanted to see Larsen put on track for supervisory positions. Concerning "Initiative," Rose's response spilled over the space on the form: "Has plenty, but does not always use it readily. Is diffident or rather intensely self-restrained in self-expression." Yet Rose believed Larsen had real executive ability, "and will use it, if left in position of responsibility." Regarding drawbacks, Rose wrote testily, "Her color is the only possible one." Overall: "I consider her ability somewhat more than average and her personality unusually *pleasing*."[56]

The committee worried about how other students would react to Larsen's presence and about what would happen during the annual week-long "inspection trip" during which the students would travel up and down the Eastern states between Baltimore and Boston visiting libraries. Would people object to rooming with Imes? Would restaurants and hotels bar her entry? Nonetheless, they considered the application a good one and asked for her grades from the Fisk registrar, who replied promptly in May. Although the grades were not stellar, the 63 in Latin would not have bothered the librarians, since they were more concerned with modern languages, and in these they had reason to believe Imes would do well. She sat for the day-long entrance exams in early June, covering History, Current Topics, French, Literature, General Information, and German.[57] Her worst performance, expectedly, was in French, a C-minus. But she got A's in Literature and Current Events, B-plus in both General Information and German, and a C-plus in History.[58] This was good enough for director Ernest Reece and his faculty, who soon informed Larsen of her acceptance. In a report to the American Library Association a year later (reprinted in *Opportunity* magazine), Rose would single out Larsen's entry into the school as that year's most important single development with respect to library work and racial "readjustment" in the United States.[59]

The spring and summer library programs of 1922, while Larsen was readying herself for library school and working full time, included an ongoing series of weekly discussions of "Modern Racial Problems," introduced by a string of prominent citizens, activists, and scholars, mostly African American, from New York, Chicago, and Washington. In early March, the forum's regular participants, led by James Weldon Johnson, decided to form a society for the study of Negro History, which the *Age* termed "epoch-making" in significance.[60] The staff regularly worked up new lists of "recommended" books on various subjects, including contemporary literature and drama.[61] The first Wednesday in April, Augusta Markowitz of the Woodstock Branch delivered a talk entitled

"The Library and the Community," and Jessie Fauset of *The Crisis* spoke on Haitian poetry. Babette Deutsch, a key member of the Provincetown Theater and the Greenwich Village rebellion of the 1910s and early 1920s, which was breaking the grip of the genteel literary establishment, then read some of her poems, and a leading children's librarian from the library school told several stories.[62]

For Music Week in early May, the assistants compiled a bibliography of black music and set out written music along with collections of folklore, poetry, and biographies of musicians. A concert in the auditorium featured music by black composers.[63] In the Children's Room, Larsen helped put together a special collection of songs and folktales, and on Thursday the fourth a storytelling hour focused on uplifting tales of black achievement, including Frank Stockton's story "The Magical Music" and a tale about the life of the Anglo-African composer Samuel Coleridge-Taylor.[64]

In early March, the library announced its plan to hold a second exhibition of "Negro arts."[65] Larsen once again served as secretary to the executive committee. The assistant chairman was none other than Mrs. E. P. Roberts—a.k.a. Ruth Logan, the daughter of Warren Logan and princess of the Tuskegee campus in the spring of Larsen's tenure there, since married to one of Harlem's most esteemed physicians. During all the years of her marriage to Elmer, Nella had to negotiate such awkward remeetings, in subordinate roles, with "race women" and "race men" she had once known in institutions from which she had been ejected.

Larsen's job began with recruiting prominent men and women to head the various committees, a task made difficult by the fact that she was a "nobody." Adah Thoms initially agreed to chair the Art Committee, at Rose's rather than Larsen's request, but later withdrew.[66] Larsen also announced meeting times and kept track of who would be absent.[67] At the evening meetings themselves, she silently took the minutes (still extant, in her hand, among the library records). The more visible honorary role of executive secretary went to the better-known Ruth Whitehurst, and so Larsen was never mentioned publicly in connection with the exhibition. Similarly, although Ernestine Rose presided over most of the planning meetings, Jesse Moorland was the official chair, so Rose's leadership was largely invisible. By contrast, Jessie Fauset resigned as chair of the Program Committee when she realized that she would be expected to help work up audiences: "This I have no time to do. And on the other hand I do not like to subject my 'talent' to such small gatherings," she sniffed. "Perhaps another year we shall be able to hit on something different."[68] Nella Larsen Imes and her colleagues picked up the slack; but Fauset got the credit, because her name was already on all the stationery and printed matter as the chair of the Program Committee.[69] But Larsen's social connections expanded as she came in contact with the cream of Harlem society through library programs and ancillary events, such as a card party and dance at the Alpha Physical Club in June to raise money for the exhibition.

Predictably, other conflicts arose during the months of planning. Several prominent people had decried the title of the 1921 show, "Negro Art Exhibit," because they objected to the notion of "Negro art." Louise Latimer, trained at Brooklyn's Pratt Institute and the National Academy of Design, who assisted in the library and was also an exhibitor, suggested "Society of Negro Artists." Rose replied that she wanted "to form a permanent art exhibit on the order of the Bohemian exhibit in the Webster library," and thus wanted a name to "sustain that idea." The committee finally settled on "Exhibit by Negro Artists."[70]

While all of this was going on, Nella's mother and stepfather moved to California, following Anna and her family. Mary, at least, was already living in Los Angeles by May 1922 when she visited a notary public there to sign the papers selling the house on Maryland Avenue in Chicago. Peter was in Chicago for the transaction but joined Mary immediately thereafter.[71] From now on, a continent separated Nella Larsen Imes from the Larsen family and she had no more direct ties to Chicago.

The exhibition, which opened on August 1, as it had the previous year, included artists at all levels of training. Ninety-six artworks by forty-two people (none of them well known today) went on display in the library's public rooms. The artists hailed from cities all down the East Coast between Boston and Washington, and from Chicago. There were posters, magazine covers, architectural drawings, oil paintings, landscapes, etchings, and books loaned by Young's Book Exchange.[72] Very few of the objects concerned "Negro" subjects—landscapes and still lifes predominated. Six of the portraits on display would later be reproduced in a December issue of *Survey Graphic,* a social work magazine with fairly wide circulation.[73] Each Thursday a special program took place with talks on art or musical performances.[74] Twenty to forty people signed the guestbook most days, success enough to set a pattern and establish a tradition of holding an annual "Negro" art exhibition in New York—later at the International House, and ultimately under the auspices of the Harmon Foundation not only in New York, but around the country.

Before the exhibition closed, Larsen had begun library school. With more than a little chutzpah and calculated dissimulation, she had barely made it in. When on September 18 she climbed the steps between the guardian lions of New York's temple of learning and entered the columned lobby to find her classroom, formal library training was still a fairly new phenomenon. Like the

Central Library building itself, the school was only eleven years old, and the profession was in the process of defining itself, battling the low pay that accompanied the feminization of the field by continually raising the bar to entry.[75] Already, Larsen knew, the American Library Association had decided the top three grades of library service should exclude anyone who had not finished college and taken a year of library school.[76] She would graduate just as a definitive report came out concluding that "professional library training should be based on a college education or its full equivalent."[77] For women like Larsen, the doors had shut.

Half of Nella's entering class of forty-two students held bachelor's degrees, and she was probably the only one without some form of high school diploma.[78] The director of the school boasted that 10 percent of the students were of "foreign birth," some having come from Scandinavia and Asia specifically to attend the school: "This, together with the fact that those born in this country unquestionably represent every prominent old-world racial strain, stamps the School with a cosmopolitan and catholic character of which it may be increasingly proud."[79]

The location of the NYPL Library School in the publishing capital of the United States, within the world's greatest public library, afforded extraordinary opportunities, and the fifteen-member faculty took full advantage of them. The list of more than seventy guest lecturers for the 1922–1923 academic year included the city's leaders in editing, publishing, literary scholarship, and library science, including people (such as Carl Van Doren) with whom Larsen would later rub shoulders at literary soirées. For fieldwork, students had access to the exceptionally diverse branch libraries but also to America's largest business and technical libraries, book auctions and rare-book sellers, binderies, art exhibitions, printing houses, readings, and performances. And the tuition was free for Larsen, since she had worked in the library system for a year.[80]

The main subjects tackled by first-year students were Cataloguing and Subject Headings, Reference Work, Book Selection, and Administration, with additional time devoted to Current Events, American Libraries, Printing, Bibliography, and Modern Literature. Students learned how to bind and repair books, how to "weed" a library, how to determine the value of different editions. Most Wednesday afternoons, the school held a "social hour," occasionally with famous authors, critics, and editors as guests.[81] Thursday night lectures brought in outside specialists on recent literary trends and new publishing fields worldwide.

Larsen got her best grades in the book selection course, which provided excellent background for an aspiring author. She learned how to judge various editions of books and heard lectures on the history and current work of the most important publishers in Great Britain and the United States. Her seminars covered current fiction and poetry, as well as literature in foreign languages. Twice a week, she attended classes on outstanding fiction writers in languages other than English. She visited and evaluated bookstores. For classes in Current Events she had to study coverage of selected issues in an array of newspapers, weeklies, and monthlies, a practice that became a habit for her throughout the 1920s.[82] Among the fourteen weeklies and five monthlies were a number that would be important to Harlem Renaissance authors: *The Independent, The Nation, The New Republic, Outlook, Saturday Review, Survey,* and *Current History.* Students studied the editorial staffs, contributors, and policies of all the journals, and chose one weekly, one monthly, and one quarterly to read regularly throughout the year—valuable professional training for a writer.

Larsen excelled in what interested her most, while settling for a passable performance in other subjects. In the first semester, she received straight A's in Book Selection; B's in Cataloguing and Subject Headings; B's in Reference; a B-plus in Classification; a B-plus in American Libraries (based entirely on the report she gave on the state library at Albany); and an A in an extra class on Book Selection. Other than the A's in Book Selection, these were essentially average and even below-average grades.[83]

In the fall of 1922 or early 1923, the Imeses moved from their Harlem apartment to a house at 51 Audubon Street, Jersey City. Without Nella's salary, the couple may not have been able to afford the rent of a nice apartment in Harlem. In any case, Nella would have no great difficulty getting to midtown Manhattan for her classes, and Elmer was not such a confirmed "city person" as Nella; perhaps he preferred living in a single-family home. It was a three-story house in a "white" section of the city, and a man named Robert S. Hartgrove rented the top floor.[84] The house still stands, close to the street on a steep slope with three large living-room windows overlooking a small garden and city sidewalk.

The move altered the Imeses' social life for the next four years, although they kept contact with their friends in Brooklyn and Manhattan, hosting small dinner or bridge parties with some regularity. They socialized chiefly with young black couples in the professional class: Louis and Corinne Wright, Alonzo DeGrate Smith, Walter and Gladys White. They almost certainly made occasional visits to Elmer's brother and sister-in-law, now living in Philadelphia, where William pastored a flock of Presbyterians.[85]

The second semester of library school included the regular coursework, but also new challenges in which race was bound to become an issue. At the beginning of the term, each student normally spent two weeks at each of two different branch libraries gaining practical experience.[86] From February 5 to February 17, Larsen worked at the Woodstock Branch, serving a predominantly Hungarian Jewish neighborhood under the wing of Augusta Markowitz, whom Larsen already knew. Larsen proved to be a quick learner and a fine librarian, particularly in reference and children's work. She struck Markowitz as calm and self-possessed, with an "excellent" attitude toward the public. She also got along extremely well with the staff, and Markowitz said she would be happy to have Larsen as a full-time employee.[87]

For the next two weeks, into early March, Nella worked at the Seward Park Branch under Alice Keats O'Connor, one of the key branch librarians in the system, who gave an even more positive report and went out of her way to praise the student. Larsen spent all her time except one evening in the Children's Room, where she did well. To the question on the report form, "Has she taken criticism well and profited by it?" O'Connor replied: "None given—it was not necessary." Larsen not only did good work but got along very well with the staff, "and there are two Southerners who had anticipated being unhappy. Mrs. Imes completely disarmed them of their prejudice." Larsen had not learned "very quickly," O'Connor admitted, "but she is not slow." Most important, O'Connor would be happy to have Mrs. Imes in her own branch.[88] For her practice work under Markowitz and O'Connor, and the report she wrote on the experience, Nella received her only A of the year in a subject other than Book Selection.[89]

Classes resumed on March 5, when Larsen started learning to bind books and records, a practice she would take up as a sort of hobby in the Twenties, keeping scrapbooks of newspaper clippings on literary issues. Classes that month also introduced students to book collecting, another of her passions in later years.[90] But the main event of the semester was the week-long "Inspection Trip" to major libraries of the Northeast.

Worried about how Larsen would be received, the registrar had contacted all the hotels where the students would be staying and was relieved to find that none of them objected to having her as a guest, for either lodging or meals. The thirty-two members of the group gathered at Grand Central Station on Friday, March 23, and boarded a train for Albany, where they set up "headquarters" in shared rooms at the comfortable Hotel Ten Eyck. That afternoon, they visited the famous New York State Library and library school, founded by Melvil Dewey, who had been thrown out of Columbia for educating women in the world's first library school. Saturday morning, the students awakened early to catch a train to Boston, where they spent three days exploring the cavernous Boston Public Library on Copley Square, the cupola-crowned collections at

Harvard, the Boston Athenaeum, the Massachusetts State Library, and the Division of Public Libraries in the State House. Next they headed to Providence to visit the libraries at Brown University, the Providence Atheneum, and the Rhode Island Historical Society. The next day, after touring the Providence Public Library and the State Library in the gleaming white-domed capitol building, the group caught a train back to New York.[91] Another social hurdle behind her, Larsen could now expect a smooth track to graduation.

That winter and spring of 1922–1923, the 135th Street Branch was humming with cultural activities. Every Saturday evening, Hubert Harrison, under the auspices of the Board of Education, gave lectures on "Literary Lights of Yesterday and Today," featuring Emerson, Macaulay, Hugo, Lincoln, Poe, Bret Harte, and others.[92] On January 10, Nella's former neighbor and colleague Sadie M. Peterson presented sculptor Augusta Savage's bust of W. E. B. Du Bois to the library in a special ceremony with a presentation speech by anthropologist Franz Boas of Columbia University; Boas returned two weeks later to give a talk entitled "Race Problems in America."[93] Every Wednesday night the Booklovers Club hosted guest lecturers in the library. Du Bois himself spoke in a packed auditorium on January 17, tracing the history of black literature from the late seventeenth century on and urging black readers to quit being ashamed of their folklore.

On February 14, Clement Wood, a well-known left-wing poet and author of the novel *Nigger,* gave an address entitled "What the Negro Can Give to Literature." (He had just published an article in *The Nation* entitled "Shall Black and White Mix? Alabama: A Study in the Race Problem," which had created a buzz among black literati.)[94] Acknowledging that many blacks were offended by his book's title, he admitted: "When I wrote that novel, I never thought of the Negro readers at all. I wrote for the white people. I painted things as they are in an effort to show my race the great difficulties that beset Negroes when they tried to rise." Noting the importance of figures like Alexander Pushkin, Henry O. Tanner, James Weldon Johnson, J. Rosamond Johnson, Claude McKay, and Jessie Fauset, he decried the comic stereotypes purveyed in the popular magazines. The Negro, he asserted, "must make every effort to build up his own literature—a realistic literature."[95] After the lecture, Walter White gave a dinner for Wood in his home and then hosted a reception for him that Nella likely attended. Two weeks after Wood's lecture, the Booklovers evening was devoted to "the best colored poets of the younger group."[96]

In mid-March, a large audience came to hear Margaret Sanger's talk "The Women of Japan." Sanger chided American women for doing little to further their own emancipation since acquiring the vote and emphasized the need to disseminate birth control information to all. Several policemen were on hand to see that she did not do so during the talk.[97] In April the forum hosted P. Dow Cunningham, an Egyptologist, who delivered an address called "The Life, Arts and Monuments of the Ancient Egyptians." If the Egyptians lived in the contemporary United States, he observed, they would be classed as Negroes; and he promised to show, in his next lecture, "pictures of King Tut's black grandmother."[98]

Things were quickly heating up in the realm of black artistic expression. Walter White had a bit part in the Ethiopian Art Theatre's version of *Salome* that spring and summer; Nella and Elmer could not have missed it. The Ethiopian Art Theatre had started out on State Street in Chicago, not far from where Larsen grew up. Legend had it that while visiting Chicago, the white director (previously instrumental in the Moscow Art Theatre productions in Greenwich Village) had been inspired by the talent of black café and cabaret entertainers along State Street; he was convinced they could form the basis of a new experimental theater movement in America. He gathered an all-black cast from the Chicago club district and opened on the city's "black Broadway" to a full, integrated house including the literary lions of the Midwest. When the troupe moved on to New York, it created a minor sensation on the Great White Way; and after another week-long stint in Harlem's Lafayette Theater, it reopened for a repertory season on Broadway, picking up folk plays by black author Willis Richardson. The group was not universally admired, but Harlem newspapers such as the *Amsterdam News* touted their success as a sign that a new era of serious black drama, and of opportunity for black performers, was in the offing.[99]

In popular entertainment, black acts were getting increasing attention from *Variety*, the main journal of the business, and female blues artists—beginning with Mamie Smith on Okeh Records in 1920—were breaking sales records in the young recording industry, surprising everyone by appealing across racial lines. In the fall of 1922, the fast-paced, dance-packed, all-black "speed show" *Liza* had introduced the Charleston to Broadway and set off a fad that would help to define the Twenties for later generations.[100] Duke Ellington had just come to New York and was playing at Barron's Exclusive Club, one of Harlem's (black-owned) glitziest; while (white-owned) Connie's Inn in the basement of the Lafayette Theater presented (black) Leonard Harper's first New York floor show. Newly arrived from Chicago's State Street and Gold Coast, he would soon make his mark on the Roaring Twenties, becoming "the preeminent creator of floor shows for nearly every black nightclub in New York City."[101] In many respects, the Jazz Age was incubated in Nella Larsen's hometown—or rather, her very neighborhood. But New York opened it to the world.

Meanwhile, in the neighborhood of her newly chosen profession, the Chicago native was being held up as a beacon of hope for black advance and interracial "adjustment." At the American Library Association's April conference in Hot Springs, Arkansas, in the featured round table on the topic "Work among Negroes," before an audience of over a hundred, Ernestine Rose delivered a bold paper entitled "Progress for the Year" that the *Amsterdam News* found significant enough to feature on May 2. Interest in Negro literature, Rose pointed out, was growing. Requests by both whites and blacks for lists of books by and about Negroes demanded new efforts by librarians they had not contemplated before. Taking the bull by the horns, she directly attacked segregated libraries, including "the purely Negro library": all limitations to Negro librarians must be broken down, and opportunities for full responsibilities in all libraries opened up. At the same time, in branches serving primarily black neighborhoods, interracial staffs should be maintained as part of the wider battle against race prejudice.

The key to the way forward, Rose announced, was indicated by the case of the Negro who had been accepted that academic year to the Library School of the New York Public Library: "Perhaps that incident in New York which seems to me most significant is the acceptance by our library school of a colored applicant on precisely the same terms as the white, and the following fact that all facilities offered by the school have been at her command."[102] Subsequent to Larsen's matriculation, Rose continued, a "colored girl" had been admitted to the Carnegie Library School in Pittsburgh. In July the new journal of the Urban League, *Opportunity*, reprinted her speech in full: "It will be more than interesting—it will be vastly significant to note the places which these two girls find open to them. Opportunities for training, it may be, will open more rapidly than suitable places of employment except in colored organizations or groups."[103] At this stage, Rose continued, it was important to ensure that those who entered the field succeed, or the enemies of the race would exploit their failure: "A single failure will clinch in many unthinking minds the old argument, that Negroes lack capacity to develop beyond a certain point. But because these hard sayings are true, there exists a very special necessity for friends of Negro advance to give prepared colored workers ample opportunity to disprove the need of such special conditions. Unless the place is open to an educated and prepared worker, how is he to prove his fitness for it? This is the road along which we are called to advance."[104]

In Larsen's class on Library Administration, the director of the school devoted the entire Thursday afternoon session on May 3 to the conference proceedings.[105] Whether he mentioned Rose's comments or not, the students and faculty would come upon them in the *Bulletin of the American Library Association* (required reading), where her statement was reprinted in full.[106]

In the professional ferment that followed her talk, the *Bulletin* duly noted, the Southerners at the conference vehemently disputed Rose's view that "the South does not know the negro" and that they were blinded by racist "sentimentality." When the session finally broke up, many participants were feeling that "the negro question was a sectional one, and that the South must approach it from its own angle"—a position that Rose never ceased attacking but that put an end to the round table's existence two years later.[107]

Larsen's grades for the second semester, it must be said, were mediocre. She got straight A's again in Book Selection, and an A for her Practice Work. Her next best subject was Reference, with B-plus across the board. But she had a C in Administration; a B-minus and two C-pluses in Bibliography; a B in Current history; and a B, C-minus, and C in Printing and Indexing. These grades put her in the bottom quarter or bottom third of the class in most subjects.[108] But she had done very well in the most crucial areas, Book Selection and Practice Work. Larsen, like at least half of her class, did not show up for the class photograph, and she would take no interest in the Alumnae Association. Neither did she bother to join the American Library Association. And like almost all the other students, she did not go on for the senior-year program (which would have earned her a diploma on top of her certificate), because it conferred no tangible benefits. As leaders of the school complained, senior-year training and a diploma were irrelevant to professional advancement at the time.[109]

Commencement came on Friday, June 8, in Room 213 of the Central Library. The words of the main speaker, James Wyer of the New York State Library, were reported in the *New York Times*. He pleaded with the graduates "for the retention of established standards of literary taste."[110] Distressed by the overwhelming flood of new and modern books, he urged librarians to preserve "the soul of the nation." "Are its traits and ideals to be ugliness, extravagance, ignorance, brutality, or will they come more and more to be simplicity, health, sweetness and light?"[111] "It is to you and to those few hundreds like you who each year go out into the work from these schools that we confidently look for light and leading."[112] As they emerged from the great lobby into the sunlight, looking over the heads of the lions onto bustling Fifth Avenue, who could have known that four years later Nella Larsen Imes would find herself embroiled in the battle Wyer had identified—yet on the other side?

[TEN]

Rooms Full of Children:
Seward Park and Harlem, 1923–1924

THE day after Commencement, a faculty member wrote a memorandum "for use in answering requests for recommendations." The memo showed that six of the thirty-one junior class students had not yet been placed, including Nella Larsen Imes. She wanted to travel abroad during the summer and hoped eventually to locate work in Newark, "but plans for the fall are uncertain."[1] As it turned out, Larsen did not go abroad, though she may have spent some time in Canada, where Elmer occasionally attended professional conferences in the summer. Technically, she still had a job in New York, being on leave from the 135th Street Branch. She hoped to find a position close to her home in Jersey City: before her leave ended on July 1, she extended it until November.[2]

She probably never found a job outside New York—perhaps because of racial discrimination—but she decided not to return to the 135th Street Branch for the time being. Instead, she sat for the library examinations for promotion to Grade 2, which took place over the course of four days in late October and early November.[3] Afterward she was appointed a Senior Assistant, and began immediately working in the Children's Department at the Seward Park Branch on the Lower East Side, for a salary of $1,317 per year.[4] The normal beginning Grade 2 salary was $1,229 annually, but library school graduates with a year's prior experience enjoyed a nearly 10 percent bump. Larsen had less than one year's experience, but she got the higher salary. A year later, when she moved to take over the Children's Room in Harlem, she got a raise to $1,488, the top salary in her grade.[5]

All three of the branch librarians who had supervised Larsen had said they would be glad to have her on their staffs; she was promoted more rapidly than most of her colleagues, and paid accordingly. Larsen's well-respected boss, Alice Keats O'Connor, had written glowingly of Larsen's service as an intern, and she had a special regard for children's work. O'Connor had begun her own career as a children's librarian, and Seward Park was considered the best place for training to direct children's departments.[6] O'Connor's high opinion of Larsen paved the way for her placement, allowing her to start at a familiar (and prized) branch, under a boss who respected her and who was widely admired through-out the system. Having worked previously at another branch, Larsen was in a position for quick promotion if she performed well. But her options for place-ment were likely limited to Jewish and black neighborhoods. Larsen also won the confidence of the highly regarded librarian in charge of the Children's Room, Harriet S. Wright, whose good report of her work would be crucial to further advancement.

Seward Park was an easier commute than Harlem from Larsen's home and, by late 1923, already a storied neighborhood—the heart of the Lower East Side. Russian Jews fleeing pogroms had been pouring into the area since the late nineteenth century, and not a few had gone on to distinguish themselves in the arts. To native-born Americans from outside the neighborhood, it bore an air of high excitement, squalor, and confusion.[7] Swarms of children roamed the neighborhood while housewives nonchalantly swept trash out of their houses right into the street. Overflowing garbage cans bordered each doorstep and an interminable line of pushcarts stood along the curb selling fish, fruit, vegeta-bles, shoestrings, ribbons, furs, and chewing gum. "Grimy men," wrote one of Larsen's colleagues, "noisily screamed their wares or haggled with equally grimy women over the price of the head or the tail of a fish. Young mothers tirelessly pushed baby-carriages up and down the sidewalk."[8] This was one point of view.

Konrad Bercovici, a gypsy author who visited the library and neighborhood while Larsen was there, noted more the flourishing artistic and intellectual life: "The whole neighborhood is teeming with young artists, the future great artists of America. . . . There is not a house, no matter how poor it be, where there is not an easel, a piano, or a violin, and where the hope of the whole family is not pinned on one of the younger set as a future genius."[9] Theaters in the area fre-quently staged plays by Ibsen, Bjørnson, Strindberg, and Chekhov, well before other theaters in New York.[10] East Broadway at Seward Park was the intellectual heart of the East Side in the 1920s. All the Jewish newspapers were there—*For-ward, The Day, Jewish Daily News, Jewish Morning Journal*—along with the cafés where writers, playwrights, and composers hung out. Other Jewish publishing operations and magazines clustered along East Broadway. Next to Seward Park, and facing this "Yiddish Park Row," was the neoclassical limestone and redbrick branch library building, with the largest circulation in the city, and on the other side of the park was America's largest public school. "Seward Park is like an open-air forum," Bercovici wrote, "where from early morning till late at night bearded men with their tool-bags under one arm and prayer-bags under the other are discussing the policies of the world, as well as the interpretation of passages in the Talmud and the Bible; while the youngsters of the neighborhood do their courting, between games of baseball and football and foot-races that are being organized by the teachers from the neighborhood schools."[11]

Nella Larsen started in the Children's Room at the library just in time for Children's Book Week, November 12–17.[12] Making her way from the subway station across the block, she could smell the all-pervading odors of pickle vats, herring, and garlic wafting over the daily battle of the housewives, who pinched and poked the merchandise in the ever-present pushcarts while sellers half-threatened, half-pleaded, "Lady, lady, don't squeeze the fish!" Rushing past, little boys snatched dill pickles out of the brine on their way to school, tucking them dripping into their blousy shirts.[13] On Saturdays, as she approached the library before it opened in the morning, Larsen would see the long line of children waiting for the doors to open, three abreast and halfway down the block along East Broadway, often finishing their breakfast rolls as they waited for first chance at the books.[14] On weekdays after school let out at three, they raced across the park for the library, where the line, practically filling the broad stairway despite the efforts of the custodian to keep them in order, extended from the street to the second floor.[15] High-ceilinged, airy, and spacious—cool in summer, warm in winter—the main reading rooms were adorned grandly with murals of Sir Galahad, Robin Hood, and Venice's Grand Canal, forming an oasis from the cramped and smelly dark rooms of the tenements.[16]

In the overburdened Children's Room, the supply of books fell far short of demand in this era before in-school libraries, and the books themselves disintegrated from overuse.[17] Alice Keats O'Connor reported in January 1924 that "the circulating books in the Children's Department are in the most pathetic condition I've ever seen them."[18] As they became completely unusable and funds could not be found to replace them, the shelves grew bare.[19] Only the enthusiasm of the "valiant" children's librarians, the director of the system wrote, maintained the goodwill of the schools and parents.[20]

After the children had crowded in, they filed past the circulation desk to return books and got the familiar greeting, "Hands, please?" Little forearms shot out, palms upward, while Larsen or another assistant inspected them for cleanliness. Further back in line, boys and girls anxiously licked their palms and rubbed them on skirts and trousers. Always a few had to be sent home; but some were allowed to dash for the water fountain in Seward Park, from which they hurried back, hands scrubbed pink and shining, "but arms and faces quite as smeared as ever."[21]

The squirming mass on the stairway subdivided as it entered the room, and the children took their places in three lines leading to the shelves for fiction, fairy stories, and "easy books." Assistants like Larsen stood at the head of each line forcibly holding the children back with outstretched arm as each in turn looked over the shelf and made a selection—the only way to prevent a free-for-all. The readers knew what they wanted and exactly where to find it. Every half-hour girl and boy pages replenished the shelves with newly returned volumes, and children would stand in line over and over again, for hours if necessary, until a copy of the book they were looking for reappeared.[22] At times, not one readable book was left by the time a hopeful borrower reached the front of the line. The librarians themselves never got used to the children's persistence: "To be eager to come day after day to a place so thronged, to wait literally for hours at a time in the hope of securing some special book—and then to do it all over again at the very earliest opportunity."[23]

Partitioned off by low bookshelves from this noisy and never-ending drama, the reading area, with cases of beautifully illustrated books that never left the library, held fine editions of *Peter Rabbit, Uncle Remus, Alice in Wonderland, Otto of the Silver Hand, The Thousand and One Nights.* Around the room were exhibits of Jewish arts and holiday traditions.[24]

To make up for the dearth of books, Larsen read stories aloud and helped to create exhibits.[25] Special story hours for older girls who had been in the country less than a year started out as picture-book hours and evolved over the months into literary reading clubs. "All the children's room staff are interested in this work," O'Connor reported, "and wish to be story-tellers."[26] Classes from the public schools visited for "book talks" during the week. On Fridays and Saturdays, story hours transpired in the dingy basement beneath the hissing furnace pipes, filled to capacity with squirming children on rickety chairs. As the smell of dill and garlic lingered in the air, the assistant librarians transported the children to the Germany of the Brothers Grimm, the America of Paul Bunyan and Uncle Remus, the Ireland of Padraic Colum, and, not least, Hans Christian Andersen's Denmark.[27]

In the boys' clubs, where the books often had to do with adventures in the Far West, the children would listen in utter silence to the careful diction of the librarian, and then, when all was over and they filed out into the main reading room, would burst out with cowboy yells and whoops. On Saturday afternoons the "tiniest tots" came for a picture-book hour, often accompanied by older brothers or sisters.[28] When the weather was good, older children listened on the roof, "enraptured," to stories by Edgar Allan Poe, Mark Twain, Bret Harte, and Louisa May Alcott.[29] Adults used the Children's Room, as well, checking out books of fairy tales or history in very simple English in order to learn the language, but also borrowing huge volumes of Dostoyevsky, Turgenev, and Tolstoy in the original Russian.[30]

In biweekly staff meetings, Larsen and the other assistants delivered book reports and discussed their work. They made tours of local settlement houses and similar institutions to foster cooperation between such agencies and the work of the library. Occasionally a representative of the Educational Alliance would come speak to them, or one from the Henry Street Settlement and its Neighborhood Playhouse.

After a while, as Larsen made her way through the park or the neighborhood, she could recognize the little girl always asking for a book about dolls, or the one fixated on Pinocchio, or the bespectacled boy always haunting "the biographical and scientific shelves."[31] Assistant children's librarians at Seward Park visited parents in their homes to get their signatures on registration forms and to introduce them to the library.[32] Often the children left their cards at the library for safekeeping, but would forget what name they'd registered under. If Larsen was at the desk, she would have to determine if Irving Berg was the same little boy as Isadore Bergowitski.[33]

Even if the librarians tended to look down on their patrons, they could hardly fail to respond to the heartfelt thank-you notes, some of them still available in the library's archives: "I send you as many kisses as there are stars in the sky"; "I send you as many kisses as there are pennies in the world."[34] Five months after Larsen left the branch, the Mothers' Club finally amassed enough money to donate a set of silver candlesticks to the library in honor of the children's librarians: "We have chosen this symbol of light as a gift to the library," they wrote, "because it brought joy and light into our life and that of our children. May this spirit of your library live forever."[35]

The development of the "Children's Room" in public libraries was a distinctly modern—and American—phenomenon, and the philosophy and practice developed in the early Twenties in New York laid down the paradigm that has been followed ever since.[36] Annie Carroll Moore, who oversaw all aspects of children's work in the branches, including the training of the librarians, believed that the greatest gift of any Children's Room was "its recreation value—to inspire a love of reading for reading's own sake for the pure joy and refreshment it gives throughout life."[37] She considered storytelling the best known technique for accomplishing this, and her model for storytelling came from a performance sponsored by Mrs. Charlotte Osgood Mason—later a patron of Langston Hughes and Zora Neale Hurston—in which the renowned English storyteller Marie Shedlock lectured on "The Fun and Philosophy of Hans Christian Andersen" and told some of his great Danish stories. "Completely captivated,"[38] Moore instituted the practice of storytelling in public libraries for the first time and began storytelling classes for assistants in the Children's Rooms of New York.

Moore "raised her methods to the level of ritual" through continuous in-service training and regular personal conferences with all children's librarians in the system.[39] She insisted that each Children's Room be adapted to its neighborhood, with decorations, projects, and events reflecting local interests. Children's librarians should combat children's shame about foreign origins, which drove a wedge between them and their parents, and instead give them pride in their heritage while also helping them acculturate to the United States.[40]

Annie Carroll Moore's columns for *The Bookman,* one of the journals Larsen followed regularly, had historic importance in the context of book publishing, for children's books had never before received such attention in "adult" literary journals. The development was part of a more general revolution in children's literature that began in New York in the years 1919 to 1926, with the cooperation of the same publishers who supported the blossoming of African American literature known at the time as the Negro Renaissance.[41] Children's books were "at best a sideline with publishers" before the 1920s, according to John Tebbel.[42] This changed about the time that Children's Book Week, promoted by the American Booksellers Association, began in November 1919.[43] Soon the Children's Rooms in New York public libraries had formed close relationships with publishers and local booksellers as they advertised Children's Book Week, made up lists of recommended children's books, set up displays of well-designed books for children, and developed programming around the new children's literature. The first specialized Children's Departments in the publishing business began in 1919 and 1922. The first Newbery Medal, established by the Children's Librarians Section of the American Library Association, was awarded in 1922 to Van Loon's *Story of Mankind,* published by the avant-garde firm Boni and Liveright, the same house that published Jean Toomer's *Cane* the following year.[44] During Children's Book Week, just as Larsen started at Seward Park, children's book design entered the modern age when C. B. Falls's *ABC Book* came out, illustrated with the author's colorful woodblock engravings—"a landmark in the history of American picture books."[45] Viking Press would later hire Falls to work on James Weldon Johnson's historic volume of poetry, *God's Trombones.*

The chief impetus for all of these developments came from the children's library movement in the NYPL, which demanded new editions and updated reprints, encouraged production of new books, and backed up professional judgment with purchasing power. Never before or since has there been such a close relationship between publishers and librarians.[46]

What books did Larsen read and recommend to the children? We cannot know precisely, but children's literature remained a point of reference for her for many years, and she quoted from it in her fiction. For younger children there were the perennially popular "read-aloud" tales of Andersen and *Mother Goose*, and new favorites like *Tales from Silver Lands* by Charles J. Finger, presenting legends and folktales from the Indians of South America, or A. A. Milne's first children's book, *When We Were Very Young* (1924), which started him on a career that would produce *Winnie the Pooh*.[47] The most popular model for girls' stories in the 1920s was the *Five Little Peppers* series by Margaret Sidney, which "described poor but worthy children, 'naturally genteel,' who were adopted or befriended by affluent gentlefolk."[48] Such tales would show children struggling bravely with hardship and family tragedy in early life and then "deliver them to a better life, with money, protection, and education." The heroines of such tales, though of lower-class background, often orphans, had good manners and "finer feelings," as well as an innate responsiveness to beauty and art that allowed them to move gracefully into higher-class circles.[49] The plot formula closely paralleled Larsen's own life story at the time.

The higher-class circles in which Elmer and Nella Imes moved in the early and mid-1920s became increasingly diverse from the time Nella began working as a librarian. Perhaps, lacking "family," Nella felt rather insignificant to much of Harlem "society," but she discovered other, more sympathetic outlets for her social and intellectual interests. Her social life gravitated more strongly toward different, more racially integrated, sometimes less straitlaced circles—and people poorly remembered in Negro Renaissance lore of later generations. These included African Americans in Greenwich Village—Vivienne Ward Stoner, Edna Thomas, Dorothy Hunt Harris—and Dorothy Peterson, who frequented the Village and apparently introduced Larsen there at about the time she was working at Seward Park. Vivienne and Elmer Stoner, good friends of Nella and Elmer, with whom they often played bridge, moved from 124th Street to Greenwich Village in 1924, where "Vi" opened a gift shop on Christopher Street.[50] The Village was much easier to reach from Larsen's home and workplace than Harlem, and she enjoyed its atmosphere.

Peterson, through whom Larsen met other young "New Negroes" with literary interests and ambitions, must have met Larsen through the library when Larsen was assisting at the 135th Street Branch in 1921–1922, for they already were close friends before Larsen returned to the 135th Street Branch in the fall of 1924. A Spanish teacher in the public school system, Peterson was an attractive, sophisticated, and polished young woman of cosmopolitan background and well-known family. Langston Hughes described her as "a charming colored girl who had grown up mostly in Puerto Rico, and who moved with such poise among these colorful celebrities that I thought when I first met her she was a white girl of the grande monde, slightly suntanned."[51] Dorothy's father, Jerome Bowers Peterson, who had been born in Greenwich Village, was widely respected as a journalist and quasi-politician with deep roots in the history of black New York. In 1884, he and T. Thomas Fortune had founded the *New York Freeman,* later renamed the *New York Age.* They were considered radicals in the late nineteenth century, and their newspaper had great influence through the post-Reconstruction period. It was a key instrument in agitating for enforcement of the New York Civil Rights Act; it helped to win equal pay for teachers, suppressed Jim Crow on streetcars, and agitated with some success, at least, for justice after the 1900 race riot. After 1904, Peterson held a series of government posts, including U.S. Consul in Puerto Cabello, Venezuela (where James Weldon Johnson also served from 1906 to 1909), and later in San Juan, Puerto Rico. Dorothy and her brother Sidney received at least three years of their education in Puerto Rico, and grew up with Spanish as a second language. They also, according to one of Dorothy's good friends, experienced a "different" type of race prejudice on the island, being "on the upper side of the line, in a land where color-caste was more rigid than at home."[52] The family returned to Brooklyn in 1916, and Peterson resumed writing occasional editorials for the *Age,* while working for the U.S. Treasury Department. He was well known in liberal groups around New York, a frequent presence at the Civic Club downtown.[53]

Dorothy Peterson had a wide circle of friends, including many who became Larsen's good friends as well. Grace Nail Johnson was one of Dorothy's correspondents in the early 1920s, and they shared books with each other. Both women had distinctly modern tastes. Dorothy sent Grace a copy of Joseph Conrad's *Nigger of the Narcissus* for summer reading in 1923: "I know you'll love it. I've read it over and over again."[54] She had a special passion for drama and was resolutely independent. Although she resided, when Larsen met her, in the family home in Brooklyn, her quarters there formed practically a separate apartment. "My attitude toward my family," she would write a sometime "boy-friend," "is one of complete independence—affection, intolerance, quarrels, sacrifice, everything on a plane of each one of us as being equal individuals with a right to do as he pleases whether it pleases the family or not."[55] Dorothy spent a lot of time socializing in Greenwich Village, an easy stop for Larsen on her way home from work, and easier to get to from New Jersey (or Brooklyn) on weekend evenings than Harlem.

Such connections with Greenwich Village were more significant before the high tide of the Harlem Renaissance than historians have so far noticed. Many informal contacts preceded the staged events of the mid-1920s and made them possible. Some blacks frequented the Village more often than Harlem in the

8. Dorothy Peterson (center), Faculty Advisor of the Spanish Club, Bushwick High School, Brooklyn, early 1920s. Yale Collection of American Literature, Beinecke Rare Book and Manuscript Library, Yale University.

early 1920s merely because they found the atmosphere more comfortable and inviting, although this involved avoiding the "Negro-hating" establishments which, to be sure, existed here as everywhere. For that matter, Greenwich Village had always been an area of black settlement. One of the first black-authored novels of the Twenties, since then totally ignored, was set in Greenwich Village, focusing on the lower-class, multiethnic youth gang culture there. Published by a major New York publisher, it was written by a teenage high school student named Harry Liscomb and titled *The Prince of Washington Square.*

Anita Thompson, another close friend of Dorothy Peterson who spent most of her time in the Village from about 1923 to 1928, has described the attraction of this environment: "Many of the people I admired and enjoyed being with were in Greenwich Village." At Lee Chumley's café, among others, whites and blacks were equally welcome, by Thompson's account, and interesting writers and artists met there. "Dorothy and James Harris lived in the village. Dorothy and Sidney Peterson, close friends of Dorothy Parker, were over in Brooklyn, but they were all such close friends that they might as well have lived in the Village; they were there so often."[56] The Harrises were friends of Franz Boas, and so he also became friends with the circle around them. Also in this group were Edna St. Vincent Millay, Eugene O'Neill, and the famed set designer Cleon Throckmorton (later involved in a number of "Negro plays"), who threw a "Cleopatra Party," where, as Thompson recalls, "he was Antony and I was Cleopatra and everyone came in costume. It was there at the party that I realized that all the pleasure, the stimulation, the newness and excitement that I felt meant that I belonged in New York."[57] This occurred in about 1924.

Thompson liked the social atmosphere in the Village more than the one in Harlem because the intellectuals were like those she had known in Los Angeles in Charles Chaplin's circle, which she had frequented along with her mother. "The group was hospitable to those black people who were in the Village at the time, the Harrises, Dorothy Peterson, Abbie Mitchell [a well-known actress] and some others. . . . But colored people suspected all white people of being so prejudiced that they were being hypocritical; that the colored people were not 'sincerely' welcome. Which was not the case. There was that suspicion and the conventions and, of course, the exclusivity of what I might call 'our families.'"[58]

Among the upper crust, attitudes to the kind of contacts Thompson describes connected with a more general prudishness and lingering Victorianism. "There was nothing simple about what respectable colored people thought were their moral standards," Thompson would recall. "The women, especially, were so prudish. . . . I got the impression they were afraid to be mistaken for an 'easy lay' even by their husbands." Her own "Hollywood liberty" in talking about sex and birth control shocked Harlem "society" women. Thompson was used to being around people discussing the Lucy Stone League and whether married women should keep their maiden names.[59] Much like Thompson, Larsen noticed that women around her felt a sense of comfort and security in the maintenance of strong boundaries between white and black, male and female, upper and lower classes. By the same token, "modernist" bohemian tendencies put the boundaries under strain, and to some young black and white artists interracial socializing in itself (formerly limited to urban vice zones such as those where Larsen had grown up) had an aura of avant-gardism, a certain shock value, the excitement of not just testing limits but achieving personal and social transformation. Many of these relationships were fleeting, superficial, or merely histrionic. Yet they were integral to the scene in which Larsen came into her own authorial voice.

Anita Thompson is the probable model for Audrey Denney in *Quicksand*.[60]

Later a part-time high-fashion model and cover girl in Paris, to whom Coco Chanel gave away dresses, she was a beautiful, long-limbed, "light-caramel" colored woman (in her own words) radiating sex appeal. She combined an easy grace and self-confidence with disregard for conventional social boundaries. She inspired infatuation as prolifically as Edna St. Vincent Millay, who she could hardly believe "'burned her candle at both ends'; she seemed to be such a nicely brought-up young woman, I imagined she went to bed at eight o'clock with a volume of Tennyson."[61] A lot of people of the more bohemian and artistic sort—white and black, American and European—liked having Anita around. She came from a "good family" with connections all over the country, Langston Hughes being one of her many cousins; but, having grown up in Hollywood, and even played bit parts in such blockbusters as *The Four Horsemen of the Apocalypse* and *The Thief of Baghdad*, she had been raised among free-thinkers, atheists, and anarchists as well as the black upper class.

Thompson had come east to New York with her mother in 1923 to be one of the many bridesmaids in the society wedding of Mae Walker—adopted daughter of A'Lelia—and then absconded to the Village, fleeing the stifling atmosphere of the haute bourgeoisie. For a while she lived in Baltimore, directing arts programs in the black public schools, but false rumors of an affair with a married man (based on the fact that they spent long hours talking politics together) sent her back to the refuge of Greenwich Village. In an apartment on Gay Street, she "settled into a life that I considered my own, and one in which I was surrounded by people whom I understood and who could understand me also."[62] Thompson later left for Paris and fell in with the Dadaists and Surrealists on the Left Bank, particularly Man Ray—her "dutch uncle" as she termed him—just as Larsen would later. But Thompson was not fleeing African Americans or her own "blackness"; she moved with ease between white and black groups that didn't mind the freedom of her ways, and ignored the notoriety it inspired. Like Denney, Thompson was also an excellent dancer—the "pony" of the chorus line for *Runnin' Wild*, when she was also a student at Columbia. She learned the Charleston from Jack Carter and tap-dancing from Bill "Bojangles" Robinson, the greatest dancer of the age. The black "stage-door johnnies" who took her out to the Cotton Club found the Columbia co-ed exotic, and the Columbia students she dated found her chorus-girl persona equally intoxicating.[63] At formal affairs, her dance cards always filled up early.

There was at least one group of Harlem's elite in which interracial socializing was practically a civic duty and the moral standards were much more "modern." This was the circle surrounding James Weldon Johnson and Walter White, of which the Imeses (like Anita Thompson) were a part. With impeccable credentials as a "race man," Johnson was above suspicion.[64] He optimistically believed that bringing artists and intellectuals together across the racial divide and winning recognition for African American literary achievement would help to knock down the color bar. According to Walter White,

> Jim and Grace [Johnson] . . . were responsible more than any others for the so-called Negro Renaissance of the early twenties. Frequently their apartment was the gathering place of writers, poets, singers, and men and women of the theater. The color line was never drawn at Jim's. Many an evening we talked until long after midnight. It was there that many who were later to do much in wiping out the color line learned to know each other as fellow human beings and fellow artists without consciousness of race.[65]

The Whites also hosted more than their share of such parties and receptions in their apartment at 90 Edgecombe Avenue, at the corner of 139th Street, and to these as well as the Johnsons' gatherings Nella was often invited.[66]

In contrast, Larsen does not seem to have been closely associated with Jessie Fauset, the literary editor of *The Crisis,* with whom she has often been paired. Society notes on Fauset's parties list everyone in attendance but make no mention of Larsen.[67] Neither did Larsen belong to Fauset's "Saturday Night Club," a group of black women with similar intellectual and cultural interests.[68] These groups were rather exclusive both racially and socially—and quite straitlaced—whereas Larsen's closest relationships tended to be with people of a more bohemian character. Langston Hughes described Fauset nicely in his autobiography as "a gracious, tan-brown lady, a little plump, with a fine smile and gentle eyes," crediting her as a "midwife" of the Harlem Renaissance.[69] Privately, however, Hughes chafed at her critical standards and the gentle pressure with which she tried to move him toward more "respectable" themes and conventional forms.[70] To Claude McKay she seemed "prim, pretty and well-dressed, and [she] talked fluently and intelligently. All the radicals liked her, although in her social viewpoint she was away over on the other side of the fence. She belonged to that closed decorous circle of Negro society, which consists of persons who live proudly like the better class of conventional whites, except that they do so on much less money."[71] Even her friends described her years later as "very prim" and "very haughty."[72] Her views are reflected in her decision in 1922 to turn down a contract to translate René Maran's *Batouala*—winner of France's prestigious Prix Goncourt and regarded by many as a landmark in black fiction. She wrote Joel Spingarn, who was encouraging her to take on the project: "I know my own milieu too well. If I should translate that book over my name, I'd never be 'respectable' again."[73]

Ethel Ray Nance, secretary to the editor of *Opportunity* magazine and a good friend of Fauset's, termed her "one of the more conventional people," singling out the decorum one found at her home with its tasteful mementos of France, where Fauset had once studied.[74] Langston Hughes, too, characterized Fauset's Sunday afternoon teas as staid and decorous, disappointingly sober, the conversation often in French: "At the Seventh Avenue apartment of Jessie Fauset, literary soirées with much poetry and but little to drink were the order of the day."[75]

Larsen almost certainly attended these "teas" on occasion, but she would leave a remarkably unflattering description based on them in her first novel, in a passage that Fauset could well have taken personally. On a hot Sunday afternoon, emotionally distracted by thoughts about a man, Helga Crane is walking down Seventh Avenue from 139th Street (about three blocks from Fauset's Seventh Avenue apartment in 1925) when she suddenly decides to attend a tea. She finds it

> boring beyond endurance, insipid drinks, dull conversation, stupid men. The aimless talk glanced from John Wellinger's lawsuit for discrimination because of race against a downtown restaurant and the advantages of living in Europe, especially France, to the significance, if any, of the Garvey movement. Then it sped to the favorite Negro dancer who had just then secured a foothold on the stage of a current white musical comedy, to other shows, to a new book touching on Negroes. Thence to costumes for a coming masquerade dance, to a new jazz song, to Yvette Dawson's engagement to a Boston lawyer who had seen her one night at a party and proposed to her the next day at noon. Then back again to racial discrimination.
>
> Why, Helga wondered, with unreasoning exasperation, didn't they find something else to talk of?[76]

Larsen does not endorse Helga's attitude here, but she could clearly empathize, and when other opportunities for social and intellectual stimulation opened up she drifted away from such affairs.

At the parties later hosted by Fauset's good friends Regina Anderson, Ethel Ray, and Louella Tucker in their apartment at 580 St. Nicholas Avenue—parties which have passed into legend—Larsen could not have been a frequent invitee, for Ray (later Nance) herself told biographer Charles R. Larson, "I had very little contact with Nella during my time in Harlem."[77] Ray was very much a part of the circle around Jessie Fauset and her sister Helen Lanning. She mentioned that Regina Anderson (who became Regina Andrews after her later marriage) had worked with Nella in the library, but there was little social contact between them. In an interview with historian David Levering Lewis, Andrews herself, who had belonged to the Writers Guild, had little to say when asked about Larsen: "I didn't know her too—too well."[78] Before she moved to 580 St. Nicholas, Regina Andrews lived with Fauset at 1945 Seventh Avenue.[79] A native of Chicago, she was married in Jessie Fauset's apartment, with Fauset as her maid of honor. In turn, Andrews served as one of the attendants at Fauset's own marriage, to which Larsen was not invited. Thus, attempts up to now to posit a close friendship or even mentoring relationship between Fauset and Larsen appear to have little basis in fact.

Fauset was much more skeptical than Larsen of relationships across the color line. To an interviewer in the late 1920s Fauset noted with satisfaction that Negroes were now finding beauty among themselves "and are becoming satisfied to stay within themselves. As enlightenment spreads the taboo against intermarriage increases."[80] Ethel Ray, whose own mother was Swedish (her black father was president of the NAACP in Duluth), avoided social contact with whites; she did not attend "downtown" parties, because she suspected Negroes were merely "on exhibit," and she did not invite whites to her home for the same reason.[81] If Ray's judgment was not entirely trustworthy, neither was it entirely off base; both she and Fauset had strong reasons for their prejudices. The point here is that Nella Larsen, Dorothy Peterson, and Anita Thompson had a different attitude, for reasons based in their own past experiences. One rarely saw white people at Jessie Fauset's soirées or those of her good friends, whereas Larsen and Peterson clearly enjoyed "mixed" company despite its cost to their reputation in some circles. Some will charge Larsen and Peterson with "self-hatred," but this is far too simple—"a dangerous half-truth," to borrow a phrase from W. E. B. Du Bois.

Larsen made friends with people whom she found amusing, who paid attention to her, who shared her iconoclasm and ironic wit, and who could help her out. She admired aesthetic discrimination, disdained "uplift" ideology as condescending and moralistic, distrusted melodramatic oppositions, and looked askance on "propaganda." Although Larsen believed blacks needed greater faith in themselves, independent of white approval or "white standards" of beauty and custom, she was little attracted to racial insularity except for brief periods which mostly ended in disillusionment, and she was impatient with even the mildest forms of racial chauvinism. Her skin color and hair texture were advantages of which she was aware, but she was not as "light-skinned" as people have often assumed—she was, according to two interviewers, the color of "brown honey" or "maple syrup." She convincingly described the harmony of dark skin, "African" features, and "nappy" hair. Her favorite African American performers in the 1920s were dark-skinned: Roland Hayes, Paul Robeson, and Ethel Waters.

She took pleasure in all-black environments but mostly lived in "mixed" ones and always had "white friends."

Larsen could speak condescendingly of uneducated blacks and patronizingly of poor whites, and she encouraged people to believe her class background higher than it was. Yet she was keenly sensitive to class snobbery, and her own blue-collar origins were a hidden touchstone for every experience. She worked to support herself for most of her life, shopped in second-hand stores, and bought balcony theater tickets to save money. She was gallant, courageous, generous, and "selfish"—an individualist who sought most to please herself, in part because of a deficit of "self," a permanent and irremediable lack.

Surely, it would be too much to expect that the intense pressure of racism in Larsen's life—as in that of other authors of her era—had not left its mark in the form of racial insecurity, doubt, even shame.[82] By common standards, Larsen tolerated white presumption and racism on a personal level to an irritating degree, even while she exposed and protested against it very incisively in her fiction. That tolerance owed much to empathy, but also to an understanding of the deep structures of racial division and a determined, devil-may-care resistance to them.

After all, Larsen had grown up in a largely, but unevenly, segregated environment where her mere presence had brought great hurt not only to herself but to those dearest to her. Her mother made inordinate sacrifices to keep and help her, but the racial mores of the United States worked relentlessly against them, and against the sort of "mirroring" relationship every child needs from her chief love object. One result was a persistent deficit of self-validation (not simply *as black* but *as Nellie Larsen*), deriving from the pressure the color line exerted on her family. She felt a need that could never be met, a relation that could not be publicly affirmed, and the need never left her.

What is striking about Larsen, however, as Barbara Johnson has written, is that she was able to analyze the problem. Moreover, she blamed it not on individuals but on the institution of race as such. She and her family had all felt the stares, the questions, the disdain, together. "Race" had exacted a terrible price from each of them, to be paid throughout their lives, both together and apart. Nor did Larsen idealize her own responses; she was highly self-critical. Her novels provide aesthetic representations of the dilemmas she herself encountered, but they could not resolve those dilemmas.[83] For that, a social revolution was needed—one she was powerless to effect. Hence her fatalism.

Larsen's attitude toward "race" as such is inherently difficult to separate from her ambivalence about her necessary relationship to African American society. She had not been raised in a situation tending to present black society as something consistently positive. The central institution of the "race" in America, the black church, was a foreign realm to her and she was never apparently religious. Black popular music she knew as the music of the saloons and brothels around Twenty-Second and State, places she had been taught to avoid while living immediately above or beside them. Although she probably had always had black friends (except during her years in Denmark), the "black community" was a community to which she had never exactly belonged until well into adulthood, and which had proven unevenly validating for her even then. Her experiences with black authority figures were just as often disillusioning as supportive in her early career, while she had considerably more support from whites than most blacks experienced, expected, or sought. Some of her most determined supporters had always been white. Despite the deep wounds of antiblack racism, then, for many reasons "white people" simply could not mean to her what they meant to the identity of most African Americans. Powerful emotional reasoning supported the individualism she valued and her ambivalence about "group" identity. And for Larsen, emotionally speaking, racism was not so much a reason to distance herself from white people as an irritating and very inconvenient fact of life—inconvenient not only for her but for the white people she cared about. She tried not to let it affect her happiness, her movements, or her ambitions, and often downplayed it in conversation—especially, on first meeting, with whites whom she wanted to win over.

The Imeses' removal from Manhattan to Jersey City may be one reason that Nella does not show up on membership lists of the official groups gathering in Harlem at the time—groups such as the Professional Woman's Luncheon Club. Formed by Sadie M. Peterson, an assistant at the 135th Street Branch library, with the aim of "blending intellectual thought and creating an interest in international affairs," this group included several people Nella knew, including Gwendolyn Bennett, Eunice Hunton, Nina Gomer Du Bois, Regina Anderson, and Lillian Alexander. But Nella was not part of it.[84]

Neither was Larsen ever, apparently, a member of the rather exclusive Writers Guild, often mentioned in Harlem Renaissance histories and reminiscences.[85] One searches the black society columns covering Jersey City and New York in vain for mention of Larsen's inclusion in women's auxiliaries, sororities, and social clubs, or attendance at parties and events to which people like Lillian Alexander, Jessie Fauset, and Regina Anderson were regularly invited.[86] She did not at all "count" until after the acceptance of her first book in 1927. "In Harlem she was a nobody," one patronizing acquaintance told David Levering Lewis in later years.[87]

That Larsen was left off some guest lists in High Harlem only emphasizes

9. *Walter White, 1924. Photographer unknown. Underwood and Underwood Studio, 1924. Yale Collection of American Literature, Beinecke Rare Book and Manuscript Library, Yale University.*

the value to her of those groups in which she was welcome and even admired. Her friendship with Walter White in 1924–1925 was particularly important. White's novel *The Fire in the Flint* finally appeared in early 1924, sparking heated controversy, and he moved quickly to fan the flames. Attacks in Southern newspapers provoked defenses from prominent New York columnists like Heywood Broun, drawing attention and boosting sales. White even lined up Konrad Bercovici to review it and then talked Carl Van Doren into having Bercovici's review placed in *The Nation,* where it would reach the prime audience for such a novel. Eugene O'Neill, T. S. Stribling, and Clement Wood all wrote White letters of support. Overall, the novel was well reviewed and went into several printings as well as translations.[88]

By this time White was already networking like an insurance salesman (his previous calling) or an NAACP organizer. Like Johnson, he cultivated relationships with a broad range of editors and publishers and was recruited as a talent scout in his own right by Viking Press when it first set sail in 1925, with Johnson's own *Book of American Negro Spirituals* as its immensely successful bellwether. Thus, Larsen's friendships with him and James Weldon Johnson connected her to literary circles of historic importance, just as they were forming in the early years of the renaissance.

As yet, however, Larsen was not regarded as one of the most likely authors of the movement. She was still living in New Jersey and working on the Lower East Side when, at a February meeting of the Writers Guild, Gwendolyn Bennett and Regina Anderson suggested that the group host a dinner in honor of the publication of Jessie Fauset's forthcoming novel, *There Is Confusion*. In the course of the conversation, someone proposed the idea of using the occasion as a means of bringing attention to the "newer school" of Negro writers, primarily members of the Guild, and Howard University professor Alain Locke was suggested as a master of ceremonies. Charles S. Johnson, editor of the Urban League's *Opportunity* magazine, spearheaded the plan and contacted Locke, envisioning him as a "dean" for the younger group.[89] In the long list of black and white intellectuals Johnson listed as prospective invitees, the names of Nella and Elmer Imes do not appear. They evidently missed what came to be known as the "debut" of the Negro Renaissance: the gathering of more than one hundred people at the Civic Club near Washington Square.

The excitement of the event reverberated through the circles in which Larsen moved and seemed to prove that the doors were opening to black contributions in literature. The meeting was historic because it gathered so many movers and shakers in one place with the explicit aim of advancing and publicizing a new approach to "Negro" literature, one based less on reaction against racism than on exploring the beauty, power, and complexity of black culture in its own right. This did not mean that social consciousness and the exposure of racism would be abandoned, for any authentic rendering of African American sensibility and experience "from the inside" would raise readers' consciousness of past and continuing injustice. Writers had their own unique role to play in the liberation of the Negro spirit. Only if "art" achieved relative independence from "propaganda" could it fulfill its distinctive functions: this was the overriding philosophy of Charles S. Johnson and Alain Locke, and Johnson organized the program to give it the greatest weight.[90]

Larsen may already have begun writing. According to Adah Thoms, Larsen during her library career "gave much time to study and writing verse."[91] If Larsen, like Jessie Fauset, experimented with poetry before coming to fiction, she must have realized that fiction offered greater opportunities for professional success and financial reward. By 1924, there were more and more indications that African Americans had opportunities in the literary arts on a scale never before known; this development encouraged many who might not otherwise have aspired to write poetry and fiction "seriously" to do so. It was the golden age of American literary publishing, in which the new houses gambled on new authors, new styles, and new audiences (including children and immigrants), and the range of publications exploded. Closely associated with the ferment in publishing, the public libraries of New York encouraged the new trends.

The stream of speakers appearing at the 135th Street Branch throughout 1924 brought the cutting edge of modern social and cultural thought to the attending patrons. In mid-March there was a lecture entitled "Negro Music of America and Africa," demonstrating the connections between African musical practices and those of the black New World. Friday evening, March 28, Alain Locke spoke on the topic of "Negro" literature, with James Weldon Johnson presiding. Beginning April 2, the Columbia anthropologist Alexander Goldenweiser, a student and colleague of Franz Boas, presented a series of monthly lectures entitled "Race and Culture." The renowned New York *World* columnist Heywood Broun, who frequently spoke out on racial injustice, appeared on April 10. That same spring, the National Ethiopian Art Theatre School opened at the library, and 140 people signed up to take classes. Directed by Anne Wolter of Carnegie Hall, who had dreamt of starting such a school for years while associated with the American Academy of Dramatic Art, the organization had some of the top theater talent in New York behind it, including Philip Loeb of the Theatre Guild as head of the Dramatic Art Department and James Weldon Johnson as treasurer.[92]

In August 1924 Konrad Bercovici, during dinner with the Whites and a Paul Robeson concert afterward, told Walter his novel would make a "magnificent play" and that the well-known critic and novelist Carl Van Vechten thought the same. By coincidence, that very day, White had received a letter from Van Vechten, one of the great talent scouts of the early twentieth century, asking White to call him so they could arrange to have a long talk.[93] Van Vechten had received a copy of *The Fire in the Flint* from Knopf, his own publisher, and was impressed. Perhaps Van Vechten, who had already been publicly touting African American music and female blues singers, saw something big in the making. In any case, on a Tuesday afternoon in late August White met with Van Vechten at the latter's apartment, and an important relationship began.[94] White quickly made his way into Van Vechten's larger entourage. The English actress Marie Doro—a great beauty of the previous generation—invited him to her soirées, where he met Sinclair Lewis and others approaching the peak of their fame. Doro held a party in honor of Walter and Gladys in early October. At another on October 16, attended by the Whites, the Knopfs, Van Vechten, the Mexican artist and writer Miguel Covarrubias, and others, George Gershwin played "Rhapsody in Blue." White, in turn, invited many of these people to his own parties and joined them at cabarets, introducing them to a broad swath of black society.[95] Just as this was taking place, Larsen was appointed head of the

Children's Room in black Harlem's library on 135th Street—a promotion that put her back in proximity to the heart of the action.[96] She was fortunate, for there had been no regular staff raises in the entire branch library system since 1920, due to lack of funds. The only way to advance was to wait for someone at a higher level to retire or move. Ernestine Rose and her colleague had put her on a fast track for promotion, to take up a leading position among Harlem librarians.

The Children's Room at 135th Street was much less crowded and hectic than that of Seward Park; it had less than half the circulation. Part of Larsen's job was to attract new patrons.[97] One of the top officials at the branch, she had responsibility for programming, supervising assistants, and buying and discarding children's books. The effect of her leadership was immediate and noticeable. More than a thousand new memberships were issued to children in Larsen's first year, and 625 new books were added to the children's shelves.[98] In fact, children's circulation accounted for about 40 percent of the total circulation of the branch that year. Just after Larsen arrived, publicity for the department began appearing for the first time in the *New York Age,* probably based verbatim on news releases written by Larsen. The Junior Literary League, a club for girls in the sixth through eighth grades, met on alternate Fridays at 7:30 P.M. throughout the winter, reading fiction, plays, and poetry. Special meetings for storytelling were held during the year, usually with outside guests reading the poetry. There was also a Senior Literary League for older girls, giving special attention to drama and aiming to produce one or two plays in the spring.[99] "Picture-Book Hour" for little children and their parents took place on Saturdays.[100]

The reading club for boys aged twelve to fifteen, besides discussing books, debating topics of current interest, and giving plays, made field trips to historical and literary landmarks.[101] The first of these was an evening at Poe Cottage in the Bronx, following a series of Saturday evening discussions of Poe's life and work.[102] When Children's Book Week began on November 15, Larsen directed her assistants in setting up displays and compiling lists of recommended books. In early December, she brought in her former supervisor from the Seward Park Branch, Harriet S. Wright, to talk about the new children's books and to suggest good ones for Christmas.[103] On Christmas Eve, at a special party, the librarians opened a dozen gift-wrapped books (sent by Annie Carroll Moore) after asking the children to speculate as a group about what the books might say.[104] The volumes stayed in the reading section, prominently displayed, for the twelve days of Christmas.

Larsen met regularly with Annie Carroll Moore and other librarians in charge of Children's Rooms at branches throughout the city. Each month, at a different

10. The Children's Room in the 135th Street Branch of the New York Public Library, circa 1926. New York Public Library Archives, The New York Public Library, Astor, Lenox and Tilden Foundations.

branch, normally on a Tuesday morning at 9:30, all the children's librarians gathered with Moore to discuss their work, current books, and job-related difficulties. As the monthly meetings rotated among all the branches in the system, the women got to know the many different neighborhoods and libraries.[105] In the process, Larsen also made useful contacts. She wrote monthly informal reports and essays on the "daily life" of the Children's Room and the state of the book collection at the 135th Street Branch.[106]

Each month, too, she met privately with Annie Carroll Moore in Room 105 of the central library to discuss her work, and then went off to peruse the stacks of new books, all of which had typed reviews clipped to their covers.[107] In order to make informed judgments about which ones to order, she was expected to consult catalogues, study annotated lists such as "Children's Books for Christmas Presents" (compiled by the American Library Association) and "Graded List of Books for Children" (issued by the National Education Association); she

173

would also have read Moore's columns in *The Bookman* and (from 1924) the Sunday *Books* supplement of the *Herald Tribune*.[108] Choosing titles posed a special challenge for a librarian in black Harlem. When black characters showed up at all in the children's books of this era, they played menial or minstrel roles, "Sambos" or "pickaninnies," using a "dialect" never spoken on land or sea. The illustrations were humiliating. With the exception of the groundbreaking book *Upward Path: A Reader for Colored Children,* edited by M. T. Pritchard and Mary White Ovington and published by Harcourt Brace in 1920, the Uncle Remus tales were about as "liberal" as anything available at the time (except in black Sunday school readers). But even *Upward Path* was composed of excerpts from adult books that were deemed appropriate for children.

The 135th Street Library had many community-oriented activities in the late fall and winter of 1924–1925, and hosted a much greater number of regularly scheduled meetings of community groups and lectures than any other branch in the system: meetings of the Tri-Arts Club, Hubert Harrison's lecture course on literature, troops of Girl Scouts and Boy Scouts, a Choral Society, the North Harlem Community Forum, lectures sponsored by the Board of Education, classes in drama, story hours, and so forth.[109] Larsen's former boss Warren Logan—remarried since the death of his first wife—on returning from a trip abroad, was honored with a testimonial reception by the Tuskegee Association of New York.[110] He is quite possibly the model for Robert Anderson in *Quicksand,* with whom Helga Crane reconnects at a New York social function years after her service at Naxos. The Wednesday night meetings of the North Harlem Community Forum in mid-November featured NAACP publicist Herbert Seligman speaking on the topic of race prejudice, and Columbia anthropologist Franz Boas giving a talk entitled "What Is a Race?"—a lecture later published in *The Crisis.* Boas, whom Larsen may have already known through the Harrises, was a frequent guest.[111] Later meetings featured talks entitled "The Soul of Modernism" (by the Reverend Ethelred Brown), "Racial Aspects of Labor Conditions in Latin America," and "French West Africa" (by W. E. B. Du Bois).

Thursday "Book Evenings" included events such as "A Discussion of Negro Literature," moderated by Mary White Ovington and including Walter White and Paul Robeson (who was then starring in Eugene O'Neill's play *All God's Chillun Got Wings*). Konrad Bercovici, author of *Around the World in New York,* gave an address entitled "Your New York."[112] A Wednesday night "Poets Evening," with Ernestine Rose presiding, featured a series of brief poetry readings by Countee Cullen, Augusta Savage (better known as a sculptor), Sadie Peterson, and Gwendolyn Bennett, as well as a short-story reading by Eric

Walrond. Afterward the poet and critic Babette Deutsch, a leading literary figure of Greenwich Village and supporter of the Provincetown Players, joined Arthur Schomburg in congratulating the authors on their work.[113] When O'Neill's play *The Emperor Jones* was revived in the winter with Paul Robeson in the lead role, the NYPL Staff Association, to which Larsen belonged, hosted a theater party for its members that sold out the Provincetown Playhouse on December 18.[114]

All of this activity at the library benefited from and contributed to the quickening of interest in African American culture on the part of the city's intellectual communities, at the same time that Harlem's nightlife began attracting downtown patronage. There was a growing sense of exhilaration, centered around 135th Street and Seventh Avenue. The library began suggesting textbooks about writing, advising on source material, explaining how to prepare manuscripts and how to present them to editors and publishers. It developed book lists on "Negro" subjects and answered a growing volume of inquiries from white and black authors about sources on African American history and culture.[115] Ernestine Rose decided to set aside a special shelf in the reference room for "Negro" books only, out of which soon developed a Department of Negro Literature and History.[116] Besides hosting readings by aspiring young writers like Countee Cullen and Gwendolyn Bennett, the library brought in established authors and editors, both black and white, to speak with and meet the aspirants.[117] The famous "Harlem" issue of *Survey Graphic* magazine that came out in March 1925, following up on the Civic Club dinner of 1924, was to a remarkable degree a product of the networks formed at the 135th Street Branch during the years that Larsen worked there.

Several people who later became known as authors of the Harlem Renaissance met in or by way of the library, even though they lived outside Harlem in the various boroughs. Larsen's friendship with Dorothy Peterson, which began there, opened up a wide circle of friends. Harold Jackman, one member of this circle, worked as a page at the library while he was a college student and Larsen was on the staff.[118] Through Peterson and Jackman, Larsen met others, including Gwendolyn Bennett and Eric Walrond (who, like Peterson, lived in Brooklyn), Langston Hughes and Countee Cullen. She did not form many close friendships in this group, however; most of them were a decade younger than Larsen, and unmarried. Nonetheless, partly through them, she came in contact with others who would become intimate friends and play an enormous role in her life.

Larsen's own role at the 135th Street Branch during this crucial period has been obscured by her later "disappearance" from the black high society and literary circles that passed down stories of those days. It has also been clouded by the fact that she left library work in the late 1920s to pursue a literary career, and by her ambivalent relationship to the black Harlem elite. Others who retained such connections ended up getting credit and completely forgot about Larsen, or neglected to mention her.

Regina Anderson Andrews is most often identified as the mainstay at the 135th Street Branch during this period—and indeed throughout the Harlem Renaissance. But contrary to many reports, Andrews was never Ernestine Rose's "first assistant," and she worked at the branch only from April 1923 through December 1924. The library records, which have never been consulted on this issue, show that Andrews was a Grade 1 library assistant, essentially a clerk, from April 1923 to January 1924, and then a Grade 2 assistant until the end of that year, when she moved to a temporary position at the Hamilton Fish Branch on the Lower East Side. In March 1925, she moved to the Woodstock Branch, where she remained for the rest of the 1920s—not in Harlem, but in a Hungarian section of the "white" Bronx.[119] She thereafter moved among a number of branches outside Harlem as she advanced to higher-level positions, most notably Branch Librarian in Washington Heights—also a white neighborhood at the time.

Much has been made of a brief controversy that W. E. B. Du Bois stirred up over Andrews' position and pay, creating a false notion of her role at the library and of the institution's policies. Du Bois was convinced that she was being cheated of the salary and professional status she deserved, but Andrews herself knew that she was paid less than Larsen and other colleagues in the mid-1920s because she was new and had not graduated from library school. Because of her personal and family connections with Harlem's elite (her father being a friend of Du Bois and a prominent Chicago attorney), because she continued with a career in the system, and because library records have not been consulted, her role at the 135th Street Branch in the 1920s has been greatly exaggerated, while Larsen's has been almost entirely ignored.[120]

Nella Larsen was the first professionally trained black librarian in the system, but others have always been given that credit rather than her. Andrews herself was partly responsible for this imbalance, since her influential friends and colleagues gave her undue credit and she quietly declined to correct them. In an extensive videotaped interview with the Harlem librarian Jean Blackwell Hutson, for example, in which Hutson and the film director repeatedly pumped her for information about her friends and colleagues at the library in the 1920s, she never mentioned Larsen, who preceded her as an assistant there, stayed longer, and worked as her superior. Moreover, Andrews claimed that until she arrived at the 135th Street Branch, black intellectuals (including Du Bois) had barely set foot in the library; she allowed the interviewers to conclude that she was largely responsible for drumming up interest. Her testimony became a major source of later historical reconstructions. The truth is that five black and five white assistants, including Larsen, staffed the library before Andrews arrived in 1923, and activities were in full swing.[121]

When a scholar queried the director of the Schomburg Collection in 1969 for information about Larsen, the director was unable to supply any substantial information except that Larsen had attended nursing school at Lincoln Hospital and Home, had been married to a physicist named Elmer Imes, and was rumored to have begun passing in her later years. Jean Blackwell Hutson termed Larsen "the most elusive of the authors whose biographies I have tried to trace." Though committed to reclaiming the lives of New Negro personalities, she was unaware that Larsen had once worked at her own library.[122]

ELEVEN

High Bohemia:
1925

BY early 1925, Larsen began thinking seriously of becoming a novelist and asked to go on half-time at the library so she would have more time to write.[1] One Sunday evening in early February, a week before her new hours went into effect, she attended a party at the Peterson home in Brooklyn after a benefit concert for the Harlem YMCA. Everyone drifted into the kitchen and dining room, where Dorothy Harris began making strawberry shortcake; and noticing that Mrs. Peterson (who disliked Harris) was out of sorts, Nella and Elmer decided to run interference. While they were charming the elders, Eric Walrond arrived with two white people in tow—a tall man in his mid-forties with prematurely white, silky hair, and a thin, younger man with brown hair and startled eyes. They were the novelist Carl Van Vechten and his friend Donald Angus. As Dorothy Harris, still busy with the shortcake, looked on jealously, Larsen turned to Van Vechten and began chatting him up.[2]

One of the literary celebrities of New York, Van Vechten wore two or three bracelets, and when he was first introduced to a woman, he would hold her hand a moment while fixing her face in a pallid stare, as if imprinting it in his brain. (Later, he would write her name down in a little black book.) But when he smiled, two long tusks would angle out alarmingly from beneath his upper lip. In the spring of 1925, after years of scraping by on journalism and prescient but ill-paid music criticism, he was nearing the top of his fame. *Peter Whiffle,* which had established him as a novelist in 1922, was one of Elmer Imes's favorite books.[3] Van Vechten had followed it with the mildly salacious novels *The Blind Bow-Boy* (1923), *The Tattooed Countess* (1924), and *Firecrackers* (1925)—sophisticated fluff on first reading, deliberately superficial and flamboyantly decadent, but admired at the time for their veiled but unorthodox sexuality, voyeurism, and sardonic humor. With a sensibility embracing artifice, naive exaggeration, and pleasure at unintended irony, Van Vechten was the king of camp before anyone else knew what camp was. Larsen was aware of him not only through his novels and articles in fashionable literary journals like *Vanity Fair,* but more personally from Walter White and other friends, who had known him for

*11. Carl Van Vechten, summer 1927.
Photo by James L. Allen. Yale
Collection of American Literature,
Beinecke Rare Book and Manuscript
Library, Yale University.*

months. He was, for them, a unique discovery.[4] After the party at the Petersons', Harold Jackman wrote to tell him, "You are the first white man with whom I have felt perfectly at ease. You are just like a colored man! I don't know if you will consider this a compliment or not, but that's the only way I can put it."[5]

Larsen ran into Van Vechten again, along with his wife Fania Marinoff, at the NAACP Women's Auxiliary's Third Annual Spring Dance, in the packed Green Room of the Manhattan Casino the last Friday in March. It was one of the signature benefit functions of the Negro Renaissance, and despite inclement weather hundreds of people showed up in evening dress ready for a grand evening of entertainment. The club, at 155th and Eighth Avenue, was one of the largest and most elaborate dance halls in Harlem. Nella and Elmer probably sat with Dorothy Peterson, who was on the reception committee and had bought a box of seats. Grace Johnson, one of the chief organizers, took Carl and Fania to join her and Jim in their box.[6]

Fletcher Henderson led the two bands, including his Roseland Orchestra in their sharp English walking suits, and the Rainbow Orchestra, which he first introduced that night. The Roseland's big band included the startling new cornetist Louis Armstrong (recently arrived from Chicago), now at the beginning of his emergence as a soloist. Anyone listening carefully to the music that evening was hearing the emergence of a new conception of jazz in songs like "Mandy, Make Up Your Mind," and especially "Copenhagen," first recorded the preceding October. "Sugar Foot Stomp," recorded that spring, has been credited with inaugurating the New York jazz style. Armstrong was giving New York an education in swing. A bluesy, overpowering arc of sound made people stop and listen as his driving solos soared over the clipped, mechanical syncopation of the popular style and the musicians around him strove to enter the gates he opened up—including Coleman Hawkins, the first great saxophone soloist, who credited Armstrong with inspiring a new idea of what brass instruments could do.[7]

The event that night epitomized several crucial features of the Harlem Renaissance that help to explain why Nella Larsen began only then to emerge into visibility, and within a year found her voice. The jazz-accompanied NAACP dances started in 1924. The rise of the nightclub and cabaret in the early Twenties brought black music and dancing into "respectable" society as never before. It brought about and was symptomatic of a relaxing of social boundaries in the arts and a mixing of classes, races, sexes, ethnic groups unseen since the 1840s, if ever—a fact Larsen distinctly recorded in her fiction. Fletcher Henderson himself, a college-trained musician brought up on classical concert music in a middle-class Southern home, associated blues with the seedy and "low-down." When recruited to play for Ethel Waters in 1921, he hesitated because her music was "beneath" what he had been reared to produce. The queen of the notorious "shimmy," Waters forced him to remake himself musically, and while touring with her he first heard Louis Armstrong. Whether Henderson really initiated the innovations his orchestra produced or was pulled into a musical vortex, the tension between his clean, high-class demeanor and background and the novel, low-down elements of his band (especially embodied by Louis Armstrong) accounts for his success and epitomizes what was happening in the 1920s. It was the musical equivalent of the Great Migration.

No longer was popular musical entertainment confined to all-male saloons and lower-class dance halls.[8] The very fact that a high-hat organization like the Women's Auxiliary of the NAACP would put on a glamorous benefit dance for a mixed crowd of blacks and whites, to the beat of jazz—which only a few years earlier had been the music of State Street saloons and brothels—speaks volumes. In this relatively fluid and improvisational atmosphere, Nella Larsen emerges from the shadows.

Things were changing all over. At Fisk University, the students had rebelled en masse in mid-February against the old dress and social codes, still substantially the same as when Nellie had been kicked out in 1908.[9] But not all black

New Yorkers liked what they were witnessing. In the "Keeping Fit" column of the *Amsterdam News* (published in Harlem), Dr. E. Elliott Rawlins asked, "Will the women of to-day make as good wives as the wives of yesterday?" They were "running wild," smoking and drinking, dancing with men other than their husbands, craving jazz "untrammeled by the obligations of motherhood."[10] The next week, Rawlins attacked jazz itself as a "drug" akin to morphine, cocaine, or opium, undermining the social order.[11] Moreover, the paper reported, a recent Howard University study showed that births were declining among the "highest ranks" of Negroes, threatening the "extinction of the advanced section of the race." It was the duty of men to guide their women away from self-destructive "flippancies" of jazz manners and bobbed hair, toward the "high and holy function" of motherhood.[12] Cigarette-smoking, childless Nella Larsen Imes, of the short dresses and racy cabarets, took notes as she dreamed of being a novelist.

In March came the special issue of *Survey Graphic* entitled "Harlem: Mecca of the New Negro." Gracing the cover was an arresting black-and-white portrait of dark-skinned, nappy-haired Roland Hayes, whom Larsen knew from Fisk. The roster of contributors read like a reprise of the list of recent speakers at the 135th Street Library, where some of the pieces had been delivered as lectures. "There are times," editor Paul Kellogg stated in his preface, when the "subtle traces of race growth and interaction" that normally work slowly and delicately "seem suddenly to flower—and we become aware that the curtain has lifted on a new act in the drama of part or all of us. . . . If *The Survey* reads the signs aright, such a dramatic flowering of a new race-spirit is taking place close at home—among American Negroes, and the stage of that new episode is Harlem."[13]

In his introductory essay, Alain Locke wrote of a "great race-welding" taking place in the Northern city while a "transformed and transforming psychology" permeated the masses, forcing race leaders to embrace a new spirit of self-determination. "We may be witnessing the resurgence of a race," Locke hypothesized, driven by a "momentous folk movement."[14] The direction in which Locke pointed—indeed the direction of the mainstream of African American literature for much of the twentieth century—was not the direction Nella Larsen would follow. The peril of her position is evident in the *Survey Graphic* in details small and large. Accompanying James Weldon Johnson's essay "The Making of Harlem" one finds a map identifying "where Negroes live," with the addendum that "the fringe of houses in which both Negro and white tenants live is not indicated."[15]

At the 135th Street Library, as the Sunday *New York Times* reported in an extended article, a special department was taking shape to preserve and make available the literature, historical records, and art of the "Negro race." Ernestine Rose noted that although scattered collections existed at the Library of Congress, in colleges and universities, and in private collections, "the collection at the 135th Street Library should properly become one of the largest and most valuable in the country."[16] Already the library had begun building a collection not only of rare books but of art as well, including sketches of Africans by Walter Von Ruckteschell (used by Alain Locke in the *Survey Graphic*), and an enlarged copy of Meta Warrick Fuller's sculpture *Ethiopia Awakening*. The *Times* went on to highlight the many activities Larsen had going in the Children's Room.[17]

In April the library mounted an exhibition of works by the white German-born artist Winold Reiss, with originals of the portraits and illustrations used in the March *Survey Graphic*, along with many other pastel portraits of various Negro notables and "race types," including Harold Jackman as "A College Lad" wearing an impeccably tailored suit.[18] Unfortunately, as Jeffrey C. Stewart has pointed out, Reiss was "ahead of his time in these bold renderings of largely dark-skinned African Americans," not always presented in an idealized fashion.[19] At a forum hosted by the staff during the opening reception, Reiss was roundly attacked. Many of Harlem's elite, it turned out, objected to his portraits of Harlem "types," and to the fact that a white artist's work had been featured at all. Elise McDougald, one of Reiss's subjects who had also recruited people to sit for him, informed Locke that one critic "wondered if the whole art side of the issue were a 'piece of subtle propaganda to prejudice the white reader.'"[20]

Reiss's portrait of two schoolteachers raised particular ire; one man declared he "would be afraid" of the women if he should meet them in the street—whereupon one of the models for the portrait stood up to say she considered the image "a pretty good likeness" and regretted that she would frighten him.[21] Reiss's defenders accused his critics of threatening "a truly racial art with the psychological bleach of 'lily-whitism.'"[22] Such was the opinion of Alain Locke, who was including them in his forthcoming anthology, to be called *The New Negro*, solicited by A. and C. Boni. (He would also include a photograph of *Ethiopia Awakening*.) Locke's opinion has generally held up in subsequent art criticism, but, paradoxically, the racial politics of the critics would win out in terms of Reiss's "fit" with the Harlem Renaissance. He was never able to sell the portraits—or even to exhibit them, except at the library that spring—because gallery owners feared they would attract black people into their establishments and scare off white customers.[23] Furthermore, editions of *The New Negro* that have appeared since the revival of academic interest in the movement in the

1960s (the work is a standard text in courses on the Harlem Renaissance) have silently deleted Reiss's name from the title page and most of his portraits from the book.[24]

The same month that the Reiss exhibition took place, the library hosted Jean Toomer for a Thursday evening lecture, "Towards Reality." The editor of *The Bookman,* poet John Chipman Farrar (later a founder of Farrar, Straus and Giroux), introduced him to a large "mixed" audience in the auditorium after mezzo-soprano Charlotte Murray set the tone with a few spirituals.[25] Since the publication of *Cane* in 1923, Toomer had become immersed in the "Work" of Armenian mystic G. I. Gurdjieff and English literary critic A. R. Orage (Gurdjieff's chief epigone in America), and he was assembling a Gurdjieff group of African Americans. A magnetic figure, tall and slim, with light-brown skin and a trim mustache, Toomer began his lecture by taking note of *Survey Graphic*'s special issue on Harlem as "evidence of a two-fold fact, the fact that the Negro is in the process discovering himself, and of being discovered" by the culturally aware members of the white world.[26] The Negro was emerging from a "crust" of self-doubt and painful self-consciousness about his racial subjection, while overcoming a bone-deep distrust of whites born of centuries of oppression. As a result, "new facts, truths, realities, are manifest to a transformed state of being."[27]

By this time, Toomer thought of himself not as a Negro but as an American product of multiracial fusion, the first conscious member of a "new race." He nonetheless believed in the significance of the Negro awakening. Toomer prophesied that as the Negro overcame his shame about the slave past and discovered the self beneath the "crust," he would gain a greater awareness of "reality" and might succeed in uncovering "that strange thing called soul."[28] To Toomer, accepting oneself as a Negro and embracing the racial heritage came together with greater openness to "white" influences as one overcame an essentially reactionary habitual response: "Prior to the present phase, because he was denied by others, the Negro denied them and necessarily denied himself. Forced to say nay to the white world, he was negative toward his own life."[29] Hence the disdain for "slave music," blues, and jazz. It was premature, Toomer believed, to say what would be revealed in the process of discovery the Negro writers were undertaking, for to set up any model at this point could only be arbitrary and restricting: "Rather," the ex-Negro added, "I would be receptive of his reality as it emerges (being active only by way of aid to this emergence), assured that in proportion as he discovers what is real within him, he will create, and by that act create at once himself and contribute his value to America."[30] Toomer's talk was "excellent, if a trifle too highbrow for me," John Farrar reported in *The Bookman.* Yet "the audience enjoyed it and discussed questions of spirit and mind with verve."[31]

Larsen was already familiar with Toomer's theories, for she had been invited to join in his meetings beginning in the late summer of 1924, based on Gurdjieff's system of exercises and study for the "Harmonious Development of Man"—a method of rigorous self-examination intended to awaken higher consciousness of one's "real" self. Langston Hughes's chief mention of Larsen in his first autobiography—an immense influence on later accounts of the renaissance—identifies her as a participant in Toomer's meetings, which has led some to believe she was closely involved in the "Gurdjieff Work."[32] She certainly did attend some meetings, and she talked about the movement with friends over dinner or at parties—some half a dozen of her good friends were devotees between 1924 and 1930 at least—but Larsen's own comments suggest that she distanced herself from the group's abstruse psychological cultism fairly early and made fun of people for buying into what she considered a "pseudo-religion."[33] Still, the general influence of the "Work" within her circle of friends and its encouragement of artistic self-expression helped to stimulate Larsen's ambition to write fiction. Toomer's and A. R. Orage's exercises for "self-observation with nonidentification" may well have affected Larsen's approach in *Quicksand.*

Toomer's involvement with Gurdjieff has often been identified with a form of "passing," but he maintained his friendships with those blacks who shared his interests and were at least tolerant of his unorthodox view of his own racial position. He rarely discussed race during his sessions with the Gurdjieffians in the years 1924 to 1926. His Gurdjieff work did not induce him to move from Harlem to Greenwich Village. In fact, like many others involved in the Harlem Renaissance, he had never lived in Harlem; before as well as after the publication of *Cane,* when living on his own in New York, he lived in the Village. People like Dorothy Peterson and Aaron Douglas visited him often at his flat on East 10th Street.[34] The African American subgroup Toomer led in 1924 and 1925 did not, as routinely assumed, always meet in Harlem. They also gathered at Dorothy Harris' home in Greenwich Village or at Dorothy Peterson's in Brooklyn, and several of the people to whom Toomer introduced the "Work" continued with Orage's group afterward.[35] In fact, most of Larsen's friends who were deeply involved, whether black or white, became or were already a part of the Orage circle. This fact has been obscured by the presumption that the African American participants attended only all-black meetings in Harlem, under Toomer's tutelage.

Because of the vagaries of Toomer's career, a notion has taken root that

Gurdjieff's system discouraged artistic labor in favor of mystical absorption, but this is seriously mistaken. Among Toomer's manuscripts of the time are several sheets of notes for meetings in which he gave advice to aspiring black creative writers, now filed with the manuscript fragments out of which "The Negro Emergent" was composed—the basis of his library lecture. No doubt some of the participants in his weekly Friday night meetings—which included Larsen (briefly), her friend Dr. Alonzo de Grate Smith, Harold Jackman, Vivian Stoner, Wallace Thurman, Arna Bontemps, and very occasionally Charles S. Johnson and E. Franklin Frazier (when he was visiting from Atlanta), in addition to such "believers" as Dorothy Peterson, Dorothy Harris, and Aaron Douglas—attended for the intelligent conversation and advice on art.[36] Whether one participated in the meetings or not, in Nella Larsen's circle they were a common topic of conversation.

According to Aaron Douglas, Toomer taught "that we all have the potentialities of intellectual, artistic giants if we could only get to the bottom of our real selves. He claims that back deep in our natures there is a mine of unused power, a source, a hitherto little known faculty which is neither body, emotion or intellect, but is equal to the combined power of all. The key to this source is self-observation. The ultimate goal is free will."[37] Toomer's meetings stressed that all artists were on the same quest for self-discovery and understanding of "reality."[38]

Most of those who took part in the "Work" were writers, editors, artists, dancers, and actors. Some people attended meetings and demonstrations chiefly to gain new perspectives on their artistic methods. Modern-dance choreographers raved about Gurdjieff's dances. For a while Orage even conducted his meetings as creative-writing workshops. He insisted that participants should be able to communicate with all sorts of people, and some began writing for the popular market.[39] Larsen wrote her first short stories, "Freedom" and "The Wrong Man," for pulp magazines (see Chapter 12).

The New York meetings were not, as often assumed, attractive only to white people with a large disposable income and plenty of spare time, although they ultimately depended on such. Nella's friend Muriel Draper, a white interior decorator and one-time salon hostess, popular in music and art circles, was living in very straitened circumstances while hosting Orage's meetings in her barnlike room (once a stable) on East Fortieth Street in 1926. Participants would be squashing cockroaches under their heels while listening to improvised discourses on artistic self-consciousness and the psychology of nonidentification. The charismatic Orage himself, looking for all the world like a rangy Yorkshire farmer, lived frugally in a working-class Armenian neighborhood and taught in fraying clothes. The suggested contribution of $2.50 was optional, and those who could not afford it, including Aaron Douglas, were not expected to pay at all.[40] Douglas, apprenticed to Winold Reiss and groomed to take the lead in the effort to develop a distinctive "Negro" style of art, remained intensely interested for years during and after his rise to fame, as did Dorothy Peterson. Both continued with Orage's group in Greenwich Village after Toomer left town.[41] Despite its core principle of "self-observation with nonidentification," and despite Toomer's own theory of a "new race," there was no necessary contradiction between faith in the distinctiveness of African American culture and Gurdjieff's movement. One of Orage's elementary rules of thumb was to "be more so—the more like yourself you behave, the more likely you are to catch a glimpse of yourself."[42]

Toomer encouraged the Negro Renaissance in 1924–1925, when Larsen knew him, although he did not consider himself to be directly involved in it. Then Alain Locke included his work and his portrait by Winold Reiss in *The New Negro.* Toomer had in fact offered Locke, for use in his book, an essay derived from the lecture he had delivered at the library—but Locke did not want it. Instead, against Toomer's wishes, Locke used extracts from *Cane.* It was one thing, Toomer discovered, for him to have worked out a position in his own mind and shared it with his closest friends; it was quite another to project his concept into "this American world in which, as I had come to realize more and more, there was this fixed view that in this country a person must be either black or white."[43] His fame as a writer forced him into a position of either publicly identifying exclusively as a Negro or withdrawing from the world in which he would be constantly forced to make such choices. Soon he moved to the Midwest to start a new life as a man neither black nor white, and, not coincidentally, "disappeared" from the literary universe. Ultimately, he succumbed to the color line, denying there was any solid evidence that he even had Negro ancestors—a denial he knew was false. Larsen, in contrast, never stopped thinking of herself as a Negro (and a mulatto, and a Danish American), but at the heart of her fiction was one of the most incisive protests against the inhumanity of the color line and its psychic cost ever penned in American literature.

May 1, the night after Toomer's lecture at the library, marked the next big public event of the literary blossoming: the *Opportunity* literary-contest banquet in the Fifth Avenue Restaurant on 24th Street. More than three hundred people attended, including the Imeses, who sat with Dorothy Peterson and other friends. Charles S. Johnson had recruited some of the top editors and authors of the city to serve as judges, many of them already friends or acquaintances of Larsen. The contest, he hoped, would stimulate more young Negroes to write at the same time that it helped build a market for their work.[44] Mrs. Henry Goddard Leach, wife of the editor of *The Forum* magazine, had put up the first $500 in prize money, but as the dinner ended it was announced that an anonymous poetry lover had donated another $500 to double the value of each award. Finally a letter was read from the Harlem businessman and numbers king Casper Holstein presenting a $500 check for the next year's prizes, and expressing his belief that the contest would "go far toward consolidating the interests of, and bridging the gap between, the black and white races in the United States today, and particularly will it encourage among our gifted youth the ambition to scale the empyrean heights of art and literature."[45] Most of Nella's friends went on afterward to A'Lelia Walker's Harlem apartment until about 1:00 A.M., when they moved on to the YMCA dance in time for a Charleston contest, thence to the Bamville (a nightclub), and finally to a 4:30 A.M. "supper" for forty people, at which the Cotton Club band gave a thrilling jam session until past dawn.[46]

That Sunday evening, Paul Robeson and Lawrence Brown gave a program of spirituals at the Greenwich Village Theatre to a capacity crowd including the Imeses' entire circle of friends. Abandoning the "pseudo-refinement of the typical concert singer" and striving to restore the evangelical energy of the originals, Robeson and Brown began a new trend in African American concert style.[47] This New Negro method of presentation, countering the tendency since the 1890s to assimilate the spirituals to Western styles of art music, marked a rising confidence in the black aesthetic heritage.

After the concert, everyone migrated to a large and progressively unbuttoned party at Winold Reiss's studio. "One girl danced entirely nude," Van Vechten informed his wife Fania Marinoff (who had been known to do the same); "Jessie Fauset almost expired at this."[48] The culprit was a tall and slender beauty roughly Nella's age, with a cinnamon complexion and curly red hair. Nora Holt Ray, born Nora Lena Douglas in Kansas City, was the talk of the Chicago cabaret circuit and beginning to make her reputation in New York—surely one purpose of that evening's performance.[49] No one greeted the vogue of the Negro with more sophistication, audacity, and verve. She soon became Nella's friend.

Nora Ray (who later reverted to "Holt") had made her start in Larsen's old neighborhood, the near South Side "sporting" clubs of Chicago, including the Everleigh Club.[50] Widowed early on (she had been married to a rich club-owner), she was now on her fourth marriage, to the supervisor of the large restaurants for Bethlehem Steel in Pittsburgh, and living a lavish life in New York, Chicago, and points between—"the prize vamp, white or black of the world," according to Van Vechten, who was a pretty good judge.[51] "Her trail is strewn

12. *Nora Holt, early 1930s. Photographer unknown. Photographs and Prints Division, Schomburg Center for Research in Black Culture, The New York Public Library, Astor, Lenox and Tilden Foundations.*

with bones," he informed Mencken, "some of them no longer hard."[52] About this time, her husband's private investigators had discovered she was bedding down in the wee hours with a prominent New York attorney, William Patterson (later a lawyer for the Scottsboro Boys); high-profile divorce proceedings would soon begin.[53] But Ray was more than a glamorous nightclub entertainer and real-life vamp. The first black woman to hold a Master's degree in music, from the Chicago Conservatory, she had been the music critic for the *Chicago Defender* and would found the National Organization of Negro Musicians. She was an intellectual with broad interests and cosmopolitan tastes, a classic personality of the Jazz Age.

Four nights after Reiss's party, Larsen and her colleagues hosted the debut of the Negro Literary and Historical Society, officially opening the new collection housed on the third floor of the library. With Arthur Schomburg presiding in the auditorium, Hubert Harrison, an immigrant from the Virgin Islands, "stirred up a 'hornet's nest'" in the opening address when he attributed the success of the effort to the work of West Indians.[54] After a series of speeches by library officials and musical performances, Alain Locke spoke on the historical background of the current project and then presented a silver loving cup to Paul Kellogg in recognition of his work for the race as editor of *Survey Graphic*. By the late spring of 1925 the level of interest in black culture and the variety of institutions nourishing that interest seemed astonishing, and between her service at the library and her circle of friends, Nella Larsen was in the thick of it.

Walter White, for one, was encouraging her to write a novel. Three or four publishing houses had asked White to scout for them, and he was urging friends to get their work into publishable condition. "There is unlimited opportunity," he wrote to Claude McKay in Paris. "You would be amazed at the eagerness of magazine editors and book publishers to get hold of promising writers."[55]

The same day that the Negro Literary and Historical Society opened, the *Herald Tribune* announced that "the American Negro is finding his artistic voice and . . . we are on the edge, if not already in the midst, of what might not improperly be called a Negro Renaissance."[56] The following afternoon a group including Du Bois, Van Vechten, Walter White, Ridgely Torrence, the Johnson brothers, and Arthur Spingarn of the NAACP assembled at Jim and Grace Johnson's to formulate plans for a new Negro Theatre.[57] The meeting led to the founding of the Krigwa Players, based in the 135th Street Library's basement auditorium.

The next night, a Saturday, Nella and Elmer attended a small after-dinner party at Van Vechten's that included Jean Toomer, the white actress and dance instructor Rita Romilly, Lawrence Langner (co-director of the Theatre Guild),

Dorothy and Jim Harris, Dorothy Peterson, and Donald Angus. Much of the conversation no doubt centered around Gurdjieff's concepts, for at least four of these people were deeply engrossed in the "Work."[58]

Nella wasted no time in reciprocating. The very next Saturday, she and Elmer had Van Vechten to their home in Jersey City for an 8:15 dinner with the Harrises, Dorothy Peterson, and several others whom Van Vechten had not yet met. Rita Romilly had been invited but was unable to come. In the course of the dinner, Elmer told an amusing story from his experience working as an engineer in Michigan. The white owner of his company had seen how busy Elmer was and advised him to hire an assistant. So Elmer picked one of his university classmates, the best person he could think of for the job. When he mentioned the man's name, "Levy," to his boss, "The boss threw up his hands at once and said, 'Don't you know we don't take Jews here?'" Elmer apologized, hired a black man instead, and the boss was perfectly satisfied. The dinner conversation drifted to the perennial question of what African Americans should be called. A few guests, whom Van Vechten would later term the conservative, "precious type," "were all for the word 'colored.'" But he and the Imeses thought "Negro" was better. As the argument carried on, laughter began emerging from the kitchen. Elmer got up to see what was so amusing the maid. Soon he could be heard laughing with her. Then Van Vechten got up to find out what was so funny. He pleaded until Elmer told him. Now all three could be heard in chorus. "It don't matter what they call us," the maid had observed, "we're Niggers right on." Spicy fare for mixed company, but the Imeses laughed freely and often over such things when among friends.[59]

Through June, July, and August, more and more of the Imeses' social life, which usually included the Harrises and Dorothy Peterson, involved Carl Van Vechten and his good friends. Soon their circle included Isa Schindel (another Gurdjieff disciple, better known by her maiden name and pen name, Isa Glenn); Harry Block, one of the senior editors at Alfred A. Knopf; the Mexican artist Miguel Covarrubias and his wife, the dancer Rose Rolanda; and many more. On the second of July, a Thursday, they attended a late-night party at the Harrises' in the Village and stayed past 3:30 in the morning, celebrating the imminent departure of the two Dorothies (Peterson and Harris) for Paris, where they would be trying their luck with the Prieuré des Basses Loges in Fontainebleau, Gurdjieff's palatial headquarters and live-in education center. Visitors never knew until they arrived at the gate if Gurdjieff would let them in.[60]

Soon the Imeses were among those who could simply drop in on Van Vechten in the evening—on the 24th, for example, for a party that lasted past 2:00 A.M. Three nights later, a Monday, Carl decided after dinner to throw an impromptu party for his brother Ralph, a rich banker visiting from Chicago, and again invited the Imeses, along with seven others including Nora Holt Ray and Isa Schindel. Carl's bootlegger, Jack Harper, had come by that afternoon with six quarts of gin, an impressive supply in the midst of Prohibition. Some of the gin apparently survived the evening, for at the end of the week the same group gathered for a reprise.[61] Nella and Elmer ran into Van Vechten again the following Friday at an Italian dinner Jim Harris threw in the Village for A'Lelia Walker, who showed up drunk nearly two hours late, and promptly passed out.[62] As the Imeses drove Van Vechten home at midnight, they made a date to meet the next evening for a party at the Bamville, then caught the 42nd Street ferry back to New Jersey.

They stopped by for him at midnight that Saturday, but Fania wasn't dressed yet, so they went on to the club, where Fania and Carl joined them before long with his adored Nora Ray. The Bamville was a fairly high-toned club that by 1928 would become, like Small's Paradise, a main attraction for white downtowners on their first trip to Harlem. But the patronage at this point was still largely black—like the group that night, which gives some sense of the people with whom Nella and Elmer spent time that summer after Dorothy Peterson and Dorothy Harris left: Hubert Delaney, Vivienne "Vi" Stoner (another black Greenwich Villager), Emmett Scott, Jr., Dorothy Gates, Jim Harris, Crystal Bird, and Gilbert Daniel.[63]

The presence of white people at black clubs in Harlem was already frowned on by many New Yorkers—both black and white—who distrusted the motives of both the whites who came and the blacks who escorted them. It was also discouraged by the police, who for some time concentrated their raids on "black-and-tans" (clubs with "mixed" clientele). The automatic association of black-and-tans with crime and immorality, and their tendency to attract police attention, became a common excuse for barring blacks from some Harlem clubs in the 1920s—and for barring whites from some "black" clubs—despite anti-segregation statutes. Black-managed clubs were particularly prone to police harassment if they accepted "mixed" parties, but the police were not the only ones who objected. In his 1923 short story "The Stone Rebounds," Nella's friend Eric Walrond had already written about the suspicion aimed at blacks who brought white friends to Harlem nightclubs.[64] In some neighborhoods, simply walking down the street in company with a white person was like "running the gauntlet," according to George Schuyler.[65]

Larsen's feelings on the issue infuse a tense nightclub scene in *Quicksand*, where Anne Grey, Helga Crane's well-heeled friend in Harlem, gives vent to her feelings about Audrey Denney, who lives downtown on Twenty-Second Street:

"It's a wonder she hasn't some white man hanging about. The disgusting creature! . . . She ought to be ostracized."

"Why?" asked Helga curiously, noting at the same time that three of the
men in their own party had deserted and were now congregated about the offending Miss Denney.

"Because she goes about with white people," came Anne's indignant answer, "and they know she's colored."

"I'm afraid I don't quite see, Anne. Would it be all right if they didn't know
she was colored?"

. . . . .

"Why, she gives parties for white and colored people together. And she
goes to white people's parties. It's worse than disgusting, it's positively obscene."

"Oh, come, Anne, you haven't been to any of the parties, I know, so how
can you be so positive about the matter?"[66]

That white men dance with colored women at such parties particularly outrages
Anne Grey. "'Don't the colored men dance with the white women, or do they sit
about, impolitely, while the other men dance with their women?' inquired
Helga very softly, and with a slowness approaching almost to insolence. Anne's
insinuations were too revolting. She had a slightly sickish feeling, and a flash of
anger touched her. She mastered it and ignored Anne's inadequate answer."
Helga, the product of a union between a black man and a white woman who
may have once met in dance halls, has reason to feel "sickish" and angry. Ignorant of this background, Anne goes on to reveal the depth of her hatred for
Denney's "treacherous" behavior:

"She certainly ought to be ostracized. I've nothing but contempt for her, as
has every other self-respecting Negro."

The other women and the lone man left to them—Helga's own escort—all
seemingly agreed with Anne. . . . Helga gave it up. She felt that it would be
useless to tell them what she felt for the beautiful, calm, cool girl who had the
assurance, the courage, so placidly to ignore racial barriers and give her attention to people, was not contempt, but envious admiration. So she remained
silent, watching the girl.[67]

Helga's silence here reflects Larsen's own self-censure until she opened up publicly in her fiction.

Any black woman seen in the company of a white man was risking her reputation. A friend of George Schuyler's who took a white college professor to a
"Negro social affair" attended by blacks of the "upper crust . . . was snubbed and
slurred and afterwards ran across several ugly rumors reflecting on her charac-

ter and morals."[68] She would never risk it again, her status had been so lowered. When Anita Thompson asked if she could bring H. L. Mencken, at the time the famous editor of *The Smart Set* (before he founded *American Mercury*), to an Alpha social dance, the hostess was shocked: "Why, we don't have white men in our parties! We don't have white people at all! But if we did, they would have to be social equals, and no journalist would fit into our parties. . . . So don't ask to invite common white people."[69]

Larsen's friendship with Carl Van Vechten, in particular, damaged her reputation in some influential quarters and has continued to inspire aspersions on her character. Yet Larsen's best friends all felt toward him much as she did. They would not suffer the same calumny, because their more secure position in black society and their civil rights activism shielded them from the criticism of later generations.

Larsen had many reasons to relish Van Vechten's company. He was, of course, an important contact, one of the great talent scouts of the twentieth century, but his literary tastes also had much in common with hers. Having been born and raised in conservative Cedar Rapids, Iowa, a misfit of outré fascinations and budding homosexual inclinations, he was peculiarly sensitive to creative people who felt wary or misunderstood. He was an amusing, generous, and imaginative host known for his flamboyant self-parodying costumes. Around those issues that usually demand intense seriousness to the point of hypocrisy—race and sex —he was always testing boundaries, inspiring people (at risk of offending them) to loosen up. Moreover, he liked Larsen and admired her intelligence.

Sensitive about being a parvenu in the black bourgeoisie, Larsen found in Van Vechten a different conduit to recognition and self-affirmation. Moreover, Larsen and Van Vechten had plenty to talk about. As a student at the University of Chicago at the turn of the century (when Larsen was living on State Street), he had witnessed the performances of the black musical greats Bert Williams, George Walker, and Aida Overton in State Street resorts. He had even filled in at the piano once or twice at the Everleigh Sisters' brothel at Twenty-Second and Dearborn and could still remember the fountain in its foyer.[70] A reporter for the Chicago *Inter-Ocean* and the Chicago *American* between 1903 and 1906, Van Vechten was full of stories about Nella Larsen's old stomping grounds, and he had long been interested in black culture.

Nonetheless, the distrust some Harlemites felt toward him was not entirely undeserved. He told H. L. Mencken in mid-1925, "Jazz, the blues, Negro spirituals, all stimulate me enormously for the moment. Doubtless, I shall discard them too in time."[71] (He did not; in fact his interest deepened and lasted until he died.) A self-described opportunist and provocateur, he was also a compulsive cataloguer and collector. In the mid-Twenties Van Vechten's serious engagement with black culture did not prevent him from voicing stereotypical notions of Negro primitivism that were common to the era, and that he himself would repudiate later. (Nor was Larsen immune to some of the same notions.) For better or worse, Larsen's life was deeply affected by her friendship with Carl and Fania; and from the time that she grew close to them, much of her social and professional identity was connected to theirs. This fact may well damage Larsen's reputation even today, because in the minds of many Van Vechten is still regarded as the perfect example of the white cultural vampire, or at the very least a pathological voyeur. Larsen's relationship to him is widely regarded as either a symptom of her poor judgment or an elaborate confidence game. In truth, like many friendships, it was a little bit of both, yet much, much more.

Charges of voyeurism against Van Vechten are unquestionably true. Van Vechten believed in pursuing voyeurism the way a poodle believes in sniffing posts. He was a connoisseur of surfaces. Amusement, he believed, came from watching others being completely themselves in a conducive atmosphere. Mabel Dodge Luhan wrote of him, "Whimsicality was the note [things] must sound to have significance. Life was perceived to be a fastidious circus, and strange conjunctions were more prized than in the ordinary relationships touted in eternity."[72] But Van Vechten was also a closet idealist with an austere vision of his time years before the economic Crash, as Bruce Kellner has pointed out. By 1925, his fiction was already anticipating the unhappy end of the great party at which he was so enthusiastically tending bar. According to Thomas Wirth, the character Campaspe Lorillard in *The Blind Bow-Boy* expresses a core aspect of Van Vechten's philosophy: "How was it possible to read an author who never laughed? For it was only behind laughter that true tragedy could lie concealed, only the ironic author who could awaken the deeper emotions. The true tragedies of life . . . were either ridiculous or sordid. The only way to get the sense of this absurd, contradictory, and perverse existence into a book was to withdraw entirely from reality. The artist who feels the most poignantly the bitterness of life wears a persistent and sardonic smile."[73]

As Emily Bernard has written, "Van Vechten had as many detractors as supporters," and he had a way of quietly shutting people out when he was through with them.[74] With respect to those in whom he perceived great talent, however, the record is clear. Gertrude Stein, Langston Hughes, Ethel Waters, Zora Neale Hurston, and Nella Larsen could hardly have been more different from each other, but they all adored him.

For Larsen, star-struck as she surely was and intent on maneuvering herself into his fold, he was a breath of fresh air after years of loneliness, backbreaking labor, and frustration, hampered by the closed world of the black professional class on which she was partly dependent, yet among whom she was, after all, someone of minor significance and no family. Without proof of college attendance, even the sororities rejected her. She was ready to be amused, especially in the company of one of New York's most sophisticated aesthetes. Both Carl and Fania, moreover, knew what it meant to be an outsider, to be "queer" and different. They took to Larsen even more than to her husband, whom they also liked —and opened the door to a glittering world.

Van Vechten encouraged Larsen to write about African American life while he gained perspective from her and Elmer on the subject matter of his own novel-in-progress, in which a black librarian was a central character. He was convinced that Negroes' "sensitiveness"—what Toomer referred to as a "crust" —was preventing them from developing and exploiting their "racial gifts" in music and literature. The inhibition pertained especially to the more "colorful" and "exotic" aspects of black life and culture, but Van Vechten did not encourage writing about these aspects alone. Much of what he was drafting stressed the untapped drama in the lives of striving professionals like those who were inviting him into their homes. Even these realms of black life, he believed, were not being explored freely and audaciously enough because of the resistance among African Americans themselves.

In mid-September, while Nella and Elmer were traveling in Canada (probably in connection with one of Elmer's professional conferences), she wrote Van Vechten from Montreal: "I wonder if you are responsible for two books and a letter which I had from Mr. Alfred Knopf just before setting out for this wonderful wet Dominion!" They were staying in the old French quarter on Rue St. Denis: "Among the many interesting sights are the Americans with nice edges on. You will know, of course, that we are not included among these."[75] While the "Americans" in Canada were giving her the cold stare, Van Vechten was paving the way to his publisher.

Back in the world of the library, the Staff Association, under the leadership of Nella's champions Harriet Wright and Ernestine Rose, was clamoring for increased city support that summer and fall, circulating a petition and gaining the attention and even editorial support of the city's newspapers. They launched a two-month educational campaign to raise public awareness of the funding shortage. Every year 21 percent of trained library staff resigned, citing disintegrating books and the impossibility of subsisting on their salaries. At $124 per month, Larsen's salary beat that of many librarians who had been working longer than she had, but did not match that of a beginning teacher. In the Children's Rooms, shelves were bare. The librarians sought a $400 per year increase for all employees—a 25 percent raise in Larsen's case. Beginning with a mass meeting in early June, the campaign kept up into early October, and succeeded. The Board of Estimates gave the librarians all the salary they asked for and allowed more money for books beginning January 1, 1926. Nella Larsen Imes, nonetheless, took a leave of absence from October to January, and then resigned when the leave expired.[76] Drawing confidence from the remarkable surge of interest in African American literature and encouraged by acquaintances, she had decided to concentrate on writing.

She did not, however, begin by writing on "Negro themes." Had she done so, her first two stories might appear today in anthologies of African American women's writing from the first half of the twentieth century. Work by black writers that does not focus on "racial" subject matter has a way of disappearing from literary history, excluded from the canons of black and American literature. At a time when many of Larsen's friends were encouraging fiction about black life by black writers, and when the demand for such fiction was great, why did the Harlem librarian Nella Larsen Imes—or, rather "Allen Semi," her nom de plume, which reversed the spellings of her first and last names and referred to a "hybrid" identity—choose to debut with stories in which the characters, racially unidentified, were presumably white? In part, it was a characteristic choice for someone who persistently tested racial boundaries. Moreover, pulp magazines were not yet welcoming to "Negro fiction." Under a cloak of invisibility, and without immersing herself in the complications of identifiably racial themes, Larsen worked out essential motifs and narrative strategies that became her signature, and that applied as well to "white" topics as to "black." In the process she revealed secrets of her own troubled history, profound insecurity, and fragile marriage.

TWELVE

The New Negro:
Model 1926

L ARSEN'S first published short story came out in the January 1926 issue of *Young's Realistic Stories Magazine,* a pulp that was published monthly in New York by C. H. Young and that sold for twenty cents. *Young's* appealed to both men and women, specializing in stories featuring "modern women" who smoked and had affairs. It had several regular contributors with pen names like Alan Williams, Courtenay Savage, Marion La Mountain, and Janet Barrington. Class-riven love triangles, bohemian settings, and bootleg liquor figured frequently. Not uncommonly two women—one rich, one relatively poor (say, a stenographer)—would struggle for the attentions of the same man. The cover always featured a color drawing of a young white woman showing plenty of shoulder and neck, with story titles like "No Questions Asked," "A Prisoner of Passion," "Pearls for Purity," "Scorned," and "The Phantom Kiss." Such fiction appealed across racial lines and, according to E. Franklin Frazier, "helped to define the meaning of sex" for many young black women in the "demoralized" areas of Chicago's South Side, whose experiences, he added, often closely paralleled those of the pulp protagonists—as did Nella Larsen's.[1]

Larsen's first story, "The Wrong Man," strains credulity at the end but has a number of features in common with her later "serious" fiction—for example, in its style, its lavish description of women's dress, and its use of interior settings. Rendering the consciousness of a young woman (about Larsen's own age) from an obscure and poverty-stricken background, now well-off, married, and nearing middle age, it uses third-person limited narration to startling effect. Like her novels, the story derives tension from a triangulated relationship and constraints on women's sexuality—themes at the psychological core of Larsen's creative impulse.

The protagonist, Julia Romley, is neither an innocent victim nor an ideal "heroine" but has climbed, rather gallantly, from a sordid childhood to a life of comfort and relative emotional security. She has made her way in a world where she could take nothing for granted—and, much as she would like to, she cannot forget her past. Happily married, she nevertheless harbors a secret: she has never revealed that she was once the mistress of a man who financed her education in interior decorating in Chicago, making her professional rise in New York possible and thus her entry into the circles in which she met her husband. A woman of apparently perfect composure who moves gracefully in high society as if she belongs there, she is disturbed and restless beneath the calm exterior—disturbed by the hidden secret of her personal identity, restless with desire.

Competition between Julia and one of her supposedly good friends roils beneath the surface of civilized manners, provoked by the presence of an accomplished and compelling man. In the background, "the orchestra blared into something wild and impressionistic, with a primitive staccato understrain of jazz. The buzz of conversation died, strangled by the savage strains of the music. The crowd stirred, broke, coalesced into twos, and became a whirling mass."[2] This is an early version of the kind of scene that would later appear in Larsen's novels. As jazz awakens "primitive" tendencies and throws people into new configurations, a reminder of an old passion arises to threaten Julia's carefully ordered life: "Ralph Tyler, risen from the past to shatter the happiness which she had grasped for herself. Must she begin all over again?" Professional independence has led to marriage into the upper echelons and entrée into an "envied gay life in one of Long Island's most exclusive sets. Yes, life had been good to her at last, better than she had ever dreamed. Was she about to lose everything,—love, wealth and position?" This was classic material for *Young's* magazine, but it also expresses Larsen's own secret fears.

Infusing the atmosphere is the motif of a child's dream world that is bound to vanish—"the people, the music, the color, and these lovely rooms, like a princess's ball in a fairy tale."[3] Observing the crowded ballroom, Julia recites a popular counting rhyme that girls often used when playing jump-rope, a rhyme in which each phrase indicates a potential future husband:

> Rich man, poor man,
> Beggar man, thief;
> Doctor, lawyer,
> Indian chief.[4]

The occasional blending of the "real" adult world with the realm of fairy stories and raw chance is a characteristic feature of Larsen's approach to fiction. She was fascinated by the way different dimensions of experience occasionally overlap, threatening a sudden dissolution of boundaries or a fatal transformation.

Julia (much like Larsen herself) cannot distinguish her love for her husband from the security and position he represents. As she obsesses over the possibility that Ralph Tyler will unmask her, she feels "suddenly weary and beaten. It was hopeless. And she had been so happy! Just a faint shadow of uneasiness, at first, which had gradually faded as the years slipped away."[5]

Julia's essential psychology, her basic insecurity yet outward calm and elegance, is a self-revelation on Larsen's part, the imaginative working-out of her own private nightmares. Neither is it inconceivable that at some point in her life Larsen had found herself in a position like that of Julia Romley at the end of girlhood: "when a girl has been sick and starving on the streets, anything can happen to her."[6] It was no stretch for Larsen to imagine this situation, which had been at least her mother's if never her own.

What makes the story unbelievable—the fact that Julia tells her secret to the "wrong man" and asks him to say nothing to her husband—resonates with Larsen's insecurity at this point in life, less than seven years into her marriage and her involvement with the New Negro elite. Julia's confidence in her secure and happy life is so fragile that she nearly self-destructs. The Ralph Tyler she meets at the party, a former schoolmate of her husband, looks so much like the Ralph Tyler she once loved that only on close inspection at the very end of the tale, when he expresses complete ignorance of her, does Julia suddenly realize he is the "wrong man." The incredible nature of this narrative climax is an index of the author's secret compulsions and inarticulate fears—her fear, particularly, that the new life she was enjoying in the mid-1920s could not last, that it was all a sort of fairy tale.

Her next story, "Freedom," appeared in *Young's* that April. Again using third-person limited narration, Larsen imagined the mindset of a man who deserts his mistress of three years and after two years of wandering, unable to stop thinking of her, learns that she died in childbirth the day he left her. As the story opens, the unnamed protagonist wants release from the woman with whom he is obsessed. Outwardly fastidious and self-controlled, he cannot rid himself of the notion of an organic "depravity" in her character that both entrances and appalls him. This is much like the allure that Helga Crane possesses for James Vayle in Larsen's first novel, and also resembles the prevailing suspicion that illegitimate mulattos were marked by organic depravity—a suspicion to which Larsen was exquisitely sensitive. As in "The Wrong Man," the woman seems, on the surface, independent and self-centered, mysterious, manipulative, and remote—yet is utterly dependent at the same time. The story is so claustrophobic in its focus on the mind of the male deserter that it creates an intense aura of expressionistic compulsion. It originates in personal nightmare and fantasy bred by familial insecurity and division. (Within two years the Imes marriage would reach the breaking point, where Nella's presence could quickly set Elmer's teeth on edge. He came to regard her as a "selfish little beast.") Moreover, the story inspires a profound concern with the dependence of women and the centrality of sexual subjection in their lives—sexual allure being a woman's chief tool for achieving some fleeting comfort in a male-dominated universe, at the same time that childbirth was a trap, a source of profound dread. Such themes, central to all of Larsen's surviving fiction save one tale she practically plagiarized, were classic elements of Scandinavia's "modern breakthrough," with which Larsen had become familiar in Denmark, but they also resonate powerfully with her own emotional history.

Larsen deliberately stresses the unknowability of the woman who both is and is not the center of the story, who remains in essence invisible throughout. We know of her only through the consciousness of the protagonist; and since the story begins as the man is leaving her, she is never physically present. We never know what she actually looks like; we're told only that the man believes she wears a "disguise" of outward beauty covering an "inert mind" and not the beauty of soul he had imagined: "He suspected, too, a touch of depravity; perhaps, only physical, but more likely mental as well." He thinks of her as "a creature irresistibly given to pleasure at no matter what cost. A sybarite! A parasite too!" Believing that she saps him physically and spiritually, he imagines her "flitting from mate to mate" after his departure, yet he cannot help feeling troubled and guilty about leaving her. Drawn by animal passion, he projects onto her a depravity and predatory sexuality that may be his own.[7]

The story's psychological complexity resides partly in the fact that we often are told not what the man directly "thinks" or "wants" but rather what he thinks he wants to think or imagines he had once felt. These are techniques Stephen Crane had explored at the turn of the century, now ratcheted up with the unconscious drives and elliptical suggestion characteristic of modernist fiction. Larsen is experimenting with ways of representing suppressed desire and psychic disavowal, scapegoating as self-defense. She reveals how we sequester, in intricate labyrinths of the mind, those abject stirrings that make us feel guilty. In the name of orderly identity, we make the other bear the guilt. We wash our hands of them—they deserve their fate; there is nothing we can do. We bury them. Yet they return, ghostly and unremitting, demanding acknowledgment and reconciliation.

After two years away, the protagonist learns that his mistress died in childbirth the very day he left her. As if his desertion itself caused her death, he is racked with guilt and blames her for victimizing him by dying. He then imaginatively re-creates their relationship as a loving one, forgetting that they ever parted. The story starts to read like a psychological thriller by Poe. Suddenly it is *she* who has deserted *him*. "He sat waiting for her. He seemed to remember that she had promised to come. . . . Why didn't she come? . . . A nameless dread seized him; she would not come! In the agony of his disappointment, he did not see that the fire had died and the candles had sputtered out. He sat wrapped in immeasurable sadness. He knew that she would not come." Finally, enveloped in his delusion, he decides to go to her. He opens a French window and steps out, "down to the pavement a hundred feet below."[8]

Nearly as unbelievable as the conclusion to "The Wrong Man," this dénouement is driven by the psychological, expressionistic algebra of the story—something out of Eugene O'Neill rather than Ibsen or Bernard Shaw. "Freedom," ironic title and all, is a tale purely about the costs of psychological repression and unabsolved guilt, and perhaps imaginative vengeance against those who had deserted Larsen in her life, or against the one who would essentially do so three years later, setting off Larsen's own neurotic descent and "disappearance." It is as if she saw what was coming and tried to confront it, to ward it off by giving it aesthetic form. Already we see the essentially fatalistic quality of Larsen's narrative imagination. That her stories fit some of the formulas of fiction marketed to young, unmarried working-class women is no argument against their spiritual authenticity.

Whatever nightmares Larsen indulged through her "hack writing," on the surface of her life everything seemed swell. She had a full social calendar in the spring of 1926. The annual benefit dance of the NAACP took place at the Manhattan Casino on Friday, March 19, lasting well into the morning.[9] The next night, Nella and Elmer attended a gleeful housewarming at Dorothy and Jim Harris' new apartment on Gay Street in the Village, where they saw the Robesons, Evelyn Preer, Harry Block, Covarrubias, Dorothy Peterson, and others of the cosmopolitan arts community.[10] These were the glitterati of the Harlem Renaissance. Evelyn Preer, former member of the Ethiopian Art Theatre and like Larsen a product of Chicago public schools, was one of the two most famous black actresses of the period, with a major role opposite the "blacked-up" Lenore Ulric in David Belasco's latest Broadway hit, *Lulu Belle*. This play followed the rise of a beautiful colored waif from the streets of Harlem through cabaret chorus lines to the high society of Paris—almost exactly the story of the celebrated black dancer and singer Josephine Baker. Staging all-black scenes from New York and employing many black performers for important roles in a mixed cast, for all its flaws (and they were considerable) the play seemed to many a milestone in black performance history.[11] Paul Robeson was by this point one of the great celebrities of the decade, having starred in O'Neill's controversial drama of interracial marriage, *All God's Chillun Got Wings,* and the revival of *The Emperor Jones.* In the winter and early spring of 1926, he was touring in the North, performing spirituals, carrying on an affair with a "white girl" and contemplating divorce.[12]

In late April or early May, Harold Jackman recruited Nella to help show the famous Polish anthropologist Bronislaw Malinowski around the "Black Metropolis." Paul Robeson's wife, Eslanda ("Essie"), who had studied with Malinowski at the London School of Economics, made the contacts for him in Harlem. He wanted particularly to see the dancing at the just-opened Savoy Ballroom, and Jackman asked Larsen to be Malinowski's dancing partner. When the knock came at the door of Jackman's apartment at the appointed time, they opened it and a tall, thin, clean-shaven white man introduced himself in a clipped European accent. Behind the bowing Malinowski stood a mustached and mop-headed American whom a star-struck Jackman recognized immediately as the celebrated philosopher John Dewey.[13]

Either Jackman or Robeson chose Larsen as Malinowski's partner for the evening because she danced well, she could keep up an intelligent conversation with a charismatic conversationalist, and she could bear up under the stares and whispered comments in the newly opened "Home of Happy Feet," one of Harlem's most beautiful ballrooms. By going out for the evening to dance with a white foreigner of middle age, unaccompanied by her husband, Nella would be making herself vulnerable to all sorts of innuendo.

The block-long Savoy was big enough, however, to get lost in. Just opened in mid-March on Lenox Avenue between 140th and 141st streets, it was the first grand dance palace in Harlem. Coming into the lobby, one saw a huge cut-glass chandelier lighting a marble staircase that led up to the blue and orange ballroom, half-carpeted, and furnished with plush settees, tables, and chairs where patrons could rest between dances and observe the crowd. Spotlights cast varied hues over the dancers and two alternating orchestras. Men without partners, like John Dewey that night, could hire a "hostess" for twenty-five cents a dance.[14]

There was more to Malinowski's interest in the Harlem club scene than a touristic adventure. He considered the United States an ideal place to test current theories of race and culture, to unite "knowledge of the human organism and race with that of culture." This was a challenge to the American anthropologists at Columbia who, under Franz Boas, argued that "race" and culture were not organically related. Malinowski suspected otherwise and felt that the issue had only been approached "emotionally" so far. He considered it one of the greatest scientific issues of the age. Britain's failure to apply scientific anthropology, he believed, had led to "deplorable" results in Ireland, and threatened to do the same in Africa and other parts of the empire. Applying biology and physiology to racial problems might or might not be useful, but it was important to find out. "The question of race, the mixing of races, of human Mendelism, might be studied within the United States. Here also we have an experiment on a gigantic scale of forceful acculturation of one race by another."[15] Larsen's personal history in itself should have wreaked havoc on Malinowski's notions.

Before sailing from London, he had suggested in a long conversation with Essie Robeson that "segregation without degradation" might be the best solution for the races in the United States—that is, setting aside a separate area of the country for Negroes. Robeson argued strenuously against this notion, insisting that black Americans would never accept being set off in a separate state or states. She even wrote up a formal essay on the topic and gave it to Malinowski shortly before his departure from London. Pairing the anthropologist with Larsen was, deliberately or not, a challenge to his proposed solution to the "race problem."[16]

Shocked by the prejudice against blacks in the United States, Malinowski could not fathom why all persons with "a drop of coloured blood" were considered Negroes. When he got to Atlanta, he wrote his wife that he had spoken to "sev'l professional niggs.—all as bitter as can be and rightly so." "The most puzzling part of it all is that the Mulatto is classed with the Negro and thus a solidarity is created, through which naturally the light skinned break through in education and achievement and are yet pushed back constantly."[17]

Malinowski's reflections help to set in relief one of the great differences between his thinking and that of Franz Boas, who emphasized that cultures are not wholly self-contained but always "in process," and who traced the diffusion of cultural elements across ethnic and social boundaries. In contrast, Malinowski aspired to refine his theory of "cultures" as unified organisms, self-contained within discrete environments; the hypothesis that culture and "race" were inherently connected derived in part from this theoretical aspiration. If each culture was an organic unit, "mixing" was likely to provoke conflict and degeneration. Fox-trotting that night under the lights at the Savoy, where would Malinowski's dance partner fit into his scheme? His extant correspondence doesn't say. After all, he was unlikely to inform his wife that he had gone out dancing with a young, decidedly attractive "mulatto."

Jean Toomer was leading a revived, chiefly African American subgroup in the Gurdjieff Work. Aaron Douglas, Eric Walrond, Dorothy Peterson, Dorothy Harris, Vivienne Stoner, Harold Jackman, Wallace Thurman, Charles S. Johnson, Alonzo Smith, and a man named Franklin Nichols were all involved in the weekly meetings, mostly held in Brooklyn or Greenwich Village that spring and early summer, but not Nella, apparently, nor Carl.[18]

On May 1, a Saturday, Nella and Elmer attended the second *Opportunity* Contest Dinner at the Fifth Avenue Restaurant, orchestrated by Charles S. Johnson. Editor, critic, and author John Macy, who presided, set the keynote for the evening with a paean to the universality of art. "Let our emphasis be right. We rejoice because *good work* has been done, not that good work has been done by *Negroes*. It is the beauty of the poem that counts, not the fact that it was written by a Negro. I don't want to hear about Roland Hayes, the Negro tenor. The man whose singing charms and thrills us is Roland Hayes, the *tenor*." He then weighed in on the other side. "All artists in the world must express intensely their race, nation, time, family, personality." Why should Countee Cullen marvel that God had made a poet black? "What is curious about it? We do not write verses with our skin or sing with our hair. Art belongs to everybody who can make it and enjoy it."[19] Among the four hundred people listening, in addition to a blushing Countee Cullen, were many of the country's top writers and editors, who had served as judges on integrated panels.

Most of the Imeses' friends gathered for a party afterward at Rudolph and Jane Fisher's. The Imeses may have joined the party of twenty that went on after that to Small's Paradise and stayed nearly till sunrise. Wednesday the fifth, the Imeses joined a party at stage director Dudley Murphy's with much of their usual circle—the Harrises, Lloyd and Edna Thomas (then acting with Evelyn Preer in *Lulu Belle*), the Whites, Van Vechten, singer Taylor Gordon, Rita Romilly, and Harry Block.[20]

It was a gay life. On June 11, a cool, bright Friday, Nella and Elmer went to Van Vechten's after dinner, meeting up there with Walter White, James Weldon Johnson, banking heir Eddie Wasserman, Donald Angus, Rudolph ("Bud") Fisher, and Zora Neale Hurston. They all headed out to the New World cabaret —the renamed and reopened Fifth Avenue Small's—where they ran into other friends, including a party with Eric Walrond. Hurston would make this the setting for part of her now-celebrated essay, "How It Feels To Be Colored Me," not inconceivably based on this very episode.[21]

Nella and Elmer went out to Bordentown Manual Training School for Commencement Day in June (Bordentown, near Trenton, was the only such school in the North exclusively for Negroes); and the following week Grace Valentine, wife of the school's principal, stayed with them for a couple of days in Jersey City, no doubt taking in some Manhattan cabarets over the weekend.[22] Then in early July, Nella and Elmer spent some more time out of town, getting back on the eleventh in hopes of making it to a party at Dorothy Peterson's. They had been on the road all night and then up all day. Nella lay down for a nap and didn't wake up until 11:00 P.M. "Consternation," she wrote Carl apologetically the next morning. She had dressed quickly and rushed with Elmer to Brooklyn, getting there at 1:00 A.M. "All for nothing. You were gone. Very sick ever since."[23]

There were other cabaret parties that summer. Elmer and Nella met up with Zora Hurston and Van Vechten the following Saturday for an evening that started at the New World and ended at 4:00 A.M. at the Nest, one of the smarter cellar clubs on 133rd between Lenox and Seventh avenues, attracting prize-fighters and show biz personalities, and the scene of fierce jam sessions into the wee hours. Musicians migrated there after their "regular" jobs in downtown cabarets and formal Harlem clubs, and competed against each other in "cutting" contests.[24]

All of Nella's friends by now knew about the novel Van Vechten had been writing and wondered how they might figure in it, or worried that he would leave them out. "Everyone is on tip-toe," Nella wrote, after spotting an advertisement in the July issue of *American Mercury*. Elmer had told her, "'Your people' [a witticism meaning "Negroes"] don't buy books, but that's one they are all going to buy."[25] James Weldon Johnson, Walter White, and Rudolph Fisher had read the manuscript and praised it. White thought it would be a "sensation in Harlem." The ending, with a spectacularly decadent scene set in the Black Venus nightclub—based on Small's Paradise—Fisher considered a "knockout."[26] But the main story line centered on a troubled romance between a librarian at the 135th Street Branch of the New York Public Library—an admirer, like Larsen, of Gertrude Stein's story "Melanctha"—and an aspiring black fiction writer who could not think of a subject to write about.

Nella was doing some writing of her own that summer. By July she was about halfway into a novel when Van Vechten found out about it. He wrote her a note asking if she had forgotten him. "Forget you?" she wrote, "D'you know any more jokes?" He had earlier expressed faith in her talent and wanted to know what she was writing. "I must say," she wrote, "you're a trusting soul. How do these things get about? It's the awful Truth. But who knows if I'll ever get through with the damned thing. Certainly not I." She guarded herself with low expectations: "The thing might turn out to be utter rot. When I first started, I honestly thought it was really good, now, something more than half way, I'm afraid it's frightfully bad. Too, I'm getting rather bored with it. I wonder how many half-finished novels there are knocking about the world."[27]

Albert and Charles Boni, publishers of *The New Negro,* had put up a $1,000 prize for the best novel by a Negro. She initially thought of submitting her manuscript to them, but then she heard they were disappointed in the submissions. Rather than seeing this as an attractive opportunity to win a prize, Larsen decided that although "it would be nice to get a thousand dollars" and the publicity, she did not wish "to be merely the best of a bad lot." "It is being whispered about that anything literate is sure to be awarded the honor. That's discouraging."[28] She asked Carl for his opinion, adding, "I like Knopf. He does things so well, sends them out looking attractive,—nice type, bindings, title pages, and everything,—but, he seems very hard to please, (see Mr. Llewelyn Powys and hear Miss Jessie Fauset). True, good makeups deserve good books."[29] Van Vechten almost certainly encouraged her to think in terms of Knopf. Three weeks later she had "definitely decided against the Bonis, even if Knopf won't have me. In that case, I think I'll try the Viking Press"—the new house Walter White had been talking up.[30] The Bonis never did get a novel their judges considered worthy of the prize.

As Nella was writing her own novel and thinking of publishers, she got caught up in a minor ruckus about White's recent novel, *Flight.* In the July issue of *Opportunity,* young Frank Horne—a sometime member of the Imeses' and Whites' social set—published a highly negative review of *Flight,* several months after White had had an advance copy sent to Nella and Elmer. The indignant novelist dashed off an irate letter to Charles S. Johnson with a copy of Llewellyn Jones's highly favorable review from the *Chicago Evening Post,* asking if he shouldn't be upset when a white critic of such standing could write so favorably of *Flight* "and then in a Negro magazine there appears a piece like the one to which I take exception?"[31] After further vituperation from White, Johnson decided to go the extra mile in making peace, soliciting a full response to Horne's review from "Mrs. Nella Imes, who writes well and has a most extraordinarily wide acquaintance with past and current literature."[32]

Larsen's letter was virtually made to order for Walter White. In fact, she mailed him a copy of it—two single-spaced pages, signed "Allen L. Semi"—when she was done, apologizing for her bad typing and adding, "I have not said all I wanted to, nor what I have said as effectively as I would like."[33] Her critique of Horne's review, taking the same tack as White's initial letter to Johnson, was scathing, condescending, and self-dramatizing. But her decision to parade her knowledge of recent fiction, the better to accuse Horne of being behind the times, reveals the sort of work she took as a model while working on her own novel that summer and fall.

Her chief point of attack was exactly White's—that Horne did not know enough about modern fiction to write an informed review of *Flight,* which she attempted to put in the company of the best recent European and American novels. The truth is that much of Horne's criticism was valid: White's characters are flat and his protagonist Mimi Daquin unconvincing, in part because of creaky staging and plot machinery. Hounded out of the black community early on because of a "love child" and then built over the course of the novel into a kind of stock image of the rich white woman with the world at her feet, Mimi suddenly becomes conscious, Horne charged, "of the essential artistry and beauty of her own 'race,' as expressed in the voice of Roland Hayes," and completely changes her life. "And so," Horne lamented, "the climax meant to be intense and sweeping, strikes a hollow, blatant note."[34] The problem is not (as Larsen charges Horne with arguing) that it is implausible for a woman who is "passing" to choose blackness over the advantages of whiteness, but that White fails to build Mimi Daquin into a three-dimensional character and then present her "conversion" in a convincing fashion. Moreover, Horne believed, White did not satisfactorily deal with the dénouement: How will Mimi be accepted back into the black fold? What mental and psychological adjustments will she have to undergo, in view of all her past experience in both the black and the white worlds? Reading Larsen's own novel *Passing* after reading *Flight* is like moving into a whole new dimension of fictional technique, linguistic control, and psychological understanding. Her review is therefore most interesting as a revelation of her own literary bearings.

Horne had conceded, Larsen points out, that Mimi Daquin was (in Horne's words) "a character worthy of a novel," deserving treatment "of a kind to place her beside Maria Chapdelaine, Mattie Frome and Salammbo." Why, Larsen asks, does Horne turn to these outmoded fictional models as points of comparison? Why use them "to disparage the sensitive, rebellious, modern Mimi? . . . Would not Galsworthy's unsurpassable Irene Forsyte, or Jacobsen's Maria Grubbe have been more effective for purposes of comparison as well as for disparagement?"[35] The characters Larsen privileges violate conventions of marriage, filial obedience, and female sexuality more radically than either Mimi Daquin or the characters named by Horne. The reference to the heroine of *Marie Grubbe,* by the Danish novelist Jens Peter Jacobsen, is notable because although Jacobsen was a pivotal figure in recent Danish literature, British and American writers were barely aware of him and practically never mentioned his work.[36] (Moreover, his uses of narrative point of view and scenic technique strongly resemble Larsen's.) Horne's charge that White did not provide a satisfying dénouement was, in Larsen's view, obtusely old-fashioned: "Authors do not supply imaginations, they expect their readers to have their own, and, to use them. Judging by present day standards of fiction, the ending of *Flight* is the perfect one. . . . For others of this type, I refer your reviewer to Sherwood Anderson's *Dark Laughter,* to Carl Van Vechten's *Firecrackers,* to Joseph Hergesheimer's *Tubal Cain.*"[37]

As for Horne's complaints about the awkwardness of White's prose, Larsen's original letter gave the retort (excised from the published version) that even after two readings, "these sins escaped me. . . . Even the opening sentence, so particularly cited, still seems to me all right. But then, I have been recently reading Huysmans, Conrad, Proust, and Thomas Mann. Naturally these things would not irritate me as they would an admirer of Louis Hemon and Mrs. Wharton. Too, there's Galsworthy, who opens his latest novel with a sentence of some thirty-odd words." The truth is that Nella's own methods compare much better to the models she mentions than do Walter White's, although her final judgment, comparing *Flight* with White's first novel, is defensible: "To my mind, warped as I have confessed by the Europeans and the American moderns, *Flight* is a far superior piece of work than *The Fire in the Flint*. Less dramatic, it is more fastidious and required more understanding, keener insight. Actions and words count less and the poetic conception of the character, the psychology of the scene more, than in the earlier novel."[38] White, "eternally grateful" for her "magnificent answer" to Horne, admitted more than he knew when he wrote: "You understood 'Mimi' even better than I did. I shan't soon forget this generous act of yours."[39] Larsen cagily submitted her letter under the same pseudonym she had used for her two pulp stories, but magazines generally require that letters to the editor bear the name of the author, and so it was published, with abridgments, over the name "Nella Imes."

White's vanity was not the only thing at stake in the controversy—although it was thoroughly displayed in his handling of the whole affair. He had learned from the fracas over *The Fire in the Flint* that controversy was good publicity. If you could get some respected critic to respond to a negative review on your behalf, it might keep people talking and even provoke further fireworks. But the little dogfight over *Flight* was nothing compared to the storm that was building around *Nigger Heaven*.

Nella received her advance copy of the novel early on the afternoon of Friday, August 6, and wrote Van Vechten immediately. Elmer was off in "the country" and she had a dreary weekend in store, planning to stay hidden at home because she'd just had her hair cut and looked like "the wrath of god." "But, I am more than compensated," she purred. "'Nigger Heaven' arrived a few minutes ago. . . . Therefore I shall have a wonderful time." She approached the reading like a courtesan preparing for a night of pleasure: "I'm terribly excited. Too, almost incited to forgo the ritual which the reading of particular books always demand from me, a Houbigant scented bath, the donning of my best green crepe de chine pajamas, fresh flowers on the bedside table, piles of freshly covered pillows and my nicest bed cover,—and sit right down to it. But no, impatient as I am, I shall make it a ceremony. Not to do so would be blasphemous. . . . Thanks and other things will follow after the pleasure. Just now, everything waits but that pleasure."[40]

By placing the abortive relationship between an aspiring black novelist, Byron Kasson, and a frustrated black librarian (named Mary Love) at the center of the novel, Van Vechten was trying to suggest the potential of a black literary universe begging to be born—a universe comprising the black underworld, the glamorous as well as "low-down" cabarets, the striving middle class and struggling young professionals, individuals who passed as white, Harlem's everyday working people, white interlopers and "friends of the Negro" as well as slummers and mediocre writers looking for "material," black vamps and "sweetmen," blues women and jazz men. Van Vechten even included practical advice to aspiring authors, specifying the need to send a stamped self-addressed envelope with submitted manuscripts, describing the typical rejection slip, and explaining why rejections are so common. Lacking Van Vechten's usual light touch and wicked satire, the core narrative managed to work in plenty of propaganda for the black bourgeoisie and against white prejudice while providing what amounted to an annotated bibliography of African American literature, a running advertisement for the New Negro writers, and a tourist guide to Harlem. Attempting (unsuccessfully) to patch together examples of all these different types of fiction around the central romantic tragedy, spiced up with sensational scenes of sadomasochism and a title guaranteed to shock, *Nigger Heaven* became a kind of Rorschach test of New Negro literary taste.

If Larsen saw anything of herself in the character Mary Love, she did not say so. (According Bruce Kellner, the "physical model" for the character was Dorothy Peterson.)[41] Mary is likely a composite, but the contents of her bookshelf are Nella Larsen's: James Branch Cabell, Anatole France, Jean Cocteau, Louis Bromfield, Aldous Huxley, Sherwood Anderson, Somerset Maugham, Elinor Wylie, James Gibbons Huneker, and inscribed copies of James Weldon Johnson's *Fifty Years and Other Poems,* Toomer's *Cane,* McKay's *Harlem Shadows,* White's *The Fire in the Flint,* Du Bois's *Souls of Black Folk,* Jessie Fauset's *There Is Confusion.* On her writing table are books from the library "to keep abreast with the best of the modern output."[42] Like Larsen, Mary Love is aloof and intensely self-restrained; though a good dancer, she never allows herself to "let go." She feels torn between a "white" side and a "black" side—among whites she has a "white psychology" and among blacks a "black" one—and is never completely comfortable in either world, rather like the protagonist of *Quicksand,* Larsen's first, semi-autobiographical novel. (Indeed, Larsen was given to speaking of having different racial "sides" herself.) With her light-skinned roommate Olive,

Mary "took in most of the good plays and musical entertainments, revues and song recitals alike, downtown, usually sitting in the balcony to save expense, although Olive was light enough and Mary's features were sufficiently Latin so that they were not rudely received when they asked at the box-office for places in the orchestra."[43] One of Larsen's later friends noted that Nella always bought balcony tickets to save money.

Larsen read *Nigger Heaven* three times before writing Van Vechten her predictably gushing response:

> Was it you or another who told me of the shocked horror of one of your friends because "Carl Van Vechten knows a Negro"? Well! What will she say when she reads this shy story, with its air of deceptive simplicity and discovers that Carl Van Vechten knows the Negroe?
>
> It is a fine tale, this story of the deterioration and subsequent ruin of a weakling who blames all his troubles on that old scapegoat, the race problem. Dangerous too. But with what exquisite balance you have avoided the propagandistic pitfall. But of course, *you* would. Like your Lasca Sartoris, who so superbly breasts the flood of racial predjudices (black and white).
>
> I like that. I mean your dispassionate way of simply proceeding with the tale, getting on to the tragic denouement, merely stating thus and so is the case, and leaving it at that,—in effect, if the reader is a doubting Thomas, let him draw back and be damned to him. And yet, how forceful it is.[44]

Then Larsen hedged a moment: "I don't think that, just now, I can tell you all that I feel about the book, because I really don't know myself." She would not let it "swerve" her allegiance to his earlier novels, *Peter Whiffle* and *Firecrackers.* What got in the way was a feeling of racial loyalty, perhaps a nervousness about what Van Vechten was up to. "You see, it's too close, too true, as if you had undressed the lot of us and turned on a strong light. Too, I feel a kind of despair. Why, oh why, couldn't we have done something as big as this for ourselves? Fear, I suppose. It is big," she confided, in a lingo typical of the Twenties, "big in its pity, big in its cruelties."

Her husband, too, liked the book: "Elmer is very enthusiastic about it. I don't believe he expected to like it—why I don't know for he was the one who discovered Peter [Whiffle] and worried me and Walter to death one summer until we read it—and was amazed to find that he did. He thinks it shows the same understanding and deep insight as [Marmaduke Pickthall's] Saïd the Fisherman." She concludes somewhat incongruously:

> Well, I filled three pages without saying how marvelous this result of your imagination and instructive perception working together. The scenes, the de-

scriptions, the conversations are spontaneous as life. The whole thing moves easily and surely. And, how you have caught the spirit inherent in us, the urge, the sweet craving for happiness—and the bitter knowledge of unfulfillment, and our blindness to the reason. And the mixedness of things, the savagery under the sophistication. But surely I've written too much.[45]

Indeed she had. Was she just telling Van Vechten what she knew he wanted to hear, or was she giving her honest opinion after three readings? Probably a bit of both, but she continued to reassure him for years that it was a fine book.

There is no doubt, in retrospect, that the novel fell short of what Larsen claimed for it, but any suspicion that she was simply buttering up a potential patron whom she secretly disdained—as some scholars stubbornly insist—does not fly. Those who did not like *Nigger Heaven* had no trouble making their feelings known, and they had plenty of support. People like Jessie Fauset, Countee Cullen, and Regina Anderson stopped speaking to Van Vechten and cut him off their guest lists. Larsen's close friends did exactly the opposite.

Lillian Alexander, who had objected to the novel based on reviews she read when it came out, wrote Elmer Imes to apologize, because after finally reading the book she realized how "dumb" the criticism of it was:

Really the book is an epic—to me—(and I rarely rave over anything or anybody) and is revealing in every line of Negro wants, needs, failures and why, aspirations and the vicious circle that prevents their realization.

And it is true at the same time. Most folks choke over the prologue but I just drank it in because you know how well I know my Lenox and Seventh Avenues and how I walk up and down them drinking in the magnificent comedy and the dire tragedy and woe encountered in every block. Except for some of his obscure slang, Carl knows Nigger Heaven almost (?) as well as I! Love to Nella and when shall we see you both?[46]

Sadie Delaney Tandy, Nella's former colleague and friend at the library, wrote an unsolicited letter to Van Vechten saying that she had awaited the appearance of the novel with misgivings because of the title but was "happily disappointed after reading it. . . . Much credit is due you, and I wish the book much success, which it rightly deserves."[47] Rudolph Fisher's sister Pearle spoofed the criticism of the novel and of its title in her column "This Harlem" in the *Baltimore Afro-American*.[48]

The most important novelists of the renaissance warmly praised *Nigger Heaven*—Walter White, Langston Hughes, James Weldon Johnson, Rudolph Fisher, Wallace Thurman, and Eric Walrond among them. Alain Locke thought it "brought us a step nearer the flush level of Negro material in American art."

"Only another flight (of stairs, not Walter's either)," he wrote Langston Hughes, "and we will have our real Negro novel."[49] Two years later Gwendolyn Bennett was still praising the novel: "Whether you are a person who likes *Nigger Heaven* or not you must admit that this book paved the way for a good bit of the writing that Negroes themselves are doing today," she wrote in her column for *Opportunity*. "But then you see we've always liked *Nigger Heaven* regardless of what many of our friends have said or thought about it."[50] Charles Chesnutt, the *éminence grise* of African American fiction, wrote Van Vechten a long, warm letter after receiving his free copy and went on to defend the novel in print. Nora Holt, a.k.a. Lasca Sartoris, wrote from Paris in her telegraphic style: "Great! . . . Have loaned my copy to several Harlemites here who were antagonistic to the title. After reading it, they are quite *mad* over it especially your treatment of subject."[51] There was nothing duplicitous in Larsen's statements about *Nigger Heaven*. Yet it must be said that the novel reads today as merely a well-intended, opportunistic mishmash of fictional elements that never quite cohere, alternately pedantic, amusing, propagandistic, and sensation-mongering. Perhaps, as with Walter White's novel, Larsen did not *want* to be too critical.

Elmer and Nella dropped in on Carl and his wife after dinner on the twenty-fifth of August and got to know Fania better while Carl was nursing a cold. They stayed until midnight, partly talking books. "I can't tell you how much we enjoyed our last visit in your home," Nella wrote later. "Fania Marinoff is delightful, in appearance and manner—like a princess out of a modern fairy tale."[52] The phrase, one Larsen liked to use, was strikingly apropos. Four years older than Nella, "Fanny" (her childhood name) Marinoff had been born in Odessa, Russia, the thirteenth child in a Jewish family. She lost her mother while a baby, and her father remarried a devout Jewish woman, moved the family to America when Fanny was about five, and settled in Boston's Salem Street tenements. Fanny grew up in the streets, hawking matches for pennies all day even before starting school. She got a thrill out of doing what was not allowed: "Secretly I disobeyed. On Sabbath I went to Gentile sewing parties; on Pesach I ate bread when no one saw me; on Yom Kippur I ate."[53]

Resented by her stepmother, she was sent to live with a brother in Denver, but his wife hated Fanny and worked her as a kitchen slave from the age of seven, later farming her out as a servant to pay her room and board. Her brother Jack, a radical Socialist, began taking her to meetings to recite "heavy poems" of social revolt to audiences of tradesmen, shopgirls, and small storekeepers, and she found that she enjoyed performance. At eight or nine, already living practically on her own, she became a waitress in a boarding house and met a woman who ran a school for the dramatic arts. By the age of twelve, after free training there, a brief stint in a Denver opera, and free lessons from a school of oratory, Fanny joined a traveling stock company and began touring Western villages and towns, getting paid only in board, occasionally trading tickets for food. When the troupe folded in Crete, Nebraska, leaving her stranded, a woman from the company took her to Omaha, where the troupe reorganized, only to disband again in Ogallala. Petite Fanny, in her early teens, took a dishwashing and waitress job until she earned enough to get back to Denver, and promptly jumped back into traveling theater.

While acting and drumming up audiences, she used her sewing skills as assistant wardrobe mistress. Finally she changed her name to Fania (in 1911), hopped with a show to New York, and drifted into vaudeville. By about 1912, when she met the newly divorced, barely solvent theater and music critic Carl Van Vechten, she was "a darksome and delightful slip of a girl," as a columnist called her, with a rising reputation on the stage.[54] In 1914, the year they married, she made her debut in the motion pictures and went on to become a princess of the silver screen, notably as Trina in *Life's Whirlpool* (1916), a silent film adaptation of Frank Norris' *McTeague*. In the early years of marriage, her earnings chiefly supported the ménage. She lived a rich life without children, largely on her own terms—traveling alone often, staying overnight with friends, making her own living. In the fall of 1926, she was admired by all for her dramatic looks, stylish outfits, intelligence, and personal charm, and was performing in live dramas on WEAF Radio every Sunday evening.[55]

Nella and Fania had many things in common. Close in age, they had both escaped childhood trauma, crowded slums, and the hatred of stepparents who wanted to be rid of them. Just as "Nellie" had become "Nella" in puberty, so "Fanny" had changed her name to "Fania" as she invented a life for herself independent of her family. Raised in squalor, with a sporadic formal education, Marinoff now moved easily in the *beau monde* with confidence and grace. She kept her maiden name, and she was used to taking care of herself. One acquaintance described her at this time as "a bewitching creature five feet six, exquisite figure, dark eyes, fascinating face with a head full of jet black hair and keen feet!"[56] Actually, as Bruce Kellner points out, she was a few inches shorter than this—exactly the same height as Nella Imes. Expert seamstresses, the two women liked to exchange clothes and "work over" dresses together. They had similar tastes in fashion, to the extent that Marinoff modeled at one point for the artist Mary Mackinnon in one of Nella's high-fashion dresses called the "Golden Forest," designed by Paul Poiret, the avant-garde Parisian couturier credited with ending the reign of the corset.[57]

While Elmer was away at an engineering conference, Nella sent Carl some of his scientific articles (on the practical applications of quantum theory) and professional correspondence to "give a clearer idea of what his work really is." She archly enclosed a copy of Harry Stillwell Edwards' novel *Eneas Africanus,* "which I think is even more interesting than my husband's writings."[58] The book was "plantation school" fiction of the deepest dye, extreme if unintended testimony to the racial delusions to which upper-class white Southerners were prone. It tells of the eight-year odyssey of a faithful servant, Eneas, who sets out to save a precious heirloom wedding cup from advancing Union troops in the waning months of the Civil War, gets lost, wanders throughout the South—in the meantime marrying, having numerous children, becoming an itinerant preacher, and winning a fortune by racing his master's colt—and returns just in time for the wedding of his master's daughter. Disdaining emancipation to the end, he pledges his wife and children to the master's family. The book, in the words of its preface, memorializes a "vanishing type, dear to the hearts of the Southerners, young and old," with sidelight on the "Southerners themselves, kind of heart, tolerant and appreciative of the humor and pathos of the Negro's life."[59] Published by a small press in Macon, Georgia, in 1920, it was a sort of collectors' item for the Imeses. Nella knew it would appeal to Van Vechten's sardonic sense of humor, an attribute she shared with him and her husband.

Dorothy Peterson returned on the seventh of September from a summer in France, "anxious to see the reviews" of *Nigger Heaven.* Having saved duplicates for her, Larsen promptly took them to Dorothy in Brooklyn.[60] Peterson and Larsen had special reason to interest themselves in the furor surrounding the novel, for the most critical reviews in the African American newspapers were as much attacks on them as on Van Vechten.

On the first of September the *Amsterdam News* had published an extensive screed entitled "Homo Africanus Harlemi," by the Afro-Caribbean socialist critic and educator Hubert H. Harrison. "The author of this breach of the peace," it began, "has been well and favorably known to Harlem's new and nocturnal aristocracy of 'brains' and booze. He has been wined and dined by the seekers after salvation by publicity, by the pundits of 'advancement' and by the white pen-pushers who manufacture retail prominence for the smart snobbies of the New York Renaissance—'New York Negro type, Model 1926.'"[61]

Larsen was implicated in Harrison's litany of abuse. "'Nigger Heaven'—the title and the theme should be highly appreciated by Van Vechten's dusky hosts—and hostesses—over whose bottles he imbibed the conception of Harlem, which is here exhibited." After attacking Van Vechten as a literary "pansy," Harrison concluded by returning to a long-running feud with the likes of James Weldon Johnson and Langston Hughes:

The futile footing of our "intellectual" ephemeridae is fairly well indicated in the character of Byron Kasson, which is (like the other chief characters), a composite of elements to be found in the real Harlem. . . . One thing, however, Van Vechten has achieved and we thank him for it—he has risen up like a German submarine to throw the fear of "Nigger Heaven" into "the whole crowd of timorous and flocking birds" who hover around in Harlem dreaming that they are writing "Negro" literature, because Van Vechten's kind has coddled them at pink-teas and literary contests.[62]

Johnson shrugged it off: "I was amused by Hubert Harrison's article in the New York Amsterdam News. Harrison was not reviewing the book, he was, perhaps unconsciously 'reviewing' the people in Harlem he doesn't like."[63] Nella had written Van Vechten at the same time, "Hubert Harrison. Ugh! More about him another time."[64]

In early October Larsen was still consoling, flattering, and encouraging Van Vechten. "Surely Nigger Heaven is the most reviewed book of this season. . . . The more I think of it, the more I believe that it would make a corking good play, and be well received too. Why don't you?"[65] No friend of Van Vechten was giving him more caresses over Nigger Heaven than Nella Imes. Toward the end of September, in a letter inviting "My dear Carl" to her house for dinner, Nella responded to several of the reviews: "I liked Burton Rascoe's review. He did you much better than the Blind Bow Boy in 1923. I was just re-reading his review of that, before your letter came."[66]

On the last Sunday in September, a glorious fall afternoon, Nella fixed dinner for six. Alonzo Smith brought Carl with him from Manhattan. Dr. George C. ("Chester" or "G.C.B.") Booth—a friend and business partner of Elmer and of Walter White—and his wife Gussie were the other guests. John Davis (Jessie Fauset's replacement as literary editor of The Crisis) showed up with some friends following the meal, and the conversation drifted to a new idea that either Larsen or Van Vechten proposed: a bookshop should be opened in Harlem, with Nella in charge. The group developed the notion that a budding Negro market for books could be nurtured in Harlem itself, under black direction, in concert with the renaissance. The evening ended at about eleven, when Nella and Elmer drove Van Vechten down to the Forty-Second Street ferry, but the idea kept percolating.

Two days later, trying to raise money for a business venture, Elmer dropped in on Van Vechten to ask for a letter of introduction to Lawrence Langner (a patent lawyer and co-director of the Theatre Guild). Exactly which "business" Elmer wanted help with is unspecified in Van Vechten's diary, but a trading corporation in which he was a stockholder, along with Walter White, Paul Robeson,

Hubert ("Hap") Delaney, Alonzo Smith, Emmett Scott, Jr., Louis T. Wright, A. J. Ayer, Chester Booth, and others, had held an urgent meeting at Booth's home in Harlem on the fifteenth of September, to discuss setting up a permanent office.[67]

This is probably also about the time that Elmer changed jobs, leaving Burrows Magnetic Equipment Company to become a research engineer for Edward A. Everett, a manufacturer of railroad equipment in Manhattan. Elmer was by now a fairly renowned physicist of international reputation. His research on practical applications of quantum theory to electromagnetic radiation had many potential uses in railroad switching mechanisms, signaling equipment, and the like. At his new job he devoted most of his time to laboratory work aimed at developing new patents for such devices. He apparently was also paid very well—at least $6,000 a year.[68]

In the meantime, Nella was on fire with the bookshop idea. "I've been unable to sleep since Sunday," she wrote Van Vechten three days later, "so excited about the book shop." On Tuesday she had spent the day in New York talking to people about it, notably at the NAACP offices downtown:

> To everyone except Walter I merely said that a friend of mine was thinking of opening a book shop in Harlem. You will be interested to learn that Walter has been bitten by the same idea almost. . . . That['s] why I told *him* about it being your plan. We had a very good talk together, in the midst of which we became so excited that we were seized with the desire to rush up to Harlem and evict a poor music shop keeper on Seventh Avenue and 135th Street . . . but the phone rang and the music shop keeps.[69]

White was thinking of consulting with his contacts at Doubleday about the idea. (They had a "Negro" book exhibit at the time in their bookshop at Pennsylvania Station.) James Weldon Johnson had already talked with publishers about the need for wider distribution of books in Harlem and they were well disposed to work with a reliable person or agency. Secretaries of the YMCA and YWCA, Nella felt, would welcome it, advertise it, and order books through it. The 135th Street Branch would also advertise the shop and order books through it, as others already did through the bookstores in their neighborhoods. And books they needed immediately they would purchase on the spot (as when visiting lecturers came and their books were all checked out). Nella was already planning a trip to Harlem to ask around at churches and schools. "I'm sure the ministers will be glad to help. . . . And Bibles!" Gussie Booth's father, minister of St. Philip's Episcopal Church, said that during religious holidays and for confirmations parishioners would buy dozens of prayer books. And Chester Booth, Nella said, would "whoop it up and also advise all his patients to buy certain books on care of the teeth . . . (he has a huge practice)." Several other doctors promised to order through the store. "Several friends of mine who buy from twenty to forty books a year promised patronage, and one who buys a book a week."[70]

Two days later Walter White had an even more ambitious idea. Why not start a "Negro" version of the new Book-of-the-Month Club and operate it out of the store? "It occurred to me that, being really the only Negro book shop in the country, it might well become a national thing, drawing its customers from every part of the country."[71] The venture's "niche" would be those people, mostly black, who were particularly interested in books by or about the Negro. Once Nella had established this base, White suggested, she could probably interest her customers in novels by Willa Cather, Sherwood Anderson, "and others who are not distinctly racial."[72] She could get mailing lists from people like James Weldon Johnson and Charles S. Johnson. White offered to help, adding that Carl had just telephoned and wanted to see him: "I suspect he wants to tell me about the book shop."[73]

Van Vechten, however, had cooled on the idea and, somewhat alarmed by the alacrity with which Larsen and White had seriously taken it up, backed off. Probably the financial risk had sobered him; he was a conservative investor. He must have written Larsen to this effect, for her next letter, precisely a week later, concedes, "Oh, I do understand that the bookshop is only a vision. But, it's an exciting one. Inciting too." In the meantime, she had gone back to her novel: "Celebrated the return by destroying a good half of what was completed. It *was* awful."[74] Walter White didn't seem to think so, having written her that he admired particularly the way she handled the scene between her "heroine" and the principal of the school where she worked.[75] But it is not clear that White had read very far into the book. If he responded any further at this early stage, he did so in person.

In the midst of the flap over *Nigger Heaven* the October issue of *Opportunity* came out, containing James Weldon Johnson's laudatory review of that novel and Frank Horne's sharp response to Nella Imes's "charmingly energetic partizanship" for Walter White's *Flight*. Feeling that in White's case Nella had mistaken "the *intention* for the accomplishment, the *conception* for the expression," Horne apparently suspected that Mr. White himself was behind her letter: "She truly frightens me at times by the clarity of insight she has as to the *intentions* of Mr. White." Without budging from his position, Horne closed with a firm handshake extended across Nella to his friend Walter: "This interest she displays as well as that which has come to my ears from other quarters have been most gratifying. But I remain quite incorrigible. I firmly assert that Mr. White is a jolly fine fellow, but I as vehemently insist that he has not written a jolly fine book."[76] If White was hoping for more fireworks, Horne effectively put an end to the show, in which Nella's part seemed a bit silly. White tried to keep it going with a fatuous, insulting letter of his own responding to Horne's response to Nella's response to Horne's review of White's book, but even though Johnson published the letter in the December issue of *Opportunity,* the tempest blew over with little effect, except on Larsen's opinion of White's ill-disguised vanity (on which more anon).[77]

On the sixteenth of October, Elmer and Nella went to a small housewarming party at Vi and Elmer Stoner's new place on Christopher Street in the Village, meeting up with the Harrises, Dorothy Peterson, and Van Vechten, whom the Imeses' drove home at 3 A.M. on their way back to Jersey City.[78] Meanwhile, Gladys White had landed a role in Laurence Stallings' opera *Deep River,* which opened on Broadway on October 4.[79] It was Gladys' professional acting debut, in a cast of one hundred that included ten African Americans—another sign of the race's "progress," as any mixed cast in serious drama was then thought to be. On October 24, a Sunday, the Imeses again went out to Dorothy Peterson's for a party, and again ran into Van Vechten, Elmer and Vi Stoner, Gwendolyn Bennett, and Frank Horne. The Imeses with Van Vechten and the Stoners then migrated to the Stoners' for more drinks until 1:30 in the morning.[80]

The controversy over *Nigger Heaven* continued unabated as Larsen drafted her first novel (then entitled "Cloudy Amber"), and Larsen never tired of following it. At the end of October, the 135th Street Branch hosted a discussion of *Nigger Heaven* at its first "book evening" of the season. In her letter inviting the author, Ernestine Rose archly inquired, "Why not take this occasion to find out the truth about the Library, which you have used in your book quite freely, and, forgive me for saying so,—with almost complete unaccuracy."[81] Knowing what he was in for, Van Vechten declined, as did all of his friends. Clarissa Scott Delaney (Emmett Scott's daughter, just married to Elmer's friend Hubert Delaney) presided. By 8:15 the auditorium was packed, and after Delaney's introductory remarks Harlem journalists and others began a series of acrid denunciations of Van Vechten and his black friends. According to the *Pittsburgh Courier,* a nationally circulated black newspaper whose chief correspondents lived in New York, "They were all bitterly scored."[82] Yet about the same time, Van Vechten was nominated for the Spingarn Medal of the NAACP, the organization's highest honor. Nella told him to refuse the nomination: "If you got it, you'd be lynched—by Negroes. Take my advice, refuse it, graciously but firmly."[83] Supposedly, he had already been hanged in effigy at 135th Street and Seventh Avenue.

On November 4, Elmer and Nella again went to Carl and Fania's for dinner; afterward, Rebecca West and Konrad Bercovici dropped in, followed by Lawrence Langner and his wife Armina Marshall, and then the South Carolinians DuBose and Dorothy Heyward—staying until 2:00 in the morning.[84] It was the Heywards' first experience of meeting "educated" Negroes on such informal terms. At one point the conversation turned to a play the Heywards had just co-written, a dramatization of DuBose's novel of the Charleston waterfront, *Porgy*. Shortly after midnight, Carl pulled out his copy of the novel and DuBose inscribed it to him: "In memory of this night and new friends."[85]

"Yes, we did have a good time at your house last Thursday," Nella later wrote, "I enjoyed every minute of the whole SEVEN hours. We almost spent the night, didn't we? Isn't Mr. Heyward interesting to meet?—and natural? You know, theoretically, I hate all Southerners 'as a matter of principle,' but actually, I have never yet met one that I didn't like. I'm terribly anxious about his play. I mean I hope that he is able to get the people he wants to do it."[86] Originally the play was supposed to be produced that fall, but the Heywards wanted black actors (rather than whites in blackface) and the director claimed to be having difficulty finding enough black talent with extensive experience in "serious" drama. The director was losing interest and the fate of the play was in doubt.[87]

On Sunday, the seventh of November, Rudolph and Jane Fisher were at the Imeses' home for dinner. They tuned the radio to WEAF, just in time to learn they had missed Fania Marinoff performing in *The School for Scandal*—an appropriate title for the hullabaloo in which they were all implicated.[88] As if in direct response to James Weldon Johnson's defense of *Nigger Heaven* in the October *Opportunity*, Floyd Calvin in the *Pittsburgh Courier* used the book, as Hubert Harrison had, to flay Van Vechten's friends:

> It is clear that Mr. Van Vechten tried to give a faithful picture of the set he associated with. His descriptions are at least accurate, for one can see he was writing what he saw. . . . But we do not blame Mr. Van Vechten for the wave of "Niggerism" which this book has caused. . . . We blame those Negroes who were practically Mr. Van Vechten's guides in Harlem while gathering his material, who were in position to stifle the influence of the work on its initial appearance, had they had the courage and interest of the race at heart as they have so often claimed.[89]

Soon after Calvin's column appeared, Van Vechten sent a copy of it to Nella, along with some other clippings. She had just returned from "a tiresome visit in Philadelphia among the ultra-religious"—meaning Grace and William Lloyd Imes, whose opinion of *Nigger Heaven* was identical to that of Calvin. "Thanks awfully for the clippings," she replied. "They are pathetically amusing. Have you noticed that when Nordics talk against the admission of Negroes to their homes, etc., it is rank predjudice, but when we take the same attitude about white folks it is race loyalty? I met Floyd Calvin some five years ago just once. He is a fool, a boor and a snob."[90]

The review that stung Van Vechten most deeply was Dr. Du Bois's in *The Crisis.* "Carl Van Vechten's *Nigger Heaven* is a blow in the face," he began, and the rhetoric escalated in ferocity from there. "It is an affront to the hospitality of black folk and to the intelligence of white."[91] Since Du Bois had never been hospitable to Van Vechten, Walter White wrote to ask on behalf of his friends: "Is such a dictum literary criticism or is it a matter solely for the consideration of those who have shown hospitality to Mr. Van Vechten?"[92]

Du Bois's position derived in part from a late-Victorian aesthetic sensibility and, as Emily Bernard has suggested, his well-known contempt for homosexuality. "Life to [Van Vechten] is just one damned orgy after another, with hate, hurt, gin and sadism," he snarled.[93] Yet also motivating Du Bois's review was an often justified aversion to certain tendencies of the time, including the white "invasion" of Harlem, the flourishing nightclub culture that obscured what black life in Harlem was mainly about, and (as Du Bois saw it) the corruption of young black talent by white cultural vampires—Carl Van Vechten being the most visible and energetic of them. Since the play *Lulu Belle* and the appearance of *Nigger Heaven,* the "white trade" in Harlem was building into a nightly avalanche. Citing the popularity of those works, Anita Handy—daughter of the "father of the blues," W. C. Handy—had become a professional tour guide to the black mecca's Nordic pilgrims. She was prepared, said her blue-enveloped mailers, "to carry you through Harlem as you would go slumming through Chinatown." In fact, Dorothy Peterson learned, she was married to a "Chinaman" and got the idea from him.[94]

Du Bois's larger point concerned white hegemony over the culture industry, but the instigation was partly intra-racial cultural politics. Langston Hughes, of whom Du Bois was fond, had declared his independence from elder black (and white) critics in "The Negro Artist and the Racial Mountain," a black bohemian manifesto declaring allegiance to the spirit of jazz and blues and a rejection of the assimilationist impulses of the black bourgeoisie. Hughes's opponents, on the other hand, accused him of "selling out" to the whites. His first book of poems, published that year by Knopf, had carried a preface by Van Vechten.

White decadents, in Du Bois's view, were co-opting the Negro Renaissance, and the appearance of *Nigger Heaven* gave him the chance to open up.[95] In his heart of hearts, Van Vechten feared that Du Bois—whose intelligence he deeply respected—might have a point. Despite the assurances of his friends, he was never confident that in this novel he had done a good thing, and when the Theatre Guild approached him in early 1927 about producing a dramatic version of *Nigger Heaven* by one of New York's top directors—a production certain to make lots of money—he waved it off.[96] He began despairing that he would never be able to write again, and in fact soon he would abandon fiction writing forever, even as his dedication to the long-term cause of the Negro changed and deepened. It appears that he wanted to make up for his mistakes.

On Sunday the fourteenth of November, the Imeses went nightclubbing in New York, meeting up with the Whites for a while, and then headed to the downtown apartment of Harry Block, senior editor at Alfred A. Knopf. While chatting with Walter over a drink, Nella mentioned that she was just finishing her manuscript of 35,000 words and facing the horror of typing it. White suggested that his secretary, Carrie Overton, might be able to help out. Completely incompetent as a typist, Larsen reminded White the next day and threw herself on his mercy—or rather Overton's: "I'm very anxious about this. You might tell her that I'm a *very* nice person and very helpless—excite her pity."[97] Happy to repay a debt, Walter wrote Nella back the next day that Overton had promised to help. He then invited Nella, with Elmer, to dinner for later in the week—but not Sunday, "for that is the maid's day off and we do want you to have a good meal."[98] Unlike Gladys, Nella usually cooked and cleaned her own house. But she had no children to raise, and Gladys was a month pregnant with her second child—a remarkably rare condition among Nella Larsen's women friends.

On the twenty-fourth, at the request of the publisher, Larsen wrote out a brief biographical narrative for use in publicity. It responded directly to a series of questions about the author's past life, "human-interest material," hobbies, prominent friends who might write blurb material, education, and whether a spouse should be mentioned or kept secret. In stylish script, Nella wrote out a story revealing the close parallels between her life and that of Helga Crane. It left out her public health nursing and teaching at Lincoln to create a more streamlined narrative of her career, and it withheld the name of her husband.

> Nella Larsen is a mulatto, the daughter of a Danish lady and a Negro from the Virgin Islands, formerly the Danish West Indies. When she was two years old her father died, and shortly afterward her mother married a man of her own race and nationality.
>
> Her formal education began at the age of eight. She and her half sister— child of the second marriage—attended a small private school, whose pupils were mostly the children of German or Scandinavian parents.

When she was sixteen she went alone to Denmark to visit relatives of her mothers in Copenhagen where she remained for three years.

On her return to America she entered a training school for nurses in New York City and after graduating accepted a position as Head Nurse of the hospital at Tuskegee Institute,—the school founded by Booker T. Washington—, but her dislike of conditions there, and the school authorities dislike of her appearance and manner were both so intense that after a year they parted with mutual disgust and relief.

When she returned to New York she applied for admission to the Library School of the New York Public Library, and was accepted as an experiment, it being entirely contrary to the policy of the school to admitted [sic] negroes. On graduating she worked as an assistant and later as Childrens Librarian in the New York Public Library until January 1926.

She is married. Her husband, a PhD., University of Michigan, is a research physicist and employed by an engineering development corporation.

Her hobbies are bridge and collecting Van Vechteniana.[99]

The closing phrase, in a promotional bio that she knew might end up in advertising or jacket copy, poked a finger in the eye of critics like Calvin, Harrison, and Du Bois.

On the first Saturday in December, Larsen and Dorothy Peterson visited Van Vechten during the day, Nella bringing the newly typed manuscript, "Cloudy Amber," for Van Vechten to read. He advised her about the possibility of rejection and worried about her reaction if it should be turned down. He read it that very evening after dinner, finding it, as he recorded in his daybook, "in many ways remarkable."[100] He wrote Nella about it within the next day or so, giving a number of detailed comments and offering to take the book personally to Knopf. She responded with thanks on the seventh, adding:

> I was intending to write you anyway to say what should have been said Saturday, but I am not good at saying these things.
>
> This. If the Knopfs don't take the thing, I will, of course be disappointed, but, nothing more. Not surprised, or shocked, or cross. And, I am more grateful to you than I know how to say, for reading it and taking it to them, regardless of the outcome. I realize very well that any author, black, white, or green, would thank his stars for such favor from such source. And, certainly, had I been told, in the not so distant past, that I was to fall into such good fortune, I should have considered the prophet a little mad, to put it mildly.

She knew that Van Vechten was concerned that a rejection might hurt her feelings and harm their friendship. Still stinging from Du Bois's recent attack on him, during their conversation on the fourth he must have alluded to the review, but she reassured him: "So, even if, because of the thing's lack of merit, or of publishing conditions, they don't take it, I won't feel that you have 'violated my hospitality',—which, incidentally, has been returned seventy times seven—, but that you have gone out of your way to do me a great kindness, which leaves me eternally in your debt."[101]

Even if the manuscript failed at Knopf, Larsen could have submitted it to Viking or another press through Walter White. She was not dependent on Van Vechten; but Knopf was her top choice because of its prestige. It was the preeminent American publisher of modern fiction, while Viking was still new and untried, Boni and Liveright (where Nella's acquaintance T. R. Smith was the talent scout) had a reputation for publishing outré titles and "sex books" along with the occasional modern classic, and Harcourt Brace was considered rather conventional. These were the chief presses that had so far shown interest in African American creative writing, and Knopf was easily the most prestigious for a debut novel. It also packaged them most handsomely.

Van Vechten worried about the novel's brevity and thought the title should be changed. Nella did not disagree: "The truth is that I got awfully tired of it about the middle of the Copenhagen episode. That and the last chapter ought to be longer. I should hate terribly to have to write even one more word for the damned thing, but I suppose I could if I absolutely had to. I don't think the title is so good either." She closed by reiterating her gratitude for his interest: "Yours for further 'violation of hospitality,' or as George Gershwin (wasn't it) put it 'Do it again.'"[102]

THIRTEEN

Quicksand

L IKE many debut novels, *Quicksand* was largely autobiographical, and like many ethnic novels focused on the life of an individual, it explored the consequences of choices the author had forgone.[1] Larsen had never before exposed so much of her past or of her inner life, except possibly to Elmer. Here she gave vent to all her rage against the forces she had fought against so long—not, however, by following the life of a great heroine either triumphing over racism or being crushed by it. Helga Crane is a "mixed" person in more ways than one: often less than admirable; exquisitely sensitive and intelligent yet quiet; craving acceptance yet outwardly aloof or seemingly arrogant; of lower-class background yet to all appearances comfortable and well bred; sensuous yet intensely self-restrained and unsure of what would bring her happiness; defiant of restrictions yet willing at times to be used if it helps her get what she wants out of a relationship. To the extent that this is a self-portrait, it is a highly critical one, possibly an indication of the effect of "self-observation with nonidentification," shorn of its metaphysical trappings. Yet the fact that the approach to the main character is naturalistic and unmelodramatic intensifies the force of the attack on social institutions in which Larsen herself had for so long been trapped. Only with knowledge of Larsen's past and current connections can one appreciate the sheer audacity of the novel from its opening page. By the same token, if novelists live most intensely in the act of creating their fictions, and if Larsen revealed little of herself outside her stories, then examining *Quicksand* and its composition as a chapter in her life may have its rewards. Here Larsen emerges from the shadows and, finding her voice, provides an unprecedented vision of her world.

What dismays many readers of *Quicksand* is Helga Crane's sudden break from one mode of life to a completely different one at the end of the novel. Critics charge that Larsen does not provide sufficient narrative preparation for Helga's sudden conversion to Christianity and marriage to a Southern preacher. That is to say, Helga's personality lacks unity and coherence—it lacks identity. This common judgment is only a more intense expression of the sense that at any point in her life, if not for a perverse flaw in her personality, Helga might have settled into one of the social niches offered her—in Naxos, in Copenhagen, in Harlem, even in the rural South. She might, that is, have made the adjustments that bring identity and recognition. Instead, she disappears.

In the early months of 1927, Larsen made revisions to her manuscript, apparently at the request of editors at Knopf.[2] Van Vechten's concern that the book was too short, combined with hers that it was "too thin," particularly in the Copenhagen episodes and the conclusion, suggests that this is where the revisions concentrated as she expanded the manuscript from 35,000 to about 56,000 words. Van Vechten's reservations about the title "Cloudy Amber" inspired a new one, "Quicksand," shifting the focus from the color of the protagonist and the "clouds" obscuring her life, or the appearance of a semiprecious jewel, to the motif of disappearance, of being swallowed up without a trace. Nella dedicated the book to her husband, "E.S.I." but chose to use her maiden name—Nella Larsen—as author, perhaps influenced by the many accomplished women she now knew who had kept their maiden names. One result is that in future years she would be known by two names, Larsen and Imes.

For an epigraph, Larsen chose four lines from Langston Hughes's poem "Cross":

> My old man died in a fine big house.
> My ma died in a shack.
> I wonder where I'm gonna die,
> Being neither white nor black?[3]

The theme of "mulatto" tragedy had a long history in American fiction, but Larsen's book veered sharply away from the conventions of novels by both blacks and whites centering on mixed-race protagonists. This may have had less to do with a conscious decision to undermine the old models than with the fact that, as far as "race" literature is concerned, the models available to Larsen bore no resemblance to her personal history. With few exceptions (most notably *Our Nig*, by Harriet E. Wilson, which also was autobiographical), in fiction about mulattos the mother was black and the father a wealthy white man—a convention that has largely been maintained to the present day. Even in recent fiction featuring "colored" children of unions between black men and white women, the woman is typically rich, or a slaveholder, or from a wealthy family. The many biracial children born over the generations to working-class and servant-class interracial couples remain largely absent from American literature. The very epigraph to *Quicksand* fits poorly with Helga Crane's story.

If Larsen did not have many literary models of mulatto fiction to follow, her broad reading certainly played a central role in how she developed the work. Her crucial literary allusions are to Ibsen, Anatole France, and the Greek classics. Her technical strategies derive from writers whom most American scholars would call the later naturalists but whom many at the time would have considered modernists. Her novel reverberates powerfully in theme and method with landmarks of the Scandinavian "modern breakthrough" such as Ibsen's dramas and Jacobsen's *Marie Grubbe,* as well as with John Galsworthy's *Forsyte Saga,* quite possibly her favorite fiction at the time. The theme of a passionate woman's inability to fulfill her nature, and that of a marriage based on a lie, pervaded Ibsen's most famous plays as well as Jacobsen's and Galsworthy's masterpieces, which had a strong impact on Larsen's general aesthetic sensibility. Jacobsen's practice of leaving out narrative linkages between scenes and minimizing dependence on action apparently influenced her. Developing chapters as distinct dramatic scenes, which in turn can be easily grouped into "acts," she used an essentially dramatic technique of narrative development and revelation of character—one reason that contemporary reviewers found her novel clipped and spare, leaving much unstated. Yet she does not rely chiefly on dialogue; much of the interest resides in what might be called the drama of perception filtered through the consciousness of Helga Crane. "The psychology of the scene" and the "poetic conception of the character" count more than actions and words, to borrow Larsen's own phrasing from her defense of Walter White's *Flight.*[4]

When Larsen shifts from Helga as the central consciousness (therefore "subjective," prone to error) to a more "objective" narrative mode, it is usually to dramatize Helga's relation to her immediate environment. Portions of the book's first paragraph might have come out of the opening chapter of *Marie Grubbe.* Jacobsen preferred an indirect method of rendering a character's personality, using evocative imagery in place of psychological analysis, describing the environment and clothing (particularly women's dress) as an index of character and situation. In the opening of her novel, too, Larsen employs aspects of the arabesque—repetitive interlocking patterns of imagery or even syntax—which Jacobsen picked up from Poe and passed on to the French symbolists of the 1890s. The style, rhythm, and syntax match the arabesque and orientalist images:

> Helga Crane sat alone in her room, which at that hour, eight in the evening, was in soft gloom. Only a single reading lamp, dimmed by a great black and red shade, made a pool of light on the blue Chinese carpet, on the bright covers of the books which she had taken down from their long shelves, on the white pages of the opened one selected, on the shining brass bowl crowded with many-colored nasturtiums beside her on the low table, and on the oriental silk which covered the stool at her slim feet. It was a comfortable room,

furnished with rare and intensely personal taste, flooded with Southern sun in the day, but shadowy just then with the drawn curtains and the single shaded light. Large, too. So large that the spot where Helga sat was a small oasis in a desert of darkness. And eerily quiet. (*Quicksand,* p. 1)

Continuing the orientalist motif, Larsen has Helga reading Marmaduke Pickthall's *Saïd the Fisherman,* the book from Knopf's Blue Jade Library that Van Vechten had recommended and that Nella and Elmer admired.

The essential narrative pattern is that of a labyrinth, to which Larsen alludes by opening her novel in a place called "Naxos." In classical mythology, Ariadne is a Cretan princess who helps Theseus to escape the Labyrinth built by her father, King Minos, and whom Theseus then abandons on the remote island of Naxos. According to the most common conclusion of the legend, Dionysus finds Ariadne, marries her, and makes her immortal. Plutarch gives a different ending, however, in which Theseus leaves Ariadne pregnant and she dies in childbirth. Meanwhile, Theseus sails to Delos and institutes a dance called the *Geranos,* the "Crane," named after the bird whose movements resemble the twistings and turnings of the Labyrinth.[5] The Labyrinth might well serve as a figure for the prison of race and gender from which Helga Crane is never able to emerge. Indeed, the Labyrinth was originally constructed to hide a creature of "mixed" and forbidden origins—a monster known as the Minotaur that is half man, half bull—to which King Minos' wife Pasiphaë gave birth after having intercourse with a bull. According to Ovid's famous version in *The Metamorphoses,* "In [Minos'] absence the monstrous child which the queen had borne, to the disgrace of the king's family, had grown up, and the strange hybrid creature had revealed his wife's disgusting love affair to everyone. Minos determined to rid his home of this shameful sight, by shutting the monster away in an enclosure of elaborate and involved design, where it could not be seen."[6]

Helga Crane's story is in one sense a figure of the labyrinth in the form of an attempt to escape it, and Helga parallels the Minotaur whom the labyrinth was intended to hide. Yet just as the Minotaur is a kind of double of his half-sister Ariadne in some interpretations, so Helga Crane's story resembles that of Ariadne with its alternate endings. The version of the myth that says Dionysus/Bacchus (god of vegetation) marries Ariadne and makes her immortal fits Helga's hopes when, after a religious orgy of "almost Bacchic vehemence," she goes off with Reverend Pleasant Green. It turns out, however, that Plutarch's version of the myth is the correct one in relation to Helga Crane's fate. She is not saved in the end, but rather left in childbed, possibly to die. The myth also resonates with the relationship between Helga's parents, dealing as it does with a daughter who falls in love with a man of another people, cutting her links to her father, and then suffers abandonment. The novel, with its allusions and narrative structure, identifies the mother's and daughter's predicaments as intertwined, as products of the same race and gender system.

In her treatment of Naxos, transparently based on Tuskegee, Larsen presented the most bitter fictional indictment of that institution prior to Ralph Ellison's *Invisible Man,* and she had more to risk in offering it than Ellison would more than two decades later. Helga's alienated position, which she attributes to her family background, enables an acute perception of the contradictions and hypocrisies around her: "The dean was a woman from one of the 'first families'—a great 'race' woman; she, Helga Crane, a despised mulatto, but something intuitive, some unanalyzed driving spirit of loyalty to the inherent racial need for gorgeousness told her that bright colors *were* fitting and that dark-complexioned people *should* wear yellow, green, and red" (*Quicksand,* p. 18). In what may be the first fictional attack on popular hair-straightening techniques (the major source of A'Lelia Walker's fortune), Helga finds herself wondering "just what form of vanity it was that had induced an intelligent girl like Margaret Creighton to turn what was probably nice, live, crinkly hair, perfectly suited to her smooth dark skin and agreeable round features, into a dead straight, greasy, ugly mass" (p. 14). Larsen's attack on "race women" and "race men" (but never on "the race"—that is, never on black people as such) is partly enabled by her perspective as an outsider; like Helga Crane, she is a "despised mulatto." Larsen's defiant stance toward the institution of race is not a form of "color blindness" but precisely the opposite: it both derives from and enables her genuine appreciation of human differences that reductive "race" thinking brutalizes on a procrustean bed.

Both at Naxos and in Harlem, Helga's mulatto appearance and European manners, combined with her unspeakable origins, bring status to those for whom she serves as a subordinate partner or retainer. Robert Anderson, the director of Naxos, suggests that she is needed at the institute for her "dignity and breeding," but Helga reacts indignantly to his assumptions: "The joke is on you, Dr. Anderson. My father was a gambler who deserted my mother, a white immigrant. It is even uncertain that they were married. As I said at first, I don't belong here" (p. 21). According to the text, these comments come from a "lacerated pride." In reaction against the pain of losing her mother and suffering the racism of her white relatives, then enduring the subordination to a black elite that disdains miscegenation but nonetheless mimics the white elite, Helga has developed her own sense of ethnic honor.

Shortly after her interchange with Anderson, Helga feels shame for betraying her mother: "She had outraged her own pride, and she had terribly wronged her mother by her insidious implication" (p. 23). Helga's sense of personal integrity, bound up with her relation to her mother, makes her relationship to "whiteness" and "blackness" different from that of her black friends. This is not a pride in "white blood"; it is a psychologically necessary identification with the one woman who had loved her but whom "race" had defined as utterly different from her. What accommodation can she make to this institution, which pits itself directly against the most primary of human bonds?

Returning to Chicago to seek shelter and aid from her kindly uncle after her abrupt resignation from Naxos, Helga discovers too late that he has remarried: she knows what to expect of his new wife but must be dragged through the ordeal of rejection. More directly than anywhere else, here we see how "race" trumps "family" in the American context. After Helga introduces herself as Peter Nilssen's niece, his sister's daughter, she feels the wife's latent antagonism followed by a completely specious denial of their family connection:

> "Oh, yes! I remember about you now. I'd forgotten for a moment. *Well,* he isn't exactly your uncle, is he? Your mother wasn't married, was she? I mean, to your father?"
>
> "I—I don't know," stammered the girl, feeling pushed down to the uttermost depths of ignominy.
>
> "Of course she wasn't." (*Quicksand*, p. 28)

As Helga, frozen in shame, struggles to find the doorknob, her aunt adds: "And please remember that my husband is not your uncle. No indeed! Why, that, that would make me your aunt! He's not—" (p. 29). The precision and realism of Larsen's dramatic presentation gives us the best insight we have into her own private agonies—which is not to infer that she had precisely this experience—and a unique perspective on the intricacies of racial subjection in both "black" and "white" environments.

Larsen quickly shifts Helga to an all-black environment in which the same underlying rule of the color line holds. We can see from Helga's interactions with Mrs. Hayes-Rore, the "'race' woman" who takes the girl under her wing, and later with the woman's niece Anne Grey, that the price of acceptance into their society is a sort of "passing" that causes suffocation and self-contempt. Like the people of Naxos, Mrs. Hayes-Rore values having Helga as a secretary because of the young woman's looks and refinement. At first, this bodes well for Helga, and as they come to know each other, the older woman asks how a girl like Helga could so easily pick up and travel from Chicago to New York with a stranger. Won't Helga's "people" object, or at least make inquiries? To the simple answer that she has no "people"—"You see, there's only me"—Mrs. Hayes-Rore responds that everyone has "people": "If you didn't have people, you wouldn't be living" (p. 38). Helga finally confides to the older woman the mystery of her lack of family—a mystery almost identical to Nella Larsen's—first mockingly and then with "that sore sensation of revolt, and again the torment which she had gone through loomed before her as something brutal and undeserved" (p. 39). As Helga speaks, now tearfully baring her grief and rage, Hayes-Rore turns her head completely away, and their faces suddenly harden. "It was almost as if they had slipped on masks. The girl wished to hide her turbulent feeling and to appear indifferent to Mrs. Hayes-Rore's opinion of her story. The woman felt that the story, dealing as it did with race intermingling and possibly adultery, was beyond definite discussion. For among black people, as among white people, it is tacitly understood that these things are not mentioned—and therefore they do not exist" (p. 39).

Helga's introduction to elite black society is predicated on her denial of her mother—her denial of the very "people" that Mrs. Hayes-Rore insists everyone must have in order to exist. Before arriving at Anne Grey's home in Harlem, Mrs. Hayes-Rore advises Helga not to mention that her "people are white" —"Colored people won't understand it, and after all it's your own business" (p. 41). She will introduce Helga with the half-truth that the girl's mother is dead, allowing Helga, in effect, to "pass." Helga, in gratitude, reaches out to take the woman's "slightly soiled hand." In later years, Helga has only to close her eyes to remember her introduction to Anne Grey under the shadow of this half-truth, having "her hand grasped in quick sympathy" and feeling "like a criminal" (p. 42).

After moving in with Anne, Helga eagerly acclimates herself to her new environment, the first place she has felt truly at home. Larsen's early descriptions of Anne Grey from Helga's point of view are admiring and unconstrained. Beyond Anne Grey's elegantly comfortable life, Helga equally revels in black Harlem's diversity and expressive styles. Larsen left eloquent witness of her appreciation for the beauty of black life apart from white intrusion, and of the feeling of satisfaction within an all-black world:

> She lost that tantalizing oppression of loneliness and isolation which always, it seemed, had been a part of her existence. But, while the continuously gorgeous panorama of Harlem fascinated her, thrilled her, the sober mad rush of white New York failed entirely to stir her. Like thousands of other Harlem dwellers, she patronized its shops, its theaters, its art galleries, and its restaurants, and read its papers, without considering herself a part of the monster. And she was satisfied, unenvious. For her this Harlem was enough. Of that

white world, so distant, so near, she asked only indifference. No, not at all did she crave, from those pale and powerful people, awareness. Sinister folk, she considered them, who had stolen her birthright. Their past contribution to her life, which had been but shame and grief, she had hidden away from brown folk in a locked closet, "never," she told herself, "to be reopened." (*Quicksand*, p. 45)

In exchange for her new sense of belonging, Helga has locked her mother away. Briefly she feels free. But the next chapter begins with the revelation that within Helga Crane, "in a deep recess, crouched discontent. . . . She felt shut in, trapped." Helga needs something she cannot name, "something vaguely familiar" (p. 47).

Anne Grey's obsession with the race problem particularly distresses Helga. Although Helga has suffered from white racism more intensely than any of the race women in this novel, Anne's racial ardor begins to feel oppressive to her. Anne's wholesale contempt for all whites buttresses the color line and betrays a kind of self-hatred, given that she "aped their clothes, their manners, and their gracious ways of living"—even preferred their music (p. 48). Her name, Anne Grey, suggests the dependence of her own "black" identity on an abject whiteness within ("Miss Anne" being a derogatory term for a white woman).

Larsen draws a distinct connection between Anne Grey's abhorrence of interracial intimacy, her condescending attitude to common black folk, and her rejection of vernacular culture. Moreover, Larsen attributes similar attitudes to James Vayle, Helga's erstwhile fiancé who fits so naturally into the Naxos "mold." Anne's status and self-regard depend as much on racial segregation as on class stratification within the black community, both of which have deeply wounded Helga Crane. Thus, the "sisterhood" between the two women is powerfully challenged by their quite different structural and psychological relationships to the color line.

The difference Helga feels from Anne grows acute in a cabaret scene featuring the beautiful and enchanting Audrey Denney, who frequents mixed society and dates both black and white men. Audrey and Helga are similarly dressed— Audrey in an extremely *"décolleté"* apricot dress and Helga in a "cobwebby black net touched with orange" that Anne thinks "too *décolleté*" (pp. 60, 56). (Later, in Denmark, Helga will be dressed much like Audrey.) Anne comments that the dress gives Helga the look of "something about to fly," provoking Helga's choice of the garment. Effectively, Helga Crane wears something like Audrey's dress covered in a net that restrains flight. Whereas Helga silently admires Audrey Denney's confidence in ignoring racial barriers, Anne finds Audrey "positively obscene" for inviting whites to her parties and for going to theirs. Interracial dancing disgusts her. Yet Anne is no more "black" than Audrey, who radiates racial and sexual self-confidence through appreciation for jazz and an ability to dance with sensuous pleasure.

At this period of Helga's growing alienation from black Harlem, her white uncle sends her $5,000, with the suggestion that she go to Copenhagen and visit her Aunt Katrina, who has always wanted to keep Helga in Denmark. Suddenly the allure of her "white" inheritance feels irresistible, at the same time that a hatred for black people grows powerful within her. "It was as if she were shut up, boxed up, with hundreds of her race, closed up with that something in the racial character which had always been, to her, inexplicable, alien. Why, she demanded in fierce rebellion, should she be yoked to these despised black folk?" (pp. 54–55). But this racial self-hatred is not so simple, for it provokes intense feelings of guilt and self-loathing. Her feelings of entrapment conflict with conscience and political identification: "'They're my own people, my own people,' she kept repeating over and over to herself. It was no good. The feeling could not be routed" (p. 55). In contrast to the method of Walter White or Jessie Fauset, Larsen's treatment of Helga Crane hinges on irresolvable ambivalence and a highly sophisticated approach to the conflict between psychological drives and moral imperatives. No racial or ethnic self-flattery here.

Larsen neither justifies nor condemns Helga Crane in her struggle, but clinically probes the divisions and contradictions of her character. As Mr. Darling, Helga's black employer at a New York insurance company, approaches her cubicle, Helga feels intensely guilty for her thoughts: "Panic seized her. She'd have to get out" (p. 55). Courteous and thoughtful, Mr. Darling excuses her from work, urging her not to hurry. Helga, recognizing the kindness of his gesture, "had the grace to feel ashamed, but there was no softening her determination. The necessity for being alone was too urgent. She hated him and all the others too much" (p. 55). Outdoors, Helga is bitter with self-reproach for her feelings, yet at the same time, "She rejoiced too. She didn't, in spite of her racial markings, belong to these dark segregated people. She was different. She felt it. It wasn't merely a matter of color. It was something broader, deeper, that made folk kin" (p. 55). The narrative will ultimately undermine her new perspective, but not by directing the heroine into a comfortable accommodation with the racial order.

The labyrinth takes on a new twist in Denmark, the native country of Helga's mother. In contrast to Helga's Danish relatives, a white American family could scarcely conceive of arranging a marriage between their mulatto niece and a white artist as a means of advancing their class position. Helga's uncle in the United States effectively disowned her to avoid estranging his wife. In the United States, Helga must hide her connection to her white mother and learn to mix only with Negroes. But aboard the steamer that Helga takes to Copenhagen, a white Danish purser asks her to dine with him, remembering her from the earlier trip she took with her mother. Only outside her own country can Helga be publicly identified with the woman who gave birth to her, loved her, and raised her.

Europeans' fascination with Helga as "exotic" and "savage," emphasizing, even exaggerating, her racial difference, contrasts with the attitude of American whites in the novel. Larsen makes this point explicitly in one of Helga's first comparative cultural observations after meeting members of Copenhagen's high society: "'How odd,' she thought sleepily, 'and how different from America!'" (p. 72). Their use of her also connects with the specifically Danish customs of matchmaking and marriage: "And was she to be treated like a secluded young miss, a Danish *frøkken,* not to be consulted personally even on matters affecting her personally?" (pp. 71–72). Helga was kicked out of her white family in America; her Scandinavian aunt and uncle are, in contrast, intent on looking after her.

Other attitudes also distinguish Danes from Americans. Aunt Katrina (Fru Dahl) tells Helga, "If you've got any brains at all they came from your father"— a pointed contradiction to American racial views of so-called mulattos (p. 78). Fru Dahl unapologetically probes Helga about her feelings toward the artist Axel Olsen, and his toward her; this is the elder woman's traditional role—to explore marriage possibilities. The chapters on Denmark, overall, are an impressive—and unique—comparative study of European and American cultures from the perspective of a young mulatto woman shuttling between them.

Whether or not Helga Crane's aborted romance with Axel Olsen draws from an episode in Larsen's own life, it comments on contemporary events, most notably the sudden fame of Josephine Baker beginning in 1926, when she danced into every Frenchman's heart wearing nothing but a skirt of bananas in the Revue Nègre, produced by Carl Van Vechten's friend Caroline Reagan and managed by his young lover Donald Angus. An instant sex symbol who played to French colonial fantasies with undisputed talent, Baker was supposedly turning away repeated offers of concubinage and marriage from French nobility, according to rumors proudly reported in the black New York papers that summer. Then again, there was Nella's unstoppable friend Nora Holt (she had dropped the name "Ray" by now). In Paris from fall 1926 until spring 1927, she had bleached her red hair and made a sensation on the cabaret circuit as "La Créole Blonde," thanks in part to Van Vechten's advice about clubs and his mailings of the latest songs.[7]

A central feature of this section of *Quicksand* is aimed at demonstrating how

Helga has internalized American views of miscegenation that her Danish relatives cannot comprehend. Helga asks her aunt whether she doesn't think mixed marriage is wrong "in fact as well as principle," to which Fru Dahl replies that it is a foolish question: Danes do not think of such things in relation to individuals. To her aunt, Helga also reveals the reason she could not think of marrying a white man. Such marriages "brought only trouble—to the children—as she herself knew but too well from bitter experience" (p. 78). Fru Dahl cannot understand this reasoning.

Axel Olsen eventually asks for Helga's hand in marriage, but only after she has innocently ignored his hints that he would like to have an affair with her—European artists traditionally formed temporary liaisons with their models, who most often came from lower-class backgrounds. Axel attributes Helga's unresponsiveness to a strategy of playing hard to get—accusing her of having the warm impulsive nature of an African but the "soul of a prostitute," selling herself to the highest bidder (p. 87). Helga responds to his insult in kind, telling him that she is not for sale to any white man. She goes on to explain that she fears he might grow ashamed of a marriage with a black woman, and that he might come to hate black people, as her mother did.

Axel's differences from white American men appear in his very incredulity about her fears: "I have offered you marriage, Helga Crane, and you answer me with some strange talk of race and shame. What nonsense is this?" (p. 88). Helga is at a loss to explain something that in the United States would go without saying. Even Uncle Poul cannot understand her reasoning, what he calls "this foolishness about race": "It can't be just that. You're too sensible" (p. 91).

Crucial to Helga's change in position is the black vaudeville act she witnesses with Axel at a theater known as the Circus, a scene rendered with such psychological precision that one can't help thinking it is based on Larsen's experience. Watching the show, Helga initially feels "shamed, betrayed, as if these pale pink and white people among whom she lived had suddenly been invited to look upon something in her which she had hidden away and wanted to forget" (p. 83). As the only person with a racial connection to the black performers, Helga feels exposed. A part of herself she has locked away (her black father, the "gay, suave scoundrel") is here brought out for the amusement of European whites, for whom it epitomizes just what they are not. Suddenly Helga sees her relationship to them in a new light: she once imagined she had finally found her people, but she now realizes that their interest in her is predicated on her not being "one of them." This recognition precipitates an intense feeling of alienation from those around her, along with a growing feeling of connection with the father she has locked away, and a desire to reclaim her blackness.

Larsen's uses of Copenhagen pointedly revise the uses of Europe as an inter-racial haven in earlier American novels with black or mulatto heroines—novels that tend to ignore the class lines so important in Europe, or rather deploy them to stress the gentility of the heroine or hero. Engagement or marriage to an aris-tocrat reveals the lack of prejudices of the "highest" people in Europe, thus serv-ing up white Americanism as a betrayal of civilized behavior while showing that the American Negro is as refined as the "best" Europeans.[8] For Helga, Europe does not offer freedom from racism; it merely displays a different kind of rac-ism. Like a Scandinavian modernist, Larsen foregrounds the snobbishness of the Scandinavian bourgeoisie, their obsession with class status, and the role of the exchange of women through marriage in cementing class ties. Moreover, in *Quicksand* the protagonist's return to the United States does not represent a sac-rifice of happiness for the sake of heroic racial uplift, as in other novels. Helga Crane's repatriation and her brief commitment to uplift in the South lead merely to a more disastrous dead end.

Just as Helga felt on arriving in Copenhagen that she had finally come home, she feels the same emotion on returning to Harlem, but the feeling proves no more permanent than it did in Denmark. Her friendship with Anne Grey wanes because Anne distrusts and patronizes Helga for having lived too long with Nordics and for being too tolerant of them. James Vayle, whom she has met up with again in New York, insists that she was "always a little different" from Ne-groes (p. 102). As he expresses his distaste for the interracial social scene of New York, and more particularly for the sight of a black woman talking to a white man at a party, Helga probes him "with polite contempt" until he exposes the heart of his dissatisfaction: "You know as well as I do, Helga, that it's the colored girls these men come up here to see. They wouldn't think of bringing their wives" (pp. 102, 103). In fact, however, they *have* brought their wives (as Helga quickly points out): one of these women is dancing with a Negro even as Vayle speaks. Larsen directs her satire not just at stereotypes of interracial intimacy, but also at the common ethic of racial "ownership" of women's sexuality. Vayle presents a eugenicist argument, according to which middle-class Negroes have a duty to propagate the race: "Don't you see that if we—I mean people like us—don't have children, the others will still have. That's one of the things that's the matter with us. The race is sterile at the top" (p. 103).

Vayle's contention that white men come to Harlem seeking affairs with black women is particularly ironic, since Helga very soon finds herself in the arms of Robert Anderson, who is married to her erstwhile best friend Anne. Helga loses all her envy of Anne's recent marriage, even as she hopes for a romantic rendez-vous with Robert, who has kissed her passionately. As Helga becomes fully conscious of her desires, Larsen returns to the metaphor of the labyrinth: "Abruptly one Sunday in a crowded room . . . she knew that she couldn't go [back to Copenhagen], that she hadn't since that kiss intended to go without exploring to the end that unfamiliar path into which she had strayed. . . . A species of fatalism fastened on her" (p. 106). Yet Anderson does not offer the recognition she craves. Abandoned "forever" like Ariadne, Helga looks into an "endless stretch of dreary years" that is her only conceivable future (p. 108).

At this point the novel veers far from Larsen's own experience. It seems likely, as I have pointed out earlier, that after spending 1908–1909 in Denmark Larsen returned briefly to the United States and then went back to live in Copenhagen until 1912; but such a return would merely have muddled the plot in *Quicksand* and drawn the story out. (Helga intends to return to Copenhagen but ends up changing her mind.) Instead, Larsen invented a whole new trajectory for Helga Crane's life and appended it to the narrative that brings Helga back to Harlem at the peak of the Negro Renaissance.

Anderson's rejection of Helga drives her to a nervous breakdown. In a distressed state, thinly clad and drenched with rainwater, she stumbles into a Pentecostal service in a storefront church. Accosted by the women as a "scarlet 'oman" (a term that recalls Axel's comment that Helga has "the soul of a prostitute"), Helga is easily hypnotized by a hymn that urges the surrender of the self to God. The scene is erotically charged with "Bacchic vehemence." It precisely parallels a famous scene in Ovid's *Ars Amatoria* (Art of Love) in which Bacchus, accompanied by his maenads and satyrs, arrives to "save" Ariadne after her desertion by Theseus on Naxos. Yet this will prove a false salvation, for in reality Helga's surrender to faith is merely a kind of "passing," her religion "a kind of protective coloring, shielding her from the cruel light of an unbearable reality" (*Quicksand*, p. 126). Moreover, she uses her "deliberate allure" to snare the Reverend Pleasant Green, Larsen's grotesque stand-in for Bacchus. Looking for some "Power" to help her, she decides to "make sure of both things, God and man" (p. 117). She still, that is to say, has the "soul of a prostitute"—like Mary Magdalene, as the final literary allusion of the text will suggest.

Before long, Helga's experience as a pastor's wife in the Deep South disabuses her of her romantic and condescending views of the "folk." Attempting the sort of racial uplift she had earlier rejected, she finds her efforts both wrongheaded and unsatisfying. The black women of her new community do not need her uplift; they tend, rather, to look down on her while pitying her husband. Helga retreats increasingly into herself until, after the birth of her fourth child, she nearly dies. She emerges from the ordeal without a shred of respect for her husband, her faith gone. In this state, and pregnant for the fifth time, she asks a nurse to read her Anatole France's story "The Procurator of Judaea."

During the period in which Larsen was writing her novel, this tale was republished in English translation in a handsome edition of France's most famous stories, brought out by Dodd, Mead in 1926. Larsen may have learned of the book through her friend Eddie Wasserman, a great fan of the French author. Anatole France, in his last years, had befriended Wasserman, and in a short time they had grown very close. Wasserman even published his reminiscences of their time together in an essay in *The Bookman* in 1925, around the time Larsen met him and at a time when she read *The Bookman* regularly. She may have thought of this essay while writing, for it includes an allusion to Ariadne's mother and her monstrous coupling with a bull. "One day," Wasserman remembered, "when we were talking of women, [Anatole France] remarked that Pasiphae was less reprehensible than Lady Macbeth, for she at least had had physical pleasure in her sin." This is the sort of pleasure Helga Crane wants to believe her mother enjoyed with her father.[9]

"The Procurator of Judaea" concerns, in part, the way Roman society depended on the control of sexuality to reproduce racialized subjects for the imperial state. It is composed of two conversations between Pontius Pilate and Aelius Lamia, an old acquaintance from the days when Pilate had been the procurator of Judaea. Pilate speaks of how hard the job was, the Jews being rebellious and contemptuous of Romans, whom they considered an unclean race. For his part, Pilate thought the Jews barbarous and stupid. A cosmopolitan wanderer and Epicurean philosopher, Aelius Lamia is more tolerant of the Jews and begins to reminisce about the beauty of the Jewish women, particularly a dancer who joined the group surrounding Jesus—clearly Mary Magdalene. Pilate reproves Lamia for adultery and miscegenation. In his view, sex between Romans and people of other nations is wrong: "Marriage from the patrician point of view is a sacred tie; it is one of the institutions which are the support of Rome. As to foreign women and slaves, such relations as one may enter into with them would be of little account were it not that they habituate the body to a humiliating effeminacy. . . . What, above all, I blame in you is that you have not married in compliance with the law and given children to the Republic, as every good citizen is bound to do."[10] Pilate's patriarchal view of women and sex is inextricable from his racism and his abhorrence of race mixing—attitudes mirrored by the Jews themselves. In what Larsen terms the "supremely ironic" ending of the tale, Lamia speaks of the charismatic Jewish healer offering salvation across ethnic and national lines, whom Pilate executed at the request of the

Jews. Larsen quotes Pilate's reply: "Jesus? . . . Jesus—of Nazareth? I cannot call him to mind" (*Quicksand*, p. 132).

Larsen's late revisions and additions to her novel, while departing from a plot based in her own experience, increasingly explored the meaning of that experience in terms of how racial order depends on a policing of boundaries and sexuality while mandating the disappearance of the person who cannot assimilate to one side or the other of the color line.

Quicksand ends with Helga Crane in childbed, feeling asphyxiated once again, knowing that she must escape or die. But the thought of leaving her children holds her fatally in place: "To leave them would be a tearing agony, a rending of deepest fibers. She felt that through all the rest of her lifetime she would be hearing their cry of 'Mummy, Mummy, Mummy,' through sleepless nights. No. She couldn't desert them" (*Quicksand*, p. 135). The voice Helga hears is her own, crying for the Danish mother whom "race" in America has stolen from her. The reason Helga Crane cannot save herself in this conclusion (a conclusion that has disappointed so many readers and critics) has everything to do with American society's suppression of attachments that contradict the color line.

Helga takes responsibility for her catastrophe and abstains from self-pity. To many, she may seem more pathetic than tragic, her fate just another turn of the screw. But what she suffers is out of all proportion to her flaws; it seems inexorable as well. Larsen thus lines up with the naturalist Ibsen rather than with the classical dramatists, for in her novels fate is not above and independent of human institutions but largely determined by them.

In relation to Larsen's psyche, the most revealing departure of Helga Crane's story from the author's is the fact that Larsen's mother did not die when Nella was fifteen. Instead, at age sixteen Nella was sent to Fisk (the "Devon" of *Quicksand*). Following her expulsion she moved to Denmark, and from that point on was banished from her immediate family. In constructing the plot of *Quicksand*, Nella spared her mother by killing her off. Moreover, rather than giving Helga a half-sister who kept living with the mother into adulthood, Larsen made all of Helga's siblings stepbrothers and stepsisters, brought to the family by the white husband. Thus, Nella preserved her mother's love—and her love for her mother—in a realm apart, the landscape of grief, while unleashing her rage against the racial order that separated them.

Unlike Helga Crane, Larsen managed to escape the labyrinth into a much freer and more cosmopolitan social niche, in no small part through marriage to the man to whom her novel was dedicated, a man much like Dr. Anderson. She wrote and revised *Quicksand* even as she was working her way into circles where she felt valuable, understood, and at home, and these circles defied the constraints of racial, gendered, and sexual entrapment, and to some extent class rigidity, that bedevil Helga Crane. Through Helga, Larsen indirectly accessed the trauma she had suffered but could never overcome and explored a terrible alternative to her own life trajectory, ending with no opportunities for self-expression. Yet, in the process, she also wrenched her narrative out of its generally realistic development, for the reader has difficulty accepting Helga's sudden transformation in the revival scene, an episode seemingly imported from expressionist drama. Some of the most astute and admiring reviewers would balk at this aspect of the novel, feeling that a woman as modern and intelligent as Helga Crane would find some other way out of her predicament.

If Larsen had based her narrative more closely on her own experience through 1927, *Quicksand* would have had an essentially comic pattern, with the protagonist eventually triumphing over the forces of inherited convention and achieving the twin goals of self-expression and emotional fulfillment in a new social configuration. But such a dénouement would not have fit Larsen's notions about the most compelling forms of modern literary expression. Moreover, it would have dulled the point of her attack on a suffocating society, and frustrated her release, in the act of writing, from "the feeling of smallness which had hedged her in, first during her sorry, unchildlike childhood among hostile white folk in Chicago, and later during her uncomfortable sojourn among snobbish black folk" (p. 46). Larsen's creative passion lay in bravely exposing all the forces that had hemmed her in for so long. *Quicksand* marks the threshold where a woman whose being forms the radical "other" to the racial order disappears—or rather, is perpetually sacrificed on the altar of the color line.

In place of the Oedipal drama and the incest taboo (both ubiquitous in "tragic mulatto" literary tradition), Larsen turns to a female-centered drama figuring the abandonment of women, death in childbirth, the enslavement of the body to procreation of racialized subjects alienated from themselves and their mothers by national ideologies of racial and class identity. Never embracing Jean Toomer's dream of a "new race," neither does Larsen simply dismiss race as a fiction, for she recognizes it as a formative feature of modern experience. Rather, she exposes the violence of racialization as such in the effort to make it ethically insupportable, like fate in classical drama: an affront to humanity.

FOURTEEN

In the Mecca:
1927

ALL the time that Larsen was writing and revising her novel, the continuing fierce battles over the direction of black literature occupied her attention. She followed the debates in the newspapers and literary journals devotedly and spent much of her time with people who were involved or implicated. She combed the black newspapers and clipped out articles and reviews, mailing duplicates to Van Vechten for his scrapbook. When Langston Hughes's book of blues poems, *Fine Clothes to the Jew,* came out at the beginning of the year the response was immediate and, in the black newspapers, mostly ferocious: "About as fine a collection of piffling trash as is to be found under the covers of any book," wrote J. A. Rogers in the *Pittsburgh Courier.* "But, of course, this book, like *The Weary Blues,* is designed for white readers, with their preconceived notions about Negroes."[1] The dedication to Van Vechten was a provocation lost on nobody.

In late February Hughes met with *Courier* editor Floyd Calvin in the Knopf offices on Fifth Avenue to discuss his work and the furor surrounding it. Hughes said he feared only that black critics' hostility to his work would "frighten younger writers away from writing about themselves." Calvin then turned to Nella's friend Harry Block, "the one responsible for the firm's accepting Hughes' book," who "said the firm is wholly in sympathy with the kind of work Mr. Hughes is doing and believes he is doing a good work, and published his poems because of it."[2] Calvin was furious with Knopf for publishing the book at all.

Hughes answered his critics with a two-part essay in the *Courier,* "Those Bad New Negroes: A Critique on Critics," in which he accused his enemies of thinking that whites were better than blacks, believing that "what white people think about Negroes is more important than what Negroes think about themselves," being nouveau riche snobs, and lacking "culture." People often complained, he noted, that the young writers didn't write about the "best" colored people:

> But I fear for them if ever a really powerful work is done about their lives. Such a story would show not only their excellencies but their pseudo-culture as well, their slavish devotion to Nordic standards, their snobbishness, their

detachment from the Negro masses and their vast sense of importance to themselves. A book like that from a Negro writer, even though true and beautiful, would be more thoroughly disliked than the stories of low-class Negroes now being written. And it would be more wrathfully damned than *Nigger Heaven*, at present vibrating throughout the land in its eleventh edition.[3]

Larsen believed that the novel she had just turned in to Knopf was precisely such a book.

"Heaven forbid that I should ever be bitten by the desire to write another novel!" she wrote Carl in early March. "Except, perhaps, one to dedicate to you. For, why should Langston Hughes be the only one to enjoy notoriety for the sake of his convictions?"[4]

Both Elmer and Nella expected her book to be reviled in the fashion that Hughes predicted. "Elmer says," she remarked to Carl, "that if I do get the present one published that 'your people' will run me out of these United States. (He didn't use the words 'your people' either, in referring to them.)"[5] Larsen identified the cultural politics of her work completely with those of Van Vechten and Hughes.

She and Elmer joined Carl and Fania for a private dinner on Washington's birthday, after which others arrived for a party that lasted until 3:00 A.M., including Lenore Ulric (star of *Lulu Belle*) and John Vandercook, who was writing a historical novel called *Black Majesty* based on the revolution in Haiti and the reign of King Christophe.[6] "The most pleasant and interesting party we have been to for a long time," Nella wrote Carl afterward. "Comfortable and congenial too."[7] On the sixteenth of March, Fania and Carl hosted a much larger party, with a much larger range of show biz and literary personalities, including Eleanor Wylie and William Rose Benét, Lawrence Langner and Armina Marshall, Grace and Jim Johnson, Louise Bryant and William Bullitt, photographer Nickolas Muray, and Nora Holt, who sang.[8] Years later, Langner remembered meeting a number of memorable people at such parties, including James Weldon Johnson, "the red-haired singer Nora Holt, half-Scotch, half Negro, who was the toast of Paris and the Riviera," and "the attractive writer of Negro novels, Nella Larsen."[9] Van Vechten, "wearing a magnificent cerise and gold mandarin robe," would amuse himself by going from guest to guest offering drinks while affectionately pinching derrieres or biting people on the neck with his monstrous teeth. Meanwhile, Fania "darted about amidst her guests like a tropical humming bird, and was even more gorgeously caparisoned."[10]

Knopf's office called the day after the midweek soirée to tell Nella her book had been accepted and they were sending it back to be put in shape for the printer. On Friday, Elmer wrote Carl to thank him "for getting [Nella] settled about the book" and for "the wonderful party Wednesday night. I almost went out on my ear so I may not have told you exactly how I felt about it. Nella applies the adjective gorgeous. I guess it means what I am trying to say."[11] Two days later they met again at a birthday party Rita Romilly threw for Fania, with people like Winold Reiss, Covarrubias, and the Johnsons.[12]

A week later, Nella and Elmer attended a large party at Van Vechten's in honor of the visiting French writer Paul Morand, which Geraldyn Dismond found notable enough to mention in her society column for the *Pittsburgh Courier*.[13] With a book accepted by Knopf, Nella was now important enough to be noticed. Two nights after Van Vechten's party, it was the Langners' turn to host almost exactly the same group, as well as Scott and Zelda Fitzgerald.[14]

Morand would remember these occasions in his book *Black Magic* (published as *Magie Noir* in 1928 and then in translation by Viking in 1929), although he could only regret "all the dilution of blood, . . . adulterated unions and inextricable adventures" that had made African Americans a new people.[15] A surrealist fantasy, with cannibal feasts, no less ("their Negro guts, used to hunger as they were to excess, were being gorged. . . . They gulped his eyes"),[16] *Black Magic* represents the apotheosis of the theory of Negro atavism. The book's three sections, centered on the United States, the West Indies, and Africa, are united by the thesis that beneath all habiliments of "white" civilization, assimilation, and racial mixture, even the whitest of Negroes is, deep down, a full-blooded African and can find fulfillment only in harmony with the primal rhythms of life, sex and "feeding," sleeping and waking. "She envied the blood of such strength that neither poisonous bites of wild beasts, nor the terrible African diseases could spoil it. What a difference from the American Negroes with their half-colours, their teeth rotten beneath the gold, their flabby bellies, and all the tares of cross-breeding."[17]

These passages are only slightly more offensive than Morand's descriptions of black Harlemites on the subway in his book *New York* (1930), also based on the 1927 visit. "Clinging with long hooking hands to the leather straps, and chewing their gum, they remind one of the great apes of Equatorial Africa."[18] On the sidewalks he found equally inspiring sights: "Young Negresses, precociously mature, dash wildly along, swinging their bodies harmoniously, on atrociously noisy roller-skates, with an animal swiftness, a warlike zest, something savage and triumphant; they seem like the black virgins of some African revolution of the future."[19] Taking a brief break from his primitivist fantasy, he would remember "Nella Larsen" in *New York* as a member of the "small 'intelligentsia' [of blacks] in contact with similar white groups," helping to force the "respect and sympathy" of the city through art and literature.[20] It can be wondered whether Morand considered this a worthwhile project.

Elmer and Nella were now traveling in one of the roaringest party circuits of the Twenties. The affairs they attended were often depicted in fiction of the period under various disguises—notably (and negatively) in novels by Clement Wood, Maxwell Bodenheim, and Thomas Wolfe. If people like Langner, Langston Hughes, Walter White, and James Weldon Johnson portrayed Van Vechten's parties in the most glowing terms in their memoirs, white authors who resented Van Vechten more often found them insidious and decadent beneath the glamour, particularly if they regarded themselves as more genuinely interested in "the race."[21] The interracial camaraderie seemed a bit self-conscious, and the occasional petting outré.

Several black writers who did not really know Van Vechten had precisely this impression, and their disdain for him carried over into their impressions of those who partied with him, tinged with a distinct undertone of sexual malaise: "When they were down there flirting with Carl Van Vechten," boasted Sterling Brown (who had an enormous influence on later literary historians), "I was down south talking to Big Boy [a blues musician whom Brown immortalized in verse]. One of the most conceited things I can say is that I am proud that I have never shaken that rascal's hand. . . . He corrupted the Harlem Renaissance and was a terrible influence on them. He was a voyeur. He was looking at these Negroes and they were acting the fools for him. And the foolisher they acted, the more he recorded them."[22] Arthur Huff Fauset—who, like Brown, did not live in or near New York during the period—came to the same conclusions: "Old and young hopefuls fell over each other catering to his whims—he was their liege lord, not only a brilliant literary light, but enormously rich, and that endowed him with power to promote the interests of aspiring young Blacks willing to pay him homage."[23] Van Vechten's parties would never have attracted so much bile if they had been all-white affairs. But they were not just occasions for whites and blacks to meet one another. Major figures of the New Negro movement first met each other through Van Vechten, sometimes at dinners deliberately planned for the purpose.[24]

Not all of Larsen's social life revolved around such parties, of course. Dorothy Peterson was still her mainstay, along with Dorothy Hunt Harris, with whom she often played bridge. The Imeses also saw a lot of the Stoners, and they had several good friends connected with the Bordentown Manual Training School. William R. Valentine, a Harvard graduate highly respected up and down the Eastern Seaboard, was the principal, and his wife Grace was a friend of Nella and Dorothy. The Valentines had a wide circle of friends in the New York boroughs who on special weekends often went out to the school's campus on the banks of the Delaware. Commencement weekend and the spring tennis tournament were considered regular social occasions for the black New York elite. In summer, the Bordentown campus became a vacation spot for black New Yorkers of the Petersons' set. Frances O. Grant, a French teacher at Bordentown, was a good friend of Nella Larsen and Dorothy Peterson, as was Crystal Bird, head of Bordentown's English department.

A native of Boston, Bird had previously worked for the YWCA in Chicago and, in 1918, became the first black woman to serve as the YWCA's National Girls' Work Secretary for Colored Girls. She was an old friend of Grace Johnson and Lucile Miller, and Nella had known her even before she met Dorothy Peterson. After being jilted by Roland Hayes in 1927, Bird reportedly collected $35,000 for not filing a breach-of-promise suit against him. She would later surprise Nella by marrying Jessie Fauset's half-brother, Arthur Huff Fauset.[25]

Then there were Gussie and Chester Booth. Gussie, née Estelle Bishop, was the daughter of the Episcopal priest of Harlem's toniest congregation, and sister-in-law of Grace Valentine. Chester had been a Captain in World War I and ran one of the largest dental practices in Harlem; by 1927 he was succumbing to the alcoholism that would kill him in 1929.[26] Rudolph Fisher, a radiologist, and his wife Jane also became a part of the Imeses' social group after he moved up from Washington. Talented, like Elmer Imes, at comic repartee, tall and handsome, he was one of the most brilliant short-story writers of the renaissance and working on his first novel just as Nella was finishing hers. Alonzo de Grate Smith, the only pediatrician in Harlem and an outpatient physician at Harlem Hospital, was an amateur artist (he did paintings, pencil sketches, pastels), and shared offices with Fisher at 2352 Seventh Avenue. He also wrote regular columns entitled "Health in the Home" and "Better Babies" for Harlem newspapers. Vernon Ayer, Nella's personal physician, was Alonzo's best friend and would be the best man at his wedding in 1928.[27]

The friendships among the Imeses' friends generally predated their friendships with Nella and often went back to family connections. Furthermore, nearly all of her black friends were college graduates belonging to sororities and fraternities. Nella once tried to join a sorority, with Dorothy's encouragement, but she was barred for lack of proof that she had gone to college.[28] Although Nella's best friend, Peterson was closer to Dorothy Harris than to Nella until the late 1920s. Nella never shared intimate details of her past with any of them, although they knew she had grown up in a white family in Chicago and bore deep inner wounds that made it hard for her to open up. Nella was always a bit remote; she could be drawn out in certain company, but even Dorothy Peterson felt that she knew very little about Larsen's personal history.

The people who didn't know Larsen well tended to assume—because of the company she kept, her appearance, speech, and manner—that she had a privileged background, perhaps in a city where they had not lived. For example, the artist and writer Bruce Nugent, who'd been born in D.C., figured her for an "Old Philadelphian." In old age, Nugent told biographer Thadious Davis that Larsen's "manners were something that people who don't have, but admire, resent not having."[29] Yet these manners came not from an aristocratic background but from a carefully cultivated method of emotional self-defense. Nella shared with Helga Crane "that faint hint of offishness which . . . repelled advances, an arrogance that stirred in people a peculiar irritation. . . . The self-sufficient uninterested manner adopted instinctively as a protective measure for her acute sensitiveness, in her child days, clung to her."[30]

By mid-March 1927 the Imeses were getting ready to cross the Hudson and resettle in Harlem. Nella was reading stories for the *Opportunity* contest—"sifting" them for the judges to cull the hopeless cases. "Very diverting. One contains this prize, 'I have decided to *cast* my *Rubikorn* with you.' (The italics are mine)."[31] By the sixth of April they were "half-way settled" in Apartment 5A at 236 West 135th Street, around the corner from the 135th Street Library.[32] It was a five-room flat on the fifth floor, facing the street. Nella decorated the living room to give, as a reporter described it, "the air of a Greenwich Village studio with its vari-colored pillows, paintings, books and more books, flowers, large and small vases," and "an autographed portrait" of Carl Van Vechten, among other furnishings.[33]

Looking out over one of the main crosstown thoroughfares of the black metropolis, it was very noisy, as Nella immediately discovered. She had an even greater worry just after the move, writing Van Vechten: "Almost I had nervous prostration because in the move I thought I had lost your letters—and that possibly Elmer had found them."[34] Just what Nella was afraid Elmer would have learned from Carl's letters is unclear. Nella never gave them to Dorothy and Carl, despite at least one promise to do so as they collected manuscripts in the 1940s. It is very unlikely that Nella and Carl had any sort of romantic or sexual relationship, but his letters to women—and theirs to him—sometimes playfully hinted at such.

Geraldyn Dismond found the Imeses' move important enough to announce in her column for the *Pittsburgh Courier:* "One hundred and thirty-fifth street is going social. And by the way, Mrs. Imes' book will soon be off the press."[35] She was wrong about the book. *Quicksand* would not appear until early 1928.

Nella and Elmer lost no time jumping into the nearby nightlife. On the sixth of April, a Wednesday, they attended the benefit costume ball for the Fort Valley Industrial School, an institute in Georgia run by Dorothy Harris' father. The ball was the sort of social phantasmagoria that could only have taken place in the Harlem of the Twenties. Planned by Jimmy Harris and held at the Renaissance Casino, "Harlem's Monument" on Seventh Avenue, the benefit attracted all of the Imeses' friends—the Johnsons, the Whites, Edna and Lloyd Thomas, the Fishers—along with a large contingent of young men (mostly white) in drag. Geraldyn Dismond described some of the costumes for her readers, and enthused over the "Lacedaemonians everywhere," "Ladies lost in envy," literati, intelligentsia, "jazzers from the Savoy," and "a vamp in shimmering black chiffon that he made himself."[36]

Several black newspapers took the Harrises to task for sullying the reputation of an upstanding institution. Larsen clipped out a disapproving editorial from the *New York News:*

> Most unfortunate was the adverse advertising given the splendid Fort Valley Industrial School, by the ball recently staged at the Renaissance Casino. . . . When the Black and Tan Ball, which was featured principally by the denizens, many of them abnormal and their colored associates of similar unsavory reputation, was staged, it gave chills to the sincere friends of Fort Valley. It is most unfortunate that colored men and women seeking the Bohemian life of the great art center of Gotham, should not choose for their companions the very highest and best type of that quarter. . . . The discarded froth of Caucasian society cannot lift them or their race in the respect and confidence of the Caucasian world.[37]

The event seemed to bear out the "venomous attack made by a recent and perverted writer upon the morals of Harlem society in his salacious novel." In the same vein, the *Chicago Whip* savaged the "degenerate" and "depraved" spectacle. Perverted cross-dressers, mostly white, "threw consternation into the black people whose men for the most part are 'he' men through and through. Such spectacles cannot escape condemnation behind the pretense of art, nor behind the sable shades of Bohemian convention. . . . It is some more of Van Vechten's 'Nigger Heaven' and Van Vechten was among those present." Those who attended "awoke to the fact that the much talked of understanding of the literary and artistic cults of white and black races of New York is in fact an unholy alliance of thrill seekers, revelers, debauchers, and despoilers whose ideals have been perverted somewhere in the 'Village' or maybe on 'Main Street.'"[38] The reference to Sinclair Lewis' novel *Main Street*—then banned in Boston, among other places—gives a good idea of how literary references helped to define the field of racial, cultural, and sexual politics for the black bourgeoisie.

On the tenth of April, a Sunday, Carnegie Hall hosted the U.S. premiere of George Antheil's *Jazz Symphony* and his spectacular *Ballet Mécanique*. Nora Holt came up from Philadelphia for it; all of the Imeses' friends were there, and several performed in it. After a string quartet and sonata to warm up the audience, the stage went dark. When the lights came back on, they revealed a backdrop with two enormous Negro figures painted black and blue and doing the Charleston. In front were twenty-nine black musicians—the band from Connie's Inn—conducted by Antheil and Harlem's Allie Ross. Banjos, saxophones, trumpets, four pianos, and a hugely appreciative audience filled the hall with vibrant sound and an electric mood of anticipation.

After a short intermission came the piece everyone was waiting for: the *Ballet*. It was more shattering than anyone could have imagined, even with the help of reports on the earlier premiere in Paris. Ten grand pianos stood in a great horseshoe led by one mechanical piano. Two great tables held mechanical devices to imitate factory whistles, roaring elevated trains, canning machinery, and the like. There were two airplane propellers, four bass drums, and eight xylophones, all conducted by Eugene Goossens, an acquaintance of the Imeses. Max Ewing and Colin McPhee, two of Nella's other friends, were featured pianists. (Aaron Copland was another.) "Noise in all its glory beat upon the audience which finally went mad and joined in the screaming and whistling," Dismond reported. "A timid few hurried from the hall as the rhythmic pounding thundered on and on and the hysteria of the gallery rose. . . . When you felt that surely another moment was beyond your endurance the drums beat in quiet succession and the Ballet Mécanique was over."[39] A'Lelia Walker was heard to say, "Thank goodness, I will be dead before this becomes the vogue."[40] After the *Ballet*, Donald Friede, the producer, gave a big supper party at Club Deauville, with music by the Connie's Inn band, conducted by W. C. Handy. About five hundred people came, "including *all* the Negroes," according to Van Vechten, but some forty left in protest when the very dark, and married, Paul Robeson danced with the very white, and single, Muriel Draper.[41]

Larsen woke up the next day to glorious spring weather, with buds bursting and bulbs blossoming in the parks, and Van Vechten dropped in on her in the afternoon.[42] The Antheil concert must have been a main topic of conversation Wednesday night, April 13, when Nella had Carl, Donald Angus, Jim and Grace

Johnson, Crystal Bird, and Dorothy Peterson for dinner to show off her new apartment on her birthday. After dinner, Rudolph and Jane Fisher, Dorothy Harris, Covarrubias, Harry Block, Gussie Booth, Vi Stoner, and others came in, staying until about 3:00 in the morning.[43] The following week, Nella, Elmer, and Dorothy went to Carl's for cocktails, and then on the twenty-fifth Donald Angus hosted a party they attended with many others. Harry Block, Dorothy Peterson, Nella, Elmer, and Carl all went out to a Greek restaurant in the midst of it and then to Carl's for "a drink and a chat" until midnight.[44] The next morning Nella came to his place to visit with his African American maid and cook, Meda Frye, staying an hour. As she left, she walked with Carl to his bank and then back to his apartment before taking the subway home.[45] From the time of the move to Harlem, Larsen and Van Vechten began seeing each other constantly, often several times a week—usually but not always with Elmer present.

One topic of conversation was Gertrude Stein's collection of novellas, *Three Lives* (1911), including "Melanctha," recently republished by Albert and Charles Boni in the United States. Van Vechten wrote Stein in May that he had been recommending "Melanctha" to friends, and added, "Nella Imes, one of the most intelligent people I know (you will see her in Paris next winter) says it is the best Negro story she has ever read (she is Negro herself)."[46] Nella had many friends who had visited Paris and paid Stein a visit—particularly Nora Holt, whom Stein liked immediately ("she is tender and I like her postal cards. I guess she is having a good time alright but then it is easy anybody would like her, I don't know it's quite tender").[47]

The Imeses caught many of the signature events of the season. Geraldyn Dismond spotted them on Friday, May 6, at the opening of Club Vo-De-O, next to the Alhambra Theatre.[48] Before the *Opportunity* contest dinner on the afternoon of May 7, Elmer and Nella picked up Carl for a cocktail party at Dorothy Peterson's, where much of Dorothy's circle congregated—Dorothy Harris, Sidney Peterson, Mr. Peterson, Bruce Nugent, Harry Block, and so forth. Dorothy had reserved a table at the dinner for the group.[49] They showed up late, loud, and "slightly soused" for the big event, drawing stares and much unfavorable comment.[50] Bruce Nugent wore evening clothes but no socks, necktie, or collar, and his blue shirt was unbuttoned halfway down his chest. The portion of his supposedly ongoing novel published recently in *Fire!!* (an avant-garde art quarterly that produced only one issue), flamboyantly omnisexual and freely dropping names of well-known acquaintances, was notorious.[51] Presiding over the dinner was John Dewey, who introduced the various speakers.[52] After the event, at midnight, Nella, Elmer, and Grace Valentine went home with Carl before calling it a night.[53]

The very next day, a Sunday, Van Vechten and Jack Stephens, a white librarian friend visiting from the Midwest, went uptown in the afternoon to visit with Nella and Elmer and ended up staying for dinner. Then much of their party from the day before showed up, including Dorothy Peterson and Grace Valentine, and they carried on until nearly midnight. Three days after that, much of the group went to the MacDowell Club "to hear Crystal Bird murder Spirituals," in the words of Van Vechten, and Elmer and Nella went home with him, staying again until the late evening. He hosted a cocktail party two days later, a Friday, with Nella and Elmer and much of their usual group. In the midst of it, Nella, Dorothy, Harry Block, and Walter White left for a show, but returned afterward as the party continued deep into the wee hours. Sunday of the same weekend, Nella and Elmer had Van Vechten and Colin McPhee, among others, for cocktails in the afternoon.[54] The following Thursday, Nella and Elmer attended Eddie Wasserman's farewell party for Taylor Gordon and Rosamond Johnson, who were preparing to spiritualize Europe. Afterward all except Eddie and Louise Hellström went over to Carl's place, where, he wrote in his diary, "we have a gay party and everybody takes off their clothes."[55] The next day, Lindbergh started his flight to Paris.

Hubert Harrison thought he saw where it was all leading. His article "Cabaret School of Negro Writers Does Not Represent One-Tenth of Race," published on May 28, could only have intended Nella Imes as one of its targets, plus all "the colored cognoscenti, Harlem's high intelligentsia," who were entertaining white decadents with the sort of thing they expected out of Harlem.[56] Those who had opened their homes to the whites, Harrison sneered, ended up following where the whites led—chiefly to cabarets. This, of course, was greatly exaggerated. Much of the entertainment took place in people's homes—for example, the next day Dorothy Peterson had her friends over for a quiet Decoration Day dinner.[57] And at least in Nella's and Dorothy's case, much of the "cabareting" was connected with benefit functions. Van Vechten could afford to go out to cabarets every night, perhaps, but people like Elmer and Nella could not.

Yet these charges were really incidental to the main issue: the cultural politics of contemporary black literature. Harrison's point of view, adopted by much of Harlem's middle class and clergy, would inform later histories written about the Harlem Renaissance. But Harrison's predictive powers for what constituted real literary achievement—achievement buried under the piffle of the "cabaret school" (Exhibit A: Langston Hughes)—have had less staying power: "In prose genuine masters like John Matheus and real critics like Frank Horne were swamped by the turrid tide of trumpery pish-posh and could hardly be heard for the babel of callow cackling. Many who began with sound artistic impulses but weak wills, like Zora Neale Hurston and Helene Johnson were soon swimming with the tide of tenth-rate marketers."[58]

There was a brief hiatus in the socializing in early June, when something happened to Nella's face. She wrote Van Vechten that she wouldn't be able to see anyone for a while, because she had gotten her "face and neck pretty well splattered up with hot grease. The result being that all tied and bandaged up as I am I'm really not presentable." Confined to the house, she just hoped she would emerge unspotted. "Maybe, I will take myself to the country for some weeks, when the doctors decide that I'll heal all right without further attention. I'm not sure yet."[59] She must have been overestimating the damage or else telling a fib, for only eight days later she and Elmer visited Carl after dinner and stayed until nearly three.[60] Soon thereafter, Elmer took off for a work-related retreat at a resort in French Lick, Indiana. He "had a comfortable and successful trip," according to Nella. "Not the slightest suspicion of unpleasantness. Even his presence at the dance tripping it with Nordic ladies seemed not to cause any remark."[61]

When Elmer was out of town (a common occurrence), Carl often took it upon himself, with Elmer's approval and even at his request, to keep Nella company and escort her around.[62] One evening, Carl gave her an unexpected call from Ethel Waters' place on 137th Street, where Ethel, along with her mother and aunt, were feeding him a home-cooked meal of baked ham and stringbeans, "topped off with iced tea and lemon meringue pie."[63] Ethel had not eaten much at one of Carl's recent dinners, featuring cold borscht ("enough to chill your gizzard for a week") and other exotic delicacies ("the caviar looked like buckshot to me and didn't taste much better"), so he had asked her what she liked to eat, and she invited him over to find out.[64] After the meal, Carl decided it was time for Nella and Ethel to meet each other. When Nella arrived at the apartment, she and Ethel seemed to hit it off, for at about midnight, Ethel and her partner Earl Dancer, Nella, and Carl drove down to Carl's place and carried on until 1:30.[65] As Ethel and Nella parted, Nella invited her for tea the next Monday afternoon, and Ethel said she'd be happy to come.[66]

"Sweet Mama Stringbean," as Waters was first known in the business, for her long slender form, began her career in black musical theater and tent shows singing minstrel and "coon" songs along with vaudeville and ragtime to all-black audiences. But she was "essentially a blues singer," as Randall Cherry points out.[67] She had moved to New York about 1919 and started singing in Edmond's Cellar, a Harlem honky-tonk, entering the recording industry at the same time and becoming one of the first black recording stars. In live performance, she held her audience not with the vivacious charm and sprightly movement of a Florence Mills, but with a seemingly innate poise and subtle, understated movement, emanating power in reserve.[68] Elegant, almost languorous even in her signature move, the shimmy, she exuded at the same time a sort of mock-innocent sophistication perfectly in tune with the spirit of the decade.

For the "tea," Nella invited Dorothy Peterson and a white friend from library school, Mary Skinner, "a rather interesting girl from Chicago, who was sailing that night" (probably for Cairo, Egypt, where she worked in a library). They waited and waited for Waters, who never appeared. When Gussie Booth phoned, Nella invited her up. "Finally, at seven o'clock we ate the cakes and sandwiches. I was very disappointed because I felt sure it was going to be a success. Everything was just right. Mary Skinner who is good-looking, rich and intelligent knows the secret of being friendly without being patronizing. Dorothy really wanted to meet her [Waters], and had intended, if things fell out that way, to ask her to go over to Brooklyn with me and Elmer on Friday night. Gussie knows nothing about her—and doesn't care, so she would have been perfectly natural."[69] Nella asked Carl, who had returned to Chicago for a few days, to see if he could find out what happened.

Something may have come up; then again, Waters may have simply changed her mind about Larsen. She was well known for her prickly personality and was particularly competitive toward other women. Carl and Fania became Ethel's "dearest friends," but she did not generally like his other black friends. She told him "he'd been hanging around" too much "with dictys who tried to be as much like white people as possible."[70] She may well have regarded Larsen in this light, although they later socialized together. Certainly, Larsen—who was embarrassed about her class background, particularly since her mother was white—would have seemed quite "dicty" (upper-class) to Waters, as she did to most people upon first acquaintance.

The ever-moody Ethel Waters, moreover, was growing suspicious of admirers who wanted to become her friend. At the very time she had Van Vechten over to dinner, she later wrote, "I was getting the first hints that theatrical fame was not all pie à la mode. . . . When you become a celebrity some people act as though you have turned into a walking Christmas tree. They try to pick presents and annuities off you."[71]

While Elmer, the two Dorothys, and Carl were away in late June, Larsen took advantage of the break in her social life to get some writing done, and by the end of the month had finished "a kind of a short story" of about 6,000 words, which she was thinking of sending to *Harper's*, "though I'm not at all sure its quite the type." "Now that it's done," she meditated, "I'm inclined to believe that I've squandered an idea that would have made a novel."[72] The story, possibly an early version of *Passing,* was never published.

The Whites' social life had shifted gear with the birth of their second child in June and, soon thereafter, their departure for a year in France funded by a Guggenheim Fellowship. By this time, however, Nella and Dorothy were growing away from Walter and Gladys, finding them rather full of themselves. Walter was a chronic and incurable name-dropper (although, to be sure, he knew a lot of people with big names), and he and Gladys seemed to be growing condescending toward some of their old friends while they chummed with the likes of Clarence Darrow. Van Vechten was always irritated by Walter's practice of calling famous people by their first names from the moment he met them, as if to show he could. Speaking of big names, they had named their boy Carl Darrow White, and had given at least two of the "Carls" they knew—including Van Vechten—the idea that the child had been named specifically for them. (The other Carl was a black surgeon, then living in Chicago.) Nella was rather dismissive about the whole thing, and most ungracious. "Gladys called up to inquire why I hadn't called to gaze upon the son and heir (?)," she wrote the new "godfather." "I congratulated her effusively on its being a boy. 'Yes,' she said triumphantly, 'Walter wanted a boy to *carry on This name.*' [double-underlining on *This name*] There are only five pages of Whites in the New York telephone directory alone. And two in the Brooklyn one. Now if it had been Van Vechten, or Imes—."[73] The story contains an inside joke, for by now Nella knew that after the birth and naming of the son, the Whites had changed their mind, largely, it seems, because of criticism for naming the boy after white people. Nella came upon a black entertainment and scandal sheet published in Chicago entitled *The Light and Heebie Jeebies,* which sarcastically observed: "We consider such criticism captious. Parents do not only have the right to name their children after whom they wish, but, in this instance, Mr. and Mrs. White have shown that they are good old-fashioned Negroes. In slavery times most Negroes were named after friendly white folk, the only apparent difference between then and now being that there were not so many distinguished Negroes to be named after in the days when the clanking of chains was the music for sorrow songs."[74]

Trying to head off such criticism and save his image as a "race man," Walter had written to his brother on the twentieth, after Gladys got back from the hospital: "Since I sent you the announcement of the birth, reading 'Carl Darrow White,' there has been so much insistence that, against my wishes, the name Walter has been added going immediately in front of the Carl."[75] Walter wrote Carl Roberts that his wife, the attending surgeon (Louis Wright), his in-laws, his mother, and "some other people" had prevailed on him to change the name. In a sworn affidavit to the New York Department of Health, however, he put it somewhat differently: "Through an error the full name of Walter Carl Darrow White was not given by the attending physician, Dr. Louis T. Wright."[76] (Years later, when Walter divorced Gladys and married a white woman, Walter junior repudiated him by dropping the names "Walter" and "White," to become Carl Darrow.) In the meantime, Van Vechten had bought his supposed namesake a forty-three-dollar silver cup from Tiffany, engraved with the baby's original name, and made a special trip to the Whites' apartment to present it. Nella found out the truth first, but decided to wait until the Whites had sailed to show Carl the new name cards.[77] Dorothy, Nella, and Carl traded epistolary witticisms about this little episode for some weeks thereafter.

The Gurdjieff Work also provoked Larsen's mirth. While Dorothy Peterson was at the Prieuré and Dorothy Harris prepared to join her, Eddie Wasserman sent Nella *Twilight Sleep*, a "beautiful satire on all these pseudo religions. If I were courageous enough I would send it to Dorothy Harris when she sails next Wednesday."[78] When she did sail, Harris called Carl in advance to tell him, as Nella archly noted in a letter to Peterson, "maybe next year she would have time to look after her friends having spent so much time in her soul this year."[79] Harris held a party the night before she left, but "none of us"—Carl, Elmer, Harry, or Nella—were invited; apparently she wanted to be spared the witticisms. Later, in a letter to Peterson of July 19, Nella related Elmer's wry comment, "remember Katherine Mansfield," before closing, "and behave yourself."[80]

The moral instruction may have had to do with Peterson's romance with Jean Toomer, but "remember Katherine Mansfield" referred to the tubercular British writer who had died at the Prieuré in 1923. Mansfield believed that as a result of Gurdjieff's teachings, she had broken through to a new level of consciousness: "I could not write my old stories again, or any more like them: and not because I do not see the same detail as before, but because somehow or other the pattern is different. The old details now make another pattern; and this perception of a new pattern is what I call a creative attitude towards life."[81] In these comments published by A. R. Orage, which created a stir in British and American literary circles, Mansfield had sounded exactly like Jean Toomer, the "senior American" at the Prieuré in the summer of 1927: "*There were other ways of dividing up the world.*"[82] After watching a dance performance, "The Initiation of the Priestess," Mansfield fell into a fit of bloody coughing on her way to bed and died.[83] The Gurdjieffians did not grieve, however, for she had achieved her "purpose," "that process of self-annihilation which is necessary to the spiritual rebirth."[84] Dorothy was used to jibes from Elmer, Nella, and Carl about her spiritual exercises. Later in the summer she wrote Carl: "The early part of my stay was spent at a place that I am quite sure would have no special interest for you, except, perhaps, as a source for inventing vilifying stories, which I hope to escape listening to next year."[85] Fond hope.

Nella had sent Dorothy off with a design and instructions on purchasing material for a new coat she wanted to have made for her in Paris. She changed her mind about the material a few times and then told Dorothy to forget about it if she hadn't already bought the material, for she'd seen one in New York she wanted. She also asked for some handkerchiefs and a copy of Joyce's *Ulysses,* "if possible and convenient."[86] Still banned in the United States, *Ulysses* would have to be bought at Sylvia Beach's bookshop Shakespeare and Company, on the Left Bank, and essentially smuggled back to the States. Clearly Larsen wanted to keep up with the latest in modern literature, but she was also by now something of a book collector. She always, like her fictional protagonists, liked "nice things."

While Dorothy was away, Nella kept her informed about potential romantic prospects in New York, chiefly Harry Block. "I had quite a talk with Harry," she wrote in mid-July. "I think he's much interested in you. You'd better write to him a time or two, in a more or less intimate manner."[87] Apparently Dorothy responded to the advice, for that fall she and Harry would be an "item," experiencing the thrills of interracial romance in the Jazz Age. Nella also had her eye on Alonzo Smith for Dorothy: "I mentioned that you had tried hard to invite him over but that he wasn't at his office or at his apartment. He said that he hopes you are having a pleasant time . . . and that he'll see more of you this winter than in winters past."[88]

Nella's long letter to Dorothy in early July reveals how their lives had intertwined and how close they had grown to friends made through Van Vechten. In the month of July, Nella was constantly busy with this group. On July 3, Nella had Carl over for Sunday dinner, after which Harry Block came in and they all went out to hear the great blues singer Clara Smith.[89] On the fourth Fania returned from abroad, bringing Nella "a quaint little hammered brass box for cigarettes, or what-not."[90] On the fifth, Dorothy Harris called and then came up to Harlem with "Jimmie" to play bridge with Nella and Elmer. On the sixth, Eddie Wasserman threw a "night party" to welcome Fania home, with bright lights from the world of publishing and theater.[91] On the seventh or eighth, Nella and Elmer went to a small tea party at Muriel Draper's, and on the ninth she went to a stadium concert with Sidney Peterson. The next day, Van Vechten and Fania had Nella and Elmer to dinner, with Colin McPhee and Isa Schindel. Witter Bynner, Harry Block, Mark Mooring (a young producer), and Sidney Peterson came up afterward. Isa hadn't seen Carl since Dorothy's birthday party, and she filled the group in on a dinner Dorothy Peterson had hosted for her Gurdjieffian friends (at which Nella had not been present.) "So we had another g. [Gurdjieff] meeting. It was terribly funny, because Isa was quite cool, in spite of the devastating things that all the men plus Fania and I said to her."[92]

Slightly older than Nella, widowed and well-heeled, dark-haired Isa Glenn had grown up the daughter of a mayor of Atlanta. She was also a cousin of James McNeill Whistler and had studied painting in his Paris studio. She had later married a dashing West Point graduate, S. Bayard Schindel. Early in the marriage they'd lived in the Philippines and other outposts of American empire in Asia.[93] Her amazing but now completely forgotten first novel, *Heat,* had been published by Knopf in 1926, and like Hughes's *Fine Clothes to the Jew* bore a dust jacket by Covarrubias and a dedication to Van Vechten. An anti-imperialist story set during the Filipino American War, it criticized both the brutal military form of imperialism and its more altruistic "uplift" accompaniment, focusing in part on a single white American woman who comes to teach in a "native" school only to grow disillusioned with the whole notion of uplift. Glenn also critiques the lure of the "exotic"—a dangerous illusion for Western romantics innately connected with male fantasies of sexual exploitation. The effect of imperialism on whites, as *Heat* presents the case, is soul-rot and corruption; and on the displaced native peoples, misery and hatred for their overlords. When the novel closes, Tom Vernay, the chief male character, has gone "native" and married an abusive Filipino woman who despises him. A former prostitute and rebel sympathizer, she gets the novel's last word.

Glenn's several subsequent novels, psychologically intricate and always keenly attentive to the etiquette of race, often featured clever women who maneuvered for whatever power they could over their own lives, in conditions over which they had little control; the books also satirized the ideal of the Southern "lady." Remarkable as they are in their expert dissection of the intersections of race, gender, class, and sexuality, they have so far been completely lost to literary history. Like Nella Larsen, though before her, Glenn-Schindel used her maiden name as a nom de plume and became best known by it.

On the eleventh of July, Nella, Elmer, Eddie, Carl, Fania, Harry, Muriel Draper, and Isa made up a party (noted by the Harlem papers) to attend the Broadway opening of Ethel Waters' new show, *Africana.*[94] They sat in the middle of the fourth row, as Walter Winchell noted the next day, and cheered enthusiastically.[95] Waters "threw the house into fits of laughter" in a burlesque on Josephine Baker and the Italian count reputed to have offered her marriage—a skit for which Waters was soon served a warning by La Baker's attorney that they might sue.[96] Featuring saucy numbers like "Shake That Thing," "Take Your

Black Bottom Outside," and "My Special Friend Is in Town," *Africana* was Waters' first Broadway musical, sending her toward stardom while Florence Mills was abroad knocking out London audiences. "Some of it was excruciatingly funny," Nella reported to Dorothy. "I thought Harry would have to be carried out."[97] Afterward, she went backstage with her friends to congratulate Ethel and found her in tears because she hadn't changed clothes in time for the finale.[98] "It was a good, fast show," Waters remembered later, "and gave the theater-going ofays of Broadway their first long look at me."[99]

With her book in press, Larsen's reputation was growing. The author of an article on Ethel Waters in the *Pittsburgh Courier* reported that she had entertained the new star, not realizing that Waters had never shown up for her "tea."[100] Waters (or Earl Dancer) had used Nella's name to boost the singer's prestige. Nella was equally amused by an advertisement in the *Chicago Defender* puffing Howe's Bookshop and tea room in Harlem with the report that "Miss Dorothy Peterson Brooklyn society maid and Mrs. Elmer Imes, Harlem matron *and novelist* find our lunches very superior."[101] "(To what)," Nella added archly in the note to her friend. Harry Block asked her to read a book in Danish for Knopf and give him a judgment on it, for which she was paid five dollars.[102] Harpers sent her an advance copy of Countee Cullen's *Copper Sun* in July on Walter White's recommendation, with the idea that she might recommend it to friends and perhaps librarians.[103] She was not, however, sufficiently impressed, writing Dorothy: "It's fair. Just that."[104] As in fiction, her tastes in poetry tended more to the modernist styles.

If Larsen was getting a bit snooty in her judgments, she was not alone in suspecting that the standards for writing by African Americans had fallen. Alain Locke, Claude McKay, and Charles Chesnutt were among the many who thought as much. With the Negro vogue still on an upward arc, publishers were on the prowl for new manuscripts by black authors. "Dorothy," Nella wrote her friend, "you'd better write some poetry, or something. I've met a man from Macmillan's who asked me to look out for any Negro stuff and send them to him."[105]

Concerning "The Caucasian Storms Harlem," by Rudolph Fisher, she wrote Dorothy merely that he "has a fairish article in the Mercury about Harlem, called 'The Caucasian Invasion.' It's mostly about cabarets."[106] Fisher's essay reflected on the change in Harlem's cabaret culture since the early 1920s, when few whites ventured into the black clubs. He was at once dismayed and heartened by the phenomenon, for it seemed to suggest that whites were appreciating African American culture as never before. He wondered, as the *New York Age* summarized his meditation at the time, if Nordics were finally tuning in to the Negroes' wavelength. "Whatever the answer to this riddle of humanity it would indicate that the experiment of turning black into white may be tried also in the reverse direction. Time only can show what the result will prove to be. In the meanwhile, the effect of a Harlem cabaret course on the average Nordic should prove a mollifying and enlightening influence, in softening the asperities of a Puritan conscience wedded to the chase for the Almighty Dollar."[107] More common than this overly optimistic assessment were editorials fulminating against the Nordic invasion and the proliferation of nightclubs in general.

Harlem vogue or no, in the midst of a heat wave ("I haven't had on clothes for days") Larsen was sweltering in her fifth-floor walk-up on the mecca's busiest cross-street. Keeping the windows open for breezes, she was assailed by all the noise, shouting, and laughter that carried on late into the night. "I'm still looking for a place to move. Mrs. Beasley [a neighbor] is looking too. Its really rather ridiculous I suppose but—. Right now when I look out into the Harlem streets," she wrote Peterson facetiously, "I feel just like Helga Crane in my novel. Furious at being connected with all these niggers."[108] She wasn't alone. Numerous black professionals, including W. E. B. Du Bois, would soon flee the congested core of Harlem for places further north. But Larsen had no intention of leaving Harlem. A couple of weeks later she thought she'd found a place—in the same building, downstairs, "second floor back"; "not so noisy—but [double-underline in original] more accessible."[109] From her perch near 135th and Seventh Avenue, she could keep in touch with people and enjoy what Harlem had to offer.

Friends came up to see her occasionally, and she ran into others out on the town, including the era's stars. "I saw Roland [Hayes]—at a cabaret—recently," she informed Dorothy. After dropping their friend Crystal Bird, "he seems to have fallen violently in love with a very unsophisticated looking little girl of the Jewish persuasion—judging by appearances."[110] Nella dropped in on the Whites while they were packing for a trip to France on July 18th. "They intend to look you up," she warned Dorothy, "and you have my *very* deepest sympathy."[111] (As it turned out, Dorothy would write Carl, "Somehow or other I missed seeing your godson when he passed thru Paris. I think perhaps his father is passing for French or maybe French colonial or something like that.")[112]

By now Peterson's closest friend, Larsen kept her up-to-date on all the gossip, including the fact that Zora Hurston had married "some doctor in Chicago."[113] Not even Dorothy Harris was now so close to Peterson. As Harris prepared to sail for Paris, Larsen was the one who told her where the other Dorothy would be. Always an outsider, Nella was finding a place of intimacy with another woman, and it made a difference in her personality of which even she was

13. Larsen at her needle, summer 1927. Photo by James L. Allen. Library of Congress, Washington, D.C.

14. Portrait of Nella Larsen, summer 1927. Photo by James L. Allen. Yale Collection of American Literature, Beinecke Rare Book and Manuscript Library, Yale University.

aware. "I do miss you very much and that is remarkable!! because I'm not in the habit of missing people."[114] Letting down her guard, she was coming to depend on Peterson's friendship. She had found someone she could trust and, just as important, had found within herself the ability to trust. Evidently, this was becoming less true of her husband. "Elmer says I'm a selfish little beast. Etc. Etc."[115] In fact, Elmer was spending a fair amount of time away, and he may already have been philandering.

Imes felt frustrated by what he regarded as his wife's self-indulgence. She had quit her library job to write, but while partying hard was not getting much accomplished, and the household income had dropped precipitously. Nella told Dorothy that she was going to eliminate her social life because she had to "work like a nigger. I *must* make some money [triple underscore on the word "must"]. Almost I've decided too to sell my house and spend a couple of years abroad. Elmer too, of course. Why don't you too?"[116] She did not, however, follow through on the thought. This is the first mention of a house that Larsen may have purchased in her own right outside New York. She definitely spent time in the country north of the city in the late 1920s and after, and in later years her friends believed she had a house somewhere near Danbury, Connecticut.[117]

In late July or early August, Larsen sat for a series of portraits by a twenty-year-old black photographer, James L. Allen, who had been photographing prominent intellectuals and artists. He had already exhibited his work at the New York Camera Club, the 135th Street Library, and a special exhibition organized by Wallace Thurman on 136th Street in May; and he was slated to enter the Royal Photographers' exhibition in London that September.[118] He prided himself on capturing the varied skin tones of African Americans, and preferred soft-focus shots. The two portraits he took of Nella Larsen that survive include one nearly full-length profile of her sitting in a chair in a luxurious dark "oriental"-style dress, darkly shadowed, head down, evidently sewing. She wears her hair in a bun, a few stray hairs feathering her soft face, which appears meditative, reposed, far away. The other is a head-and-shoulders shot taken close up from her left. Her face is half-turned, strikingly attractive, young and bright; and her eyes gaze intelligently straight into the camera, focused more clearly than the rest of the face, revealing something, a quickness of perception, "a look." Briefly she seems to be all there, modern, alert, not haughty but sure of herself. It is one of James Allen's most memorable photographs.

On Thursday the twenty-first, she and Elmer went to the heavyweight fight between Jack Dempsey and Jack Sharkey at Yankee Stadium. They had first-rate seats, thanks to tickets from Elmer's boss. Nella was "quite enthusiastic about it—the crowds they say are marvelous."[119] Although Dempsey's carefully managed image had attracted women to the sport (and brought million-dollar gates), it remained unusual for women to attend boxing matches. With a ring built over second base, the ballfield and stands were jam-packed and roaring by the time the principals were introduced—just after Mayor Jimmy Walker—at 10:00 P.M. It turned out to be a very strange fight. The night was humid and misty, with a cloud of mosquitoes and gnats hovering over the lighted ring as the spectators settled in. For the first six rounds, Sharkey seemed in control, and Dempsey was wearing down. He began going hard to Sharkey's body, often below the belt. In the seventh round, after a clinch, Dempsey fought loose and threw a hard punch half a foot below the belt. While Sharkey protested to the referee, Dempsey struck again, even lower. Doubled over and backing away, Sharkey looked to the referee for a call of foul, leaving his chin an open target, and Dempsey nailed it on the point with his trademark left hook. Sharkey went down flat on his face at full length, his body quivering and writhing as the referee counted him out.[120] With the entire crowd on its feet, petite Nella (like most of the women) probably could only see the backs of the people in front of her and hear the roar at the fight's climax. Dempsey would go on to fight Gene Tunney in one of the most famous bouts ever, the climax of the era in boxing.

A night or two after the fight, Vivienne Stoner—whose marriage was in trouble—came up to visit Nella, bringing along a young friend named Julian Langner, whom Nella immediately liked. He was "by way of being a *real* person," having "been everywhere and seen everything," rather like a character in her fiction. But Nella was ill for several days after that, confined to the apartment until Sunday, July 31, when Carl and Fania had her and Elmer over to dinner to meet his sister and niece.[121]

On the third of August, she and her friends finally went to see *Rang Tang,* a black musical comedy by Flournoy Miller and Aubrey Lyle that had been running for three weeks. While it had some funny scenes trading on old "coon show" qualities, "as one watched it," James Weldon Johnson reflected, "the thought arose that perhaps the traditional pattern of Negro musical comedy was a bit worn."[122] It was becoming harder to laugh at some of the old routines. Increasingly, the best shows of the Twenties in New York would get their laughs by self-consciously spoofing those routines and racial stereotypes. The times demanded irony and sophistication, double entendres, turning old images inside out—as in Flo Mills's "I'm a Little Blackbird" performed in white tails, or Ethel Waters' burlesques of Josephine Baker and *Lulu Belle.*

Throughout August, Nella's round of dinners and parties carried on much as before. On the twentieth, while all Harlem was gay with flags for a black Elks convention, she had the photographer "Jimmie" Allen over, with Colin McPhee, Crystal Bird, and Van Vechten, who was promoting Allen's career. Presumably, they admired the pictures Allen had taken of her. After dinner Vi Stoner and Julian Langner came in, and they talked till 1:00 A.M.[123] The very next night, Nella and Elmer, with Ethel Waters and Earl Dancer, spent the evening at Carl and Fania's, where Aaron Douglas had recently repainted the bathroom with one of his trademark murals, of the sort soon to begin appearing on the walls of nightclubs, the 135th Street Library, and eventually the library at Fisk.[124] Whatever misunderstanding had arisen between Ethel and Nella was over.

Van Vechten and downtown friends would drop in for a friendly chat in the evening now and then, as did Vi Stoner and Crystal Bird. Nella was not so close to the other "name" writers of the Harlem Renaissance, which explains why she is rarely mentioned in their correspondence or memoirs. She ran into Langston Hughes and Zora Neale Hurston, for instance, mostly at larger gatherings in Harlem, at Van Vechten's, or at Eddie Wasserman's in the Village.[125]

Dorothy Peterson returned from France in September and caught up with Larsen immediately. Toward the end of September, when they stopped over at Van Vechten's newly redecorated apartment on 55th Street, Nella and Fania exchanged dresses.[126] It seems likely that this is when Nella loaned Fania the Golden Forest, by Poiret.[127]

When Club Ebony, a new black-owned cabaret, opened on the fifth of October, the Imeses gathered beforehand at Van Vechten's with Fania, Carl, Eddie, and Eddie's friend Olga Hilliard; they went as a party and took a table together. Lloyd Thomas, the manager, and his wife Edna were good friends of this group.[128] It was a vintage Twenties opening, much commented upon in the Harlem papers—"by far the smartest affair of the budding season," according to one reporter, who noticed Nella and Elmer there.[129] Florence Mills, just back from Europe, was the guest of honor, and Lenore Ulric, of *Lulu Belle* fame, came as the special guest of Edna Thomas, who had just replaced Evelyn Preer in the play.[130] Aaron Douglas had painted the club's interior in warm blues, oranges, blacks, and yellows, depicting tropical settings, African drummers and dancers, a banjo player, and a cakewalker, in a sort of visual history of black music and dance. On the main panel, a background of modern skyscrapers set off silhouettes of contemporary black performers—not a few of whom were in the audience.[131] Thick velvet carpets and red damask upholstery gave a sumptuous feeling to the place. On the packed dance floor, Mac Rae and his Ten Ebony Stompers managed to "stomp right down," although there was scarcely an inch of free space. "Way late," maybe 4:00 A.M., odors of fried chicken, corn fritters, bacon, scallops, waffles, and steak came wafting from the kitchen.[132]

As a black-owned cabaret, Club Ebony represented an attempt to keep the wealth derived from black entertainment in the black community. The quality of the owners and managers also symbolized the transformation of the saloon's back room into a respectable place of entertainment, for owners Gardner Pinckett and Lloyd Thomas were both highly regarded men of "society," not the "sporting class." And here, at their opening, came the elite of Harlem, Atlantic City, Greenwich Village, Washington, and Philadelphia.[133] Most important, before the opening of Club Ebony and the reopening of the Bamboo Inn the same night with a black manager and waiters (it had previously been staffed with Chinese), the only two "bigtime" Harlem clubs owned and managed by black men were Small's Paradise and the Nest.[134] Moreover, in the decoration of the club, Pinckett and Thomas gave Aaron Douglas his first opportunity to display his work on a large scale. With a name inspired by Gwendolyn Bennett's "Ebony Flute" column for *Opportunity,* Club Ebony would bring black popular entertainment, jazz, and "high art" together in true renaissance fashion.[135] It was never intended, however, as an all-black club. Like the new Bamboo Inn, the managers wanted to attract both white and black trade, and to bring money from downtown into Harlem. The gala opening raised hopes that blacks might take over a "new economic field."[136]

Arriving with Van Vechten at such affairs, however, was inherently a daring move. Not long before, the *Pittsburgh Courier* had quoted Elmer's esteemed brother at length attacking *Nigger Heaven,* Van Vechten, and his black friends for giving Harlem a bad name and encouraging immorality. Nella clipped the article out for Van Vechten's scrapbook.[137] On the first of the month, Terence E. Williams, manager of the Uptown Legal Bureau, had launched a similar attack on black women who were hanging around with Nordics, especially the "'queer' folks from Greenwich Village." Finding the Village too small for them, these outcasts of the white race had begun invading Harlem, aided and abetted by a few young black women. "While our men are showing what fine mettle they are made of, in every possible endeavor, these indiscreet females of the species are out there in the cabarets, these big fashion balls, escorted by the Nordics, these so-called ultras or whatever they are, razing to the very ground a structure of true, clean living that all the world adores."[138] Of course, Williams had certain particular (though unnamed) women in mind: "Carl Van Vechten came to Harlem and had a time of his life. We have often heard some of our dear, lovely creatures speak about 'Carl.' They showed him a time of splendor and he went into the finest homes and admitted that these Negroes really knew how to entertain, and then, at the final turn of the road, what did he say about them, about these ladies possessing this 'poise and finesse'—'Nigger Heaven.'"[139]

The day after Club Ebony's opening, producer Aubrey Lyle took advantage of a celebrity banquet for Florence Mills to speak out against Van Vechten and his friends. Under a banner headline, the *Pittsburgh Courier* reported his tirade in full that Saturday. Worried that Mills, "representing our highest and best," might be "gobbled up by a flattering Van Vechten and made to feature disgusting vulgarity," Lyle bitterly scored all those promoting the blues and the man who was singing the praises of Ethel Waters and Clara Smith.[140] Almost simultaneously, the *New York Telegraph* took aim at Waters herself: "Massa Carl Van Vechten's favorite colored girl is smutting her stuff in a joy-joint of her own" on West 54th Street, sneered Robert Garland, "singing of her adventures from the neck down. . . . The secrets of her boudoir leave me cold."[141]

When the Dark Tower, A'Lelia Walker's new "tea room," opened on October

15, Harlem had yet another black-owned and black-operated club, later to become legendary. A large room overlooking the back garden of Walker's 136th Street townhouse had been fitted up "after the Greenwich Village fashion," with a specially made cabinet holding books by black authors, and hand-painted verses by Langston Hughes ("The Weary Blues") and Countee Cullen ("The Dark Tower") on two of the gold-and-buff walls. A sky-blue Victrola complemented the dark-rose tints on the tables, chairs, and piano. Wine-colored candlesticks and special silverware graced the tables, with napkins inscribed "The Dark Tower." It was all very elegant and classy.

Invitations to the opening went out to only a select group of the "literati and elite of Harlem," and Nella Larsen Imes does not appear among the invitees and attendees listed in the society columns. Similarly, in reports of subsequent parties held at the Dark Tower during the club's brief life, Nella's name does not appear in the often long lists of participants. "Members only and those whom they wish to bring will be accepted," read the initial formal invitations.[142] Ironically, the fact that Larsen did not socialize much with A'Lelia Walker—for which Walker, not Larsen, is chiefly responsible—has been attributed to Larsen's supposed snobbishness and class pretensions.[143] In actuality, the converse was the case.

Ignored by the "colored aristocracy" because of her mother's lowly origins (as a washerwoman) and the source of her wealth (popular hair-straightening products), Walker turned to artists, entertainers, and white Broadway types to achieve "entree into the tiny closed circles which had refused the ambitious A'Lelia," according to Bruce Nugent. If she could befriend them, "they might in turn leave the sacred doors a little ajar," or even sponsor her "among their friends in the restricted groups."[144] Larsen was not in a position to do this. Walker often invited Van Vechten to her homes but not his friend Nella Imes.

The Dark Tower did not last long as an artist's hangout, however, and young artists never, according to Nugent, felt quite at home there. "The New Negro made one or two loyal attempts to try to support the place, the misplaced idea of the place, but they could not afford it. A'Lelia gave several soirees there to which were asked all of white social New York, and visiting royalty and Rothschilds. Slowly but surely the place began to fail. Finally A'Lelia in a rash of disgust (the artists had let her down, they didn't come and anyhow she was loosing [sic] money on the joint) closed it, less than a year after its gala opening. Such was the brief life of the 'Dark Tower.'"[145] In the fall of 1929 it reopened under different management as a traditional tea room.[146] But it went into legend as one of the great hangouts for black bohemians throughout the Harlem Renaissance.

It is possible that, like Carl and Fania, Nella was invited to the opening of the Dark Tower but missed it because of a party for DuBose and Dorothy Heyward the same night, in honor of the new play *Porgy* that had opened on the tenth under the auspices of Lawrence Langner's Theatre Guild.[147] Nella had been at Carl and Fania's on the fourteenth for cocktails, and was spending a lot of time with the Langners and others connected with the Guild; thus it seems likely that she spent the night of the fifteenth, as Van Vechten and Marinoff did, at the party in honor of the playwrights, whom she had met some months before.

Porgy had opened on October 10 at the Guild Theatre to rave reviews and much excitement among the black intelligentsia. Rather than using its own top talent and tinting their skins brown, as was often the practice in the past, the Guild had hired black actors, many of whom had never had a chance on Broadway or in front of mixed audiences. The script itself was rather dry, long, and clumsy, but the directing of Rouben Mamoulian, formerly of the Moscow Art Players, together with the brilliant acting, made it a great play in performance, according to the Harlem critics.[148] Cleon Throckmorton's set designs didn't hurt either. *Porgy* put *Lulu Belle* to shame and proved to Broadway that the "Negro" had arrived as a serious contender for dramatic honors. As James Weldon Johnson put it, "Here was more than the achievement of one or two individuals who might be set down as exceptions. Here was a large company giving a first-rate, even performance, with eight or ten reaching a high mark. The evidence was massive and indisputable. *Porgy* was one of the great theatrical successes of the decade."[149] Moreover, it "loomed high above every Negro drama that had ever been produced."[150] Everyone in Larsen's and Dorothy Peterson's circle thought the play a breakthrough. The young writers Bruce Nugent, Wallace Thurman, and Dorothy West actually had bit parts as denizens of Catfish Row—Thurman because he wanted to learn how to write plays. Like many theatrical phenomena of the time, too, the production had a benefit function. The band in the third and fourth scenes, readers of the program learned, was from the Jenkins Orphanage in Charleston, "part of the actual aggregation described in the lodge parade of Mr. Heyward's novel. Anyone interested in assisting this southern negro orphanage can communicate with them through the office of the Theatre Guild."[151]

The day after the party for the Heywards, Larsen went down to Van Vechten's early in the afternoon to help Fania make over a dress—probably Nella's Poiret dress, which Fania would wear for a large portrait soon begun by the artist Mary Mackinnon. (The painting, which went on tour with others by Mackinnon later in the year, would hang prominently in Marinoff's and Van Vechten's drawing rooms for decades thereafter.)[152] Then the two women left together for a party at the home of Tom Smith, Liveright's top editor. When they came back hours later, they cooked supper for Carl and Eddie Wasserman, and then Lawrence Langner came in to try to entice the group to another party, but since Carl had sworn off parties for a while, the group broke up about midnight and Nella went home to bed.[153]

That fall was a bittersweet one for New York's black theatrical world. While *Porgy* seemed to mark a milestone, the "Negro Ambassador to the World," Florence Mills, died suddenly of appendicitis. With a sweet and wholesome charisma, Mills had represented the pride and aspiration of black America to the world.[154] The ninety-eight-pound body lay in state for a week in a chapel at Seventh Avenue and 137th Street while thousands came to pay their respects. Swathed in silk and lace within a massive casket of hand-hammered bronze (reputedly a replica of the late Rudolph Valentino's), the "dainty little comedienne, singer and dancer" was poised by funeral directors for her last, and most lavish, performance. On Sunday, November 6, a splendid sunny day, thousands of people of all races thronged Harlem. The Mi-Tee Monarch Band headed the march down Seventh Avenue to 125th Street, over to Lenox Avenue and up to the church on 137th, with a uniformed group of Elks following as escorts. Next came nine cars bursting with floral tributes, including one gigantic arrangement (rumor had it) from the Prince of Wales, eight feet high and four feet broad. The casket, blanketed with roses, was followed by eighteen flower girls in sober gray, and then came the honorary pallbearers, male and female, mostly from the theatrical world. Scores of women fainted during the procession and one musician died of a heart attack. In the church, tributes cabled from all over Europe and the United States were read, including telegrams from James Weldon Johnson, Nora Holt, the Knopfs, and Bill "Bojangles" Robinson. After the service the cortège swung down Seventh Avenue to Woodlawn Cemetery under police escort. As it neared 142nd Street a low-circling plane released a flock of blackbirds, recalling Mills's song "I'm a Little Blackbird." At the cemetery another plane released flowers over the grave and the mourners.[155]

In histories written later in the twentieth century, Mills's death has occasionally been interpreted as a warning bell to the Harlem Renaissance, but it did not seem that way to most people at the time, certainly not to Nella Larsen and her friends. The outpouring of grief and love, as the black Harlem papers presented it, exemplified the ability of art to triumph over the color line.[156] Ethel Waters, one of the honorary pallbearers, looked to James Weldon Johnson like Flo's successor. Josephine Baker was the greatest star in Europe and was setting off a "suntan" craze on the beaches of France that has yet to end. Nora Holt was the biggest draw in Chicago. *Porgy*, produced by Lawrence Langner's group with several of Nella's friends in the cast, was the hit of Broadway. The first week of November, Paul Robeson and Lawrence Brown gave their first Paris recital of spirituals from Jim Johnson's *Book of American Negro Spirituals* to a packed house (including James Joyce and Sylvia Beach), with encore after encore.[157] *God's Trombones*, illustrated by Aaron Douglas, was in its second edition and getting excellent reviews; Johnson's *Autobiography of an Ex-Colored Man* had been republished. Walter White was on a Guggenheim Fellowship in France. First novels by Nella Larsen and Rudolph Fisher were in press at Knopf, New York's most prestigious publishing house. Her literary career was just getting started. She was accepted among some of the most fascinating and famous people in New York. She was having fun. Everything was looking up.

FIFTEEN

Year of Arrival:
1928

AS Nella rose from "nobody," at best the wife of Dr. Elmer Imes, to "somebody," a Knopf author named Nella Larsen, she grew more confident. The extraordinary developments in her life, accelerated after the move to Harlem, profoundly altered the dynamic of her marriage. Elmer's status still derived chiefly from traditional black institutional connections—Fisk, family, fraternity—and from his job, while hers derived increasingly from her writing and her reputation within the high bohemia of Manhattan modernism. As the year 1928 began, the renaissance—or was it just a fad?—seemed unstoppable. *Vanity Fair*'s January cover featured a collage-like illustration inspired by "Harlem" entertainment—a black chorus line, a banjo player in a tuxedo, and sheet music for "Nigger Heaven Blues." The Negro was in vogue, as Langston Hughes would later famously recall, and partly as a consequence of the vogue Larsen was being catapulted from obscurity right over her social betters in black New York—in a manner of speaking.

The higher echelons of the colored aristocracy, after all, considered the theater and artistic types from Greenwich Village with whom Larsen associated rejects from white society—a judgment that held some measure of truth, for many of them, like Marinoff and Van Vechten, had been outcasts on their native turf and had fled their middle-American homes or wretched backgrounds to find each other and create supportive communities in New York, independent of family and former social designation. If relations with such people looked treasonous or arrogant to some, they felt to Larsen like the long-awaited discovery of the people among whom she belonged—like the homecoming of a princess in a modern fairy tale. She inhabited a highly unusual niche.

Voyagers from outside found it completely disorienting. Visiting James Weldon Johnson in his downtown NAACP office, DuBose Heyward had difficulty absorbing the vision of the impressive Negro surrounded by busy stenographers and assistants, with white people waiting to speak to him. He was even more astounded when Grace Johnson came in and joined right into the conversation about current intellectual issues and how they related to Heyward's play. "What would grannie have said?" he wrote his sister afterward.[1]

Another white Southerner, the critic Hunter Stagg, came up from Richmond in early February. One of his first stops was Nella Imes's apartment, to which Carl Van Vechten brought him, along with the actor Tom Rutherford, on the first Friday in February. Like Rutherford, he had movie-star good looks and an open, yet discriminating mind. After Elmer arrived, the five of them left for the newly opened Sugar Cane, the Lulu Belle, and the Nest to take in the new acts, finally going home at dawn.[2] "I liked your friends very much," Nella wrote Carl a few days later, "Dorothy P. said she'll be glad to have them in her box Friday night" at the NAACP benefit dance.[3] Hunter Stagg had helped to edit *The Reviewer*, an important outlet for the first stage of the "Southern Renascence"; his meetings with the black intelligentsia of Harlem made an impression on him even stronger than that of the cabarets. Later Nella wrote Carl to add, "I did have a very exciting time while Hunter Stagg was here. I think he's perfectly grand, etc., etc. But alas! thinking back, I'm afraid I failed to take advantage of my opportunities; and as everyone knows it can never happen again,—never the exact mood, that delightful feeling of,—oh—er—pleasure."[4] Stagg was at least equally impressed by Nella Imes and would write, after reading *Quicksand* in May, "Nella is a woman of sense, thank goodness, and I am anxious to see what she will do next."[5]

While *Porgy* continued packing in audiences, black playwrights that winter tried to figure out how they could successfully break into Broadway with "serious" drama. On Monday, the sixth of February, Nella and Elmer, along with Dorothy and other black friends, attended the opening of *Meek Mose*, a "folk play" written, produced, and directed by Harlemites Lester A. Walton and Frank Wilson (one of *Porgy's* stars and winner of *Opportunity's* playwriting contest in 1926). Millionaire banker Otto Kahn, who had bankrolled Earl Dancer's *Africana*, was there, along with Mayor Jimmy Walker, the great German director Max Reinhardt, and critic Alexander Woollcott. Black alderman Fred R. Moore had a box with R. R. Moton (who had come up from Tuskegee on a visit), Dr. and Mrs. (Ruth Logan) E. P. Roberts, and Lester Walton's wife. Introduced by his Civil Service Commissioner, the black politician Ferdinand Q. Morton, Mayor Walker even got up after the second act to give a speech in support of the play, predicting a long run and complimenting the race on its cultural advances.[6] Many hopes rode on the production.

They did not outlast the final scene. In the play, the black citizens of Mexia, Texas, struggle against rising white envy of their economic progress. When whites begin condemnation proceedings to force the blacks out of their fine neighborhood into a swamp, the blacks divide into two groups, one militant and the other accommodating. Under Meek Mose, the accommodationist "church" people move, infuriating the militant faction; but just as the rage of the mob against Mose reaches its height, oil is discovered in the new "colored" section, fortuitously bearing out his favorite dictum, "The meek shall inherit the earth."[7] Even the best choral work on Broadway couldn't save this plot.[8]

Wilson foundered in the attempt to fit a politically conscious story of contemporary black Southern experience (which *Porgy* was not) within the thematic frame of Christian meekness as one of the prized inheritances of the race. Rollo Wilson attacked it in the *Pittsburgh Courier*: "The show is propaganda, simple and unadorned, for white supremacy," he lamented.[9] Percy Hammond in the *Herald Tribune* termed it "a mess of oversweet theatrical marmalade."[10] Larsen was equally caustic: "Frank Wilson ought to be shot for offering a receptive public anything like."[11]

Two days later, Van Vechten surprised her with a gorgeous bouquet commemorating the third anniversary of their first meeting. She made herself some tea and sat down to luxuriate. "Dear Carl, I was *so* surprised. They are lovely and you are a dear to think of me. Of course I had immediately to make tea—a nice China tea—so that I might enjoy them to the veriest fullest. I do thank you and I'm so pleased and they are such a grand colour."[12] Nella may not have known that Van Vechten always sent his more cherished friends a note or gift on the date he had recorded meeting them. For Nella, this was the first time, and it shows how his regard for her had grown in the three years since she had turned her attention to him at the Petersons' in Brooklyn.

Carl, Nella, and Elmer were together again for dinner Friday night at Eddie Wasserman's birthday party before setting off as a group for the NAACP dance at the Manhattan Casino. The people with Nella and Elmer that night were primarily theatrical, including Avery Hopwood, one of the most successful American playwrights and Carl's dearest friend except for Fania.[13] Amid Palm Beach décor, the dancing went on far into Saturday morning to the music of Ford Dabney's fifteen-piece jazz band from *Rang Tang*.[14]

On February 15, a Wednesday, Van Vechten dropped in on Nella in the afternoon while Elmer was at work.[15] Carl was about to go on a tour out West, first to Chicago to settle family business surrounding the death of his sister-in-law, Fannie, through whom he would inherit a million dollars in trust. (The bulk of the estate went to his niece Duane Van Vechten.)[16] While this was a major windfall, his business in Chicago was gloomy and awkward, for the death was unexpected. Nella and his good friends in New York who had known Fannie's daughter Duane apparently planned to go to church to mourn. Nella wrote him a long, thoughtful letter on February 18.

> Carl dear:
>
> I am sorry. And please say so to Duane for me, if you think its all right to do so.
>
> Donald [Angus] called up. I had almost completed a date to go to church on Sunday night when I remembered that I didn't know how to locate Tom Rutherford, so that will have to wait until you get back.[17]

Unaware that Carl was on the verge of departing for Chicago, Elmer had planned to go to see him that afternoon, until Nella filled him in:

> He's having a very amusing time with the French [*heavily revised and censored*] Nigger Heaven. I think I'm going to try laboring through it. Also Elmer was deploring the fact that he hadn't seen Fania since she came back. I *think* he sent her a valentine with a shine on it. Not entirely sure about this, he may have changed his mind and sent a pretty one.
>
> I am going into retreat. I do want to finish my book in the next two months. What I lack is self driving power. How do you do it?
>
> It has been a nice three years. I think you're the grandest friend that I've ever had, and I do hope that I will never do anything to merit the withdrawal of your friendship. I don't, of course, see, now, any immediate way to get myself off the red ink side of your ledger, but I'm not really worrying about that because you do understand everything.
>
> Our very best love for you, and the hope that things wont be too difficult and distressing for you. Please say hello to Nora for me and tell her that I'm always going to write her and never do. Will some day.
>
> Nella[18]

At the Apex Club on 35th Street near State, Chicago's swankiest new resort, Nora Holt, as hostess, was working the house and vamping like nobody's business, according to Van Vechten: "A scion of one of the richest Chicago families is violently in love with Nora. He is considerably wilder than Avery [Hopwood]. —We have written the headlines if this scandal breaks!"[19] Larsen had begun the first version of the novel that would eventually be *Passing*, in which the "black" Clare Kendry, married to a white millionaire, bumps into an old friend while both women are "passing" on the roof-level restaurant of the "Drayton Hotel" in Chicago—a structure based on the Drake Hotel in Chicago, where Van Vechten had been staying during his trip.

Elmer wrote Carl in early March to thank him for sending what he termed the "lynching of Nigger Heaven"—the bowdlerized French translation. "A great many Frenchmen must be convinced that Harlem associations made you a bit more than a little mad. It won't hurt, however."[20] He and Nella had also received a copy of John Vandercook's new novel, *Black Majesty*—probably sent at the author's request—which Elmer found "quite wonderful." He was reminded of the prophecy in *Nigger Heaven* that if black authors did not get busy using "racial" material, white authors would beat them to it. "Too bad some of 'our group' couldn't have done it. In the meantime McKay's book is simply terrible—as bad as Wilson's play—in quite another way."[21]

McKay's *Home to Harlem* takes its readers on a detailed tour of what he termed the "underworld" of black working-class life, among the buffet flats (hangouts serving liquor at all hours) and speakeasies frequented by single black men. McKay deliberately defied the critics who insisted black art should serve racial uplift, partly because he thought they knew nothing about art, and partly because he disagreed with their politics. The novel centers on the adventures of Jake, a longshoreman who deserted from the U.S. Army during World War I. On his first night back in Harlem he picks up a charming occasional prostitute who likes him so much she returns his payment for her services. Jake spends much of the rest of the novel hoping to find his beautiful "brownskin" again, while McKay introduces us to a spectrum of black working-class men, first in Harlem, then on the railroad and in cities where men who "run the road" stop between runs. Throughout, blues music provides a steady backbeat, distilling the rhythms and "melancholy-comic" quality of the black working-man's response to existence.[22] Believing that the future of the race depended on those (mostly dark-skinned and lower-class) people who were still in touch with their "primitive" selves, McKay depicted their lives unapologetically while bitterly castigating the "superior" pretensions of the African American bourgeoisie.[23] The matter-of-fact treatment of carefree sex and casual prostitution earned McKay a reputation for staking out the "lowest" ground of the Negro Renaissance. When *Home to Harlem* became a bestseller, its critics felt vindicated in their judgment that this was the sort of black fiction white readers wanted, and McKay shared in the obloquy showered upon *Nigger Heaven*, which many thought McKay had tried to emulate. Larsen's *Quicksand*, scheduled to come out at the end of the month, would seem to them just the antidote they were looking for. The reaction against McKay so conditioned responses to *Quicksand* that it blinded most readers to Larsen's main concerns, and she would go down to posterity, paired with Jessie Fauset, as an apologist for the light-skinned black elite.

Nella herself was sick again, for the fourth or fifth time since Christmas, according to Elmer: "You must help me get her to go to California when you come back," he said to Carl. "It would never do for you both to be there at the same time!"[24] Carl wrote Nella in early March but, still sick with "the grip," she took a week to respond, on Thursday the fifteenth: "No news in Harlem." She had nearly given up on the novel she had started. "I am having the most hellish time with my novel (not Quicksand). I've torn it all up and now face the prospect of starting all over again—if at all."[25] She had heard from the Whites, however, prompting some cutting wit: "A letter from Gladys enclosing a snap shot of your name sake on the back of which (the picture not the baby) is written 'Brother at six months.' I surmised that this poor infant has had so many names that now he is simply Brother. When he's about six and starting to school and they are compelled to call him something else, you'll see that it will be Walter."[26] She was right, of course; in fact, the Whites were already referring to the baby as Walter. Calling him "Brother" in her note to Nella was Gladys' way of avoiding embarrassment. Eventually a Frenchman helped the Whites out of their difficulty by referring to him as "le pigeon," and for years afterward he was called "Pidge."

Harlem was not entirely without gossipworthy news. W. E. B. Du Bois was nearing his sixtieth birthday, and a committee was sending out letters "asking people to subscribe $50 and $100 towards a purse of $2500 as a gift. Some nerve I say. I'm about to celebrate a birthday too and I felt like writing and telling them that I could use $2500 myself. In fact I think it will do me more good at thirty-five than him at sixty."[27] The reaction of the almost-thirty-seven-year-old Nella Larsen may seem ungracious, but $2,500 was an enormous sum at the time. A $50 donation (equivalent to $550 today) would have been nearly half a month's salary for an assistant librarian, and to all appearances Du Bois was living well on his $5,000 a year NAACP salary, in a special double flat at the prestigious Dunbar Apartments. What Nella did not know was that he still owed $3,000 to friends who had bailed him out of a $2,500 debt to Jessie Fauset and her sister in 1926, and his daughter Yolande was due to wed Countee Cullen in April, an event that demanded extraordinary reserves in every way.[28]

Van Vechten returned from his trip on the seventeenth of March, about the time that the first prepublication copies of Quicksand arrived. That day Larsen signed at least three personal copies and mailed them: "For dear Carl and Fania / with my love / Nella"; "For Eddie / in memory of his parties"; and "For Dorothy Peterson, This sad tale of a girl who came to a bad end."[29] A few days later she mailed copies to Nora Holt and Avery Hopwood.[30] Her Harlem friends received copies as well, often when they dropped in on her.[31] She had reason to glow at the style of the book's modern appearance: a beautiful light green dust-jacket with orange and black horizontal bands covered a cloth binding in bright orange with black scoring along the borders. The dimensions were typical for Knopf novels at the time, as was the Caslon typeface, which the colophon identified as that used for the first printed copies of the Declaration of Independence. The inside front flap, carrying a description of the tale, could not have been written by Larsen but may have had her prior approval:

> This is almost the only Negro novel of recent years which is wholly free from the curse of propaganda. Miss Larsen has an interesting story to tell, and she tells it in a thoroughly charming and civilized fashion. Her heroine is beset by problems, but they are the problems of the individual and not of a class or of a race. She meets them in Chicago, New York, Copenhagen, New York again, and finally once more in the South; and she confronts them like a human being—that is to say, with a certain gallantry and a pitiful inadequacy. It is a human, not a sociological, tragedy. Miss Larsen's first book is distinguished for the quality of its writing, for its wisdom, and for its unfailing interest.[32]

The description is remarkable for downplaying the "racial" subject matter. The Knopf marketing staff had declined even to use details from the "author's statement" they had solicited, which revealed the close correspondence between Larsen's life and that of her protagonist. Nor, in the jacket copy, did they attempt to piggy-back the book on the popularity of other "Negro" titles. The back flap carried merely an advertisement for *American Mercury* and the back of the jacket a list of "Distinguished Borzoi Fiction / Spring 1928"—including novels by Thomas Mann, Joseph Hergesheimer, Elinor Wylie, Isa Glenn, Max Brod, and Sigrid Undset. Heady company, indeed. These were exactly the kind of contemporary authors Larsen most admired. With review copies that were mailed to the press, Knopf included her autobiographical statement and the James Allen portrait in which she sits in a comfortable dark robe looking down, seemingly absorbed in sewing.

Nella and Elmer's social life picked up as soon as Van Vechten got home. They attended a small after-dinner party at his apartment on Tuesday, the twentieth, with Avery Hopwood, H. L. Mencken, and a friend named Raymond von Hofmannstal. Then, when Duane Van Vechten, the recent heiress, came to New York in early April, they attended a small dinner party for her, along with Carl's closest friends (and sometime lovers), Donald Angus and Avery Hopwood. "Gave a party for Duane last night," he reported to Fania, who was out of town. "I had snails because I didn't think the Imes would eat them and Avery and I could have plenty but everybody except Duane ate them!"[33] The next day, he began rereading *Quicksand* "with great pleasure"—which he no doubt communicated to Alfred and Blanche Knopf, as well as Emily Clark of *The Reviewer,* when he had them to dinner that night.[34] He continued reading the novel "with growing enthusiasm" over the next two days and then wrote Nella his sincere congratulations.

Officially released on the last day of March, *Quicksand* had received little immediate notice, and Larsen was feeling low. She and her friends probably searched through all the newspapers of early April, largely in vain. She responded on Tuesday, April 10: "It is impossible for me to tell how much your letter cheered a poor coloured child who for some reason or other has been feeling blue over that same old book. Its really the nicest letter I ever had."[35] One reason she felt low was probably the very first review, which came out in the *New York Times* on April 8, entitled "A Mulatto Girl." Despite the heading, the anonymous reviewer took his or her lead from the jacket copy, suggesting that race was not the central concern of the novel. With trepidation, the debut novelist read,

> "Quicksand" is not part of the tradition which began long ago when Mrs. Stowe pictured for us Simon Legree beating Uncle Tom, nor is it very much in the tradition which began recently when Van Vechten pictured for us the bright lights and social subtleties of Harlem. Miss Larsen cannot help being aware that the negro problem is a real one, cannot help being aware that negro exhibitionism, in the manner of *Nigger Heaven,* is a vivid and interesting spectacle; but she is most of all aware that a novelist's business is primarily with individuals and not with classes, and she confines herself to the life of Helga Crane.[36]

As Larsen read on, the review kept her in suspense, giving a workmanlike summary of the plot. Finally, in the last paragraph, came the judgment: "This is an articulate, sympathetic first novel, which tells its story and projects its heroine in a lucid, unexaggerated manner. In places, perhaps, it is a little lacking in fire, in vitality one finds it more convincing than moving. But it has a dignity which few first novels have and a wider outlook upon life than most negro ones."[37] This was far from a thumbs-down, but if most debut novelists dream of rave receptions, it didn't exactly fit the bill. The caveat that the book lacks "fire" seems connected with a blindness to the social criticism inherent in the work: Nella and Elmer thought the book bristled with social defiance. The greater letdown, however, was that Larsen would have to wait a full month for more reviews to start coming out. The sole exception was George Schuyler's piece in the *Pittsburgh Courier,* on April 14.

In the meantime, she had other things on her mind, particularly a party she threw on the wedding day of Yolande Du Bois and Countee Cullen, Monday,

April 9. The marriage of the great race leader's daughter to the lyric star of the Negro Renaissance promised to be one of the great social spectacles of late-Twenties Harlem, and all over the Eastern Seaboard the black elite pined for one of the 1,300 engraved invitations certifying that they "counted." Dr. and Mrs. Imes received one of them—chiefly because of Elmer's membership in the Boulé and the Fisk Club. Living close to the church and the reception site, they invited "a few of the thousand and one invited guests"—and some who were not invited to the wedding—to come for a cocktail "before proceeding to the solemnities." "Any time between four and five-thirty," she wrote Eddie Wasserman, "you can wet your whistle at 236 West 135th Street."[38]

Wasserman did not attend the party, because he was not invited to the wedding. As it turned out, Nella and Elmer didn't go to the wedding either. "People kept coming in and then deciding not to go on to the wedding, so we were here until eight o'clock. Then we went out to dinner. It was very amusing too because the sandwiches kept getting fewer and fewer and I kept rescuing them from hungry guests and saying firmly 'You'll have to leave some for Eddie Wasserman and some one else.' Then when you didn't appear they accused me of trying to save the food."[39] The church had practically filled up by 4:00 P.M. anyway, and not long after that the church doors had to be locked and the police called in to keep back the crowd.[40]

If Larsen was disappointed with the slow pace at which reviews of *Quicksand* were coming out, she had to be gratified by the inclusion of her portrait in a photography exhibit at the 135th Street Library. James L. Allen had chosen to represent his work with portraits of Paul Robeson, Aaron Douglas, Edna Thomas, Harold Jackman, James Weldon Johnson, Countee Cullen, Langston Hughes, Walter White, J. Rosamond Johnson, Alain Locke, Carl Van Vechten, and "Mrs. Elmer Imes." This put her in the company of the premier talents of the renaissance, and the portraits stayed on exhibit until the middle of May—perfect timing for Nella's book.[41]

On April 14, George Schuyler's review came out in the *Pittsburgh Courier.* Here, Schuyler assured his audience, was not a story of "bull-dikers, faggots, slums, cabarets, prostitution, [and] gin parties," but a tale of Negroes like the people "we know." "One may disagree with the author in some of her insinuations and assumptions, and to many—as to me—the heroine, Helga Crane, will appear unreal and incredible, and yet the story smacks of biography and is very well done. Few Negroes have written with the objectivity that characterizes this first novel. And few of them have etched character as successfully as Nella Larsen."[42] Unlike the *Times* reviewer, Schuyler noticed the attack on some sectors of the black bourgeoisie—an attack that might cause some readers to recoil.

Langston Hughes also appreciated Larsen's effort and took the trouble to send his congratulations, even though she had not sent him a copy of the novel. "Thanks for your letter," she responded. "It cheered me very much. I fear the book is having a very hard time, and am therefore grateful for any kind words." "You will be interested to know," she continued, "that Floyd Calvin says that the only part of the book worth printing is the verse of your poetry."[43] No fan of Hughes, Calvin probably caught the drift of *Quicksand*'s cultural politics better than most.

The same day Larsen wrote to Hughes, she sent some astonishing news to Van Vechten:

> On May thirteenth, Sunday, The *Women's Auxilliary* of the N.A.A.C.P. *is going to give a tea for me!!!* [two underscores on the phrase *Women's Auxilliary* and six on the word *me*] The good God only knows why. I hope you will get an invitation because this will be a time when I will need all of my friends. You will be very pleased to know that I was very gracious about accepting, though I wanted very much to have the pleasure of refusing. I acted as if nothing had happened, and declared myself very flattered. I dread breaking the news to Elmer, because I'm sure he'll be so furious that he'll have a convulsion of some sort.
>
> I hope I did the wise thing to accept.[44]

The Women's Auxiliary, or "Committee of One Hundred Women," included some of Larsen's good friends—Lillian Alexander, Dorothy Peterson, Grace Johnson—but also many of the women she had implicitly criticized.

Yet these aspects of *Quicksand* were completely overshadowed, for many readers, by the novel's middle- and upper-class settings. The resentment against McKay's *Home to Harlem* and Van Vechten's *Nigger Heaven* framed the reception of Larsen's tale. In her "Ebony Flute" column for the May issue of *Opportunity*, Gwendolyn Bennett knowingly predicted, "Many folks will be interested to hear that this book does not set as its tempo that of the Harlem cabaret—this is the story of the struggle of an interesting cultured Negro woman against her environment. Negroes who are squeamish about writers exposing our worst side will be relieved that Harlem night-life is more or less submerged by this author in the psychological struggle of the heroine."[45] The novel's incisive social critique and attack on racial subjection went almost completely unnoticed. Even when partially recognized, they were quickly buried beneath other concerns—chiefly old notions of mulattos suffering from instinctive conflict between "white blood" and "black blood" and a fixation on what sort of Negroes were "represented" in the novel.

On May 7, Nella and Elmer moved into "Uncle Tom's Cabin" (Elmer's term), a top-floor flat in the Dunbar apartment complex, facing Seventh Avenue. They paid $200 down and about $60 per month (nearly half of which went to "up-keep" and the other half to payment of principal and interest) for Apartment 6N, 2588 Seventh Avenue.[46] Matthew Henson, the Arctic explorer, lived on the second floor of the same building. On the shop-level ground floor, a spacious Madame C. J. Walker Beauty Parlor was preparing to open. There was also a grocery (the "Victory Store") and a new bank, Dunbar National, founded by John D. Rockefeller with a black management and staff.

Now famous as the residence of many celebrated figures of the "New Negro" era, the Paul Laurence Dunbar "garden apartments"—named, in appropriate renaissance style, for the famous black poet—originally grew out of a philanthropic plan for housing families of the working class in and around New York.[47] Beginning with a $50-per-room down payment, tenants would acquire stock in the corporation that owned the complex through a lease-to-own arrangement, with moderate monthly payments over a set term, at the end of which each tenant would become owner of his or her apartment. Rockefeller essentially underwrote the whole project after purchasing one of the largest unoccupied plots of land remaining in Manhattan, the old "Ontario Field" between 149th and 150th streets and Seventh and Eighth avenues.

If the financial scheme was devised by Rockefeller, the architectural genius behind the project was Andrew J. Thomas, a self-taught architect who had grown up in tenements and wanted to make the advantages of luxury apartment houses, with light and air and courtyards, available to people of modest means.[48] Beginning in Jackson Heights, Queens, he created a new type of apartment complex, using a whole city block and arranging buildings in clusters around central courtyards, much like college quadrangles, but with separate entrances to each unit and no corridors. Each courtyard had space for gardens and playground equipment.[49] In some buildings, shops, beauty parlors, and medical offices took up the first floor. Every apartment had plenty of light and air. Like the apartment building itself, each flat also lacked the traditional corridor separating rooms. One entered a typical four-room apartment from the outside landing through a small vestibule to the kitchen. Beyond this, there was a small breakfast nook, and an adjoining living room that was about ten feet by fourteen feet. The two bedrooms (roughly nine feet by twelve) opened off the living room, with a bathroom between them.[50]

Rockefeller and the Urban Leaguers who approached him about applying the garden apartment concept to Harlem had planned to provide low-rent housing and the incentives of ownership to working-class blacks. But the project was quickly seized upon by members of the Talented Tenth—Harlem's upper crust—seeking refuge from the deteriorating conditions around them. Perhaps working-class blacks, surviving on much less than white workers, could not have afforded the rent. But after those Harlemites who met with Rockefeller decided in favor of the cooperative arrangement, it was virtually a foregone conclusion that the apartments would house middle-class government workers, professionals, and business people.[51]

Quiet and self-enclosed, the complex created a sense of community among residents, but its design also served to wall it off from the surrounding neighborhoods and form an exclusive enclave. Two guards policed the grounds at night and one in the daytime, members of a special constabulary commissioned by the New York Police Department. No music was allowed after 10:00 P.M. if any neighbor wanted quiet.[52] W. E. B. Du Bois, looking for an escape from the offensive behavior and rent parties of his tenant-neighbors on St. Nicholas Avenue, managed to cut a special deal allowing him to buy two four-room apartments.[53] "Directory of Tenant-Owners Reads Like Blue Book of Accomplished Persons," read the subtitle of a February 1928 *Amsterdam News* article on the complex: "What is believed to be the greatest aggregation of Negro intellect, both of local and national repute, is now housed in one single aristocratic colony."[54] The colony had its own newspaper, a club room for older children, and a free nursery and daycare for younger ones.[55] At night wrought-iron lanterns with frosted glass lighted up the gardens. Truly, the Imeses had arrived.

The Thursday after the move, largely settled into the new place, Nella went to Van Vechten's for dinner and then to the theater to see Mae West in *Diamond Lil*. After the play, they went to a party at Eddie Wasserman's, meeting up with Elmer, Fania, and many others of their usual circle.[56] Two days later, the *Chicago Defender* carried a notice of Larsen's book under Allen's shadowy portrait of her. The caption read:

MISS NELLA LARSEN BIDS FOR LITERARY LAURELS—Hitherto unknown, whose new novel, *Quicksands* (Alfred A. Knopf & Co., New York), has been highly rated by critics. Miss Larsen, who deals with the subject of racial crossings, does one of the most interesting bits to be published since Miss Jessie Fauset wrote *There Is Confusion. Quicksands* is written somewhat on the same style as Miss Fauset's book, but lacks much of the interest of the latter. Unusual interest centers around this book because of the fact that so little has been and is known of the author. Many persons are of the opinion that much of her life is reflected in *Quicksands,* her first novel.[57]

How fitting that the first review of Larsen's novel in her hometown would emphasize questions about the identity of the "unknown" author, who had been raised within blocks of the *Defender* office.

There was quite a bit of curiosity about the woman who had suddenly, it seemed, made a dramatic entrance onto the stage of the Negro Renaissance. That month of May, the *Amsterdam News* carried a feature article on its editorial page entitled "New Author Unearthed Right Here in Harlem." Thelma Berlack, who had interviewed Larsen before the move to the Dunbar Apartments, described her subject as five foot two and 122 pounds, and even, somewhat astonishingly, specified her age: thirty-five. (Larsen was actually thirty-seven.) Most of the article consists of the biography of this mystery woman —"'Madame X,' or whatever you want to call her"—provided in the interview in response to Berlack's questions. Berlack specifies that Larsen went to high school in Chicago, then spent one year at Fisk and three at the University of Copenhagen. Oddly, however, Nella said she had "lived East only twelve years"— that is, since 1916, when she had returned to Lincoln Hospital from Tuskegee. Otherwise, the biographical summary follows what we know: assistant superintendent at Lincoln, "social service work for the Board of Health," assistant children's librarian at the Seward Park Branch, and children's librarian at the West 135th Street Branch of the New York Public Library. Carl Van Vechten, she said, had "discovered" her as a writer—"and in her living room is an autographed photograph of him. Five months in her head and six weeks on the typewriter is the time it took her to write her book." She had promised to write two more novels for Knopf, "neither . . . to be of the propaganda type."

Berlack found Larsen "a modern woman, for she smokes, wears her dresses short, does not believe in religion, churches and the like, and feels that people of the artistic type have a definite chance to help solve the race problem." Her hobbies were housekeeping, sewing, and playing bridge. Most curiously, the name "Imes" never appears in the article and Elmer is never named: "For nine years she has been married to a man who holds a Ph.D. degree in physics from the University of Michigan. He is employed downtown by an engineering company." And as for her own family, "The only relatives she has in this country are her mother, who is white, and a half-sister. They live in California. Her father, a Danish West Indian, died before she was old enough to know much about him. All of his people live in Denmark."[58] Evidently, Nella did not consider her stepfather a relative at this point. He was still very much alive in California, though probably separated from her mother.

On the afternoon of Sunday, May 20, Elmer Imes escorted his wife to the

Walker Studio for the NAACP tea in her honor, rescheduled from the thirteenth. Fully one hundred people packed the flower-decked room, bright with daisies, roses, jonquils, sweet peas, dogwood, and lilies. Nella's old Lincoln colleague Lucile Miller had made up the punch table charmingly in green and yellow. As Larsen looked over the well-dressed crowd, she saw many friends, new and old, sporting blue-and-white beribboned name cards—Adah Thoms, Grace Johnson, Corinne Wright, Dorothy Harris, Harold Jackman, Edna and Lloyd Thomas, "Bud" and Jane Fisher, Aaron and Alta Douglas, Carl Van Vechten and Fania Marinoff, Donald Angus, and many, many more. Neither Jessie Fauset nor Regina Anderson attended, nor did any of Nella's old Tuskegee acquaintances such as Ruth Logan Roberts.

Roberta Bosley, Larsen's former neighbor on 135th Street, started the festivities off with two spirituals, accompanied on the piano. The famed team of J. Rosamond Johnson and Taylor Gordon, home from European triumphs, followed with two numbers "in their inimitable style," and then Inez Richardson Wilson, chair of the Women's Committee, delivered an introduction for the committee's delegate to the national conference at Los Angeles and for three entrants in their Popularity Contest, the winner of which would get free round-trip tickets to California (Zora Neale Hurston was one of the entrants). Finally James Weldon Johnson stepped up to introduce Larsen, giving a brief speech on the significance of the literary movement and claiming that, as the Women's Page reporter for *Amsterdam News* phrased it, "there should be a real place for the woman novelist of the group, as she had such a complete background of achievement to her credit in the upward climb of the race." "Mrs. Imes" then spoke about her reasons for writing her novel. After what Van Vechten described as her "charming speech," autographed copies of *Quicksand* were sold while six ladies of the committee served the punch and cakes. It was what Dorothy Peterson might term a "kack party"—as "dicty" as could be. Nella Larsen Imes reveled in it.[59] Afterward, Carl, Fania, and Donald joined Nella and Elmer in their new apartment for supper and stayed until eleven.[60]

The buzz in black Manhattan was not entirely positive. Dorothy Peterson's father, Jerome, who had extensive contacts across Greater New York because of his political and journalistic background, reported that some women objected to Helga Crane and felt the book reflected badly on black women. They would have preferred a happy ending. "This adverse criticism," however, only confirmed Jerome Peterson's opinion that Larsen had "achieved distinction in the dissection of feminine character." People also objected to the fact that her "treatment of the ministry in the book is somewhat in the nature of an indictment."[61] Elmer's family surely felt stung, as did the many black New Yorkers with strong ties to Tuskegee. At Tuskegee itself, Elmer's cousin G. Lake Imes, who knew Nella from her work there, was still head of the seminary.

Soon reviews of *Quicksand* began appearing in a steady, if modest, stream. On the ninth of May came a paragraph in *The Nation,* a weekly followed by most of Larsen's friends, combining miscomprehension with sympathetic critique. The author, Alice Beals Parsons, began with the hoary notion that the novel was about "a mulatto who is dragged one way by her Negro blood and another by her white. . . . The motivation of this character is not always convincingly explained; the intention of the book is not even always clear; but it is a mine of information about one human being."[62]

On Sunday the thirteenth, a substantial, signed review by Roark Bradford appeared in the prestigious *New York Herald Tribune Books.* He was an odd choice, in that his own novel *Ol' Man Adam an' His Chillun* had just come out, with his confession that it was the "nigger," not the "Negro," that interested him. A stereotype-laden, rather outdated "folk" novel—the sort often termed "sympathetic" in those days—*Ol' Man Adam* is remembered today, if at all, as the story on which the play *Green Pastures* would be based. Peering through the lenses of past literary treatments of "mulatto" melodrama, Bradford finds that Larsen maintains the "wistful feeling" of a character torn between the "comforts of civilized culture" and the "rumble of old Africa," until, alone with Robert Anderson for a moment in Harlem, "savagery tears at her heart; the black blood chokes the white, and Africa rumbles through her veins." In Bradford's opinion, the novel fell off after this, into "odors" of "burnt cork, mostly." But ending on a highly positive note, he stressed the measured tone of Larsen's approach: "She is quite sensitive to Negro life, but she isn't hysterical about it. There is a saneness about her writing that, in these hysterical literary times, more than compensates for her faults."[63] Again, any comfort provided by the mildly positive tone of the review was vitiated by its simplemindedness.

On the fifteenth of May, the *Baltimore Afro-American* ran a cropped version of the Allen portrait with the caption, "COLORED OR WHITE," and a brief review on the editorial page. Like the *Defender,* the *Afro-American* seemed to find the identity of the author the chief source of interest, but this critic knew more about her. "In some respects," the review began, "this book is an autobiography. The author is a New York woman. Her real name, Mrs. Elmer Imes. Her mother is Danish and her father was colored, but her step-father is white." Like Roark Bradford, the critic reduces Helga's conflict to a battle of "bloods." Her "white blood will not let her be satisfied amid the military discipline of a southern school where she is a teacher, nor yet in Harlem, where jim crow is absent. . . . In

Copenhagen, Denmark, . . . it's the colored blood which rebels and causes her to refuse marriage offers of aristocratic Danes." Like Helga Crane, the review continues, "Mrs. Imes has lived in Denmark as well as in the U.S. She has taught at Tuskegee." But unlike Helga, it adds in mild disapproval, "she did not wed a preacher and have children faster than she ought to." Clearly the issue of racial "representativeness" remained uppermost in the critic's mind: "After the super-sex stories like *Rainbow Round My Shoulder* and *Home to Harlem*, *Quicksand* is a refreshing story, built on the proposition that there is something else in Negro life besides jazz and cabarets."[64] The pattern set by these early reviews in the *Times Book Review*, the *Defender*, *Herald Tribune Books*, and the *Afro-American* would rarely waver over the next several months. *Quicksand* suffered the fate of many books ahead of their time: people tried to fit it into patterns to which they were accustomed and, not always satisfied with the fit, found the novel wanting.[65]

Ruth L. Yates, on the editorial page of Floyd Calvin's *Pittsburgh Courier*, objected that Larsen portrayed only three groups of Negroes: "Southern hypocrites, the Bohemian set of Harlem," and "the uneducated." "Perhaps if Helga Crane had been placed with other groups of Negroes she would have been able to find happiness. Too much stress has been placed upon the illiterate Negro, the jazz-crazed Negro and the Negro who thinks that the white man is next to almighty. There are other classes of Negroes. Why not use them as examples once in a while?"[66] This would give incentive to Negroes and acquaint "the white race" with the fact that the "uncultured Negro" does not represent them all.[67] This response applies exactly the same criteria that had been used in the *Courier* against Langston Hughes. Yates completely suppresses a central strain of the novel, found in Larsen's treatment of Anne Grey (who is no bohemian and does not like jazz), Robert Anderson, and Mrs. Hayes-Rore. Intrigued, like others, by the parallels between the lives of the author and heroine, the reviewer objects to the unhappy ending. After all, "Miss Larsen seems to have been able to master the emotions which made Helga Crane restless, unsatisfied and misfit in the various social groups."[68] If Yates found the novel lacking because it did not treat positively the "best" of the race, others (mainly white) found, on the contrary, that it dwelt too much on the neuroses of an intellectual "New Negro" removed from the lives of more genuinely "black" subjects—a complaint that has had a long shelf life.[69]

Not all the reviews reduced the novel to the drama of warring blood. In the *Boston Evening Transcript*, an admiring reviewer praised Larsen's "tragedy of mistaken values, a tragedy that is independent of social rank and racial distinction. *Quicksand* proves quite definitely that a colored author can blend successfully the ever-moving history of the American negro with the broad, universal problems that cling to humanity as a whole."[70]

In the June issue of *The Crisis* Larsen finally found unstinted praise from none other than W. E. B. Du Bois, who reviewed *Quicksand* directly in contrast with McKay's *Home to Harlem.*

> Mrs. Imes, writing under the pen name of Nella Larsen, has done a fine, thoughtful and courageous piece of work in her novel. It is, on the whole, the best piece of fiction that Negro America has produced since the heyday of Chesnutt, and stands easily with Jessie Fauset's *There Is Confusion,* in its subtle comprehension of the curious cross currents that swirl about the black American.
>
> Claude McKay's *Home to Harlem,* on the other hand, for the most part nauseates me, and after the dirtier parts of its filth I feel distinctly like taking a bath.

Du Bois's enthusiasm for the novel can hardly be uncoupled from his wish to steer African American novelists away from the example of McKay, who "has used every art and emphasis to paint drunkenness, fighting, lascivious sexual promiscuity and utter absence of restraint in as bold and as bright colors as he can." He unquestionably connected this emphasis with the influence of Carl Van Vechten, charging McKay with catering to "a certain decadent section of the white American world, centered particularly in New York."

That Larsen serves as Du Bois's foil for the sort of literature demanded by white decadents is only one irony of the review, an irony that would reappear in much later literary criticism. And yet, identifying with his subject, Du Bois makes the unusually astute comment that "there is no 'happy ending' and yet the theme is not defeatist. . . . Helga Crane sinks at last still master of her whimsical, unsatisfied soul. In the end she will be beaten down even to death but she never will utterly surrender to hypocrisy and convention." Projecting yet further his own notion of the sort of black fiction needed, he continued, puzzlingly, that "Helga is typical of the new, honest, young fighting Negro woman—the one on whom 'race' sits negligibly and Life is always first and its wandering path is but darkened, not obliterated by the shadow of the Veil. White folk will not like this book. It is not near nasty enough for New York columnists. It is too sincere for the South and middle West. Therefore, buy it and make Mrs. Imes write many more novels."[71]

By pitting her work directly against McKay's on a stage where he could extensively iterate his objections to current directions of black fiction, Du Bois effectively subordinated Larsen's novel to his own agenda even as he raised it to the highest place in the African American canon. Perhaps no review shows so clearly how much the reception of *Quicksand* was framed by the battle between partisans of the "cabaret school" and those who identified with racial "uplift." This conflict, in turn, was framed in polarized racial terms that could only submerge important aspects of Larsen's novel: "White folk," we are assured, "will not like this book."

It is true that white people did not like the book; it is also true that black people did not like the book. But it is equally true that both black people and white people—most particularly white decadents like Carl Van Vechten—*did* like the book. One white critic, of rather more mixed feelings, was Eda Lou Walton, who wrote an extended review for *Opportunity,* the rival of *The Crisis* for cultural and artistic leadership of the renaissance. Walton was an assistant professor of modern poetry at New York University, author of a book of interpretations of Navajo and Blackfoot songs, and one of Countee Cullen's former teachers at NYU. She was a tough critic, with some knowledge of recent fiction on and by African Americans. Walton, notably, drew attention right away to the sexual aspect of the novel: "To tell the story of a cultivated and sensitive woman's defeat through her own sex-desire is a difficult task. When the woman is a mulatto and beset by hereditary, social and racial forces over which she has little control and into which she cannot fit, her character is so complex that any analysis of it takes a mature imagination. This, I believe, Miss Larsen is too young to have."[72] Walton's chief complaint is that the different aspects of Helga Crane's character do not cohere—she lacks, that is, a consistent self: "The character is not quite of one pattern." The complaint might have been made of Nella Larsen herself: "Now it is Helga, the aesthete, the impulsively intelligent girl whom we feel; now it is Helga, the mulatto, suffering from an inferiority complex about her mixed ancestry, her lack of social status."[73] What Walton terms a lack of realism or of psychological unity seems, in the context of Larsen's own life story, very close to self-revelation.

Unfortunately, Walton's comments quickly became even more damning. "Besides the difficulty of incomplete characterization there is the fault of fine-writing in the worst sense of that word. The opening paragraph is a good example of that elaborateness of uninteresting detail into which Miss Larsen plunges in order to assure us that her Helga is cultured and modern."[74] Walton failed to perceive the intensely personal design of Helga's room at Naxos—the way the design reflects Helga's personality and mental outlook. For Walton, the setting becomes merely a status-oriented display of sophistication motivated by the author's inferiority complex, rather than a means of delineating Helga Crane's eccentricity in the context of Naxos. Larsen would suffer from this kind of miscomprehension throughout the twentieth century. Yet Walton is probably right to complain, as others did, about Helga's sudden decision to marry Mr. Pleasant Green. While concluding with a belief in the author's potential, Walton finds her lacking when compared with other writers: "She has not in this first book anything of the usual richness and fullness of character presentation, or the zestful interest in life in Harlem that other novelists of Negro life have given us."[75] Would *Quicksand,* Larsen might well have wondered, ever be taken on its own terms?

There was still room for hope. In a piece written for her column "Book Chat" and released to newspapers in early August, Mary White Ovington, a founder of the NAACP whose critical judgment Larsen respected, gave one of the more attentive and admiring reviews, focusing on the power of Larsen's depiction of Helga Crane. Ovington was one of the few reviewers who avoided trying to subordinate the novel either to some theory of racial essences or to the battle between the "cabaret school" and the "conservatives"; and she was virtually the only one who paid close attention to the verbal as well as psychological texture of the novel—the extent to which its meanings are carried in subtle representations of perception and in the spare dialogue, rather than in overt action. She praised the "finished style, beautiful in its choice of words and its sureness of imagery." The secondary figures may be indistinct and the ending a bit unreal, but "Helga is clear, unforgettable. As she sits on the bedside idly dangling a mule across her bare toes, telling the astonished friend who comes in to see if she is ill, 'I am not going to be late to my class, I'm not going there at all,' we like her and applaud her reckless courage. We want greatly to learn what she will do next. She is a real person, one who will be long remembered by those who are interested in the literature of the colored race: and, we hope, by many others who are interested in literature with whatever race it may deal."[76] This was the most perceptive critical assessment the book would receive until the late 1970s.[77] I have yet to find a single newspaper that chose to print it.

Throughout June, Larsen's social life continued to center around Van Vechten and Dorothy Peterson and their various friends, with frequent dinners and cocktail parties. She also became friendly with Bill "Bojangles" Robinson through Van Vechten. Robinson had been a headliner in vaudeville for years, but with *Blackbirds of 1928* he lit up Broadway and rocketed to fame as "the greatest tap-dancer in the world."[78] Nella saw his work up close at a Van Vechten party in honor of Nora Holt, where he danced and Nora sang. Nora, for that matter, was becoming a rather good friend of Nella's, staying overnight with her when she visited New York in the midst of complicated divorce proceedings.[79] Another woman who became a regular part of Larsen's life at this time was Elizabeth Shaffer, Van Vechten's niece. One day in June, Larsen inscribed a copy of *Quicksand* for her: "To Elizabeth Shaffer, This sorry tale of a girl who got what she wanted."[80]

On the first of July, news came that Avery Hopwood had died in the ocean at Nice, evidently of a heart attack—quite possibly alcohol- and drug-induced. Only Fania and Donald Angus had been closer to Carl, to whom Nella wrote an exquisitely thoughtful letter on July 3:

> I have been reading a little in Peter Whiffle this morning. Do you remember the last time I saw Avery, at dinner at your house a night or two before he sailed, you told me that some of Peter was about him,—especially the Bermuda part? How well you have managed there to capture and fix some quality of his charm. And how fortunate—now.
>
> Fania too, I know is very sorrowful about this.
>
> Thanks to you both for letting me know Avery—and love
>
> > Nella

The Imeses' marriage was on the rack by now. Increasingly, Nella went out without Elmer, or he was out of town. On the fifteenth of August, he dropped in on Van Vechten: "in trouble—for dinner." In the course of the evening sixteen more people showed up and partied, but not Nella. That Friday afternoon, she went alone to see Carl, evidently about her marriage problems.[81] The relationship remained troubled at least into early September, when Elmer locked Nella out for a day and half, just as she was trying to finish her book. Nonetheless, they kept up a front of compatibility, hosting a Sunday dinner on the twenty-sixth of August, visiting with friends. When Dorothy Peterson moved at the end of August to 320 Second Avenue, down by Stuyvesant Park and the East Village, Elmer and Nella went together for lunch and an informal housewarming.[82]

The troubles were partly financial and partly job-related. Elmer's position had become precarious due to a drastic slowdown in railroad purchasing that forced major cutbacks at his company. To make matters worse, the laboratory had developed a string of products far beyond the capacity of the factory production schedule. Elmer's research department risked being shut down, temporarily at least, and he was frantically searching for alternatives—no easy job for a black research engineer and physicist in 1928.[83] He was thinking, specifically, of a faculty position at Fisk—a place to which Larsen had no desire to move. Moreover, he may already have begun an affair with the school's white publicity director, who visited New York frequently to raise funds and had a number of good friends (Lillian Alexander, Frances Grant, Victoria Bishop) in common with Nella. Larsen poured her fears and anxieties into the center of consciousness in her second novel: a woman worried about her husband's professional dissatisfaction in New York and his possible affair with an old friend who is "white."

Larsen wrote Van Vechten as soon as she was done with her manuscript, "I have this day completed your novel 'Nig.' That is, it has only to be copied. Thank God, Glory Halleluja Amen!"[84] At the same time, she was thinking of entering the Harmon Foundation Award competition in literature, a contest to encourage black writers. On August 25 she wrote George Haynes of the Foundation—an old friend and fraternity brother of Elmer's and another Dunbar resident—to ask for an application.[85] That very day, the *New York Age* reported that there had been so few entries by the original deadline, August 15, that the organizers had extended it to September 10.[86] "Looking back on the years output of Negro Literature," she wrote Van Vechten, "I don't see why I shouldn't have a look in. There's only Claude McKay besides—Rudolph is just too late—and the Harmon Foundation is in some way tied up with the uplift so maybe 'Home to Harlem' won't get a very warm welcome."[87] She was completely ignoring W. E. B. Du Bois and Jessie Fauset, both of whom were candidates for the award that year. She clearly interpreted the award as a prize for the best novel of 1928, which was an error, for the award was actually intended to recognize outstanding overall achievement in literature. This put her at a considerable disadvantage with regard to McKay, Du Bois, and Fauset.

On the nomination form, Lillian Alexander signed as the person "proposing" Nella's candidacy, although Larsen filled out the rest of the application herself, backdating it to August 10 just in case (the form specified August 15 as the deadline), and listing James Weldon Johnson, Jerome Peterson, and Eddie Wasserman as references. She asked Van Vechten if she could use him as a reference, but may have decided that his travels would make it difficult for him to write a recommendation.

As Nella was finishing her new novel, she was also thinking of leaving Knopf. On August 28, the day after the lunch at Dorothy's, she went to talk to Carl about it, saying she wanted to go to Viking Press, which apparently was after her manuscript. Viking had done a magnificent job with James Weldon Johnson's poetry collection *God's Trombones,* which featured gorgeous woodblock display lettering by C. B. Falls (famous for the *ABC Book*) and drawings by Aaron Douglas. Carl tried to dissuade her.[88] She wrote him on September 3:

I did tell you that I meant to do as you advised me?

I have had a very hellish week, but have finished my manuscript. This in spite of having been locked out for a day and a half, and sudden death. I wasn't, however, able to make a carbon copy. I did try, but just couldn't do it.

I don't suppose, or expect that at this eleventh hour you will have time to read it. And I realize that its my fault entirely. The C.P.T. [Colored People's Time] will be the descrution [destruction] of us all. And I'm sorry and disappointed.

But, I may type it again, as it does seem very badly done—even to me. Perhaps after another going over, the typing will look better. In that case I could send you a copy, if you'd not mind too much being bothered on a holiday. Do let me know exactly how you feel about it.[89]

Carl was setting off for Europe in just two days, however, and he never did see the manuscript that became *Passing* until its publication the following spring.

Nella made it to the September 5 sendoff party for Carl in the royal suite of the *S.S. Mauretania,* to which nearly all his New York friends came. As they drank up at least a case of champagne, Witter Bynner composed some verse in honor of the occasion. And the festivities ended with panache: "In the final moments, Nora Holt belted out *My Daddy Rocks Me with One Steady Roll.* When she finished, an unidentified Southern lady tottered up to her to confide, 'How well you sing spirituals, my dear.'"[90]

Two weeks later, Crystal Bird and her sister went abroad—"On the forty thousand Hay[e]s dollars, I suppose," Nella would write (referring to the money Roland had given to Crystal in their out-of-court settlement).[91] She and Dorothy Peterson sent them off in proper style. "Nella and I gave a Kack party up at the Walker Studio for them," Dorothy wrote Carl. Donald Angus and Dorothy's boyfriend, Harry Block, "were afraid of the kacks ['dicty' Negroes] and wouldn't come—Eddie who is partly kack himself came for the earlier part of the evening —and Elizabeth came in late after the theatre—all the rest of the people were kacks and the party was a beastly bore, nothing but dancing and polite conversation."[92] Nella, who termed the party "*very very* dicty" [double underline on *very very*], noted that Blanche Knopf had also come, with Eddie: "She was particularly charming that night, and so was Elizabeth Shaffer."[93]

In one of her typical newsy letters, Nella mentioned that she had seen Jack Stevens and Tom Rutherford, and that the Whites were back from France— "Gladys White is ever so much more charming since her return."[94] The Whites took a new apartment overlooking the Hudson at 409 Edgecombe, in what Langston Hughes would call "Harlem's tallest and most exclusive apartment house."[95] Ethel Waters, having let Earl Dancer slide, had been picked up on the rebound by a new paramour in Philadelphia: "She does look well. The new man is very handsome but that is all. Still I don't believe he has the cupidity of his predecessor."

Elmer had not been feeling well for some time and, Nella thought, needed a long vacation. They were feeling the pinch of living solely on his imperiled income, and she was thinking of returning to the library, "if I can't get a job that suits and pays me better."[96] She did not mention that the couple's finances would give out quickly if Elmer lost his job, which seemed imminent.

The ever-industrious Walter White had given Nella a letter of introduction to Samuel Craig, president of the Book League of America—a new venture which sold books on a subscription basis—identifying her as "one of the best known of the younger Negro writers," and *Quicksand* as "one of the best written by any Negro author and one of the most distinguished first novels by any American author written within recent years."[97] She had, moreover, graduated from the New York Public Library's library school and "is an expert in cataloguing and manuscript reading."[98] On the very day that White wrote his letter, Elmer wrote the president of Fisk asking for a position. His New York laboratory being in jeopardy because of business troubles, he explained, he had decided to approach his alma mater because he knew the place already. He hoped to be able to continue his work there, which could put Fisk on the map in applied physics research.[99]

Armed with White's letter, Nella went in to meet Mr. Craig and David Roderick, the league's vice president, in late September. She impressed them greatly as they talked with her about plans for the company, and they asked her to come back soon, but she never did. Roderick wrote White in mid-October, trying to track her down: "I had expected to see her within a few days following that visit. I do not have her address and I am writing to see if you could forward it to me, so that I might get in touch with her again."[100] Clearly, Roderick was interested in hiring Larsen; otherwise, he could have simply let the matter drop. White immediately replied and then wrote Nella, enclosing Roderick's letter and a copy of his own, urging her to call Roderick "as soon as possible."[101] But Larsen apparently had lost interest, while Elmer had received an enthusiastic response from President Jones of Fisk. By early 1929 he would be asking for a postponement of a move there, where he was expected soon.[102]

Larsen heard good news from Knopf almost simultaneously. Soon after receiving her manuscript, Harry Block told her it was "at least four times better than Quicksand." By mid-October, it was already scheduled to come out April 19, 1929. She doubted that it was as good as Harry said it was, "because it was done much too quickly. Two months—not counting the time it did me to type it."[103]

She had also been approached for a story by the editors of a newly organized magazine, *Harlem,* under almost the same leadership as *Fire!!* It was to be a black literary review, and Nella was interested; but since they couldn't pay contributors, she decided not to submit anything. "I write so slowly and with such great reluctance that it seems a waste of time." Moreover, her ultimate goal in writing, she confessed, was "money"—something the Imes ménage needed to worry about at the moment.[104]

Larsen was not the only black intellectual to avoid entanglement in *Harlem,* and her friends would have cautioned her against it. Dorothy Peterson had helped to sponsor *Fire!!* and wanted no part of another magazine edited by Wallace Thurman. Knowing this, when her old friends Bruce Nugent and Scholley Alexander approached her about doing a theatrical page each month, they made no mention of Thurman. Next, they suggested that Scholley Alexander would be the editor and that they needed a business manager. Shortly thereafter, Peterson received a letter from Thurman—with his name on the letterhead as editor—thanking her for her support. "So you see," she wrote Van Vechten, "they are still putting things over on your poor little friend."[105] Scholley Alexander had pleaded with her to support the venture: "Bruce [Nugent] has been painfully frank about your past support of Wallace and his selfish treatment of those who have helped him gain a place in the literary world. I appreciate your reluctance in joining forces with him again—and I am well aware of the attitude of your friends—those who would resent seeing you show a misplaced loyalty once again." Alexander assured her that he would not let Wallace run amok. "If you will ask your friends to forbear—to *with-hold their criticism until they have the first issue at hand to criticize*—then you will render *yourself* and *us all* a very real service" (the phrases "first issue at hand" and "us all" are underscored twice).[106] The appeal failed. Resentful at having been "tricked," Peterson contributed nothing to *Harlem.*

Since all of this happened at the same time that the board approached Nella Larsen for a contribution, it is not surprising that she turned them down. She probably was glad in the end. All of her friends considered *Harlem* a failure, including Bruce Nugent, who wrote Dorothy after the issue came out to express his disappointment, blaming it on "Wally's" editorship. Thurman was simply impossible, he confided, and neither Scholley nor Aaron Douglas was insightful or strong enough to counteract him. (Nugent himself was touring with the cast of *Porgy* as the magazine was put together.) He was particularly concerned that

Van Vechten should not think he had been "in any way responsible for the perpetration of Harlem."[107]

Thurman's own piece for the magazine—a review essay dealing with *Quicksand*, Fisher's *Walls of Jericho*, and Captain Canot's *Adventures of an African Slaver*—castigated Larsen for creating a senseless character: "For the most part all Helga ever does is run away from certain situations and straddle the fence; so consistently, in fact, that when she does fall on the dark side the reader has lost all interest and sympathy, nor can he believe that such a thing has really happened." But Thurman asserts, "The author of *Quicksand* no doubt pleases Dr. Du Bois for she stays in her own sphere and writes about the sort of people one can invite to one's home without losing one's social prestige. She doesn't give white people the impression that all Negroes are gin drinkers, cabaret hounds and of the half world. Her Negroes are all of the upper class. And how!"[108] Thurman had given closer attention to Du Bois's review of the novel than to the novel itself.

With Van Vechten out of town, Larsen's social life had quieted down considerably. "There is, of course, nothing happening here, with you out of town. Are you ever coming back?" But Dorothy Harris still came by often; and probably in the company of Dorothy Peterson, who had a keen interest in drama, Larsen made the opening of the Civic Repertory Company's historic production of *The Cherry Orchard*, with the celebrated Russian actress Alla Nazimova as Madame Ranevsky: "I wish Fania could have seen her," she wrote her friends in Europe. "She really was wonderful."[109]

To some African Americans interested in the arts, if not to Wallace Thurman, Nella Larsen was one of the heralds of a new day in literature. Bruce Nugent, playing with the *Porgy* company at the Blackstone Theatre in Chicago, added a postscript to a letter to Dorothy Peterson on November 22: "Tell Nella that she is quite a hit out here."[110] A couple of weeks later, Larsen was a guest of honor at the first of the season's "intimate talks on the theatre" at the Hotel Warwick, in a discussion entitled "The Negro as Dramatic Material."[111] And in late November the *New York Age* held her up as a pioneer of a new direction in the representation of African Americans. The "only remedy" to the current flood of books and plays portraying the "lower" life of Harlem, the writer believed, was to write plays showing "another side of Negro life and better books."

Something has been accomplished along these lines by two or three of our writers, who have shown sound psychology in their character drawing and carried their stories to a logical conclusion. But the big success is yet to come along these lines. The writers who have already given us *Quicksand, There Is*

Confusion, Flight, and *The Walls of Jericho,* may be looked for to follow up these early successes by a fuller and higher conception of the life and aspirations of the race, which will command general attention.[112]

The "positive" response to *Quicksand* continued to be based on a class bias and an ethos of uplift that were ironically at odds with Larsen's whole point of view. (Nearly six decades would pass before critics and writers gave the novel a closer look.) Perhaps she would shock readers out of their complacency with a new work dedicated to the "devil" Van Vechten and his wife—a tale she had daringly entitled "Nig."

[SIXTEEN]

Passing

I F *Quicksand,* as its epigraph implies, is about a woman "neither white nor black," *Passing*—which shed the manuscript title "Nig" at the book stage, possibly at Knopf's urging after the flak over the title *Nigger Heaven*—is about the disturbance generated by a woman *both* white *and* black. With her combination of skin color, social positioning, and racial background, Clare Kendry is, literally, both a black white woman and a white black woman. Classwise she has been both "low" and "high." Clare's childhood resonates strongly with Larsen's own in important details. But rather than recounting the tale from Clare's point of view, or that of an omniscient narrator, Larsen filters the narrator's perceptions of Clare through the clouded perspective of Irene Redfield, the other main character, thereby leaving Clare a mystery.

It would be a mistake to think of either of these two women in *Passing* as based specifically on Larsen or any of her friends, but elements of her character can easily be discerned in both Irene, who is referred to throughout the novel by her married name, and Clare, who is referred to by her maiden name. The two women are not exactly alter egos, but Larsen clearly develops them as complex doubles. As Mae Gwendolyn Henderson has pointed out, whenever Clare utters her opposite's name, she drops the *I* and uses the form '*Rene.*[1] Not that Imes/ Larsen divided herself into these two characters; rather, she drew upon her own emotional life and personal habits in developing them. Irene's marriage anxieties and concern for "safety" resonate with Larsen's own in 1928 and 1929, but Clare is the character she most admires, and the one who preserves the most creative and destructive aspects of her personality rooted in youth: her "having" nature, her mysteriousness, her indifference to traditional moral expectations, her gallantry, her attitude to the color line and essential ambivalence about racial loyalty as such, her peculiar adaptation to the racism of individuals on whom she relies, and her capacity for heights and depths of feeling that those who prize security within conventional social mores can never know.

Larsen developed *Passing* much like a play, symmetrically formed into three parts, or acts—Encounter, Reencounter, and Finale—each consisting of four chapters, or scenes. She probably worked out the basic story line first, including the history of her main characters, and then deliberately broke it up with a brief flashback (a modern cinematic technique, as a contemporary reviewer noted) in the first chapter recalling Clare's childhood and then a long flashback beginning in the second chapter that takes up nearly a third of the novel. Riffing brilliantly on the nature of passing in the novel's very exposition, she withholds any mention of race or color until well into Chapter 2, where, with feigned nonchalance, she drops the veil: "Did that woman, could that woman, somehow know that here before her very eyes on the roof of the Drayton sat a Negro? Absurd! Impossible! White people were so stupid about such things for all that they usually asserted that they were able to tell."[2] Up to this point, one has had no way of knowing that Irene is black. The greater irony is that neither Irene nor the reader suspects that the other woman is a Negro, too—a fact all the more telling in that she is a childhood friend of Irene's. Some things, we will learn, Irene prefers not to remember. As a result, our knowledge is blocked.

In *Passing*, Larsen returns to some of the methods she used in her early short story "Freedom"—techniques for treating abjection, fetishism, and psychic disavowal through ingenious use of the third-person limited point of view. By funneling our perceptions of Clare and nearly all of the action of the novel through Irene as the center of consciousness, Larsen makes Irene's defense against the psychic disturbance Clare generates inseparable from our understanding. Irene must do away with Clare, and erase this erasure, to maintain the order of her world, while "forgetting" her own role in this North American ritual. Yet the reader is left with no evidence on which to convict her. *Passing* is an extraordinary novel in many respects, but it is extraordinary above all for its treatment of the psychology of disavowal.

The novel opens with Irene going through her mail and coming upon a letter from her childhood acquaintance. Provoked by Clare's boldness and unconventionality, Irene is reminded of the "pale small girl," "stepping always on the edge of danger," whom she had once known (*Passing*, p. 4). This first view of Clare reflects fragments of Larsen's own remembered childhood: a young girl, assistant to a dressmaker, sits on a ragged blue sofa in a working-class apartment on Chicago's South Side, sewing pieces of bright red cloth to make a dress for a Christmas party. Her powerfully built, alcoholic father abuses and threatens her because she has kept some of her earnings for herself. "But . . . she had made up her mind to wear a new dress. So, in spite of certain unpleasantness and possible danger, she had taken the money to buy the material for that pathetic little red frock" (p. 5). Clare—like Larsen—loves to dress up, has a highly developed fashion sense, and speaks in a low, "slightly husky" voice. Going out to dance, she wears her hair, again like Larsen, in a tight bun at the nape of her neck. When Irene encounters her on the roof of the Drayton Hotel, she is wearing a frock of green, Larsen's favorite fabric color.

Reference is never made to Clare's mother, but her father dies in a "silly saloon fight" when Clare is fifteen—the same age as Helga Crane when her mother dies in *Quicksand,* and one year younger than Larsen was when her family moved to "white" Englewood and sent her off to Fisk. As the daughter of an illegitimate mulatto janitor, taken in by white aunts on Chicago's West Side after her father's death, Clare, like Helga Crane, grows up betwixt and between —on the lines dividing black and white, as well as the middle and lower classes. This position has helped her to develop an extraordinary awareness of the hypocrisy around her (an awareness she has to muffle in order to get by), a furtive insight into other people's thoughts and actions, and a lack of allegiance to the kind of collective wisdom that cements group identities. As a result, Clare is essentially amoral, apolitical, and mysterious, lacking reference to the world around her, to borrow a phrase Hawthorne used to describe Hester Prynne's Pearl. Inciting both entranced admiration and dread, when she suddenly reappears as a beautiful and sophisticated adult, she is the nearly perfect human embodiment of a fetish.

Nearly a third of the novel recounts Irene's disturbing memories of two encounters in Chicago in 1925, when Clare suddenly reentered the margins of her life. In the first, Irene has escaped the summer heat by "passing" in a rooftop restaurant of the Drayton Hotel, when a "white" woman seated nearby begins staring and then comes over to ask if they mightn't know each other. Irene, cycling mentally through all the white women she has known, is at a loss until Clare finally identifies herself and then sits down to talk. Had Irene not been thinking of the woman as white, she would have had less trouble remembering her. "Black" Clare is now a wealthy white woman with two children; but she longs to reconnect with Irene. After the conversation, which Irene finds vaguely disturbing, being both attracted to and repulsed by Clare, she is determined not to renew the friendship. But Clare manages to inveigle Irene into visiting her hotel apartment, where she has also invited another old acquaintance, Gertrude, who "married white" but whom Irene disdains. When Clare's husband, Jack Bellew, comes in, the three women engage spontaneously in an elaborate performance to keep Clare's racial background a secret while Jack freely expresses his racist notions and calls his wife by the pet name "Nig." The suspense, danger, hilarity, suppressed indignation, and barely controlled hysteria of the scene all hinge on the potential revelation of the marriage as a mixed one, with both Irene and Gertrude cooperating to keep the secret. Larsen deliberately develops the scene to make the deception as difficult as possible. Clare orchestrates the entire shadow-play and looks on dispassionately as it unfolds. Outraged, Irene departs feeling all the more determined never to speak to her again.

Part Two returns to the present (1927) where the book opened. Irene is at home, opening her mail. Determined not to respond to Clare's renewed attempt to connect and to experience the Negro world, this time in Harlem, she finds herself nonetheless seduced when Clare comes in person to visit her, barging into the Redfield home off Seventh Avenue just as Irene is fretting over the state of her marriage. From this point a correspondence develops between the desire of her husband Brian to move to Brazil, where (they believe) there is no color line, and Clare's determination to move freely between the white and black worlds, even if it should mean Jack's discovery of her secret and the destruction of her marriage. Ultimately, these two threats to Irene's psychological security and social mores—in short, her identity—merge when she becomes convinced that Brian and Clare have fallen in love.

In Part Three, "Finale," Irene becomes more determined than ever to prevent Clare from becoming "black" again, since this would spell the end of the Bellew marriage and leave Clare free to win Brian from her. She hopes for some way of conveying to Clare's husband that his wife has been taking up with Negroes (but not that she *is* Negro), which she believes would lead him to take Clare away from New York and out of Irene's life. But when Irene bumps into Jack on the street while out with a visibly black friend, out of race loyalty to Clare (to "protect" a racial sister who is passing) she pretends she doesn't know him. Unable to come up with a way of keeping Clare on the white side of the color line, Irene now wishes her dead. She gets her wish in the final scene, when Clare "falls" out of a window at a party in a sixth-floor Harlem apartment. Larsen's masterful use of the third-person limited point of view justifies itself most brilliantly in the resolution, which leaves Irene both saved and damned, a tragic villain.

With an audacity even greater than that in *Quicksand,* Larsen addresses the core of her argument with the black middle and professional classes. White racism in *Passing* is blatant—up close and personal in the figure of Jack Bellew. Larsen uses Jack to ratchet up the tension in the middle of the story, to throw sympathy toward Irene and to make Clare's moral position untenable; and then she bores into Irene's consciousness with a nurse's precision—not merciless, but strict—to discover the roots and effects of the issue, the nature of a malady that Irene herself cannot acknowledge.

As the bare plot outline reveals, *Passing* overturned prior conventions of black-authored novels of passing and put to confusion nearly all the tendencies to racial idealization common in both white- and black-authored texts on the topic. Judith Berzon has pointed out that the chief difference between black-authored and white-authored passing fiction is "the emphasis in black novels on racial pride."[3] The "whiteness" of the passing mulatto, far from being a mere appeal to white empathy, is employed to mark a boundary for the consolidation of Negro identity, as the passing protagonist either "sells his birthright for a mess of pottage" or finally repudiates passing, chooses black over white identity after recognizing the moral bankruptcy of white identity, and thus affirms the ethical triumph of black race loyalty.[4] At a time when segregation of the races was growing ever more universal and absolute, Hazel Carby has pointed out, "the mulatto figure was a recognition of the difference between and separateness of the races at the same time as it was a product of a sexual relationship between white and black."[5] That sexual relationship, however, was supposed to be either all of the past or a purely exploitative affair, a matter of white male sexual predation. In *Passing,* everything is different. As Mary Condé has pointed out, "What is powerful and unexpected" in *Passing* "is the sympathy which Larsen shows not for Irene, who remains true to her racial origins except for brief excursions, but for Clare, who betrays them."[6]

Critics have often found fault with the novel's ending, seeing Clare's death as a melodramatic and unrealistic means by which Larsen extricated herself from a narrative corner into which she had painted herself. But the scene uses the techniques of expressionism (a mode, as in O'Neill's drama, that borrows from melodrama and eschews verisimilitude) and is necessary for setting up the real focus of the novel's ending, which is not Clare's death but the drama of disavowal, the covering up of those processes by which threats to identity are done away with. Corresponding to complaints about the ending is the common charge that the novel is weakened by its very attention to passing and to a supposed tragic mulatto—hackneyed conventions allegedly dictated by the need (or pathetic desire) to appeal to a white audience. According to this way of thinking, *Passing* only "passes" as a novel about passing (in Condé's witty phrase), and Larsen lacked the courage to address openly her "real" concerns. Cowed by white audience expectations and driven by her own class pretensions to write about genteel mulattos, Larsen supposedly "masked" her most subversive themes and ultimately "paid a price," as Cheryl A. Wall once put it: "Passing is and ever was a losing game."[7] The conventions of tragic mulatto fiction, as Nathan Huggins argued long ago, allegedly overwhelmed her.[8] On the contrary, Larsen uses her titular subject matter to blast wide holes in established convention, and the mysterious murder of the white/black woman is absolutely essential to the novel.

Clare Kendry is not a "tragic mulatto." In Larsen's terms she is not even a mulatto. Larsen never applies this term to her, and when she did use the word (rarely) in relation to herself, it was as a way of specifying that she had a white parent (which Clare does not). Clare undergoes no tragic struggle over a discovery that she is black, nor is she tragically prevented from marrying a white suitor because of the unbreachable barrier separating the races. To Clare, there is nothing tragic about being black. She makes no profound sacrifices, no deeply ethical choice for one race over the other. Her choices are entirely selfish and epicurean; she does what pleases her.

Larsen even develops minor characters to deliberately fumigate the torrid atmosphere around the "tragedy" of interracial love. The marriage between (black) Gertrude and (white) Fred Martin breaks with all prior (and, as far as I know, subsequent) models in American literature. The family's ordinariness comically trespasses against the general American mysticism about "miscegenation." Gertrude, though light enough to pass, is anything but a beautiful, exquisitely mannered, slender exotic. She is a rather awkward and ill-mannered woman with "stout legs in sleazy stockings," plump hands incompetently manicured, and a broad (white) face. "Her husband—what was his name?—had been in school with her and had been quite well aware, as had his family and most of his friends, that she was a Negro. It hadn't, Irene knew, seemed to matter to him then" (*Passing*, pp. 166–167). Neither, she soon learns, does it now. The couple is contentedly married and quite boringly middle class, Fred owning a small butcher shop. And Gertrude is far more concerned about the color of their children than her husband is.

Whereas racial convention dictates that the mulatto character be welcomed back into the fold (or die sadly in despair over her racial stigma), Clare is never particularly welcome among her black friends (and she is anything but sad about being black). This estrangement long precedes Irene's concerns about Brian's attraction to Clare. It even precedes Clare's decision to pass, being chiefly due to Clare's lowly class origins and abject parentage. Indeed, during childhood Clare was always kept at arm's length or regarded as a charity case by the black people she knew. "Clare had never been exactly one of the group" (p. 154), and after her "disappearance" to Chicago's white West Side because of her father's death, her former acquaintances quickly forgot about her.

The charge that Clare has turned "traitor" by passing, that she feels no racial allegiance, is, to say the least, hypocritical. Clare's outcast status was merely reaffirmed after she was taken in by her racist white aunts. They treated her, she bitterly recalls, like a servant: "But do you realize, 'Rene, that if it hadn't been for them, I shouldn't have had a home in the world?" (p. 158). They were the only "people" she had. She explicitly identifies her motive for passing, namely a desire for the sorts of things her black friends had. But in pursuit of these things she was barred within the black community by her abject background—a direct inversion of the usual convention in which the passer longs to have what whites have and blackness entails severe deprivation. Even living with her poverty-stricken white aunts on the West Side, with her "blackness" hidden (at their insistence), Clare might not have made up her mind to remain "white" except for the way her black friends treated her as her clothes grew more and more shabby and she grew resentful.

"You had all the things I wanted and never had had," she tells Irene. "It made me all the more determined to get them, and others" (p. 159). Clare decided to pass not because blackness *as such* represented victimization and powerlessness, but because of the class dynamics of social mobility in a racially segregated world.

Clare had an easier time making her way in white society than in black society, because whites placed less emphasis on family background. Irene, curious about passing, queries her on this issue.

> "What about background? Family, I mean. Surely you can't just drop down on people from nowhere and expect them to receive you with open arms, can you?"
>
> "Almost," Clare asserted. "You'd be surprised, 'Rene, how much easier that is with white people than with us. Maybe because there are so many more of them, or maybe because they are secure and so don't have to bother. I've never quite decided."
>
> Irene was inclined to be incredulous. "You mean that you didn't have to explain where you came from? It seems impossible."
>
> Clare cast a glance of repressed amusement across the table at her. "As a matter of fact, I didn't." (*Passing*, pp. 37–38)

A mocking quality, the sardonic remnant of a suffering outlived, often invests Clare's reminiscences of how the black community—with the exception of Irene's father—regarded her in her youth.

Clare does not suffer from what bell hooks has called the "terror" of whiteness in the African American imagination.[9] To Clare, whiteness in itself is really rather banal. Having lived with whites on intimate terms, she has a less mythic view of them and of her relations with them than does Irene. One corollary of that different structure of feeling is a relative nonchalance (not unlike Larsen's own) about the racial barrier that most Americans religiously sustain. Clare is irritating in large part because she does not have the proper feelings about racial difference; she flouts the protocols of race.[10]

In Jessie Fauset's *Plum Bun*, written simultaneously with *Passing*, the passer ignores her black acquaintances and pretends not to recognize them in public. Larsen dramatizes the opposite in Clare's experience: "Once I met Margaret Hammer in Marshall Field's. I'd have spoken, was on the very point of doing it, but she cut me dead. My dear 'Rene, I assure you that from the way she looked through me, even I was uncertain whether I was actually there in the flesh or not" (*Passing*, p. 154). Margaret's behavior buttressed racial difference and hid personal relationship; if Clare had become white, as her friends assumed merely on the basis of having seen her with white men, then she could not be acknowledged. She was "dead" to black society. Clare's desire to breach this barrier of racial etiquette was squelched. The experience was so searing that she decided not to risk another: "I remember it clearly, too clearly. It was that very thing which, in a way, finally decided me not to go out and see you one last time before I went away to stay. . . . I felt I shouldn't be able to bear that. I mean if any of you, your mother or the boys or—Oh, well, I just felt I'd rather not know it if you did. And so I stayed away" (*Passing*, p. 155). There is a curious silence here about what Irene's family might have said to her, but Clare seems to imply awareness that they suspected her on sexual grounds, that they believed she had been sleeping with white men. Clare's suspicions are, of course, correct.

The greater difficulty of being accepted within the black bourgeois world, in order to pursue her ambitions there, is what finally drives Clare to the white side. When she decides later that she wants to rejoin Negro life as a result of her reencounter with Irene, her white identity walls her off from this; Irene will not let her return. Wishing to live freely, Clare attends a "black" party at the home of the Freelands and falls to her death, landing in white snow—where, in effect, Irene has decided she belongs.

The question in this mystery story is not, "Who killed Clare Kendry?" but why did Larsen decline to represent the act itself? Why did she keep the "truth" sequestered? Her choice followed, with fatal logic, an essential thematic pattern established throughout the narrative. The novel gives innumerable instances in which Irene hides the truth of her knowledge or beliefs about Clare; yet Clare always knows exactly what Irene is not telling. When they meet in Chicago, she tells Irene, "I'll wager you've never given me a thought." And the narrator comments: "It was true, of course. After the first speculations and indictments, Clare had gone completely from Irene's thoughts. And from the thoughts of others too" (*Passing*, p. 28).

In the brief period before this happened, however, the group shared rumors that Clare was prostituting herself to white men. "There would follow insincere regrets, and somebody would say: 'Poor girl, I suppose it's true enough, but what can you expect. Look at her father'"—evidently an allusion to the fact that her father was the illegitimate son of a white man (pp. 26–27). Irene shared in these opinions, although she pretends, almost immediately after they come back to mind, to have forgotten entirely what the group said of Clare at the time. "Oh, 'Rene!" Clare cries mockingly, "of course you remember! But I won't make you tell me, because I know just as well as if I'd been there and heard every unkind word" (p. 29). Irene rationalizes her clique's attitude to Clare with thoughts of Clare's "selfishness" and furtiveness. The passage provides yet one more instance of Larsen's concern with the specific ignominy and moral taint of suspected illegitimacy combined with interracial parentage, and the secrecy around it.

Irene's presuppositions about Clare repeatedly prove wrong. The rumors that Clare was a mistress or prostitute are contradicted when we learn that she married as soon as she left her aunts' home. Irene worries awkwardly about how to get out of asking Clare what she has been doing for the twelve years since her "disappearance," reasoning that "if things with Clare were as she—as they all—had suspected, wouldn't it be more tactful to seem to forget to inquire how she had spent those twelve years?" (p. 32). A few paragraphs later, we learn that Clare married at eighteen and has a ten-year-old daughter; the "mystery" of what she has been doing is solved. Later, trying to dissuade Clare from attending an NAACP-style dance, to keep her on the "white" side of the line, Irene warns that Clare might be mistaken for a lady of easy virtue, "and that wouldn't be too pleasant" (*Passing*, p. 127). Clare laughs at the bitter irony, which Irene does not notice: "Thanks. I never have been" (p. 128).

After their first reencounter in Chicago, Irene suspects Clare intentionally failed to mention her married name out of fear that Irene would expose her; she seizes on this as a rationale not to tell her father of meeting Clare, and to cancel her appointment to see her again. The next day, Clare calls, presses Irene into coming to see her, and then exclaims, "Oh, yes! The name's Bellew. Mrs. John Bellew" (p. 52). Irene has a whole series of suspicions and stereotypes in her mind about Clare that she uses to rationalize shutting her out, making her "disappear" again. Yet Clare proves again and again to possess an uncanny knowledge of those suspicions. She knows precisely where she always stood in relation to the circle of her old acquaintances.

Clare's background is not just the opposite of what is "proper"; it is the excluded and unintelligible, what is known in psychoanalytic terms as the "abject." Her father was not only an illegitimate mulatto but a janitor who had committed some obscure crime against social convention. Men used him as a warning to boys "not to end up like Bob Kendry," but the nature of his disgrace remains a secret. Irene has even forgotten that Clare's aunts were white.

Clare haunts the domain of the black community as its outer limit. Her "cat-like" qualities—her alternate warmth and coldness, her selfishness and lack of allegiance, her ability to scratch and longing for affection—derive from child-hood. When Irene opens her letter at the beginning of the novel, it seems "sly," "out of place and alien." All of these descriptors derive almost verbatim from Carl Van Vechten's writing about cats—not only *The Tiger in the House* (one of the great "cat books" of all time) but, just as tellingly, *Peter Whiffle*. Particularly in view of Larsen's statement that *Passing* was "his" book, it is worth having a look at what he thought of the species.

Cats, Van Vechten asserted, though highly individualistic, are all independent, "amorous," and "mystic."[11] They revert to the wild state more easily than any other domestic animal, having "a strong racial instinct which survives to be awakened when it is called."[12] Cat-haters consider them "sly and deceitful, thieving and ungrateful, fickle and cruel"—all qualities Irene projects onto Clare. Hence the misnomer "catty," which by right should be applied only to "some gracious and graceful female, dignified and reserved, redolent of beauty and charm and the mystery of love."[13] Wherever a cat may live, he "lives there on his own terms, and never sacrifices his own comfort or his own well-being for the sake of the stupid folk with whom he comes in contact. Thus he is the most satisfactory of friends."[14] Indeed, what Clare offers Irene is nothing but friendship, and what she asks for is very minor indeed—merely a return to the "race." But Irene disdains the lack of anything "sacrificial" in Clare's personality or her attitude to race.

The qualities Van Vechten finds in the cat match not only Clare's personality but, to a remarkable extent, Nella Larsen's, including her political leanings: "If men and women would become more feline, . . . I think it would prove the salvation of the human race. Certainly it would end war, for cats will not fight for an ideal in the mass, having no faith in mass ideals, although a single cat will fight to the death for his own ideals, his freedom of speech and expression. The dog and the horse, on the other hand, perpetuate war, by group thinking, group acting, and serve further to encourage popular belief in that monstrous panacea, universal brotherhood."[15]

The cat's "racial" memory of past persecution accounts for its unique attunement to the "mystery of life and nature," which in turn explains its personality and its association with occult powers. Near the close of *Peter Whiffle*, as the novel's hero approaches death, he grows oracular: "The great secret is the cat's secret, to do what one *has* to do. Let IT do it, let IT, whatever IT is, flow through you."[16] Bespeaking a personality both "selfish" and oblivious to danger or social boundaries, the cat's secret is an irreligious, secular, anarchic spirituality.

Clare's catlike quality and association with "heights and depths," "unfathomable" expressions, are part of an imagistic structure that features dangerous chasms, walls, and precipices—all classic tropes for the color line in American culture. Clare's constant tempting of danger is a high-wire act, a deft adventure—or "misadventure" in the closing terms of the novel—on the edge of the abyss between white and black. Irene is shocked to find that Clare is "capable of heights and depths of feeling that she, Irene Redfield, had never known. Indeed, never cared to know." Clare's attitudes to danger, and to race, Irene cannot comprehend. "Between them the barrier was just as high, just as broad, and just as firm as if in Clare did not run that strain of black blood. In truth, it was higher, broader, and firmer" (*Passing*, pp. 110–111). Without reducing the novel to its racial thematics, one can fairly say that the barrier is "higher, broader, and firmer" than that between black and white because, if Clare genuinely misses the ways in which Negroes cultivate their lives, she disdains the racial barrier that most blacks and whites revere. Irene is determined from the beginning of the novel "to maintain unbroken between them the wall that Clare had raised." Yet the wall had been raised, early and repeatedly, not by Clare but by Irene. Without any loyalty to *race*, Clare likes the company of African Americans; she likes black culture and expression.

Irene's loyalty to race forces her to keep the passer's secret, and to try to keep the passer out of black society, even when she believes that informing on Clare would save her own marriage: "She was caught between two allegiances, different, yet the same. Herself. Her race. Race! The thing that bound and suffocated her." No matter what steps she took, "something would be crushed. A person or the race" (p. 180). In what way would the "race" be crushed by exposing the passer? Clearly, the unmasking would destroy not the actual people of the "race," but only an abstraction to which Irene's psyche is desperately attached. The sacrifice would be the artifice of the boundary—a boundary that Irene already knows is artificial but that she psychically requires nonetheless, and must therefore buttress as if it were foundational, or sacred. What is the relative value of a person as against the "race" in this sense? What is the moral meaning of race?

As these disquieting questions knock for the first time, briefly, Irene wishes she were not a Negro. Color-line thinking is such that most readers will automatically assume this means Irene wants to be white, but Larsen does not phrase it this way. Not wanting to be a Negro is not the same as wanting to be white; it is more like a desire to exist outside American notions of race—dangerous territory for Irene Redfield. As Samira Kawash puts it, Irene's race loyalty is "less a loyalty to the dignity of her race than it is a loyalty to the very principle of race, insofar as it is the condition of order, predictability, and security in her life."[17]

The immense attraction Irene feels for Clare alternates (as Kawash has also emphasized) with repulsion.[18] Clare becomes an eroticized, fetishized element in Irene's fantasy life, a woman of occult powers who is "almost too good looking" and represents precisely what Irene must banish psychologically in order to secure her identity.[19] (Like the body of the protagonist's wife in "Freedom," Clare's exquisitely beautiful face seems, to Irene, a mask hiding something decadent or morally repugnant within.) In this respect, Irene is much like Jack Bellew, whose pet name for Clare, "Nig," reveals the eroticization of the racial boundary. Jack needs his "Nig," Judith Butler has argued, as the "spectre of a racial ambiguity that he must subordinate and deny" to sustain his racial identity.[20] The same can be said of Irene, whose phobic insistence that Clare remain "white" expresses her need for absolute difference.[21] One cannot go freely back and forth. Deriving from the invisible crossroads between blackness and whiteness, upper and lower classes, a place "out of bounds" in social terms, Clare inhabits a symbolically central position in the psyches of both Jack and Irene.

Readings, beginning with that of Deborah E. McDowell, which emphasize a lesbian attraction between Irene and Clare have done much to bring serious attention to the novel, suggesting that Clare represents a threat to Irene's sexual identity—that Irene must blot her out or fend off recognition of her own illicit sexual desires.[22] Such interpretations have plenty of textual support. But the anxieties Clare arouses in Irene, however eroticized, invariably concern her racial identity as much as her sexual orientation. During the "tea" in Clare's hotel room, after one of Jack's viciously racist comments, Irene finds Clare's "peculiar eyes fixed on her with an expression so dark and deep and unfathomable that she had for a short moment the sensation of gazing into the eyes of some creature utterly strange and apart. A faint sense of danger brushed her, like the breath of a cold fog" (*Passing*, p. 69). This look remains with Irene later that night. "Frowning out into the dark rain," she ponders "that look on Clare's incredibly beautiful face. She couldn't, however, come to any conclusion about its meaning, try as she might" (p. 79). Critics such as Deborah McDowell and David Blackmore have rightly identified the strong hint of an erotic dimension to these moments, and in Clare's flirtatious gestures as well. When Irene tries to impress on her the danger of coming even briefly to see Irene in Harlem, Clare replies: "You mean you don't want me, 'Rene?" (p. 117).

Clare's unfathomable and mysterious nature, hinged to her beauty and repulsiveness, is as much spiritual as physical, connected with her attitude to danger, the disallowed. When Clare repudiates any desire for safety, "for another flying second [Irene] had that suspicion of Clare's ability for a quality of feeling that was to her strange, and even repugnant" (p. 118). The contact zone between socially polarized "races" inevitably bears an erotic charge. Irene herself recognizes this fact in other aspects of her experience. At the Negro Welfare League dance, the white author Hugh Wentworth (partly based, perhaps, on William Seabrook and partly on Van Vechten) becomes spellbound by Clare, striving to determine the "name, status, and race of the blonde beauty out of the fairytale" (p. 137).[23] A discussion follows about the difficulty of telling "white" from "black" and about the nature of interracial sexual attraction. Wentworth wonders why white women prefer to dance with Negro men at such affairs: "They're always raving about the good looks of some Negro, preferably an unusually dark one" (pp. 138–139). Irene agrees: they feel excitement, "the sort of things you feel in the presence of something strange, and even, perhaps, a bit repugnant to you; something so different that it's really at the opposite end of the pole from all your accustomed notions of beauty." She adds, "And I know coloured girls who've experienced the same thing—the other way round, naturally" (p. 139). Her terms—"strangeness," "repugnance," attraction to otherness or transgression—express exactly her own feelings about Clare.

The connection comes up again when Irene discusses passing with Brian: "It's funny about 'passing.' We disapprove of it and at the same time condone it. It excites our contempt and yet we rather admire it. We shy away from it with an odd kind of revulsion, but we protect it." Brian immediately identifies this psychological complex with the sexual impulse to race-mixing on the part of both whites and blacks, attributing it to the instinct of the "race" to survive and expand.

Irene's racial anxieties account for the symbolic parallelism between Clare and Brazil that forms a basic structural element of *Passing*. Larsen set up two parallel narratives in Irene's emotional world: as Clare comes closer and closer to Irene and her family, Brian grows increasingly restive and Irene grows more and more fearful of Brian's "increasing inclination to tear himself and his possessions loose from their proper settings" (*Passing*, p. 193). This threat she terms "Brazil." At one point Brian, angry that Irene will not let him talk to their sons about racism and the reasons for lynching, strikes back with the statement: "I wanted to get them out of this hellish place [the United States] years ago. You wouldn't let me. I gave up the idea, because you objected. Don't expect me to give up everything" (p. 232). Irene wonders if "everything" means "Clare."

The threat of "Brazil" folds decisively into the threat of "Clare" in the opening scene of Act Three, "Finale." Hence the parallelism between Clare and Brazil, as opposed to Irene's intense identification with the United States.[24] Not only does Clare replace Brazil as the apple of Brian's eye (Irene fears), but her own husband actually made his fortune in that country. Jack left Brazil, however, out of repugnance for all the "niggers" and the mixing between white and black. Since racial identity is more fluid in Brazil than in the United States (according to Jack and Brian's belief), passing is simply not an issue there.[25] That Irene regards Brazil as a threat and, like Jack, insists on her "American" identity has much to do with her allegiance to American racial ideology.

The threat of Brazil is displaced by the threat of Clare as the novel approaches its crisis, Irene worrying about Brian's restlessness and thinking, "If I could only be sure that at bottom it's just Brazil." His increased brooding and outbursts of temper fill Irene with "foreboding dread": "It was as if he had stepped out beyond her reach into some section, strange and walled, where she could not get at him" (*Passing*, p. 214). Within the metaphorical landscape of *Passing*, Brian has joined Clare in Irene's consciousness. "He was discontented, yet there were times when she felt that he was possessed of some intense secret satisfaction, like a cat who had stolen the cream" (p. 214). Brian becomes identified metaphorically with catlike Clare, who in this particular construction is the "cream" he has perhaps stolen from Jack. The identification does not end with the feline metaphor, "strangeness," and walls, however. At the opening of the next chapter Irene notices an "unfathomable expression" in Brian's eyes and learns that Clare appeared for her tea party while Irene was asleep. One can be an agnostic about what is really going on between Brian and Clare; what is important to this novel is what is going on in Irene.

Clare may have many resonances with the young Nella Larsen, but when it came to the present, the character of Irene in the closing chapter served as the conduit of Larsen's darkest emotions. She may well have written the final scene, set in an apartment much like her own, while she was locked out. Such appears to be the meaning behind her cryptic statement to Van Vechten after the "hellish week" in which she finished her manuscript, "in spite of having been locked out for a day and a half, and sudden death."[26] It was Larsen who had been locked out, and Clare who had suddenly died, ejected from a sixth-floor "garden apartment" with a layout much like Larsen's own. The only garden apartment complex in Harlem was the one in which the Imeses lived; and they lived on the sixth floor.

Readers are apt to let Irene off the hook for Clare's demise, a telling effect of Larsen's strategy and of her major theme. Because we can perceive only what Irene allows herself to remember, we get no account of what "really" happened. For this reason, and because disappointment with the novel has derived chiefly from its ending, the scene deserves a careful inspection.

Completely nonchalant when Jack appears in a rage, Clare stands perfectly composed, seemingly "unaware of any danger or uncaring." In fact, she has already told Irene that if Jack learns her "secret" and divorces her, any responsibility for her child—the only thing that keeps her from revealing her race and provoking a divorce—will be taken out of her hands. The last thing Irene wants is for Jack to know that Clare is black and to divorce her. After Jack roars at Clare, "So you're a nigger, a damned dirty nigger," Clare stands by the window smiling. She perches, after all, on the verge of "freedom."

> It was that smile that maddened Irene. She ran across the room, her terror tinged with ferocity, and laid a hand on Clare's bare arm. One thought possessed her. She couldn't have Clare Kendry cast aside by Bellew. She couldn't have her free.
>
> Before them stood John Bellew, speechless now in his hurt and anger. Beyond them the little huddle of other people, and Brian stepping out from among them.
>
> What happened next, Irene Redfield never afterwards allowed herself to remember. Never clearly.
>
> One moment Clare had been there, a vital glowing thing, like a flame of red and gold. The next she was gone. (*Passing*, p. 209)

As unique as Irene's panic at the thought of Clare being "free" and turning black again is Larsen's presentation of Jack Bellew, who deeply loves his wife still, despite his racism. His love, primal, animal-like, comes head to head with his racism. As Clare "disappears" through the window, "There was a gasp of horror, and above it a sound not quite human, like a beast in agony. 'Nig! My God! Nig!'" (p. 209).

Larsen could easily have played this scene differently. She could have made him shed all feeling for Clare, or have made him overtly responsible for Clare's death, or have had Clare fall off balance in reaction to his accusation. There would be no reason for Irene not to remember that; indeed, it would exactly fulfill her hopes by doing away with Clare without staining her own conscience. But it would not fulfill Larsen's design; indeed, it would fold the novel within a predictable pattern and abandon the theme of disavowal. What is even more important than the fact of Clare's death or the issue of who "causes" it is Larsen's emphasis on the conspiracy of silence and blindness about how it came about. The cause of Clare's death will never be accepted into consciousness.

We have little reason to believe that Clare jumped or fell, or to believe that Jack touched her; Irene would have remembered these things. The reason we don't see precisely what "happened" is that we only know events by way of Irene, and what happened is something she refuses to remember. (Moreover, in stepping out from the "huddle" of people across the room as Irene rushes toward Clare, Brian blocks their view.) We've been given examples throughout the novel of Irene's tendency to avoid remembering uncomfortable aspects of her relationship to Clare, to avoid acknowledging her or her husband, to suppress the truth.

While all the other people at the party rush downstairs, concerned about Clare, Irene sits down, stunned.

> Gone! The mocking daring, the gallantry of her pose, the ringing bells of her laughter.
>
> Irene wasn't sorry. She was amazed, incredulous almost.
>
> What would the others think? That Clare had fallen? That she had deliberately leaned backward? Certainly one or the other. Not—
>
> But she mustn't, she warned herself, think of that. She was too tired, and too shocked. And, indeed, both were true. She was utterly weary, and she was violently staggered. But her thoughts reeled on. If only she could be as free of mental as she was of bodily vigour; could only put from her memory the vision of her hand on Clare's arm!
>
> "It was an accident, a terrible accident," she muttered fiercely. "It *was*." (*Passing*, pp. 210–211)

These are nothing if not the thoughts of the guilty, rendered with terrifying precision. I quote them at length here to emphasize Larsen's means of showing precisely how certain "mysteries" come to be so mysterious.

For the remainder of the novel, Irene's actions are those of a woman scared to death that she will be found out, and not knowing how to account for herself.

> People were coming up the stairs. Through the still open door their steps and talk sounded nearer, nearer.
>
> Quickly she stood up and went noiselessly into the bedroom and closed the door softly behind her.
>
> Her thoughts raced. Ought she to have stayed? Should she go back out there to them? But there would be questions. She hadn't thought of them, of

afterwards, of this. She had thought of nothing in that sudden moment of action. (*Passing*, p. 211)

The psychology of the guilty here anticipates that rendered by Richard Wright in *Native Son* after Bigger Thomas kills the white Mary Dalton and his girlfriend Bessie, wishing to "blot them out" to cover his shame and fear, and then worries about being caught.

> In the midst of her wonderings and questionings came a thought so terrifying, so horrible, that she had had to grasp hold of the banister to save herself from pitching downwards. A cold perspiration drenched her shaking body. Her breath came short in sharp and painful gasps.
> What if Clare was not dead? (*Passing*, pp. 212–213)

When Felise informs her that Clare is dead, "Irene struggled against the sob of thankfulness that rose in her throat" (p. 214). Her body begins heaving in convulsive sobs, not of grief as her friends think, but of relief.

None of the characters wants to consider that Irene, literally, might have had a "hand" in Clare's death. Frozen in "stark craven fear" when asked what she knows, she is saved when an officer breaks in, before she can respond, to ask if Jack had given Clare a shove, as Brian suggested (p. 214). Brian has good reason to shift any suspicion away from his wife and the mother of his children. Just what he really believes, what he saw, is an open question. Deeply shaken, as Irene sobs with relief over Clare's death, he makes "a slight perfunctory attempt to comfort her" (p. 215). Jack, she notices, is the only person gone, suggesting the police may have taken him as a suspect—which would compound the sense of guilt she would have to bear and initiate a criminal investigation. "As she began to work it out in her numbed mind, she was shaken with another hideous trembling. Not that! Oh, not that!" She assures the officer that Jack could not have been at fault, that Clare "just fell, before anybody could stop her. I—" Then she faints, and "everything was dark" (p. 216).

When the woman on the boundary is done away with, thereby securing the boundary, no one will be at fault. (It is a theme Jean Toomer had also treated, more lyrically and less subtly, in his story "Becky," in *Cane*.) There will be no conscious memory of the crime, only a vacant space where the life of the black white woman passed through. "Centuries after," reads the novel's concluding paragraph, "she heard the strange man saying, 'Death by misadventure, I'm inclined to believe. Let's go up and have another look at that window'" (p. 216). So speak biographers and historians.

After the second printing of the novel, this final paragraph mysteriously disappeared.[27] No one knows why.

SEVENTEEN

A Star in Harlem:
1929

A S *Passing* went through production, Larsen began to enjoy a small measure of celebrity. At the 135th Street Library, *Quicksand* was in "continuous demand,"[1] and she was lined up to give a lecture there at the end of January, publicized throughout the library system, on "what present-day negro writers are saying, and how."[2] On the first or second of January, she learned that she had won the Harmon Foundation's bronze medal (for second place), with a $100 honorarium.[3] On the fifth, the announcements came out in the *New York Age*, and these were soon followed by scores of notices and articles in newspapers across the country. The January issue of *Opportunity* featured James Allen's most flattering portrait of her (identified as "Nella Larsen" rather than "Nella Imes") on the first page of its lead essay, Alain Locke's "1928: A Retrospective Review."

The "Negrophile movement" had become a fad and was possibly at its high tide, Locke announced, yet after the tide subsided real achievements would remain. Larsen's "study of the cultural conflict of mixed ancestry is truly a social document of importance," he asserted, "a living, moving picture of a type not often in the foreground of Negro fiction, and here treated perhaps for the first time with adequacy."[4] Larsen's stinging critique of *Black Sadie* by T. Bowyer Campbell led off the review section of the same issue. "The tale opens in the south with a rape and closes in New York with a murder. Every strangeness, every crudity, every laxity, which by ancient superstition has been ascribed to the black man, Mr. Campbell has incorporated into this story—and some others." The white characters, Larsen acknowledged, were no better than the black, but "they are not set down as thieving, sexually immoral, and brutal." Campbell showed little skill as a stylist or narrator, and yet, "in spite of its twaddle concerning the inherent qualities of the Negro" and its stylistic affectations, the novel was partly redeemed by the character of Sadie, whom Larsen found "interesting and forceful"—a "delightfully sunny person" in the midst of an almost gruesome tale. Larsen could not suppress her arch sense of humor in the closing advice: "Often its very inaccuracies make much of the book very amusing—especially to the Negro reader. Don't miss it."[5]

In the Harmon Foundation contest, Larsen had beat out W. E. B. Du Bois, Jessie Fauset, Arthur Huff Fauset, Georgia Douglas Johnson, and the poet Leslie Pinckney Hill, most of them far more experienced writers. Claude McKay had won the gold medal, barely, for achievements throughout his career rather than for the merits of *Home to Harlem.*

The decision had not been easy, and since the choice of McKay over Larsen has been attributed to the prejudices of the judges, it is worth pointing out that the "primitivism" and "low-life realism" of *Home to Harlem* had, if anything, harmed McKay's case. Moreover, several of the judges admitted personal prejudice against him because of his notoriously difficult personality. The correspondence between the various judges and George E. Haynes, who conducted the contest, reveals clearly that McKay won the gold award because candidates were to be considered, as Haynes informed them beforehand, "from the point of view of the ensemble of their achievement rather than on the basis of any one composition."[6] W. D. Howe (a publisher) and William Stanley Braithwaite both rated Larsen first on the sheer strength of *Quicksand.* Braithwaite, a genteel black Bostonian best known as a poetry anthologist, was determined to prevent McKay from receiving the award. He may have had a personal vendetta against McKay (who considered him "the Booker T. Washington of American poetry—a bred-in-the-bone sycophant"),[7] but he particularly detested *Home to Harlem,* and he quickly fired off a protest to George Haynes after learning McKay had won the gold medal, objecting that McKay should be judged on the work he had submitted, not on his overall output or "literary genius."[8] This rationale conflicted with the terms of the contest, but Haynes communicated it to the other judges and asked if they would like to reconsider. While several of the judges considered *Quicksand* excellent and disliked McKay, they were not swayed. Even the publisher W. D. Howe, who had initially rated Larsen first and admitted a prejudice against "low-life realism," acceded to the majority.[9] The original vote thus stood. It is unlikely that Larsen felt short-changed, since she had suspected from the beginning that her main chance against McKay would lie in the prejudice against him on the part of "uplifters."

Larsen came down with the flu in late January and had to cancel her speaking date at the library, a misfortune notable enough to be reported in the *Amsterdam News.*[10] Hearing about it in Montreal while touring with *Porgy,* Bruce Nugent wrote Dorothy Peterson to ask how she was doing and wish her good luck.[11] That very day or the next, at Van Vechten's urging, Larsen sent a letter and a copy of *Quicksand* to Gertrude Stein:

I have often talked with our friend Carl Van Vechten about you. Particularly about you and Melanctha, which I have read many times. And always I get from it some new thing a truly great story. I never cease to wonder how you came to write it and just why and not some one of us should so accurately have caught the spirit of this race of mine.

Carl asked me to send you my poor first book, and I am doing so. Please dont think me too presumptuous.[12]

Stein thought this a "charming letter," and wrote to Van Vechten about it almost immediately: "It touched me a lot."[13] She would write Larsen as soon as she received the copy of *Quicksand,* and she remembered Larsen's letter for years as her favorite correspondence concerning "Melanctha."[14]

Larsen might well have returned again and again to "Melanctha," one of three novellas focusing on working-class women in Stein's *Three Lives,* and the one in which Stein first explored the modernist style that made her famous. An extraordinarily nuanced story of emotional power struggles and triangulated relationships, "Melanctha" comes to focus on anxieties over the control of female sexuality. A boundary figure whose free spirit and sensuous appeal inspire intense infatuation and yet fear in those to whom she becomes passionately attached, Melanctha is abandoned by one friend after another because of her "wandering" across the lines of female and racial propriety, ultimately dying alone in a home for consumptives. Stein's studied deployment of racial stereotypes as rote clichés, strings of words periodically trotted out but perpetually failing to describe the personalities to whom they attach, destabilizes habitual modes of "placing" people. As a female *Bildungsroman* focusing on a young mulatto of tormented childhood, unwanted by father and mother, repeatedly alienated from intense relationships by her own need for and fear of intimacy, as well as by the threat her "wandering" poses to the security of identities bounded by convention, "Melanctha" has much in common with Larsen's fiction, right down to its pathetic conclusion.

On Lincoln's birthday, Larsen starred in the Harmon Awards ceremony at the Mother A.M.E. Zion Church on 137th Street. Claude McKay, off in Morocco, had asked James Weldon Johnson to stand in for him. Rabbi Stephen Wise, a popular orator closely connected to the founding of the NAACP, gave the keynote address: "We gather here tonight to rejoice in the spirit of comradeship that there are those of the negro race entitled to high awards by reason of distinction and through promise of lofty achievement yet to be. . . . Was it not Lincoln, who as much as any other human has led us to see that liberation from without means little unless it be supplemented by self-liberation?"[15] The publicity photo that went to newspapers shows Nella in a formal dress shaking the

15. Larsen receiving the Harmon Award bronze medal, 1929. From left to right, Helen Harmon, Nella Larsen, Channing H. Tobias, James Weldon Johnson (standing in for Claude McKay), George E. Haynes, and unidentified man. Copyright © Bettmann/ Corbis.

hand of Helen Harmon (daughter of the late donor) and appearing very uncomfortable while Johnson, Channing Tobias, and George E. Haynes look on. Reports of the awards came out in newspapers across the nation.

The *Nashville Tennessean* duly noted that three of the twelve winners were Fisk graduates, including Nella Larsen Imes, who, the writer averred, "has lived much of her life abroad, having been adopted as a child by a Norwegian woman."[16] Journalistic integrity had its limits. The Harmon Foundation press release clearly stated that the author's mother was Danish and that Larsen had lived for three years with her family in Denmark. As the evident capital of the "New South," white Nashville wanted to trumpet the superiority of its black institutions over those of Atlanta and Washington, but pride in Fisk always depended on the unspoken observances of the color line. There were certain things the public did not need to know.

While *Passing* neared its publication date, another black-authored novel about passing came out in mid-February: Jessie Fauset's *Plum Bun,* published by Frederick A. Stokes. Walter White suggested to Mary Mackay of the firm's publicity department that they send a free copy to "Mrs. Nella Larsen Imes," and even thanked her for following his advice: "I am sure it is a copy well invested."[17] (He and Gladys dined at the Imeses' apartment the same night, along with Van Vechten, Marinoff, and Corinne Wright.)[18] Evidently, however, Larsen was unimpressed. Of course, *Plum Bun* may have seemed to steal some of *Passing*'s thunder, but its form and approach could hardly have been more different —they were even diametrically opposed. If Larsen found it lacking, she was far from alone among her circle of friends. Van Vechten, also receiving an advance copy at White's suggestion, found it an "idiotic book."[19] Harold Jackman, in a letter to Countee Cullen, called it "lousy, absolutely terrible. Really, I don't see how the publishers could take it. Jessie doesn't know men, she doesn't write prose well; it is bad, bad, bad."[20]

Subtitled "A Novel without a Moral"—in a direct slap, apparently, at *Nigger Heaven* (which had been reviewed positively in the *New York Age* under the heading "A Novel with a Moral") and possibly also at Claude McKay's *Banjo* (subtitled "A Story without a Plot")—*Plum Bun* exemplified the sort of idealism, optimism, and pride of race that some African Americans believed the white publishing industry would not accept in "Negro fiction."[21] Larsen's novel almost exactly inverts *Plum Bun*'s narrative logic and structural resolutions. While the goal of passing, for Fauset's protagonist, is to get what white people have and to be "free," in Larsen's novel Clare Kendry passes in order to get what her more well-off black friends have, for her family background precludes her moving into their class position within the carefully policed boundaries of respectable black society. In Larsen's novel, Clare's closest black friend is determined to prevent her return to the "race," and does not want Clare "free"—that is, black. Fauset's protagonist Angela Murray / Angèle Mory (French for "Dead Angel"—her "white" name) ignores her black sister when they pass each other in public, whereas Clare finds her former black friends "cut [her] dead," and Irene does not even recognize her when they meet again in Chicago. Fauset's Angèle is reborn as Angela Murray (her real name) after happily rejoining the race at the end of *Plum Bun.* Clare Kendry dies, evidently at the hands of her friend, just as she becomes publicly "black" again.

Even more coincidentally, Angela's true love, Anthony Cross / Cruz, passes for most of Fauset's novel as a white Brazilian before revealing that he is actually

African American.[22] Since the lynching of his African American father, he has vowed never to entangle himself with whites; luckily, like him, Angela is just becoming resolutely "black" again as she gives up passing, making her a suitable mate. Whereas Clare Kendry dies during a Christmas party at the hands of the jealous wife of an African American who wants to become a Brazilian, Angela is resurrected as she crosses back over to blackness and her "Brazilian" mate becomes African American, appearing at her door, literally, as a Christmas present. Whereas Larsen uses the passing character to explore Irene's feelings of attraction and repulsion regarding a woman both black and white—whose brazen border-crossings threaten the boundaries on which Irene's secure life has been carefully built—Fauset glorifies the security that comes from keeping racial boundaries intact and women's sexuality subordinated to them. *Passing*, not unlike Stein's "Melanctha," practically inverts the patterns of the classic romance in its basic structure.[23] *Plum Bun* finds those patterns congenial, and rightly so, for they had emerged in the context of legitimating racial, and bourgeois, concepts of the early modern nation.

Stokes got no statement from Nella Larsen to go with the publicity flyers that went out to NAACP members and other potential readers, bearing blurbs by the likes of Du Bois, Countee Cullen, and George Schuyler, as well as several well-known white authors. She did, however, attend a Sunday afternoon tea at Club Caroline in Fauset's honor, sponsored by the Saturday Night Club in mid-February. While members of the club presided over the tea tables, Ruth Logan Roberts directed the evening's program of formal concert music and uplifting speeches. Then, according to the *New York Age,* W. E. B. Du Bois "spoke in the warmest appreciation" of Fauset's attempts "to picture in her novels, normal, decent, self-respecting colored people."[24] Fauset followed with words of thanks to her friends and publishers, and particularly to her sister. The audience of 135 included the cream of black society in the Greater New York area, and a smattering of friends from New Jersey and Philadelphia.

On March 15, a balmy Friday heralding spring, Nella and Elmer had dinner at Eddie Wasserman's with Van Vechten, Marinoff, Lawrence Langner, and Armina Marshall before heading all together, along with Blanche Knopf, to a concert by the Peruvian contralto Marguerite d'Alvarez and then the NAACP ball celebrating the twentieth anniversary of the organization's founding.[25] The star-studded floor show began at eleven at the Renaissance Casino, with Bill "Bojangles" Robinson as the master of ceremonies, and the chorines from *Blackbirds* handing out favors. The "Struttin' Drum Major," J. Mardo Brown, from the hit musical *Show Boat* headed the lineup, followed by the Palmer Brothers' harmonizing trio from Connie's Inn. Adelaide Hall sang, and the whole audience joined in on the chorus when Aida Ward and Bojangles sang a duet of "I Can't Give You Anything but Love," from the *Blackbirds* show. The era's terpsichorean stars, many from the *Blackbirds* revue, filled out the bill—Earl "Snakeships" Tucker, Eddie Rector, Pegleg Bates, and of course Bojangles himself. Afterward, the regular dancing started, lasting until 3:00 A.M.[26] It was Nella's last big fling before going back to work as a substitute at the Fort Washington Branch Library, beginning Monday, the eighteenth.[27]

Also in early March, Larsen spoke at the 135th Street Branch in one of an ongoing series of programs for library school students of Columbia, Pratt Institute, and the training class of the NYPL, and she attended various lectures and recitals.[28] Dorothy Peterson, meanwhile, was busy during her free time directing the new Negro Experimental Theatre in the "Play House" of the 135th Street Branch.[29]

Elmer, who was expected to start at Fisk in the fall, was angling for a position at the University of Michigan. He wrote President Jones at Fisk that he wanted a one-year postponement so that he could spend a year doing research in Ann Arbor. This would also give the current physics professor, a veteran of many years' standing, a chance to adjust to the idea of having a younger man come in over him at a considerably higher salary. (Elmer was demanding $5,000 per year—astronomical by traditional Fisk standards.) Moreover, Elmer wrote, he was "tied down with consulting contracts which I cannot afford to break. . . . Mrs. Imes appreciates the possibility of Library work should we come to Fisk, but does not quite reconcile herself to a 25 percent drop in my contributions to the budget. This is not vital, but I mention it as part of my policy of absolute frankness with you."[30] Jones agreed to the arrangement and added that Nella would be welcome to start at Fisk and move into a house near campus while Elmer was in Ann Arbor.[31]

Nella had no interest in moving to Fisk, but just what else she might do seemed unclear. Elmer, meanwhile, got bad news from Michigan: they could not take him for only one year unless he would accept a $2,500 fellowship, which he considered inadequate. Moreover, legal entanglements over patent infringements would keep him on the job at Edward A. Everett for some months, so he could not, he claimed, go to Fisk until fall of 1930. He would, however, be willing to accept an appointment and to attend occasional functions.[32] On May 4, Jones sent him a letter officially appointing him head of the Department of Physics, with the understanding that he would begin his "resident work" in fall 1930, and in the meantime visit occasionally to help organize the department. He would have a salary of $4,500 for the 1930–1931 academic year, and get a raise of $500 the next.[33]

With her second novel in press and no major project under way, Nella went back to work full time all that spring, moving, after a week at Fort Washington on the northern tip of Manhattan, to the Rivington Street Branch on the Lower East Side, where she would work through the end of June for $135 per month.[34] It was a neighborhood primarily Italian and Jewish, not far from Seward Park. Because of work, Nella missed out on much of her usual socializing that spring. Among the many events surrounding the much-anticipated wedding on April 3 of Jessie Fauset to Herbert Harris (an officer of Victory Life Insurance Company), Larsen did not make it to any of the showers or smaller parties, but she was invited to a ladies' bridge party for thirty-two co-hosted by Regina Andrews in honor of Fauset and an out-of-town visitor.[35]

Almost simultaneously, the first prepublication copies of *Passing* arrived from Knopf (its official publication date was April 26). Opening the package, Larsen found that the dust jacket had a striking tan-and-red patterned design in handsome Art Deco style, while the dimensions, typography, and binding made it a perfect pair with *Quicksand*. To *Quicksand*'s orange cloth with black scoring, *Passing* sported a black cloth with orange scoring in an identical design. Priced at $2.00, the book's dimensions and Caslon type were typical for Knopf novels—including Van Vechten's *Nigger Heaven*, and appropriately so in view of Larsen's bold dedication, "To Carl Van Vechten and Fania Marinoff," centered a bit above the middle of the page and spread out over four lines in large type. (Late twentieth-century editions of *Passing* would progressively shrink the dedication to the point of near-illegibility.) The inside front flap of the dust jacket reprinted most of Larsen's 1926 biographical statement for Knopf's Publicity Department, discretely dropping her attack on Tuskegee, as well as any mention of her marriage, and adding a line about *Quicksand* and the Harmon Award.[36]

Larsen either sent or took a copy of the book immediately to Carl and Fania's apartment with the humble inscription:

Dears:—
    Please take this little book as a slight indication of my great thanks and appreciation for all the good and lovely things which you have done and made possible for me.

Nella

April 3, 1929[37]

Carl got home that day at about 5:00 in the afternoon and found the book waiting for him. He sat down immediately to have a look at it: "Read it absorbedly," he wrote in his daybook, "till I have to go out to dinner. . . . Home at 1 & finish

Passing, an extraordinary story, extraordinarily told. I go to bed & sleep badly. I am so excited."[38]

The next morning he woke up at 8:30, dressed, and headed immediately to the Knopf offices two blocks away on Fifty-Seventh Street. "I stir Blanche & Alfred up about Nella Larsen's *Passing,* making quite a scene." He dropped in to the *American Mercury* editorial offices next door and talked the book up to George Jean Nathan, and then headed for Goldfarb's florists, where he ordered a bouquet for Nella. "Then to Dorothy Peterson's for lunch. Nella is there."[39]

The Knopfs went into action immediately. To no other book of the Twenties had Van Vechten responded so fervently. Right after his unusual eruption in her office, Blanche arranged for a tea on the eighteenth at the Sherry-Netherland Hotel, one of New York's finest, and began sending out invitations to friends of Larsen and to literary lights of the city that very day.[40] Alfred rounded up the marketing people and scheduled a special meeting about the book. The following Wednesday, April 10, just after lunch, Nella headed for Knopf's headquarters in the elegant Hecksher Building, a slender Flemish Gothic skyscraper rising from the southwest corner of Fifth Avenue and 57th Street, filled with high-class offices and the brand-new Museum of Modern Art. She could not have missed the glass case near the elevator bank filled with Knopf's beautiful new books of the season, including her own. They drew everyone's attention.[41]

After Nella arrived, Blanche, Alfred, Harry Block, and two salesmen gathered with her; Carl came in soon after, and they began to work out a special marketing strategy in which his enthusiasm for the book would play a key role.[42] They would emphasize the "sensational" quality of the story, but keep people in suspense as to the nature of the sensation they would experience. Since most potential readers would never pick up a black-authored novel in a bookstore, they would learn that *Passing* was a "Negro novel" only after being drawn in by the tantalizing hoopla surrounding it. The sales representatives were to make a special effort with the major bookstores in both New York and Chicago. Van Vechten was to provide help with advertising copy; a paper "belly band" encircling the middle of the dust jacket, with a Van Vechten blurb in large bold letters, would be added to dramatize the book in display windows and set it apart as one of *the* books of the season. This was no "niche" marketing scheme; they would aim for the broadest possible readership. The Knopfs were rolling out the red carpet for the book's official entry on April 26.

The bright-green belly band on the tan-and-red jacket set off the bold black lettering: "'A strangely provocative story, superbly told. The sensational implications of PASSING should make this book one of the most widely discussed on the Spring list.'—Carl Van Vechten."[43] The April 13 issue of *Publishers Weekly* carried a full-page advertisement for *Passing*: "An ASTONISHING and SENSATIONAL Novel that will be widely advertised." Alfred Knopf had written a special advertising letter, printed in full in an eye-catching hourglass design over his personal signature: "*Passing* is a novel on a theme so explosive that for a long time the advisability of its publication was seriously debated," he puffed disingenuously. "But the complete artistry of its telling and the poignant interest of the story itself imperatively demanded that the book see the light of day." Then followed a nice fiction loosely based on the events of April 3 and 4:

> I sent an advance copy of *Passing* to a well known novelist. He started to read it before dinner. He expected guests. They came. They started dinner but he did not sit down at table until he had finished the book. He could not tear himself away from it. Next morning he came to my office. I was in a long conference. He waited an hour to see me. Then he told me how the book had held him and he said: "If you don't sell this book in a big way, you are not the publisher I think you are. It is a sensational story brilliantly told. It carried me away and it will hold the interest of any man or woman you can persuade to read the first few pages."[44]

The key was to persuade booksellers skeptical about the sales potential of "Negro" fiction to order multiple copies and display the book prominently, and then get members of the general public to open the cover of a volume they might normally overlook.

Blanche Knopf received an endorsement of the novel from James Weldon Johnson on the same day: "I read Passing at one sitting. It is a startlingly good story. It is written with weight and with power, and beauty. Anyone who wishes to get an insider view of life just over the color line on the Negro's side, and who wishes to know something about the practice of crossing the line into the white world should read this story by Miss Larsen."[45]

Knopf's Publicity Department mailed out a special news release announcing that on Thursday the eighteenth, Larsen would be guest of honor at a tea given by Blanche Knopf at the Sherry-Netherland. "Among those who will be present are: Emonie Sachs, Isa Glenn, Irita Van Doren, Muriel Draper, Fannie Hurst, Freddie Washington, Mr. & Mrs. William B. Seabrook, Mr. & Mrs. Peter Arno, Carl Van Vechten, Arthur B. Spingarn, Sinclair Lewis, Dr. Henry Seidel Canby, and Miguel Covarrubias."[46] Meanwhile, Dorothy Peterson planned a more informal tea at the family home, and Eddie Wasserman began making plans for a large party at his place in Larsen's honor for the evening before the book's official publication.

Also on April 13, Larsen's thirty-eighth birthday, an article by Mary Rennels appeared in the New York *Telegram*'s literary gossip column—appropriately entitled "Behind the Backs of Books and Authors"—based on an interview with Larsen. It gave Larsen's opinions on everything from Carl Van Vechten's work to antiracist activism. Rennels combined partial misrepresentations with naive renderings of Larsen's typically barbed tongue-in-cheek ironic quips, and faithful reporting of mildly alarming indiscretions. More than just "behind the back," the article amounted to an unintentional and partly self-inflicted stab in the back. Larsen quickly set out to control the damage.

> Carl dear:—
>
> I *am* so upset.
>
> I'll never be interviewed again!
>
> Walter called up yesterday to protest because Mary Rennels "said I said" that I didn't believe in propaganda.
>
> Three Harlem Negroes have registered their protests (one very bel[l]igerently and indignantly) because I am reported to have stated that its perfectly all right to send Negroes around to the back door.
>
> Tonight when we got the damned paper Elmer rose in the air because he thinks I was "trying to pose as a silly uplifter of the race."
>
> All these things are nothing—
>
> But when I read that I had referred to you as a devil I almost had a stroke of paralysis. I do think the phrase is awfully clever—as she evidently did—But about you! That's really too thick.
>
> I don't know at all what to do about it. I could die of rage and mortification. In fact I see no way out except suicide.
>
> Please come to my parties anyway.[47]

Rennels had reported that "her favorite authors are Galsworthy and Carl Van Vechten, the latter 'to some of us is a savior, to others a devil'"—certainly nothing for Van Vechten to be upset about. Countee Cullen had far more reason to be piqued for being called "another Edna St. Vincent Millay 'with something left out.'" She named Roland Hayes and Paul Robeson as the artistic leaders of the race.

To any self-respecting New Negro, the Nella Larsen portrayed in the article was an unprepossessing character, to say the least:

> Her voice is like a muted violin. You have to listen for it. She is proud of her poise. She laughingly admits it is acquired. Underneath her satin surface Nordic and West Indian are struggling. It hurts one way and helps another. She doesn't mind being shooed up the employe[e]s' entrance in hotels, because her Nordic side waits for such a situation; her negro side understands it.

Nella Larsen's philosophy toward life is answered:—"I don't have any way of approaching life. . . . It does things to me instead." She admits she is a fatalist if you point it out to her.

The "unforgivable sin" is being bored. She selects only amusing and natural people, not too intellectual. She would never pass because "with my economic status it's better to be a negro. So many things are excused them. The chained and downtrodden negro is a picture that came out of the civil war."

She seemed to completely dismiss group agitation for social change: "She is convinced recognition and liberation will come to the negro only through individual effort." Although, according to Rennels, Larsen had the uplift of the Negro "buried near her heart," Rennels quoted Larsen as saying that "propaganda isn't the way to accomplish it"—certainly an infuriating opinion to Walter White, with whom she was to share a stage the night after the report came out.

Rennels' article gave the impression that Larsen was a shallow materialist, "not quite sure what she wants to be spiritually," although "books, money, and travel would satisfy her materially. . . . She would like to be twenty-five years younger. She wants things—beautiful and rich things." In fact, she seemed not much different from her tragic antiheroines. Although she loved children, she evidently did not want to be trapped raising them: "Her years as a children's librarian in New York (she is in the Ghetto now) may be escape from her desire for the luxury of ten children."[48]

The Knopfs also arranged for the journalist Marion L. Starkey to interview Larsen and Walter White—who had just published *Rope and Faggot*, on lynching—in the library of the firm's office suite. Sunk deep in an overstuffed couch, the two authors chaffed each other about their new books, and a talkative Larsen carried the conversation "vivaciously" according to Starkey, who found her strikingly attractive, with skin the color of "brown honey." "She is petite and chic and duskily lovely and has lustrous eyes. Her Scandinavian strain shows chiefly in the strong and beautiful modeling of her heart-shaped face."[49]

Starkey's article (never published) consisted almost entirely of quotations from Larsen. They are worth reproducing at length, as they give some sense of the author's occasionally wacky charm, unbuttoned opinions, and ability to perform for a mixed audience. But they should be taken with a grain of salt, since they are self-conscious publicity work.

"Why I really shouldn't wonder," said Nella Larson, tamping the cigarette Walter White had just given her with her slim brown fingers, "if right now the unknown Negro author of genuine ability hasn't an easier road to recognition than the unknown white writer.

"Of course it wouldn't do to make a dogmatic statement to that effect. I don't know that anyone, least of all myself, has ever taken a census to demonstrate that Negro writers have no difficulties with editors. Naturally, they must have.

"But for myself, I have had almost no trouble ever in getting placed, and that seems to be the experience of all my own immediate circle of writing friends. Editors not only welcome us, they actually seem to be on the lookout for us.

"They seem eager to give us an opportunity to show ourselves to the world as we appear to each other, and not as we formerly appeared in magazine literature, as a strange race of blackface comedians engaged in putting on a perpetual minstrel show. It may be just a fad on their part, but I think it's an awfully good fad."[50]

Both White and Larsen were very upbeat, and despite the topic of White's new book, he was "much disposed to change the subject" when Starkey tried to bring up the topic of lynching. "And so was Miss Larson who never, if she can help it, reads about lynchings or Jersey torch murders or subway suicides, who fears that she has no great aptitude for the sociological and economic problems involved in the race question."

Larsen preferred to talk about the position of black writers. Even if the current interest on the part of publishers was just a fad, it was one with "a much needed educational effect. Until recently it was almost impossible for a Negro to sell a veracious story of Negro life. The only Negro stories that were considered at all were the burlesques."

When asked if she meant tales like those of Joel Chandler Harris' Uncle Remus, Larsen was taken aback:

"Uncle Remus?" her lovely eyes widened. "Oh dear, no. I love Uncle Remus. Not one word against B'rer Rabbit and B'rer Fox and Tar Baby. . . . No, I was thinking rather of the Octavus Roy Cohen sort of thing.

. . . . .

"But now the tide is turning. White writers themselves are painting much truer pictures of us. Do you know Julia Peterkin in 'Black April' and 'Scarlet Sister Mary'? I love 'Black April'—all but that awful part about April's feet. And then there's DuBose Heyward and T. S. Stribling—oh, we owe a great deal to white authors.

"But more important is this being encouraged to express ourselves. We have Claude McKay the West Indian—'Home to Harlem' and poems, our Dr. W. E. B. Du Bois, Jean Toomer, Countee Cullen the poet . . . and Jessie Redmon Fauset—'There Is Confusion,' oh yes, and Walter White here with 'Fire in the Flint' and 'Flight.'

"Even if the fad for our writings passes presently, as it is bound to do I suppose, we will in the meantime have laid the foundation for our permanent contribution to American culture."

A prescient statement. For all her hopefulness, Larsen was not naive about the current "vogue." Nor did she expect it to have deep and far-reaching social effects in the near future. Yet literature had its place in the broad front of Negro self-expression and its long-term impact on the national culture.

On the ultimate contribution that Negro authors would make to American literature, Larsen took self-contradictory positions. For someone who could be withering about "twaddle concerning the inherent qualities of the Negro" (as in her review of *Black Sadie*), she seems more than susceptible to such twaddle herself. "Once we have done writing so much about our problems and sorrows," she professes, black writers' main contribution will be "our vitality, our native sunniness of temperament."

"This aspect of the Negro is very vivid to me, because, as you know, I am half Danish, and for a considerable part of my life, first when I was a very small child, then when I was 17 to 21, I was brought up in Copenhagen where I got well-acquainted with the Scandinavian half of myself.

"They are wonderful people, the Scandinavians, intelligent, broadminded, and yet in spite of all that they are on the whole a strangely unhappy lot. It's hard to understand it."

"Perhaps," suggested Mr. White, "they read Ibsen too much."

"Oh, I shouldn't wonder, Walter!" laughed Miss Larson in her husky contralto. "Too much Ibsen. Of course, that accounts for everything. But no, I mean it. They really seemed to me an unhappy people. And so many suicides as there are in those Northern countries!

"I can't see why. They have had peace and prosperity for so long. But perhaps that is exactly it. Perhaps they have had too much. Possibly the best of their future is all behind them, as the saying goes, and they have little that is dramatic and interesting to look forward to.

"And perhaps that partly explains why we are so happy, because everything still lies ahead of us. For all their troubles do you often hear of a Negro committing suicide? So seldom! Our folk do have good times in spite of everything. Work all day, hard grinding labor, and still ready to laugh half the night through. I don't think there's a race in the world with more capacity for sheer enjoyment.

"Who can tell what achievement we have ahead of us, what we shall make of ourselves in America? Oh, I think it's a wonderful thing to belong to the Negro race! No matter what adjustments, what sufferings are yet to come, the very worst, surely, the blackest part of the shadow lies all behind us. We are going forward into the light.

"Do you know, speaking of my gloomy Scandinavian half-brothers, I shouldn't wonder if, once we have done with all these problems that Walter spends his time investigating, we won't be the influence that keeps American literature prevailingly sunny-tempered in the end.

"We may supply just that tendency needed to counteract the gloom of those frightfully intellectual Scandinavians who are busy raising crops of problem novels out in the mid-Western prairies. The black influence in American literature will be in the end the influence of the sun."

Abruptly realizing how optimistic and stereotypical all of this sounded, and how utterly remote from her own writing, Larsen "suddenly announced that for herself she is a very morbid, easily depressed sort of person, and that the hero-ine of 'Passing' dies at the end. "Though does that make my book a tragedy? Don't most people do that in the end?"

The voluble author had single-handedly, and somewhat unwittingly, talked herself into a corner. Someone decided to turn the interview more in the direc-tion of racial barriers and interracial social relations, on which Larsen also had plenty to say.

"I have no enthusiasm for barriers," said Miss Larson, "but I do know that colored people are happier as a whole in their own society. It's not so much that there is prejudice, but that race is race wherever you go and whichever race you belong to, and you're happier among your own kind. Negroes who mingle freely in white society are, in my experience, looked on rather askance in Harlem."

She made it clear that she and Elmer Imes could be counted among those who "mingled freely":

"For myself I have never in my life suffered any real unpleasantness because of my race, and my husband, whose experience is simply amazing, has been so pleasantly received everywhere that he claims and I think believes that there is no such thing as the color line. Here in the North of course.

.....

"In his work he is thrown exclusively with whites, belongs to their techni-cal societies, attends their dinners. Why he's even been to conventions in At-lantic City where we are expressly not welcomed—and has never met with anything but hospitality and good fellowship.

"It isn't that he 'passes.' Not in that sense. He is fully as dark as I—wouldn't you judge so, Walter? It is merely that he has never had anything but kindness from whites in his life, expects nothing else, gets nothing else."

Running out of time, Larsen turned down an offer of another cigarette and got up to head back to the library, pulling her "smart little black hat over her blue-black hair." The usually loquacious Walter, who had sat silent through practically the entire interview, gamely wished her good luck with *Passing*, adding "I hope it's a best seller. I hope it's banned in Boston."

"It won't be," said Miss Larson. "I'm much too innocuous to get banned anywhere. And don't go insinuating things against Boston. I love Boston.

"I don't think there's any place in the world where a colored person can come and go with more complete absence of embarrassment. People are delightful there. I have so many friends who feel just the same way, who have a very special feeling for Boston.

"And what about all those tables of yours in the back of that lynching book? Ever since lynchings have been recorded there's not been one in Massachusetts, and only two in New England. You talk to me about Boston!"

If there is such a thing as conversational sleight of hand, this mildly inebrious interview suggests that Larsen was a master at it.

A diaphanous self-parody runs alongside the quasi-ethnological observations, which are perpetually undermined by threads of doubt. It is vintage Twenties chatter, outrageously downplaying the reality of Northern racism, yet testifying to it in the negative at the same time. Though she couldn't bear to read about lynchings, Larsen remembered even the statistics on individual states in the back of White's biography of "Judge Lynch." Though she had never experienced racism first hand, implicitly she had never known a place where a black person could move about with complete "lack of embarrassment." (Boston was merely the closest approximation.) And though she had had no problem placing her work, she neglected to mention that her publishers had yet to encounter much luck selling it—a point that went for black-authored writing generally, as she well knew.

"I know it's going to be a best seller this time," Walter shouted after her as she made for the door, donning her smart cloche hat. Starkey closed her article with Larsen's game reply: "'Oh no. The best seller is always next time. Goodbye both, and my love to Boston.' And Nella Larson had gone out into the gray and silver April afternoon."

She knew how to charm. Larsen was neither naively uttering a lot of nonsense, nor, in the simplest sense, pulling the wool over her interlocutor's eyes—

although she was, to be sure, wearing a mask, avoiding unpleasant subjects, being irresponsible. A warmth and sincerity invests her very posing, expressed partly in self-mockery. One is hard-put to identify the line between the "real" and the make-believe. The light-hearted camaraderie, recklessness, and good-humored sophistication carry the performance along in literal spite of the boundaries of racial difference that so often make every gesture and word too self-conscious, too heavy with accumulated baggage. "Conversational weight-lifting," Larsen had termed it in *Passing*.

On April 14 Larsen joined Walter White again, this time literally onstage, as an invited speaker for "Authors' Night" at the St. George Playhouse in Brooklyn, announced in the *New York Times*. They addressed a large, virtually all-white audience, she on "Negro Authors" and he on "Lynching."[51] This was yet more of the marketing campaign the Knopfs were orchestrating for the two authors, and on its heels came the series of celebrations leading up to the official publication of *Passing*.

On the seventeenth, Dorothy Peterson's tea party brought together many of Larsen's closest friends. Just back from Europe, Crystal Bird joined Dorothy in politely receiving the guests—Inez Wilson, Corinne Wright, Dorothy and Jimmy Harris, Alta and Aaron Douglas, Van Vechten, Eddie Wasserman, Harry Block, Sally and Ernest Alexander, Grace Johnson, Max Ewing, Muriel Draper, Gladys White, Harold Jackman, Marion Beasley, Eunice Carter, Richmond Barthé, and a few others.[52] The guest lists of such events help to pinpoint Larsen's unique position in the complex fabric of Manhattan high life, always straddling social and cultural divisions.

The next day, the eighteenth, Carl picked up Nella and Elizabeth Shaffer, his niece, and took them to the "tea"—actually a cocktail party—that Blanche Knopf was hosting in Nella's honor at the Sherry-Netherland Hotel. No entering the back door on this occasion. A liveried doorman welcomed them into the resplendent lobby, and an elegant Art Deco elevator swept them to the sixth floor, where, in Room 6E, New York's most powerful woman publisher received them. The throng of supporters included Irita Van Doren, author William Seabrook and Marjorie Worthington, Isa Glenn, Grace Johnson, Walter White, Dorothy Harris, Emily Clark, Harry Block, Eddie Wasserman, and plenty of others whom Blanche Knopf could always call on to help launch a book.[53]

A week later came a more extravagant and unbuttoned reprise, Eddie Wasserman's *thé dansant* at his home on East Thirtieth Street,[54] on the eve of *Passing*'s official publication. In arranging the event, Wasserman remembered Nella's inscription in his copy of *Quicksand*: "For Eddie, in memory of his parties."[55] The phenomenon of the *thé dansant* dated back to about 1912, when club managers began offering afternoon dances, or "tango teas," for women on their own, with paid male partners (gigolos) provided by the host.[56] For the featured entertainment, Wasserman played off this idea by hiring none other than Gladys Bentley. A cross-dresser, and the main draw at Harlem's Clam House, La Bentley typically performed in top hat and tails. Accompanying herself on piano, she specialized in outrageous ad libs of popular tunes, turning the most tender ballads into raunchy anthems to which her audiences gaily sang along.[57]

As Fania and Carl prepared to leave for another summer in Europe, Lawrence Langner and Armina Marshall threw a party for them on the first Saturday in May. The sixteen guests included Elmer and Nella, who drove the guests of honor home at 4:00 A.M. But when Carl and Fania sailed on the *Majestic* the following Friday, Nella could only wire them a morning telegram: "Love and affection and the best time ever for you both but dont stay away too long."[58] Elmer made it to Pier 59 to see them off, but Nella had to work.[59] She faced a long and lonely summer, with Elmer planning to spend it mostly in Ann Arbor and Canada, and Fania and Carl abroad until late August.

When the NAACP Women's Auxiliary held an elegant Sunday evening party at the Walker Studio in honor of Walter White's *Rope and Faggot,* "Miss Nella Larsen" appeared as one of the specially invited guests, along with Jessie Fauset and Aaron Douglas. Each made a short speech, after which White spoke of the experiences that went into his "biography of Judge Lynch." Larsen, Fauset, Douglas, and White autographed books for sale during the refreshment period.[60]

Thinking of Larsen, Van Vechten wrote to Alfred Knopf from Europe, urging him to keep up the marketing campaign for *Passing.* Knopf soon replied: "PASSING has now sold about 3,500 copies and I have just ordered a small third printing. The sale incidentally is confined almost entirely to New York—I am rather surprised that Chicago has evinced no interest in the book at all although I tried to get the more important booksellers there to push it."[61] It was no easy task getting the general public to buy a black-authored novel. It was not easy to get even the Negro public interested; white-authored novels, even on Negro subjects, generally outstripped black-authored novels in popularity at the 135th Street Library.[62]

By late May a number of reviews had come out, largely favorable, and for the most part more insightful than those of *Quicksand* had been. In the *New York Times Book Review,* Larsen was praised for her "good, firm, tangible prose" and the unity of her tale. Larsen avoided sensationalizing black life or pandering to mere curiosity about black difference, according to this and other white reviewers: "Unlike other negro novelists, and white novelists who write about negroes, she does not give her following a bath in primitive emotionalism. She is not seeking the key to the soul of her race in the saxophone to the exclusion of all else." Rather, Larsen focused on presenting the psychological conflicts within her two chief characters, filtered through the point of view of Irene Redfield. "Not only has *Passing* the unity imparted by keeping the action to within the perceptive limits of one person; it also has a time unity, gained by employing the 'flashback' method of the motion picture. Miss Larsen is quite adroit at tracing the involved processes of a mind that is divided against itself, that fights between the dictates of reason and desire." But the critic found the ending of the novel completely unconvincing, a way of solving most of the narrative problems Larsen had set for herself by "sweeping them out of existence" with Clare's death. Too, Clare seemed too beautiful to be true; but perhaps that was merely because the reader saw her through Irene's eyes. All in all the novel was an effective one on an important problem, and "the fact that it is by a girl who is partly of negro blood adds to the effectiveness."[63]

On the same day that the *Times* ran its review, Margaret Cheney Dawson's review appeared in Irita Van Doren's *Herald Tribune Books*. Dawson, too, praised the way Larsen avoided sensationalizing racial difference for the titillation of white readers, taking the manners of her characters for granted, with no concessions to white ignorance. Yet much of the review hinged on how the book would strike white readers. Dawson admired Larsen's presentation of the story through Irene Redfield's point of view, and the way she developed Irene's conflicted response to Clare as the novel's chief element, which whites would find especially interesting. While the narrative style was disappointingly sober and unimpassioned for a "black" novel, "that strange excitement arising from the mere mention of race, as from the word sex, holds one's interest to the end."[64]

A mixed review in the New York *Sun* on the first of May criticized Larsen's style for overwrought elegance and the "impeccable refinement" of Irene and Clare's conversation, but found the book earnest and courageous in the way it addressed the "dilemma of mixed race." Hobbled by popular racial theories of the time, the critic found justified resentment of whites' hypocrisy toward the "mixed race" for which they were responsible, offset by allusions to the "powerful call of the negro blood which decisively binds the near-white grandchild or great-grandchild of the black man to the more primitive race."[65]

Larsen's spirits were lifted when William Seabrook's review appeared in the prestigious *Saturday Review*. Much admired for a recent book on voodoo in Haiti—"the best book of the year on a Negro subject," according to Aubrey Bowser in the *Amsterdam News*[66]—Seabrook started out with high praise: "Negro writers seldom possess a sense of form comparable to that of Miss Nella Larsen. Her new novel, *Passing,* is classically pure in outline, single in theme and in impression, and for these reasons—if for no others—powerful in its catastrophe." Yet Seabrook was annoyed by the restrictions of the narrative point of view, wanting to see Clare directly, or at least to perceive her through a more interesting "device-character" than Irene. "As it is, we are impatient with Irene Redfield's tortures because they cut off our view of Clare." He found the style occasionally overwrought or "literary," which he attributed to Larsen's consciousness of writing for a mixed audience, including whites who were likely to be "either uncomprehending or hostile. But there is a great deal less of this self-consciousness in Miss Larsen than in most writers of her race. She has produced a work so fine, sensitive, and distinguished that it rises above race categories and becomes that rare object, a good novel."[67] In a letter written to Van Vechten in mid-June, Nella called this a "marvelous review. . . . Quite the best and most perceptive, though a bit too eulogistic."[68] One wonders if she was being sincere, particularly since she had met Seabrook through Van Vechten.

While flawed in its critique of Larsen's use of Irene, Seabrook's review certainly beat that of Aubrey Bowser for the *Amsterdam News* on June 5, which naively assumed that Irene's feelings about Clare expressed those of the author. Bowser was convinced that Clare had affairs with white men before her marriage and "stole" Brian Redfield. He complained of narrative sloppiness, oblivious to the flashback strategy Larsen used to begin the novel: "The story opens with a letter from Clare Kendry to Irene Redfield. Three chapters later Irene receives another letter from Clare, but 'she couldn't remember ever having a letter from her before.'" More pathetically, Bowser criticized Larsen for succumbing "to the grudge that most Negroes have against a Negro who goes over the race line and cannot stay there. The grudge is justifiable, for a person should be either one thing or the other, but it hampers the story-teller. . . . Thus her heroine, like most of the chief characters in race-line novels, is portrayed as a despicable character."[69] Not only did Bowser interpret Irene's perceptions and self-justifications as the author's own; he agreed with them.

Esther Hyman, writing for *The Bookman's* June number, was also thrown off by Irene's point of view, faulting Larsen for "lack of sympathy with a very real problem. Irene's passionate devotion to the Negro race to which she only partly belongs is a natural enough defensive instinct; but Clare's case is as real, and infinitely more deserving of compassion. . . . If Miss Larsen had presented Clare directly, instead of obliquely through Irene, she would have made of her a more satisfying character. As it is, her problem is never clearly stated and in the end is evaded."[70] Larsen's groundbreaking approach to the psychology of the color line repeatedly confounded the critics, both black and white.

By late June it seemed indeed as if *Passing,* while winning Larsen some notoriety, would find few attentive readers. But Dr. Du Bois came through again, with a glowing review in the July *Crisis:* "Nella Larsen's *Passing* is one of the finest novels of the year." Noting that Jessie Fauset and Walter White had recently used passing as a subject, Du Bois comments that Larsen attempted an entirely different kind of fiction from theirs. "She explains just what 'passing' is: the psychology of the thing; the reaction of it on friend and enemy. It is a difficult task, but she attacks the problem fearlessly and with consummate art. The great problem is under what circumstances would a person take a step like this and how would they feel about it? And how would their fellows feel?" Clare, he points out, "has been rather brutally kicked into the white world, and has married a white man, almost in self-defense. She has a daughter, but she is lonesome and eyes her playmate Irene with fierce joy." Recounting the conflict between "the race-conscious Puritan, Irene," and "the lonesome hedonist, Clare," Du Bois put his finger on the heart of the drama and concluded: "If the American Negro renaissance gives us many more books like this, with its sincerity, its simplicity and charm, we can soon with equanimity drop the word 'Negro.' Meantime, your job is clear. Buy the book."[71] The great race man had moved Larsen to the top of the reading list.

Through late May and a hot June, Larsen was not without diversions in addition to her library work. The Langners gave Elmer and her tickets for the Theatre Guild plays that season, and they "had a perfect orgy of theatre going."[72] Larsen ran into Rita Romilly several times and had a three-and-a-half-hour lunch with her one day: "What we, who never had much to say to each other talked about for all those hours the good god only knows."[73] She was spending a fair amount of her leisure time with lonely Dorothy Peterson in her apartment at 320 Second Avenue; Dorothy's brother Sidney, who had been living with her, moved to the outskirts of Harlem to live with his (white) Jewish fiancée, a fellow medical student at Columbia. The Whites, however, had cut Nella out of their social life after Dorothy told Walter that Nella had said "he dedicated his first book to Gladys, his second to Jane, but that he feared to dedicate the third to his son, because then we would discover what the infant's name really is. So that's that!"[74]

Nella had other sources of amusement, however, as her long newsy letter to Van Vechten gossiped in mid-June: "I went to lunch the other day with some people that I know very little (fays). In the course of our talk it developed that they would have been keenly disappointed had they discovered that I was not born in the jungle of the Virgin Isles, so I entertained them with quaint stories of my childhood in the bush, and my reaction to the tom-tom undertones in jazz. It was a *swell* luncheon."[75] At the same time, she was "seeing quite a good deal" of the trim and handsome Colin Hackforth-Jones, a twenty-four-year-old Englishman she had met at one of the Langners' parties. "He is a nice person to take one around, dances well, is amusing and seems not to have any race consciousness at all."[76] Fully fourteen years her junior, Hackforth-Jones was an Oxford graduate and aspiring novelist, in New York at the time because his father, a prosperous stockbroker, had sent him to work with associates on Wall Street to learn the business.[77] Elmer was mostly unavailable, and Nella did not expect to see much of him. "I shall be, as always, at home this summer, mostly alone I think. Elmer is planning to go to Canada and later to Ann Arbor, I believe." Clearly, they were communicating with difficulty. After ten years of marriage, he was losing interest in her, awakening fears of abandonment that resonated with early memories.

She could have traveled, herself, that summer. She'd received an insulting offer to tour the South and gather material on black plantation life for a *Forbes* writer — "all expenses paid and a whole hundred dollars for the work. The south in the summer on Negro Plantations (whatever they are) and in Jim Crow cars, all for a hundred dollars: I felt it was a shame to take the money."[78] She had more tempting opportunities, however. Both the new *Liberty* magazine and the prestigious *Forum* asked her for short stories, offering between $200 and $250 for 1,500–2,000 words. She stopped working at the library at the end of June and set to work, but found it hard to write. She always felt "seedy" in the summer, she confessed to Van Vechten. Moreover, "I can't write short stories."[79] Nonetheless, it must have been at this time that she cranked out the tale "Sanctuary" — a rewriting of Sheila Kaye-Smith's "Mrs. Adis" transposed from England to the American South — and a story, never published, entitled "Charity."

Elmer was gone most weekends, but Colin Hackforth-Jones kept escorting Larsen through July, to "places like the Ritz, the Roosevelt and the Pennsylvania and Biltmore roofs. . . . But I'm about fed up on it. That is I'm awfully tired of being stared at."[80] And he was, after all, no replacement for her husband. Through Hackforth-Jones, she and Dorothy met a young Spanish poet (unnamed in Larsen's correspondence) who was studying English at Columbia. He was Federico García Lorca, and in time would be known as one of the great poets of the twentieth century.

Hackforth-Jones, a Spanish major, had met Lorca while a student in Granada back in 1926–1927 and they had become fast friends. Then one day in June 1929, during the time he was escorting Larsen around, the Englishman spotted Lorca in a Manhattan restaurant, which led to a joyous revival of their friendship.[81] Dorothy Peterson soon "picked up" Lorca for the summer, according to Nella, who called him "a charming Spanish musician and poet.... He really is delightful. Sings and plays. Thats beautifully fragile old fifteenth and sixteenth century things. I can't tell anything about his poetry because it hasn't been translated. We have both received letters from his mother ... to visit her in Granada."[82]

In his letters home, Lorca discreetly made no mention of Dorothy Peterson, in whose Second Avenue apartment he attended at least one of the parties he described (identifying the apartment as Larsen's in his correspondence); but he was utterly taken with "a famous Negro writer of the American literary vanguard, Nella Larsen," who introduced him to Harlem. For an entire evening, probably with Dorothy's help, they conversed in French, since Larsen spoke no Spanish and he barely could speak English. Some of his infatuation is attributable to the romantic haze of half-understood conversation in a language neither interlocutor could speak well, abetted by Larsen's good looks, pleasing low voice, and newly acquired literary reputation.

> This writer is an exquisite woman, full of kindness and that melancholy of the Negroes, so profound and so moving.
>
> She had a party at her house where there were only Negroes. This is now the second time that I've been with her—she interests me enormously.
>
> During the last party, I was the only white person there. She lives on Second Avenue, and from her windows one can see all of New York lit up. It was nighttime, and the sky was cross-hatched by the long beams of searchlights. The Negroes sang and danced.

The spirituals reminded him of the Cante Jondo (the "deep song" of the Gypsies, and the source of flamenco), which he played and sang to their encouragement. They made him repeat several of them four or five times. "The Negroes are such good people. When they said goodbye, they all hugged me and the writer gave me her books with wonderful inscriptions, which was a great honor, since it's something she never does." Larsen also took him to a black cabaret, where he was constantly reminded of his mother, "for the place seemed to be right out of those movies that scare her."[83] In early August Lorca drafted "El rey de Harlem" (The King of Harlem) and "Norma y paraíso de los negros" (Standards and Paradise of the Blacks)—both later to become cantos of *El Poeta en Nueva York* (The Poet in New York).[84]

Lorca considered spirituals an American equivalent to the Gypsy songs that had previously inspired his poetry, and he believed the very soul of America was in the melancholy and spirituality of blacks. Without the art of the Negro, American culture would be nothing but mechanism and automatism.[85] This conviction, colored though it was with a kind of romantic surrealist enthusiasm for "exotic" races, would stay with him into the Thirties. In an interview four years later, he trembled with intensity as he recounted his experience of Harlem: "In New York, you can find people from all over the world; but the Chinese, Armenians, Russians, and Germans will always be foreigners. Everyone except the Negroes. Without a doubt, they exercise enormous influence in North America, and despite what everyone says, they are the most spiritual and delicate people of that world."[86] It was the Negroes, he was convinced, who set the true aesthetic standards and patterns of North America, above all through the music that had sustained them, and continued to sustain them, in an alien world.

"It has been a hot, a hectic, and rather amusing summer," Larsen wrote Van Vechten at the end of July. One source of amusement was Sidney Peterson's marriage to "that girl, Edith Sproul. Quite much excitement about it. The Graphic, the News, and the Mirror seems [sic] to have interviewed all members of both families concerning the desirability, advisability and legitimacy of the marriage. She, however, seems a sensible enough creature and quite old enough to know [her] own mind, if not exactly what she was doing. So much for that!"[87] The couple had been seeing each other since at least January and were married without fanfare at the municipal chapel by a deputy city clerk.[88] Edith was twenty-one. Her father, a New York photographer, approved of the match, which created a minor sensation as part of what seemed to the Harlem papers a "wave of intermarriage" in the late 1920s.[89] The "wave" apparently consisted of two or three such marriages, including that of Kip and Alice Rhinelander, to which Larsen made brief allusion in *Passing*. Having won her earlier case against an annulment, Alice had filed for divorce by now and was suing her father-in-law for "alienation of affection."

The evening of the very day that Larsen posted her letter to Van Vechten, she attended Dorothy's reception for the bride and groom, without Elmer, on one of the hottest nights of the year. Dorothy's more intimate black friends made up the group, along with Edith's father and brother. "We lolled about," reported Geraldyn Dismond, "drank endless cocktails a la [Richard] Bruce, and iced teas, ate numbers of French sandwiches and admired the beautiful Mrs. Peterson, who wore a dark blue sleeveless gown, and amber beads the color of her hair, and the groom who has acquired a mustache and glasses."[90] The marriage, unfortunately, would not last much longer than the Rhinelanders'.

Inspired by the heat, Nella was learning to swim, joining a surge of black New Yorkers taking to the beach.[91] "Bathing and other beach sports have become a fad with Harlemites this summer," the *New York Age* reported.[92] The suntan vogue, meanwhile, had finally hit the beaches of North America after a three-year incubation in French resorts, inaugurated simultaneously with Josephine Baker's celebrity and the fascination with olive-skinned South Sea islanders—for which La Baker passed in her first film role. Everyone was getting browner. "Jimmie [Harris] is in town as black as the ace of spades," Larsen cracked. "However sun-tan being very fashionable I suppose it's all right. On Fifth Avenue one can't tell the fays from the niggers these days, which is just as well."[93] Some African American reporters hoped the whole phenomenon would teach white Americans the folly of their prejudices and wreak havoc on the Jim Crow laws.[94]

Taylor Gordon's picaresque autobiography *Born To Be* was having a rough career in the black press; and it seemed that the foreword by Van Vechten, introduction by Muriel Draper, and illustrations by Covarrubias weren't helping any. "The dunning of Taylor Gordon's book is very amusing what with you, Muriel and Miguel all included. I should hazard that it will be a howling success, though I am beginning to feel," Larsen confessed, "that the reading public is getting rather bored with Negro books."[95] One wondered how long the cultural "amalgamation" would continue. The "fad" had already outlasted most and seemed bound to end. Nonetheless, James Weldon Johnson won a Rosenwald Fellowship to take a year's leave from the NAACP and work on his writing ("Isn't that grand?"), Langston Hughes had a novel in press, and King Vidor's much awaited, "all-Negro" film *Hallelujah!* was about to come out.[96] Vidor was quoted in the black press as saying that he was "trying to do for Negro talent what we did for the doughboy in *The Big Parade*."[97] *Hallelujah!* was the first all-colored talkie, starring Nina Mae McKinney, a pretty, bright-eyed Harlemite whom Vidor had picked out of the *Blackbirds* chorus.

In July Larsen decided to have another go at the Harmon Award, in hopes of winning the gold medal. Lillian Alexander nominated her, as before, listing Van Vechten, W. E. B. Du Bois, and Dorothy Peterson as references. After Du Bois's glowing review of *Passing,* Alexander and Larsen had reason to think he would enthusiastically endorse her, but he had two other friends in the race—Georgia Douglas Johnson (with whom he was carrying on a long-term affair) and Leslie Pinckney Hill, director of the State Normal College in Cheyney, Pennsylvania. Hill was clearly his top choice, deserving of "exceptional recognition. . . . His last poem on Toussaint L'Ouverture is to my mind a masterpiece." He was considerably less enthusiastic about Georgia Douglas Johnson and about Larsen, of whom he wrote simply, "I regard her work as important and outstanding."[98]

Van Vechten showed more enthusiasm. Both of her novels, he wrote, "are written with an insight into character, an intensity of development, and in a fine English style that proclaims the true novelist. Both objectively and subjectively, they are a psychological advance over any previous work by a Negro novelist." He was endorsing her "because she is probably the most interesting and the most promising of the young writers of her race." This, knowing that his friend Walter White was also entering the competition that year; even his well-known admiration for Langston Hughes's work did not, at that moment, match his judgment of Larsen's fiction. At this point, Van Vechten considered Larsen a professional novelist. Whereas Lillian Alexander's nomination identified Nella's occupation as "housewife" and Dorothy Peterson termed her a "librarian," Van Vechten stated unequivocally, "She is an author."[99]

Yet Dorothy Peterson's recommendation is the most intriguing, listing three published short stories—"Freedom," "Tea," and "The Wrong Man," all from 1926—and two unpublished stories—"Sanctuary" and "Charity." "Tea" has never been found, and Larsen herself never listed it as a published work. "Sanctuary" would appear soon in *The Forum*, but "Charity" remains unknown. Peterson stressed Larsen's past experience and cosmopolitanism, "her education and life in Europe and America, her travel, her work in different fields—as nurse, librarian, teacher etc., her broad contact with many different classes of native and foreign races with an ability to understand and portray all these sympathetically." Moreover, Larsen's psychological perceptiveness made her stand out: "I endorse this candidate because I feel that her honest and logical presentation of modern problems, her keen insight into human motives particularly her gift for interpreting feminine psychology, combined with her gift for clear and beautiful writing, all form a definite force for better understanding in race relations and raise the artistic standards of Negro writers."[100] As others who could vouch for the candidate, Peterson listed Du Bois, Eddie Wasserman, Harry Block, Alice Dunbar-Nelson, and James Weldon Johnson. She could not perhaps have known that Dunbar-Nelson was in Georgia Douglas Johnson's corner and James Weldon Johnson was going all out for his understudy Walter White.

Nella and Elmer made up part of a small celebration at Eddie Wasserman's when Fania and Carl returned in late August. On the twenty-third, Nella visited their apartment and Van Vechten asked her to write in an autograph book he had begun abroad. She was the first person he asked in New York. She made up a piece of amusing doggerel that displays her inveterate attraction to inversion, the literary trope of chiasmus, and ironic sexual innuendo. "Dear Carl," she wrote,

Here's hoping you live as long as you want to
And want to as long as you live;
If I'm asleep and you want to, wake me.
If I'm awake and don't want to, make me.

—Nella Larsen Imes

It was by far the sauciest autograph anyone wrote for him, a campy caress for a friend whose extramarital affairs were always with men.[101]

On the twenty-fourth Nella and Elmer took Fania and Carl to see *Hallelujah!* at the Lafayette Theatre in Harlem, one of the big events of the season.[102] Vidor had given serious leading roles to good-looking black actors, and respectfully spotlighted amazing performances of folksong and folkdance. But the film, which featured a lusty temptress, a philandering preacher, and orgiastic church scenes (by then de rigueur in black "folk theater"), was not far removed from old patterns. Vidor thought he had inoculated the film against racist opposition by using no white people in the cast and by showing "the black man building his own life along lines different from those of the whites"—not wearing evening clothes, not going to college, not attending the theater.[103] The Southern Film Association banned the film nonetheless, ensuring its financial failure.[104] Nina Mae McKinney's performance impressed Larsen's group, however, and her name was quickly added to Van Vechten's guest list.

Life in the segregated South loomed threateningly on the horizon for Nella Larsen by the late summer of 1929. Elmer had changed his mind about waiting to go to Fisk. He wrote President Jones on August 15, saying that as soon as he had mentioned to his employers that he might leave, they had turned against him; he would be jobless as of September first.[105] Jones responded that he would gladly have Imes come in the fall, but the Board of Trustees had already met and approved a budget with no salary for him, and they had very few students in the Physics Department as yet. Jones asked if he could join part time for the coming year, helping to plan what should be done with the new science building, Bennett Hall.[106] Apparently they worked out a deal, for Imes would receive $3,012.85 for 1929–1930, despite not being in permanent residence or teaching that year.[107]

Jones was making a concerted effort to recruit top black talent from the Negro Renaissance as part of a revitalization of the university, and he was succeeding to a remarkable extent. Charles S. Johnson, editor of *Opportunity* and a major orchestrator of the Harlem Renaissance in literature, had already signed on. Elmer attended his going-away party, while thinking over his own position.

Nella wanted none of it, but Fisk was Elmer's safety net. And there were other attractions there. On the fifth of September, he dropped in on Van Vechten with a "hard luck story," and soon thereafter left for Nashville.[108] The marriage had become a charade. Elmer had spent most weekends away all summer, and planned to be gone into October. "He needs it," Nella rationalized. "As usual I shall be here."[109]

At Fisk, he got a more than warm reception. Ethel Bedient Gilbert, the dedicated, popular, and immensely gifted Director of Publicity and Finance who had almost single-handedly made possible the school's new recruiting and building efforts, welcomed him into her home and lifted his spirits. "We have just had a fine two weeks visit from Elmer Imes," she wrote her old friend Walter White, savoring the afterglow. "I had the pleasure of 'putting him up' and the night he left was like the parlor grate with the fire gone out."[110] Had the word gotten out to greater Nashville, a firestorm would have raked the institution. And it couldn't afford that.

When Gilbert had arrived in 1928, the school faced a $110,000 deficit—staggering in proportion to the school's resources at the time. She had reorganized the publicity and finance operations to make fundraising continuous, had wiped out the debt, and was building up a million-dollar endowment in the belief that "Fisk represents a big idea that will not be completely put over in America for scores of years."[111] Traveling tirelessly, and totally committed to the "idea" of Fisk, she succeeded spectacularly in attracting support from philanthropic foundations and well-heeled New Englanders. As a result, Fisk by the late 1920s and early 1930s was able to hire stars of the Negro Renaissance—people like Charles Johnson, James Weldon Johnson, Elmer Imes, Aaron Douglas, Arthur Schomburg, E. Franklin Frazier, St. Elmo Brady, and Alain Locke—at twice the salary top faculty members (almost all white) had previously made, and could provide them with brand-new faculty houses, built to order next to campus. By 1929 Gilbert was near the top of the organizational chart of the university, yet at the same time was regarded as the students' most valuable ally in their push for greater self-governance. If some of the older administrators feared her zealousness and "radicalism," no one could deny the magnitude of her contribution. Whiteness was only one attribute she had that Nella did not. Except for her racial identity, Ethel Gilbert was much more in line with the Imes family traditions.

Elmer had returned to New York by the tenth of October, but Nella continued to socialize as much without as with him.[112] On the sixteenth she had Eddie Wasserman, Van Vechten, and Marinoff over for dinner; along with Corinne Wright, who came in after the meal, they stayed till midnight.[113] On the twentieth, Carl came by with an aspiring young actor (white) from Chicago, Nicholas J. Nelson, and together with Nella they headed out to the Cotton Club, where they were turned away, to their shock, for being a mixed party.

Infuriated, they walked to Pod's and Jerry's, a tiny joint with dim lighting and a sprinkling of tables with red-and-white-checked tablecloths, a small bar at one end of the room, and some of the best music in Harlem.[114] Everything in the club cost a dollar. It was the throne room of the king of Harlem stride piano, Willie the Lion Smith (himself married to a white woman), who came on at midnight. Here the managers made a point of seating the black and white patrons indiscriminately. When whites objected, "Pod" (Charles Holingsworth) would call a cab and tell the driver to take them to Connie's Inn two blocks away. Still upset about the Cotton Club incident, Nick Nelson got drunk and made himself "obnoxious" until Carl managed to get rid of him. Carl took Nella home at about 1:30.[115] The next morning, his fifteenth wedding anniversary, as soon as he got up he went to Goldfarb's and had flowers sent to her—consolation for a disappointing evening.[116]

One might wonder why Carl Van Vechten and Nella Larsen, two aficionados of Harlem nightlife, tried to get into the Cotton Club, which famously excluded blacks. But from the Harlem newspapers one learns that the Cotton Club was not always off limits to black patrons. Its policies often changed without notice —in part because of police intimidation of "black and tans"—and in the spring and summer of 1929 blacks had been allowed in. Racial restrictions on entry into Harlem haunts—of whites into "black" clubs and blacks into "white" clubs —were often adopted because there were police raids on places allowing blacks and whites to dance together.[117]

On November 2 Dorothy had Nella for lunch, along with other friends—including the handsome actor Tom Rutherford, who was developing an interest in Dorothy. Afterward, Nella and Carl stopped in Greenwich Village looking for his old friend Bob Chanler and had a chat with the owner of "some very beautiful cats in a window," then took a bus uptown together.[118] About this time, Carl gave Nella a copy of Taylor Gordon's *Born To Be,* which she read for the second time, finding it still "amazing" and "amuzing."[119] Elmer liked it, too. Larsen praised Carl's introduction and wrote that she was "working on a piece about Mr. Carl Van Vechten which I think will be called 'Toward Nigger Heaven.'" She wanted to interview him within the next week or so.[120]

On the tenth, she learned from the newspapers that Nick Nelson, of the awkward night at the Cotton Club and Pod's and Jerry's, had been killed, prompting her to write Carl glibly: "If it had happened the night he was up here think what a grand time you and I would have had as witnesses. Poor dear. I suppose his tremendous inferiority complex was what finished him."[121] Nelson had been leaving a Greenwich Village speakeasy with friends when he got into a fight with a bartender and was knocked against a wall. A policeman found him in a coma at 29th and Broadway, and he died the next day of a fractured skull.[122] The corpses were beginning to pile up.

Now that the Imeses were buffered by Elmer's guarantee of a job at Fisk, the stock market crash had little immediate effect on Nella's life, but she could see major changes on the near horizon. The last thing she wanted was to move to Nashville, leaving behind the New York writer's life and the best friends she had ever had, to be with a husband who little cared for her. She may have suspected already that he was in love with another woman. She applied for a Guggenheim Fellowship in early November. If Elmer went south, she would try to get away to Europe.

Giving her present occupations as "hack writing," "housework," and "sewing," she proposed to write a novel "laid partly in the United States and partly in Europe. The theme will be the difference in intellectual and physical freedom for the Negro—and the effect on him—between Europe, especially the Latin countries Spain and France. I have never been in these countries and therefore feel that I am not prepared without visiting them to judge attitudes and reactions of my hero in a foreign and favorable or more unfavorable environment. My plan is, travel and residence in Europe, principally the South of France and Spain, while completing the novel."[123] She hoped to begin the fellowship in September 1930.

On Thanksgiving, Elmer and Nella had dinner at Carl and Fania's, with Eddie Wasserman, Edna Kenton, Donald Angus, Tom Rutherford, Miguel Covarrubias, and Rose Rolanda—all staying late into the night.[124] Three of them were involved in the last big NAACP benefit of the 1920s, a Broadway celebration of the Negro Renaissance to raise money for civil rights work. Nella and Elmer were "patrons." Through Van Vechten, Lawrence Langner had promised the free use of a theater, subject to the Theatre Guild's approval. Contents of the program, designed by Aaron Douglas, would include new caricatures by Covarrubias, a new essay by Van Vechten, and a slightly altered excerpt from *Quicksand*.[125]

Eerily blurring the line between fiction and reality, Larsen's description of a "renaissance-style" ball appeared under the title, "Moving Mosaic, or N.A.A.C.P. Dance, 1929":

There was sooty black, shiny black, taupe, mahogany, bronze, copper, gold, orange, yellow, peach, ivory, white. There was white hair, gray hair, yellow hair, red hair, brown hair, straightened hair, crinkly hair, woolly hair. Black eyes in white faces, brown eyes in black faces, green eyes in yellow faces, blue eyes in tan faces, gray eyes in brown faces. Young men, old men, black men, white men, flapper women, older women, pink women, golden women, fat men, thin men, tall men, short men, stately women, small women, slim women, stout women, ambling lazily to a melody or twisting their bodies to a sudden streaming rhythm or shaking themselves to the thump of unseen tom-toms. Africa, Europe, and a pinch of Asia in a fantastic motly of ugliness and beauty.[126]

Van Vechten's essay, "Keep A-Inchin' Along," recorded the expansion of black entertainment, the decline of blackface, and the transformation of casting since he had first begun attending the "Negro Theatre" thirty years before. Whereas Dunbar and Chesnutt had then been "lonely eminences" in the field of literature, now "there is scarcely a publishing house of any standing which does not advertise the name of at least one Negro author." In 1906, blacks "lived modestly around Fifty-third and Fifty-ninth Streets"; "Now the negro is installed in Harlem, the largest Negro city in the world," with banks, churches, newspapers, theaters, clubs, libraries, a YMCA, and much more. "These are a few of the bald facts. What they signify you may determine for yourself."[127] Walter White's words on the same page projected how very different the country would be without the work of the NAACP over the previous thirty years: one or two hundred lynchings every year, no voting rights in the South, residential segregation encoded into law in most cities. The night's gathering was "both a seal upon the past and a happy omen for the future of the Negro and the white man in their common country."[128]

The December benefit raised more than $2,700, not bad for that gloomy month, although vacant seats could be seen in the orchestra.[129] Heywood Broun emceed a show at the Forrest Theatre on Forty-Ninth Street, featuring Broadway stars like Duke Ellington, George Gershwin, and Fredi Washington along with blues singers Clara Smith and Alberta Hunter.[130] Afterward, a large crowd of the principals and audience moved en masse to the Walker Studio, where, Geraldyn Dismond reported, "whoopee appropriate for so auspicious an occasion continued until dawn."[131]

Fad or no, on the eve of the Thirties, you couldn't tell Nella Larsen or her friends that the "movement" was a failure; and they never bought into the lugubrious assessments that gained force in the Great Depression. But Larsen never expected a fashionable, if much-fractured, artistic movement to break the chains of centuries. If it was a fad, in Larsen's words, it was "an awfully good fad," and would leave a legacy. If the vogue soon passed, as Larsen believed it was "bound to do," black authors would "in the meantime have laid the foundations for our permanent contribution to American culture"—a point that is now indisputable. If there was a Negro Vogue, there was also a Negro Renaissance. Maybe they were only inchin' along, but they were never going back to where they'd been.

EIGHTEEN

Trouble in Mind:
1930

BY January 1930, Nella Larsen was regarded as one of the chief figures of the Negro Renaissance and its premier novelist. On New Year's Day, the *Amsterdam News* listed the Harmon awards won by Claude McKay, Nella Larsen, and Channing Tobias, along with the honoring of the explorer Matthew Henson, as the outstanding events of the previous year.[1] She was mentioned as being a prominent hostess for the Harmon Exhibit of Fine Arts by Negroes at the International House on Riverside Drive. And she had an illustrated short story in the new issue of *The Forum,* one of America's most prestigious monthly magazines of literature and current events.

Handsomely decorated and illustrated on every page, with a circulation of 100,000, *The Forum* was a venue for measured debate over important controversies. It also solicited fiction by distinguished contemporary authors as a special feature.[2] Larsen was the first black author to place fiction there, in an issue that included articles by Eleanor Roosevelt, André Maurois, E. B. White, Howard Mumford Jones, Will Durant, and AE (George W. Russell). Specially commissioned woodblock illustrations and display decorations by Winold Reiss accompanied her story, "Sanctuary."

A folk story of the Deep South and a tale of racial solidarity overcoming intraracial animosities, "Sanctuary" differed markedly from all of Larsen's previous fiction. As Charles R. Larson has pointed out, "Nowhere else in her published work has Larsen made such an emphatic statement about blackness." Moreover, "It is the sole piece of dialect fiction that Larsen published during her career."[3]

The narrative is simple enough. On a strip of desolate land along the Southern coast, a desperate young man named Jim Hammer stops at the cottage of a friend's mother, Annie Poole, seeking protection from the law. Although he has shot someone and Annie dislikes him, for the sake of his friendship with her son she agrees to hide him from the "white folks," putting him in her clean feather bed and covering him with fresh laundry. The sheriff comes to the house bearing the dead body of her son, whom Jim shot during a burglary. But Annie lets the sheriff leave none the wiser, and then addresses her son's murderer: "Git outen mah feather baid, Jim Hammer, an' outen mah house, an' don' nevah stop thankin' yo' Jesus he done gib you dat black face."[4]

In terms of its psychology and narrative technique, "Sanctuary" is not nearly as complex, subtle, or original as Larsen's earlier published work; and the dialect does not always ring true. It appears that Larsen, like many authors after their first or second book, was trying to get away from autobiographically based fiction. She turned, disastrously, to unfamiliar subject matter and lifted the story from an eight-year-old piece of fiction by Sheila Kaye-Smith set in Sussex, England.

Kaye-Smith's tale, entitled "Mrs. Adis," tells the story of a lower-class fugitive fleeing the keepers of a nearby castle estate after killing the son of the woman who harbors him. The similarities between the stories are undeniable, with racial difference in Larsen's story substituting for class difference in Kaye-Smith's. Not only is the plot identical, but aspects of setting, description, and even dialogue are nearly direct "samples" imported from "Mrs. Adis." Could Larsen have been toying with a sort of deconstruction of racial difference by making an "English" tale into a "Negro" one? Turning from her "mulatto" and "passing" fictions to one more purely "black," and appealing to the demand for authentic folk fiction, she suggested the artificiality of such literary distinctions.

Yet there is something self-destructive about this act of near-plagiary, as if, disoriented by her sudden fame and the glamour of her new social world, Larsen subconsciously had to puncture the fairy tale, much like the protagonist of her very first short story, "The Wrong Man." "Mrs. Adis" was not exactly an obscure work. It had appeared first in January 1922 in *The Century,* a widely circulated magazine that was much like *The Forum* (and that merged with *The Forum* in 1930). It had been published again in 1926 by Harper and Brothers, in a well-known collection of Kaye-Smith's short fiction entitled *Joanna Godden Married and Other Stories.* If Larsen thought the change in location and racial identity of the characters would disguise her debt to Kaye-Smith, she quickly learned otherwise. Letters were soon pouring into the office of *The Forum's* editor, Henry Goddard Leach.

Knowing that the gossip would soon begin, Elmer visited Van Vechten on the afternoon of January 18 to tell him that Nella had been accused of plagiarism.[5] *The Forum* had already written to request an explanation, and Larsen showed the letter to Dorothy Peterson, along with a draft of her reply.[6] Dorothy's brother Sidney looked up the similarities between "Sanctuary" and "Mrs. Adis" and began pointing them out to others. The news was soon all over literary Harlem.

On January 25 Harold Jackman wrote Countee Cullen, who was in Europe, "Literary dirt: Nella Imes has a story in the *Forum* for this month called *Sanctuary*. It has been found out—at least Sidney Peterson was the first to my knowledge to discover this—that it is an exact blue print of a story by Sheila Kaye-Smith called *Mrs. Adis* which is in a book called *Joanna Godden Married and Other Stories*. The only difference is that Nella has made a racial story out of hers, but the procedure is the same as Kaye-Smith's, and Anne and Sidney have found that the dialogue in some places is almost identical. If you can get ahold of the *Forum* and the Smith book do so and compare them."[7] Two weeks later, Jackman reported that the buzz was far from over: "No one who has heard about Nella Larsen's steal has quite gotten over it. By the way I sent the *Forum* to you. You can probably get the Smith book from the library. . . . Do try and get it and compare the two."[8]

Nella scrambled to defend herself, claiming that she had heard the rudiments of the story from an old woman in the geriatric ward of Lincoln Hospital fifteen years earlier. But literary Harlem was having none of it. When Countee Cullen cautioned Harold Jackman not to judge "poor Nell" too hastily, Jackman retorted,

> Poor Nell is right; it is poor, sad Nell. Boy, that gal has used some of the identical words Miss Smith uses in her *Mrs. Adis,* and as for the dialogue, little Nell, I'll call her this time, has just changed it to make it colored. The technique and method is identical—description, dialogue, dénouement, are incontestably congruent. . . . Is it known? I'll say it is. All literary Harlem knows about it, and I hear that the *Forum* has gotten word of it and has written Nella about it. Nella's benefactor, Carl Van Vechten, is trying to justify his protégée but his arguments are so weak and in this case *so* stupid.[9]

If she didn't manage to convince Jackman and other Harlemites of her innocence, she did convince not only Van Vechten but the *Forum* editors, whom she sent four rough drafts demonstrating how she had worked the story out from plot outline to final product. In the April issue, under a representative reader's complaint and an editorial commentary that pointed improbably to "similar coincidences in history" (the invention of the incandescent bulb by two men unknown to each other, the working out of the theory of natural selection independently by A. R. Wallace and Charles Darwin), they printed in full "The Author's Explanation." An elderly woman named Mrs. Christopher, Larsen claimed, had told her the story in Lincoln Hospital sometime between 1912 and 1915. More recently, in talking the story over with friends, she had discovered that this was an old and common folktale with "many variations: sometimes it is the woman's brother, husband, son, lover, preacher, beloved master, or even her father, mother, sister, or daughter who is killed. A Negro sociologist tells me that there are literally hundreds of these stories. Anyone could have written it up at any time."[10] Larsen maintained that she had originally intended to change the story in order to use Harlem as the setting, "but that little old Negro countrywoman was so vivid before me that I wanted to get her down just as I remembered her."[11] This story won't wash. As Harold Jackman insisted, the parallels between "Sanctuary" and "Mrs. Adis" are simply too detailed. Throughout the early months of 1930, the scandal and ignominy hung over Larsen's head. Her closest friends did not desert her, but her general reputation in Harlem plummeted.

The plagiary scandal was not her only disappointment. About the first of the year, Larsen learned that the judges for the Harmon Foundation had decided not to award a gold medal in literature, and since she had won the bronze for 1928, she was ineligible for the 1929 bronze, which went to Walter White.[12] Larsen received the news with evident composure, but Walter White felt so short-changed that he wrote indignant letters to both the foundation and Joel Spingarn, unaware that Spingarn had played a role in the decision and hoping Spingarn could sway the committee to change its mind. Spingarn wrote White not to give the matter another thought, that it was best to pay no attention to literary prizes at all.[13]

While Nella was weathering attacks on her character over the "Sanctuary" scandal, Elmer left for Fisk in early February, to remain there until the end of March, supposedly pressing the interests of the Physics Department in the construction and furnishing of the new science building. He asked Van Vechten to "cheer Nella up occasionally. She seemed a little blue about my leaving."[14] He did not know that by now Nella had learned of his affair with Ethel Gilbert in Nashville, for she was keeping mum about it in hopes that it would not permanently affect the marriage.

Larsen was devastated by the revelation of Elmer's affair. She already knew Gilbert, who often visited with Lillian Alexander in New York and had a number of other good friends that were also friends of Larsen's. Coming in the midst of the attacks on her (which she knew had merit), it stirred the half-buried ghosts of her childhood. She had been gradually estranged from her mother and pushed out of her home by the advent of Peter Larsen and then Anna, white people who had stolen her birthright. That early loss to a triangulated relationship had stamped her personality with fears that expressed themselves in anxious, insecure attachments on the one hand and vehement assertions of self-sufficiency on the other—the ability to cut people off suddenly and irrevocably.[15] Larsen's relationship with her older, more established husband, anxiety-ridden though it always was, had allowed her to build a sense of emotional security. Now that relationship, not unlike those she had created in fiction, was approaching a crisis.

Larsen talked to no one about the affair, which only magnified her loneliness while she continued to put up a brave face at her usual round of social functions, knowing that people were talking behind her back. She grew increasingly dependent emotionally on Van Vechten, the one acquaintance who had publicly defended her, while her best friend, Dorothy Peterson, was devoting herself full time to a budding career on the stage in what promised to be a major event of the season, Marc Connelly's play *The Green Pastures*. Through all of this turmoil, however, Larsen was also working on a new novel—a "white" novel, as she would call it later. Part of her ambition was to explore new subject matter previously off limits to African American writers, who were expected to stick to writing about their "own" people and the lives they presumably knew best.

Nora Holt was back in New York by mid-January, and Nella saw her frequently, often in company with Van Vechten.[16] In fact, Larsen still enjoyed a fairly rich social life, albeit without Elmer and usually escorted by Carl.[17] Her friendships with the Johnsons, the Wrights, the Whites, and others had survived the *Forum* scandal. At the end of February, escorted by Van Vechten, she attended a "high" Harlem Sunday afternoon tea given by Victoria Bishop (Gussie Booth's sister) for friends from Atlantic City; also present were old friends like Gussie Booth, Walter White, James Weldon Johnson, Crystal Bird, Corinne Wright, Hubert Delany, and Jane Fisher. The next night, she enjoyed a more intimate yet decorous party thrown by the Whites for Sonia Jones, a violinist from Cleveland, with Nora Holt, Corinne Wright, Charles Studin, Taylor Gordon, Grace Johnson, Aaron and Alta Douglas, and Van Vechten.[18] Then, on the twenty-fifth, came the dress rehearsal for *The Green Pastures* at the Mansfield Theatre, which Nella attended with largely the same group. The twenty-sixth was the long-awaited opening night.[19]

Dorothy Peterson had been granted a year's leave from teaching beginning the first of February while trying out and then rehearsing for the part of "Cain's girl" in the play, a minor but substantial role.[20] Based on Roark Bradford's problematic novel *Ol' Man Adam and His Chillun*, a story setting the history of ancient Israel in the context of a rather stereotypical idyll of Southern black folklife, the play employed an all-black cast of nearly one hundred, including the famous Hall Johnson choir, and depended on the quality of the acting to avoid debacle. Leading the cast as "De Lawd" was the dignified Richard B. Harrison, until then a professional elocutionist from Chicago, aging in obscurity with little outlet for his talents, and with him Daniel L. Haynes, best known for his role in the film *Hallelujah!* Larsen, who attended the play with the Petersons —Jerome, Sidney, and Edith (Sidney's wife)—knew several people in the cast, most notably Dorothy and Inez Richardson Wilson. The set design by Robert Edmond Jones—whose work with "Negro plays" went back to Ridgely Torrence's productions of 1917 and included the famous Provincetown Players productions—provided striking backdrops and huge moving platforms to help render the forty-year pilgrimage to Canaan.

By all accounts, no one was quite ready for what they witnessed that cold Wednesday evening. The actors held the large opening-night audience in thrall for nearly three hours, the *New York Age* reported, "and not even the hardboiled newspaper reporters left their seats until the final curtain." Harrison, in a magnificent performance on which everything depended, dominated the show. In the expansive scenes featuring massed groupings on an enormous treadmill to portray the exodus, the play managed to convey the impression of a horde of men, women, and children plodding over the desert, "faint, exhausted, but not discouraged, singing as they went 'I am bound for the promised land' in a full-throated chorus" that sent chills up the spine as it resounded through the auditorium.[21] In scene after scene, the lighting and staging provided fresh surprises in synchrony with sublime spirituals that blended perfectly with the action, knitting the entire performance together and magically merging African American expression with the epic experience of the ancient Israelites.[22]

Afterward, Nella went to Dorothy's apartment on Second Avenue for a small party, but for her it was not an entirely congenial crowd. She covered her insecurities with ill-concealed conceit. Harold Jackman ran into her there and wrote Countee Cullen vitriolically, "You should have heard painful Nella Imes tell about a cocktail party on Park Avenue, and a luncheon date here [the tea she had attended]; she thinks she is so much hell—I could have strangled her that night. . . . I have been so broke I haven't been going anywhere."[23] It seems that some of Nella's old Harlem friendships were wearing thin.

She still had supporters, however. The evening after the *Green Pastures* debut, she had dinner at Van Vechten's with Nora Holt and Witter Bynner. After dinner, Nina Mae McKinney, of *Hallelujah!* fame, under a new long-term contract with Metro-Goldwyn-Mayer, showed up with Tom Rutherford and the black performer Louis Cole.[24] (Home on a visit from Hollywood, McKinney was then starring in a show at the Lafayette Theatre.) Nora and Nina sang, and Louis Cole danced. More than that, however, they talked "for hours on end about The Green Pastures," Carl informed Fania. "Indeed, no one talks about anything else."[25] Nella herself was ecstatic about the play; that and Van Vechten's solicitude kept her cheered up in the midst of her more private fears and sorrows. Knowing she was down—she had cried on his shoulder lately—he sent her a surprise gift in early March, prompting another gush of gratitude:

> You are so sweet! When I look at those beautiful glasses I feel so contrite and so mean. After all I do believe that some people love me even if some times I feel entirely alone. And the people—the very few people who are nice to me are so grand and worth so much more than all the others that I really should abase myself, not because I merit your regard but because it is there.
>
> This poor coloured child has done very little work during the past week. But then "Green Pastures" only happens once (or twice perhaps) in a life time. I have felt like dancing in the streets.[26]

There were, at least, a few things to be glad about.

Despite the scandal in *The Forum,* the Knopfs had kept their confidence in Larsen and were expecting a book from her in due time. Blanche asked her to come into the offices on the fifth of March "to meet an African savage," as Larsen facetiously put it. The occasion was actually a party for a new Knopf author, Bata Kindai Amgoza Ibn Lobagola, of Benin (supposedly), and a number of Knopf authors and literary lights attended—James Weldon Johnson, Van Vechten, H. L. Mencken, Henry Seidel Canby, and Dashiell Hammett among them.[27] The guest of honor, a onetime vaudeville entertainer now making a living as a "lecturer" on African customs, had published some memoirs in *Scribner's* in 1929, and the Knopfs were bringing out a book-length version with the sensational title *Lobagola: An African Savage's Own Story.* This was clearly an attempt to cash in on the current interest in exotic customs in places untouched by the hand of Europe. The publishers made much of Lobagola's being a "savage" from a part of Africa supposedly never visited by whites, although Lobagola described himself as a "Black Jew" descended from people who had left the Holy Land after the destruction of Herod's Temple and wandered across the Sahara to the rain forests of Benin. In truth, he was born Joseph Howard Lee in Baltimore, and had latched on to the African-prince persona as a career move.[28] The book was picaresque pseudo-autobiography, almost unedited, bristling with the author's social-anthropological observations about "West African" customs and his cross-cultural adventures in Africa, Eu-

16. Nella Larsen, circa 1930. Photo by Ben Pinchot. Yale Collection of American Literature, Beinecke Rare Book and Manuscript Library, Yale University. Reproduced by permission of the Pinchot estate.

rope, and the United States. Few reviewers were fooled, however, and it seems unlikely that Larsen or her friends were. The anthropologist Melville Herskovits would give a scathing review of the book in *The Nation* that Larsen almost certainly saw in late July, by which time Lobagola was under indictment for sodomy with a fifteen-year-old boy in the Bronx, a member of one of his enthralled high school audiences.[29]

About the fifteenth of March, Larsen learned from the Guggenheim Foundation that she had won a fellowship, one of the country's most prestigious prizes for a creative writer. She called Van Vechten immediately to share the excitement, and that afternoon he sent her flowers from Goldfarb's.[30] One of eight creative writing fellows that year (Thomas Wolfe was another), she was only the fourth black writer to win a Guggenheim.[31] Not everyone was pleased, however, by Larsen's good fortune. Harold Jackman wrote Countee Cullen again: "It is known all over Harlem that Nella Larsen stole Sheila Kaye Smith's story, and now that Nella has been awarded a Guggenheim Fellowship everyone is quite sorry, especially when such people like Langston Hughes and Bud Fisher are on the horizon."[32]

Finally, at the end of March, Elmer returned to town for a short visit. Nella still carried on as if she knew nothing of his romance in Nashville. They talked over plans for his permanent move and what they would do about a home there. President Jones of Fisk sent Elmer a letter on the third of April with blueprints and a questionnaire concerning the sort of house they would like. Construction would begin in the late spring, after approval by the trustees. Elmer and Nella chose the plan for an English cottage in stone and stucco, with beams showing in the upper story, and began working on a detailed floor plan that would allow them to live practically in separate spheres. Whether Nella would really be a permanent resident even after her fellowship, however, remained up in the air.[33]

By mid-April, she was once again on her own. On the eleventh, she had a quiet dinner with Carl and Fania. Then Fania's dearest friend, Regina Wallace, came in, and Carl took Nella out to see the play *Street Scene,* in its second year at the Ambassador Theatre just off Broadway on Forty-Ninth Street.[34] On her birthday, the thirteenth, she received a gift Carl and Fania had bought at Vantine's (a shop specializing in "oriental" furnishings) the day of the dinner.

Dears:

The most beautiful thanks that I know how to say to you both for remembering my birthday so exquisitely. And Carl dear had already taken me to the theatre, which I had already taken as my birthday remembrance!

You are and have always been so lovely and so kind to me, doing so much to make life lovely and exciting, beside the big thing of your really and truly being, that it is difficult to see how in the world other people who don't know you even exist.

My love to you and
Thanks and
Thanks and
Thanks.

Nella[35]

Nella might well have been wondering how *she* could exist without Carl and Fania at this point. When they threw a party for David and Richard Plunkett Green and Ruth Baldwin—visitors from London—on Friday, the eighteenth, she was at their apartment again, along with such bright lights as the popular black singer Adelaide Hall, Langston Hughes, the Johnsons, the painter Marsden Hartley, Jack Carter (who had played "Crown" in *Porgy*), the Whites, Blanche Knopf, Nora Holt, Rose McLendon, Lloyd and Edna Thomas, Olivia Wyndham, Dorothy Peterson, Bruce Nugent, and Eddie Wasserman. Gladys Bentley provided the entertainment.[36] Two nights later Nella was on Eddie Wasserman's guest list for a Sunday supper party for twelve, including much of the same group plus his French friend Baron von Rothschild. After dinner the group migrated to a party at Taylor Gordon's.[37]

Again on the twenty-ninth of April, Fania and Carl had Nella for a private dinner. Then the three went together to the dentist's (where Carl had a decaying tooth worked on) and continued to the Broadway opening of the new cinema spectacular, *All Quiet on the Western Front*.[38] On the second of May, the evening of the NAACP Spring Dance, Nella had dinner at Van Vechten's again before going with him and friends to the dance at Caspar Holstein's Saratoga Club, where the crowd was huge, the band Luis Russell's orchestra, and the temperature "unbearably hot." Nora Holt was a headliner of the floor show that began at midnight, but the heat and crowd made for an uncomfortable evening in the relatively cramped space (compared to dance palaces like the Manhattan Casino). One could feel the Great Depression clamping down on the glamour of the Twenties. Was the last dance near?

The NAACP, however, was feeling its oats politically. It was in the midst of turning the tide in an all-out battle against confirmation of Judge John J. Parker of North Carolina to be an associate justice of the Supreme Court. Walter White, acting field secretary while James Weldon Johnson was on leave, had seized on the issue to mobilize blacks across the country to unite regardless of party affiliation against the Hoover administration's "lily white" policies. Ef-

17. Carl Van Vechten and Fania Marinoff, May 29, 1930. Photo by Nickolas Muray. Carl Van Vechten Papers, The New York Public Library, Astor, Lenox and Tilden Foundations. Copyright © Nickolas Muray Photo Archives.

fectively using Parker's comments in a 1920 election campaign against black political participation, White's efforts, combined with those of organized labor, had succeeded in intimidating enough Republican senators to seriously imperil Parker's confirmation. On May 7, the Parker nomination was defeated in the Senate on a 41-to-39 vote. Although comments on the Senate floor generally revolved around Parker's decisions on labor matters, White hailed the decision as striking proof of the way in which black unity and organized effort could be marshaled in defense of civil rights.[39] It was a stunning victory, widely celebrated in Larsen's circle of friends. But Larsen's mind was focused on more personal matters.

"This little note is to say that tomorrow I am leaving for Nashville, a dutiful wife going down to visit her husband," Nella wrote Carl on the eleventh of May. "It will only be for about two weeks or so. I do hope that you will not be gone by the time I get back. . . . Have been working like a coloured person and to very little purpose I'm afraid."[40] She did not tell Van Vechten the full story about her dread of Fisk.

She of course knew that she would run into her husband's lover there, an attractive and immensely popular administrator, particularly well liked by students and black faculty. To make matters worse, a number of professors at Fisk had been there in 1908, when the faculty had voted to expel Nella, precipitating a major crisis in her adolescence. Some of the newer faculty members had been students while she was there, including Elmer's friend St. Elmo Brady, who now headed the Chemistry Department.[41]

Elmer, on the other hand, strode around campus with the confidence of a man fully at home. He had been teaching at Fisk only a decade earlier and still had strong connections to the faculty and administration. Paul Cravath, chairman of the Board of Trustees, held him in high esteem and even had him out to his place on Long Island on weekends. Elmer's aunt, Mabel Lewis Imes, the last of the original Jubilee Singers, still visited campus each spring for special ceremonies in which she was celebrated and sang. On Jubilee Day the school newspaper ritually printed her "Jubilee Message," recalling the brave early years, when the school seemed to rise on faith alone and men like Ulysses S. Grant addressed the graduates.[42] William Lloyd Imes was considered one of the school's most distinguished alumni to enter the ministry.

Elmer came in with one of the highest salaries of any faculty member. No one except the president made more. In 1930–1931, Elmer Imes, James Weldon Johnson, St. Elmo Brady, Charles S. Johnson, and Homer L. Morris (head of the Economics Department) were the top-paid faculty, all making $5,000 a year and living in university housing. (President Jones made $6,000.) In comparison,

Dora Scribner, after thirty-nine years' experience, received $1,850. In Elmer's own field, Augustus F. Shaw, the preceding head of the Physics Department, with thirty-six years' service to the university but no Ph.D., made exactly half of Elmer's salary.[43] Elmer was a key member of President Jones's new cadre of black research professors intended to take over leadership of the school and put Fisk at the forefront of black education in the United States.[44]

Jones believed strongly in the notion of a Fisk "family"—one reason for providing nice homes to please the wives of the most distinguished professors. He wanted "Mrs. Imes" to settle on campus, and even offered her a position in the new library that was going up across from the chapel in the center of campus. It would house a special "Negro collection," mainly selected and overseen by Arthur Schomburg, and already Aaron Douglas was on site painting magnificent murals in the third-floor rooms intended to hold it.[45] But this was all small consolation to Nella, whose career might well be ruined by the loss of contacts in New York and the need to settle in to the helpmeet functions of the faculty wife —at Fisk, of all places—a role for which she was magnificently ill-suited.

Dorothy Peterson was the first person to write her, passing along news about *The Green Pastures'* continued run and about their mutual friends. When Nella wrote "home," she put the best possible face on Nashville and acted as if it was all new to her, despite the fact that her friends knew perfectly well she had once attended Fisk. Apparently, things were not as bad as expected. In a highly affected letter to Carl and Fania, she sounded upbeat and outrageously condescending about black Nashville:

> It really is quite delightful here. Beautiful country and handsome men. I am staying in a fascinating old house with lovely old furniture and delicate faded chintzes and lots of books.
>
> Carl would adore the Negro streets. They look just like stage settings. And the Negroes themselves! I've never seen anything quite so true to whats expected. Mostly black and good humoured and apparently quite shiftless, frightfully clean and decked out in the most appalling colours, but some how just right. Terribly poor.
>
> The poor whites are also exactly as expected but not so amusing. Rather, tragic and depressing.

She expected to start home within the next few days:

> Elmer wanted me to come down and I rather thought it was the diplomatic thing to do. Now that I've been nice and everything I think that's all that can be expected.
>
> Fisk is very delightful with a rather interesting faculty. Mixed. The nicest

men are two handsome Southerners and an Austrian and a rather remarkable Negro chemist. Ground and buildings are quite lovely.[46]

Fisk, indeed, had probably never looked better.

The new $400,000 library was nearing completion in the center of campus while new science buildings arose on its west flank, forming a large, well-kept quadrangle with the imposing Art Deco library in the middle, its central tower rising nearly to the height of Jubilee Hall's main cupola. The spacious campus green, with neat pathways crossing the turf, conveyed the calm of an elite New England college, enhanced by the surpassing beauty and soft air of the Middle Tennessee spring. But Nella had no intention of staying until the heat set in, and she was back in New York by the beginning of June.

On the third, a Tuesday, she dropped in on Carl and Fania a little after five and stayed for dinner, along with James Weldon Johnson. Then Carl took them both to the dress rehearsal for *The Garrick Gaieties* at the Guild Theatre, where they saw the Langners and other stage-oriented friends.[47] It was a fast, bright, mischievous show with plenty of "nice dirt"; its scoffing libretto took aim at popular targets, from Walter Winchell to modern sex mores, including a satire on Junior League women who donated their services at fundraising sales of bed mattresses.[48] Nella spent the following weekend out of town at the tony village of Briarcliff Manor, fifty miles north of the city, site of a famous lodge and pleasant cottages—and returned the Monday after to find pictures and clippings Van Vechten had sent her. "As for last Tuesday at your house it was simply marvelous. I keep saying over and over to myself 'Didn't we have fun!' I have had lots of good times at 150 West Fifty-fifth street but I dont remember any time better than that. Perhaps because it was all so spontaneous and sincere."[49]

Van Vechten was actually trying to give up on the hectic social life and heavy drinking that were wrecking his marriage, not to mention his health. Fania took a Panama Pacific liner to Los Angeles to try out for talking films while he packed for a trip to Europe alone.[50] Nella was one of the very few people who knew of his imminent departure for France. "I havent told anyone about your sailing—except Elmer of course who is too far away to be indiscreet."[51] She was hunting around for a Witter Bynner poem he wanted—perhaps the one Bynner had written for the going-away party two years before aboard the *S.S. Mauretania*. He and Fania wanted to get away quietly to their separate destinations. While they were gone, his farewell to the Twenties—with not a few harsh renunciations of hollow friends and drunken excitements, but with admiring salutes to the people, music, and dancing of Harlem—would come out in the book *Parties*.[52]

Practically a clipping bureau in her own right since library school, Nella kept Van Vechten up to date on the literary gossip around New York, including notices of her "own things," current events and issues in the black community, and recent reviews of publications on the "Negro." When Gilmore Millen's *Sweet Man* was published by Grosset and Dunlap in early July, she bought a copy and began scanning the newspapers to rake up reviews. "I do think it is one of the most extraordinary books I have read—fascinating too—I have been going about doing a lot of proselyting for it. It has not yet been reviewed in the black press. We are all holding our breaths waiting to see just what will be what. If they do howl—and I expect they will—Well! After all the Negroes may be what they will consider low. But think of the white people in that book!"[53]

A more important new book, however, was James Weldon Johnson's history of black culture in New York, still an indispensable and highly readable narrative. Nella "went straight through Black Manhattan one afternoon without one weary second," she wrote Jim and Grace. "I especially like the chapters which deal with Florence Mills and the Negro Church and Dr. Du Bois. And the Garvey chapter—oh, most especially the Garvey chapter. And—but I like them all. And the last!" She liked the form of the work, moreover, and above all its tone: "Its unusual restraint, no whining, and no bragging give it great dignity and grace. To me it has a rare quality—of breadth, and yet fineness—that reminds me of Walter Pater in his less tired moments. The Renaissance essays. And curiously enough this holds for the matter as well as the method."[54]

A week earlier she had written Van Vechten, with equal flattery, "My one fault with it, is that he failed to include Nigger Heaven as one of the big influences on Harlem and its artistic life during the last five years."[55] This was the sort of thing she knew Carl lapped up, but it also coincided, ironically, with the harshest judgments about the novel's effect on black New York. The difference was that Larsen considered *Nigger Heaven* a highly positive influence.

In Harlem, the main controversy that summer had to do with the insulting arrangements for transporting black "Gold Star Mothers"—mothers and widows of men slain in World War I—on their government-sponsored pilgrimage to France. According to reports in the black press, the black women would be sailing on a slow freight vessel at a cost of $100 per person, while white Gold Star mothers sailed on passenger ships for $175 apiece. James Weldon Johnson, "meditating upon heaven and hell and democracy and war and America," was inspired to throw other work aside and write a riposte in verse, "Saint Peter Relates an Incident of the Resurrection Day," which was published almost immediately in book form by Viking.[56] Walter White led an NAACP drive to persuade the women to boycott the trip and petition the War Department for fair treatment. The War Department, of course, vehemently denied that accommodations for the black women were in any way inferior to those for the white women and defended the plan of shipping the ladies separately as most "comfortable for all concerned."[57] This time, White's protests drew plenty of attention in New York but to little effect.

"The N.A.A.C.P. and Mr. White are in the papers again," Nella related cynically. "Some foolishness about the Negro Gold Star Mothers being discriminated against by the government and steamship lines on the pilgrimage to France. The government, the steamship companies, the New York hotels and Mr. White are being quoted on the subject daily. A long cry from the Parker case eh? What next?"[58] At a City Hall rally broadcast on WNYC radio, New York politicians and black leaders blasted the federal government while paying homage to the women, who sailed for France that Saturday, boycott or no. While taking the War Department to task, all praised Mayor Walker and Joseph McKee, president of the city aldermen, for their "freedom from racial prejudice."[59] Larsen suspected White of political opportunism.

Sidney Peterson had moved back in with Dorothy, his wife having left him. Nella confided skeptically, "Sidney claims it's a matter of incompatibility, and that race had *nothing* to do with it (?)." She wasn't one to believe that interracial unions had much chance in the America of her day. In the meantime, her own miscegenating husband was back home "and looking very well."[60] His bond to Ethel Gilbert would prove far happier and more durable than his union with Nella. After all, intraracial marriages could be as fragile as any. Even Inez Richardson Wilson, one of the *grandes dames* of the NAACP Women's Auxiliary, and now of *Green Pastures* fame, had moved out on her husband and in with Nella's friends Edna and Lloyd Thomas. In contrast, Carl and Fania were together again, she having joined him in Europe.

Aside from the Petersons, for social entertainment while Elmer and Carl were away, Nella mainly relied on the Valentines and Crystal Bird. And even when Elmer came to town, he would soon leave for Paul Cravath's place on Long Island. "I wasn't invited, but I can't go anywhere anyway because I haven't finished that damned book." She had little else to do. "You are missing nothing," she assured Carl, "no new plays, no parties, no amusing people."[61]

The next day, she wrote Langston Hughes to congratulate him on his new novel. "I read Not Without Laughter some ten days ago and have been intending to get the letter off ever since. But its been too hot to hold a pen. And I 'seen' your picture in the paper Sunday. You have done what I always contended impossible. Made middle class Negroes interesting (or any other kind of middle class people) And your prose is lovely."[62] Hughes had tried to depict, as he himself said, "more or less typical small-town life in any town outside of the South —the average, small Main Street town."[63] The texture of black working-class life had never been rendered with such unapologetic tenderness and fidelity as in this novel centering on the life of young James "Sandy" Rodgers. Hughes exposed, with searing authority, the everyday wounds of racism in the South and Midwest between the turn of the century and World War I, and the long prehistory of racial terror. Popular music and black religion provide his characters with competing forms of saving grace, while the conflict between the "sinners" and the "saved" in Sandy's family provides the chief source of rising tension in the novel and its thematic focus. The conflict is finally resolved when Aunt Harriett, the "Princess of the Blues," who made her name on State Street in Chicago, insists on Sandy's continuing his education; he must, as his "dicty" Aunt Tempy might have said, "get ahead—all of us niggers are too far back in this white man's country to let any brains go to waste."[64]

One is driven to ask why Nella Larsen, who had grown up largely in the midst of the very honky-tonk world Hughes described—who walked the very streets his characters walked in the later chapters of his novel—never had the wherewithal to write about this world. Since she was always evasive about the details of her past life, it seems clear that she was ashamed of her lowly origins in the vice district of Chicago, ashamed in a special way, for she dreaded that people would think her the daughter of a white prostitute. Yet, just as important, as a member of a white immigrant family, she had no entrée into the world of the blues or of the black church. If she could never be white like her mother and sister, neither could she ever be black in quite the same way that Langston Hughes and his characters were black. Hers was a netherworld, unrecognizable historically and too painful to dredge up. Self-effacing and silent, she had never, after all, really belonged there. She had been in it but never of it. And she didn't like to look back.

Her own name was being paired with that of Hughes in the black press in the wake of his novel. Theophilus Lewis, in his "Harlem Sketch Book" column for the *Amsterdam News,* asked what posterity's verdict would be on the current crop of "Big Negroes," and imagined an equivalent to Thomas Gray's "Elegy in a Country Churchyard."[65] On the twenty-third of July (a week after memorializing Van Vechten and White), he printed a "second canto" of three quatrains— one each for Langston Hughes, Nella Larsen, and Alain Locke:

> Langston Hughes.
> Here lies Langston Hughes,
> He burnt out his fuse

> Before he could write
> Another "Weary Blues."
>
> Nella Larsen.
>
> Here sleeps Nella Larsen,
> Who "passed" just in time
> To be a candidate
> For a Heavenly Guggenheim.
>
> Alain Leroy Locke.
>
> Here nods Dr. Alain Locke.
> Shut up, if you please!
> He's buried in a bucket
> Of Phi Beta Kappa keys.[66]

In the same issue of the newspaper, Aubrey Bowser raved about *Not without Laughter* as exactly the sort of novel black America needed. The problem with most fiction by Negroes, he complained, was that it was not "Negro literature," because it was written for white people. If a large Negro audience could only be built up, he argued, "Our Fishers, McKays and Larsens would write things twice as good as anything they have done."[67] Larsen was still considered one of the major authors of the race. The storm about "Sanctuary" had blown over. With the Guggenheim as encouragement and support, she had her sights set on a professional career as a novelist, something no black writer had yet achieved.

She had written Van Vechten already that she planned to leave the States on the first of October and spend "at least two years in Europe."[68] Elmer was spending the summer mainly in Ann Arbor doing research. Steeling herself to confront him about his affair and agonizing over the fate of their relationship, she grew ill as she awaited a brief visit in early August. Elmer found her in bad shape, though he still did not know why. On the fourteenth of August, back in Ann Arbor again, he wrote President Jones at Fisk, "I was disturbed at finding Mrs. Imes quite far from well and spent a while in New York trying to help her get comfortable. I left her in the country and am returning to New York next week. She will probably sail about the 20th of September, but it may be the first of October, in which case I shall probably ask to be late in returning to Nashville."[69] Two days later, Nella wrote Van Vechten, who was still in the dark about Elmer's affair, "I am better. I came back in town yesterday to be here for the papers Sunday, because of course I am crazy to see what they have to say [about *Parties*]. Elmer is still in Ann Arbor. I expect him back next Thursday or Friday."[70] During that return visit, she finally told Elmer that she knew of his affair and that she had decided to leave him.[71]

Stunned, Elmer admitted that he was in love with Ethel Gilbert but assured

Nella that he still cared about her and did not want a divorce. He talked her into postponing any final decision, and on the twenty-sixth of August he wrote President Jones that she was feeling much better and would probably sail on the nineteenth of September—in time for him to get back to Fisk before the start of classes.[72] They were giving up their lease on the apartment in Harlem, and he would come to Fisk as soon as he had closed the place up. He let Jones believe that Larsen would join him at Fisk after she returned from Europe in a year or so. There was, after all, no reason to make an irrevocable decision before she left; perhaps the time away would help her think things through—and she would be free to do as she wished abroad. The marriage was now "open."

She had in fact booked a berth on the S.S. *Patria*, sailing to Lisbon September 19. From there she planned to journey by rail to Barcelona and then take the ferry across to Palma, Mallorca. The following spring, she would move on, by way of Marseilles and Toulon, where William Seabrook lived, to Paris for the summer and early fall. Of her marriage agonies she breathed not a word to friends. Since Van Vechten and Marinoff would return to New York on the seventeenth, she would barely have time to look in on them before sailing.[73]

Still she kept Van Vechten up to date on the new shows in Harlem, the doings of friends, and the reception of his book when it came out in August. Dorothy Peterson would be going back to teach in September while continuing in *The Green Pastures'* long run. Sidney had moved out again and taken an apartment in Greenwich Village. Crystal Bird was "training that voice of hers again" in hopes of a lucky break, and Tom Rutherford had finally found an acting job with a stock company in Westfield, New Jersey—apparently the same group Langston Hughes was working with at the time, under Jasper Deeter's leadership.[74]

Van Vechten was wondering about his beloved Nora Holt, never a dependable correspondent. "I can't seem to learn a word about Nora Ray," Nella responded. "Nor can Dorothy. Saw Harold Jackman at her house last night and asked him to dig up her whereabouts and doings."[75] Finally Nora called her on a Wednesday evening in early September. She had arrived the day before by way of Atlantic City, divorced at last. They made a lunch date, but after an hour and ten minutes of waiting in the lobby of the McAlpen Hotel, Larsen gave up on her and dined alone.[76] Was it a snub, or just typical of Nora Holt's casual approach to commitments, relationships, and appointments? They were soon enough on warm terms again, but all evidence suggests that the chief basis of their relationship was the friendship of each with Van Vechten.

For Nella, it had been a "rotten summer" all around.[77] Moreover, the Depression was taking its toll, the optimism of the renaissance growing thin. Newspapers reported that lynchings were on the rise. "The winter or I should say summer sports have set in with a vengeance. People are being lynched everywhere, even in places like Indianapolis."[78] She was more than ready to get away, but not before Carl and Fania's return.

They arrived on the seventeenth of September. On the eighteenth, Nella and Elmer went to their apartment for dinner and talked about their thoughts of separating.[79] The night of the seventeenth, Elmer had written a letter to Carl that he posted the next morning. It began by saying he was glad that Carl and Fania were back,

> especially because Nella has so wanted to see you.
>
> If she does see you she may ask your advice about a very delicate matter and in case she does I wish you to read the enclosed note before you decide what to say to her.
>
> The question is with regard to our future—this for identification. I think that her and my interests are the same in the matter and am only taking this method so that you may know certain phases which she may omit in talking with you.[80]

Within the envelope was another sealed envelope marked, "Please destroy if not necessary to use."

[NINETEEN]

A Novelist on Her Own:
1930–1932

T HE morning of September 19, Elmer drove Larsen down to the Thirty-First Street Pier in Brooklyn in time to board by nine A.M.—far too early to expect friends to show up and say goodbye. The *Patria* cast off at noon and, under fair skies with gentle winds, cruised up the coast toward Boston to take on more passengers.[1] While Nella settled into her first-class cabin, Carl Van Vechten, in his Fifty-Fifth Street apartment, read the letter from Elmer posted the day before and then opened the sealed envelope enclosed with it. In cramped, penciled script Elmer had written:

Dear Carl—

Early in the year and quite by accident Nella became possessed of information which pointed decidedly to the fact that I was at the time very much interested in another girl. Like the sweet little sport she is she decided to keep along and not say anything about it, feeling that no matter what happened nothing could change our relationship. Of course this created a situation beyond even her ability to carry off. A great many things were misinterpreted and a great many conclusions come to—at least prematurely.

About three weeks ago she decided that she must talk it over and has taken the attitude that she is to eliminate herself—That it is best all the way around. I had by no means got that far—just what might have happened I do not know, but I do know that there was never any question of deserting her or of shirking any responsibility toward her. I am sure that no matter what new thing may have come into my life, Nella has her own place and if it had ever seemed advisable—as it doubtless would have seemed—to talk to her about it, this would have been as to a friend asking what we should do under the circumstances.

What I want you to know is the stage setting—the fact that she knew and I did not know that she knew and that therefore she has made herself unduly miserable and has perhaps come to wrong conclusions as to what is immediately necessary to do. It is not necessary for her to feel that there is any question of her "going it alone" or being under necessity of taking steps of any sort to guarantee support. I want to do all for her that I can and be everything to her that she will let me be. I am not denying that I am very much in love with the other girl—very much indeed, but she does not expect or wish me to forget to love Nella. A quite involved situation—but possible if we can be clear headed.

If I am to work and do the things I must do for myself there can be no publicity—My job would be gone in ten minutes and I wouldn't be able to do anything for anybody. I have asked Nella not to do anything or make any hard and fast decisions until I see her next summer.

I hope that you can see the situation in this way and help her—and me us in our thinking.

Affectionately,
Elmer[2]

Such complications were nothing new to Van Vechten; it seemed that people were constantly bringing their marital problems to him. He considered sexual infidelity a silly reason for ending a marriage if two people still loved each other.[3] He advised Nella to keep the affair to herself and take time to think over what she wanted to do; in the meantime, she should make the most of her trip and enjoy her freedom.

After docking in Boston briefly, the *Patria* cast off for the eight-day voyage past the Azores to land at Lisbon, its ultimate destination Marseilles.[4] The first people to extend themselves to Nella on the boat were a couple of white Virginians living in Nice, which appealed to her love of irony. White Southerners out of their native element, she was coming to believe, felt more comfortable with Negroes than most white Northerners, and made better company. Later she made friends with a Portuguese diplomat and his wife, who offered to introduce her to Lisbon—not a bad start to her adventure. Like a character in one of her own stories, Larsen moved easily in the *beau monde* and conveyed to many the impression that she belonged there. Yet she partook of it with the anxious joy of one who never knew when she might be pitched out.

The *Patria* steamed into port the afternoon of Sunday, September 28, and Nella checked into the Avenida Palace Hotel, one of the city's finest. On Lisbon's grandest boulevard and bordering the theater district, it was a place that visiting American celebrities and upper-class British tourists patronized—ideal if you did not know Portuguese. She got the best room with bath, which, with meals, cost ten dollars a day.[5] Monday she cabled Dorothy and sent Carl and Fania a postcard with an interior view of the church of the Mosteiro do Jerónimos (a sixteenth-century monument of messianic imperialism), showing the cenotaphs of Vasco da Gama and poet Luis de Camões: "Arrived! Very amusing trip.

18. Nella Larsen, passport photo, 1930. U.S. Department of State. Courtesy of Charles R. Larson.

Letter follows this. Millions of churches in this place. Also millions of men ready for—anything."[6]

She had an amusing four-day stay in Lisbon: "A fascinating city. I have never had such a good time any place."[7] She was surprised to find it cleaner than any city she knew in North America, while the brilliant blue skies of October set off the pastel-hued houses.[8] Her friends from the ship introduced her to their friends and took her to dinner and the theater. Never a fan of exhibits, she avoided the museums and art galleries but was fascinated by the Moorish palaces perched on hilltops, some even higher than King Christophe's Sans Souci in Haiti: "Curious African trait that to build in such inaccessible places."[9] Her amateur ethnography was, admittedly, rather hit-or-miss.

The racial composition of the population particularly intrigued Larsen. "About fifty per cent of the population are as dark or darker than I am. And a large majority have distinctly negroid features. There are, too, a few Negroes, pure black. They seem, however, to arouse no comment or curiosity (except in me)." She thought she detected the pre-Moorish Roman presence in many physiognomies: "Those who aren't heavy African featured have that sharp disdainful profile of the later day Romans. But it doesn't seem to be confined to the better families. Some of the well born people I've met are dark and heavy while many of the servants and peasants have the distinctly roman patrician face."[10]

Thinking over what to do about Elmer's affair, Nella decided to follow Carl's advice and "do and *say* nothing about it. In fact I hadn't—except to Dorothy. And she understands that its all rather indefinite and somewhat precarious." On the other hand, she had determined to put all she could into her writing. She longed to make her name and living as a novelist, regardless of how things turned out with Elmer. No black woman had yet been able to support herself as a creative writer, but she would give it her best shot: "I really mean to work like a nigger. Thinking it over," she wrote, astonishingly,

> I've come to the conclusion that I've never expended any real honest-to-God-labour on anything in my life (except floors and woodwork) and perhaps that's not being quite fair either to myself or the very few people who—.
> I shall be writing you both very often, but not as often as I shall think of you
>
> with
> love
> Nella[11]

Nella's cables and letters to Dorothy and Elmer do not survive, but Elmer attested to Van Vechten that she was cabling him often.

Wednesday night she went out with some Southerners from the American consulate, and on Thursday she took the train from Lisbon to Madrid—a change of plans, possibly due to political and labor unrest in the south of Spain, including major strikes. The Spanish capital she "simply adored." She then headed northeast to Barcelona and boarded the night packet for Mallorca, which cast off at nine P.M. for the ten-hour crossing, one of the celebrated experiences of the Mediterranean. The passengers awakened at first light and gathered on deck as the geographic outposts of the island came in sight—steep, volcanic peaks and peninsulas catching the sunlight and plunging into the brilliant greenish blue of the sea, bearing exotic names: Dragonera Islet, Mola de Andraitx, Cap Andritxol, the Bay of Santa Ponsa, and the Cape of Cala Figuera. Then the island flattened out and the steamer turned a corner, passed the Fort of San Carlos, and entered the immense Bay of Palma and its port.

The awakening city spread out in warm golden-brown hues, an eight-mile amphitheater embracing the turquoise harbor. Circular Bellver Castle caught the light crowning the summit of a wooded hill on the left, overlooking the district of El Terreno, where rows of villas and their attached gardens descended the terraced hillside toward three modern tourist hotels overlooking the water. In the center of the panorama, fronting the docks, the ancient Customs building and old houses and shops stood beneath a towering medieval city wall. On the right, a broad, walled mount immediately bordering the bay displayed the magnificent thirteenth-century cathedral, its huge "Mirador" portal facing the water and great spires pricking the sky above the city. Just left of this vision, on the same rise, the Almudaina Palace of the Moorish kings, usurped by Spanish royalty, brooded in the morning shadow of the cathedral's towers.[12]

As Larsen came off the dock and onto the quay, the aroma of coffee and chocolate emanated from the nearby shops and cafés, suffused with the sweet scent of Mallorcan pastries, *ensamaidas.* After still-European Barcelona, the palm-dotted city had a distinctly North African ambience, redolent of orange trees and lemons.[13]

The island was enjoying its first real tourist boom, becoming one of the premier destinations in that part of the world as British tourists discovered they could live well on as little as ten pounds a month. The Brits vastly outnumbered visitors from other countries, making it a comfortable place for Americans knowing little Spanish, Italian, or French—perhaps one reason Lawrence Langner and Armina Marshall had recommended it to Nella.[14] The area boasted some of the finest hotels in the Mediterranean, all built within the previous two decades.[15]

Nella checked in first to the Hotel Calamayor, on the seaside around the corner from the bay and at least a mile from trendy El Terreno—peaceful but lonely and boring for a woman of Larsen's temperament. She promptly moved to the Hotel Reina Victoria in the heart of El Terreno's British colony, and began looking for a more permanent address.[16] The Victoria was twice the size of the Calamayor and twice as expensive—the most expensive hostelry in Mallorca at the time, and famous for having one of the best chefs in Europe running the kitchen.[17] She had barely settled in when she came down with pneumonia—a remarkable achievement in Mallorca at that time of year. On the twentieth of October, recovered from her illness, she wrote Henry Allen Moe of the Guggenheim Foundation: "I should like to relate the series of misadventures that got me here. But since I did finally arrive—and quite safely I won't do so. Besides, everything seems merely funny now that I am very happily settled in a very beautiful spot. Comfortable room, good food, heavenly weather—and quiet. So quiet that I have already put pen to paper, or rather paper in the typewriter."[18] She did not mention that she was not yet working on the novel outlined in her fellowship proposal but rather a different one begun earlier, concerning a love triangle in the New Jersey suburbs—a "white book," as she termed it, involving a philandering husband and a jealous wife.

She was pleased with her location and the excellent food but admitted to Moe that her Spanish was not up to speed. "However, that, I suppose will soon

19. Hotel Reina Victoria, circa 1931. After a month in the hotel, Larsen moved to a house halfway up the hill between the hotel and Bellver Castle in the background. Jaime Escalas, Mallorca: Colección de 64 fotografías. Palma de Mallorca: Galerias Costa, 1932.

adjust itself." Actually, it is unlikely that her Spanish (or Mallorquin, a variation of Catalan) improved appreciably, because her social life centered entirely in the British, American, and German expatriate community. Her own hotel seemed "to be full of decaying Englishmen and spreading German ladies."[19] One could easily get around El Terreno without Spanish.

The Reina Victoria clung to a rugged ledge of rock along the shoreline. From the upper garden terrace and the seaside rooms, one had a glorious view of Palma across the bay. Professional photographers took panoramic shots from here for postcards and publicity pamphlets. The British-American Club was not far away, and the Hotel Mediterraneo stood a couple of hundred yards up the shore. Right behind the hotel, Larsen could pick up the tram past the Tennis Club and the Nautical Club into central Palma to roam the elegant shops along the Passeig Borne or wander among the historic buildings and baths in the old Arabian quarter behind the cathedral.

On the hillside above her hotel, beneath the castle grounds, perched the haphazardly sited villas and peasants' homes, the latter with vegetable gardens in the yards, ranked in loose rows by four parallel streets that effectively terraced the hillside. Gertrude Stein had lived just up the hill and to the left about three blocks. (The house still stands.)[20] Bernard Shaw had lived in the neighborhood. Larsen was excited to learn that John Galsworthy had wintered here the previous year and was expected back in December, and that Somerset Maugham was another sometime visitor. She had her sights set on a more permanent lodging in the neighborhood.

On the eleventh of November, she took one of the nearly obligatory pilgrimages of the island. Only ten miles northwest of Palma, on a picturesque route that passed through olive groves and then ascended through craggy gorges into the mountains, lay the village of Valldemossa and its Carthusian monastery. Here George Sand and an ailing Frédéric Chopin had spent several unhappy months, described in Sand's book *Un Hiver à Majorque* (A Winter in Mallorca). Secularized in the early nineteenth century, the monastery's cells had been converted into spare, rentable apartments. The medieval pharmacy remained intact, with ancient containers of esoteric remedies still crowding the open shelves.[21]

From the cells of Chopin and Sand, Larsen strolled out onto an exquisite garden patio with vine-covered arbors, neatly pruned orange trees, and a vista over the green hills to the south. "It is quite beautiful," Larsen wrote to Carl, "and the rooms are said to be preserved as they were then. If I hadn't been afraid of landing in a Spanish jail I certainly would have stolen some original manuscripts of Chopins for you. They were only sketches and studies I suppose but really it was criminal the way they were lying loose."[22]

Finally, on the twelfth of November, she wrote a long letter to Van Vechten, who had sent several cards.

> You would have heard from me again but like an idiot I came here and promptly proceeded to get very sick with pneumonia. All right now, I hope. . . .
>
> Please say to Mrs. Langner that Mallorca is all that she told me. I have never seen such gorgeous country. Marvelous weather, too. Like our best June days. . . .
>
> I am trying to make up my mind to take a house. I can get a very good one and a servant for fifty-five dollars a month. Food for the two of us will come to about thirty dollars a month. The only thing is that I have to take the house for six months and how do I know what I'll want to do next May?

She had already met a slightly colored friend of Nora Holt's whom she suspected of passing as an Egyptian. And another passing couple she had met on the boat from Barcelona she suspected only when they asked if she knew Carl Van Vechten.

She was keeping up with the literary news, critically as ever ("I was quite shocked at Sinclair Lewis getting the Nobel Prize. How come?"), and with the gossip of New York, partly thanks to Carl's cards. "I was even more shocked at Meda's going [Meda was Van Vechten's maid and cook]. And Rebecca West's marriage."[23]

The next day, having made up her mind about the house, Larsen wrote again, saying she was ready to "settle down to a long siege of work." She had talked the landlord into a five-month lease that would let her out at the first of May, since the writers and artists began migrating north in April. On a narrow, quiet street high on a hill above the bay, the house was virtually a brand-new villa built for visitors, "the most modern in the place," with fine furniture. It was large enough, too, for visiting guests; she hoped Carl and Fania would come stay with her. At 32 Jose Villalonga, unlike all the neighboring buildings it was sited at an angle to the street to face the cathedral of Palma and fully exploit the view, which was spectacular day and night. Just up the hill from Larsen's house was the stone gate to the main walkway up to Bellver Castle and its grounds, a broad, steep path through the pines with fabulous vistas of the bay.[24]

Haunting the bar at the British-American club, she was getting to know her way about and scoping out members of the colony. "There is a Lord Douglas staying here. He has remnants of fine looks. I'm awfully curious about him, but of course one can't go up to him and say 'Pardon me but are you the Lord Douglas who slept with Oscar Wilde?' no more than one can drop into a conversation about the Winston Churchill libel suit. Not with this man who has more than his share of the English stand offish manner and a quite ferocious look in his handsome eyes." "Oh yes," she added, "the friend (Egyptian?) of Nora's is the bartender at the American Bar in the English Club. He was bartender at Monte Carlo at the place where she sang."[25]

Still a newcomer, however, Larsen was a bit lonely. A married African American woman on her own among British and German tourists and artists, without a single acquaintance on the island, Larsen would need time to find people who would open up to her. She took advantage of her solitude to write. "I *think* my book, my white book is really good. Perhaps being a bit lonely is doing me good, or rather doing what I'm trying to do, good. I wish I'd taken your advice about a European address. But, then you're always right. However, I'm now permanently located for at least five months."[26]

Nora Holt, currently in Chicago, heard immediately from Van Vechten that Nella had met an old friend of hers and asked him for Larsen's address, writing in a typically telegraphic flourish, "What a grand event Nella to meet Don, he is grand one and she must bring back with her.—He's a scream."[27] Holt was on her way west—way west—from Chicago, ultimately for an engagement in Shanghai, and planned on continuing in the same direction for a round-the-world tour. She hoped to meet up with Nella in Europe.[28]

Elmer, battling the architect and worrying the trustees over Fisk's new Physics Building, was living in two rooms in a shared faculty house. Smoke and grime spewing from the smokestack of the power plant just down the hill seeped in everywhere at that time of year. Early in December he mailed Nella some books for Christmas and a check to help cover her expenses. "The last letter says that she has taken a house in the stylish settlement Terreno, with cook and maid of all work for $55.00 a month."[29] One would think the Guggenheim stipend of $2,500 would be enough for a place as cheap as Mallorca; but, Elmer wrote, "I am rather holding my breath and my pocketbook for Nella's needs. She has seemed to need a great deal so far." And she wasn't expressing much gratitude, informing Dorothy Peterson that Dorothy and Carl were her "best correspondents."[30] On the other hand, Ethel Gilbert was all that Elmer could desire in a companion, and he wanted Carl and Fania to meet her when she came to New York. "She has more enthusiasm to the square inch than anyone I know and fits her work better."[31]

Elmer knew few details of his wife's life in Mallorca except what he needed to know to send money, stockings, and books. More than two months passed before Van Vechten received another letter from her. She wrote Henry Allen Moe in early January, informing him of her change of address and asking for a six-month extension of the fellowship, letting on that she was living quietly and cheaply and making the most of her time.

> The work goes fairly well. A little slower than is usual with me. But—I like it. Of course that means nothing because I really can't tell if its good or not. But the way I hope and pray that it is is like a physical pain almost. I do so want to be famous.
>
> I am wondering if it will be possible for me to have a short extension of three or six months.
>
> Palma is very beautiful—and so peaceful. Not many tourists come here these days. Perhaps it's to[o] inconv[en]ient to reach.[32]

The truth is that Palma was enjoying a remarkable surge in tourism that winter.

Just two weeks after the letter to Moe, Larsen wrote Van Vechten: "I know it's been a coon's age since I wrote to you, but life here is so hectic that its almost impossible to find time to sleep. I haven't been to Capri, but I doubt if it could have been even in its great days more amuseing than this." Galsworthy and Somerset Maugham had been around in December. The Irish novelist Liam O'Flaherty (very depressed and contemplating suicide) had spent two weeks in El Terreno in early to mid-January, "and painted the whole place,—well, purple."[33]

Around early January, Nella had motored to the fishing village of Deyá, forty-six miles past Valldemossa on some of the most spectacular roads of the island, curving along cliffs high above the sea, to meet Robert Graves and his Circe, Laura Riding. A strange, brooding couple (Riding jealously dominated the household), they accepted few guests at their small stone cottage a mile out of town; presumably Larsen had been ushered by one of their select friends.[34]

She had also begun dating "a delightful young English-Scotsman . . . who appeared suddenly at my house one evening offering me a gold and green enamel cigarette lighter which he informed me I'd forgotten in the American Bar. Well, I had been in the bar. But I'd never seen the lighter before. We both knew this. But I took it, and thanked him for bothering, returning it some days later because as I told him I'd noticed he'd been using matches ever since he'd brought me the lighter." Flattered by the attention, especially after she learned of his background, Larsen preened affectedly for Van Vechten. "It develops that he's rather important. Terribly good-looking, filthy rich, a rather famous polo player and all that. Anyway he's been very convenient for opening doors, picking up handkerchiefs—and such things. Besides, he thinks we look awfully well together because he's so tall and blond and I'm so little and brown."[35] Suddenly Larsen's plans for the summer had changed to include a two-month stay in Scotland.

A likely candidate for Larsen's "English-Scotsman" is Norman Cameron, a tall and handsome Oxford graduate from Scotland, born in 1905. He had entered the civil service in Nigeria in August of 1929 and left disillusioned about eighteen months later, going straight to Mallorca. Already an intimate of Robert Graves and Laura Riding, whom he had known since the late 1920s, he would certainly have known a near neighbor of Larsen's whose husband served in Nigeria, and he was a good friend of the English painter John Aldridge, a resident of El Terreno, and his partner Lucie Brown, both of whom belonged to the very small circle always welcome by Graves and Riding in Deyá. Cameron was a dashing bachelor, a "liberal" on matters of race who detested the racism and segregationist mores of the colonial regime in Nigeria (one reason he left there) and was attracted to black women, as his letters to Graves of 1929–1930 reveal.

He had come into a large inheritance just before his trip to Nigeria—and burned through it in the next several years, in part by spending lavishly on Mallorca and buying expensive gifts for his friends there. By all accounts he lived a bohemian life, partying and drinking hard, which eventually caught up with him. He wrote excellent poetry and produced superb translations of Baudelaire and Rimbaud, as well as of Henri Murger's *Vie de Bohème,* a work close to his heart. Living first around Palma (surely in an El Terreno hotel), he eventually bought property and moved to Deyá in April 1931.[36]

Larsen's color helped her stand out in an attractive, exotic way among her new British and European acquaintances. Being a Knopf author from Harlem, intimate with the famed sophisticates of New York, and a Guggenheim Fellow couldn't have hurt, either. She had soon enough broken into the toniest circle of the English-speaking expatriate colony. A "Lady Newton," whom Larsen identi-fied as the wife of the governor of Nigeria (although no governor of Nigeria ever carried that name), was wintering in a house nearby. "She's about thirty-eight or so—doesn't look it—very well dressed, very clever and witty, gives aw-fully good parties and seems to have taken quite a shine to me, for some reason or other."[37]

Her nearest neighbors were a young English couple,

> both so handsome that they might have stepped out of a Michael Arlen book. They're amusing too. Most of the time they're both a few sheets in the wind.
>
> Then there's a pair of German dancers who've been wintering here because she's been sick. They are not too bad—especially her. She's awfully young, in-clined to take a drop too much and then—well, then—she's liable to wake up in anybody's bed. No wonder she's been sick. But she is amusing and a pretty little thing.[38]

Nearly forty years old—though she didn't look it—Larsen found many of her acquaintances "young things," it seems, and she took pleasure in the attentions paid her by younger men, especially. She did not see much of the rather few Americans on the island, though there was one who came to her house "con-stantly"—"a nice young thing from Richmond, Virginia." He was a friend of Tom Rutherford named Archer Jones, a gay man, who also knew Hunter Stagg. "He's quite good-looking and wouldn't be too bad if he weren't suffering from acute intellectualism. You did say once, didn't you, that the only people South-erners spoke to away from home were Negroes. Right again!"[39]

By mid-January, Larsen was trying to finish typing her novel, now entitled "Crowning Mercy," but she found it hard to get much work done. After striking up with her dashing polo player, she had begun taking riding lessons and found it painful to sit at a typewriter: "After hours in the saddle its hard to sit on a chair—for a beginner—. I never knew before what a tender portion of the anatomy the kenetta is." No longer lonely, she was having a wonderful time. "It is fun you know dashing about all night from one place on the island to another with people to whom time means nothing. Besides shocking the natives."[40]

The expatriates and the native Mallorquins lived practically in parallel worlds, with few contacts other than those of employer-servant or client-salesperson. Mallorcan women stayed indoors most of the time, and when they ventured out they wore veils and long black dresses. They would never be found in a bar or astride a horse. And of all the expatriates, the North American women were particularly scandalous in the eyes of the locals, as a feature article in Palma's chief newspaper, *La Ultima Hora,* pointed out the day before Larsen penned her letter to Van Vechten.[41]

By now Larsen was firming up her plans for the new year, intending to stop in Nice after leaving Palma toward the end of April. Bill and Margaret George of New York—apparently the passing couple she had met at sea who had asked if she knew Carl Van Vechten—lived there and had invited her to stop with them on her way to Paris. She would try to see William Seabrook in Toulon and then go on to the French capital, with a side trip to Scotland in June and July, no doubt with her English-Scotsman. Around October she planned to return to Mallorca: "Its comfortable and I like it."

She wrote Gertrude Stein on January 26, 1931, as she plotted out her itinerary, mentioning that every letter from Carl Van Vechten—one of Stein's most loyal and longstanding friends—referred to Stein. But, Nella added rather obsequiously, she didn't need to be reminded to try to see the *grande dame* of high modernism; it was one of her main reasons, she claimed, for visiting Paris. She then described her life in Mallorca in a way completely contradicting what she had just written Carl, and probably tailored for Stein, whom she knew had given up on Mallorca after less than a year to return to Paris. Larsen had thought, she wrote, that quiet Mallorca would be a good place to get work done:

> It seems not. After this I shall know that live cities are the places in which to do live things—or is it living?—which is perhaps a good thing to find out as well as the fact that the less time one has the more one accomplishes. I can quite understand why—apart from his illness—Chopin and George Sand were so unhappy here. Its marvelously beautiful—and brutal. And the people are so terribly placid, a resigned unhappy placidness. Even the children. Perhaps because they're so old and tired and everything has happened to them.
>
> Or it may be just that I've got a nostalgia, a yen to see the teeming streets of Harlem and hear some real laughter.[42]

Much of the letter was intended to prick Stein's interest; but, affected as it is, it probably only conveyed the author's desire to flatter and impress.

Larsen was hoping to visit Stein at her famous apartment on the rue de Fleurus in May. With warm messages of introduction from Van Vechten, whom Stein adored, Larsen had little reason to fear being turned away, but as it turned out Stein would be gone while Larsen was in Paris. She asked if Nella might not either stay longer or return to Paris in the fall. Disappointed, Larsen wrote back somewhat dejectedly, "Life is like that. I've just had a note from Carl berating me for not having seen you." But she claimed she would make another trip to Paris in the fall: "I should go back there, anyway, to see you, because I don't know when I'll get over again."[43]

By the first of March, Larsen was eager to leave Mallorca. She made no more mention of her English-Scotsman, and the trip to Scotland for June and July was off the calendar. She had apparently suffered a significant personal disappointment. (It may be relevant that, at just about this time, Norman Cameron had taken up with a young German woman living with Graves and Riding, and he moved to Deyá at the beginning of April.) A few months later she would be telling Dorothy Peterson in Paris that she didn't want to return to Mallorca because she was "afraid of islands."[44] The third of March, she wrote Carl, "There is no news in these parts, except that I am well. And, thank God! hoping to get away from here by the fifteenth of April at the very latest."[45] She was already giving her future address as Guaranty Trust Company of New York, Place de la Concorde, Paris—although her rental contract required her to pay for lodging through the month of April and she would not leave Mallorca for another month and a half. She claimed the heat was a difficulty: the weather was getting "devilish hot" and a white dress that Fania and Carl had given her, she wrote, was "one of my joys."[46]

She had just spent an entire Sunday reading, and relishing, George Schuyler's satirical novel *Black No More*—a gift from Van Vechten. "I was crazy about it," Larsen wrote, "the material I mean—especially Garvey and our friends of the N.A.[A.]C.P. (Don't tell them) and the *ending!*"[47] Marcus Garvey appeared as Santop Licorice, who had been "for fifteen years very profitably advocating the emigration of all the American Negroes to Africa. He had not, of course, gone there himself and had not the slightest intention of going so far from the fleshpots, but he told the other Negroes to go."[48] The novel hilariously, and for the most part good-naturedly, caricatured several of Larsen's friends and acquaintances. W. E. B. Du Bois featured as "Shakespeare Agamemnon Beard," editor of *The Dilemma:* "Like most Negro leaders he deified the black woman but abstained from employing aught save octoroons. . . . He bitterly denounced the

Nordics for debauching Negro women while taking care to hire comely yellow stenographers with weak resistance." James Weldon Johnson, as Dr. Napoleon Wellington Jackson, had the task of writing "long and indignant letters to public officials and legislators whenever a Negro was mistreated, demanding justice, fair play and other legal guarantees vouchsafed no whites except bloated plutocrats fallen miraculously afoul of the law, and to speak to sex-starved matrons who yearned to help the Negro stand erect." Walter White was Walter Williams, "a tall, heavy-set white man with pale blue eyes" and a remote Negro ancestor, decrying the loss of Negro solidarity and race pride; and R. R. Moton of Tuskegee was Colonel Mortimer Roberts, principal of the Dusky River Agricultural Institute, "the acknowledged leader of the conservative Negroes (most of whom had nothing to conserve)," whose speech "conveyed to most white people an impression of rugged simplicity and sincerity, which was very fortunate since Colonel Roberts maintained his school through their contributions."[49]

Schuyler presented greed and sexual desire as the two great driving forces of American society, deeply intertwined at the racial border. The origin of American racial institutions, he believed, lay in economic history going back to the early years of American settlement, when race-mixing had to be repressed—or, where it could not be repressed, disavowed—to preserve a slave system dependent on racial division. Racial distinction became a source of economic gain and erotic fantasy while the actual extent of miscegenation was hidden behind the luster of racial purity. The novel hugely appealed to Larsen's own sardonic feelings about the workings of the color line, and her utter disdain for it. "I didn't, however, think it was so well done as it might be," she confessed. "I should love to have seen the reviews in the nigger papers. Dorothy sent me two from the ofays."[50]

Learning belatedly that Langston Hughes, one of her favorite black authors, had won a Harmon award, she wrote him her tardy congratulations:

> News comes slow to this backwater so I'm afraid it['s] rather late to offer congratulations, and I suspect that you've already spent the five hundred. Only I hope not, and that you will be coming to Paris this summer. Do! I've been struggling with the Spanish language for months and am about to give it up and try the French instead. . . .
>
> The work goes, so-so.
> And yours?
> Congratulations!
> And you did deserve it.[51]

Increasingly lonely in El Terreno, Nella was expecting to see Carl and Fania soon in France, an event she awaited with bated breath: "I shall literally fall on your neck and kiss you." On the twentieth of March, she sent Fania a happy-birthday cable, and two days later wrote, "Now, I am looking forward to getting away from here; in fact, I don't see how I'm going to stand it for the next three weeks, but I've got to. All the amusing people have gone, and really I've never been so lonely in my life. I could almost weep from boredom. I do hope I'm not going to be quite so forlorn in Paris."[52] Archer Jones, evidently her last good friend, had left—she suspected for bad behavior. "It's a little way they have here if one is too gay, or gets too tight too often."[53]

Adding to her disappointment was the news from Henry Allen Moe that her appeal for an extension of the fellowship had been turned down. The foundation, after all, wanted to give as many people an opportunity as possible, as Larsen understood, "especially in these hard times. My husband writes that America is quite a different place these days owing to the tightness of money there."[54] Indeed, Fisk was feeling the pinch, and students were beginning to drop out.

For Larsen, however, the Depression seemed as remote and abstract as the political turmoil in Spain. "Life goes on here as it has for hundreds of years," she reported, "placid and monotonous; but I shall be getting away in a week or two. The Spanish fleet is in the bay. Its officers are very nice but not exciting or amusing."[55] Actually, the Spanish monarchy was hanging by a thread, and the fleet was probably in the bay in case of trouble with Catalan nationalists and the feared anarchists of Barcelona. In less than two weeks, a historic election would decide whether Spain was to become a republic. Some feared that King Alfonso would defend his throne with armed force and spark a bloody revolution.[56]

Seemingly oblivious to all of this, Larsen was rewriting her novel and lining up her itinerary for the coming months, planning to leave Mallorca just as the elections would be taking place. She tried to learn from Walter White how to reach the literary agent William Aspenwall Bradley in Paris, to see if he knew how to contact Claude McKay in Morocco—a place she hoped to visit in the fall with Dorothy Peterson.[57] She also wrote William Seabrook to ask if she could stop in on him in Toulon on her way to Paris. The Georges were expecting her for a couple of days in Nice.

She had shown her novel to a "play-writing friend," who told her candidly that he thought "it was *rotten.* And on re-reading it I came to the conclusion that he was right, though I was sure that there was good stuff in it. Since then I have sweated blood over it. Perhaps that's just as well. I remember you always say that easy writing makes bad reading."[58] Set in a New Jersey suburb, the novel focused on a love triangle. The protagonist was a woman in her second marriage. Her husband, also previously divorced, remained in love with his first wife, who bore him a child after the divorce. Driven by jealousy and an ungovernable sexual appetite, the main character wants to get even with her husband and his sister, who interferes in their marital squabbles. She goes to the first wife to try to get her husband back but is rebuffed, and so turns to an affair with another man, who turns out to be merely taking advantage of her. "Baffled in her search for love," as a reader for Knopf would put it, in a sudden moment of inspiration she secretly poisons her "lover" and the novel closes when she attends his funeral.[59]

The lurid narrative of interlocking love triangles in which all of the characters are pathetic, unsympathetic, or worse (according to the reader at Knopf), the novel may well have expressed Larsen's frustrations and anxieties of 1930–1931, when she was involved in interlocking love triangles of her own, and when the future of her marriage to Elmer remained ambiguous. It also tapped the seemingly bottomless reservoirs of her obsession with triangular relationships, female sexual competition, and under-requited love.

Van Vechten, probably the only important man in her life who had never let her down, still felt insecure about what he had done in *Nigger Heaven* and asked her yet again what she really thought of it. Predictably, she reassured him. "Yes, of course 'Nigger Heaven' is a good book. An American who lives in the south of France, Antibes, was in the other night and was very curious to know my opinion of it. I gave it to him. The thing that he could not believe was that there is as much snobbery among Negroes as the booke seems to imply!"[60]

She had received a long newsy letter from Fania, and another from Isa Glenn. Dorothy Peterson reported on the NAACP Spring Dance—one of the last of the era, since they were beginning to lose money. James Weldon Johnson surprised Larsen by announcing his resignation from the NAACP to take a faculty post at Fisk—its first chair in Creative Writing: "I can't quite understand why, but it will perhaps be very good for him to get away from the uplift and to have a good deal more leisure to do the things he wants and ought to do."[61]

She had been reading a novel—*Mulatto Johnny*, by the Frenchman Alin Laubreaux. Originally titled *Yan-le-Métis*, it had recently been translated into English. She liked it very much, "though it isn't quite done. But maybe that's the translation." Set primarily in New Caledonia and Australia, the novel focuses on a "half-caste" islander beloved by his Breton father but separated from him by race. After Yan, or "Mulatto Johnny," commits an accidental homicide, his father gives him his life savings to help him escape from the law. Living between the races for most of the novel, Yan longs to be united with his father but must ultimately accept his position as a *Canaque* (a Kanaka, or Melanesian) because it is the only one that other people will acknowledge. Though heroic, courageous, richly emotional, and physically godlike, he is essentially a simple-minded "primitive." A broad and passionate indictment of racism and colonialism, the novel nonetheless turns on popular notions of black and Polynesian "fatalism" versus white historical consciousness, "colored" sensuality and harmony with nature versus white rationalism.[62] But Larsen was not entirely immune to its ethnographic assumptions.

It was probably the last book she read, other than her own sweat-stained manuscript, before packing up to leave Mallorca in the heat of the excitement over the birth of the Spanish Republic. For the municipal elections held April 12, citizens of Palma began lining up early in the morning under the eyes of mounted police and Civil Guards. Voting in great numbers, they delivered the socialists and republicans a solid majority, with Catalan nationalists and Mallorcan regionalists making important gains. Virtually all the major cities of Spain gave the republicans—many of whose leaders, including the presidential candidate, were in jail for a December rebellion—a smashing victory. For a while it appeared that Catalonia, including the Balearic Isles, would seek autonomy. King Alfonso ordered all the Captains-General of Spain to Madrid, and an armed revolution seemed possible. Civil Guards, armed to the teeth, appeared in Seville and the capital out of nowhere and began firing on mobs. On the fourteenth, the Second Republic was born.

In Palma, crowds destroyed small chapels around the city and tore down or defaced any emblems referring to the monarchy. Students marched through the streets chanting. The monument to monk Ramón Llull, a longstanding city landmark, was decapitated. In El Terreno, a couple of blocks from Larsen's house, signs for the Calle de Alfonso XIII were summarily changed to read "Avenida del 14 Abril."

On the fifteenth, a Catalan Republic was proclaimed in Barcelona, and plans for renewed autonomy for the Balearic Isles were circulated. From the first hours of the morning Palma erupted in jubilation. All the commercial establishments, even cafés, closed. From her front windows and porch Larsen could see the streets teeming with animated crowds. She could hear the fanfare in the harbor as the royal colors were struck and watch the flag of the republic hoisted on all the ships. To her, it looked like a revolution. Larsen wondered when it would end and the shops reopen, while her maid prowled the neighborhood for people willing to sell food out of their gardens.[63] "Why do the papers always say that these things are done with utmost peace and quiet?" she would ask a month later. "I was simply terrified. I don't care if I never see Spain again."[64]

"This is to say that I am leaving here by the next French boat," she wrote Henry Allen Moe on the twenty-first, "which I hope will be to-day though that is quite uncertain as the political situation here is very critical, though one reads in the papers that it is perfectly peaceful. I suppose the papers always say these things. The fact is that everything is at a stand-still, no taxis, buses, trains, and few boats are running." The shops were all closed, and for the past week Larsen and her maid had been living on whatever they had in the house—which could not have been much, since the custom was to shop each day for that day's meals —or what they could buy directly from the gardens of the neighboring peasants. "The populace seem to think that republic means an eternal holiday. . . . It has been, however, very interesting."[65]

Finally she got on a boat to Marseilles, probably at 10:00 A.M. the very day she wrote Moe, arriving in the French port at seven the next morning.[66] From Marseilles, she went to Nice and was picked up by the Georges. Bill George, a very fair African American well known in the higher circles of the black bourgeoisie, had made his fortune managing nightclubs in Chicago and New York; he was a kind of pioneer in the field, associated early on with the Nest in Harlem, and manager of the Apex Club in Chicago when it opened with Nora Holt as hostess in 1927. A friend of both Van Vechten and Holt, he had actually lived in Nora's house on Prairie Avenue before marrying and moving to Nice in 1928–1929.[67] His bride, the former Margaret Carter Gibbs, was so light-skinned that when Van Vechten met Bill in January 1929, he noted in his diary that he had "just married a white woman."[68] A former dancer, reputed to be one of the original "Florodora Girls," she was the mother of the actor Jack Carter, best known as "Crown" in *Porgy*.[69] Larsen knew Jack, and apparently had met the Georges on her way to Mallorca.

They had a villa in the fashionable village of Cimiez, high above Nice, known for its cooling breezes in summer and for the nearby ruins of an old Roman town. "I can't make out whether they pass or not," Larsen reported, "or simply say nothing about it. Evidently they have a sufficient portion of the world's good, a big house in a good neighborhood with counts, lords, and American millionaires for neighbors. They entertain all sorts of people including the aforesaid kind, as well as people like Sid Chaplin and Rex Ingram, and seem always to be in the Paris Herald, Riviera society section. Their garden is lovely and their cars very swell."[70]

They were not actually "always" in the Riviera section of the Paris *Herald,* but they were featured in a prominent article on the twenty-second of April, the day that Larsen would have been on the road to meet them. It reported that the Georges had just entertained at a buffet dinner in their "lovely villa," with guests including the Comte and Comtesse Raymond de Mondauban, Mrs. Gould Jennings, Princess Sabiha Feridoun Ben Ayad, Izzet Polakewics, Madame Izzet Pasha, and Rechad Bey, consul of Turkey for the Riviera.[71] "They took me everywhere and introduced me to everyone who was left," Larsen gushed, although "it was a bit after the season. The whole thing was very interesting and amusing."[72]

On the twenty-seventh Nella rode out of Nice with the Georges in one of their swell cars, climbing the corniches—roads carved into the cliffs with glorious views over the Mediterranean Sea—en route to Monte Carlo. She won big in the palatial casino, and picked up a postcard depicting it to write Fania and Carl: "Won gangs of money here today."[73]

She stayed a few more days above Nice before heading to Paris, where she arrived in pouring rain on the morning of April second and checked into the Hotel Rovaro. It was not quite the Ritz, but it came close: a first-class six-story hotel, built in 1927 of tan limestone, with elegant Art Deco décor and its own Bar Américain. In its Restaurant à la Fine Fourchette, lunch cost between twenty-five and thirty francs, and dinners upward of one hundred and twenty-five. Rooms ran from sixty to seventy-five francs a night, a very pretty centime in those days.[74] The building still stands at 44 rue Brunel, in the Seventeenth Arrondissement. Close to the Champs-Elysées and not far from the Bois de Boulogne, yet away from the buzz, Larsen felt lucky to find "such a decent place," since the rooms of Paris were filling up with visitors for the International Colonial Exposition. This vast display of artifacts from Europe's African, Asian, and New World colonies would create a sensation in the city for the next seven months: more than 33 million people would stream through its numerous pavilions.[75]

Larsen had much to look forward to. Letters from Dorothy Peterson and Eddie Wasserman told her they would be coming to Paris in the next month. It still looked like Van Vechten and Marinoff would be coming; he wrote to Gertrude Stein, "You should be seeing Nella Imes soon and you will like that and so will she."[76] Anita Thompson, Larsen's old acquaintance from Harlem and Greenwich Village, was in Paris, living near Montparnasse, though very soon to leave for Morocco. She was also trying her hand at writing, and had a book in the works that she wanted to bring out in time for the exposition, as she informed Walter White while asking for a blurb: "I need not insist that color interest will run high during that season."[77]

According to Thompson, African Americans in Paris at the time spread out across the city, meeting up with each other on friendly terms, gathering for special occasions like Louis Cole's swank birthday parties or to hear a string quartet by Clarence Cameron White at the Ecole Normale de Musique (not far from Larsen's hotel), but not settling near one another: "The Negroes in Paris were scattered, according to their education, their occupations. They saw each other by accident or when they wanted to, not in close black groups."[78] This had been true for Gwendolyn Bennett, Walter White, and Countee Cullen as well. It was certainly what Larsen experienced. She never thought of moving to Montmartre, the center of Paris' black colonial population.

She did visit there, however, soon after her arrival. She was introduced to Paris' "Nigger Heaven," as she called it, by Josephine Baker's understudy, "an interesting child of twenty-one who has lived in Europe since she was three years old. Speaks every language—and English with an accent. Rather pretty—but bum legs. Too bad, because she can sing."[79] Baker was starring at the Casino de Paris in *Paris qui remue* (Bustling Paris) a show capitalizing on the Colonial Exposition. It had little to do with Paris, actually, but drew most of its material from erotic fantasies about the colonies in Martinique, Algeria, Indochina, and Africa. In her first number, "La Petite Tonkinoise," Baker came onstage as the delicious Vietnamese mistress of a French colonist.[80]

By this time La Baker, the "Jazz Cleopatra," had pretty well taken Paris, along with the Casino de Paris, from the French star Mistinguett. But her shows rarely portrayed her as African American. Indeed, she had been chosen Queen of the Colonial Exposition despite objections to her lack of fluency in French (or any African language), her slick black hair, and her American citizenship.[81]

One night, a male friend took Larsen to the Théâtre de la Madeleine to see Sacha Guitry and his wife Yvonne Printemps in Guitry's play about Franz Hals. "Would you believe it," she wrote Carl, "I'd never seen them before. Fortunately, I wasn't disappointed. But the man with me assured me they were rotten."[82] The next night, Friday the eighth, she took in a new Roland Hayes concert at the Salle Pleyel, with a program ranging from sixteenth-century Italian melodies to Negro spirituals. A discriminating listener, she found his spirituals "terrible" but his German *Lieder* "inexpressibly wonderful. The audience interested me very much. They were so tremendously receptive." The reviewer for the Paris *Herald* agreed with Larsen: "Though many expected to be taken by the spirituals," the audience was most captivated by the Schubert selections and Beethoven's "Adelaide."[83] Spirituals did not lend themselves best to the concert hall and grand piano. This was an opinion that Larsen knew Van Vechten shared, preferring the more evangelical style of Paul Robeson—although both Van Vechten and Larsen admired Hayes's singing in other modes.

On May 10, a Sunday, Larsen visited Bricktop's, the famous Montmartre club owned and managed by red-headed African American Ada Louise Smith, who had grown up on State Street during Larsen's girlhood. The club of choice for many American celebrities, Bricktop's was small, with about a dozen tables, featuring a glass floor lit from below and a bar and benches along the walls.[84] The night Nella showed up, Bricktop was not in, however, "and the whole thing was pretty dull. An off-night perhaps." But Larsen did get to see her old Harlem acquaintance Louis Cole. He was now Bricktop's piano player, "looking quite handsome" and with a "rather interesting following."[85] She almost certainly returned several times during her cold but happy five months in Paris.

The following day, Larsen lunched with "Willie" Seabrook and his wife Marjorie Worthington—another woman Van Vechten was encouraging to write novels—at their hotel. She had met Seabrook in New York with his first wife, Katie, and he had reviewed *Passing* quite favorably for the *Saturday Review,* so she was prepared to like him. He was also at the peak of his fame. *Ladies' Home Journal* had just paid $30,000 for the serial rights to his new book, *Jungle Ways,* and he was proceeding to destroy himself with alcohol in a lavish suite overlooking the courtyard at the Ritz.[86]

He wasn't unlike one of Larsen's fictional characters—tall, tanned, ruggedly handsome, the kind who had "been everywhere and done everything." But according to Man Ray he was quite unassuming about his celebrity. His first bestseller, *Adventures in Arabia,* cashed in on the orientalist craze in the years when young American women swooned over Rudolph Valentino as the "son of the sheik." Later came *The Magic Island* (1929), a sort of participant-observer journalistic documentary of Haitian culture, with the focus on voodoo. Introducing the term "zombie" to the American vocabulary, it had been a hit in Harlem (although today one would prefer to think otherwise). Even Aubrey Bowser of the *Amsterdam News* had called it "the best book of the year on a Negro subject" and Seabrook "a personified miracle"—a white Southerner who had "purged himself" of racial prejudice.[87] At the same time, Nancy Cunard was writing a scathing, and largely deserved, denunciation of him in a letter to Walter White.[88] When Seabrook was in Paris, his usual Montparnasse address became a regular stopping-place for the famous and notorious of all descriptions.[89]

Riding high on the Negro vogue, Seabrook had taken up the project that became *Jungle Ways* after Paul Morand urged him to go to Africa and "get inside" a "cannibal" culture. According to his publisher's advertisements, "Morand, Cocteau, Maurois say that not four living Americans can write as well as William Seabrook."[90] Few would agree today, but such enthusiasm was more than commercial hype; Man Ray, for example, considered Seabrook superior to Hemingway, because his adventures were not merely "so much raw material for a literary career. . . . In earlier days he might have been a sort of Marco Polo. There was no literary pretense about Seabrook."[91] If he embroidered his tales, that only made them better.

Jungle Ways is chock full of "the unexpurgated truth about the life and customs . . . of the real savages," according to the advertisements. Seabrook's goal in Africa had been to partake in a cannibal feast and witness a human sacrifice before such rituals disappeared from the repertoire of the world's cultures. He even included detailed recipes for cooking people. "The barbecue method," Seabrook averred, was not practiced by those with whom he had lived; slow-roasting worked best, "turning frequently and basting with fresh palm oil, to which you begin adding the ordinary condiments." His friend "Fire Helmet" attested that "as a matter of personal choice, the palm of the hand was the most tender and delicious morsel of all."[92] At the climax of the "cannibal" episode of the book, in a weird set piece, Seabrook finally sits down to a roasted rump steak of human being, with rice and a bottle of wine.

Years later, in his autobiography, Seabrook would admit that the closest he ever came to a cannibal feast was a dinner of ape meat—until he'd returned to France. Back in Paris, some friends had arranged for him to eat the flesh of a corpse spirited out of a hospital, which had become the basis of the description of his first taste of human rump in *Jungle Ways*. After going to the "heart of darkness" to experience the most secret rituals of the world's last true savages, he had returned to the City of Light to feast on the body of a Frenchman in an aristocrat's courtyard.[93]

Knowing this, as Larsen could not have, one reads the solemn conclusion of *Jungle Ways* as farce. Turning meditative, the author observes that the Eiffel Tower, and the Paramount and Chrysler towers, are "strangely like proud gigantic replicas of Habbe altars, and at their base a people as fantastic and bewildering . . . as ever were the Habbe—a people who also seem mad, but who, despite their seeming madness and despite backyard horrors as hideous in their different way as those of Sangha, yet believe too in a religion of life and worship life after their fashion."[94]

Seabrook's own fetishism was a kind of benign sadism, which he made no attempt to hide from friends. Much of the time in Paris he kept a nude woman chained to the banister of his staircase.[95] Tolerant of his "sickness," which Seabrook considered intimately bound to his desire to write, Marjorie Worthington appeased him for a while by going around with a metal cylinder locked around her neck so tightly she could barely swallow or lower her chin.

"I did like them both tremendously," Nella reported to Carl after her lunch with them. "They will be here a week or two, so I shall be seeing them again. . . . And listen to this! Rose Wheeler is giving a tea for them and me and Roland Hayes on Friday afternoon. I look forward to that with—well with everything."[96] She was to be fêted with the celebrities of the hour.

Larsen had met Arthur and Rose Wheeler in New York through Van Vechten. Now residing mainly in France, they lived well on the fortune Arthur had amassed on Wall Street before retiring, at an early age, just in time to avoid ruin. "They radiated wealth," Man Ray would remember, describing Rose as "a dark little woman, smartly groomed."[97] Anita Thompson portrayed Arthur as "a square man with a round belly and an appetite for good things."[98] It was Arthur Wheeler who had talked Man Ray into trying his hand at cinema and put up the money for the film *Emak Bakia,* a nonnarrative "cine-poem" shot in and around the Wheeler's estate of the same name (Basque for "Leave Me Alone") near Biarritz, while Rose sped the artist around in her Mercedes race car.[99]

It was probably from the Wheelers that Nella learned Anita Thompson had just left for Morocco, staying temporarily with Claude McKay in Tangier and writing a book. (There was no sex involved. She found him too fat, and he was chiefly interested, she suspected, in the Arab boys.)[100] Thompson considered Man Ray her "surrogate father." He had introduced her to the Wheelers, "big-hearted people" in her memory, "a great couple to know. They were warm and intelligent, and I spent many happy hours with them."[101] After placing a "lynching" story in a London publication, she was writing a book about her family, and while Arthur encouraged her, he felt she shouldn't write on "racial" subjects. Light-skinned as she was, she'd live more comfortably, he believed, if she forgot about such things. Nonetheless, he agreed to fund her while she lived in Morocco and wrote her book. Like a lot of men, he had a crush on Thompson, and one day while out for a walk offered her $1,000 extra to sleep with him. She turned him down in good humor, and when they got back to the Wheelers' apartment suite, he promptly told his wife. "Why, I don't blame Anita," Rose responded, "I wouldn't sleep with you for a thousand dollars myself."[102] They shared a belly laugh and remained warm friends for years afterward.

Very friendly to Nella, and to other African Americans they knew from home, the Wheelers could introduce Larsen to some of the most famous artists in Paris at the time. Larsen loved their apartment. "Mann Ray did it for them. Incidently he is going to do some pictures of me."[103] Both Van Vechten and Nora

Holt were friends of Man Ray's. In 1930 and 1931, Van Vechten kept the artist supplied with the latest jazz records, in return for which Man Ray sent him his latest photographs; on the second of February, he had written Carl, "If you want anyone's picture write me."[104] Before long, Nella would be one of the artist's nearest neighbors and apparently on warm terms with him. But any portrait of her, which may well have been taken, has yet to surface from the scattered heaps of Man Ray's massive and disorganized photographic remains.[105]

Only two weeks in Paris, Larsen had been getting around. She had even been to the home of William Aspenwall Bradley, agent for most of the celebrated British and American authors in postwar France. "I never felt so stupid and uncomfortable in my life. I knew he was—or is—a very important person but honest to God! I had no more idea what he did than an octopus. However, they were very nice and I guess I managed well enough because I've been invited again. You can bet I made it my business to extract the necessary information from the first person I ran into who could tell me."[106]

Although many white American tourists brought their prejudices with them and tried to get the French restaurateurs to draw the color line, Larsen's experience, and that of the black people she knew, contradicts the popular belief that black and white Americans avoided each other in Paris.[107] "Tom Rutherford seems to have friends all over the globe," Nella wrote Carl. "Yesterday Mrs. Arthur Garfield Hayes (ex) almost fell into my arms telling me she felt as if she'd known me all my life because Tom had talked so much about me."[108]

She had other friends on the way. Willie Seabrook had told her that Eddie Wasserman had taken a place in Villefranche, and the card Wasserman had already mailed probably informed her that he would soon be coming to Paris, where he expected to see her. By early June, however, she knew that Van Vechten had decided against coming over. He was happy and comfortable in his New York apartment, and Fania was rehearsing for three plays in the summer stock theater Lawrence Langner had organized in Westport.[109]

The last Sunday in May, Larsen attended a concert featuring, among others, Clarence Cameron White, an African American composer she knew from New York and socialized with at least a little in Paris. She was proud of the fact that his performance was by far the best of the evening.[110]

Larsen had moved in late May to a cheaper hotel, nearer her friends. The Hotel Paris-Dinard, in the Sixth Arrondissement, rented luxuriously furnished rooms for thirty-five francs and up—still high-class, but not as dear as the Rovaro. On a quiet street a couple of blocks from the northwest corner of the Luxembourg Gardens, it gave Larsen access to all the attractions of the Left Bank and made searching for an apartment there much easier.[111]

Very soon, she had located more permanent digs in a classy building on the south side of the rue Campagne Première, near the heart of Montparnasse. She could hardly have done better, and the chances are that her connection with the Wheelers had something to do with it. Man Ray lived in an apartment on the first floor just inside the entrance, and Larsen was taking over that of another American artist, Paul Burlin, for the three months from July through September. The building had been designed and completed in 1911 expressly for artists, and was just around the corner from the American Students' and Artists' Club. Four stories tall with two very high apartments to each story, it sported an elegant Art Nouveau façade and enormous northwest-facing windows that maximized the natural light for the benefit of the artists' studios. Each apartment had two floors connected by an internal staircase, with the studio on the main floor along with a dining room and kitchen. Above, a living room with a loggia overlooking the studio connected with the bedrooms and bathrooms. With an elevator and central heating, gas, and electricity, the building was very up-to-date, and well out of the reach of most artists. When Man Ray wrote Marcel Duchamp to tell him he had taken an apartment there, Duchamp replied, "A studio in that building is a remarkable thing."[112]

But Larsen could not move in until the first of July, and for the time being she remained situated between St. Sulpice and the Luxembourg Palace, waiting to hear from Blanche Knopf about the verdict on her manuscript. She finally gave the Colonial Exposition a try—the biggest happening Paris had seen in some time, and a major event in European thinking about race, art, and the relationship between colony and metropole.

Larsen may have gone for the opening of the American exhibit on May 26, "the most brilliant Franco-American fête Paris has seen in years," according to the Paris *Herald*.[113] Just what a replica of Mount Vernon, complete with transplanted rosebushes and a scenic railway where the Potomac would be (but no slave cabins, of course), had to do with the French Empire no one seems to have bothered to ask. The United States was one of five nations represented at the fair, but the great structures of the exposition were the huge replicas of the temple of Angkor Wat (three years in the making), the Hova royal palace, the great mosque of Djenné in West Africa, and a Marrakesh palace. Built on 250 acres around Lake Daumesnil in and near the Bois de Vincennes (now the site of Paris' main zoo), the show even included an entire West African village in which people went about their daily lives, stopping now and then to break into a "native" dance—a feature of such fairs going back to Copenhagen's Tivoli and Chicago's Midway Plaisance of the 1890s.[114] Larsen's verdict: "To my mind, very dull. But then my mind is peculiar. Everybody else seems to think it swell."[115]

Everyone except the Surrealists, that is, who came out with a manifesto at about the same time entitled "Ne visitez pas l'Exposition Coloniale" (Don't Visit the Colonial Exposition). They reviled the exposition as a colossal propaganda event intended to pump up pride in the empire—"possessions" stolen from the peoples of Africa and Asia—and to recruit men to the colonial army.[116]

As Phyllis Rose has suggested, while Josephine Baker's show at the Casino de Paris "showed the colonies as sexual resources" throughout the season, the exposition showed them as "natural and cultural resources."[117] Part of the point was to keep the French people's minds off their miseries as unemployment rose to staggering levels.

The governor-general of the exposition, on the other hand, regarded the colonies as offering "in all the domains of the spirit, to its engineers, its *savants,* its artists, its philosophers, a vast unknown territory to prospect. Thus colonization, born of the spirit of domination, appears in the final analysis as an instrument of peace. It is the *deus ex machina* that will permit Western civilization to escape suicide, and, better yet, to regenerate itself."[118] Larsen's blasé response—expressing neither political outrage nor naive admiration, but simple boredom—reveals her usual sardonic response to such idealizations and her epicurean, apolitical sensibility. Not to mention her complete independence of mind.

The event attracted thousands of people from the colonies during a period when tourism in general was falling off. Paris needed the boost. The city's unionized musicians and performers, hit hard by the slowdown, even got entertainer Texas Guinan and her girls deported before they could disembark from their ship in Le Havre. The Americans in Paris were all worked up about it, Nella reported rather drily, but the French nightclub acts did not need competition from Broadway's queen of "Whoopee."[119]

Willie Seabrook and Marjorie Worthington had gone back to Toulon but kept up their correspondence with Larsen and invited her to visit later in the summer. Eric Walrond had recently stopped to see them. "I think I shall go," Nella confided, "if my finances hold out. Or if I can prevail upon my husband to supplement them." She had now read *Jungle Ways,* which she "was crazy about. . . . It was fascinating. And there were some very beautifully written passages in it. I did think, though, that it was one of the saddest books I have ever read"—sad, because it purported to document cultures that French imperialism and "progress" were stamping out.[120]

Elmer had practically stopped corresponding. "I heard from him the other day for the first time in four months. And then only to berate me for having spent as much money as I have. Before I sailed he promised to come over when school closed. Now, I do not know. It seems pretty doubtful. I have a suspicion that he will do as he did the most of last summer—that is, spend his vacation with Mrs. Gilbert. I don't care about that. But I do object to being left short of money."[121] Actually, he was planning to come over *with* Mrs. Gilbert, as she would learn soon enough.

About the seventeenth of June, Nella picked up a copy of James Weldon Johnson's new book of poetry provoked by the Gold Star Mothers controversy, *Saint Peter Relates an Incident of the Resurrection Day,* "in a delightful shop here where they know all about Jim Johnson"—surely Sylvia Beach's Shakespeare and Company—and wrote him her congratulations on the back of a postcard showing Cézanne's painting *La Neige fondante* (Melting Snow).[122]

On the first of July, Larsen moved into her new apartment at 31 bis, rue Campagne Première, and began familiarizing herself more with the neighborhood. Campagne Première runs between Boulevard Montparnasse on the northeast and Boulevard Raspail on the Southwest. Larsen's building—just near the corner of Boulevard Raspail, with a view of Montparnasse Cemetery and the broad, tree-lined Boulevard Edgar Quinet—was quiet yet well located in relation to the famous artists' hangouts of the late 1920s and early 1930s. The block between rue Campagne Première and rue Boissonade (to the east) contained hundreds of artists' studios in which Americans had been living since the 1870s.[123] In the summer, particularly July and August, many of the French deserted Paris, and the art academies also closed—one reason Larsen was able to find such a prime studio for the third quarter of the rental year.

At the northern end of the street, on the corner of Boulevard Montparnasse, was the famous Jockey Bar, owned by Hilaire Hiler, a white American painter who decorated the exterior with stylized pictures of cowboys and Indians, and the inside with old posters. He also played piano.[124] Nora Holt had performed here between dates in 1926, and Chicago-born Archibald Motley had done a famous painting of the place in 1929.[125] Hiler was a friend of the black painters Palmer Hayden and Hale Woodruff, whom Larsen surely met, since Woodruff was still in Paris that summer and often at the club.[126] Most of the artistic and literary folk of the neighborhood hung out here, and Man Ray's old flame, Kiki de Montparnasse, still sang naughty French songs in her inimitable deadpan style, passing a hat around and browbeating customers for tips she promptly shared with the "less favored performers."[127]

In the middle of the block on rue Campagne Première was Chez Rosalie, a restaurant for down-at-the-heels artists, filled with long wooden tables and rough benches.[128] Also in the neighborhood were Le Dôme and La Rotonde, a big café on the corner of Boulevard Raspail. Man Ray often frequented the Dingo, which was more intimate and low key. La Jungle, about two blocks from Larsen's address, was a club that had recently gone "black fashion."[129]

Eddie Wasserman came up to Paris about the time of Larsen's move and they lunched together. On the Fourth of July, she went out with him, Katie Seabrook (Willie's first wife), and Clarence Cameron White. "Nella is grand, just finishing a book," Eddie reported to Van Vechten.[130] They were both also at Louis Cole's birthday party on the fifth—a big occasion among the smart crowd of Americans in Paris. After the party, Miguel Covarrubias, another recent arrival, showed his new film on Bali, featuring dancers who were then performing at the Colonial Exposition.

Finally, about the second week of July, Dorothy and Sidney Peterson arrived, occasioning a joyful reunion. Dorothy and Nella "were almost moved to kiss each other," she informed Van Vechten, "which has only happened twice in our lives, you know." Eddie Wasserman hosted a "grand luncheon party" in the Petersons' honor and that of Miguel Covarrubias and Rose Rolando. Countee Cullen, summering in Paris, came by to read a play he had co-written with Arna Bontemps, entitled "God Sends Sunday"—an early version of *Saint Louis Woman*.[131] And Katie Seabrook threw a cocktail party to celebrate Dorothy's arrival.

Katie had divorced Willie, but not before accompanying him to Africa on the trip that resulted in *Jungle Ways*. Born Katherine Edmondson, she was the daughter of a Coca-Cola executive, raised in Atlanta as a member of one of the "best and oldest local families," though she was by no means a "Society Girl."[132] When Seabrook decided in 1915 to help the French in World War I, Katie went with him and worked as a volunteer nurse while he joined the ambulance corps in the Field Service.[133] After he was gassed, they returned to Georgia, where he (or rather, as he pointed out, his black foreman) ran a cotton plantation briefly, but they soon grew restless and moved to Greenwich Village. While Willie tried to get a writing career started, Katie co-owned a popular café called "126," on Waverly Place. This is where Van Vechten, Dorothy Peterson, and probably Nella first got to know the adventurous Katie Seabrook. Although she had not been with Willie for his more exotic and imaginary exploits, she had traveled overland from Ivory Coast through present-day Burkina Faso (Ouagadougou and Ouahigouya) and up to Timbuktu—a rather epic journey in those days. Back in Paris, she was an equally adventurous hostess known for wild parties in honor of her New York friends.[134]

The night of the twelfth, while Katie, Dorothy, and Nella were out on the town, hitting the bars of Montmartre, they stopped to pick up a postcard. On the back of a photograph of the flamboyant, gothic Tour Saint-Jacques (looking not unlike a phallus sporting a French tickler), they each inscribed a message for Van Vechten and then dropped the card in a postbox:

> 12 Midnight. 12 July
> 3 Nice girls out
> together.
>   —Nella
> This is the most phallic picture we could find.—Katie
> And all tight, tight, tight.—Dorothy[135]

On the photograph each had signed her name next to one of the gargoyles jutting out from the peak of the erection.

"Our apartment is perfectly marvelous," Dorothy enthused a week later, "and from the high studio window, we look down the Boulevard Edgar-Quinet with it's five lovely rows of trees. We have what is known as a view, altho at present it is quite cluttered with French servant girls off for Sunday afternoon with their lovers, who with one hand clutch their funny little hats always a size too small and with the other hand grab the girl by the neck as tho she were going to take her first chance and run away. French girls must be different from others—huh? Nella's busy working but sends her love."[136] Larsen had begun yet another novel, probably the one she had originally proposed to the Guggenheim Foundation. Soon Dorothy, too, would be starting one.

Elmer was due to arrive on the twentieth, as a cable from his brother informed them. With Ethel Gilbert in tow, he stopped in New York the week of July 5, and the Alexanders gave a dinner and bridge party in their honor. The *Amsterdam News* identified Elmer's colleague as "Mrs. Susan Gilbert," a married "instructor of German" who was sailing, like Elmer, on the *S.S. Saint Louis* to Europe. Apparently calling Gilbert a German instructor was a ruse to explain why they were both going to Austria and Germany at the same time on the same ocean liner.[137] Lillian Alexander, Ethel Gilbert's good friend, probably knew exactly what was going on. But to Van Vechten, whom Elmer visited without Gilbert the day before sailing, he never let on that they were traveling together.[138]

Elmer and Ethel did not stop long in Paris—where Dorothy Peterson first met Gilbert—before taking off for a tour of Bavaria, Austria, and northern Italy. Carl received a brief postcard from Elmer: "The girls did not go although I arranged a house for three weeks in Munich."[139] It seems very unlikely, however, that Elmer intended for Nella and Dorothy to come with him. In fact, they were expecting a visit from Harold Jackman while he was gone.

20. Dorothy Peterson in Paris, August 1931. Yale Collection of American Literature, Beinecke Rare Book and Manuscript Library, Yale University.

Jackman had sailed on the first of August on the *Ile de France* and planned to spend several days in Paris "to see the Exposition and to visit Dorothy and Nella," as he put it,[140] before continuing to Toulon as guest of Princess Violette Murat, granddaughter of Napoleon III. Well known to Harlem from previous visits there, Murat had been ordered out of Toulon for "debauching all the young sailors," according to Eddie Wasserman; so in the summer of 1931 she converted an old mosquito-boat submarine chaser into a "yacht" and moved into the harbor, practically beneath Seabrook's window.[141] Jackman was spending his fifth summer in Europe as her guest.[142]

Elmer was due to leave Europe on the ninth of September, in time to get back to Fisk before school started. President Jones expected Nella to accompany Elmer or to follow soon after, as he knew her Guggenheim was to end then; but Larsen had no intention of going back before Christmas. Dorothy, just released from *The Green Pastures,* was on leave from teaching until January, and since the weather was turning chilly in Paris they began looking south. "We probably go back to Spain soon," Nella informed her friends.[143]

Nella and Dorothy were having the time of their lives and apparently never did get down to Toulon to visit with Willie Seabrook and Marjorie Worthington. A steady procession of old friends kept showing up in town, providing occasions for merry reunions. One would hardly know that the Depression was on. Just as Hale Woodruff and Eric Walrond left, Aaron Douglas was due to appear, on a fellowship.[144] Dorothy's old friend Ed Morgan was around and about. Eddie Wasserman still came up occasionally from Villefranche for nights on the town. In fact, a lot of Americans—including Ernest Hemingway and F. Scott Fitzgerald—passed through in late August and early September, and the clubs of Montparnasse and Montmartre enjoyed a surge of business reminiscent of the previous decade.[145] Several new clubs opened up or reopened near Larsen's apartment in August, including the African Habib Benglia's Le Train Bleu, featuring sensational entertainment with Benglia in a witch-doctor costume, West Indian women in colorful Creole attire, and African girls clad only in loincloths.[146] "We are living a wild life here," Nella reported at the end of August.[147] Interracial dancing was a big drawing card that season, according to J. A. Rogers, who also noted the presence in Paris of Nella Larsen Imes for readers of his column back home.[148]

She fell sick soon thereafter, about the same time she would have heard from Blanche Knopf that her manuscript, "Mirage," had been turned down.[149] The reader's report, by an in-house editor named Abbott but also signed by Blanche, found the end of the novel "very well done," rising above a conventional dénouement, but the story in general merely a "conventional love triangle." "The woman is very impulsive, jealous and stupid, and the husband is a perfectly awful character, but drawn in an obscure way so that it is difficult to see why two women are so crazy over him." However unlikable, the main character was at least vividly drawn. The "chief defect" of the novel lay in the "passive and shadowy characterization" of the husband. "The book ought to be rewritten to bring him out and perhaps to excite some sympathy for the sex-mad wife who deserves nothing but derision as she exists here."[150]

Nella herself seemed mad, in the opinion of Elmer, who had to suddenly cancel his passage to New York and write a hurried note to President Jones at Fisk explaining that he would be late for the beginning of the semester. "This is done on account of Mrs. Imes' health which is causing us both a great deal of anxiety. As the result of her illness last winter her chest is in very bad condition and the last few weeks of unseasonably wet cold weather is responsible for a cold that is regarded as serious. She is quite frightened and discouraged by minor hemorrhages and it seems best for me to stay with her until she is definitely better."[151] Since Jones was expecting Nella to come to Fisk with him, Elmer concocted a story that she would have to stay in Europe for some time to recover. Quite possibly, he too had expected her to come home with him. Her fellowship, after all, had ended, leaving him to pay her bills. These, however, were a bit mitigated by the partnership with Dorothy. "We have arranged a companion for her and the present thought is to establish her for the next few months at Malaga (Spain) where the mild climate will likely help her get back to normal. At least her Paris physician thinks this is best and she rather agrees."[152] The "Paris physician" was surely an invention; Nella had been planning all year to go back to Spain in the fall.

In her letters to Van Vechten she made no mention of being sick, though when it came to the Guggenheim Foundation she used illness as an excuse for not having written before the end of September to thank them for her expiring fellowship. "I have not quite finished my work," she informed Henry Allen Moe, "but now that things seem quieter there I mean to go back to Spain, where the weather is pleasanter and leaving [sic] cheaper, and get on with it."[153] To Van Vechten the next day she merely wrote, on a card probably picked up at the Jardin des Plantes, "We leave here (Dorothy and I) next week for Spain and North Africa where we hope to get warm again."[154]

Dorothy had originally wanted to go to Mallorca, having heard so much about it from Nella, but Nella now insisted that she was "afraid of islands." Then Dorothy's friend Ed Morgan, who had stayed in Málaga, recommended that town for its climate and ambience.[155] Already becoming popular among the

British as a winter resort, Málaga in its habits, customs, geography, and climate was just about the most "southern" place in Spain other than Mallorca—a town of whitewashed houses overlooking the turquoise sea, elaborate patios and luxuriant tropical flowers, goats in the street and, according to an American travel guide of the time, "a predominance of men, women, and children with the most ambiguous complexions."[156]

Nella and Dorothy took a house, the Villa Mercedes, and settled in very happily, according to Dorothy, who soon began writing a novel.[157] They quickly made friends in the British "colony" and, with Dorothy for company, Nella practically ceased writing her occasional long, newsy letters to New York. One finds only postcards after this. They made frequent trips to nearby Gibraltar with their English friends, finding it a "merry spot" with exotic Indian stores, a nice place for a day's shopping, and visits to aromatic cafés.[158] Occasionally Nella wished for more privacy. When news of Van Vechten's *Sacred and Profane Memories* began coming out, Nella took a moment to write a card: "Carlo dear! We have just had a clipping about your forthcoming book. I hope I live to see it. Today I am having (Thank god!!) a day to myself, D. having gone to Gibraltar with some of our Eng. friends. My best & dearest & sincerest love to you both & every good wish & all thanks for everything." On the face of the postcard was a medieval illustration from the *Roman de la rose* with the caption, "Lover attains the rose" and Nella's comment, "I think of you like this. Am I wrong?"[159]

Toward the end of November, Nella and Dorothy decided to cross over from Gibraltar and see the Spanish tip of North Africa—Tangier, Tetuán, and other old Moorish towns of Spanish Morocco. Nella sent Fania and Carl a card on the twenty-sixth: "Darlings! We have been reading such nice things in the October papers about Fania. Tomorrow we go to Africa."[160] Claude McKay had, by now, returned to New York after several years abroad, but Anita Thompson was still in Tangier and an excellent guide.

Thompson had moved out of McKay's house after three weeks to a place in the Arab quarter and quickly adopted mostly Arab styles of furnishing and cooking. Friendly with the women of the neighborhood, she occasionally even went to market fully covered and veiled like the Muslims, which she preferred to being gaped at in European cities. By the time Nella and Dorothy appeared, however, she may have already moved into the rear quarters of an old palace owned by a blond and blue-eyed friend, born in Tangier to the owner of the Grand Hotel and married to a French naval officer. The palace sat on a high peninsula above the Straits of Gibraltar.[161]

Tangier was a uniquely international town, governed by thirteen legations from different countries, with a dual justice system featuring both Arab and European-style courts. The Moroccan brand of slavery was still openly practiced and "a very real part of life," according to Thompson. Wealthy Arabs bought young West African concubines and servants and raised them in their households almost as family members.[162]

On the twenty-ninth of November, Nella and Dorothy moved on from Tangier to Tetuán. Nella wrote Van Vechten two days later, "The deeper we go into Africa the colder it gets." She and Dorothy had "already bought good old fashioned woolen b-v-d's. But it is simply fascinating."[163] In Tetuán, Dorothy picked up a "grand Arabian boy friend" after spending an afternoon visiting him in Nella's company and learning that she "bore a fatal resemblance to Queen Sofia of Albania, who, I judge, was a former girlfriend. He is marvellously good looking and I am coming back to Tetuan next summer to visit him."[164]

They were back in Málaga by the eleventh of December, when Dorothy wrote home to say she looked entirely different:

> What with my skin ten shades darker and my hair ten times whiter, added to my former good looks, I am now a quite charming old lady. Then too, I have had an operation and as I've been told that no woman is really interesting until she's had her operation, I now claim the added attraction of interest. My operation was very serious, lasting two hours, during which I suffered agonies but behaved very bravely. My doctor's name was Heliotrope Ramos and the head nurse Nella Larsen.[165]

The "operation"—she had her ears pierced—had been inspired by the "gorgeous earrings" Nella and Dorothy kept finding while poking around old jewelry shops in the back streets of Málaga.

They worked more on their books for a week or two and then, before Christmas, set off on a circuit of Andalusia's interior, in which the Moorish past remained as palpable as anywhere in Europe. First they visited Granada eighty miles away, mainly to see the Alhambra. (If they visited García Lorca's mother, they left no record of it.) They picked up cards here for friends back home, then pushed on to Córdoba and Seville, ancient capitals of Andalusia.[166]

Back in Málaga and counting the remaining days with regret, they began writing again—Dorothy finishing her first manuscript and actually beginning another. "It sounds like an epidemic, doesn't it?" she wrote Jean Toomer. "But it just happened that I was in a less unhappy state than I'd been in for years, I was freer to do things I wanted—and I needed to work—and there were things I had to say. So that's how it happened."[167]

Nella, a happy influence on Dorothy, was working hard to complete the novel for which she had been awarded the Guggenheim and dreading the complications and decisions that awaited her in New York and Nashville. Full of regret and bright memories bound to fade, just after the beginning of the New Year Dorothy sailed from Gibraltar.[168] Nella seems to have waited and sailed a week or so later, alone, savoring the last days of her freedom.

TWENTY

The Crack-Up:
1932–1933

THE New York to which Nella Larsen returned in mid to late January 1932 was not the city she had left in the fall of 1930. The Empire State Building, with a triumphant marble and brass lobby designed by Winold Reiss, had colonized Midtown with the spirit of the Twenties just as everything went gray. Three years after the stock market crash, the great glittering NAACP balls were a thing of the past. Carl Van Vechten had quit drinking and quit writing, having taken up photography. Although serious interest in black literature and art continued, even broadened, there was no more Negro vogue; in fact, there were no more vogues. Black professionals struggled to pay their rent and keep food on the table while the poor went hungry in freezing flats, missions, and relief agencies. Panhandlers haunted every corner and entryway. Breadlines snaked around city blocks. Many writers and artists had left town in the struggle to earn a living or the search for cheaper rent. The Dunbar apartments were emptying out, and abandoned dogs roamed the neighborhood, biting a score of people every week. Even in the Imeses' former building, no apartment was safe from break-ins, and single women felt targeted.[1] Nella no longer had a permanent home in New York, and Elmer had by now been in residence at Fisk for well over a year. All of Nella's books and furnishings were in Nashville with him.

Nonetheless, Mrs. Imes was fortunate. Her husband had a secure job, still paying $5,000 per year. They had little reason to fear that he would lose it, unless of course Nella let the cat out of the bag about his outrageous affair. But the last thing she wanted to do was to join him in Nashville, where she was expected soon.

Dorothy Peterson moved in with her father again at the old homestead in Brooklyn, and Nella stopped there with her, ostensibly for a few days before continuing to Nashville. Van Vechten's niece Elizabeth Shaffer Hull and her new husband, Jim (both aspiring authors), had sublet Dorothy's apartment on Second Avenue until May, and Dorothy and Nella often visited them there. Soon Elizabeth was one of Nella's best friends, although Elizabeth would remain closer to Dorothy into the 1940s. Elizabeth wrote Grace Johnson on February 2 about how well both of the returned travelers seemed. Dorothy had let her hair go gray and looked "very handsome indeed. Nella is lovely and I am so glad she is back."[2] They were full of amusing stories, Carl informed the Johnsons.[3]

Dorothy soon returned to what she called the "nightmare" of teaching, cherishing the memory of "one of the most interesting episodes in my long and varied life."[4] Fania was busy in a series of plays throughout the winter and spring, and contributing devotedly to various relief efforts for unemployed performers. Elizabeth and Jim Hull were both writing books; Nella would drop in on them occasionally for company and cocktails. "Nella was here the other night," Elizabeth wrote her uncle in early February. "She got tight. She loves you."[5] After a year and a half away, however, her relationship with him was not what it had once been. Doubtless, Nella also saw a good deal of Dorothy Harris—now remarried and renamed Dorothy Harris Wolfe—and caught up with Grace Valentine. But the reunion with her husband she kept putting off.

Instead of packing up to leave town, in fact, Larsen began scouting for an apartment of her own in Manhattan, mainly around Greenwich Village. She found one by late February, in an attractive brownstone on West Eleventh just off Fifth Avenue. Dorothy called it a "charming little apartment," in a "very swanky" neighborhood.[6] Just two doors away from the recently constructed main building of the New School for Social Research, on a quiet but not lonesome street, it was also relatively safe for a woman on her own. And, if she liked, Nella could easily attend evening lectures and readings only a few steps from home.

The first Saturday in March, as part of a program for "interracial amity," Professor Treadwell Smith of Columbia Teachers College took a group of whites to Harlem, where Romare Bearden's parents gave a party in their home on 131st Street. Larsen and Rudolph Fisher "spoke very delightfully" on the arts, by Dorothy Peterson's report.[7] The next night, Dorothy and Nella went to hear Paul Robeson in a farewell recital at Town Hall (he was going abroad) and had a "nice chat" with him after the show.[8]

Nella spent some time at Bordentown in March, and may have been hoping to get a position there, while Elmer's colleagues and supervisors at Fisk wondered when they would see her in Nashville. Week after week, she kept putting them off. Even Dorothy began worrying about when she would ever leave and wrote Grace Johnson in mid-April, saying that soon after moving into the new apartment Nella had contracted a "touch of pleurisy" that

> kept her in bed for a week—then getting up inopportunely for various parties that she had no business attending, put her back in bed again and again.

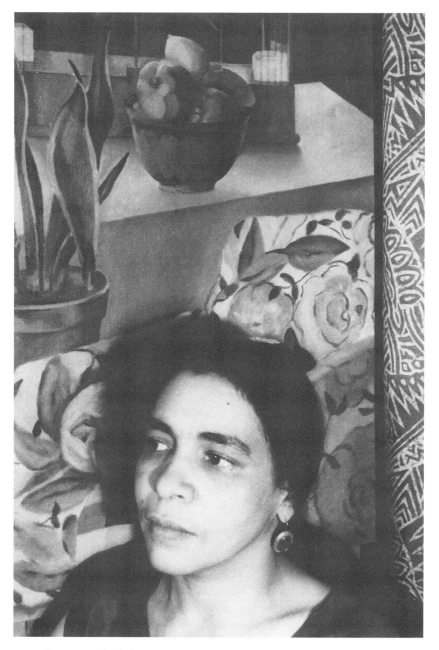

21. *Nella Larsen, back from Europe, March 26, 1932. Photo by Carl Van Vechten. Yale Collection of American Literature, Beinecke Rare Book and Manuscript Library, Yale University. Reproduced by permission of the Carl Van Vechten Trust.*

22. Sidney Peterson, Nella Larsen, and Dorothy Peterson, in Carl Van Vechten's apartment, March 26, 1932. Photo by Carl Van Vechten. Yale Collection of American Literature, Beinecke Rare Book and Manuscript Library, Yale University. Reproduced by permission of the Carl Van Vechten Trust.

However, she really plans leaving for Nashville next week, so you will be seeing her quite soon. Do drop her a line in the mean time for her illness has left her quite depressed. Perhaps if you let her know that you, at least, were looking forward to her visit, it would provide the impetus for a definite date for her departure, as in her present state she seems inclined to put it off from day to day until she regains her strength.[9]

Nella's letters to others at this time, however, make no mention of illness. What chiefly kept her in New York was the thought of a living nightmare in Nashville that she was not ready to enter.

On March 26, she sat for a series of photographs Van Vechten took of her, Dorothy, and Sidney individually and as a group. A couple of days later, apparently while she was at his apartment, Carl gave her a copy of his latest book, an anthology of previously published essays entitled *Sacred and Profane Memories.* "It is a particularly delightful volume for me to have just now when I am away from my books and have been so long denied the pleasure of looking into them when and where I wished."[10] By the tenth of April she had received the photo-graphs Carl had taken. Van Vechten feared she would be disappointed, but if she was, she did not let on: "From your letter I got the idea you are not awfully pleased with them. Why? I think they are very unusual and extraordinarily in-teresting. And they are so like me. The group pictures are charming. And Sid-ney's are quite wonderful. But I am afraid that—though they are more beautiful —I don't like Dorothy's as much as I do my own."[11] In truth, the portraits are peculiar; the angle is odd and the busy background nearly overwhelms the sub-ject, while the light throws a heavy shadow from Larsen's face and shoulders against the post-Impressionist painting that dominates the frame. Nella herself looks pensive, attractive, and still several years younger than her actual age of nearly forty-one.

On the thirteenth, Fania and Carl gave a birthday dinner for her, cake and all —as they had done in years past. "It meant a great deal to me, more this year than ever. And please thank Edith [Ramsey, the cook] for the nice dinner and beautiful cake—I really must learn her surname." She renewed her acquaintance with Hunter Stagg, who was up from Richmond—"not so handsome as I re-membered him," she admitted, "but infinitely more charming."[12] She had yet to reciprocate their frequent hospitality because she found her sparsely furnished apartment "so bleak and small and depressing. I hate having people see it." She was reading Mabel Dodge Luhan's *Lorenzo in Taos* (an account of D. H. Law-rence's sojourn in New Mexico) at Carl's insistence, and it was making her "a bit woozy in the head. Can't make out if it's D.H. or Mrs. Luhan, or myself. But it is rather an amazing book."[13]

Other things were weighing more heavily on her mind, however. Possibly prompted by a letter from Grace shortly after Dorothy's letter to Nashville, she had finally made arrangements to take a train to Cleveland and then hazard an airplane to Nashville. The flight would cut her travel time from thirty-six hours to eighteen, for only five dollars more in ticket fare. Costing no more than she would spend on meals if she took a train the whole way (as she told Carl and Fania), it also avoided the insult and injury of Jim Crow accommodations (something she did not mention).[14]

Finally she left, in the first week of May, arriving as the dogwoods and azaleas were shedding their petals and the rhododendrons were blooming. One could not but appreciate the beauty of a middle Tennessee spring. On the fourteenth of May, she wrote Carl with apparent cheer: "Well here I am, and have been for a week. And it really is rather exciting, weather, people, and country." Grace and Jim Johnson had taken her under their wing.

Already, Grace had escorted her on a "Southern" adventure in the small city

23. *James Weldon and Grace Nail Johnson in Carl Van Vechten's apartment, 1931. Photo by Carl Van Vechten. Photographs and Prints Division, Schomburg Center for Research in Black Culture, The New York Public Library, Astor, Lenox and Tilden Foundations. Reproduced by permission of the Carl Van Vechten Trust.*

of Murfreesboro, between Nashville and Chattanooga: "You will be amused that I who have never tried this much discussed 'passing' stunt have waited until I reached the deep south to put it over. Grace Johnson and I drove about fifty miles south of here the other day and then walked into the best restaurant in a rather conservative town . . . and demanded lunch and got it, plus all the service in the world and an invitation to return. Everybody here seems to think that quite a stunt. Jim told me to be sure to tell you."[15] Indeed, it is hard to imagine how Larsen pulled it off, unless she used some of her newly acquired Spanish to pass as a "white" foreigner.

The Johnsons seemed happy and well settled in their newly built Cape Cod–style home. With them, and with Charles S. Johnson running the Sociology Department, the Negro Renaissance had taken root at Fisk. The new university library, opened just after Larsen had gone abroad, now graced the center of the campus, and held a special "Negro" collection built up by Arthur Schomburg himself, who had just returned to New York after a year in residence. Aaron Douglas' murals of black history covered the high walls of the third-floor reading room. Roland Hayes had also been on campus, and from there he had gone down to Georgia to see the man who had once owned his mother. Finding the old slaveholder and his wife sick and poor and about to lose all that was left of the plantation, the house in which they were living, Hayes "did a very ironical thing," as Nella pointed out. "Like the heroes in all the stories he kept the mor[t]gage from being foreclosed and did all the other proper things."[16] The New South had plenty of good stories yet to be told, as the Agrarians at Vanderbilt were fond of insisting, though some of the best were beyond their ken.

Jim Johnson, the first African American to hold a professorship in Creative Writing (the Spence Chair at Fisk), was teaching a course on recent black literature, and almost immediately asked Nella to talk to his students. "Jim's class is interesting and very much alive," she told Carl. "I visited twice and made a pretty bad speech on one occasion."[17] Her reports to Elizabeth Hull were even more upbeat, as Elizabeth informed Grace: "Nella says Jim's course is great and inspiring. I would love to hear the lectures. I wish I could come down next winter for a little while. It sounds like such an interesting place."[18]

President Jones was urging Nella to live in Nashville at least part of each year, and offered "to build the kind of house I want, but I haven't made up my mind about it. There seems to be a lot of gossip floating about. But then, there's always gossip everywhere."[19] She was barely letting on to the extent of her distress. In this case, the gossip was devastating.

Elmer's relationship with Ethel Gilbert was so well known it would hardly qualify as an open secret. He escorted her regularly to college functions and wrote letters to her daily when she was out of town, typed by his student secretary.[20] Neither Elmer nor Ethel was inclined to hide the relationship on campus, although they avoided open displays of affection. In mid-April, President Jones had called Gilbert to his office for a long talk, leading to "an opening up of all the rumors regarding her reputed lack of loyalty to the administration, her associations with Dr. Imes, etc.," as Jones wrote trustee Paul Cravath.[21] Believing in frankness and honesty, she resented suggestions that she should keep up "appearances." Moreover, she was tired of spending so much time on the road and wanted a regular home at Fisk, "and free evenings where she can read, entertain, etc." In short, she wanted to settle down near Elmer and her beloved students.

Cravath, the chairman of the board, was in her corner; she was practically irreplaceable and her dedication to the institution unsurpassable. Cravath himself had advised her "to press the matter" of having a house or nice apartment for 1932–1933 and had even offered to help furnish the house. Jones, however, resisted the idea of providing homes for "divided families," to which Gilbert protested: "We have 'undivided families' on the campus who would not in a thousand years provide the kind of center for students you so much desire on the campus. This is my home and these students represent to me my work, my children, my religion, all of my earthly ambition. I want a way to serve them without killing me. I think I have been patient and believe that I am next in line."[22]

Indeed, her imagined floor plan included one enormous room in the downstairs that could accommodate up to fifty students at a time, with a large informal dining table and chairs at one end for quiet study and group meals. "My frame of mind isn't always pleasant when I give every waking moment to Fisk, use every ounce of energy and all the ingenuity I have to serve Fisk's interests and see everywhere the comfort go to newer comers."[23] It is clear that the rumors of her affair with Elmer had done nothing to reduce her popularity with the students. And she was planning to stay in Nashville over the summer. In contrast, Nella was leaving behind an esteemed place in the cosmopolitan world of high bohemia and returning to the scene of humiliations past and present. Her correspondence scarcely hints of her distress. But the drama of a classic love triangle had reached its third act, in which, from the campus point of view, she was destined to play the villain.

She had not been at Fisk more than two weeks when Elmer cabled Carl in desperation: "Please wire convenient telephone apartment this or tomorrow evening."[24] There is little question that the call had to do with Nella. Less than two weeks later she was back in New York. In mid-June, Elmer would thank Carl for "listening so patiently to my telephone talk last May." Nella, he confessed, "has the most ungodly ability to keep me in an unpleasant stew, which can only end in further estrangement. However she considers that she has the whip hand and thinks that this is what she wants."[25] She still loved Elmer and could not bear the thought of having lost his heart to Ethel Gilbert; but knowing the power his interracial affair had given her, she was going to make him pay. There was little that he could do about it. By now she seems to have agreed to the house, but she would maintain a residence in New York until it was done, and she was planning on a trip abroad.

Back in New York for the summer, while Elmer was mostly in Ann Arbor, Larsen attempted to keep up a semblance of her usual New York routine, but her behavior was getting erratic. On the twenty-fifth of July, she renewed her passport.[26] Dorothy, now back in her apartment on Second Avenue, got out of school at the end of June. Vi Stoner, who had been away, was back in town and lobbying to move in with her, and Dorothy Harris Wolfe was also in town. Elizabeth and Jim Hull, their marriage already in trouble, had moved out to a farm in Pomfret, Connecticut, but still came into the city now and then. Jim's first book, for children, came out in August, and Nella started "going to all the libraries" and talking it up to the children's librarians.[27]

In mid-July, Van Vechten had Nella, Dorothy, and several others sit for him again—Nella on the eleventh. In this series of photos, Larsen looks more remote than ever, even when staring straight into the camera. She wears a flower-print dress with a low neckline and a pair of simple earrings—no necklace. Without the hint of a smile, or any attempt at "prettiness," she gives nothing away. Her hair, suddenly very thin, is drawn back over her ears in what must be a tight bun, close to the skull. The mouth is solemn and the large dark eyes, under extremely thick black brows, are ringed with shadow. Much less attractive, in a conventional sense, than any of the early photographs that have surfaced, these images are nevertheless distinctly haunting.

Larsen said she loved them. "The more I look at the pictures the more I like them. Everyone who has seen them thinks they are simply amazing. I took them to Dorothys that very night, I was so crazy about them. She and Grace Valentine —who was here just for a minute—both wanted one of Va:20—the one Donald likes. I think—perhaps—it's the one I like best also. . . . I am certain I never had had any pictures half so lovely or so interesting."[28] In the one her friends preferred, her bare head is half-turned to the left; her eyes glance yet further left, drawing attention to the contrast between the whites of her large eyes and the broad black brows that curve sharply down to parallel the corner of the eye. Whatever she is looking at evokes neither pleasure nor excitement but a sort of calm, melancholy curiosity. In another portrait she looks down into the camera, hat on, with an unreadable expression, self-possessed, apart.

By now the new home in Nashville was nearly finished—"the most attractive house that has yet been built on campus," President Jones boasted to Chairman Cravath—and it was time for the lady of the house to take possession.[29] It was (and is) a handsome two-story Tudor-style home with a gray stone-and-stucco exterior on Morena Street, near the southwest corner of the campus, about a block from the Johnsons' house and close to Elmer's classrooms and lab. A pretty tree-lined walk led to the front door. Inside was a slate-tiled entryway leading to a comfortable living room with a fireplace at one end and a small library in one corner. Off the living room, through French doors, one entered the dining room, which connected in turn with the spacious kitchen and breakfast room. Mahogany trim and shelves through much of the ground floor contributed to its soft elegance, while the kitchen, with bright red walls and black trim (at Nella's request), suggested an artistic temperament, a flare for dramatic

24. Nella Larsen, April 17, 1932. Photo by Carl Van Vechten. Yale Collection of American Literature, Beinecke Rare Book and Manuscript Library, Yale University. Reproduced by permission of the Carl Van Vechten Trust.

25. *Professor Elmer S. Imes, 1930s. Photographer unknown. Fisk University Archives, Nashville, Tennessee.*

statement.[30] Elmer had designed the second floor so that he and Nella could live separate lives, although he also had in mind the possibility of his mother coming for long visits. The stairwell separated the master suite, with its own bathroom and study, from two other bedrooms, which shared a bath.[31]

By Columbus Day, Nella was in residence. She drove to Nashville with a young white friend named Tom Mabry, a handsome, thirty-year-old aspiring writer and literary scholar from Clarksville, Tennessee, who was trying to get a job at Fisk and to work with James Weldon Johnson. The Johnsons had hosted him at their place in Great Barrington, Massachusetts, earlier in the season.[32] They may have been partially responsible for hooking Larsen up with him, knowing that both were going to Nashville at about the same time. A mutual friend years later remembered Mabry and Larsen telling him about how, along the way between New York and Nashville, Larsen passed as white whenever they stopped at a hotel, despite the fact that Nella was, as the friend put it, "rather dark for success at that."[33] In the 1930s, before the advent of interstate highways, it took several days to drive from New York to Nashville, and the couple had

26. Central campus of Fisk University, 1931. The new library is the tall building in the center, and Bennett Hall is the low, square building to the left behind it. Jubilee Hall with its pointed cupola is in the distant background, just to the right of the library. The chapel is on the far right. Fisk University Archives, Nashville, Tennessee.

plenty of time to get to know each other better. Both were undergoing life-defining transformations.

An unusual young Southerner by any measure, Mabry soon became one of Larsen's closest friends at Fisk. They probably knew each other already, for Mabry also knew Carl Van Vechten, Muriel Draper, and Walter White, and he had worked for Alfred and Blanche Knopf in the mid-1920s.[34] Van Vechten, who photographed him several times, included him on his select list of "Famous Beauties of the XXth Century."[35] When in New York, Mabry often went to Draper's "salon" meetings. Early in the year he had written Draper about his disastrous attempt to host a "wild party" at his cabin near Nashville and introduce James Weldon Johnson and Langston Hughes (who was coming through town at the time) to Vanderbilt University's men and women of letters. "I nearly got thrown out of Vanderbilt and altogether there was a pretty mess. Johnson was amused at it and I was goddamn sore."[36] With the letter he had enclosed a now

409

infamous letter Allen Tate had written him, declining the invitation and strenuously objecting to the party itself. The problem came down to the prospect of
interracial marriage. "Johnson and Hughes are both very interesting writers,"
wrote Tate, "and as such I would like to meet them. This would be possible in
New York, London, or Paris, but here such a meeting would be ambiguous. My
theory of the racial relations is this: there should be no social intercourse between the races unless we are willing for that to lead to marriage. This interesting theory is not original with me. It was expounded to me by the colored man
who milks our cow. . . . These unfortunate limitations of the social system we
must expect to be removed only in heaven where there are no distinctions of
color and no marriage or giving in marriage."[37]

Deeply offended, Mabry shot a letter right back at Tate:

> Doubtless you would include yourself among those Southerners who could
> find it possible to sneak into the nauseous parties certain foolish people give
> in "New York, London, or Paris" where negroes are invited merely because it
> is considered smart. Such parties I do not attend. To do so would be a patron-
> age of the negro intolerable to any person having the least respect for him. . . .
> Whether or not marriage will ever be the "solution" I do not know. Certainly
> a more vicious assimilation is going on because of the attitudes of people like
> yourself. . . . To defend an economic and social domination upon the idea of
> respect for the subject race seems to me to be an inexcusable bungling of
> words and emotions.

Moreover, Tate's retreat to "art" and denial of "larger forces" was the self-indulgence of a frivolous and fatuous mind.[38] In his remarkable reply to Mabry's
striking rebuke, Tate admitted to "moral lassitude" and said he wanted to remain Mabry's friend.[39]

Draper had brought the case to the attention of Walter White and urged
Mabry to contact him for advice about his future. Then, in a phone conversation in August, White asked him for an account of his life and how he had
become interested in the "race problem." In a long and vivid letter, Mabry related that he had been born and raised in a conventional bourgeois family in
Clarksville, Tennessee, and had accepted the Southern axioms about the Negro's
place until he was sixteen, when, on his way to enter college at Harvard in 1921,
he stopped in Chicago and went to see *The Emperor Jones*. Upon taking his seat,
he discovered that he was next to two Negroes. "In horror and dismay," he ordered his seat changed. But he found himself enthralled by the play and the acting of Charles Gilpin in the title role. "Suddenly the absurdity of my position as
a human being flashed over me and I was profoundly ashamed. That was the

27. Thomas Dabney Mabry, early 1930s. Photo by Carl Van Vechten. Yale Collection of American Literature, Beinecke Rare Book and Manuscript Library, Yale University. Reproduced by permission of the Carl Van Vechten Trust.

beginning of the 'problem' for me. As years passed I thought about it more and more frequently, discovering gradually its sinister side as I had already discovered its ridiculous side." After graduating from Harvard in 1925, he lived part of each year in New York until his father died in 1929. He worked for two years in an art gallery owned by John Becker, specializing in modern French painting, but an interest in Negro education grew within him. In 1931, he reviewed *I'll Take My Stand,* the Agrarian cultural manifesto. "Suddenly [I] realized that what interested me most was the problem of Negro education in the South. I felt impelled to make a stand against the reactionary selfishness of the New Agrarians. I decided to return South." After winning a graduate fellowship at Vanderbilt, he settled in to the Agrarians' very home, and was working on his Master's degree when he learned that James Weldon Johnson had accepted the Spence Chair in Creative Writing at Fisk.

Having met Johnson in New York, he called on him in Nashville and invited him to the party that he had planned, to which he had also "naively" invited a number of his friends and professors at Vanderbilt, as well as President Jones of Fisk (who did in fact attend). Not only had Tate responded with the letter already mentioned, but he had sent copies of that letter to other members of the Vanderbilt faculty and even to a magazine editor in New York, for publication. Suddenly, Vanderbilt colleagues who had initially accepted invitations to the party, even knowing that Johnson would be there, informed Mabry that they would not come. The head of the English Department, a Southern "liberal" on race matters, called Mabry in to see him and asserted that "he could under no circumstances recommend me to a position anywhere if I persisted in having Mr. Johnson come to my house; . . . that of course Mr. Johnson should not be informed of the real reason for the party's being called off; that it would be a good thing if Mr. Johnson could be got to lecture to one of my courses in Vanderbilt."[40] Suddenly Mabry had found himself "the center of a whispering campaign." If Larsen felt isolated on the Fisk campus and under duress, Mabry felt rather the same in relation to "white" Nashville. In the coming months, they became much attached to each other.

In the summer of 1932, Dr. Jones of Fisk had offered Mabry a part-time assistantship under Johnson, to begin in January 1933, and the head of Vanderbilt's English Department offered him an assistantship as well. Neither paid enough to live on, and Mabry hoped to combine the two, but this went against the policy at Vanderbilt. When Jones tried to get Vanderbilt to make an exception, the department head refused and told Mabry, "Holding the ideas you do, you would have to go the whole way, in a social sense, if you do any work there." Maintaining social relationships with Negroes might destroy his usefulness to

Vanderbilt students, who would repudiate him. As a result, Mabry repudiated the fellowship and assistantship at Vanderbilt. He was left with no immediate alternative for supporting himself or developing an academic career. "I realize that by going to Fisk I am making an irrevocable step," he had written Walter White, "and I do not wish to do this from indignation merely, nor should I like to behead myself academically."[41]

White, who thought Mabry "one of the finest spirits I have met in a long time,"[42] immediately wrote Johnson about Mabry's situation. Johnson replied, from Great Barrington, "I have never met a finer young man than Mr. Mabry, and as a young Southerner, he is entirely unique in my experience. I have wanted, and still very much want him associated with me in my work at Fisk." But at present that did not seem best for Mabry. "I should like to be of some service in this matter," Johnson continued, "not only because of Mr. Mabry's sincerity and high courage, but also because of my deep personal regard for him."[43] White and Johnson began trying to gain Mabry a position at Smith College, whose president was an NAACP board member.

Mabry, however, did not want to go north if that meant giving up the opportunity to teach with Johnson at Fisk, and it turned out that Smith College, suffering from the Depression, could not afford to hire him. Ironically, even as he drove to Nashville with Nella Larsen, who was secretly concerned about her own future security, the post-Agrarian Tom Mabry was mentally preparing himself to go into farming to support himself. Without the Johnsons in Nashville to welcome her, Larsen was thrown largely on the companionship of Mabry and of Elmer, such as it was, and the hospitality of Esther Jones, the wife of Fisk's president and a friend of Grace Johnson's.

Ethel Gilbert had left campus for the time being and was living in the Woodstock Hotel in Manhattan, feeling "terribly lonely," according to Jones.[44] The Woodstock had been her New York hostelry for fifteen years, as she wrote Grace at the time, mainly because it was on top of Times Square and the theater district, next door to Town Hall, "and because Fisk students are treated when they come just as Mrs. Rockefeller and Mr. Cravath are." She had taken a room until Christmas and was catching up with some of her New York friends—not a few of whom were also Nella Larsen's good friends, such as Walter White and Frances Grant. On October 18, Gilbert wrote Grace Johnson that she had "had a grand old powwow with Sally Alexander last night"—the same woman who had twice nominated Nella for the Harmon awards.[45] It was particularly humiliating for Larsen that all her acquaintances would soon know, if they did not already, that Ethel Gilbert had to all intents and purposes wrested Elmer away from her, even as Nella went to live with him.

The Fisk community had been speculating from the time of Larsen's appearance on campus about whether her marriage would last. People had been freely discussing the affair between Elmer and Ethel for months; and, somewhat astonishingly, they largely approved of it. A reporter for the Baltimore *Afro-American* found, a year later, that although the top white administrators had wanted to end the affair and reunite Elmer with his wife, none of the blacks on campus had found the relationship scandalous, chiefly because of their high regard for Ethel Gilbert.

> Their hearts are full of warm admiration for this white woman. She was, they say, thoroughly genuine in spirit and in deed to the cause to which she had given herself. . . . "You can understand," explained an important member of the Fisk faculty, . . . "that a mixed faculty never establishes a complete rapport." He was grave as he spoke. "We look to one another and so do the whites. We take it for granted that the whites have an understanding in respect to social relationships. There is seldom one of these whites who is not discounted by us. Mrs. Gilbert was perhaps the one white member of the Fisk faculty who had the complete confidence of our members of the faculty and of the student body. It was not conceivable to us that she would ever betray us in word or deed or thought. We believed that she would rebuke any white member of the faculty who might attempt to whisper to her a private opinion concerning us."[46]

Gilbert was also extremely popular with students, to whom she often donated or "loaned" money out of her meager salary. She continually pressed the administration to allow more student self-government—an issue that was highly sensitive because of the predominance of whites in the higher administrative posts. Elmer, as well, was a highly regarded, even romantic figure on campus, and had often been seen escorting Gilbert. Thus, most people at Fisk had great respect not only for Elmer and Ethel individually, but for their relationship. And Nella was almost certainly aware of this.

President Jones, however, had pressed Elmer hard about bringing Nella to Fisk and reconciling with her. She arrived on campus, then, in an excruciating position relative to the racial politics of the campus community—and displaced, ironically enough, by a white woman. Esther Jones, who knew perfectly well about the relationship between Elmer and Ethel, and wanted it to end, took Nella under her wing in the Johnsons' absence.[47] They attended a recital together soon after Nella's arrival, and talked over an "unpleasant interlude" concerning a servant whom Esther had recommended to Grace Johnson and who had not worked out. "The whole matter is just between ourselves," Esther wrote to Grace, "for the girl has had the good sense to say *nothing* to me nor to N.L.I. She scarcely *could* you know under the circumstances. Neither have we said a word to her. All we wanted was simply your frank reaction—that we now have and the matter is definitely closed. I am glad, at least that you are not worrying about the future and feel sure you'll be able to locate someone who will have more—what do they call it?—'staying power'—isn't it?!"[48] In mid-November she wrote Grace again: "The Imes[es] are gradually getting settled in the little grey house with the red roof—I *do hope it works!*"[49]

Whatever problems Grace had with her student maid paled next to the ones that Nella Imes had with her student help. These were students who had already known and in some cases worked for Elmer, who knew of his affection for Ethel Gilbert and approved of it. Frankie Lea Houchins, Elmer's secretary during the time that Nella was in Mallorca, knew of his frustration over his wife's demands for money and silk stockings, and her comments to Thadious Davis decades later make no bones of the fact that she sympathized with him.[50]

When Nella came to settle into the new house, Houchins became her employee, and the tension between them must have been palpable. Houchins' comments about Larsen fifty years later are the most damning anyone ever made about her character, suggesting a haughty, racist, and extremely neurotic virago—not at all the person Dorothy Peterson, Sally Alexander, Dorothy Harris, and Carl Van Vechten knew, nor the person who could write such novels as *Quicksand* and *Passing.* In *Quicksand,* for example, one of Helga Crane's complaints against the dean of women at Naxos is that she forbids the students from wearing bright colors, while Helga believes that black people should wear yellow, red, and green, that the beauty of dark complexions is best brought out by colorful outfits; yet Houchins said Nella complained in Nashville about "'niggers' wearing loud colors."[51] In *Passing,* one of the things that irks Irene Redfield about Clare Kendry Bellew is her friendliness toward the domestic help, which blurs the social distinctions so important to Irene. Clare does not deal with Irene's maid as an "underling." Similarly, Nella herself occasionally visited socially with Marinoff and Van Vechten's black housekeeper, Meda Frye, in the late 1920s. But according to Houchins, Larsen, in Davis' words, "renamed each of her domestic helpers and called them versions of names that whites stereotypically associated with rural or working-class blacks." They retaliated by calling her "Nellie" behind her back.[52]

Not all of Larsen's domestic help, however, seems to have been so ill-treated. She made special provisions for the last maid she employed. Recommending her to the Johnsons, she wrote Grace, "I am quite certain I will not be here next year. And I know that you will be pleased with her. I shall pay her—say for a little vacation—when I go; so that she will not feel that she must set about making arrangements at once, but can wait to talk with you when you return."[53] She spoke so enthusiastically about a particular cook to Walter White that in 1934, when he was working with Poppy Cannon on a "Negro" cookbook, he wrote Nella to ask if she would talk to Cannon about the "marvelous cook" she knew in Nashville.[54]

Houchins also claimed that Larsen disliked both of the Johnsons, a charge that is inconsistent with all other evidence of her feelings toward Jim, at least, and inconsistent with what her closest friends of the time knew.[55] She may have felt guarded resentment toward Grace Johnson, who condescended to her and insisted on calling her "Nellie." Coming from one of black Harlem's "first families," Grace was used to being deferred to. However, Larsen always regarded James Weldon Johnson with great respect, as her correspondence not only with him but with her other friends reveals. She never forgot his birthday. Moreover, her two other closest friends at Fisk, Tom Mabry and Edward Donahoe, were fervent admirers of Johnson.

If the rest of the community at Fisk did not consider Larsen, as one of them put it, "as important as the other writers at Fisk,"[56] both Donahoe and Mabry—who were about a decade younger than Nella—recognized her as one of the chief novelists of the Negro Renaissance. Larsen knew Donahoe, like Mabry, already; he had worked at the *American Mercury* and in the editorial department of Knopf in the mid to late 1920s and knew many of her friends, including the Johnsons, Walter and Gladys White, Muriel Draper, Harry Block, Van Vechten, and Langston Hughes.[57] Touring Europe when Nella arrived with Mabry at Fisk in October, he wrote Grace Johnson, "How pleasant it will be to have the Imes[es] so near you in Nashville. Remember me to them when you see them. (I read *Quicksands* and found it very moving.)"[58] Donahoe came from a wealthy Oklahoma family and spent a lot of time knocking about between his home in Ponca City and New York, while trying to become a novelist. Van Vechten left a damning description of him as a preface to the correspondence he had saved from Donahoe: "The autobiography of a spoiled, self-indulgent boy . . . supported by his father, or his mother's money . . . often drunk, who believed he was writing a novel . . . which was to be dedicated to me. He had a certain wit, some charm, but no intelligence. I became acquainted with him through James Weldon Johnson and other Negro friends. He has always been staunchly pro-Negro, tho otherwise he is somewhat of a snob (of a peculiar kind)."[59] Written in 1954 to gloss letters chiefly of the late 1930s and 1940s, these comments do not necessarily reflect Van Vechten's attitude toward Donahoe in the early 1930s, but other details tend to support the description—particularly the tendency to

28. *Edward Donahoe, 1930s. Photo by Charles Henri Ford. Carl Van Vechten Papers, The New York Public Library, Astor, Lenox and Tilden Foundations.*

drunkenness, and his "pro-Negro" sensibility. Donahoe remained intensely interested in black culture and civil rights throughout the 1930s. Grace Johnson continued to correspond with Donahoe for many years. He had ended up in Nashville as a result of his friendship with Mabry. The two men had lived together early in 1932 in a log cabin at the Harpeth Hills Hunt Club in Brentwood, just outside Nashville, and together had hosted the interracial party that had so offended the Agrarians.

By early December President Jones, with the encouragement of Johnson, had worked out an arrangement by which Mabry would work three days a week, assisting Johnson in two English courses and taking charge of a class called "The Teaching of English"—all for what Jones termed "a very minute stipend."[60] Soon, however, another possibility opened up for Mabry at Fisk. Ethel Gilbert, still in New York, wrote Jones a letter of resignation on December 15. Though she had no job in sight and numerous obligations to others, she felt she must resign to save the university "further embarrassment. . . . The reason for my leaving as far as the general public is concerned can be that I cannot do road work and you must have some one who can. The less said by anyone the better. I want no defense of me from anybody, no apology for me. Making a living will be difficult at best."[61] Gilbert was still planning to travel with the choir during their winter tour, and Jones tried to talk her into withdrawing her resignation, or at least remaining technically on the staff until the end of the academic year; but in the meantime he began looking for a replacement, favoring an "able man" who would be willing to do the extensive "fieldwork" required to raise funds, chiefly in the North and East. The man he settled on was Tom Mabry.[62]

Throughout this period there is a long silence between Nella Larsen and her friends in New York. She sent a telegram to Van Vechten for Thanksgiving, but that was it. On the eleventh of February 1933, he wrote Grace Johnson, "I haven't heard one word from Nella Larsen Imes since she left N.Y. Does she want me to forget her?"[63] Larsen did not respond until after she had received a wire from him and Fania on her birthday in April, and even then it was by telegram nearly a month later. The long silence was a sign of depression. "Thanks to you and Fania for birthday telegram it was sweet of you to remember me I do mean to write but life is pretty terrible these days however I cant say I wasnt warned."[64] In June she wired them again, somewhat pathetically, three days before his birthday: "Dear Carl will you and Fania please come down and eat your birthday dinner with Jim at my house. I have two bedrooms and separate bath at your disposal and it would be great to see you."[65] Elmer, obviously, was out of town. And, unknown to Nella, Ethel Gilbert was pregnant.

Larsen gained some respite from her agony in her friendship with Edward Donahoe. They took a trip one day to Muscle Shoals, Alabama, the birthplace of blues musician and composer W. C. Handy: "We motored in my mother's majestic old Lincoln," Donahoe informed Langston Hughes much later. "Nella brought some sandwiches. I brought a quart of liquor and the set-ups for highballs. At Columbia Tennessee I had to 'pass' at a Negro restaurant. We had a very exciting trip, I assure you."[66] In an interview with Thadious Davis, John Becker told of a story Donahoe had related about an evening drive in Nashville when the police started following his car. "Larsen panicked and hid on the floor . . . In the excitement, she became hysterical."[67] After all, a black woman cruising around Nashville at night in the car of a white man could mean only one thing. And a scandal of that sort could irreparably damage her divorce case against Elmer.

Distraught as she was, Larsen nonetheless continued writing. Indeed, as Thadious Davis has pointed out, she seems to have spent most of her time at home. In a 1984 interview with Davis, Frankie Lea Houchins, who typed the novel-length manuscript "Fall Fever" for Larsen, gave the only description of it we have, saying that, in Davis' words, it "focused on a woman's deception by her husband and a sexually aggressive, menopausal woman's efforts to attract the other woman's husband to her bed." Houchins found the story, in her own word, "disgusting."[68] "Fall Fever" was actually a rewrite of the novel Larsen had written in Spain and France, then entitled "Mirage." The negative reader's report on that manuscript includes a plot summary that partly matches Houchins', although the reader found nothing "disgusting" about it. On the twenty-ninth of July, Nella wrote Dorothy Peterson: "Incidentally I've been doing some work on Mirage. I've never looked at it since we celebrated its departure to the U.S.A. in Paris. In May—or June, I gave it to Edward [Donahoe] to read. He said it was *terrible.* Early this month, I took a look at it, and I give you my word it was worse than that. It was appalling (two L's?) The stuff was good. But the *writing!* So I've done it all over, except that chapter which made you so ill, and the last. And I've changed the name to Fall Fever."[69]

Not only the novel's subject matter but also Larsen's manner of writing struck Frankie Lea Houchins as odd and contributed to the general impression that she was a madwoman, exacerbating her alienation.[70] She used long strips of lead rather than pen or pencil, which allowed her to write continuously without having to constantly sharpen a pencil or mar her manuscript with cross-outs and corrections that would make it difficult to proofread or type.

By the spring and summer of 1933, Larsen clearly was going over the edge. Elmer was the love of her life and, for more than a dozen years, her security. Now he had put her in a humiliating position, and divorce seemed inevitable. Yet if she accused him in court of adultery he would immediately lose his job and his career would be shattered. And she couldn't go anywhere else yet, because the divorce laws were such that if she left Tennessee, Elmer would gain the upper hand against her in court. She faced the possibility of being forced back into the job market in the depths of the Depression. Financial security aside, emotionally the situation was even worse. His betrayal of her in favor of a white woman who, like Elmer, "belonged" at Fisk raised all the old ghosts of her childhood. She had only Mabry and Donahoe, also outsiders. Most people on campus regarded her as a disturbed recluse, if not a freak.

Elmer's mother came to visit in the late spring and got so upset that she refused to return as long as Nella was in the house.[71] Houchins told Thadious Davis that Nella's "nerves were frazzled; she would pace the floor and pull out her hair by the handfuls. Afterwards, she refused to go out or be seen."[72] Once, when Houchins was driving her to town, "the car hit a bump crossing a railroad track" and Larsen "claimed I was trying to kill her, and insisted I take her back. She was a strange person."[73] In another incident, according to Houchins, Larsen "feigned suicide by cutting her wrists and smearing blood over the house."[74] In the spring of 1933, according to "official" reports on campus, she fell down some steps and broke her leg, but the story whispered about campus was that she had jumped from a window to do herself harm.[75] According to Houchins, who may well have contributed to the "whispering," she had jumped out of a first-floor window into an area where new landscaping work would have broken her fall, and it was all a ruse to build a divorce case against Elmer.[76]

Indeed, Larsen's main reason for remaining in Nashville at this point was to strengthen her position for alimony. The marriage was dead. In late June, Ethel Gilbert contacted officials at Fisk about withdrawing her resignation, despite the fact that when Jones had urged her to take her job back in February she had refused.[77] What had changed, it seems, is that she believed Nella would soon be out of the way.

The last ten days in June, Elmer went to Memphis to visit his mother, who was seriously ill, and tried to talk her into coming to Nashville, but she refused. Nella wrote Carl and Fania the twenty-sixth of June, "Do forgive me dearest, but life has been so damned complicated, and there was no point or reason writing to say that." She played down the true level of her distress, however.

> It is comfortable here and the house is rather nice. And it has been marvelous having the Johnsons for neighbors. We have had some gay times together.
>
> Pretty hot in these parts, but it could be worse. Certainly better—but one can't have everything. I do hate not seeing you again, but you both have all my love and all my good wishes and all my thanks for everything.[78]

She had written yet another novel, this time with her friend Edward Donahoe. "He did the men and I the women. It was rather fun to do." To Dorothy Peterson she wrote that the title was "Adrian and Evadne"; it was "a perfectly silly thing, and there are no characters in the book who have these names." They had sent it to Brandt and Brandt, Donahoe's agents. Moreover, she had pulled out the novel she had started when Dorothy was with her in Málaga, "and on going over it I think its mostly pretty good. We'll probably do it together, Edward the men and I the women. How do you like 'The Gilded Palm Tree' for a title?" Larsen felt she was "getting good on titles all of a sudden."[79]

She had never been so busy with her writing, no doubt because she had practically nothing else to do. After Jim's birthday and the start of vacation, the Johnsons went back East for the summer. Larsen's friendships with Donahoe and Tom Mabry had developed both personally and professionally—Donahoe had even brought his mother to visit her and Grace Johnson one evening at Nella's house—but neither of them was continuously in Nashville. Donahoe frequently spent time in New York or Oklahoma, and Mabry spent a fair amount of time on the road; over the summer vacation he went to Europe and did some hiking and climbing in the Tyrol.[80] She kept in contact with both men through correspondence.[81] Donahoe spent the months of July and August in Oklahoma. Larsen was not in a position to get into a serious romantic relationship, or at least a sexual relationship, with anyone as yet, because, if discovered, it would ruin her.

Besides, the heat was such that all one wanted to do was keep still and cool. Nashville was "hot as hell" in July, as she informed Dorothy—"good writing weather." In addition to finishing "Fall Fever," she had begun yet another novel of her own, with a working title of "The Wingless Hour," from a Swinburne stanza:

> Can ye beat off one wave with prayer
> Can ye move mountains? bid the flower
> Take flight and turn to a bird in the air?
> Can ye hold fast for shine or shower
> One wingless hour?[82]

Far from being discouraged about publishing opportunities, Larsen seems to have been rather upbeat. She was thinking of sending both of her single-authored novels to Brandt and Brandt, although in 1932 she had already promised Harry Block at Knopf that she would let him see her next two novels first.[83] Nothing, however, came of any of the projects she mentions at this time. Brandt and Brandt have no record or memory of having worked with her,[84] and the surviving editorial files for Knopf contain no readers' reports for novels after "Mirage."

In July, as usual, Elmer went to Ann Arbor for his summer research project. By now the divorce had been decided upon, for he was planning on vacating the house for good, and wanted his mother to move to Nashville about August first. He asked President Jones for an apartment at Fisk, to save expenses and make "easier housekeeping for Mother and me"—and to make it less likely that Nella would "return to upset things."[85] Nella was to take the furniture to New York with her. "She will of course delay as long as possible," he wrote to Jones. "In the meantime I am going to ask you to do a very generous thing by allowing me to have mother brought to the apartment which I have arranged to take furnished from Mrs. Gilbert. . . . Miss Van Buren will keep house for Mother and take care of her." He could not afford to continue paying for the house as well as the apartment, but Larsen was holding out on him: "Apparently the only hitch in the program of immediate and final separation is my inability to meet some rather ambitious financial demands. . . . She has agreed to leave on certain conditions which I couldn't quite meet but am trying to modify quietly and honorably."[86]

A week after Elmer wrote Jones, Nella wrote Dorothy:

> About the divorce.—I've about come to the conclusion to get it here. It can be done *discreetly* in *ten* days for a hundred dollars or so. Can you imagine that? There are about eight grounds for divorce in Tennessee—1 Adultery. 2 Desertion for two years. 3 Failure of wife to remove to the state if husband is living and working in Tennessee (Note these last two. It explains a lot, especially why I am here still after coming for a mere visit). 4 Habitual drunkenness contracted after marriage. 5 Non-support. 6 Commission of a crime. 7 Bigamy. 8 Cruelty.
>
>   As I see it you pays your money and you takes your choice. And that's that. Much simpler, don't you think, to get it here quietly, quickly, and cheaply, and be done with it? No waiting around to establish residence. No hanging about to have the decree made final. A session with a good lawyer, a morning in court. And then finis![87]

Larsen chose cruelty. Divorcing Elmer on the grounds of adultery could imperil his career and deprive her of future support.[88]

Larsen stayed on alone in Nashville through the month of August, perhaps trying to force Elmer to kick her out, which would aid her court case. Since most of her friends were gone, she made her old nursing colleague from Lincoln, Lucile Miller, her confidante. Miller was Grace Johnson's dearest friend and had moved to Nashville with the Johnsons. She had not gone East with them that summer, however, apparently because of illness. She was on a liquid diet at the Meharry Medical College hospital—a black institution right next to the Fisk campus—where Larsen visited her regularly. "Yes," Esther Jones wrote Grace in mid-August, "N.L.I. has quite made Miss Miller her confidante recently and has I am sure been very kind to her.—As Miss M. certainly has also been to N. I fear N. however, as she can, has—well—you know her so I won't elaborate!!"[89]

At about the same time, Larsen herself wrote Grace, mainly to update her on Lucile's condition, which was "a great deal better" than when the Johnsons had left.

> Everyone has been very kind and she has had the very best of attention. Miss Little has seen to that, and has proved herself a real friend, sympathetic and understanding, as well as a very efficient administrator. One never knows, does one? when one is going to meet and need the people one meets so casually along the road of life. . . . She has lovely flowers from almost everyone on the campus, and she has had no opportunity to become blue or lonesome. I think, too, that she has made some pleasant friends among the members of the staff. Nice for her during the coming school year.[90]

Larsen, silent about her own troubles, was also looking after the Johnsons' house while mentally preparing to leave her own.

On the thirtieth of August, the marriage ended in the first circuit court of Davidson County, Tennessee, "it appearing to the court that the defendant has been guilty of such cruel and inhuman conduct towards complainant as renders it unsafe and improper for her to cohabit with him and be under his dominion and control, and that he has offered such indignities to her person as to render her condition intolerable and thereby forced her to withdraw and that he has abandoned the complainant and turned her out of doors and refused and neglected to provide for her." One can imagine Elmer's indignation while standing to hear Judge A. G. Rutherford speak the judgment. He had, however, already agreed on terms that would be very difficult for him. For the first year, Nella would get roughly half his annual salary in alimony—$375 immediately, and $175 a month through August of 1934. Thereafter he would have to pay her $150 a month. (His monthly salary at the time was about $375 per month.) She would get all the furniture she wanted out of the house, and he would pay to pack it, store it, and ship it to New York, in addition to paying all court costs and her attorney's fees.[91]

To Elmer, it seemed a bitter harvest, but at last he was free. And he had Ethel. Nella was all alone. With a shrug of the shoulders and numbness in her heart, she went to see old friends in Chicago.

TWENTY-ONE

Letting Go:
1933–1937

L ARSEN remained in Nashville four or five days packing and settling her affairs, and then slipped out of town. She told no one on campus about the divorce except Tom Mabry—not even Lucile Miller, who had known of her intentions.[1] Arriving in Chicago on the third of September, she stopped for at least a week with her old friends the Mayos, now living within a few blocks of the State Street address at which Larsen had spent some of her youth. In the depths of the Depression and suffering a late heat wave, the city was nonetheless bursting with visitors to the World's Fair. Nella had "business affairs" of an undisclosed nature to settle in Chicago; whatever they were, they required money, for she believed that after taking care of them she would have "a few pennies" left from Elmer's initial alimony payment that she planned to put into an annuity "for safety's sake."[2]

Putting on a brave face, Larsen met a series of old acquaintances in Chicago, mainly people she had met in New York and who were in town for the fair, including Dorothy Harris' parents and sister.[3] Between the heat and crowds, the World's Fair was difficult enough to enjoy, but it was also "just about as boring as the Paris Colonial Exposition. I said then I would never go inside one of the things again. Well, I did. And it was exactly the same."[4]

On the sixth of September she wrote Dorothy Peterson: "I divorced Elmer last Wednesday very easily quickly and quietly. He is getting married tomorrow in Wellington Ohio. The new Mrs. Imes (or shall I say the second) will live in the North while he works in the South. It wont be so much different from last year. She was on [the] road a great deal and he was always away meeting her places. So much for that!"[5]

Though putting on a show of indifference, Larsen was far from being able to put the marriage behind her even in the familiar landscape of childhood. She could only try to distract herself with other things. Toward the end of the letter she came back to a painful admission: "There is nothing else to tell. Oh! Yes! Elmer expects to be a father along in February or March of next year. Isnt that swell!"[6] Actually, Elmer and Ethel Gilbert never did marry, officially, and the child must have miscarried or been given up for adoption.

Larsen may have been thinking that she herself would remarry before long. She wrote Dorothy that she had not "decided anything about my name yet. I wonder if there is much use in changing it back and then changing it again." She may not have had anyone in particular in mind, but Edward Donahoe was a possible prospect, and Nella was very attracted to Tom Mabry.

Larsen returned to New York about the thirteenth of September. It is not clear where she initially went to stay—possibly with Dorothy—but she had apparently long since given up the apartment on Eleventh Street.[7] By the beginning of December, she was giving her mailing address as the Bordentown Manual Training School, where the Valentines and Frances Grant could keep her company, so she may have gone there until she could find a place of her own in the city. Soon she settled in at 320 Second Avenue, apparently taking over Dorothy's apartment.[8]

A half-block from Stuyvesant Park in the comparative calm of the East Village, it was a typical four-story apartment building in a middle-class neighborhood now dominated by hospitals. Dorothy was back in Brooklyn at 380 Monroe Street and redecorating her living quarters, which constituted practically a separate apartment.[9]

After all her domestic turbulence and alienation at Fisk, Nella was glad to reestablish contact with her network of New York acquaintances—particularly those who were closer to her than to Elmer. She had the additional excitement of male friends such as Tom Mabry and Edward Donahoe competing for her affections, now that her marriage was over.

When James Weldon Johnson's autobiography *Along This Way* came out, Nella and Dorothy sent a joint telegram to him at Fisk: "Dear Jim you are the man of the hour here. We have been dancing in the streets with pride because of you Terribly flattering to be able to say that we know you well. . . . But honestly its a grand book Love to you and Grace."[10] He responded immediately, asking them to send him "any comments about *Along This Way* that you may come across."[11]

On October 7 one of the major black newspapers of the Eastern Seaboard, the Baltimore *Afro-American*, which had been taking a bead on Fisk, carried the headline "New York Novelist Divorces Fisk Professor." On the first page above the fold appeared one of James Allen's photographs of Larsen, head bowed, with the caption "Broke Leg—Now She's Divorced." A series of subheads highlighted Larsen's purported "jump" from a window and the resignation of her husband's

29. 320 Second Avenue (center), New York City, circa 1941. Larsen moved here after her divorce in 1933. Dorothy Peterson had an apartment in the same building in the late 1920s and early 1930s, which Elizabeth Shaffer sublet in 1931–1932. "Tax" Department Photo Collection, Courtesy New York City Municipal Archives.

"friendly comforter." The article baldly exploited the scandal of the Imes divorce, based chiefly on rumors at Fisk. "Last spring the campus was startled by the story that Mrs. Imes had fallen down the steps and broken her leg. But the story that was whispered was that she had jumped or had fallen out of a window and done herself bodily harm." The article later mentions that Larsen "spent the winter of 1931 with Dorothy Peterson, New York school teacher, in La

Palma, Majorca. . . . She was then said to be working on a novel which she termed 'Mirage.'"[12] The partly mangled yet in some respects very precise facts seem to indicate that the source of the story was close to the couple, quite probably one of the students who worked for the Imeses.

Not long after, a staff reporter for the Associated Negro Press called to interview Larsen in New York to learn more about the scandal. Unable to avoid the publicity, she agreed to talk, but remained reticent and diplomatic, minimizing her personal loss and refusing to indict either Elmer or Ethel Gilbert. The article appeared October 21 in the *Afro-American* with the headline "Love Triangle behind Fisk Univ. Divorce." It went into much greater detail about the relationship between Elmer and Ethel Gilbert than the report of October 7: "For over a year now the Fisk University community has freely discussed a love affair between Mrs. Gilbert and Professor Imes, but none of them thinks it was scandalous."[13] In contrast to the usual attitude toward interracial affairs, the campus community had warmly supported the relationship. The key to this anomaly was the extraordinary regard in which the students and black faculty had held Ethel Gilbert well before Elmer's arrival on campus, and their high regard for him as well.

The reporter waxed melodramatic in reporting Gilbert's devotion to the campus and students: "She had given not only all of herself, but all of her goods, to help 'the poor.' Her salary checks went to indigent students in the form of 'loans.'" Anecdotes of Gilbert's generosity concluded with the assertion that "the students of Fisk lost when Mrs. Gilbert lost the means to her check. And when the last one came, she did not have money enough to get away. 'Won't you buy some of my furniture?' she asked a colored friend. She was nearly penniless."[14] In contrast, as one of the boldface headings pointed out, Mrs. Imes would receive $150 per month from her ex-husband—close to a schoolteacher's full-time salary. And this at a time when many black schoolteachers, not to mention doctors, druggists, and lawyers, could not find work.

Mrs. Imes's "reticence" stood in contrast to Gilbert's martyrdom, although Nella had comported herself with remarkable self-possession in response to the reporter's prying questions.

Today, even though she has lost her husband, the celebrated novelist holds no rancor against either party. "Love is that way."

"There may be two or even three sides in this matter," states Mrs. Imes, "but I am not interested in sides. Important to me, was getting the divorce—the situation demanded it, and the exercise of care lest imprudent tongues speculate on the situation to the discredit and the injury of the university."

"We parted quite amiably," she says earnestly, "and I should be surprised to learn that Dr. Imes had subsequently made any unflattering allegations."

In a period of musing, the novelist admits that she had lost something, and that her life has been disrupted, perhaps because of "weakness" and "shifti-ness."[15]

The article ended with the unflattering repetition of the story that she had at one point "jumped from a window and injured herself," which had been passed off by the administration as a fall down some stairs. Sympathizing with the black students and faculty, the reporter lamented the loss of Gilbert to the school, and blamed it, implicitly, on the mostly white administration's insistence that Elmer's wife settle on campus.

On the very day that Larsen was absorbing the impact of the article, she helped celebrate Carl and Fania's nineteenth wedding anniversary in a party at their apartment. "She is looking well," Carl assured Jim Johnson.[16] Inside, she was aching. "Yesterday I saw Nella from lunch on until midnight," Elizabeth Hull, also recently divorced, wrote Grace Johnson three weeks later. "We and Malú [wife of Harry Block] had lunch, then Nella and I spent the afternoon together, had dinner together and then went to Carl's in the evening. Both Nella and I are ready for any insane asylum that will take us in. Grace, what do two gals do that are in love? I thought cold reason and all that might get me over it, but it doesnt and I am in love with that old man of mine. . . . Aren't people, especially love sick people, messes?"[17]

Larsen did have some distractions from her love sickness. Walter White had recruited her to an organization he had founded in response to a renewed wave of lynchings. The lynching of two white men in San Jose, followed by the California governor's public approval of the action, created a furor that White sought to exploit and brought valuable allies to the NAACP's longstanding campaign to secure national legislation. On December fourth, the Independent Writers' Committee against Lynching—independent, that is, of the Communist Party, which was wrangling with the NAACP over the defense of the Scottsboro Boys—met for the first time at the NAACP offices in Harlem, and Larsen was one of ninety-seven people invited. She was named assistant secretary (under Suzanne LaFollette, the titular secretary), while Harry Hansen, the well-known columnist and critic, took the post of chairman. In their first public actions they sent telegrams calling on President Roosevelt to speak out against the "wave of lynchings and mob violence now sweeping the country" and assailing the governor of California for approving of the recent mob action in his state; they followed up with a news release that was picked up by the New York Times the day after the meeting. More than eighty writers, journalists, editors, and publishers —mostly associated with the Negro Renaissance of the Twenties—signed the telegrams.[18]

The group's larger aim was passage of federal legislation against lynching. The central committee, to which Larsen belonged, supplied writers with information to raise awareness and nurture interest, soon reflected in articles, fiction, plays, and artworks that appeared throughout the mid-1930s.[19] Like the International Labor Defense, the Writers' League against Lynching exemplifies how, contrary to common wisdom, networks formed in the 1920s in connection with the Negro Renaissance continued functioning well into the 1930s, often to support legal, social, and political activism.

Most of Larsen's acquaintances remained intensely interested in and fairly upbeat about what they saw as continued advances in black cultural representation, even as African Americans were suffering from the effects of the Great Depression. The economic situation of most African Americans was indeed dire, as Gwendolyn Bennett pointed out in an article of March 12. "The one bright spot in the otherwise depressing picture is the situation of the nurse"—a profession to which Larsen could always return if necessary.[20]

Despite the extreme destitution in Harlem particularly, the Depression left Larsen and some others of her group relatively untouched. Several of her black friends in the performing arts were remarkably successful in the mid-1930s, and Dorothy Peterson remained safely employed in the public schools, in addition to having the family home in Brooklyn mortgage-free. Walter Winchell reported that Ethel Waters, then starring on Broadway in the topical revue *As Thousands Cheer,* enjoyed the highest income of any star on the American stage.[21] The critic Brooks Atkinson raved: "Ethel Waters takes full control of the audience and the show whenever she appears. Her abandon to the ruddy tune of 'Heat Wave Hits New York,' her rowdy comedy as the wife of a stage-struck 'Green Pastures' actor and her pathos in a deep-toned song about a lynching ['Suppertime'] give some notion of the broad range she can encompass in musical shows."[22] Equally spectacular and significant, to Larsen's circle, was the new opera *Four Saints in Three Acts.*

A "baroque fantasy" with a score by Virgil Thomson and libretto by Gertrude Stein, this avant-garde opera focused on the lives of seventeenth-century Spanish saints. Florine Stettheimer designed a bizarrely ethereal cellophane set and costumes with Baroque motifs. Thomson, meanwhile, won financial support through the circles surrounding Van Vechten and the salon of Kirk and Constance Austin, where Van Vechten, Marinoff, Edna Thomas, Muriel Draper, and others (possibly including Larsen) gathered in the early 1930s, often moving on to the Harlem nightclubs after their meetings.[23] During one of these outings, while watching a performance by Jimmie Daniels—a young singer, dancer, and nightclub host with whom Larsen was friendly—Thomson had gotten the idea of using an all-black cast for his opera, and a member of Edna Thomas' circle hooked him up with Eva Jessye's choral group in Harlem.[24]

By mid-December 1933, rehearsals had begun in the basement of St. Philip's Episcopal Church on 137th Street. Encouraged by a press agent, a sense of excitement grew throughout the winter. For the performers, the opera offered a departure from the musical comedy, vaudeville, church music, and nightclub acts to which they were normally limited. For the young actor and director John Houseman, it offered a career-defining introduction to theater production. And to the audience, it would offer rapture.

Larsen almost certainly missed the famous opening night at Hartford's Wadsworth Athenaeum—reports suggest that only whites were allowed in the audience, and a separate performance was subsequently put on for Hartford's black community—although she may have tuned in to the radio broadcast of the opening over WABC.[25] But she would not have missed the New York opening on February 20. The reviews of the Hartford performance had been ecstatic, and many of her friends had been present. Van Vechten, who had carried a typewriter to Hartford, could hardly contain himself. He wrote James Weldon Johnson, who was in Nashville, almost immediately.[26] In another letter published in the *New York Times* he called the performance "about as perfect as would seem humanly possible."[27] Walter White asked Du Bois if he would commission Carl to write a piece, with photos, for *The Crisis* when the show came to New York.[28] Most reports concluded that it was a historic theatrical event and not to be missed.

On February 20, packed with an integrated, 1,400-member audience of "quite unbearably dazzling intelligence" (according to a review in the *Herald Tribune*), the Forty-Fourth Street Theatre hosted the Manhattan premiere. It did not disappoint. The reporter for the *New York Age*, Vera E. Johns, termed it "rapturous entertainment to eye and ear. . . . I am not yet arrived at what seems to be thoughts deeper than the ocean and a century ahead of time, or is it a half million years back? All that now stands clearly before me is that Miss Stein conceived a beautiful poetic dream of art and with the aid of real artists like Virgil Thomson and Florine Stettheimer, she created it in living pictures for human eyes to see and human ears to hear." Whoever thought to use an all-Negro cast was a genius, Johns proudly continued, for "only our people could have so wholly thrown their very souls into those lines that one could swear they understood the meaning of them." Moreover, to her satisfaction the program and publicity had made no mention of the race of the players, comporting with the opera's use of colored artists for the first time in an "act for art's sake without prejudice to creed or color. . . . Gertrude Stein has laid a sane and solid foundation for the advancement of the Negro in art for art's sake—that universal art that is free and only bounded by the ability of the artist."[29]

The truth is that both Stein and Stettheimer had initially resisted the use of black performers because of the translucent costumes. Stein worried that the dark bodies would show through too boldly and suggest something erotic and "futuristic," while Stettheimer believed dark skin would clash with the color of the costumes; at one point she even suggested painting the singers' faces white. Thomson was also prepared to have the singers appear in whiteface if the "religious devotion of the public" was offended by the idea of Negroes playing the roles of saints. This proved not to be a problem, but at Florine Stettheimer's insistence, the performers wore white gloves.[30]

The night after the New York opening of *Four Saints* came the premiere of John Wesley's play *They Shall Not Die*, based on the Scottsboro case. The Scottsboro Boys were nine young blacks, ranging in age from twelve to twenty-one, who'd been accused of raping two white women in a freight car, and Wesley's work was a propaganda play intended to build sympathy for the defendants. It pilloried the NAACP and lauded the International Labor Defense, the Communist-affiliated group that had taken over the defense of the accused. Clearly, Broadway had not turned its back on the Negro. Between Waters' performance in *As Thousands Cheer* (featuring soon-to-be classics like "Suppertime" and "Heat Wave"), the ongoing tour of *The Green Pastures, Four Saints in Three Acts,* and *They Shall Not Die*, it seemed to Larsen and her friends that there was as much interest as ever in African American subjects and creativity. A new "Negro" play, *Stevedore*, starring Nella's friends Edna Thomas and Jack Carter, was also going into production under the auspices of the left-wing Theatre Union, a production company formed by an interracial renaissance-era group including the likes of Sherwood Anderson, Countee Cullen, Waldo Frank, Mary Heaton Vorse, Cleon Throckmorton, Elmer Rice, Stephen Vincent Benét, and Rose McClendon. Some of the scenes borrowed from reports of the 1919 race riots in Chicago and East St. Louis.[31] This is also when Zora Neale Hurston's first novel, *Jonah's Gourd Vine,* came out from Lippincott; and Langston Hughes's first short story collection, *The Ways of White Folks*, was in press at Knopf. About the same time, the black composer William Grant Still was awarded a Guggenheim Foundation grant. "There is very much more REAL SOLID evidence of a 'Negro Renaissance,'" Van Vechten trumpeted to Jim Johnson, "than there was in 1926–27."[32] Larsen was almost certainly continuing to

30. *Edna Thomas, June 18, 1932. Photo by Carl Van Vechten. Yale Collection of American Literature, Beinecke Rare Book and Manuscript Library, Yale University. Reproduced by permission of the Carl Van Vechten Trust.*

write and trying to place her work, but growing increasingly concerned at her lack of success.

She spent a good bit of her social life in Greenwich Village, where Elizabeth Hull lived and worked. Edna Thomas, whose stage career was finally beginning to blossom and who was widely admired by both black and white sophisticates, also lived in the Village, with both her husband Lloyd and her lover Olivia Wyndham, and was becoming one of Larsen's closest associates. By now Larsen was most widely known and referred to as "Nella Larsen," even by friends who had formerly called her Nella Imes.

Nella and Dorothy both came to know Mary McCarthy about this time. McCarthy, just twenty-one or twenty-two and recently graduated from Vassar, lived with her husband Harold Johnsrud, a left-wing actor and playwright, in an apartment on Beekman Place in the Village and was particularly friendly with Dorothy and Sidney Peterson. When Nella and Dorothy, and occasionally Sidney, came to visit, Mary and Harold would nervously usher them "past the elevator boys," worried about racial insults. "They were high up in the black bourgeoisie. Nella Larsen told stories that always contained the sentence 'And there I was in the fullest of full evening dress.'"[33] McCarthy seems to have become especially fond of the less affected and more securely elite Petersons, who were both living in Brooklyn at the time: "We liked them, not simply because they were black, and were proud of the friendship."[34]

Both Nella and Dorothy saw a good deal of Tom Mabry and Edward Donahoe when either or both of them were in town—Mabry keeping an apartment at 190 East End Avenue, on the Upper East Side, and Donahoe usually lodging at the Hotel Brevoort in the Village.[35] Donahoe was in town until February, just hanging out, while Mabry drove back and forth between Nashville and New York on Fisk fundraising business. Both men by now were fairly well integrated into Larsen's social circles—those surrounding Walter White, Van Vechten, Peterson, the Stettheimer sisters, and Muriel Draper.

Toward the end of February, Dorothy Peterson wrote Jean Toomer about a steamily developing relationship between Mabry, Donahoe, and Larsen, skillfully narrating it like a tale out of *The Decameron*.

> Having to amuse myself in my own way throughout this eternal wintry weather, I have developed a horrible habit of meddling in other people's affairs which turns out to be instructive and interesting. When I was young, and more or less charming my own life provided me with intrigue and excitement. But now gray hair and wrinkles have brought that to an end. But, on the other hand, a friend of mine whose name for present purposes shall be Capricetta becomes more charming and alluring as time passes and also more and more

involved in romantic friendships and love affairs. The present one concerns a feud between two handsome young men, friends, who came to her spiritual and mental rescue while she was suffering the harrowing experiences of pre-divorce proceedings in a little college town where all three of them seemed to be "culturally and intellectually marooned." Now that Capricetta is free of her husband and all three, re-encountering in New York, enjoy a great amount of freedom from the conventionality of the college campus where their friendship started, the question of sex has entered, and the two handsome young men find that they are in love with Capricetta. The young man who is rich loves her and wants her to marry him. The young man who is the more charming would like to have a temporary affair. Alas! she is quite mad about the charming one, although she leads the rich one on for obvious reasons. The rich man becomes, of course, very jealous. The charming one acts like a bastard. And then they dash about the country, the two men, from New York to Tennessee where the charming one works, and then to Oklahoma where the rich one lives, and then to New York—demanding explanations of each other and of her. Then they all run away from each other—then they all run after each other and the way it will end will be that she will be left entirely alone without money or love or them—and since the rich one is not completely stupid nor the charming one a complete knave the men will become friends and forgive each other, and poor Capricetta will find no consolation, until more intrigue turns up.[36]

On the rebound from the triangular relationship in which she had been so badly burned, Larsen was playing with fire—or flying into it.

Donahoe's and Mabry's romantic interests in Larsen may have been closely related to their prior interest in the cause of black civil rights; indeed, on racial issues they were more openly militant than she. The very day that Peterson wrote Toomer, Mabry wrote Ettie Stettheimer from Nashville in anger and despair about government abuse of farmers, profiteering by the Federal Housing Committee, the suffocating effects of segregation, and a recent lynching.[37]

Donahoe wrote Langston Hughes in March to congratulate him on recent stories published in *Esquire* and the *New Yorker*. Too many Negro writers, he believed, had been "conciliatory"; the bitter hatred for whites Hughes expressed in his stories provided an original departure.[38] He also scored Allen Tate's recent rantings in the *American Review* supporting segregation and white supremacy. Unfortunately, Donahoe's and Mabry's letters to Larsen do not survive, but this letter to Hughes indicates that Donahoe, who had left New York in early February, intended to return specifically for a party Dorothy Peterson would be giving in April.

Direct evidence of Larsen's doings after 1933 grows increasingly spotty, but it is clear that she remained closest to Peterson and Van Vechten, while her connections to Harlem as such diminished, perhaps because her Harlem friends had been closer to Elmer. When Walter White threw a party for his visiting sister, he invited Dorothy Peterson, but not Nella. Carl and Fania once again had Nella over for her birthday dinner on April 13. "I can't tell you how happy you made me last Friday night," she wrote them the following Wednesday. "It was the pleasantest birthday I have had for many a year—and I am glad that it happened to be this particular year."[39] When James Weldon Johnson fell gravely ill at Fisk in the early summer, Nella wrote to wish him well.[40] In addition to Van Vechten, Elizabeth Hull also remained very close to both Nella and Dorothy, and one can presume with some confidence that Nella visited Elizabeth at her small farm in Connecticut.

At some point in 1934, Larsen visited the midtown Madison Avenue art gallery of John Becker, Tom Mabry's former employer. Becker remembered the occasion years later: "I was busy and asked her to lunch the next day. Then when she left I turned to my secretary and said 'Now where can I take her?' I was told I was a damn fool, and that I should have thought of this first: the Ritz was suggested. But the Ritz was not my province. So I took Nella to Michel's, a speakeasy on 52nd Street. The following day Michel appeared in my gallery to admonish me not to repeat the performance. He had nothing against Negroes etc. but many southern customers etc."[41] The incident reminds us that Larsen's frequent social forays in "mixed" groups remained highly unusual and somewhat audacious in the larger scheme of things.

Donahoe remained a good friend, and almost certainly a romantic interest. Spending part of the summer in Michigan, he wrote Langston Hughes in August 1934 that he could be reached through Nella or Dorothy and related the tale of his and Nella's trip to Muscle Shoals of the year before.[42] One can't help reading his account of how he had passed for "colored" in a Negro restaurant as something of a boast, written to a man he wanted to impress with his racial progressivism. In the same letter he asked Hughes to write sometime about interracial relationships other than those based on cynicism or exploitation. Having earlier praised Hughes for some of his most incisive stories on whites' relations with blacks as they appeared in top magazines, now he had read them collected in *The Ways of White Folks,* just published by Knopf, and was aching to hear of some good white people—like, of course, himself. One of Allen Tate's protégés at Vanderbilt, reading Hughes's book, had pointed to the piece "Slave on the Block" to argue that Negroes obviously didn't care for people like Donahoe and Tom Mabry any more than white Southerners did. Constantly attacked even by Southern liberals, Donahoe argued, people like Tom and him should be acknowledged: "it isn't easy for such people in Nashville."[43] Indeed, Mabry had given up on Nashville and moved to New York about this time.[44]

In September the play *Judgment Day* opened at the Belasco Theatre, with Fania Marinoff in a key role; Nella and Dorothy sent a joint telegram from Brooklyn to reach her in her dressing room, presumably as they prepared to head to the theater themselves: "All our love and hopes and good wishes for a grand success."[45] The play, by Elmer Rice, was a courtroom drama in which several patriots in a southeastern European country go on trial for plotting to assassinate a fascist-style dictator, clearly based on Hitler and Mussolini. At the end, the judge shoots the dictator and then kills himself, setting off a counterrevolution. Critics had difficulty determining whether the show was intended as melodrama, lampoon, or burlesque, but agreed with Brooks Atkinson that "as a pyrotechnical opera singer Fania Marinoff introduces a flourish of good comedy in the second act."[46]

By early October, literary New York was abuzz with the news that Gertrude Stein would be visiting, in a celebrated tour of the United States largely planned by her chief promoter, Carl Van Vechten. She and her partner, Alice B. Toklas, arrived on October 24 and began a round of dinners and parties, often involving prominent African Americans, including Larsen and her friends. "Carl was giving us parties," Toklas would later write, "to meet his Negro friends, who somewhat scandalized me by their outspokenness."[47] On the tenth, while briefly in town, Carl invited Nella, and through her Dorothy and Sidney Peterson, to the party he had set for Sunday, November 18, shortly before Stein and Toklas would be pushing on to Chicago.[48] On the same day he wrote Stein, "The party for 9 P.M. November 18 is shaping magnificently. I hope you will have it happily with a spoon."[49] She responded, "We like New York best and New York is you, and that is that."[50] James Weldon Johnson, Walter White, and Beatrice Robinson-Wayne (who had played Saint Theresa in *Four Saints*) were among the other guests. Finally, Stein and Larsen had the chance to meet. The former still cherished Larsen's kind words about "Melanctha," but we have no record of how they got along, only Stein's more general reflection on the joyousness of the visit: "Carl what a good time we had in your New York, what a good time, there never was or has been such as you gave us, never ever in the whole wide world it was marvelous every moment, and I really cannot believe only it was all true . . . my dearest dear Carl we did have such a happy time I cannot tell it to you often enough and lots of love and all of our love and always all and our love, and love to Fania and remembrances to Edith and always all our love."[51] She was beginning to sound like Nella Larsen.

On the twenty-third of November, Carl had Nella over to sit for another se-

31. Nella Larsen, November 23, 1934. Photo by Carl Van Vechten. Yale Collection of American Literature, Beinecke Rare Book and Manuscript Library, Yale University. Reproduced by permission of the Carl Van Vechten Trust.

ries of portraits. Compared to the photographs of 1932, she seems to have aged considerably. Sporting a small derby-style hat and posed against a patterned backdrop suggesting mental vertigo, she appears to have put on weight; her face looks tired, even depressed.[52] One notices none of the theatrical affect of her earlier portraits, yet in the best of them she appears strong, self-contained.

There was plenty to be depressed about that winter. A growing sense of absolute desperation and slow-burning rage seemed to permeate Harlem. The renaissance seemed far off by now. In December, within four days of each other, two stars of the movement died: Wallace Thurman on Welfare Island, completely destitute, of tuberculosis and alcoholism; and Rudolph Fisher, Larsen's old friend, of intestinal cancer resulting from his work in radiology. It was also about this time, incidentally, that Larsen's mother and stepfather separated; but this did not bring Mary and Nella together again.

The Writers League against Lynching, in which Larsen continued to serve as assistant secretary, remained active; in January 1935 it sent telegrams signed by 150 people to President Franklin D. Roosevelt and U.S. Senator Huey Long protesting the lynching of Jerome Wilson in Louisiana. The signers included most of the writers connected with the Negro vogue of the Twenties: Sherwood Anderson, Stephen Vincent Benét, Heywood Broun, James Branch Cabell, Marc Connelly, Edna Ferber, DuBose Heyward, Fannie Hurst, Alfred Knopf, Sinclair Lewis, George Jean Nathan, Carl Van Vechten, Oswald Garrison Villard, and Zona Gale.[53] Simultaneously, led by Walter White, the group organized an explosive exhibit called "An Art Commentary on Lynching." The Jacques Seligmann Galleries agreed to host the show, but then got nervous and pulled out. This, of course, only raised the level of interest. Finally the Arthur U. Newton Galleries on East Fifty-Seventh Street signed on, and the exhibit opened on February 15, 1935, for a run of two weeks. It enjoyed a strong turnout, with considerable press coverage.[54]

The next word from Nella Larsen is a telegram she and Dorothy sent the Johnsons in late February, congratulating them on their anniversary: "Tonight we dined with Tennesseans one man a painter who had discovered Jim for himself with Gods Trombones asked if we knew Jim we looked at each other not only with pride but with shame realizing that February was at its end but please at this late date take our blessings and admiration and all of our love and take Elizabeths too who adores you both and will curse us if she finds we have not included her."[55]

Larsen continued to think of herself as a novelist, and Dorothy had a writing project in mind as well. She informed the son of the late Richard B. Harrison, who lived in Chicago, about her desire to write a biography of "de Lawd" of *The*

Green Pastures, listing James Weldon Johnson as a reference, as well as "Miss Nella Larsen, the novelist, author of Quicksand and Passing," who "has also read several of my unpublished manuscripts and will give you any further information that you may require."[56] Through 1935, Larsen's most intimate friends apparently remained Dorothy Peterson, Carl Van Vechten, and Elizabeth Hull. The paper trail virtually disappears after this, however; and it seems that by 1937 she practically stopped communicating with Van Vechten and Peterson.

The nature of Nella's relationship with Dorothy and Carl, and not coincidentally of Dorothy and Carl's relationship with each other, had been gradually shifting. Nella, after all, had been off the scene much of the time since 1930, involved in her own intrigues and corresponding rarely. In the year and a half she spent abroad, and then the year she spent at Fisk, she had had little contact with Van Vechten, rarely even writing him. During the same period, Dorothy and Carl grew closer to each other. Larsen had befriended Carl's niece Elizabeth Hull, but Elizabeth was always more intimate with Dorothy than with the secretive Nella Larsen, whom she liked but did not know as well.

Just as Dorothy had predicted, Larsen's relationships with Edward Donahoe and Tom Mabry ended sometime after the summer of 1934, probably in early 1935. Just as she had predicted, as well, Donahoe and Mabry remained good friends after splitting up with Nella.[57] In March, Mabry was named executive secretary of the Museum of Modern Art, where he would remain until 1939 — after that, moving to Kentucky to farm.[58] Again Larsen had lost out in a triangular relationship; and in some ways it must have felt as if the same thing was happening in her relationships with Carl and Dorothy. For the crisis of abandonment in relation to the two competing men in her life could only have been exacerbated by the sense that she was being displaced in the affections of her most devoted friends by those very friends. By 1940, Van Vechten was addressing Peterson with the moniker "Woojums," a term he reserved for only his very dearest woman friends, such as Gertrude Stein, Alice B. Toklas, and Aileen Pringle.

The correspondence between Dorothy, Nella, Carl, and Elizabeth Hull indicates that Dorothy at this time became closer to Carl than Nella was, and vice versa. Moreover, Donahoe became increasingly a part of the circle around Van Vechten and Muriel Draper (as he would write Grace Nail Johnson in the summer of 1938), just as Larsen removed herself from it.[59] Precisely at this time, Dorothy and Carl lost all contact with Nella; she shut them out of her life. Van Vechten was never able to figure out why, although he continued trying desperately to reestablish contact with Larsen right through the 1940s and 1950s, and met for lunch with Dorothy Peterson and Harold Jackman every year on the anniversary of the date he and Donald Angus had met them all at Dorothy's house in 1925. At these lunches, thoughts of their missing friend surely came up. Donald Angus told Bruce Kellner many years later that "nobody ever knew" why she had cut them off.[60]

The surviving correspondence between Van Vechten and Peterson does not say what happened; in fact, it is strangely silent on just this issue. They both felt almost simultaneously cut out of Larsen's life, and were clearly sorry about that and worried about her, but they felt they could do nothing about it. Larsen, who had learned early to fear intimacy and to expect rejection, had opened up to them as to no one else in her adult life, save, presumably, Elmer Imes. The fact that she abandoned them both simultaneously, while their own friendship intensified, holds the clue to what happened. She had grown emotionally dependent on each of them and now she felt threatened; they had grown more intimate with each other than with her. She felt vague premonitions. And so she walked out and closed the door, giving them up before they could, as she feared, give her up.

Since Dorothy Peterson and Carl Van Vechten played key roles in developing the archive of the Harlem Renaissance, this emotional drama inescapably shapes the mystery around the life of Nella Larsen. One of the last pieces of correspondence Nella wrote Carl was a small, plain white card dropped off at his apartment on his twenty-second wedding anniversary in 1936, reading simply "Love—Nella."

On the nineteenth of August, Elizabeth Hull wrote her uncle,

> I received a very queer letter from Nella, but maybe again the mails are at fault, although in this case I dont think so. She tells me in her letter she understands completely why I didnt help her out and that she should have learned you shouldnt ask friends for things and that although it has taken her such a long time to admit it she now feels she owes me an apology for writing that letter asking for help. She must have written the first letter to me in New York and I never got it. Frankly, I just think she didnt write it. I am so sure she did not that I have completely ignored the one I did get. What do you think? If I had ever been asked to help Nella in any way I would have done so. I tried all winter unsuccessfully to reach her, worried about her considerably, and did not hear from her at all. This mythical letter she refers to must have been sent to me in New York while I was still there. Knowing Nella I think it is silly to bring it all up, but will do so if you think I should.[61]

Clearly, by the late summer of 1936, Larsen seemed to her best friends to be losing her grip. At the same time, she had been strengthening other relationships in the sophisticated group of which Edna Thomas was a central figure.

This group included Edna's husband Lloyd, known chiefly as a nightclub manager; her lover Olivia Wyndham, an Englishwoman of noble birth; Fredi Washington, an African American singer, dancer, and actress so light-skinned she often had to wear makeup to play "Negro" roles; dancer and club host Jimmie Daniels; British editor, critic, and filmmaker Kenneth Macpherson, who was particularly tight with Daniels; and Andrew Meyer, a student of literature at New York University who worked on Wall Street.[62] Both Fredi Washington and Edna Thomas were in the midst of forming the Negro Actors Guild, founded in December 1937 to aid black entertainers and actors. Washington was the executive director and Thomas one of several vice presidents. (Others included Ethel Waters, Frank Wilson, Louis Armstrong, Duke Ellington, Paul Robeson, and James Weldon Johnson.)[63] Fredi (originally Freddie) Washington had begun her professional rise in the mid-1920s, often under the stage name "Edith Warren," when she stepped out from the Club Alabam Revue to be leading lady of *Black Boy* on Broadway, opposite Paul Robeson. Intellectually inclined, she surprised white critics and stagehands by reading *American Mercury* between acts—something considered out of character for a chorus girl.[64] She had played substantial roles in several of the celebrated "Negro" plays since. But in the new circle to which Larsen had gravitated, Edna Thomas was by all odds the most magnetic and extraordinary figure, one of the great personalities of the city—and of black performance history—who in the decades since has been all but forgotten.

Thomas was widely admired in both Harlem and Greenwich Village, considered by many a grand lady of the theater, although her opportunities had always been cruelly limited by her "color" (in fact, she was so light-skinned that, like Fredi, she was forced to wear tan makeup when she played "Negro" roles). She supported her husband Lloyd during the desperate Thirties, although they lived separate lives and Edna's true love was Olivia Wyndham, who lived with them.[65] The Thomases and Wyndham had moved in the mid-1930s from their apartment in Greenwich Village to 1890 Seventh Avenue, a middle-class address in Harlem, evidently because of Thomas' position in the Harlem unit of the Federal Theater Project. Both apartments were common gathering places for black and white intellectuals.

Born to a single mother in Virginia in 1886, Thomas had limited knowledge of her family. Her mother had been a twelve-year-old nursemaid in Virginia when she'd been raped by a white employer while she was caring for his three-year-old girl. A year after Edna's birth, her mother moved with her to Philadelphia and became established in a "respectable negro section" of the city, where a grandmother mainly cared for the little girl.[66] According to Edna, she was cru-

32. Two "Eddies": Edna Thomas and Edward Wasserman, at Wasserman's Port Washington cottage, July 1, 1936. Photographer unknown. Carl Van Vechten Papers, New York Public Library. Reproduced by permission of the Carl Van Vechten Trust.

elly abused by playmates for being illegitimate and for having blue eyes, golden hair, and nearly "white" skin. Until the age of eleven, "They all called me a half-white bastard," she told an interviewer in 1935 or 1936.

The mother finally married at the age of twenty-five, but according to Thomas was always promiscuous, taking up with both white and "colored" men, until she died at the age of thirty-eight. Her grandmother had also had two children, including Edna's mother, by white men early in life, and her (later) black husband was in jail during Edna's youth for murdering a black coachman. As if her bastard origins were not bad enough, the neighborhood children abused her for being the granddaughter of a murderer. Thomas had grown up in abject poverty on the border of "respectable" black society, alienated from any nourishing community or extended family. But she had somehow managed to develop a remarkable poise and seeming security that made her alluring to both whites and blacks as she grew to womanhood. After two years of high school, she married into a "higher" status at age sixteen and subsequently went through two abortions, feeling that she could not afford children. After ten years, her first husband, who came from a "respectable" black family, died of alcoholism following their divorce.[67]

Through the influence of her grandmother and father-in-law, Edna had developed "a strong feeling for the betterment of the negroes." As she matured, she "frequented high society, both white and colored. I never felt any social discrimination."[68]

Thomas had as much experience as almost any active black female actor of the time. She had begun her career with solo recitals and concerts as the "Lady from Louisiana," singing "Creole" songs, spirituals, and popular local-color songs like "Suwanee River."[69] With the advent of the Negro Renaissance, however, she had begun acting. She joined the original Ethiopian Art Theatre in Chicago under Raymond O'Neill, which moved to New York in the early Twenties and raised awareness of the possibilities of "Negro drama." In addition to years of work with the Alhambra Players and the Lafayette Players, she played Bess in *Porgy* and Ruby Lee in *Lulu Belle,* plus lead roles in O'Neill's *The Dreamy Kid* (1925), Hall Johnson's *Run, Little Chillun* (1933), and *Stevedore* (1934). She had also worked with Dorothy Peterson's Harlem Experimental Theatre in the late 1920s. She even had a budding film career, singing off-camera for Greta Garbo's character in *Romance* and playing Zeba in the 1936 film version of *The Green Pastures.*[70]

In the midst of her 1920s stage career, she fell in love with the black talent manager Lloyd Thomas and pursued him until they married. They were happy for several years, when Larsen first came to know them, until he began seeing younger women while she was away on tour. Although they remained married, lived together, and respected each other, their romantic and sexual relationship ended. Around 1930, however, Olivia Wyndham, recently arrived from England and introduced to black society by A'Lelia Walker, fell violently in love with Edna and pursued her relentlessly until, in her own words, she "yielded."

> I had avoided her because white women are unfaithful. She was persistent, to the point of annoyance. She finally came to my house and I had the most exciting sex experience of my life. It has gone on for five years because it's so very satisfactory.
>
> Pamela [Olivia Wyndham] is one of the finest women I have ever known. She has come to be very, very dear to me, not just for sex alone. It's just a very great love. She is tender and gentle as I have never known any one else to be.[71]

Although she believed she never would have entered into lesbian relationships if her husband had been faithful to her, Edna found the relationship with Wyndham completely fulfilling.

Nine years younger than Edna Thomas, Olivia Wyndham had fallen in love with her the moment they met, and began living with her in 1930. Like Thomas, she had hazel eyes and stood five foot six, but carried 131 pounds, twenty pounds more than Thomas, on a stocky frame that a sex researcher of the mid-1930s called "masculine" in both appearance and bearing.[72] Quiet and poised, with the "undeniable bearing of a woman of breeding," she had a round face with a small pointed chin, heavy dark eyebrows, and a large nose. "At forty she is plodding along without particular ambitions or desire for change and [feeling] vaguely that her life has been rather futile and unproductive." But she practically worshiped Edna Thomas: "She has a very beautiful nature. Everybody adores her. She radiates goodness and sweetness." In their sexual relationship, Wyndham always took the initiative and would not allow Thomas to reciprocate, believing her "too pure."[73]

With Thomas, Wyndham, Meyer, and others, Larsen moved between the East Village, Greenwich Village, the midtown galleries, and Harlem—visiting Jimmie Daniels' club, dancing at the Savoy, catching Billie Holiday at the Hot Cha. Andrew Meyer described his impression of Larsen years later, to biographer Thadious Davis, as a "cultured, matured woman," "friendly and outgoing," but "a bit of a snob about non-intellectuals."[74] She was still trying to write, but apparently without any success in placing her work. The summers of 1935 and 1936 she spent at the farmhouse that Wyndham and Thomas owned in Sandy Hook,

Connecticut—a large home with plenty of rooms for guests. Set amid twenty acres of rolling fields and woods, it was a perfect retreat from the city.[75]

Also in 1936, as Thadious Davis discovered, Larsen spent a lot of time with Andrew Meyer's mother, who had just moved to New York and who became a "frequent companion" of Larsen's during the daytime. They went to movies, shops, and galleries together almost daily, according to Andrew. He remembered that they saw *Camille*, starring Greta Garbo, twice in New York because it was one of Larsen's favorite films.[76] It is easy to see why, focusing as it does on the tragedy of a beautiful French courtesan who had climbed her way from obscurity into the most glamorous circles of eighteenth-century Paris, only to find herself, as she aged, losing the love of her paramour to another woman and abandoned to poverty and loneliness. Filled with the classic motifs of female vulnerability in a male-dominated society that Larsen had always found irresistible, the film had the added attraction of being based on the play *La Dame aux Camélias*, by the French "mulatto" Alexandre Dumas, *fils*, a much-celebrated figure in African American intellectual circles.

Always attracted to women who were self-sufficient, glamorous, and intellectually inclined, Larsen found in Thomas' group a new magnet of attention. This also kept her close to some of the most exciting midcentury events in black performance history. From 1935 on, Thomas was deeply involved in the "Harlem" unit of the Federal Theater Project, starring throughout the spring and summer of 1936 opposite Jack Carter in a now-famous version of *Macbeth* directed by Orson Welles. The production played on parallels Welles perceived between the story of Haiti's King Christophe and that of Shakespeare's Scottish king. Costumes and settings were designed with late eighteenth-century Haiti in mind, and for the witches Welles brought in black West Indian drummers and an authentic "witch-doctor."[77]

After heated controversy leading up to the opening, and much distrust in the community (culminating in a mugging of Orson Welles), the "Voodoo *Macbeth*," as Harlemites termed it, became a sensation, and Edna Thomas' reputation soared. While not all critics praised the production (some calling it too wild in its adaptation of the original, others too "traditional," i.e., "white"), according to Simon Callow, "the beau monde took up the show in a big way, as did theatre people."[78] Jack Carter and Edna Thomas became the toast of Larsen's New York.[79]

In the evening Larsen frequently visited Edna Thomas, Olivia Wyndham, and Lloyd Thomas or accompanied them to affairs associated with black literature and performing arts, including benefits for the Negro Actors Guild and parties to support the magazine *Challenge,* edited by Dorothy West. One such occasion brought her back in contact with Bryher (Winifred Ellerman), the Englishwoman married to the British editor and filmmaker Kenneth Macpherson but romantically connected with the poet Hilda Doolittle, known as H.D. One Thursday night in late November or early December 1936, Bryher wrote H.D.: "Nella Larsen came up, and Edna Thomas, and her husband, and Olivia Wyndham. I fell into the Larssen's arms, and she into mine. She is so quiet, and so interesting." Worried that H.D. might think a romantic interest was developing, she reassured her, inventing children for Larsen: "But do not worry, she is elderly, with two grown up, over twenty sons. She is rather ill too. Alas, she has the Danish intensity, lived there, as tiny pup, with very dark skin, and it must be intensely difficult for her. We hope to meet again. You'll remember her books."[80] Macpherson had sent them Larsen's novels, along with others by African Americans, during a New York stay in 1929.

By now Macpherson was editing a London-based journal Bryher had bought, *Life and Letters Today.* They had come to New York in part to recruit African American contributors and allies, while he also wrote a column about the New York scene. Macpherson's interest in African American culture dated to the late 1920s and had never let up; in 1929, he edited a special issue of the magazine *Close Up* on black cinema, and in Nancy Cunard's mammoth anthology of 1934, *Negro,* he had proposed the formation of an autonomous black film union, the Confederated Negro Socialist Cinema, with its own academy along the lines of the State School of Cinema in Moscow.[81] Larsen almost certainly knew Bryher and Macpherson from their visit to New York in 1934, when Carl Van Vechten had introduced them to all his friends and they had spent much time in Harlem.[82]

Macpherson absolutely adored Harlem, "the spiritual home of all dope lovers —among which I count myself; though my dope doesn't have to be sniffed smoked or injected!! I never suspected for a moment the whole place would get me so hard! . . . I'll never lose the thing that it has—its sheer and utter fantastic beauty! That, to me, is summit and bedrock—it is ultimate. Nothing better *could* be done!"[83] He was furious with Bryher over her initial repugnance for Harlem, which Bryher vividly expressed to H.D.: "Marianne [Moore] got Dog's number and said 'Well, to see Harlem before visiting us is like going to the Zoo before visiting the British Museum, which of course is quite correct.'"[84] Bryher and Macpherson had come close to divorce over the dispute in the winter of 1934–1935, when Larsen first met them.

By 1936 Bryher's feelings about Harlem had moderated, and she attended a number of parties there and elsewhere in support of African American literature and arts during the winter of 1936–1937. Nella would meet her again before long at a Saturday-night party hosted by former Harvard professor Isaac Watkins to raise money for *Challenge*. Bryher reported again to H.D.: "I met, on the one hand, apparently, a former slightly colored partner of Mistinguette, and on the other, a very learned gentleman who had been to Bali, a curator of the Metropolitan Museum of Art, and my dear 'Miss Nelly.' She tells me she was brought up in Denmark, the only dark child in the family and town, is a color hearer, loathes music, because people always insisted that [as] a negro she must sing, and is particularly interested in the Skandinavian influences on Beowulf."[85] Edna Thomas had also been there, "the greatest Negro actress living (it's so sad, she is all but white)."

The next day, the poet Elinor Wylie had called up to tell Bryher she'd had a "terrific row" with Nella after Bryher had left the party. As Bryher reported:

> Miss Nelly had watched me edging up towards Eleanor (whom I should not at all mind as a girl friend) and Miss Nelly had decided that just wouldn't do, I was her property. And am I enjoying this drama? Together with the fact that as I left, Lady Macbeth [Edna Thomas] for no known reason, leapt upon me, "mousled and towsled me" to use Wycherley's phrase, as I have seldom been mousled and towseled, I suspect to provoke her friend sitting glumly on sofa. Pup [H.D.'s sixteen-year-old daughter Perdita]—little wretch—giggled in corner, and then we all quoted Lenin to a completely strange young man, who wanted to know why Britons were not communists.[86]

Bryher soon returned to Europe, without Macpherson; but even as Macpherson became closely attached to Edna Thomas and Olivia Wyndham, he continued supplying gossip about Nella, Edna, and Olivia to Bryher and H.D.

Early in 1937, either H.D. or Bryher sent Larsen a copy of H.D.'s recent children's book, *The Hedgehog*—a beautiful volume published in a limited edition of three hundred copies in 1936 by London's Curwin Press, with woodcut illustrations by George Plank.[87] Larsen was "inarticulate with pleasure," Macpherson reported, "'deeply touched' as the late Royal Family used to say."[88]

It seems that she had become partly entangled, as well, in the relationship between Thomas and Wyndham. She spent a great deal of time with them and Macpherson, who had grown quite close to them both, not only in New York but also at Minedo (the house in Connecticut), where Larsen liked to write. Macpherson spoke of the group as if they were family, urging Bryher to come back to New York:

It's too mistaken of you to stay over there when here is so alive and everyone is so fond of you. They all talk of you, and wish you back, — as to the writing, Elinore says she sent three letters, . . . Miss Nellie, retiring behind many shy protestations, says she has been preparing a letter for weeks, so no doubt a soul-confession will reach you in due course. . . . Edna, who has a writing inhibition as bad as my own, spends nearly all her time hanging raptly over the wash machine which whirs and chugs in the most satisfying way. She loves it like a toy, and Olivia, screaming as ever, "My *God,* do you *realize . . .* ?" times it and discovers the household wash saves four hours a week! She spilt a glass of gin into it in her excitement, which didn't seem to do any harm to the washing, so we used it as a christening and called it madame Santa-Bryher.[89]

Later in the month of February, Wyndham and Thomas briefly separated, and Larsen began meddling while Macpherson wrung his hands in dismay. In the end, however, Wyndham and Thomas reunited and left for Minedo together, leaving Larsen embarrassed if not bereft. Macpherson related the events in a tantalizing letter: "After 3 days Olivia wrote Jimmie [Daniels] that being separated was 'breaking my life and my heart—not that they are important— but I feel Eddie so needs me.' And asked him to intercede and discourage Eddie from listening to 'bad dramatized advice.' That night she was back & they went off to Minedo together. So that was that."[90] The "bad advice" seems to have come from Larsen, as will soon be evident. Although it is conceivable that Larsen had her own designs on Edna Thomas, nothing in the correspondence suggests this, and Macpherson would have no reason to disguise such motives in a letter to Bryher. Perhaps at issue was the fact that Thomas was on track for an executive position in the Theater Project—a development of significance for all black performers—and her openly lesbian relationship with Wyndham could jeopardize that.[91]

The flap did not quite end Larsen's relationship with the ménage, but she evidently began to withdraw—and to crack up even further, helped along by a growing drinking problem that could only have exacerbated her depression.

Edna, Olivia, and Macpherson (Larsen's link to Bryher and H.D.) now regarded Nella as a problem. At least, one gathers as much from Macpherson's report:

At 1890, peace is restored. It is not known quite what happened, but Edna, who is very strong, and so utterly pure in thought and belief, stated her case in such a way that nothing came of the flurry. It must have been magnificently handled. Olivia, who is of the two, perhaps my greater darling, met the occasion as only a "great lady" could. She was admirable. They are together again, firmly, and all we hear of Miss Nellie is that she has just sold a short story she wrote at Minedo for $450. But I am glad about it because I feel that these very special people should NOT break up something that took great courage, love and strength to bring about.[92]

Any story that Larsen sold at the time has yet to turn up; it seems likely that she was trying to cover a growing crisis. In fact, this was not the only instance in which someone mistakenly believed she had placed some work during the winter of 1937. Arna Bontemps wrote Langston Hughes from Huntsville, Alabama, in January: "Nella's husband came out to say hello while passing through. Says that her ofay novel has been accepted. That is the book that I am eager to see succeed. It would further liberate the Negro novelist, don't you think?"[93] So far, no black writer had succeeded in publishing a "white novel." Far from regarding Larsen's effort as a sign of turning away from the race, her colleagues interpreted it as a brave attempt to break down the color bar. But her lack of success in placing her work, combined with the rebuff of her effort to distance Thomas from Wyndham, caused the increasingly unstable Larsen to withdraw from her friends.

Despite the fracas with Wyndham, it does not appear that Thomas or Wyndham shut Larsen out; the suggestion that Edna had handled the situation "magnificently" may be borne out by the fact that Macpherson still thought of Larsen as a potential contributor to *Life and Letters Today*.[94] After this, however, there is no more mention of Nella Larsen in the correspondence among Macpherson, Bryher, and H.D.

The ruckus in the Wyndham-Thomas ménage and its dénouement drastically affected Larsen. Just afterward, she told all her friends that she was "taking a cruise to South America, the name of the boat, and the date of sailing," as Elizabeth Hull informed Grace and Jim Johnson on April 22; "but she is in town, incognito or something. She is way past my understanding."[95] A few days later, on the back of a postcard, Carl wrote Grace: "The report that Nella is in Brazil is slightly exaggerated."[96] The front of the postcard displayed a Van Vechten photograph of Edward Donahoe, who had just published a novel called *Madness in the Heart* and was soon to marry an old friend.

Larsen did send Carl a birthday telegram a little after noon on June 17 from Newtown, Connecticut, the nearest telegraph office to Minedo, so it is possible that she stayed at the farm part of that summer. Her last written words to Van Vechten read, "All good wishes love and affection / Nella."[97] After that, silence.

At the end of July, Dorothy Peterson threw a party to celebrate Sidney's return from Puerto Rico, where he was working for the U.S. Department of Health, and to fête her houseguest Frances Grant. She invited many of her old friends, including the Valentines, Claude McKay, Elizabeth Hull, Aaron Douglas, and Carl Van Vechten, but not Nella.[98] Peterson soon lost contact with her.

In the fall of 1937 Larsen thought of reconnecting with at least some of her friends—Edna Thomas, Andrew Meyer, and others. She called several of them with the message, "I arrive at once"—as if, apparently, returning from South America. And then she failed to appear. Professor Davis relates, "When Andrew Meyer and Edna Thomas later compared the messages, they became concerned. Meyer had been in bed with a collapsed lung when Larsen phoned with the promise of delivering him a 'basket of good mysteries,' which she had selected from her collection. He was unaware then that she had telephoned her message of immediate arrival to everyone he knew who also knew her."[99] After convalescing, he walked to her apartment and rang the doorbell, which still bore her name, but she never answered. As he turned away to go home, he noticed the curtain move and became convinced that she was in the apartment. Later, Edna Thomas told him that Larsen had taken to drugs.[100] After this, Andrew Meyer and all of his acquaintances lost contact with her. She had entered another path.

The suspicion of a growing drug and/or alcohol dependency beginning in the mid- to late 1930s seems to have merit, and was clearly linked to Larsen's withdrawal from friends. Her erratic behavior, discreetly alluded to by people like Thomas, Meyer, and Elizabeth Hull, seems partly attributable to substance abuse. One later good friend who helped to draw her out of seclusion in the mid-1940s would also suggest, guardedly, that Larsen had not wanted people "bothering her" because of drug and alcohol habits.[101]

As circumstances would have it, Larsen's withdrawal from the writing life coincided exactly with the arrival of Richard Wright in New York, his virtual takeover of *Challenge* magazine (retitled *New Challenge*), and the triumph of his view of the Harlem Renaissance as a movement of bourgeois Negro writers bowing and scraping, "prim and decorous ambassadors who went a-begging to white America.... For the most part these artistic ambassadors were received as though they were French poodles who do clever tricks."[102]

According to Wright, "White America never offered these Negro writers any serious criticism," and the role of Negro writing in American life was accidental, taking the form of kitchen humor or "the fruits of that foul soil which was the result of a liaison between inferiority-complexed Negro 'geniuses' and burnt-out white Bohemians with money."[103] In the same issue of *New Challenge*, Alain Locke himself repudiated the "spiritual truancy and social irresponsibility" of writers who, he alleged, had addressed themselves to "faddist Negrophiles"; they should, rather, have addressed the black masses, with fiction of the folk, "racial reverence," and "sacrificial social devotion."[104] These essays marked a major turn in African American literary history and the criticism about it. Larsen's fiction could no longer be taken seriously. For nearly fifty years it was all but dismissed as irrelevant to black people, to American culture, and to literary history. She would not be heard from again.

[TWENTY-TWO]

The Recluse on Second Avenue:
1938–1944

ENTIRELY withdrawn from friends, Nella Larsen virtually disappeared for four years. Dorothy, Sidney, and Carl worried about her but recognized that for some reason she had cut them off. Elmer had no contact with her except through alimony payments. City directories did not list her name.

Dorothy and Carl drew closer than ever, and both remained very much interested in the black cultural scene. Dorothy was technical director of Langston Hughes's Harlem Suitcase Theatre, launched in the spring of 1938, and Van Vechten one of its key supporters.[1] Each year on the anniversary of their meeting, they would get together for lunch, often with Harold Jackman, and wonder about Nella. In the fall of 1938, Edward Donahoe chaired a panel entitled "The Negro in American Literature" at the League of American Writers conference—a panel that many of Nella's old friends attended. Donahoe informed Grace Johnson that Jessie Fauset gave a talk on the 1920s, "when she, Nella, Walter White et al. were first publishing their novels. Then Langston read two poems."[2] The door was still very much open for Nella to join her old acquaintances, to reminisce about the past or to plan new projects.

But one of the most important of her friends was gone. James Weldon Johnson died in a car accident at a railroad crossing in Maine—with Grace driving—in June 1938, an event Larsen had to have known about. There were few people, possibly none, she admired more. He had also been one of her staunchest literary mentors and supporters. He had introduced her at the NAACP tea in her honor, stood next to her on the dais when she received the Harmon Award, cited her work in speeches, greeted her when she arrived reluctantly in Nashville, and introduced her to his students as one of the key authors of the Negro Renaissance. Her friendship with Jim, both in Harlem and at Fisk, had been a point of pride and comfort during intense passages of her life. The funeral took place June 30 at the Salem Methodist Episcopal Church, with Countee Cullen's father presiding. The crowd of 2,500 apparently did not include Nella—at least, no one spotted her. Nor, evidently, did she come out for the memorial tribute on August 3 at Horace Mann Auditorium.

Sidney Peterson, now remarried and holding a Ph.D. from Harvard, was working as an epidemiologist in Puerto Rico for the Department of Public Health. When he returned to New York in late 1938, he dropped by 320 Second Avenue to see Nella, but he could not find her on the residents' list in the foyer, "so she must have moved or changed her name," Dorothy speculated, "which worries me because someone should at least know where she is."[3] Unlisted in the city directory, she could not be found.

Carl and Dorothy were busy at the time with a joint project: she was turning a wall of her Brooklyn house into a gallery for Carl's photographs of African Americans—the Jerome Bowers Peterson Memorial Collection of Celebrated Negroes, as it would come to be called. Dorothy spent much of her spare time in 1939 framing and mounting the collection of eighty-four images, which, after she had arranged them at home, she exhibited at Wadleigh High School, where she taught. Curiously, the collection did not initially include a portrait of Nella Larsen.

Other activities and events would occasionally remind the old friends of the excitement of the renaissance. One night they attended *Mamba's Daughters*, starring Ethel Waters as Hagar in the dramatic adaptation of DuBose Heyward's 1929 novel. Waters had been so moved by the novel that she insisted Heyward adapt it to the stage for her. Utterly absorbed in her role, which drained her every night, she made it a smash hit. "I have never been so completely thrilled in the theatre since the opening night of Porgy," Dorothy wrote Carl, "and you remember that for those times that also was historically important. But last night was an advance of 100 years over Porgy in the matter of theatre and Negroes-in-the-theatre and everything. . . . If the number of times I went to see Porgy has anything to do with the number of times I shall see Mamba, I think I shall have to stop framing pictures."[4] On Saturday, January 14, 1939, Dorothy went to a party for Ethel in honor of *Mamba's* success, and "practically everybody from the old parties . . . was there."[5] The NAACP had even revived its custom of holding a big annual dance. But Nella Larsen was nowhere to be seen.

Elmer revived a sporadic correspondence with Van Vechten by inviting him to give a speech on "Jim the man" at Fisk's memorial tribute to Johnson during the campus arts festival in the spring of 1939. Carl was unable to attend but wrote a speech that moved Fania to tears when he shared it with her. Elmer delivered it himself at the ceremony. The bond of their friendship, despite the lapse in years, remained unbroken. "I do not blame Fania for crying," Elmer wrote to Carl. "No one could have done it better."[6] Elmer was no longer happy at Fisk: "I can't work up very much enthusiasm about the place and ought to have been out of it a long time ago," he confided. Still concerned about Nella,

Carl tried to find out if Elmer knew anything about her. But not even Elmer had her new address.

Since his "secret marriage" to Ethel Gilbert (the union was never affirmed legally), after his divorce and her move to New York, Elmer spent summers and holidays in Manhattan at Ethel's apartment. He avoided most of the literary acquaintances he and Nella had shared, although he continued to see the Bishops as well as Lillian Alexander, who was a close friend of Ethel's. When Elmer came to New York over the Christmas holiday in 1939–1940, he telephoned Carl, who asked him about Nella. Carl relayed to Dorothy Peterson that Elmer "hasnt the slightest idea" about Nella's doings or whereabouts. "You see, he sends money to a bank and NEVER is allowed to have her address and he knows nobody who has seen her."[7] Two months later Elmer wrote Carl again: "Nella seems to be OK as evidenced by typewritten and addressless note a few days ago about money. I replied in care of her bank which was the only way I could think of to reach her, since her note implied that she had not received a letter addressed to 320 Second Avenue in January (and not returned because of non-delivery.)"[8] "I had a letter from Elmer about Nella," Carl wrote Dorothy shortly afterward. "She is still at 320 Second Ave!"[9] Actually, Elmer's letter does not indicate that Nella still lived at that address. She had merely moved across the street, into a more modest apartment at 315 Second Avenue, making it impossible for old friends to track her down. The residents of 320 would have known where to find her. For more than three years, her best friends did not.

Today, 315 Second Avenue is a home for recovering drug addicts and the mentally disabled, affiliated with local medical centers. A narrow four-story brick building wedged between larger structures and almost directly facing 320 Second Avenue, it is just north of Eighteenth Street, a block from Stuyvesant Square. Bordering the park at that time were several hospitals, most of them now long closed or relocated: the Salvation Army's William Booth Memorial Hospital, Beth Israel, Manhattan General at 307 Second Avenue, St. Andrew's Convalescent Hospital, and the New York Infirmary for Women and Children—the latter founded in the mid-nineteenth century by America's first female M.D., staffed entirely by women, and one of the first hospitals in New York to offer training to black nurses as well as white.[10] Many of the brownstones in the area housed doctors.

Nella's new home, Apartment 1D, was in the rear on the first floor—a large one-room studio with a separate kitchen and a bathroom. She lined the walls with books and beautiful objects from her travels in Europe—vases, antiques, her grandmother's silver candlesticks.[11] Here she shut herself off from the world. One is reminded of Helga Crane's room in Naxos—a cross between a quiet oasis and a bibliophile's cocoon.

After this, the correspondence between Dorothy and Carl grows very discreet when mentioning their friend. In the wake of Jim Johnson's death, Carl had conceived the project of memorializing him with a comprehensive collection of correspondence, books, and manuscripts associated with the Negro Renaissance, and had recruited Dorothy to help him. The project developed into an unpaid career for both of them. Aware that their letters would end up in the collection, Dorothy, especially, became very circumspect out of concern for the reputations of her friends. Moreover, she stipulated that her letters from this period be sealed for decades; they have only recently been made available to scholars. It is clear from what correspondence does mention Nella that every now and then Dorothy and Carl heard more about her than they would set down in writing. "Elmer has not been indiscreet enough to announce his marriage to me," Carl confided to Dorothy at the end of July 1940. "By the way did you hear what Tom had to say about Nella?"[12] "Tom" may well have been Tom Mabry, whom Van Vechten could easily have seen at the Museum of Modern Art. He was still single and active in the arts community; later he would resign from the museum, marry, and go back to the land as a full-time farmer in south-central Kentucky, raising Herefords and writing some finely chiseled, prizewinning short stories for venues like the *Kenyon Review*.[13]

The mystery of Nella Larsen continued to exercise Carl particularly—in part because he wanted her cooperation for the James Weldon Johnson Collection, but also because he retained strong feelings for her and Elmer. In the fall of 1940, he came across a letter concerning Nella in the course of his cataloguing, and shared it with Dorothy (the writer and recipient were not identified in their exchange). She responded: "I think the letter is very interesting because it indicates a more intimate knowledge of her and her past than I ever had and I think that I was probably as close to her as anyone could be. I did know that her father was a West Indian—at least she told me so once—I did not know that she had ever attended the University of Copenhagen, I seem to remember that she said she had no college training—at least when she was being considered for one of the Negro sororities, she could produce no evidence of college attendance."[14] Dorothy no longer took anything Nella had told her about her life on faith, and Nella had told her very little about it. Yet no one knew Nella better than Elmer, Dorothy, and Carl. When Langston Hughes's *The Big Sea* came out from Knopf —a book that would have an immense impact on all later histories of the Harlem Renaissance—the chief mention of Larsen was the erroneous statement that she was one of a handful of Toomer's followers in the Gurdjieff Work. Indeed, none of the significant memoirists or interviewees of the Negro Renaissance—Hughes, Arna Bontemps, Sterling Brown, Dorothy West, Ethel Ray Nance, even Bruce Nugent—had really known Nella Larsen.

While Nella was growing increasingly absent, Elmer was growing desperately ill. By the fall of 1940, a spreading cancer racked him with constant pain. In early November a series of X-ray treatments at maximum dosage supposedly cured the primary lesion, in his throat. But he then developed backaches, supposedly from an injured nerve. By Christmas he was severely crippled and in constant agony. In the late spring of 1941, he could keep comfortable only under sedation, and his doctors realized that the cancer had invaded his spine. He flew to New York on the sixth of June and checked into Memorial Hospital for diagnosis and treatment. Although the outlook was grim, he tried to keep up his spirits. Emaciated and nearly helpless, he wanted Carl to visit him, but not to notify Nella: "I think it would cheer me to see you. I am taking care that Nella does not know I am here."[15]

Almost immediately, Fania, who was about to go to California, came to visit, bringing a radio as a gift to help distract Elmer from his unremitting pain. He had always had a soft spot for her. Carl came not long after, and Dorothy visited once before leaving for a vacation in Puerto Rico. To both of them, when the subject of Nella came up, Elmer said "very definitely" that "he never wanted to see her again."[16] He mentioned to Dorothy that he was still paying alimony, at what Dorothy termed "a terrific sacrifice."[17] Elmer wrote Carl on the fourteenth of June that the visit had done him "a lot of good. It is so grand to have good friends—even if I haven't always seemed to show it about mine." He had, after all, distanced himself from the friends he held most in common with Nella; and it was a joy to know that they still embraced him. He was feeling more comfortable and cheerful. "In a way a sentence has been lifted—by the promise of permanent relief and perhaps total cure."[18] Five days later he wrote again to thank Carl for a bouquet of mountain laurel and to give his new visiting hours. "If you have any books you don't mind bringing, bring one or two, but don't buy any." As a hint, he mentioned that a friend had brought him *Peter Whiffle*, "knowing that I re-read it every now and then and I am finding it as fascinating as ever but a little hard to hold in the edition we have."[19]

The correspondence grows increasingly painful to read. Carl wrote Dorothy in Puerto Rico that Ethel Gilbert told him, when he called in early July, there was little hope. "He is losing weight and is in great pain and the doctors say he is infected through and through, even his lungs. He is feeling rather hopeless too and doesnt seem to want to see people."[20] On the nineteenth of July, having received more cards and a phone message from Fania and Carl, Elmer wrote again, a gentleman to the end: "They do so many things to me that I don't seem to have 'get up' enough to acknowledge notes and courtesies. . . . There seems to be slow but definite progress in the right direction."[21] The radio, he added, was his joy. A month later, Carl wrote: "No word of Elmer."[22]

On September 11 Elmer finally passed away. Nella was informed immediately (apparently through an old friend she shared with Ethel but not Carl and Dorothy), and even invited Ethel to come visit her, according to Lillian Alexander.[23] She did not attend the funeral, however. Elmer would not have wanted her there, and she had no desire to run into people she had been avoiding, particularly Elmer's family. Carl skipped the funeral because he didn't think he would know anyone there, but Dorothy decided at the last minute to attend with her old friend, and Ethel's, Frances Grant. She sent him a report:

> It was way out in Queens at the Fresh Pond Crematory and the Rev. Shelton Hale Bishop (one of whose sisters Gussie is in an insane asylum) read the services. Shelton's other sister Victoria seems to be best friend to Mrs. Gilbert. Pres. Jones of Fisk was there—a group of Elmer's old friends, Dr. W. E. B. Du Bois, Mrs. Gilbert's sister, and Augustus Granville Dill. The first part of the funeral was held in a tiny chapel upstairs in the Crematory and then those who wished to go were invited down below to see the body "committed to the ground."[24]

Frances did not want to stay, so she and Dorothy had left at that point. Carl wrote to Dorothy afterward, sorry that he had not gone, but he had not known she would be there: "Elmer's funeral sounds terribly dismal. . . . If Nella pops up, please let me know at once."[25] Dorothy expected Nella to call either her or Carl soon "to verify Elmer's death," but the call never came, and both of them grew increasingly distressed, if not annoyed with her.[26]

Ethel Gilbert wrote Dorothy after the funeral, in the midst of closing up the apartment she had shared with Elmer, to give her new address and to encourage Dorothy to get in touch with her. "I am very grateful to her," Dorothy wrote Carl, "for making Elmer's last years happier than Nella would have done for him. She says, 'I simply cannot picture a world without Elmer' which shows pretty much how she felt about him." But Dorothy barely knew her, having seen her only three times in her life, and could not bring herself to respond: "I haven't answered because I don't know what to call her. I'm not going to say 'Dear Ethel Gilbert' and I don't know her well enough to say 'Dear Ethel' and she'll probably be insulted if I say 'Dear Mrs. Gilbert,' so what can I do?"[27]

Dorothy held nothing against Ethel for taking Elmer away from Nella, but they had little basis for a relationship. Nella, on the other hand, was still very much on her mind; and even more, it seems, on Carl's. "Dear Osa," he wrote Dorothy, using a new term of endearment, "Grace writes that Elmer wanted to see Nella, at the last! Did he? I think you'd better see Mrs. G. *at least once.*"[28] Later in the month of October, he wrote Dorothy again, complaining that she had never answered his question. He had even been going back through old files looking up materials on Nella.[29] It turned out that Frances Grant had started the rumor about Elmer wanting to see Nella, having misinterpreted something that Ethel Gilbert had said to her. Dorothy was sure of it, particularly after Birdie Bird (Crystal's sister and an old friend of Nella, Dorothy, and Frances) had spent the weekend with Dorothy and implied that Frances had started the rumor.[30] Carl's obsession with clearing up the mystery of Nella's relationship with Elmer in his final days indicates how concerned Carl was about her.

He, more than anyone, was determined to make contact with her again, and he needed Dorothy's help. By this time, he had surely given up on reestablishing the close friendship they had once had. He did not know what had happened. But he himself was known for suddenly cutting people out of his life, and in Nella's case he was getting a taste of his own medicine. It seems clear that he still cared about her, yet he also wanted her to contribute her papers to the James Weldon Johnson Memorial Collection. Neither he nor Dorothy, nor anyone they asked, had the vaguest idea of where she was living. Her failure to resurface even after Elmer's death seemed to put a cap on their hopes of reconnecting. For them, she had vanished.

On the eve of Christmas 1941, Dorothy went out shopping with Anita Thompson, the prototype of Audrey Denney in *Quicksand,* who had just escaped (barely) the Nazi conquest of Europe. They were catching up on each other's lives while browsing the busy First Avenue Market near Tenth Street, when out of the milling crowd of Christmas shoppers a phantom appeared. Dorothy described the encounter for Carl:

> I suddenly saw Nella Larsen. I stopped her and spoke to her.—She asked me to come and see her—said she was living at 315 Second Avenue—although I doubt it—and swore she had just heard of Elmer's death 2 days ago—and of Jim's a week ago. She didn't tell me who had brought her the news. She said she hadn't been getting a penny from Elmer for years, although when I saw him in June he told me he was still paying alimony at a terrific sacrifice. I told her that and she just shrugged her shoulders and said Elmer was always like that. She didn't seem at all moved by his death nor the pain he had gone through.

Anita Thompson, who had not seen Nella since Morocco in 1931 and remembered her as an attractive, keen-witted, graceful young woman, thought she looked "at least eighty years old and a little mad."[31] Eager to keep the conversation going, worried that Nella would fade from view again, Dorothy asked her if she had any clothes to give her—"(we always used to exchange clothes) and she said, 'Yes,' she was lousy with clothes and would give me anything I needed, even a fur coat."[32] And then Nella receded into the crowd.

Soon thereafter, Carl met with Lillian Alexander and told her what Dorothy had said. Lillian insisted that Nella had been "notified about Elmer's death at once and even invited Mrs. Gilbert over to talk about it. She also said Elmer had given Nella his last dollar."[33] Carl was suddenly reminded of the 1930 plagiary charge and asked Dorothy how it had all shaken out.[34] That Elmer had given Nella his last dollar was not strictly true. Nella is never mentioned in Elmer's will.[35] But the fact that he continued making large alimony payments to the bitter end seems certain. In essence, Elmer's payments had helped fund Nella's descent into the abyss. Just as cruelly, his death helped to draw her out of it.

Following Elmer's death, if not before, Nella probably began working at least part time in one of the neighboring hospitals—St. Andrew's, Booth, Beth Israel, or the Women's Infirmary. A later nursing colleague told Charles Larson in the 1980s that Nella had worked in a nursing home before entering the city hospital system in 1944.[36] Without Elmer's alimony checks, she needed to do something to support herself.

Now that Dorothy Peterson and Carl Van Vechten had reestablished contact with her, Larsen began to emerge, albeit rarely and tentatively, from hiding. She remained withdrawn from her literary friends, having closed the door on that aspect of her life, but she made contact with Corinne Wright between the time that Dorothy had spotted her and the summer of 1942. Dorothy may very well have been able to speak to her on the phone, but no correspondence between them survives. Both Carl and Dorothy were intent on getting her cooperation for the James Weldon Johnson Collection, but they knew better than to press her—they might lose all contact again. Now, at least, they had her address.

On June 17 the 115th Street Branch Library, where Regina Andrews was head librarian, held a memorial birthday celebration for James Weldon Johnson, with Lucile Miller handling the invitation list.[37] The organizers had gathered mementos, manuscripts, and pictures from Johnson's friends for display, and had planned a series of presentations in the library's "Little Theatre."[38] Van Vechten, who was asked to speak, sent his regrets and a letter to be read, having already committed to something else for his own birthday on the same date. Neither did

Dorothy Peterson make it. Many of Johnson's friends and colleagues of the renaissance years were there, however. Fannie Hurst spoke, followed by Carl Van Doren and then Johnson's former secretary, Richetta Randolph. W. C. Handy spoke on Johnson's feeling for the blues; the Juanita Hall Singers performed his poem "The Creation"; and A. Sybil Gowdy recited his "Saint Peter Relates an Incident of the Resurrection Day." This was followed by a medley of songs. Johnson, the tribute implied, had been a renaissance in his own right. Several other friends spoke, including Walter White and the NAACP pro bono lawyer Arthur Garfield Hayes.[39] Harold Jackman wrote Carl the next day: "Last night I went to the library. Beautiful was the word for the tribute to Mr. Johnson. And who do you suppose was there? Nella."[40]

Carl pounced on his opportunity, asking for more information. "No," Harold replied, "I didn't have a chance to talk to Nella. I did greet her, however. She came with Corinne Wright and her daughter and Sadie Tandy."[41] Wright and Tandy were, of course, two of Nella's earliest acquaintances in Harlem, but they had never been close to Peterson or Van Vechten. A week later, Carl wrote Dorothy: "Did you go to the Library on June 17 and see Nella?"[42] Shortly thereafter, Dorothy was able to reach Nella, in person or by phone, and invited her to come visit. On a card sent July 11 to Dorothy, Carl added a postscript: "Did Nella come over?"[43] Whether she did or not, she promised at about this time to give her papers to the James Weldon Johnson Memorial Collection.

Throughout the summer, Carl and Dorothy worked intensively on organizing the documents coming in from their renaissance acquaintances, to be housed in the Sterling Library at Yale. They vicariously relived the events of the 1920s as they opened the packages and shared old correspondence of their own. "I think Jean Toomer's letters are also of the highest interest as a document," Carl commented. "His love-making I find rather algebraic. Was he more HUMAN in the flesh?" Dorothy wrote Jessie Fauset in August; three months later (she tells Carl) she received a reply: "[Jessie] sentimentalizes over our 'past' and promises to look for and send me some of her poetry in MS. The novels have been lost and she has none of those. . . . It is amazing the casual way she speaks of losing ms."[44] But Jessie was more forthcoming than Nella, whom both Dorothy and Carl considered the more important writer. They themselves were among the few people who had saved—or even received—letters from her. No one knew anything about her relatives. Her past was a cipher. The paucity of documents concerning her was the most troubling lacuna of the burgeoning archive. In August, Carl wrote Larsen to remind her of her promise, enclosing a leaflet about the collection. A month later he informed Dorothy: "No reply."[45]

By late October, with the help of Roberta Bosley, Dorothy was busy making arrangements for a dinner at the Port Arthur Restaurant in Chinatown, hosted by the James Weldon Johnson Literary Guild that Bosley had founded. The event was organized partly to honor Van Vechten but chiefly to spread the word about the James Weldon Johnson Collection. Dorothy assured Carl that she had explicitly asked Bosley to send Nella an invitation.[46] The *Amsterdam News* reported on the program in advance as one of the top social events of the season.[47] Practically everyone from the old social set was going—Nora Holt, Blanche Knopf, Muriel Draper, Fania, Essie Robeson, Geraldyn Dismond (now Holland), Walter White, Fannie Hurst, Edna and Lloyd Thomas, Harold Jackman, Zora Neale Hurston, Sidney Peterson and his new wife Vera, Grace Johnson, and many more—but Larsen never responded. Even Countee Cullen, who had finally gotten over his anger at Van Vechten for *Nigger Heaven,* showed up. W. C. Handy spoke of Van Vechten's insight as a music critic and sang, with friends, Langston Hughes's "Go and Get the Enemy Blues"; Canada Lee, one of the race's new stars, read a poem in doggerel verse by Hughes dedicated to Van Vechten. The young poet Margaret Walker, who had just won the Yale Younger Poets Series award, chosen by Stephen Vincent Benét, was also honored, along with J. Saunders Redding, author of the memoir *No Day of Triumph.* The two were seen as symbols of the notion that the spirit of the renaissance lived on.[48]

Walter White was at the peak of his fame as leader of the NAACP. A. Philip Randolph's March on Washington Movement attracted broad support; White had been a main speaker at the huge rally held in Madison Square Garden the preceding June. Marian Anderson was haggling with the Daughters of the American Revolution about arrangements for a concert in Constitution Hall at which they had asked her to perform, two years after their refusal to allow her to perform there had inspired a famous protest performance at the Lincoln Memorial. Ethel Waters and Paul Robeson were both starring in recent films considered historic by black film critics at the time—*Tales of New York* and *Cabin in the Sky.* The film version of Richard Wright's *Native Son*—the bestseller and critical sensation of 1940—was in theaters, stirring up controversy. And many of Nella's old acquaintances, including Carl and Dorothy, were working at the Stage Door Canteen, an integrated nightclub for servicemen on Times Square: the Negro Renaissance meets World War II.

Although Larsen continued to keep her distance, Dorothy and Carl maintained loose contact with her, trying to woo her out of her shell and get their hands on her papers. In the spring of 1943, Dorothy moved from Brooklyn, following the death of her father, to 233 East Fiftieth Street. Either by phone or post, she gave Nella her new address. One Saturday, June 19—out of the blue—Nella stopped by to visit her and stayed until Dorothy had to leave to do some shopping on her way to work at the Stage Door Canteen. "We left together and she took me down to her apartment on 2nd Ave opposite where I used to live and she gave me Vincent Sheehan's new book for my birthday."[49] The next day, Nella came back again and stayed until Dorothy had to go out. "I don't know when she's coming back again. She loosened up and told me more about herself than she has here-tofore and was comparatively lucid."[50]

That Nella came on a weekend suggests that she was working somewhere during the week, but Dorothy committed little of what she knew to paper. She may have had other brief exchanges with Nella after this, but for the most part the contact stopped, and she seems to have avoided discussing Nella in her written correspondence with Van Vechten because she was concerned about her friend's reputation in years to come. If Nella briefly considered reopening the door to her old acquaintances and the world of letters, she soon changed her mind. Meanwhile, they struggled to put her back in the pantheon.

In February 1944, Dorothy was working once again on the Jerome Bowers Peterson Collection—this time for an exhibit at the old 135th Street Branch Library. Now Nella was represented in the group, but Dorothy was at a loss when it came to compiling a biographical placard to accompany the portrait. Clearly, Nella was no longer speaking to her. "I have put very little information on it," she confessed to Carl, "because there is so little about her that I am sure of. A friend of hers from Chicago told me that she was born in Chicago and went to school there—I have heard Lucile Miller talk to her about their days in training at Lincoln and I have heard Elmer speak of her library training. She was working in the N.Y. Public Libraries when I knew her and I have visited her at work. So all that is fairly accurate."[51] Carl couldn't be of much help, but he thought Elmer "should definitely be mentioned."[52] He suggested that the Schomburg Collection at the New York Public Library might have some information—but the Schomburg had almost nothing on Larsen. Ernestine Rose had retired to Connecticut; none of the librarians whom Larsen had worked with remained. And rumors in Harlem suggested, inaccurately, that Nella had started "passing" downtown. Of course, Larsen could not have passed. Apparently, some people had forgotten what she looked like.

But it turns out that just as Dorothy was trying to write her capsule biography, Nella was completing her first week in a new job—as a nurse to some of the city's poorest residents, on the Lower East Side.

[TWENTY-THREE]

Nella Larsen Imes, R.N.

TWO miles south of Larsen's apartment, Gouverneur Hospital looked out across South Street onto the East River, from what had once been shipyards and a market area called Gouverneur Slip. You could see it from the Brooklyn Bridge. It was two blocks from the still-active Henry Street Settlement, five or six from the Seward Park Library. The nearest subway station was at Seward Park, but Larsen probably took the bus, since it was more direct and stopped right by her apartment. When Larsen started work on the fourteenth of February 1944, the work crews constructing FDR Drive on Manhattan's eastern shore were wending their way up from the south, laying roadbed with rubble from blitzed London that had come back as ship ballast.

There are always nursing shortages, it seems; but World War II had made the problem acute for the city hospital system by 1944. All sorts of former nurses came back into the profession as hospitals offered refresher courses, their ranks depleted by the enlistment drives of the Red Cross. City hospitals previously inhospitable to black nurses began hiring them in numbers all over Manhattan. To Larsen, the municipal hospitals were more attractive than the "voluntary" or private hospitals because they came under the civil service system. Few private hospitals employed black nurses, whereas the city hospitals were not only hiring them but paying them according to seniority and advancing them to supervisory positions. Larsen began as a staff nurse at the standard annual pay of $1,620, but within a year she was promoted to Chief Nurse—one of five—and given one of the highest raises in the hospital, leapfrogging over women who had been working years longer. For the rest of her life, her abilities were recognized and she pulled down top salaries by city hospital nursing standards. She also found the work rewarding. It drew her out of the spiral of depression and (possibly) addiction, gave structure to her existence, and supplied endless human drama in which she played a valued role.

Literary scholars tend to look down on nursing, and our ignorance about what nurses do is evident in the way we routinely refer to Larsen's return to the profession as a "surrender," a "disappearance," an act of self-burial, a "retreat" to a secure wifely or motherly role as a helpmate to doctors. The gap between literary and historical studies and the health professions is so wide that when one

463

33. *Gouverneur Hospital viewed from the East River, circa 1941. The turn-of-the-century structure (with curved balconies) at 621 Water Street still stands, but the hospital moved to new quarters on nearby Madison Street in the 1970s. The more recent building to the right is a dispensary. "Tax" Department Photo Collection, Courtesy New York City Municipal Archives.*

tries to do any kind of research into the history of those professions, or of specific institutions, one immediately discovers a vast historiographic silence, not to mention an almost total lack of curiosity.

Conversely, from a hospital point of view, fame in the literary realm is a rather limited phenomenon. Few of Larsen's colleagues, black or white, were aware that she had been a well-known novelist, and she did not talk much about that phase of her life except with two good friends. Avid readers bestowing highest praise will occasionally say that a book "literally saved my life"—meaning usually that it made them see things in a new way or pulled them out of depression. But modern hospitals save lives on a daily basis. Most working-class American women, before Larsen began working at Gouverneur Hospital, gave birth at home with minimal medical supervision and virtually no prenatal care;

464

not surprisingly, they and their babies died at a rate we would find intolerable today. Ten times as many women died giving birth in 1940 as in 1962. When Larsen got her nurse's license in 1915, more than one in ten children died before their first birthday; in 1940, the figure was about one in twenty; and in 1962, following the discovery of antibiotics, it was about one in forty.[1] Hospital nursing was partly responsible for this improvement. Moreover, nursing paid better than any other career open to women who lacked a college degree—better even than most professions open to college graduates who had been out of the workforce for fifteen years.

Larsen had not placed a piece of fiction for fourteen years at the point she started at Gouverneur; it was time to try something else. (The blues singer Alberta Hunter, like Larsen, turned to nursing when her singing career failed, working as a practical nurse at Goldwater Hospital. She would be "rediscovered," like Larsen, in the 1970s.) A downtown hospital was a logical choice for someone living near Stuyvesant Park, and integrating the supervisory levels of hospital nursing outside "black" neighborhoods had special meaning in the mid-1940s, when even the armed services were just beginning to accept integration on a limited scale.

Since Larsen's return to nursing has been figured by literary scholars as a disappearance or retreat, motivated by lack of courage or dedication, and since her working at Gouverneur rather than Harlem Hospital has been attributed to a warped value system—fear of being absorbed into the desperation of Harlem, or embarrassment about her fall in status because of an overemphasis on appearances and possessions—it is particularly important to try to describe the place and work to which Larsen devoted herself between 1944 and 1961.[2]

The only city hospital on the East Side below Twenty-Sixth Street, Gouverneur served an immigrant working-class and "underclass" neighborhood with a diverse ethnic population consisting chiefly of aging Jews, young Puerto Rican families, African Americans, Italians, and "Bowery bums" of all descriptions. Its difficulties were much like those of the near South Side of Chicago in Larsen's childhood, or of Harlem in the 1940s, but the residents of this area had far less political clout than the residents of those sections, because they did not form a settled and cohesive social group. In the 1930s, the Lower East Side had become a warren of misery and crime. The Jewish immigrants and second-generation families who could afford to had moved out across the East River to Brownsville or up to the Bronx, while, as always, the poorest new immigrants—mainly from Puerto Rico—moved into the decaying tenement buildings still standing from the previous century.

Traditionally, municipal hospitals were neighborhood institutions established specifically to serve the indigent population.[3] Gouverneur was the smallest in the system, with two hundred beds, and the physical plant, completed in 1908, was rapidly aging like the slums around it. It was already a throwback to an earlier era. Two parallel wings, each five stories high, extended toward the East River from a central administration building with an impressive Renaissance-style façade on the Water Street side. Between the two wings stood an old police station converted into an ambulance bay. The end of each wing facing the river over South Street was a semicircle, with broad fire escapes that in the warm months served as porches or balconies, replete with wooden rocking chairs, where patients could catch a breeze and watch the river traffic. It had the same kind of large, open, window-lined wards Larsen had known at Lincoln Hospital three decades earlier.

Gouverneur appeared in the newspapers most often as a result of assaults and shootings, or near-drownings in the East River—attempted suicides, cars careening off the Brooklyn or Williamsburg Bridge. During Larsen's shift many a shooting or beating victim, sometimes already dead, appeared in the emergency room. There were numerous admissions of children who had toppled off fire escapes and roof parapets in the summer, or who had been caught in fires while their mothers were out shopping for food, or who had fallen out of third- and fourth-floor kitchen windows into air shafts while a caretaker, usually a slightly older brother or sister, wasn't paying attention. Another news report concerned an old woman admitted to the hospital one evening who had allegedly thrown her life savings out with the garbage in a fit of dementia; it was discovered that she'd been living in an apartment bare of any furnishings save two wooden chairs, which she pulled together at night for a bed. Still another story told of a retired doctor, known for treating penniless sick people for free, who was badly beaten in his apartment during a burglary and subsequently brought to the emergency room on a night when Larsen was supervising.[4]

The hospital's social service department particularly addressed itself to rehabilitating men from the Bowery and the waterfront flophouses—blackened rookeries clustered around the bridge anchorages and snaking along the shoreline—with clothing so threadbare that when the men left the hospital it could not be salvaged. A quarter of the patients discharged from Gouverneur were older than sixty-five, and many of them were mentally ill.[5] Each year the hospital held a clothing drive for the poor, placing a letter in the *New York Times* and other papers that would reach prosperous donors.

Had Larsen been hired to work at Harlem Hospital, chances are that we would know far more about her during the latter twenty years of her life, because the well-known Harlem residents later interviewed for information about the Harlem Renaissance would have known something about her. Instead, so far as they were concerned, she dropped out of sight and mostly out of mind. That she did not work in Harlem has given some the impression that she was avoiding black people, but if Gouverneur was not a "black" hospital, neither was it a "white" one. The neighborhood's population was 8 percent black—just slightly under the average for New York as a whole. This was certainly greater than that of most "nonblack" neighborhoods today, but municipal hospitals served a black clientele three times as large as the black percentage of the population as a whole.[6] Photographs of Gouverneur's halls and wards show plenty of black patients and nurses.

Most of the doctors were Jewish, not a few of them veterans of World War I, others recent refugees from Europe. The director of the outpatient clinic, Dr. Siegfried Boxer, was a graduate of the University of Vienna who had fled the Nazis in 1940.[7] Some were at Gouverneur because no one else would hire them, others because they had lived in the neighborhood since youth and remained devoted to it.

At the time Larsen started, Gouverneur had forty-three Registered Nurses, of whom five were Chief Nurses and eighteen were Licensed Practical Nurses. The turnover rate was high, and within only a year Larsen had been promoted to Chief Nurse after two of them resigned. She was appointed Night Supervisor, in charge of the whole hospital from evening to early morning. The colleague with whom Larsen eventually became closest was a forty-year-old African American named Alice Carper. Daughter of a jackleg preacher (one with no church of his own who declaimed on street corners), she'd been educated at Hampton Institute and was now a widow with a son. She lived in Brooklyn and was hired a month after Nella. For ten years before coming to Gouverneur, Carper had worked at Harlem Hospital, but Gouverneur was closer to her home.[8]

Another good friend was Carolyn Lane, a Czech immigrant who was promoted to Chief Nurse with Larsen and supervised the Operating Room during the day shift; she lived on West Sixteenth Street, and had been hired four years earlier. Larsen and Lane were almost always among the top-paid R.N.'s in the hospital. In 1946, a new rank of "Head Nurse" was created—essentially to assist the Chief Nurses—and Alice Carper was advanced to that position, as assistant to Larsen. By 1947–1948, only the Superintendent of Nurses had a higher salary than Larsen, and she had been in the system far longer.[9]

Chief Nurses and supervisors were not expected to do bedside nursing, and they were by no means mere helpmates to doctors. As Night Supervisor, Larsen was in charge of the hospital from afternoon until morning, but she was always willing to pitch in. "She was an excellent nurse, and an excellent supervi-

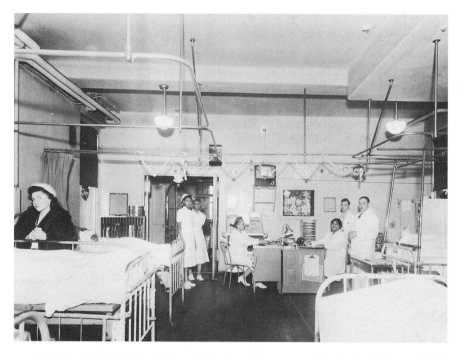

34. Male Surgical Ward and Nurses' Station, Gouverneur Hospital, mid-1940s. DPC Collection, Courtesy New York City Municipal Archives.

sor, and everybody liked her, even though she was very, very strict," according to Carper.[10] Fit and energetic, in and out of all the wards, she would pop up on all four floors of the building to be sure people were not dozing on the job. She never let herself nod on duty, and if Alice began to nod off, Nella would get upset and say something to annoy her so that she would stay awake. Intolerant of laziness or sloppy work, she could be "pretty sharp with people" who did not do things right, regardless of their position.[11] Yet she earned the affection of those who worked with her because she seasoned her discipline with respect. Often humming under her breath as she worked, she was apparently content in her duties.[12] Years after her death, when her name was mentioned, Alice Carper responded immediately, "Oh, yes, she was a *wonderful* person."[13] "Within herself she really loved people," Carper felt, "especially the sick. She would see that anything was done to help the sick."[14] According to Carolyn Lane, Nella took one young man from North Carolina under her wing and taught him to read; he in turn looked up to her almost as if she were his mother.[15] She was respected equally by hospital employees of all ethnic backgrounds, most of whom, outside the nursing staff, were Jewish.[16] Race and ethnicity seem not to have been a factor in how she dealt with people.

Dependable, highly competent, and fair, she also had an air of pride. "She held her head high," according to one colleague who spoke with Thadious Davis.[17] She kept a trim, attractive appearance and dressed with style, sporting beautiful jewelry—antique necklaces, diamond rings, jade earrings. To her regular nurse's uniform she added a striking purple cape. Colleagues considered her an unusual, dramatic character. "Nella was an actress," Carolyn Lane recalled. "She knew how to pose for a picture."[18]

Reticent about her personal life and her past, Larsen—whom all of her colleagues knew as Nella Imes—kept to herself beyond the workplace until Alice Carper and Carolyn Lane began to draw her out. Carper said she was a recluse when they first met, depressed about having lost her husband to another woman whom Carper understood to have been a kind of friend.[19] Carolyn Lane told Charles Larson that Elmer "broke Nella's heart," a blow that she thought had much to do with Larsen's general loneliness and unhappiness.[20] Carper was also under the impression that Nella did not want people "bothering her" because she did not want people to know about her drug habit.[21]

Carper began inviting her to her social affairs, and eventually Nella "was always there" when Carper had friends over, occasionally spending the night.[22] They attended matinees together at the Metropolitan Opera, sitting up high in the balcony because Nella did not like to waste money. But she often slept through the shows, because she took a narcotic to stay awake at work and would then fall asleep during the daytime. Carper laughed out loud describing how they had gone to see the musical *South Pacific* together and Larsen missed the entire show.[23]

Carolyn Lane and Alice Carper were also good friends with each other and kept in contact for decades after retirement. Larsen spoke to both of them, within limits, about her past life. Carper knew, for example, that she had been born in Chicago and had grown up with her mother. Larsen told both women that her mother was an immigrant, and Carper, at least, knew that Nella had lived in Denmark as a girl and had visited with her grandmother.[24] Carper gave biographer Thadious Davis the impression that Nella rarely spoke of her parents, but to Charles R. Larson she said, "She spoke of her mother quite a bit," and Carolyn Lane knew the names of Nella's parents.[25] Carper was unsure about Mary Larsen's nationality, however, saying at first that she thought she was German, but "now, thinking about it, it could be Denmark."[26] Similarly, Carolyn Lane told Thadious Davis that she thought Nella's mother was German but

35. Anna Larsen Gardner and Mary Larsen, in Santa Monica, circa 1950. Photographer unknown. Courtesy of the late Mildred Phillips and Charles R. Larson.

born in Denmark.[27] The confusion, as I have suggested, probably has to do with the ambiguity inherent in the national identity of people native to Schleswig-Holstein, whose lives were constantly disrupted by German and Danish take-overs. Larsen told Carper that her father was West Indian and told Lane he was a light-skinned West Indian who had been a businessman in Chicago.[28] She may have been fudging about her father's occupation, but virtually everything else she told her friends was essentially accurate. Still self-conscious about her lower-class origins and the doubt they might cast on her legitimacy, she kept a veil over the hardest facts of her childhood.

Larsen apparently spoke hardly at all about her stepfather, Peter Larsen. Pneumonia aggravated by cancer of the larynx killed him at the age of seventy-seven about a year after she began working at Gouverneur. He died intestate with exactly $1,080 in assets—all cash and personal property that went to his estranged wife.[29] He had been living in Hollywood on his modest union pension, while Mary shared a house in Santa Monica with Anna, who fell victim to multiple sclerosis and needed her aging mother's constant care. Larsen must have known about this, for even Alice Carper later knew where to find Anna's address and phone number among Nella's papers.[30]

Larsen also spoke to Lane and Carper about the exciting period of her life as a writer, and gave both women copies of her novels. Carper believed that she had continued to publish stories in magazines after her divorce to bring in extra money.[31] She mentioned her friendships with famous authors like Eugene O'Neill and her travels in Europe. Nostalgic about her years in Scandinavia, France, and Spain, she tried to talk Carper into going abroad with her, but Alice declined because she had to care for her mother and her son.[32]

Both Carper and Lane commented on Larsen's fashion sense and love of fine clothes. Carper told three different interviewers that Larsen always wore beautiful things but got them cheaply in secondhand stores and fixed them up herself. She also still wore clothes given her by old friends: "She had a lot of white friends," Carper pointed out, "and they used to give her things."[33] Bright colors attracted her; she loved green, particularly, and she could spot quality immediately.[34] Always generous with her good friends, Nella also gave Alice "nice things," including a cashmere coat.[35]

Carper was aware of Larsen's affair with alcohol. "She nipped. . . . She liked good liquor."[36] While Carper herself never smoked or drank, Nella did both, and Carper implied that she did it a bit too much. Nella especially like good brandy, and she gave her teetotaler friend a set of delicate crystal brandy glasses as well as a punchbowl and cups for eggnog at Christmastime.[37] It is not unlikely that she chose night work because she could control and cover her drinking habit better that way. But if Larsen drank heavily for one of her age and size, she did not allow it to affect her work.

She remained a first-rate supervisor, always getting among the best raises, year after year. If she was respected at Gouverneur, however, the hospital itself seemed rather sadly neglected by the city. Local community groups and health-care advocates talked as if the building might collapse at any time. In 1950 the mayor budgeted funds to build a new facility, but constant debt crises held up the project, and for the next decade the fate of the hospital was in serious doubt.[38] Citywide antitax groups joined medical authorities in calling for closure of the hospital and sending the patients uptown to Bellevue Hospital, while neighborhood groups, local physicians, and local politicians insisted that Bellevue was too far away, too large, and too alien for the at-risk population Gouverneur served, people easily lost in the cracks of the public healthcare system.

As the ground shook under Gouverneur, across the continent, in another hospital, another crack opened in Nella Larsen's life. Suffering from "senility" and generalized arteriosclerosis, on the ninth of September 1951, eighty-three-year-old Mary Larsen fell in a hallway at home and fractured her right shoulder. She was taken to Santa Monica Hospital, where she died eight days later at 6:40 A.M.[39] Anna provided biographical information to the authorities and, with the help of friends, arranged for the funeral, burying Mary next to her husband (whom she had never divorced) in Inglewood Park Cemetery. Exactly when Nella learned about this we may never know. She almost certainly missed the ceremony. The evidence is overwhelming that Anna wanted no one to know about her black half-sister, although she would, interestingly enough, mention Larsen in her will as her half-sister.[40] Surely Anna would not have wanted Nella, whom she still called "Nellie," to show up for the funeral, where Anna's "secret" would have been revealed to all and may have raised questions about her own racial identity. But Nella almost certainly learned of her mother's death before long, for she knew both the current address and phone number of Mary and Anna. And a few years later, when filling out an employment application, she would list Anna as the person to be notified in case of emergency.[41] Larsen may well have spoken with her mother occasionally on the telephone before Mary's death.

Other old acquaintances still thought of Larsen and hoped to reconnect with her. Carl Van Vechten always copied her address into his new address books and mentioned her from time to time to Dorothy Peterson, who now lived at 509 Hudson Street, near Greenwich Village, and remained on dear terms with Carl. Dorothy, Harold Jackman, and Carl continued to celebrate the anniversary of their meeting through the 1950s, until Dorothy moved to Spain late in the decade.[42] On these occasions, it seems that Carl always thought of Nella. The Mary Mackinnon portrait of Fania Marinoff in Nella's dress, always prominently displayed in Carl and Fania's apartment, also helped to keep her memory green. Her former friends Nora Holt, Bruce Nugent, Edna Thomas, and Rita Romilly all kept in touch with Carl and Fania and enjoyed reminiscing about the Twenties. In 1954 Nella came to Carl's mind again on the eighth of February (their "anniversary") as he told Dorothy of a letter that the novelist Chester Himes had sent from Mallorca: "I think you will like this one because, as I recall, you and Nella visited Majorka at the same time and Nella spent the winter there at some similar rent."[43] A slightly skewed memory, but not far off. Four days later Dorothy replied with a correction: "I would like to go to Mallorca when I retire. Nella lived there before I joined her in Europe that year, and when we left Paris we went to Málaga because Nella 'was afraid of islands.'"[44]

Three weeks before this exchange, Larsen had applied for a Social Security card for the first time. On the application, she declared her mother's maiden name as Marian Hansen and her own as Nella Marian Larsen, and said that her Second Avenue address was her permanent home.[45] Just three months later she resigned from Gouverneur for what she called "personal" reasons—an episode her friends did not mention in later interviews.[46] It was an odd time to quit: at the age of sixty-three (although the city thought she was sixty-one), with no pension, and only four months after applying for Social Security.

Larsen was quickly replaced at the hospital, but in September of the same year she was rehired—as a regular staff nurse but with her former salary. On the job application form, she wrote down Alice Carper's name as the person to notify in case of emergency.[47] It's possible that this was about the time she sold the property in Connecticut of which she had sometimes spoken, and which she told her nursing friends was destroyed or flooded in a storm before she had a chance to show it to them. Massive storms and flooding, caused by Hurricane Carol and then Hurricane Edna, hit the Mid-Atlantic and Northeast coast at the end of August and in early September, taking out many homes. Damage was especially severe around New York, New Haven, and Milford. Flood insurance was unavailable at the time, so if Larsen's home was destroyed by flooding, she would have been faced with huge repair bills and could only have collected whatever the property was worth through sale.[48] When she died nine years later, she no longer had a house, but she had over $35,000 in two savings accounts, surely more than she could have saved on her nurse's salary.

Within a year and a half of resuming at Gouverneur, Larsen advanced over the Head Nurses again to become a Supervisor—a new designation for the Chief Nurse in a unit—and before long she was back at the top of the pay scale, making $4,550 by 1956–1957. The directors of the hospital were glad to have her back.

In the course of the late 1940s and 1950s, some of the worst slums of the Lower East Side were cleared away and replaced by new public housing units separated by green lawns and areas for play. Many of the patients from Gouverneur came from such a development just across the street; but the new buildings only served to mask the deeper squalor within, and the core of the district remained largely unchanged even as signs in Spanish replaced the old Yiddish ones. In 1955, there were 43,000 families still living in crowded tenements largely devoid of light and air, and only 9,000 living in the "projects." Two-thirds of the wage earners made less than $3,000 per year.[49] Schools ran on triple sessions because of overcrowding. And many people avoided Gouverneur Hospital because it had become so dilapidated. Although the Fire Department gave the employees stellar marks for "housekeeping," the building was simply too old.

People had begun giving false addresses in order to gain admission at other city hospitals. The neighborhood leaders anticipated the building of the promised new hospital, which they identified as one of their most urgent needs. But in 1954, citing financial constraints, the Commissioner of Hospitals withdrew requests for new hospital construction.[50] A protracted political struggle ensued. The commissioner argued that with new, modern hospitals going up in Brooklyn, Queens, the Bronx, and Harlem, there was no need for a mere 400-bed hospital on the Lower East Side, where the latest developments in hospital care could not be affordably provided.[51] The Department of Health was entering a new era—in fact, the commissioner argued, it was leading the nation into that era—and the old neighborhood hospital had become a relic of a bygone time. Indeed, the huge new streamlined hospitals with space-age interiors—such as Metropolitan, which had more than 1,000 beds and a veritable army of doctors, nurses, and aides—made Gouverneur look like an old wharf house.

But political leaders and social workers on the Lower East Side were not taking the situation lying down. In 1956 they started a petition for the new Gouverneur and by June had 30,000 names. On the seventh of that month, they held a ceremony at the Water Street entrance to the hospital, where prominent city officials, mostly Jewish and probably former residents of the neighborhood, came to sign on. Nella Larsen Imes registered to vote in city elections that year for the first time. The battle would continue into the mid-1960s, and the nurses, along with other staff members, would unite in support of a new hospital. Nella voted in every city election after 1956.[52]

By then, she and Alice Carper had grown "very, very close," according to Carper, but in the fall of 1959 Carper retired, provoking a predictable response. Feeling abandoned, Larsen stopped speaking to her. "She was put out. . . . She didn't think I should leave her," Carper recalled later, "so then she sort of began to withdraw."[53] It was exactly the response Larsen had displayed repeatedly in the past when she felt—however irrationally—that she was "losing" someone. But in October, in a last sign of friendship—either a plea for reconciliation or a farewell gesture—Larsen wrote a sort of will, specifying that the money in one of her two bank accounts should go to Carper in the event of her death. Carper felt she should not keep the will: "I was foolish and I was hurt, because she hadn't given me any of her time. She wasn't speaking to me."[54] Carper sent it back. Larsen again mailed it to her, and it went back and forth several times, until Larsen finally accepted it back in the form of a registered letter dated October 8, 1959.[55] Carper and Larsen apparently hardly spoke to each other again, though Alice remained deeply concerned about her friend. Carolyn Lane did stay on at the hospital, and she along with others apparently kept Carper informed about how Nella was doing.

Things were not going well. In the late 1950s, the Joint Committee on Accreditation of Hospitals withdrew its imprimatur and approval of residency programs at Gouverneur; New York University Medical School severed its connections with the hospital; and the American Medical Association withdrew its accreditation.[56] Gouverneur was liable to close at any time, forcing Larsen to retire or start over at another hospital. And then, in early 1960, as she was on the way to work, just in front of the hospital approaching the Water Street entrance, a purse-snatcher attacked her. With the handle of her bag wrapped around her left wrist, she refused to let go, and he swung her around until, giving up, he let her fall to the pavement with a broken wrist. She picked herself up and went into the hospital, where they put her arm in a cast. She then worked her usual shift through the night before going home.[57] For weeks thereafter she wore a sling, yet never took time off from work to recover. She was "fearless," Carolyn Lane told Professor Davis.[58] She got a whopping raise of $620 that year.[59]

Yet the nurses were growing increasingly angry about the unsettled fate of their workplace. Gouverneur was not only the smallest hospital in the system, now down to 177 beds; it also had the lowest occupancy rate. In the summer of 1960, the proposed city budget for 1961 included money for acquiring a site near Seward Park and drawing up preliminary plans for a new Gouverneur Hospital, but the mayor's Commission on Health Services advised against rebuilding, saying patients would get better care at Bellevue or at voluntary hospitals in the area. The Citizens' Budget Commission urged the mayor to follow this advice, while the Commission on Health Services militated for all city hospitals to affiliate with voluntary hospitals, an arrangement that threatened the continued viability of Larsen's position.[60]

On the night of the twenty-first of November, while Larsen was supervising, the Good Neighbors Council of the Lower East Side Neighborhood Association assembled a crowd of fifty to picket the hospital with flashlights and placards demanding a "ray of hope" for a new hospital, and complaining about services and facilities.[61] Nonetheless, the Hospital Council of Greater New York decided in February that the city "cannot justify continuing to operate Gouverneur."[62] The Health Commissioner declared that the house staff of thirty physicians trained abroad was inadequate; they had all either avoided or failed the tests for "foreign medical graduates" demanded by the state Education Council.[63]

Mayor Robert Wagner continued to voice support for the new facility, but he bowed to his advisers while a new committee of physicians looked into the issue. On the fifteenth of March, 250 Lower East Side residents picketed City Hall.[64] Two days later, the city announced that Gouverneur would no longer admit patients.[65] Larsen's position changed radically.

Implicit in the fracas over Gouverneur were larger issues about the viability of the old neighborhood hospital system and the wisdom of the new "reform" program of modernization, which favored huge, impersonal institutions to maximize efficiency.[66] Part of the new program involved "paths of affiliation" between smaller city hospitals and larger voluntary ones. Following a priority list of "worst things first," the commissioner started with Gouverneur, mandating its affiliation with Beth Israel and restricting it to providing outpatient services until a new hospital could be built. Nurses, deeply angered by this arrangement, began resigning.[67] In October 1961, Gouverneur's affiliation with Beth Israel took effect.[68] On December 2, Larsen applied for a Night Supervisor position at Metropolitan, one of the mammoth new hospitals, located on First Avenue between Ninety-Seventh and Ninety-Ninth streets. Claiming to be a widow, Larsen now listed her half-sister as the person to be notified in case of emergency.[69] She was no longer speaking to Alice Carper.

Legally, Larsen had no business applying for another nursing job with the city. She should have retired in April 1961, when she turned seventy; but she was still writing on applications that she had been born in 1893. Nonetheless, she was interviewed on the eighth of December and was immediately offered a position. She would begin work in February 1962 as Night Supervisor of the Psychiatric Ward.[70] Several of her nurse friends from Gouverneur went with her.[71]

About a week before she started in her new position, Carl Van Vechten sent Dorothy Peterson a letter commemorating their first meeting in 1926. As usual, he asked about Nella. In 1959 Dorothy had moved to Seville, Spain, because she suffered from painful arthritis, needed to lower her living expenses, and loved Spanish culture; in the dry, mild climate her health improved and she became a fixture in the American community, with a Norwegian escort and a wide circle of admirers. She took a lovely apartment in the Jewish quarter that she could afford on her teacher's pension, taught English to Spanish friends and Spanish to American friends, and, according to her sister-in-law, "collected in good will and friendships."[72] Dorothy agonized over the civil rights struggle that was going on in the United States, feeling guilty for living in Spain while others were enduring social turmoil; as a Negro, she felt, she should be in America fighting the good fight.[73] But she had no qualms about the end of her relationship to Larsen. Sidney's second wife, Vera Joseph, later said that Dorothy never spoke bitterly of Nella—but on the other hand, "I don't think she ever showed regrets over a lost friendship."[74] "As for Nella," Dorothy wrote Carl, "when I first came to Spain I wrote her, but have never heard from her so I've never written again."[75]

Metropolitan Hospital was a little over six years old when Nella started there. It was a gleaming concatenation of rectangular cubes made of white concrete and glass, behind a ten-foot-high chainlink fence, and covering several square blocks along First Avenue. The third-largest city hospital (of fourteen), it had more than 1,000 beds and an occupancy rate near 100 percent.[76] Intended to serve chiefly East Harlem and the Upper East Side, it had replaced the old hospital complex on Welfare Island (now Roosevelt Island), where Wallace Thurman had died twenty years earlier. Officials in the Department of Hospitals considered it a national model of municipal hospital design and organization. About half of its nurses (including the supervisors) and virtually all of its nurse trainees were black.[77]

The fifty-bed Psychiatric Unit, which Larsen supervised, was one of very few in the municipal system. Unlike most such wards, the "Psych Unit" at Metropolitan had no alcoholics, because the hospital had a separate detoxification ward. Some of the patients were elderly people slowly losing their faculties to what would someday be called Alzheimer's disease; but they comprised people of all ages, including children. Larsen lost only two days of work to illness in her first year on the job, and after a substantial raise at the end of that year she had one of the top salaries in a long list of supervisors.[78] After a little more than a year on the job, she passed what the hospital authorities believed was her seventieth birthday, but no one noticed and she did not mention it. Nursing and reading were her entire life.

It was at about this time that she made one last, desperate attempt at reconciliation and friendship—with her half-sister Anna. She never told anyone precisely what happened, but Alice Carper, whom Larsen was avoiding, got the impression that she had traveled all the way to Santa Monica for "a very disappointing visit."[79] The details will always be foggy, because Larsen had withdrawn from her friends. "Nella went bad into depression at the end of her life," Alice told Thadious Davis; and she attributed this to the California trip. To Charles R. Larson she added that Nella "gave up the idea of having a family."[80]

36. Metropolitan Hospital, New York City, circa 1960. DPC Collection, Courtesy New York City Municipal Archives.

The rejection could have occurred over the telephone. Anna's closest friend, Mildred Phillips, knew that Anna had a "colored" half-sister (though Anna kept this a secret and was apparently unaware of Mildred's knowledge) and was caring for Anna constantly at the time because of her multiple sclerosis. She felt certain that Anna was not corresponding with Nella, because Anna was unable even to open her own mail or write a letter, having lost the use of her hands and feet, and Mildred would have known of any letters that passed between them. Mildred also felt certain that Nella had never come to visit.[81] On the other hand, Anna's son, George Gardner, Jr., and his wife still lived in the same duplex, and we have no way of knowing if they were aware of their Negro relative's existence. It is possible that Mildred would never have been told of Nella's sudden appearance. The dénouement, in any case, is chilling enough. Larsen fell into deep depression and refused to speak with friends. Both Carper and Lane had the sense that she had been turned away from the door.

At about the same time, she was turned out of yet another door. In June 1963, she was "found out" as being past the age of forced retirement. She was still entitled, however, to twenty-seven days of normal vacation leave, plus an additional week of "retirement leave" and various amounts of accrued sick leave and the like, adding up to nearly three months. The Superintendent of Nurses therefore vouched on June 11 for her application to remain on the payroll past her seventieth birthday so that Larsen could use up her leave time. Her retirement—on Social Security—would officially take effect on September 12.

Larsen listed Alice Carper again as the person to be notified in case of emergency, but she avoided seeing or talking with her. In fact, Carper had no idea that Larsen had retired. "She never retired, definitely not," Carper told Charles Larson in 1986. "I don't think she would have ever retired."[82] From Larsen's point of view, the retirement was yet another form of abandonment.

She worked her last night on the twenty-second of June, from midnight until eight o'clock A.M.[83] Now, having ended all of her social relationships, she was truly on her own. She stopped taking calls or visitors, immersed herself in reading books, and waited for the end.[84]

It came on or about Easter Sunday, 1964. According to Carper, who heard of it from the building superintendent living in the apartment in front of Nella's, Larsen had gone away somewhere for the holiday weekend and no one noticed when she came back.[85] On March 30, a Monday, the superintendent entered the apartment at 9:30 P.M., since she hadn't seen Nella for several days. What remained of Nella Larsen Imes lay face up in bed, clad in a black sweater over a blue dress, and black socks.

The first police officer to arrive found the apartment undisturbed and reported "nothing suspicious"; he wrote that the deceased had no known friends or relatives. An ambulance took the body to Bellevue Hospital, where Larsen was pronounced dead. At the city morgue, the Medical Examiner subsequently determined that the officially yet-unidentified woman had died of a heart attack brought on by arteriosclerosis and hypertension. The police searched the apartment, looking for papers identifying Larsen and any relatives or friends. They found the name and address of a female friend on Edgecombe Drive in Harlem, and she informed the police on March 31 that Nella had a relative, evidently a brother-in-law, in New York State. When they contacted him by teletyped message, however, he declined to identify or claim the body. Finally, they contacted Alice Carper, who claimed the body at the morgue on April 1 and began making funeral arrangements.[86]

By the time Carper visited the apartment and was allowed in, anxious about the "will" Larsen had once sent her, all valuables had disappeared and the apartment looked like the scene of a burglary. None of Larsen's jewelry remained, none of her vases or antiques.[87] All of her drawers had been pulled out and her papers scattered over the floor.

Carper believed the body had lain in the apartment for several days before the superintendent discovered it, although other documents suggest that Larsen died "on or about" the date her body was discovered. When interviewed by biographers in the 1980s, Carper was still furious with Larsen's former co-workers at Metropolitan Hospital for not noticing her failure to report for work. Convinced that Larsen had never retired, she did not believe that they had not seen her since saying goodbye more than eight months earlier.

Carper made funeral arrangements through Miles Funeral Home of Brooklyn, which was run by a friend of hers. She owned a family plot with four burial spaces in the "Garden of Memory" of Cypress Hills Cemetery, off the Interborough Expressway running through Brooklyn and Long Island. Her husband's body lay in one of them, and she decided to put Nella's remains in another.[88] Few people other than Nella's hospital co-workers from Gouverneur and Metropolitan knew of her death, and according to Thadious Davis, all of the flowers and cards sent to the funeral home (cards that Davis subsequently acquired) came from these former colleagues. The funeral service on April 6 was attended by more than forty people, nearly all of them nurses. Alice Carper delivered a eulogy based on what she knew about Nella, evidently supplemented by employment records and the like. Although in some cases Carper had confused the dates, by and large the biography was remarkably accurate, focusing on Larsen's career as a nurse. Only two sentences spoke of her success as an author: "Much of her time was devoted to the writing of novels, and magazine articles. Two known novels are *Quicksand* and *Passing*. Still being a dedicated nurse, she returned to the field of nursing, to help alleviate the great shortage of nurses. . . . Nella was greatly respected and loved by her co-workers and those with whom she came in contact," Carper concluded. "No task was ever too great for her to tackle. It was inspiring and encouraging the way she worked along with those in her charge. Her passing is a great loss, and she will be missed by her co-workers and many friends. God be with you, Nella."[89]

The *New York Times* carried a brief death notice the day after the funeral. The listing gave no indication of where Larsen was buried or how she had died, stating simply: "Imes—Nella Larsen, died March 30, 1964, sister of Anna Larsen Gardener of Calif."[90] The card from which this information was copied was apparently later lost. Jean Blackwell Hutson, director of the Schomburg Collec-

37. 315 Second Avenue (center), New York City, circa 1941. This is where Larsen lived the last twenty-five years of her life and died in March 1964. "Tax" Department Photo Collection, Courtesy New York City Municipal Archives.

tion, after trying to track down information about Larsen's life and death, wrote to an inquiring scholar: "In her later years, she lived down in Greenwich Village and did not come to the attention of Harlemites. Some people report that she was 'passing.' . . . Of course, in New York there are [so] many dusky complexioned people from foreign countries that among them, perhaps, she might not have been identified as a Negro. These informants said that she was found dead in Brooklyn, N.Y. several years ago, but the *New York Times* reported that there was no card for her in their morgue."[91]

Coda

Toward the end of July 2005, as the manuscript of this book was in preparation, I woke up at 4:00 A.M., drove to Indianapolis, and flew to New York to perform a final task. After eight years of working on Nella Larsen's life, I had still not visited her grave. I reached Cypress Hills Cemetery in Brooklyn by 10:30. At the cemetery office I asked how to find the gravesite in the Garden of Memory. The staff confirmed the location—section 15, block 4, lot 99D, grave 3—and gave me a map.

It took about a half-hour to walk to section 15, just next to Cypress Hills Abbey, a mostly bare hillside but a lovely spot, high above the surrounding borough. For well over an hour I walked methodically back and forth through the rows of graves, looking for the name "Imes" or "Carper." The stones in that area were modest, just horizontal slabs about eight by thirty-six inches, placed flush with the earth so the maintenance crews could mow right over them. Most were from the 1960s. Some stones were sinking and getting overgrown, and I stopped occasionally to wipe dirt or grass cuttings or spreading crabgrass off a slab in hopes of finding the one I was looking for. No luck.

As the sun rose higher, I took off my collared shirt and started over from the bottom left corner. I began to see the pattern, which was mathematical. The extreme corner of many of the stones bore a number and letter indicating the lot and grave number: 87C in this row, 97C in the next, and adjacent to that another 97C, then a 98C. Up another row, 97D, 98D, 100D. But there was no 99D, only dirt and grass, a gap in the row at the crest of the hill. Perhaps the stone had been covered already by the spreading turf. I dug with my toe for a flat rock. Bending over, I rubbed the ground with my hand, scratched the earth at a bare spot, poked. In vain. Again I walked the rows to see if I had missed something. In the early afternoon, sweating freely through my tee-shirt, I gave up and walked back to the office to make sure I had not gotten something wrong.

While I washed my hands in the outside lavatory, Valerie Swan Young, a member of the staff, brought out the record for me to see. The card bore only the name "Nella Imes"—no date of birth or death, no record of a headstone. She was there all right, in that gap at the center of the Garden of Memory, but the grave had never been marked.

Epilogue

CARL Van Vechten may have seen the listing in the *Times*. By the end of the summer, he and Dorothy Peterson, who was still in Spain, both knew that Larsen had died. But neither of them had any way of knowing about the funeral beforehand, or about the relationship between Larsen and Alice Carper, who became, in effect, Larsen's executor. Thus, Van Vechten could not get Larsen's papers for the James Weldon Johnson Collection at Yale. Carper took possession of some of Larsen's papers and belongings, including some of her "writings" and her bronze medal from the Harmon Foundation. Later, Carper lost the papers in a move, according to her own account, and in the 1980s she gave the medal to Professor Thadious Davis. The remaining items from Larsen's apartment, consisting chiefly of her books—not a few of them valuable collector's items—and furniture, were sold for sixty dollars.[1] Many of her papers were probably just thrown away.

When Carper learned that all of Nella's savings and belongings would be claimed by the state unless a relative could be found, and that she would need legal counsel to reclaim the expenses of the funeral and be reimbursed for the gravesite, she hired a lawyer and went through the papers she'd obtained from Nella's apartment, looking for the address of Anna Larsen Gardner. In one later interview she said that she called Anna on the telephone and learned that she was too infirm to make the journey to New York.[2] Alice and her lawyer, Irvin C. Maltz, sent Anna a registered letter on May 25, 1964.[3] When Anna told Mildred Phillips she had received a letter saying she would inherit some money, she reported the news with great surprise and said, "I didn't know I had a half sister" —which of course was a lie. It was the only time Phillips ever heard "Nelli" mentioned in the Larsen and Gardner homes.[4]

Anna hired a Hollywood attorney to correspond with Carper's lawyer, and then, in late April, hired a New York lawyer, Arnold A. Levin, to look after her interests in the estate.[5] Levin scrambled to locate evidence proving Anna's relationship to "Nellie" Larsen Imes, including census records of 1900 and 1920, a birth certificate for Anna, and the supposed marriage license of Mary and Peter Larsen—which turned out to be for a different couple. Levin established Nellie's birthdate as April 13, 1891.[6] In February 1965, he formally objected on Anna's behalf to the initial settling of the estate in the Surrogate's Court, which would have given everything to the state. Alice Carper had to swear an oath that Nella had said she was born in Chicago.[7] Not until March 1965 did the Surrogate judge, Joseph A. Cox, finally award what remained of Nella's estate to Anna. After lawyer's fees and reimbursements for expenses were deducted, she received $27,722 out of a gross estate of more than $36,000.[8]

The first surviving evidence that Carl Van Vechten and Dorothy Peterson knew of Larsen's death is a letter Dorothy wrote to Carl from Spain in September 1964. She shared concerns about new black separatist movements such as the Black Muslims (the Nation of Islam) and about radical assaults by both whites and blacks, from the left and the right, on integrationism. Like Carl, she felt that established authors such as Langston Hughes should "come out publicly and remind everyone of the favors and help and inspiration (as well as friendship) that he (and many others) have received from members of the so-called 'white race.'"[9] Still disillusioned from her experience with Hughes in the Harlem Suitcase Theatre, she attributed his failure to the fact that he had "absolutely no sense of gratitude" and did not like or distinguish between white people (a rather astonishing charge).

> Right now he could write a very important article "I have known many white people who . . ." and then mention Mary White Ovington, the old lady whom they called "godmother," you both, the Spingarns, the Knopfs, and many, many others whom he would know better than I would (although I would know some in the Department of Education of N.Y.C. that he would not) as well as some of the Foundations, Rosenwald, Rockefeller and others. I think maybe that if Nella were alive she would be able and willing to do such an article. But who else would dare to risk the opprobrium with which such an article would be greeted by a certain group of Negroes? Maybe Bruce Nugent? Nora? This would not have to be a huge eulogy but a simple statement of facts.[10]

By 1964, however, Nella Larsen, Bruce Nugent, and Nora Holt were almost completely forgotten, and the Negro Renaissance itself was being attacked from many directions, in no small part because of the role that whites like Van Vechten had played in it. As the integrationist ideals and practices of the early civil rights movement were displaced by the Black Power Movement, the so-called Harlem Renaissance became an example of everything that was supposedly wrong with black writers of the past and their relationships with white "patrons"—the blanket term for whites who were in any way involved with black artists of the 1920s.

Larsen herself, when her novels were remembered at all, was regarded as a member of the "rear guard" of the renaissance—an author concerned (allegedly like Jessie Fauset, with whom she would be perennially paired) with proving to rich white folks that some Negroes in America were just like them, with refined European manners and nice belongings, who ought to be allowed into white people's churches and homes. Such was the critical consensus when Larsen's novels were first reissued and began to be discussed in university classrooms in the early 1970s. Biographical speculation about her was often wildly inaccurate.

In his introduction to the 1971 Collier Books paperback edition of *Passing,* part of an important series called the African/American Library started by Charles R. Larson, Hoyt Fuller recalls the initial reception of the novel and informs the reader that, like her main characters, Larsen "had gone off to Europe for a try at rejecting her Blackness, only to return in the end to wrap it closely about her again." A footnote adds: "At one point, Miss Larsen left her husband, Dr. Elmer Imes, and went off to live in Europe. Reportedly, she considered ending her marriage and becoming the wife of an Englishman. However, she finally returned to America and to Dr. Imes."[11] Largely concerned with the issue of "assimilation" versus racial unity and the nuclear black family, this is all the biographical information Fuller provides. It harmonizes with the damning criticism he aims at the novel. Justifying the fact that recent black readers had not shown much interest in Larsen's work, he finds the novel's subject matter trivial: "Apart from the malicious delight Black people derived from having one of their own get away with such a masquerade, passing no doubt ranked very low in the essential scheme of things. Current interests lie in other, less white-oriented directions."[12] Part of the problem derives precisely from Larsen's racial pedigree, in Fuller's view. "It is all rather banal. . . . In the tradition of mulatto writers since William Wells Brown, . . . Miss Larsen dwells on the 'white' traits of her 'society Negro' characters."[13] Fuller concludes with a withering dismissal of the novel he is introducing to a new generation of readers, in the version that would be the classroom standard for fifteen years: "Without the element of intrigue and suspense injected by race, Miss Larsen's novel might have been relegated to the lost ranks of that massive body of fiction designed to titillate middle-class housewives on a long and lonely afternoon."[14]

In a far more understanding introduction to *Quicksand* for the African/American Library, Adelaide Cromwell Hill provides a more sound capsule biography based chiefly on Larsen's own for Knopf, aided by independent research, while admitting that, "in the present mood of Black Nationalism, with the Black woman trying a bit unsuccessfully to minimize her strengths in order to build those of the Black man, the themes in *Quicksand* are hard to accept."[15] Though she appreciates the way Larsen's biography shows that "Black experience can be global," and that Larsen was one of relatively few black women writers to achieve renown between the 1890s and the 1970s, Hill finally determines that Larsen failed because she rejected black identity and thus "never found herself."[16] Moreover, *Quicksand*'s style is "faded," its language "bland," and the situations it foregrounds "a trifle unreal."[17]

Such was the consensus about Larsen's fiction before black feminist critics and others began revisiting it for alternative visions of black female authorship in the African American canon. In this revisiting, the position of biracial and passing characters was still considered trivial, but now it seemed beside the point in the effort to come to grips with Larsen's "real" concerns. According to Hoyt Fuller's interpretation, Larsen had seen the error of straying from her husband and the nuclear black family; she had returned to her race. In the new feminist criticism, Larsen was legitimated by being fit into a sisterhood or black matrilineal pattern of descent extending from Phillis Wheatley to Alice Walker. In this project of reclamation, Larsen's exploration of the zone between the races, and its suppression both socially and psychologically—for which "black aesthetic" critics had dismissed her—came to seem merely a "mask," a ruse forced upon her by white people. Larsen's allegedly superficial emphasis on mulatto characters and passing had prevented her from more boldly investigating her real theme—black female sexuality, black sisterhood—and had compromised her worth as an author.

In particular, Carl Van Vechten's *Nigger Heaven* had allegedly made it "difficult to publish novels that did not fit the profile of the commercial success formula adopted by most publishers for black writers."[18] For example, Larsen had found her real story about lesbian attraction in *Passing* too dangerous to expose in a literary milieu dominated by the likes of Van Vechten and Knopf, so she'd wrapped her real concerns in the guise of the "safe and familiar plot of racial passing."[19] Through this failure of nerve, such critics said, she honors "the very value system the text implicitly satirizes" and does "the opposite of what she has promised."[20] According to this line of thinking, the best that could be said for Larsen's work was that it anticipated later, more explicit, and more satisfying treatments of black female sexuality by authors such as Toni Morrison, Alice Walker, Gloria Naylor, and Ntozake Shange.

Fitting Larsen into her proper line of descent here—which also became fundamental to the marketing of new editions of her work—had the effect of suppressing much of her experience and beliefs. This was equally true of the major attempt at biographical reclamation soon to follow. It was as if the suspicions of illegitimacy that haunted her in life because of her parentage were transmuted after her death into patterns of criticism and historical lineation. By the time Larsen's life came to seem worth investigating in depth, much of what she had said about herself—much, in fact, that she had experienced—seemed out of place. Feminist critics tended to explain it with compassionate condescension for a lost sister who was to be forgiven for her statements and embraced by the racial family she always needed.

But had this form of reclamation not come about, who knows how long we would have had to wait for the resurrection of Larsen's work? Just as Larsen, after returning from Denmark in 1912, could have been accepted only by a black nursing school, so in the late twentieth century could she have been "rescued" for the literary canon only by scholars making a place for her in a specifically African American canon defined by racial expectations formed out of the whole history of racial segregation in American life. It is not coincidental that her place was defined in familial metaphors with profound psychological resonances. In the United States, after all, race and family are joined—or so we think —at the mother's hip.

We have no place of recognition for black authors independent of their prior valorization within group parameters, and we are pervasively warned that failing to interpret them chiefly with respect to the "black tradition" and its latest authoritative canons of interpretation can only lead to egregious misunderstandings. Either Larsen is inherently not worthy of serious regard, or she merits that regard because she subverts the work of authors like Carl Van Vechten and Gertrude Stein while fitting into a continuous genetic relationship with her black "foremothers" and "daughters." And where she falls down, as the critics would have it, she falls down because she had the wrong mother, suffering as a result from delusions about her identity and culture.

The failures of understanding and imagination concerning Larsen (from which I claim no immunity myself) are the products not of bad faith or individual error but of social proscription, of a long history of racial domination, segregation, and their diverse progeny—results of and contributors to the reproduction of race and the subordination of all intimate relations to that invidious abstraction. Ultimately, however, Larsen refuses to be domesticated and puts hard questions to any form of belonging predicated on racial exclusion. In the interpretation of her life and work, in her emergence and disappearance, in the gaps of historical knowledge and the scattered remains of what has been lost, the obdurate and intricate workings of the color line reveal themselves, from the years of Jim Crow to the present day.

Abbreviations
Notes
Acknowledgments
Index

ABBREVIATIONS

Beinecke	Beinecke Rare Book and Manuscript Library, Yale University
BTWP/LOC	Booker T. Washington Papers, Library of Congress
CVV daybooks	Daybooks of Carl Van Vechten, in CVV/NYPL
CVV/JWJ	Carl Van Vechten Papers, James Weldon Johnson Memorial Collection, Yale Collection of American Literature, Beinecke Rare Book and Manuscript Library, Yale University
CVV/NYPL	Carl Van Vechten Papers, Manuscripts and Archives Division, New York Public Library, Astor, Lenox and Tilden Foundations
DPP	Dorothy Peterson Papers, Yale Collection of American Literature, Beinecke Rare Book and Manuscript Library, Yale University
Fisk	Special Collections, Fisk University Library
GNJ/JWJ	Grace Nail Johnson Correspondence, Yale Collection of American Literature, Beinecke Rare Book and Manuscript Library, Yale University
HRHRC	Harry Ransom Humanities Research Center, University of Texas, Austin
JTP	Jean Toomer Papers, Yale Collection of American Literature, Beinecke Rare Book and Manuscript Library, Yale University
JWJ Files	James Weldon Johnson Files collection, Yale Collection of American Literature, Beinecke Rare Book and Manuscript Library, Yale University
JWJ/JWJ	James Weldon Johnson Papers, Yale Collection of American Literature, Beinecke Rare Book and Manuscript Library, Yale University
LHP	Langston Hughes Papers, Yale Collection of American Literature, Beinecke Rare Book and Manuscript Library, Yale University
NYPL	New York Public Library, Astor, Lenox and Tilden Foundations
NYPL LS	New York Public Library, Library School Collection, Rare Book and Manuscript Library, Columbia University
RRMP/LC	R. R. Moton Papers, Local Correspondence, Frissell Library, Tuskegee University
Schomburg	Manuscripts, Archives, and Rare Books Division, Schomburg Center for Research in Black Culture, New York Public Library, Astor, Lenox and Tilden Foundations
SCR	Schomburg Center Records collection, Schomburg
WWPC	Walter White Personal Correspondence, NAACP Papers, Library of Congress

NOTES

1. Mary Helen Washington, "Nella Larsen: Mystery Woman of the Harlem Renaissance," *Ms.,* December 1980, p. 45.
2. T. S. Eliot, "Ben Jonson," in Eliot, *Selected Essays,* 3rd enlarged ed. (London: Faber and Faber, 1951; rpt. 1953), p. 152. Eliot is speaking of characterization in Flaubert's *L'Education sentimentale.*

1. NELLIE WALKER

1. John Dewey, quoted in Louis Menand, *The Metaphysical Club* (New York: Farrar, Straus, and Giroux, 2001), p. 319.
2. Henry Blake Fuller, "The Upward Movement in Chicago," *Atlantic Monthly* 80 (October 1897): 534.
3. Theodore Dreiser, "Cheyenne, Haunt of Misery and Crime," in *Newspaper Writings, 1892–1895,* vol. 1 of Dreiser, *Journalism,* ed. T. D. Nostwich (Philadelphia: University of Pennsylvania Press, 1988), p. 6, reprinted from Chicago *Globe,* 24 July 1892, p. 3.
4. St. Clair Drake and Horace R. Cayton, *Black Metropolis: A Study of Negro Life in a Northern City* (New York: Harcourt, Brace, 1945), vol. 1, p. 8.
5. Return of a Birth, no. 16546, Cook County, Illinois. Concerning Lyon, see listing for E. A. Lyon in the business directory section of *Lakeside Annual Directory of the City of Chicago, 1891* (Chicago: Chicago Directory Co., 1891), p. 2664, and in the general directory section, p. 1441. The birth certificate was first discovered by attorney Andrew A. Levin when developing Anna Larsen Gardner's case to inherit Nella's estate. Key to identifying this record with Nella Larsen, as Professor Davis points out, is the birthdate (which is consistent with other records, although eventually Larsen started claiming a birth year of 1893) and the fact that when Larsen was at Fisk University in 1907, her name appeared in at least one student list as "Nelly Walker Larsen" (list for First Grade in Department of Music, *Catalogue of the Officers and Students of Fisk University, 1908–1909* [Nashville: Fisk University, 1909], p. 76). Furthermore, the maiden name "Mary Hansen" (or "Hanson") matched other records of Nella's mother's name, as does the age of the mother given on the birth certificate and the marriage license application of Peter Walker and Mary Hansen. All of these records, moreover, match up with Larsen's fragmentary descriptions of her parentage and birth. Thadious M. Davis, *Nella Larsen, Novelist of the Harlem Renaissance: A Woman's Life Unveiled* (Baton Rouge: Louisiana State University Press, 1994), p. 21.
6. Charles Washburn, *Come into My Parlor: A Biography of the Aristocratic Everleigh Sisters of Chicago* (1936; rpt. New York: Arno, 1974), p. 118. For physical details of the building and related structures, I rely on the insurance atlas *Atlas of the City of Chicago: Central Business Property* (Chicago: G. W. Bromley, 1891), available in Ealey Library, University of Illinois at Chicago.

7. *Atlas of the City of Chicago*. See also the business directory section of *Lakeside Annual* (1891).

8. Dominic A. Pacyga and Ellen Skerrett, *Chicago: City of Neighborhoods* (Chicago: Loyola University Press, 1986), pp. 303–304; John J. Flinn, *Chicago, the Marvelous City of the West: A History, an Encyclopedia, and a Guide,* 2nd ed. (Chicago: Standard Guide Co., 1892), p. 579.

9. Herbert Asbury, *Gem of the Prairie: An Informal History of the Chicago Underworld* (New York: Alfred A. Knopf, 1940), p. 122.

10. *Lakeside Annual* (1891); Asbury, pp. 117–118; Lloyd Wendt and Herman Kogan, *Lords of the Levee: The Story of Bathhouse John and Hinky Dink* (Indianapolis: Bobbs-Merrill, 1943), p. 283.

11. Asbury, p. 264.

12. Ibid.

13. "Clark Street Mission," Chicago *Daily Inter Ocean,* 29 November 1891, p. 4.

14. Flinn, p. 577. See also William T. Stead, *If Christ Came to Chicago!* (Chicago: Laird and Lee, 1894), p. 257.

15. Flinn, p. 578.

16. Ibid., p. 577.

17. The death certificate for Mary Larsen gives her birthdate as 24 September 1867, and her place of birth as Copenhagen; but death certificates are notoriously unreliable, particularly for immigrants, and according to experts on Danish American genealogy, Danish immigrants were routinely said to be from "Copenhagen" even if they had been born in other regions of the country. The death certificate gives her father's name as Martin Hansen and her mother's maiden name as Karen Mandensen; but "Mandensen" is surely a typographical error, since no such surname exists in Denmark, Germany, or any of the surrounding areas. "Mortensen," on the other hand, is a common surname and the closest approximation to the name on the death certificate, which was typed by someone unconnected with the family, undoubtedly on the basis of handwritten information provided by Mary's daughter Anna, who suffered from multiple sclerosis. Mary (the Danish "Marie" being often anglicized to "Mary" in the Chicago directories and other records) Hansen probably was not born in Copenhagen. Denmark has kept amazingly precise records of births from the period, originally required within each parish, and an exhaustive search of the parish records for the city turns up no Marie or Mary Hansen born to Martin Hansen and Karen Hansen or Karen Mortensen. (Arne J. Knudby to George Hutchinson, 24 April 1997. Mr. Knudby checked all the parish registers of Copenhagen for 1867 and 1868 for Mary Hansen's birth.)

    According to Nellie Walker's birth certificate, Mary was twenty-two years old as of 13 April 1891, which puts her birthdate (assuming September 24 is correct) in 1868. This date is corroborated by a number of documents cited elsewhere: Mary and Peter Walker's marriage license application, an 1898 emigration list, an 1898 ship manifest, the 1900 census, the Chicago city directory of 1908, and the 1920 census. The 1910 census (filled out by her husband rather than herself) would put her birthdate in 1869. Thus, the preponderance of evidence indicates Mary was born on 24 September 1868.

18. Davis, p. 46; Charles R. Larson interview with Alice Carper (audiotape), 11 June 1986. Many thanks to Professor Larson for lending me his interview tape.

19. This hypothesis is strengthened by the fact that on a library school application of 1922,

Larsen wrote that she had attended school (briefly) as a child in Askov, which was just north of the German border after 1864, in a region to which many Schleswigers moved after the Prussian takeover. Supporting the possibility that Larsen had lived in such a town is the fact that she told the British author Bryher in the mid-1930s that as a small child she had lived in a Danish town. As will be pointed out later, the versions of some of the Danish children's games that Larsen translated and published in 1920 were played specifically on the Jutland peninsula in the 1890s, a fact which again supports the likelihood that Mary came from South Jutland.

20. Donald S. Connery, *The Scandinavians* (New York: Simon and Schuster, 1966), p. 96; "Schleswig-Holstein's Intricate Problem," *New York Times*, 27 October 1918, sect. 3, p. 3; W. Glyn Jones, *Denmark: A Modern History* (London: Croom Helm, 1986), pp. 34–42, 61–62; Kristian Hvidt, *Danes Go West* (Copenhagen: Rebild National Park Society, 1976), pp. 155–158; and Kristian Hvidt, *Flight to America: The Social Backgrounds of 300,000 Danish Emigrants* (New York: Academic Press, 1975).

21. Hvidt, *Danes Go West*, pp. 129, 155–158, 168; Philip S. Friedman, "The Danish Community of Chicago," *The Bridge* 8 (1985): 26 n. 3.

22. Hvidt, *Flight*, p. 116.

23. Mary's death certificate gives no date of immigration, and women had no reason to file for naturalization in those days. They automatically received citizenship through their husbands, if their husbands naturalized. The 1920 census lists her immigration date as 1886; the 1910 census, which was filled out by her second husband and is the least reliable as a source of information about Mary, lists it as 1887. See Death Certificate for Mary "Larson," File 13645, Registrar-Recorder of Los Angeles County, California; and Fourteenth Census of the United States, 1920: Population, Cook County, Enumeration District 421, Sheet 3; Thirteenth Census of the United States, 1910: Population, Cook County, Enumeration District 1386, Sheet 1B. An 1898 passenger list filled out with information she provided says she had lived in the United States twelve years, and thus corroborates the 1886 date.

24. See, e.g., Auswanderlisten VIII A1, vol. 58, Staatsarchiv, Hamburg, available on microfilm through Family History Centers of the Church of Christ of Latter-Day Saints.

25. Odd S. Lovoll, *A Century of Urban Life: The Norwegians in Chicago before 1930* (Northfield, Minn.: Norwegian-American Historical Association, 1988), p. 155. A Miss Mary Hansen, dressmaker, first appears in the Chicago city directory in 1885, and again in 1886, with a work address at 393 West Ohio; in 1887 the same woman, apparently, is listed at 345 West Erie; unlisted in 1888, she reappears at 538 Milwaukee Avenue in 1889, and continues to appear sporadically on the near North Side, in the most "Scandinavian" section of the city, into the mid-1890s and after. This probably was not Nellie Walker's mother, but it should be noted that Danish women traditionally did not take their husbands' surnames until the late nineteenth century, and the city directory normally preceded a home address with the abbreviation *h*, which it did not do for this Mary Hansen. It is therefore conceivable that Nella's mother, who was a dressmaker by 1910 and kept her finances separate from Peter's, retained her maiden name for professional purposes and worked for many years outside the home.

26. Charles R. Larson, notes from interview with Mildred Phillips, 12 February 1986. Mrs. Phillips' memory may well have faded over the years. She was eighteen when her mother told her of Mrs. Larsen's first daughter, and the families came to know each

other only after Nella's separation from the Larsens. It is easy to imagine that a "cook" became a "chauffeur" merely through a fault of memory. Similarly, Phillips, who got to know the family after Nella Larsen was settled in New York, told Professor Larson that "Nellie" had been born in New York, and that she was a nurse. This seems to be merely a slight confusion: when Phillips first heard of Larsen, Nella was living in New York, where she worked as a nurse from 1912 to 1921 and again from 1941 on.

27. Illinois Bureau of Labor Statistics, *Seventh Biennial Report, 1892; Part 1: Working Women in Chicago* (Springfield, Ill.: H. W. Rokker, 1893), p. 134.

28. Joanne J. Meyerowitz, *Women Adrift: Independent Wage Earners in Chicago, 1880–1930* (Chicago: University of Chicago Press, 1988), p. 33.

29. See *Lakeside Annual* directories for 1887–1892 and subsequent years. The 1891 business directory section lists a saloon at 2034 Armour, and the 1900 census shows a boarding house at the same address. Two Peter Walkers also appear in the 1887 directory, but the working-class Peter Walker is here listed as a carpenter at 77 North Wood. A third Peter Walker of Chicago, living in the popular health resort of Thomasville, Georgia, died April 7, 1892, as reported in Chicago newspapers; his body was returned to Chicago and buried in Oakwood Cemetery on April 12. But this man, sixty-four years old and married to Margaret Walker, with several children, was white and much older than Nellie Walker's father. See "Deaths," *Chicago Tribune,* 10 April 1892, p. 5; "Deaths," *Chicago Tribune,* 12 April 1892, p. 3; and records of Oakwood Cemetery, Chicago.

30. Thelma Berlack, "New Author Unearthed Right Here in Harlem," *Amsterdam News,* 23 May 1928, p. 16. In an autobiographical sketch for Alfred A. Knopf's publicity department, Larsen wrote, "Nella Larsen is a mulatto, the daughter of a Danish lady and a Negro from the Virgin Islands, formerly the Danish West Indies. When she was two years old her father died and shortly afterward her mother married a man of her own race and nationality." Nella Larsen Imes, 24 November 1926, Alfred A. Knopf Collection, HRHRC. The Index to Death Records for Cook County lists no Peter Walker of anywhere near the right age between 1871 and 1916, suggesting that Nellie's father may have left the county. Index to Death Records, Cook County, Bureau of Vital Statistics from 1871–1916; microfilm edition in Family History Library, Church of Christ of Latter-Day Saints.

31. By 1917, nearly all the Walkers originally of the Danish West Indies had died or moved elsewhere. Only Matilda Hortensia Walker, a "mulatto" daughter of George born in 1857, remained on the islands. She was probably a sister or first cousin of Nella Larsen's father. The genealogical information about people named Walker in the Danish West Indies is based on an exhaustive search of the 1870 census covering all of the islands; of the church records for all of the churches on St. Croix (Episcopal, Catholic, Lutheran, and Moravian); of the 1850 census for Frederiksted; of the 1857 census for Frederiksted; of the 1860 census for Frederiksted, East End, and West End on St. Croix; and of the 1917 census index for the newly acquired "U.S. Virgin Islands," in which racial designations appear. These records, or copies of them, are held in the Library of the Estate Whim on St. Croix, run by the St. Croix Landmarks Society. The census records will soon be available on compact disc from the St. Croix African Roots Project led by George F. Tyson, Svend Holsoe, Roland Roebuck, and Poul Olsen. My sincere thanks to librarian Carol Wakefield for her generosity and advice while I went through these records at Whim.

32. On racial designations in the Virgin Islands, see Gordon K. Lewis, *The Virgin Islands: A Caribbean Lilliput* (Evanston, Ill.: Northwestern University Press, 1972), pp. 29, 248; and Jeanne Perkins Harman, *The Virgins: Magic Islands* (New York: Appleton-Century, 1961), pp. 147–148.

33. "Marriage Licenses," *Chicago Tribune*, 2 July 1890, p. 3; and application for marriage license of Peter Walker and Mary Hanson, 1 July 1890, record no. 154616, Records of Cook County, Cook County Clerk. Davis mistakenly lists the date of the application as July 14 (*Nella Larsen*, p. 26).

34. Loretto Dennis Szucs, *Chicago and Cook County Sources: A Genealogical and Historical Guide* (Salt Lake City: Ancestry Publishing, 1986), pp. 239, 235.

35. A marriage certificate of 1894 for a Peter Larsen and Mary Hansen in Chicago, cited in previous studies, turns out to be for a different couple, as I will explain in Chapter 2.

36. Kevin J. Mumford, *Interzones: Black/White Sex Districts in Chicago and New York in the Early Twentieth Century* (New York: Columbia University Press, 1997), pp. 168–170.

37. My translation, from M. Salmonsen, *Brogede Minder: Fra Fyrretyve Aars Ophold i Chicago* [Varied Recollections: From Forty Years' Residence in Chicago] (Copenhagen: Gyldendal, 1913), p. 180. Salmonsen goes on to point out that there was a strong movement in Chicago to outlaw interracial marriage.

38. As W. E. B. Du Bois pointed out in 1897, the "average Negro [frowned] darkly on his fellows" who married outside the race. "In those very circles of Negroes who have a large infusion of white blood, where freedom of marriage is most strenuously advocated, . . . white wives have always been treated with disdain bordering on insult, and white husbands never received on any terms of social recognition." W. E. B. Du Bois, *The Philadelphia Negro: A Social Study* (Philadelphia: University of Pennsylvania Press, 1899), p. 359, quoted in Willard B. Gatewood, *Aristocrats of Color: The Black Elite, 1880–1920* (Bloomington: Indiana University Press, 1990), p. 179.

39. Gatewood, p. 178. In the early 1890s, interracial couples in Milwaukee and Chicago founded the Manasseh Society to combat the ostracism they faced, but even this group excluded those who were not of "high moral and intellectual standing," and it could do little to alter entrenched attitudes among Negroes, not to mention whites, who opposed interracial marriages (ibid., pp. 177–178).

40. Kevin K. Gaines, *Uplifting the Race: Black Leadership, Politics, and Culture in the Twentieth Century* (Chapel Hill: University of North Carolina Press, 1996), p. 120.

41. Quoted ibid., p. 123.

42. "No Color Line Wanted," Indianapolis *Freeman*, 25 April 1891, p. 1; see also "Indignation and Opposition," ibid., 3 April 1891, p. 5; "Where's the Race Hero," ibid., 30 May 1891, p. 1; "N.B.—" ibid., 11 April 1891, p. 1.

43. Allen H. Spear, *Black Chicago: The Making of a Negro Ghetto, 1890–1920* (Chicago: University of Chicago Press, 1967), pp. 97–98; "Aiding Their Race," Chicago *Daily Inter Ocean*, 14 May 1892, pp. 9–10.

2. INHERITING THE COLOR LINE

1. Mildred Phillips to Charles R. Larson, 11 February 1986. In the possession of Charles R. Larson.

2. The birth certificate of Anna "Lizzie" Larsen gives the address. Return of a Birth, no.

20200, State of Illinois, 23 June 1892, Cook County Clerk. This birth certificate was used by attorney Arnold A. Levin to establish Anna Larsen Gardner's relationship to Nella Larsen Imes. See Surrogate's Court file for the estate of Nella L. Imes (A2329/1964), New York County, 31 Chambers Street, New York City. Thadious M. Davis discovered the same birth certificate but inaccurately gives the year of Anna's birth as 1893; Davis, *Nella Larsen, Novelist of the Harlem Renaissance: A Woman's Life Unveiled* (Baton Rouge: Louisiana University Press, 1994), p. 29.

3. Genealogists of Danish Americans run across such transformations all the time. For example, the 1900 soundex (a specially coded name index) for the U.S. Census in Illinois reveals how commonly the Danish name "Larsen" was spelled "Larson" by officials. Occasionally, Swedes were given the Danish "Larsen" spelling by mistake. In many cases the immigrants did not consider this a matter of much importance. The name of Nella's family that year, because of the poor penmanship of the original enumerator, was spelled in the typed soundex as "Lanson," which explains why previous biographers could not find them in the 1900 census.

4. The description of the building comes from *Atlas of the City of Chicago: Central Business Property* (Chicago: G. W. Bromley, 1891).

5. Census records from 1900, 1910, and 1920 all date the marriage of Nella's mother and stepfather to 1891, which coincides with the year in which Anna Larsen was conceived. Other vital records for Peter and Mary comport with this marriage date. An 1894 marriage certificate was used by Anna's lawyer to help prove her relationship to Nella and thus acquire Nella's estate. It is also identified by Charles R. Larson and Thadious M. Davis as the certificate for Nella's mother and stepfather. But it turns out to refer to a Larsen couple different from Nella and Anna's parents: thirty-two-year-old Peter Larsen of Harland (a misspelling for Harlan), Shelby County, Iowa, and twenty-seven-year-old Marie Hansen of Chicago. The ages do not match those of Nella's mother and stepfather. Furthermore, while no records support the notion that Nella's stepfather had lived in Harlan, Iowa, a different Peter Larsen of the same age as the Peter Larsen named on the marriage certificate *did* live there. He had recently lost a wife and was on his way back to Denmark in 1894 to find a new spouse when he ran into an "old flame," twenty-seven-year-old Marie Hansen, in Chicago in 1894. They married there and moved back to Iowa, living out their lives together in the town of Ute, a Danish settlement. They are buried together in a nearby cemetery. The Marie Hansen who gave birth to Nellie Walker and who applied for marriage to Peter Walker was twenty-five when the 1894 marriage took place, not twenty-seven, the age given on the marriage certificate. Moreover, all other records of Nella's stepfather's age indicate that he would have been five years younger than the Peter on the marriage license, as well as five years younger than Peter Walker. License no. 1030237, Cook County Vital Records, Marriage Licenses, 1871–1920, Cook County Records, Chicago; Certificate of Marriage 214124, State of Illinois, 7 February 1894; Patricia Galster Braun to George Hutchinson, 11 July 1996; Mae M. Petersen to George Hutchinson, 8 May 1996; Surrogates' Court file for Nella L. Imes.

6. Mary Rennels, "Behind the Backs of Books and Authors," *New York Telegram,* 13 April 1929, sect. 2, p. 2.

7. Last Will and Testament of Anna Elizabeth Gardner, signed 3 December 1971 and filed with the Los Angeles County Clerk on 29 April 1976.

8. That so many scholars are unaware of this suggests how widespread is the ignorance about even the most basic facts of interracial family life. The problem was common in the Harlem Renaissance, as well. In 1926, Larsen's good friend Walter White wrote the anthropologist Franz Boas for clarification of a question that recurred frequently in his NAACP office: "If a child is born of one parent who is white and the other with only a small admixture of Negro blood, is it not true that the child may be black?" Boas' student Melville Herskovits answered for him: "The chances of a child born to such a couple having distinctly Negroid characteristics would be almost infinitesimal." (Walter White to Franz Boas, 9 December 1926; and Melville J. Herskovits to Walter White, 11 December 1926, WWPC.) St. Clair Drake and Horace R. Cayton: "It is impossible for the offspring of a recognizable Negro and a *pure* white person to be any darker than the Negro partner, and in all probability it will be lighter"; the same point, they added, holds for the offspring of a "white-looking" Negro (*Black Metropolis: A Study of Negro Life in a Northern City* [New York: Harcourt, Brace, 1945], vol. 1, p. 172). See also Earnest A. Hooton, "The Anthropometry of Some Small Samples of American Negroes and Negroids," in Caroline Bond Day, *A Study of Some Negro-White Families in the United States* (Cambridge, Mass.: Harvard University Press, 1932), pp. 42–107. Geneticists today come to essentially the same conclusion. Paul L. Jamison to George Hutchinson (email), 27 January 2005. In rare cases the complexion of the child could be darker than that of the "black" parent, if the white parent has some recessive alleles for a dark complexion, but for the child to be more "black" in appearance, by American standards, than those of the African-descent parent is extremely unlikely, and Mary Larsen was a fair-skinned, thin-lipped Scandinavian.

9. On almost all documents concerning Peter Larsen, including those provided by Nella herself, he is identified as a white, Danish immigrant, born about 1867. His death certificate of January 1945 gives his birthdate as 5 February 1867, which is consistent with earlier census records. Based no doubt on information supplied by Mary, it also states that he was born in Copenhagen and had lived in the United States for fifty-seven years, dating his immigration to about 1887–1888. He was a retired electric streetcar operator. (Certificate of Death for Peter Larson, dated 27 January 1945, California Department of Public Health; copy in Nella Larsen Imes files, Surrogate's Court, New York County, New York.) The U.S. Census of 1910, based on information he himself probably supplied (for reasons to be explained later), lists his age as forty-three and his place of birth as Denmark, consistent with the death certificate, but gives 1885 as his date of immigration. According to this form, he had been married for nineteen years. The 1920 census gives his age as fifty-three and 1885 as his date of immigration, and lists 1889 as his date of naturalization.

10. *Quicksand,* in *Quicksand and Passing,* ed. Deborah E. McDowell (New Brunswick, N.J.: Rutgers University Press, 1986), p. 23.

11. Donald L. Miller, *City of the Century: The Epic of Chicago and the Making of America* (New York: Simon and Schuster, 1996), p. 492.

12. Quotation from Harriet Monroe, *A Poet's Life* (New York: Macmillan, 1938), p. 121.

13. Miller, pp. 498–499; William S. McFeely, *Frederick Douglass* (New York: W. W. Norton, 1991), pp. 369–372; Linda O. McMurry, *To Keep the Waters Troubled: The Life of Ida B. Wells* (New York: Oxford University Press, 1998), pp. 199–200.

14. Miller, p. 497.

15. Quoted ibid., p. 503.
16. Ibid.
17. I conclude that this was Nella's stepfather for several reasons. On the passenger list filled out when Mary returned to her husband from Denmark in 1898, the address "325 27th Str" is given. There was no 325 Twenty-Seventh Street in Chicago, however; addresses on Twenty-Seventh Street went from 0 at the lake to 130 at South Park (where the street was cut off) and then recommenced with 330 at State Street (*Lakeside Annual Directory of the City of Chicago* [Chicago: Chicago Directory Co., 1900], p. 122). On the other hand, a driver named Peter Larson was living at 325 Twenty-Second; it seems the officers filling out the form misheard Mary or simply made a slip in penmanship. The Peter Larson, "driver," at 325 Twenty-Second was still there in 1897, but in 1899 he was gone for good, and Peter Larson, "driver," shows up in the city directory for the first time at 201 Twenty-Second Street; he remains here, with the name spelled "Larson" in 1900. As discussed in Chapter 4, the whole family is listed at this address in the 1900 census under the name "Larsen."
18. U.S. Census for 1900, schedules for Cook County.
19. Booker T. Washington, "The Standard Printed Version of the Atlanta Exposition Address," in *The Booker T. Washington Papers,* ed. Louis R. Harlan (Urbana: University of Illinois Press, 1972–1989), vol. 3, pp. 584–585.
20. David Levering Lewis, *W. E. B. Du Bois: Biography of a Race, 1868–1919* (New York: Henry Holt, 1993), p. 174.
21. Washington, "Standard Printed Version," p. 586.
22. W. E. B. Du Bois to Booker T. Washington, 24 September 1895, in *The Booker T. Washington Papers,* vol. 4, p. 26.
23. W. E. B. Du Bois, "The Conservation of Races," in Du Bois, *Pamphlets and Leaflets,* ed. Herbert Aptheker (White Plains, N.Y.: Kraus-Thompson, 1986), p. 2.
24. C. Vann Woodward, *The Strange Career of Jim Crow* (New York: Oxford University Press, 1974), pp. 71–74. The following historical reconstruction borrows liberally from Brook Thomas' excellent analysis and account in his "Introduction: The Legal Background" and the documents included in *Plessy v. Ferguson: A Brief History with Documents,* ed. Brook Thomas (Boston: Bedford Books, 1997), pp. 1–38.
25. Thomas, p. 32.
26. Ibid., p. 171.
27. Marion L. Starkey, "Negro Writers Come into Their Own," typescript, Alfred A. Knopf Collection, HRHRC.
28. Nella Larsen Imes, Application for Admission to the Library School of the New York Public Library, NYPL LS. This document was unknown to earlier biographers. Larsen gave the dates for her first stay in Denmark as 1900–1903, but this shift comported with date shifts concerning her birth and education, as will be explained later. She did not claim to have gone to school before her return to the States, and there is no reason to doubt that she lived three years abroad before starting elementary school.
29. Estimate of $115 (more than $2,500 in today's dollars), plus train fare to New York, based on passenger ticket price list for Scandinavian-America line, circa 1900, in Erhvervsarkivet, Aarhus, Denmark. See also issues of the Chicago *Arbejderen* of September 1897. The train fare was later included in the Chicago-Copenhagen round-trip fare on the Scandinavian American Line, which took over Thingvalla in 1898. See also

"DFDS rutekort," in Søren Thorsøe et al., *DFDS, 1866–1991: Ship Development through 125 Years* (Copenhagen: DFDS, 1991), p. 22; and John J. Flinn, *Chicago, the Marvelous City of the West: A History, an Encyclopedia, and a Guide,* 2nd ed. (Chicago: Standard Guide Co., 1892), p. 498.

30. The *Norge,* on which Marie and her girls came back to the United States, had capacity for 900 third-class passengers as against 150 second-class and 50 first-class. The Larsens' return ticket number, 335, indicates that they shared a third-class berth; four-bunk berths with a washstand were reserved for mothers traveling with children third class when purchased in advance. Thorsøe et al., p. 236; and Direct Emigration lists, 1898, p. 326, in Landsarkivet for Sjaelland, Copenhagen, Denmark.

31. Thorsøe et al., p. 21.

32. Henrik Cavling's description is quoted at length in Aage Heinberg, *Over Atlanten: Fra og Til Danmark Gennem Tiderne* [Across the Atlantic: From and to Denmark through the Years] (Copenhagen: J. D. Qvist, 1936), pp. 172–176; see also Martindale C. Ward, *A Trip to Chicago* (Glasgow: A. Malcolm, 1895), p. 12.

33. Heinberg, pp. 175–176, 267–277, 298. All of the "Amerikabaads" (ships to and from America) landed and departed from Larsensplads at the time. For information on the course of the voyage, see Thorsøe et al., p. 22; and brochures in the collection of the Statens Arkiver, Erhvervsarkivet, Aarhus, Denmark.

34. Mary and her girls apparently never visited Peter Larsen's family. When Nella later spoke and wrote of visiting Denmark, she said she lived with her mother's people and not her stepfather's. Peter Larsen's death certificate, filled out on the basis of information supplied by Mary, gives his parents' names as "unknown Larson," though it does give his birthplace as Copenhagen. Certificate of Death for Peter Larson, State of California Department of Public Health, filed 27 January 1945.

35. Bryher to H.D., 7 December 1936, in HD Papers, Beinecke Rare Book and Manuscript Library, Yale University. Thanks to Julia Bazar for alerting me to Bryher's letters mentioning Larsen.

36. Bryher to H.D., 13 December 1936, HD Papers.

37. "Kat efter Mus" (which Larsen calls "Cat and Rat") was recorded in three versions in Evald Tang Kristensen's pioneering collection, *Danske Börnerim, Remser og Lege* [Danish Children's Rhymes, Jingles, and Games] (Copenhagen: Karl Shønberg, 1896), p. 498. Only the version that matches Larsen's had been recorded from Jutland, and it was not noted elsewhere. The other games Larsen included in her first article, though obviously authentic, are not represented in Kristensen's work, although one or two of them seem to be related to games Kristensen's informants identified.

38. Only about 1,600 people lived in the entire parish of Malt, including Askov and Vejen. Linda Klitmøller to author, 29 September 1998, from Lokalhistorisk Arkiv for Vejen Komune, Vejen, Denmark.

39. Poster from 1898 that reads "Aschanti Tivoli Neger Landsby: 100 Indfødte fra Vest-Afrikas Guldkyst," and other publicity, newspaper clippings, in collection of Tivoli Museum, Copenhagen.

40. *København har moret sig* [How Copenhagen Has Amused Itself] (Copenhagen: Politikens Forlag, 1966), p. 118.

41. Nella Larsen Imes, "Danish Fun," *The Brownies' Book,* July 1920, p. 219.

42. Ibid.

43. "New York Passenger Arrivals, May 6, 1898," U.S. Immigration and Naturalization Service, National Archives, Washington, D.C. At each port, a list of passengers boarding at that port was made and checked by an American consul. Date of departure from Christiansand is confirmed by "Incoming Steamships," *New York Times*, 5 May 1898, p. 4.

44. "The Weather," *New York Times*, 6 May 1898, p. 1; route description based partly on Ward, p. 15.

45. "List or Manifest of Alien Immigrants for the Commissioner of Immigration," *S.S. Norge*, 6 May 1898; in "New York Passenger Arrivals, May 6, 1898," U.S. Immigration and Naturalization Service, National Archives, Washington, D.C.; Listings for Peter Larson, "driver," in *Lakeside Annual Directory of the City of Chicago* (Chicago: Chicago Directory Co., 1894, 1897).

3. STATE STREET YEARS

1. *Quicksand*, in *Quicksand and Passing*, ed. Deborah E. McDowell (New Brunswick, N.J.: Rutgers University Press, 1986), p. 23.

2. Douglas S. Massey and Nancy A. Denton, *American Apartheid: Segregation and the Making of the Underclass* (Cambridge, Mass.: Harvard University Press, 1993), p. 31.

3. Nella Larsen Imes, Author's statement for Alfred A. Knopf, 24 November 1926, in Alfred A. Knopf Collection, HRHRC.

4. Statistics from George E. Plumbe, *Chicago: Its Natural Advantages as an Industrial and Commercial Center and Market* (Chicago: Chicago Association of Commerce, 1910), pp. 58–59. School location from Business Directory in *Lakeside Annual Directory of the City of Chicago* (Chicago: Chicago City Directory Co., 1898–1900). At least two schools connected with German Lutheran churches were also near the Larsen home at 325 Twenty-Second Street: Trinity Lutheran at 159 Twenty-Fifth Place and St. Marcus Lutheran at 508 West Twenty-Third Street. South Side Danes often attended such schools, but a parochial school seems unlikely for Nella Larsen. No records from these schools remain.

5. "Our Educational System: Memorandum from Alderman Frank A. Stauber to the Citizens Association of Chicago," *Chicagoer Arbeiter-Zeitung*, 27 March 1880; reprinted in *German Workers in Chicago*, ed. Hartmut Keil and John B. Jentz (Urbana: University of Illinois Press, 1988), p. 374; "The Kindergarten Conference," *University Record* 2 (7 May 1897): 49–53. See also Michael S. Shapiro, *Child's Garden: The Kindergarten Movement from Froebel to Dewey* (University Park: Pennsylvania State University Press, 1983). See also Roberta Wollons, ed., *Kindergartens and Cultures: The Global Diffusion of an Idea* (New Haven: Yale University Press, 2000).

6. The 1899 city directory shows Peter Larson, a "driver," living at 201 Twenty-Second and gone from 325 in that year; and in the 1900 census the entire family shows up at 201. The census schedule gives the name as "Larsen" and lists Peter, Mary, "Nellie," and "Anna," with the correct birthdates of April 1891 and June 1892 for the two girls. On this sheet, Peter's and Anna's race was initially listed as "W" for white, but someone had gone back and written a "B" for black over the "W" for each of them. The older daughter, Nellie, like her mother, was listed unambiguously as white. Someone had misidentified the girls, obviously, in "correcting" the record. Peter was at work when the enumer-

ator came by, so it seems clear that the enumerator or her boss, "fixing" the original listing, surmised that Peter was black and that Mary's first husband had been white, comporting with the reversal concerning the girls' identities. Twelfth Census of the United States, Schedule No. 1: Population, Cook County, Enumeration District 46, Sheet 15A; and file for the Estate of Nella L. Imes (A2329/1964), Surrogates' Court, New York County, 31 Chambers Street, New York City.

7. *Robinson's Atlas of the City of Chicago*, 5 vols. (New York: E. Robinson, 1886), vol. 1. See listing for Elijah A. Lyon under "druggists" in the business directory sections of the *Lakeside Annual Directory of the City of Chicago* (Chicago: Chicago City Directory Co., 1892 and 1900). In 1892 he had moved around the corner from 2148 State to 200 Twenty-Second.

8. *Forty-Sixth Annual Report of the Board of Education for the Year Ending June 30, 1900* (Chicago: Board of Education, 1900), p. 269; Mary J. Herrick, *The Chicago Schools: A Social and Political History* (Beverly Hills: Sage Publications, 1971), pp. 178, 226; Edith Abbott and Sophonisba P. Brackinridge, *Truancy and Non-Attendance in the Chicago Schools* (Chicago: University of Chicago Press, 1917), p. 264, n. 1.

On a 1961 job application that allowed only one line for "elementary school" and one for "high school," Larsen would write that she had attended Moseley Grammar School beginning in 1898. She omitted other primary schools, since there was no room on the form for them. Similarly, there was room to list only one secondary school, so Larsen listed only Wendell Phillips High School, but not the Fisk University Normal School, which she had attended for just a year. (City of New York, Department of Hospitals, Application for Employment of Nella Larsen Imes, 2 December 1961). Moseley was at Michigan and Twenty-Fourth, a short walk from 201 Twenty-Second Street, where the Larsens were living by 1899. Yet 325 Twenty-Second was outside the Moseley district. We can, then, conclude confidently that Nella Larsen entered school after her return from Denmark in the spring or fall of 1898 at either a kindergarten or parochial school for children of Germans and Scandinavians in the neighborhood where she lived, and then, after the family moved, attended Moseley for most of her elementary education.

9. Twelfth Census of the United States (1900), Schedule No. 1: Population, Cook County, Enumeration District 46, Sheet 15A.

10. Herbert Asbury, *Gem of the Prairie: An Informal History of the Chicago Underworld* (New York: Alfred A. Knopf, 1940), p. 246.

11. Ibid., pp. 243–246. "Mayor Planning Three 'Levees,'" *Chicago Tribune*, 7 November 1903, p. 1. According to a 1936 biography of two famous "madams" of the 1890s, 119 houses of ill fame with 686 women "inmates" existed in the dozen blocks between Archer Avenue on the north, Twenty-Second Street on the south, Clark Street on the west, and Wabash on the east. Charles Washburn, *Come into My Parlor: A Biography of the Aristocratic Everleigh Sisters of Chicago* (New York: Knickerbocker, 1936), p. 123.

12. Washburn, p. 123; *Lakeside Annual* (1900), Business Directory; William Howland Kenney, *Chicago Jazz: A Cultural History, 1904–1930* (New York: Oxford University Press, 1993), p. 63.

13. See Twelfth Census, Enumeration District 43, Sheet 9.

14. "Chicago Again Wide Open City," *Chicago Tribune*, 27 November 1903, p. 3; "Black Belt Raid Yields Evidence," *Chicago Tribune*, 19 November 1903, p. 3.

15. Bricktop, with James Haskins, *Bricktop* (New York: Atheneum, 1983), p. 18.

16. Ibid., p. 11.
17. Ibid., p. 29.
18. Ibid., p. 18.
19. See "Saloons" in the Business Directory of *Lakeside Annual* (1900).
20. The Peter Larsen of Lizzie's 1892 birth certificate was a "teamster"; he was listed as a "driver" in the city directories of 1899 and 1900, when he was living at 201 Twenty-Second Street, while for some reason the untrustworthy census of 1900 terms him a "poultry dealer." (He does not show up in a list of poultry dealers in the Business Directory of 1900.) But by 1903 he had become a conductor on the street-railway system. The term "driver" indicates he was working on the street railways in 1899, for the men who began as "drivers" of the horse-cars became either conductors or gripmen as horse-power was phased out. And drivers were distinguished from teamsters. The location of horse-car barns is based on *Atlas of the City of Chicago: Central Business Property* (Chicago: G. W. Bromley, 1891).
21. The 1910 census gives her this occupation, and late in life, after separating from Peter Larsen and for years after his death, she supported herself "making dresses for a rather elite clientele" in California. Charles R. Larson, *Invisible Darkness: Jean Toomer and Nella Larsen* (Iowa City: University of Iowa Press, 1993), p. 117. Thirteenth Census of the United States, 1910: Population, Cook County, Enumeration District 1386, Sheet 1B. Charles R. Larson, notes from interview with Mildred Phillips, 19 February 1986.
22. Illinois Bureau of Labor Statistics, *Seventh Biennial Report, 1892; Part I: Working Women in Chicago*, pp. 45, 48.
23. Audiotape of Charles R. Larson interview with Alice Carper, 11 June 1986; letter of Nella Larsen to Dorothy Peterson, 12 July 1927, DPP; 16 October 1927 entry, CVV daybooks, CVV/NYPL.
24. *Quicksand*, p. 64.
25. Description of apartment building based on Sanford maps of Chicago, Chicago Historical Society. School information from Elementary School Register Records (card file), Colman School, 1880s–1920s; and Register for School Year Ending 1904 (microfilm), in Elementary School Registers, Reel 44, Bureau of Former Student Records, Chicago Public Schools. Students are listed alphabetically, regardless of age, so if Anna had attended Colman, her name would appear near Nellie's. In addition to the microfilm copies of the original school registers, the Bureau of Former Student Records maintains a card file that has caused some confusion. Interpreting the card on "Nellie Larson" as a registration form, Davis notes that it shows her entering Colman School in 1903 and lists Peter in the space for "father," with an "X" in the spaces for "mother" and "guardian"—suggesting to Davis that Peter was not just a stepfather, and that he was Nellie's primary caregiver. Yet the vast majority of the cards on file for the period are filled out exactly like Larsen's, with the father's name provided and X's in the spaces for "mother" and "guardian." Mothers' names appear so rarely as to suggest they were included mainly on forms for children with single mothers; guardians almost never appear. The reason for this is apparently that the name of the head of family was almost always the one listed in the cramped space on the original school registers, from which the cards were copied; stepparents are not specified as such.

On the basis of the card file, Davis concludes that Larsen had not even started school until age nine and a half, at Colman School (Davis, p. 24). The card file, however, gives no information about where a student attended school during years for which the registers are missing (as they often are). Moreover, the register does not say that Larsen entered Colman at age nine and a half; it says she registered on "9-6" (September 6) of the 1903–1904 school year, and that the enrollment registers are missing for the periods before and after that school year—specifically, from 1894 to 1903 and from 1904 to 1909. The original registers, now on microfilm, also list the "last successful vaccination date," which was 1901 for Nellie Larsen. This vaccination date is typical of her cohort and suggests nothing about when Larsen first started school. Similarly, the fragmentary documentation of Nellie Larsen's school attendance is typical.

26. See Twelfth Census (1900), Enumeration Districts 864–866.

27. Thomas Lee Philpott, *The Slum and the Ghetto: Immigrants, Blacks, and Reformers in Chicago, 1880–1930* (Belmont, Calif.: Wadsworth, 1991), pp. 147, 149–150, 123, 130; E. Franklin Frazier, *The Negro Family in Chicago* (Chicago: University of Chicago Press, 1932), pp. 111–112; and Dominic A. Pacyga and Ellen Skerrett, *Chicago: City of Neighborhoods* (Chicago: Loyola University Press, 1986), pp. 346–347.

28. See, e.g., Twelfth Census, Enumeration District 865, Sheets 11, 12, 15–16.

29. Davis, pp. 32–33.

30. *Forty-Sixth Annual Report* (1900), pp. 254–255, 269. Black instructors in public schools are listed in *Colored People's Blue Book and Business Directory of Chicago, Illinois* (Chicago: Chicago Printing Co., 1905), p. 126. The list shows one black teacher at Moseley, three at Keith School, two at Farren, and nine others scattered throughout the city, but none at Colman.

31. Frazier, p. 133. Harold Foote Gosnell also quotes one teacher from this period stating that she had "no difficulty at all about color, that is, no trouble worth mentioning," and she had started out in a mostly white school. Black teachers from the South Side "went everywhere"—that is, were assigned to schools all over the city; she herself said she had "no trouble at all with either the white children or their parents" (quoted in Gosnell, *Negro Politicians: The Rise of Negro Politics in Chicago* [Chicago: University of Chicago Press, 1967], p. 284). The main tensions had arisen between the teachers hired through the Civil Service Commission—instituted in the late 1890s—and the old political appointees. The testimony may not be typical; the chief tensions for black teachers existed not in all-white schools but in the "mixed" school districts where the in-migration of black residents was a perceived threat.

32. Fannie Barrier Williams, "Thronging the Schools," *New York Age*, 20 September 1906, p. 5.

33. "Judge Edward F. Dunne," Chicago *Broad Ax*, 1 April 1905, p. 1; Michael W. Homel, *Down from Equality: Black Chicagoans and the Public Schools, 1920–1941* (Urbana: University of Illinois Press, 1984), p. 8; Judy Jolley Mohraz, *The Separate Problem: Case Studies of Black Education in the North, 1900–1930* (New York: Greenwood Press, 1979), p. 98; Ida B. Wells, *Crusade for Justice: The Autobiography of Ida B. Wells* (Chicago: University of Chicago Press, 1970), pp. 274, 276–278.

34. The Twenty-First Street horse-car route was discontinued in the late 1890s and its barn closed. As horse-cars were phased out, the former drivers became either "gripmen" or "conductors" on cable-cars (and later electric trolleys). Peter appeared in the city direc-

tory as a "driver" until he became a "conductor" almost simultaneously with the closing of the horse-car route on Twenty-First. See George W. Hilton, *Cable Railways of Chicago* (Chicago: Electric Railway Historical Society, 1954), pp. 5–15.

35. For a memoir of the street-cars written by a man of just Nella Larsen's age who grew up on the South Side, see George T. Bryant, "The Gripman Wore a Sheepskin Coat," *Chicago History* 1 (n.s.), no. 1 (Spring 1970): 47–56.

36. Alan R. Lind, *Chicago Surface Lines: An Illustrated History,* 2nd ed. (Park Forest, Ill.: Transport History Press, 1974), p. 376.

37. "Two Views of the City Railway Controversy," *Chicago Tribune,* 12 November 1903, p. 2; "Strike Ties Up South Side Cars," 12 November 1903, p. 2; "Vote of Car Men Is for a Strike," *Chicago Tribune,* 5 November 1903, p. 2; "One More Plea, Then a Strike," *Chicago Tribune,* 9 November 1903, p. 2.

38. "Strikebreaker Ready to Come," *Chicago Tribune,* 8 November 1903, p. 3; "Wave of Strikes Threatens City," *Chicago Tribune,* 1 November 1903, p. 3; "One More Plea," p. 2; "Out Tomorrow on City Railway," *Chicago Tribune,* 11 November 1903, p. 1; "Strike Ties Up," p. 1; "Angry Strikers Ready at Dawn to Attack Cars," *Chicago Tribune,* 13 November 1903, p. 1; "Mob Attacks the Cars," ibid.

39. "Mayor Attacked as Strike's Foe," *Chicago Tribune,* 16 November 1903, pp. 1–2; "Teamsters Now Threaten City," *Chicago Tribune,* 20 November 1903, p. 2; "Army of Labor Opens Campaign," *Chicago Tribune,* 23 November 1903, p. 2.

40. "Shots Are Fired To Awe Rioters," *Chicago Tribune,* 24 November 1903, p. 2.

41. "Teamsters on War Verge," *Chicago Tribune,* 24 November 1903, p. 2; "Car Strike Over; Peace Compact Is Made at 1:15 A.M.," *Chicago Tribune,* 25 November 1903, p. 1; "Carmen at Work This Morning," *Chicago Tribune,* 26 November 1903, p. 3.

42. Georg Leidenberger, "'The Public Is the Labor Union': Working-Class Progressivism in Turn-of-the-Century Chicago," *Labor History* 36 (1995): 204–206, 207.

43. "Judge Edward F. Dunne," Chicago *Broad Ax,* 1 April 1905, p. 1; "Judge Edward F. Dunne," Chicago *Broad Ax,* 8 April 1905, p. 1. The *Broad Ax* claimed that Dunne won 75 percent of the black vote, an amazing figure for a Democrat in those years, if accurate. "The Colored Voter and Municipal Ownership," Chicago *Broad Ax,* 1 April 1905, p. 1; Leidenberger, p. 202.

44. Leidenberger, p. 207.

45. Eventually, even black men with union memberships in locals from other cities were barred from the Chicago locals. See Junius B. Wood, *The Negro in Chicago* (Chicago: Chicago Daily News, 1916), originally a series of articles in the Chicago *Daily News* (1916).

46. William M. Tuttle Jr., *Race Riot: Chicago in the Red Summer of 1919* (New York: Atheneum, 1970), p. 116; Allan H. Spear, *Black Chicago: The Making of a Negro Ghetto, 1890–1920* (Chicago: University of Chicago Press, 1967), p. 36.

47. Quoted in "Senator Ben Tillman," Chicago *Broad Ax,* 15 October 1904, p. 1.

48. Spear, p. 40.

49. John B. Andrews and W. D. P. Bliss, *History of Women in Trade Unions* (New York: Arno Press, 1974), p. 166; and Margaret Hoblitt, "A Labor Tragedy," *The Commons* 10 (May 1905): 278–280.

50. Spear, p. 39; "Colored Men," *Broad Ax,* 6 May 1905, p. 1; "The Race Issue in the Strike," *Chicago Tribune,* 13 May 1905, p. 8.

51. Spear, p. 40.
52. "Race Rioting in Chicago," Chicago *Broad Ax*, 27 May 1905, p. 1.
53. "Whose Race War Is It?" Chicago *Broad Ax*, 27 May 1905, p. 1.
54. Andrews and Bliss, p. 166; Leidenberger, p. 208.
55. Tuttle, p. 121.
56. Ibid., pp. 144–145.
57. *Proceedings: Board of Education, City of Chicago, 1904–1905* (Chicago: Board of Education, 1905), meeting of 21 June 1905, p. 781; Homel, pp. 8–10.
58. Spear, pp. 44–45; Williams, "Thronging the Schools," p. 5; Leidenberger, p. 208.
59. *Proceedings . . . 1904–1905*, minutes for 21 June 1905, p. 836. Larsen is listed as "Nellye Larson." Davis notes her registration of 5 September 1905, listed in the Wendell Phillips High School register for 1905–1906, entry no. 107 (Davis, pp. 24–25). The register is no longer open to the public.
60. Williams, "Thronging the Schools," p. 5; *1908–1909 Board of Education, City of Chicago* [a directory of the Chicago Public Schools] (Chicago: Board of Education, 1908), p. 61.
61. *1908–1909 Board of Education*, p. 61.
62. Ibid., pp. 42–43. Most of the basic textbooks for the different courses had been used since at least 1903 or 1904, except for some Ancient History texts adopted in 1906 and a "lesson" book in Geography adopted in 1908.
63. Ibid., p. 44. The only history texts listed in the Board of Education handbook, first adopted in November 1906, cover Ancient History: Botsford's *Orient, Greece, and Rome,* Myers' *Ancient History,* and West's *Ancient World.*
64. *Proceedings of the Board of Education, 1905–1906* (Chicago: Board of Education, 1906), p. 827.
65. All details concerning the reading list and composition requirements for first- and second-year high school English courses come from *Proceedings of the Board of Education, 1905–1906*, pp. 827–828.
66. Davis, p. 50. Professor Davis was able to get the grades in the mid-1980s from a later principal of Phillips. Today, officials at Phillips are unable to find any record of Larsen's having attended the school.
67. Minutes of meeting of 7 December 1904, in *Proceedings . . . 1904–1905*, p. 271. Later reports on conditions of lunch rooms show that the Phillips cafeteria remained open.
68. Homel, p. 14.
69. Ibid., p. 15.
70. *Quicksand*, p. 39.
71. Anna does not show up on the lists of students recommended for promotion from eighth grade in 1906 or 1907. She was not in school in 1909–1910, for she had not been in school all year when the 1910 census was taken.
72. Herrick, p. 114; "Calls Limit on Normal School," *Chicago Tribune*, 26 June 1906, p. 4.
73. Homel, pp. 4–7.
74. Warranty Deed dated 8 August 1907, document no. 4087047, and Trust Deed of the same date, document no. 4087048, Office of the Recorder of Deeds, Cook County Illinois. Davis, p. 40; Gosnell, pp. 281–282. On Ella Flagg Young, see especially Herrick, pp. 114–117; and Chester C. Dodge, *Reminiscences of a Schoolmaster* (Chicago: Ralph Fletcher Seymour, 1941), p. 80.
75. See alumni notes in the *Fisk Herald* for these years.

76. On expenses at Fisk, see Fisk Catalogue, 1907–1908; and C.W.S., "First Impressions," *Fisk Herald,* 25, no. 7 (April 1908): 19. On living expenses in Chicago, see J. C. Kennedy et al., *Wages and Family Budgets in the Stock-Yards District* (Chicago: University of Chicago Press, 1914). The study was based on data from 1910. Streetcar conductors for the CCR made $16.20 per week in 1908–1909, according to wage scales published in "Offers and Demands in Streetcar Row Now in Progress," *Chicago Tribune,* 8 August 1909, p. 1.

4. TURNING SOUTH

1. See Carlton J. Corliss, *Main Line of Mid-America: The Story of the Illinois Central* (New York: Creative Age Press, 1950), p. 331.
2. See "An Ignorant White Man," *Nashville Globe,* 24 April 1908, p. 1.
3. Deborah Cooney, *Speaking of Union Station: An Oral History of a Nashville Landmark* (Nashville: Williams Printing Co., 1977), pp. 53–54.
4. Don H. Doyle, *Nashville in the New South, 1880–1930* (Knoxville: University of Tennessee Press, 1985), p. 117.
5. James D. Corrothers, *In Spite of the Handicap: An Autobiography* (New York: Doran, 1916), p. 104.
6. Ibid., pp. 104–105.
7. *All About Nashville: A Complete Historical Guide Book to the City* (Nashville: Marshall and Bruce, 1912), pp. 123–125.
8. MacKinley Helm, *Angel Mo' and Her Son, Roland Hayes* (Boston: Little, Brown, 1942), pp. 81–82.
9. *Catalogue of the Officers and Students of Fisk University, 1907–1908* (Nashville: Marshall and Bruce, 1908), p. 13. The same phrasing was used in the *Catalogue* of 1906–1907.
10. *Catalogue . . . 1907–1908,* p. 18.
11. Ibid., p. 19.
12. Ibid.
13. *Catalogue of the Officers, Students, and Alumni of Fisk University, 1908–1909* (Nashville: Marshall and Bruce, 1909), p. 67; the catalogue lists students from the 1907–1908 academic year. See also letter of Mrs. M. L. Crosthwait to Ernest J. Reece, 5 May 1922, in Nella Larsen Imes file, NYPL LS. Crosthwait's letter says Larsen was in the "High School department"; this letter also lists the five-hour "academic" classes Larsen took.
14. "Labor Unions," *Fisk Herald* 25.2 (Thanksgiving 1907): 13–14.
15. "Religious Notes," ibid., pp. 18–19.
16. *Quicksand,* in Nella Larsen, *Quicksand and Passing,* ed. Deborah E. McDowell (New Brunswick: Rutgers University Press, 1986), p. 23.
17. *All About Nashville,* pp. 220–221.
18. Ibid., pp. 220–223.
19. *Catalogue . . . 1908–1909,* p. 7.
20. Ibid., pp. 66–69.
21. Many of them made between $20 and $40 per month (plus lodging, one assumes) in 1906, although President James Merrill and H. H. Wright, the top administrators, made $125 per month. American Missionary Association to Reverend J. F. Brodie, treasurer of Fisk University, 13 January 1906, James G. Merrill Papers, Folder 8, Fisk University.

22. Quoted in Thomas Elsa Jones, "Fisk University," *Southern Workman* 56 (January 1927): 10–11.
23. Quoted in Joe M. Richardson, *A History of Fisk University, 1865–1946* (University, Ala.: University of Alabama Press), p. 63. The student body at Fisk was two-thirds male.
24. Roland Hayes quoted in Helm, pp. 84, 85.
25. President James Merrill, "Report to the Trustees of Fisk University, 1907–1908," Minutes of the Board of Trustees, Fisk University, 25 June 1908, p. 320 (Special Collections, Fisk University Library).
26. Quoted in Richardson, p. 61.
27. "The History of the Normal Department at Fisk," *Fisk Herald* 25.2 (Thanksgiving 1907): 8–9.
28. *Catalogue . . . 1908–1909*, p. 17.
29. Compare *Catalogue of the Officers and Students of Fisk University, 1906–1907* (Nashville: Marshall and Bruce, 1907), pp. 37–40, with letter of Crosthwait to Reece, 5 May 1922.
30. Crosthwait to Reece, 5 May 1922; and *Catalogue . . . 1906–1907*, pp. 37–40.
31. *Catalogue . . . 1906–1907*, p. 81.
32. Ibid., p. 40.
33. *Catalogue . . . 1907–1908*, p. 76.
34. "Bells" schedule, dated 18 November 1907, in *Scrapbook of Fisk University Programs, 1904–1909*, Item 418 in vault archives, Special Collections, Fisk University Library.
35. *Catalogue . . . 1907–1908*, p. 16.
36. Merrill, "Report to the Trustees," p. 318.
37. "Religious Notes," p. 19.
38. "Public Exercises, Fri. Evening, Nov. 8, 1907," *Fisk Herald*, 25 (Christmas 1907): 10.
39. *Catalogue . . . 1907–1908*, p. 16.
40. "Cantata at Fisk during the Holidays," *Nashville Globe*, 13 December 1907, p. 1; "'From Out of the Depths' Cantata," *Nashville Globe*, 3 January 1908, p. 8.
41. "'From Out of the Depths' Cantata," p. 8.
42. College Faculty Minutes, 3 and 28 October 1907, p. 413.
43. Helm, pp. 87–88.
44. Ibid., p. 88.
45. "George Washington Social," *Fisk Herald* 25 (April 1908): 30.
46. "Personals," *Fisk Herald* 25 (March 1908): 22.
47. "Secretary Taft Visits Fisk," *Nashville Globe*, 29 May 1908, p. 1.
48. See, for example, "The Negroes and Secretary Taft," *Colored American Magazine* 14.4 (April 1908): 181–182; "Secretary Taft as a Conciliator," *Colored American Magazine* 14.5 (May 1908): 247–249; Ralph W. Tyler, "Taft and the Negro," *Colored American Magazine* 14.7 (July 1908): 397–399.
49. John Callan O'Laughlin, "Negro Vote Has Become an Important Factor," *New York Times*, 3 May 1908, sect. 5, p. 5.
50. Jones, "Fisk University," pp. 11–12.
51. Merrill, "Report to the Trustees," p. 318.
52. Letter to President and Prudential Committee of Fisk University, in Faculty Minutes, 8 June 1908, Special Collections, Fisk University.
53. Faculty response in Faculty Minutes, 10 June 1908; and College Faculty Minutes, p. 439, 13 June 1908, in Special Collections, Fisk University Library.

54. Crosthwait to Reece, 5 May 1922. The Latin and Rhetoric grades are given inaccurately as 83 and 79, respectively, in Thadious M. Davis, *Nella Larsen, Novelist of the Harlem Renaissance: A Woman's Life Unveiled* (Baton Rouge: Louisiana State University Press, 1994), p. 65.

55. The papers of Mary E. Spence, currently uncatalogued and therefore closed to scholars, might someday shed light on the controversy.

56. *Quicksand*, pp. 23–24.

5. Coming of Age in Copenhagen

1. Nella Larsen file, Alfred A. Knopf Collection, HRHRC.

2. Nella Larsen Imes file, John Simon Guggenheim Memorial Foundation.

3. Marion L. Starkey, "Negro Writers Come into Their Own," typescript in Alfred A. Knopf Collection, HRHRC.

4. Nella Larsen Imes file, NYPL LS.

5. "Amerikabaadene," *Politiken*, 15 January 1909, p. 1, my translation.

6. C. R. Vernon Gibbs, *Passenger Lines of the Western Ocean*, 2nd ed. (New York: John De Graf, 1957), p. 246; and Eugene W. Smith, *Passenger Ships of the World Past and Present* (Boston: George H. Dean, 1963), p. 227. See also "Liste over Kahyttspassagerer mod Doppeltskrue Damskit *C. F. Tietgen*," in *Book Indexes to New York Passenger Lists, April 1906–September 1920* (Washington: Immigration and Naturalization Service, 1944).

7. U.S. Immigration and Naturalization Service, Book Indexes to New York Passenger Arrivals, January 1909; and "List or Manifest of Alien Passengers for the United States Immigration Officer at Port of Arrival," *S.S. C. F. Tietgen*, 29 January 1909, National Archives. When recording family addresses, the lists always named the male head of household only.

8. The *Hellig Olav* was due in New York on Tuesday, April 16, but was held up in the last days of its voyage, which coincided with the sinking of the *Titanic*, as recorded in the "Shipping and Mails" column of the *New York Times*, 15 April 1912, p. 20; 16 April 1912, p. 20; 17 April 1912, p. 15; and 18 April 1912, p. 22. Manifests for the ship on this trip are not listed in the *Catalog of New York Ship Arrival Manifests, 1908–1924* (Washington, D.C.: Immigration and Naturalization Service, n.d.); nor do they appear in *Passenger and Crew Lists of Vessels Arriving at New York, 1897–1957*, U.S. National Archives—which is unusual in that all other Scandinavian-American Line arrivals for that year are included. The ship manifests in general during precisely this period are extremely disordered, leading one to suspect that the disruption caused by the *Titanic* disaster and by the hurried diversion of personnel to deal with the rescue and documentation of its survivors accounts for the anomaly. The *Titanic* hit an iceberg just before midnight on April 14 and sank on April 15. The *Hellig Olav* was one of the half-dozen ships nearest to it at the time, having passed through the same waters only hours earlier. The *S.S. Carpathia*, after picking up the *Titanic*'s survivors, docked in New York on the eighteenth. "Kort over Atlanterhavet med Dampskibsruterne," *Politiken*, 17 April 1912, p. 6; "Bergs Near Titanic's Path," *New York Times*, 18 April 1912, p. 7; "Titanic's Last Good-Bye," *New York Times*, 18 April 1912, p. 7; "Rescue Ship Arrives," *New York Times*, 19 April 1912, pp. 1, 5.

9. "Night of Unrest in Springfield," *Chicago Tribune*, 18 August 1908, p. 2.

10. Charles R. Larson, *Invisible Darkness: Jean Toomer and Nella Larsen* (Iowa City: University of Iowa Press, 1993), p. 187.

11. "Census Bureau Has Innovation in Advance Population Schedule," Chicago *Broad Axe*, 9 April 1910, p. 1.

12. This is attested to by one of Larsen's acquaintances of the early 1930s. See Thadious M. Davis, *Nella Larsen, Novelist of the Harlem Renaissance: A Woman's Life Unveiled* (Baton Rouge: Louisiana University Press, 1994), p. 46.

13. Ejvind Slottved (University of Copenhagen) to the author, 18 December 1997; Linda Kitmøller, director of the Local History Archive, Vejen, Denmark, conversation with the author, 2 June 1998.

14. *Quicksand*, in *Quicksand and Passing*, ed. Deborah E. McDowell (New Brunswick: Rutgers University Press, 1986), p. 63.

15. Ibid., pp. 67–68.

16. Ibid., p. 73.

17. *Vesterbro: En forstadtsbebyggelse i København*, 2 vols. (Copenhagen: Miljøministeriet, Fredningsstyrelsen, 1986), vol. 2, p. 33; and *Anmeldelse til Politiet om Beboerne*, November 1908, census listings for the fifth precinct of Copenhagen, Nos. 2, 4, and 6 Maria Kirkeplads. Larsen is not listed in any of the census records for Maria Kirkeplads. But according to Kim Melchior, a professional genealogist with expertise on Denmark, non-Danish citizens were not counted in the census (Melchior to the author, 9 April 2005). It may be impossible to find out where precisely Larsen resided.

18. *Quicksand*, p. 76.

19. The painting is reproduced in Tøve Clemmensen, *The Victorian Home of the National Museum* (Copenhagen: National Museum of Denmark, 1990), p. 21, fig. 16. See also a contemporary photograph in Palle Lauring, *Ude og Inde i København, 1850–1920* (Copenhagen: Gyldendal, 1965), pp. 48–49.

20. *Quicksand*, p. 76.

21. See 1908 Census of Copenhagen, Vesterbrogade, nos. 11–95.

22. See Peter Howard Selz, *Emil Nolde* (Garden City, N.Y.: Doubleday and Museum of Modern Art, 1963); Werner Haftmann, *Emil Nolde*, trans. Norbert Guterman (New York: Abrams, 1959); Emil Nolde, *Jahre der Kämpfe 1902–1914* (Cologne: DuMont Literatur und Kunst Verlag, 2002); Martin Urban, *Emil Nolde: Catalogue Raisonné of the Oil-Paintings*, 2 vols. (New York: Harper and Row, 1987–1990); Peter Vergo and Felicity Lunn with contributions by Ian McKeever, Hans Edvard Nørregård-Nielsen, and Manfred Reuther, *Emil Nolde* (London: Whitechapel Art Gallery, 1995); *Emil Nolde*, catalogue of exhibit at Württembergischen Kunstvereins Stuttgart and Stiftung Seebüll Ada und Emil Nolde (1987–1988).

23. *Quicksand*, pp. 82–83.

24. Steffens Linvald and Knud Sandvej, *København Har Moret Sig* (Copenhagen: Politikens Forlag, 1966), p. 134.

25. Henry T. Sampson, *The Ghost Walks: A Chronological History of Blacks in Show Business, 1865–1910* (Metuchen, N.J.: Scarecrow Press, 1988), pp. 341, 474, 478. See also postcard of Johnson and Dean, postmarked Copenhagen, 18 August 1907, photo number 6293/1966, in photograph collection of the Bredemuseum of the Nationalmuseum, Brede, Denmark.

26. Caspar Jorgensen, *Vestervold falder*, vol. 9 of Bo Bramsen, ed., *København for og nu — og aldrig* (Copenhagen: Palle Fogtdal, n.d.), pp. 272–273.

27. *Politikens Historie set indefra, 1884–1984*, vol. 2 (Copenhagen: Politikens Forlag, 1983), p. 72. The feature was quite distinct from the typical "society column" one would find in American newspapers.

28. Judith Thurman, *Isak Dinesen: The Life of a Storyteller* (New York: St. Martin's Press, 1982), pp. 7, 62. P. M. Mitchell, *A History of Danish Literature* (Copenhagen: Gyldendal, 1957), p. 191.

29. Shaw Desmond, *The Soul of Denmark* (New York: Charles Scribner's Sons, 1918), pp. 225–226, 18–19.

30. Dorothy Burton Skårdal, *The Divided Heart: Scandinavian Immigrant Experience through Literary Sources* (Lincoln: University of Nebraska Press, 1974), pp. 105–106. I have found no indication that Larsen knew many such novels, which were generally published in small editions, in Scandinavian languages, in Scandinavia.

6. A BLACK WOMAN IN WHITE

1. See, e.g., "Lawyer in Radical Stand to Oust Negro Residents," *Chicago Tribune*, 23 August 1909, p. 2; Thomas Lee Philpott, *The Slum and the Ghetto: Neighborhood Deterioration and Middle-Class Reform, Chicago, 1880–1930* (New York: Oxford University Press, 1978), p. 153; see also Allan H. Spear, *Black Chicago: The Making of a Negro Ghetto, 1890–1920* (Chicago: University of Chicago Press, 1967), pp. 11–22. Larsen may have stayed briefly with black friends; or she may have checked into the recently opened "colored" YWCA home for women in Chicago, distressed, like her later creation Helga Crane, by the "tiny" rooms, "thick cups and queer dark silver," and inwardly rebelling against the need to accept charity. The building described in *Quicksand*, however, does not match the Chicago YWCA's converted single-family house for black women on Rhodes Avenue. Rather, it resembles the tall, main building downtown, which may have accepted black residents at the time. *Quicksand*, in *Quicksand and Passing*, ed. Deborah E. McDowell (New Brunswick: Rutgers University Press, 1986), pp. 31, 29.

2. Louise De Koven Bowen, *The Colored People of Chicago: An Investigation Made for the Juvenile Protective Association* (Chicago: Juvenile Protective Association, 1913), n.p. Estelle Hill Scott, *Occupational Changes among Negroes in Chicago* (Chicago: WPA, 1939), p. 156. See also "Employment of Colored Women in Chicago," *Crisis* 1.3 (January 1911): 25–26.

3. Bowen, n.p.

4. Ibid.

5. Anna Steese Richardson, *The Girl Who Earns Her Own Living* (New York: B. W. Dodge, 1909), pp. 87–99, quotation from p. 88.

6. Scott, p. 167; Douglas S. Massey and Nancy A. Denton, *American Apartheid: Segregation and the Making of the Underclass* (Cambridge, Mass.: Harvard University Press, 1993), pp. 39–40, quotation from p. 40.

7. Darlene Clark Hine, *Black Women in White: Racial Conflict and Cooperation in the Nursing Profession* (Bloomington: Indiana University Press, 1989), p. 28; Spear, pp. 99, 100.

8. Hine, *Black Women in White*, p. 30; see also p. 53.

9. *Quicksand,* p. 40.

10. Lillian D. Wald to Clara D. Noyes, 13 August 1914. See also Lillian Wald to Chapin Brinsmade, 18 August 1914; and Clara D. Noyes to Lillian Wald, 14 August 1914. All in Lillian Wald Papers, Box 27, Folder 4.5, Rare Book and Manuscript Library, Columbia University.

11. Irma D. Minott specifies the date of Larsen's enrollment in a letter to Charles R. Larson, 13 May 1986, files of Charles R. Larson.

12. Francis J. Loperfido, *A Medical History of the Bronx* (New York: Bronx County Medical Society, 1964), p. 140. Other sources give the original name of the institution as the Society for the Relief of Worthy Indigent Colored Persons, but since Loperfido quotes from the minutes at the first meeting, his account seems more trustworthy.

13. Ibid., p. 143. The history above is drawn chiefly from Loperfido; and from Wesley Cartwright, "Brief History of the Lincoln School for Nurses," in "Negroes of New York" files, Federal Writers Project of New York, Schomburg. Other helpful sources include the typescript "History of Lincoln School for Nurses," Box 1, Folder 1, Lincoln School for Nurses Collection, Schomburg.

14. Ruth Edmonds Hill, "Black Women Oral History Project Interview with Florence Jacobs Edmonds, January 5, 1980," in *The Black Women Oral History Project,* vol. 3, ed. Ruth Edmonds Hill (Westport, Conn.: Meckler, 1991), p. 298. See also Fourteenth Census of the United States, 1920: Population, Enumeration Districts 197–199. Although the neighborhoods immediately surrounding the hospital housed chiefly German and Irish immigrant families, along with some Italians, Swiss, Russians, and Romanians, these people tended, more often than the Jewish citizens, to go to hospitals with a higher percentage of private patients, or to parochial institutions in the area. Lloyd Ultan, *The Beautiful Bronx, 1920–1950* (New Rochelle, N.Y.: Arlington House, 1979), pp. 14, 41.

15. Dorothy Levenson, "Collaboration: Building a Health Care System in the Bronx," *Bronx County Historical Society Journal* 35.2 (Fall 1998): 108; Loperfido, pp. 143, 145.

16. Vanessa Northington Gamble, *Making a Place for Ourselves: The Black Hospital Movement* (New York: Oxford University Press, 1995), pp. 10–11.

17. Hine, *Black Women in White*, p. 45.

18. Adah B. Thoms, *Pathfinders: The Progress of Colored Graduate Nurses* (1929; rpt. New York: Garland, 1985), pp. 77–78, 80; "History of the Lincoln School for Nurses," in *The Origin and History of the Lincoln School for Nurses,* pamphlet, 1961, Box 3, Lincoln School for Nurses Collection, Schomburg; Hill, "Interview with Edmonds," p. 296.

19. Benedict Fitzpatrick, *The Bronx and Its People: A History, 1609–1927,* vol. 2 (New York: Lewis Historical Publishing, 1927), p. 557; *Atlas of Borough of the Bronx* (Philadelphia: G. W. Bromley, 1921), at Bronx County Historical Society.

20. The 1915 state census lists her as "Marion Larson"; the 1917 Annual Report of Lincoln Hospital and Home lists her as "Nella Marion Larsen." *The Lincoln Hospital and Home: 78th Annual Report* (1917), p. 55, in Lincoln School for Nurses Collection, Schomburg. A Fiftieth Anniversary booklet of the school lists her among eleven 1915 graduates as "Nella Marion Larsen," but the school's 1922 annual report lists her as "Nella Marian Larsen." The only documents I have found with Larsen's own handwriting using this

middle name spell it as "Marian," which is the way she spelled it while working at Tuskegee Institute in 1915–1916, shortly after graduating from Lincoln. A later document using "Marian," in Larsen's own hand, is her 1954 application for Social Security, which also lists her mother's name as "Marian." Fiftieth Anniversary booklet, Box 1, Folder 8, Lincoln School for Nurses Collection, Schomburg; *83rd Annual Report of Lincoln Hospital and Home Training School for Nurses,* Box 2, Folder 12, ibid. (see p. 66). Nella Larsen Imes, application for Social Security account number, U.S. Social Security Administration, dated 5 January 1954.

21. *The Lincoln Hospital and Home . . . 74th Annual Report* (1913), p. 64; Box 2, Folder 10 of Lincoln School for Nurses Collection, Schomburg. The report is for the fiscal year ending September 1913—Larsen's first year at the school.

22. Ethel Johns, "A Study of the Present Status of The Negro Woman in Nursing," 1925 (typescript), Exhibit A, p. 4, Laura Spelman Rockefeller Memorial Archive, Rockefeller Archive Center, Tarrytown, New York; and "History of the Lincoln School for Nurses," p. 2; discrepancies between the Johns Report and other sources derive in part from the fact that Johns was writing in 1925, when the school had nearly ninety students. The number of students in 1912–1913 is given in the *74th Annual Report,* p. 17.

23. Johns, pp. 20–21.

24. Hill, pp. 296–297.

25. *74th Annual Report,* p. 15.

26. Hill, "Interview with Edmonds," p. 296.

27. Description based chiefly on Bertha Harmer, *Text-Book of the Principles and Practice of Nursing* (New York: Macmillan, 1922), pp. 45–184.

28. Ibid., pp. 302–304.

29. *74th Annual Report,* p. 15; and Johns, Exhibit A, p. 5.

30. Fitzpatrick, p. 557.

31. Information on nursing and medical treatments comes chiefly from Sarah Opdycke, *No One Was Turned Away: The Role of Public Hospitals in New York City since 1900* (New York: Oxford University Press, 1999), pp. 25–45; and Harmer, *Text-Book.*

32. Hill, "Interview with Edmonds," p. 296.

33. Ibid., p. 321.

34. Opdycke, p. 35. For exact figures on Lincoln's patient count during Larsen's first year, see *74th Annual Report,* pp. 5, 15.

35. Johns, Exhibit A, p. 6.

36. *74th Annual Report,* p. 16. A list of "House Officers for 1914" gives Samuels' replacement as Miss Ada J. Senhouse, who was probably, like Samuels, a graduate of the school. The New York State Census of 1915, which lists Larsen as "Marion Larson," lists Amelia Hall, a forty-year-old black Canadian woman, as Superintendent and "Adabelle Thomas," also age forty, as Assistant Superintendent. (See New York State Census of 1915, Assembly District 32, Election District 28, p. 25, Bronx County Historical Society. The census was dated 1 June 1915.) According to oral accounts, however, the superintendent of the school was always white, leading one to wonder if the census was mistaken about Amelia Hall's racial identity (just as it was about the names of Larsen and Thoms), since all the other nurses were, of course, black. The 1917 annual report lists Thoms as the school's superintendent, not acting superintendent (pp. 44–45), though perhaps it

does so merely for convenience. Larsen, in a letter published in *The Forum* magazine in 1930, wrote that the supervisor was white during most of her years as a Lincoln student ("The Author's Explanation," *Forum,* Supplement 4, 83 [April 1930]: xlii).

37. Certificate of Record of Marriage, no. 29798, for George H. Gardner and Anna Elizabeth Larsen, Will County, Illinois.

38. Adelaide Cromwell Hill, "Introduction," *Quicksand* (New York: Macmillan, 1971), p. 15.

39. Johns, p. 25.

40. Ibid., Exhibit A, p. 3. See also Opdycke, p. 38.

41. See Larsen's description of such techniques in *Quicksand* and *Passing,* in *Quicksand and Passing,* pp. 29 and 227, respectively.

42. Hill, "Interview with Edmonds," p. 296; Thoms, p. 80; "Biographical Sketch of William Lloyd Imes," in biographical file for William Lloyd Imes, Special Collections, Fisk University.

43. Thoms, pp. 79–82; "History of the Lincoln School for Nurses," p. 2; Johns, Exhibit A, p. 7. For more general information about the trends in nursing education at the time, see Isabel Hampton Robb, *Education Standards for Nurses, with Other Addresses on Nursing Subjects* (1907; rpt. New York: Garland, 1985); Isabel M. Stewart, *The Education of Nurses* (New York: Macmillan, 1943), pp. 80–81, 145–153; and Mary Adelaide Nutting, *A Sound Economic Basis for Schools of Nursing and Other Addresses* (1926; rpt. New York: Garland, 1984). *74th Annual Report,* pp. 60–63, lists the occupations of Lincoln graduates from the classes of 1900–1913.

44. Thoms, p. 83.

45. Ibid., p. 85.

46. Johns, Exhibit A, p. 3.

47. Larsen, "The Author's Explanation," p. xlii. The account seems trustworthy even though it was used to buttress Larsen's defense against a probably valid accusation of plagiarism in the writing of her story "Sanctuary."

48. Larsen, "The Author's Explanation," p. xlii.

49. *74th Annual Report,* p. 12. New York State Census, 1915, p. 26.

50. Mabel Keaton Staupers, *No Time for Prejudice: A Story of the Integration of Negroes in Nursing in the United States* (New York: Macmillan, 1961), pp. 10, 22; *74th Annual Report,* p. 16. Staupers' helpful history, it must be said, has occasional inaccuracies and presents an abridged version of Thoms's complicated career. The nursing school's annual reports are more exact.

51. The relationship seems to have turned ambivalent as Larsen went her own way and did not take on Thoms's causes as her own. Thoms took pride in Larsen's literary accomplishments publicly, but one cannot help suspecting that the author's character studies caused her private pain.

52. Thoms, p. 113. On the presumption that Larsen essentially drafted this account and that Lincoln's patients were mostly black, Davis charges that Larsen deemphasized her relationships with black patients and fellow nurses and stressed her relationships with white physicians, building the case that Larsen strove to curry favor with whites. As we have seen, however, most of the patients Larsen treated at Lincoln were white. The physicians and surgeons at the Tuskegee Institute, moreover, were black, and Larsen's experiences with them were anything but enriching. Everything Thoms wrote about Larsen

she knew from personal observation, so there is no evidence that she was simply relaying what Larsen had written about herself, despite the fact that much of Thoms's book is based on information provided by her subjects.

53. "Report of the Training School Department," *The Lincoln Hospital and Home: 78th Annual Report* (1917), n.p.

54. Johns, Appendix I, n.p.

55. See minutes of the National Association of Colored Graduate Nurses (NACGN), vol. 1, Minutes 1908–1917; vol. 2, Minutes 1917–1937; all on Reel 1 of NACGN Records, Schomburg. Larsen did not, as Davis claims, attend the national meeting in New York in August 1916, for she was still working at the Tuskegee Institute at that time. And the minutes for the conferences of 1917–1919, which list dues-paying members, do not include Larsen's name. Darlene Clark Hine points out that "the overwhelming majority of black nurses neither belonged to nor apparently identified with the NACGN" (*Black Women in White*, p. 122). According to the NACGN records, the group took in only nineteen "new members" in 1915, the year Larsen became eligible (Minutes 1915).

56. Davis claims, without documentation, that "it was through the NACGN and Lincoln's own Graduate Nurses' Home registry" that Larsen obtained her position as Head Nurse at Tuskegee (Davis, p. 88), but home registries, as the title implies, were used to place nurses in private duty positions, in people's homes. Ethel Johns was referring to the Lincoln home registry when she noted that Thoms kept a registry in New York for "negro private duty nurses" (Johns, Exhibit A, p. 21). Thoms stepped down, discouraged, from the presidency of the NACGN in 1922, and within a year the organization's headquarters and national registry were closed. Explaining in 1925 why she had abandoned "any attempt to continue organization work" for black nurses except the Lincoln alumnae, Thoms said she "cannot get them to think nationally or even racially. 'At least the number who can is so small as to be quite overwhelmed by the unthinking and selfish'" (Johns, Appendix I, n.p.).

57. R.N. License record for Nella Marian Larsen, License 12535, Archives, Office of the Professions, New York State Education Department, Albany, N.Y. Larsen's 92 in Practical Nursing, 95 in Anatomy and Physiology, 95 in Medical Nursing, 96 in Children's Nursing, 94 in Obstetrics and Gynecology, 94 in Materia Medica, 98 in Dietary Cooking, and 88 in Bacteriology and Surgery put her at the top of the charts in New York State.

58. Irma D. Minott (Executive Secretary of the Lincoln Fund) to Charles R. Larson, 13 May 1986, in the files of Charles R. Larson.

59. As of June 1915, the Superintendent of the school was Amelia Hall, a Canadian (1915 state census), and presumably Thoms was Assistant Superintendent. Evidently Hall resigned later that summer or early fall and Thoms filled in, with Larsen advancing to the Assistant position, because when John A. Kenney offered the Head Nurse position at Tuskegee to Larsen, he wrote Booker T. Washington that she was "Assistant to the Superintendent of Nurses" at Lincoln. John A. Kenney to Booker T. Washington, 21 October 1915, Hospital and Nurse Training School files, Booker T. Washington Papers, Library of Congress.

60. See Anna B. Coles, "The Howard University School of Nursing in Historical Perspective," *Black Women in the Nursing Profession: A Documentary History*, ed. Darlene Clark Hine (New York: Garland, 1985), pp. 34–36; Thoms, 112–113; John A. Kenney, "Some

Facts Concerning Negro Nurse Training Schools and Their Graduates" (1919; rpt. in *Black Women in the Nursing Profession*), p. 18.

7. REBEL WITH A CAUSE

1. John A. Kenney, "Some Special Needs," *Southern Letter* 32 (August 1915): 2.
2. Basil Joseph Mathews, *Booker T. Washington: Educator and Interracial Interpreter* (London: SCM Press, 1949), pp. 75–76, 98, quotation from p. 98.
3. *Tuskegee Student*, 13 November 1915, p. 1.
4. Darlene Clark Hine, "The Ethel Johns Report: Black Women in the Nursing Profession, 1925," *Journal of Negro History* 67 (1982): 213; Adda Eldredge, "The Need for a Sound Professional Preparation for Colored Nurses" (1930), reprinted in Darlene Clark Hine, ed., *Black Women in the Nursing Profession* (New York: Garland, 1985), pp. 77–80.
5. Darlene Clark Hine, *Black Women in White: Racial Conflict and Cooperation in the Nursing Profession* (Bloomington: Indiana University Press, 1989), pp. 49–50.
6. Hine, "The Ethel Johns Report," p. 213.
7. Johns, Exhibit M (Tuskegee), p. 2.
8. Mathews, pp. 129–130.
9. Booker T. Washington to John A. Kenney, 9 January 1914, "Hospital and Nurse Training School" files, BTWP/LOC; Emmett L. Scott to John A. Kenney, 1 August 1914, and John A. Kenney to Head Nurses, copied for Emmett J. Scott, 4 August 1914, "Hospital and Nurse Training School" files, BTWP/LOC.; Booker T. Washington to John A. Kenney, 21 October 1915, in *Booker T. Washington Papers*, ed. Louis R. Harlan (Urbana: University of Illinois Press, 1972–1989), vol. 13, p. 405.
10. Hine, *Black Women in White*, p. 56; Minutes of 1920, National Association of Colored Graduate Nurses Records, Reel 1 (Box 1, vol. 2), Schomburg.
11. Kenney to Booker T. Washington, 14 September 1915, "Hospital and Nurse Training School, Aug.–Dec. 1915" file, BTWP/LOC. Other details about the personnel problems leading to Larsen's hiring are recorded in John A. Kenney to Booker T. Washington, 2 July 1915; Booker T. Washington to Kenney, 13 July 1915; John A. Kenney to Booker T. Washington, 14 July 1915; Kenney to Booker T. Washington, 19 July 1915; Booker T. Washington to John A. Kenney, 30 July 1915; Booker T. Washington to Margaret E. Richardson, 14 September 1915; Kenney to Booker T. Washington, 5 August 1915; and Mae M. Booker to Booker T. Washington, 24 August 1915, "Hospital and Nurse Training School, Correspondence B–S, 1915." All are in BTWP/LOC.
12. Fundraising flyer, in "Executive Council, 1915" file, Reel 540, BTWP/LOC; Warren Logan to Booker T. Washington, 18 August 1915; and L. T. Beecher to Warren Logan, 13 August 1915, both in "Treasurer's Office, 1915" file, BTWP/LOC; Booker T. Washington to Warren Logan, 8 October 1915, "Treasurer's Office, Oct.–Dec. 1915" file, BTWP/LOC; Booker T. Washington to Warren Logan, 16 October 1915, "Treasurer's Office" files, BTWP/LOC.
13. Warren Logan to Booker T. Washington, 19 October 1915, "Treasurer's Office" files, BTWP/LOC.
14. John A. Kenney to Booker T. Washington, 21 October 1915, "Hospital and Nurse Training School, Aug.–Dec. 1915" file, BTWP/LOC. Washington misspells the name as "Armistead" in his handwritten notation.

15. Executive Council Minutes, 22 October 1915, BTWP/LOC.
16. Warren Logan to Booker T. Washington, 25 October 1915, "Treasurer's Office, Oct.–Dec. 1915" file, BTWP/LOC.
17. Booker T. Washington to Dr. Drew King, 10 July 1915, "Hospital and Nurse Training School, Correspondence B–S, 1915," BTWP/LOC.
18. Untitled notices, *Tuskegee Student*, 13 November 1915, p. 4.
19. John A. Kenney, memo to *Tuskegee Student* (n.d., but clearly of October 1915), "Hospital and Nurse Training School, Aug.–Dec. 1915," BTWP/LOC; and *Tuskegee Student*, 13 November 1915, p. 4.
20. J. E. Davis, "Hampton at Tuskegee," *Southern Workman* 44.10 (October 1915): 531. The money had come from a Bostonian, Elizabeth Mason, the wife of an institute trustee, in honor of her grandfather, who had been governor of Massachusetts during the Civil War. "The John A. A. Memorial Hospital and Nurse Training School," n.d.; typescript, School of Nursing files, H. B. Frissell Library, Tuskegee University.
21. *Tuskegee Normal and Industrial Institute Thirty-Fifth Annual Catalogue, 1915–1916* (Tuskegee, Ala., 1916), p. 23.
22. *Tuskegee Institute Bulletin, Annual Catalogue Edition, 1914–1915* (Tuskegee, Ala., 1915), p. 111; *Catalogue, 1915–1916*, p. 108.
23. Louis R. Harlan, *Booker T. Washington: The Wizard of Tuskegee, 1901–1915* (New York: Oxford University Press, 1983), pp. 454–455.
24. "A Press Release," 16 November 1915, in *Booker T. Washington Papers*, vol. 13, p. 452.
25. Isaac Fisher, "An Account of Washington's Funeral," in *Booker T. Washington Papers*, vol. 13, pp. 453, 454, reprinted from Montgomery *Advertiser*, 21 November 1915, p. 16.
26. Fisher, p. 455.
27. Ibid., p. 458.
28. William G. Willcox to Julius Rosenwald, 19 November 1915, in *Booker T. Washington Papers*, vol. 13, p. 459.
29. Adele Logan Alexander, "School Days, School Days: Discovering My Grandmother, Adella Hunt Logan," *Journal of the Afro-American Historical and Genealogical Society* 6.2 (Summer 1985): 65–73, quotation from p. 72. See also Adele Logan Alexander, *Homelands and Waterways: The American Journey of the Bond Family, 1846–1926* (New York: Vintage/Random House, 2000), pp. 338–339.
30. Alexander, "School Days," p. 73.
31. "Memorial Services at Tuskegee Institute," *Southern Letter* 33.1 (January 1916): 1.
32. "Health Hour," *Tuskegee Student*, 11 December 1915, n.p.; see also Kenney to Booker T. Washington, 19 October 1915, "Hospital and Nurse Training School, Aug.–Dec. 1915" files, BTWP/LOC.
33. John A. Kenney to Executive Council, 18 December 1915, "Executive Council 1915" file, BTWP/LOC.
34. John A. Kenney to Executive Council, 3 February 1916, RRMP/LC.
35. J. A. Kenney to Executive Council, 3 February 1916, RRMP/LC.
36. John A. Kenney to Mr. Logan, 15 February 1916, RRMP/LC.
37. Emmett J. Scott to John A. Kenney, E. C. Roberts, and E. T. Attwell, Box 2, Folder 1691, RRMP/LC.
38. John A. Kenney, E. C. Roberts, and E. T. Attwell to Executive Council, 2 March 1916, RRMP/LC.

39. Kenney to Executive Council, 3 April 1916, RRMP/LC.

40. J. A. Kenney to Dr. L. S. Johnston, 3 April 1916 (carbon), RRMP/LC.

41. *Quicksand,* in *Quicksand and Passing,* ed. Deborah E. McDowell (New Brunswick N.J.: Rutgers University Press, 1986), p. 19. Scholars occasionally identify Naxos with Fisk, but the military discipline, references to the black founder, and general description pertain to Tuskegee, where Larsen had taught, rather than to Fisk, where she had been a student. The school called "Devon" in *Quicksand,* where Helga Crane spends several lonely years as a boarding student, corresponds to Fisk.

42. J. A. Kenney to Executive Council, 10 April 1916, RRMP/LC.

43. See Kenney to Executive Council, 6 March 1916, 7 March 1916, and 8 March 1916, RRMP/LC.

44. Cynthia Neverdon-Morton, *Afro-American Women of the South and the Advancement of the Race, 1895–1925* (Knoxville: University of Tennessee Press, 1989), p. 133; Kenney to Executive Council, 16 March 1916, RRMP/LC.

45. For example, the club organized a series of celebrations of the Shakespeare Tercentenary beginning March 13, including several performances of plays, readings by faculty members, and music. Larsen was not part of any of these programs, and it is unlikely that she could have attended many of them (if any). "The Shakespeare Ter-Centenary," *Tuskegee Student,* 1 April 1916, p. 8; *Southern Letter* 33 (April 1916): 2.

46. "Tuskegee Woman's Club," *Tuskegee Student,* 29 April 1916, p. 1.

47. Ibid.

48. "National Association of Colored Women," *Southern Workman* 45 (September 1916): 492–493; Mathews, p. 194.

49. Executive Council Minutes, 15 October 1915, BTWP/LOC.

50. Mrs. Booker T. Washington to E. J. Scott, 3 March 1916. RRMP/LC.

51. *Quicksand,* pp. 17–18.

52. Executive Council Minutes, 23 December 1915, BTWP/LOC.

53. N. M. Larsen to Dr. Kenney, n.d., in RRMP/LC. The letter coincides with one written on the issue by the matron, C. E. Watkins, and dated 24 March 1916.

54. Kenney to Executive Council, 16 March 1916, RRMP/LC.

55. Kenney to Logan, 15 March 1916; Emmett J. Scott to Dr. R. O. Roett, 22 March 1916 (carbon) in RRMP/LC.

56. Kenney to Executive Council, 17 April 1916, RRMP/LC.

57. "Tuskegee Institute Observes Better Baby Week," *Tuskegee Student,* 18 March 1916, p. 1.

58. James E. Henderson, *Tuberculosis* (Springfield, Ill.: Hamann Print, 1914), n.p., in "Hospital and Nurse Training School, John A. Kenney, 1914" file, BTWP/LOC. See also Emmett J. Scott to John A. Kenney, 27 February 1914; and Kenney to Scott, 2 March 1914; both in BTWP/LOC.

59. Henderson, n.p.

60. "Editorials," *Southern Workman* 44.3 (March 1915): 134–135. See also A. Lyman Paey, "Hindrances to Negro Progress: Preventable Diseases and Premature Deaths," *Southern Workman* 44 (1915): 115–117.

61. Typescripts of telegrams from R. R. Moton to J. A. Kenney and Warren Logan, 1 August 1916, RRMP/LC.

62. John A. Kenney to Executive Council, 19 April 1916, RRMP/LC.

63. Mathews, p. 121.

64. Robert Russa Moton, *Finding a Way Out: An Autobiography* (1920; rpt. New York: Negro Universities Press, 1969), p. 219.

65. *Tuskegee Student*, 13 November 1915, p. 1.

66. A vivid description of the event by a faculty witness appears in Alvin J. Neely, "The First Six Years," in *Robert Russa Moton of Hampton and Tuskegee*, ed. William Hardin Hughes and Frederick D. Patterson (Chapel Hill: University of North Carolina Press, 1956), p. 113.

67. *Quicksand*, p. 4.

68. *Tuskegee Student*, 3 June 1916, p. 9.

69. Neely, p. 114.

70. Nella M. Larsen to Dr. R. R. Moton, 4 September 1916; N. M. Larsen to R. R. Moton and E. J. Scott, 9 October 1916, both in RRMP/LC.

71. John A. Kenney to "Acting Principal and Council," 18 August 1916, RRMP/LC. Kenney misspells "Larsen" as "Larcen."

72. Rupert O. Roett to J. A. Kenney, 1 September 1916, RRMP/LC.

73. Kenney and Roett to R. R. Moton, 12 September 1916, RRMP/LC.

74. Kenney to Moton, 7 October 1916, RRMP/LC.

75. Nella Marian Larsen to Dr. Kenney, 10 October 1916, RRMP/LC.

76. John A. Kenney to Dr. Moton, 14 October, 1916, RRMP/LC.

77. John A. Kenney to Miss Larsen (Copy for Dr. Moton), 16 October 1916, RRMP/LC.

78. Kenney to Executive Council, 16 October 1916, RRMP/LC.

79. Larsen to Dr. Moton and the Executive Council, 16 October 1916, RRMP/LC. The letter quoted apparently went to the council. The other note of the same day is identical except in closing "Very Truly," and having the word *"Council"* scrawled at the top—she had apparently sent this one to Moton.

80. R. R. Moton to Miss Nella N. Larsen, n.d., RRMP/LC. This might seem to imply that Moton gave her the thirty days requested in her note of the sixteenth, but that was not the case, as further correspondence with the hospital makes clear. Larsen was replaced immediately by her assistant, and the night supervisor immediately took over as acting Assistant Head Nurse.

81. R. R. Moton to Miss Janie Armstead, 17 October 1916, RRMP/LC. (The $57 for Armstead was actually $45 plus room and board.) Moton to Dr. J. A. Kenney, n.d., Box 1, Folder 1695, RRMP/LC; this letter informs Kenney that Moton has written Kyles and Armstead, and encloses his letters to them. We can be sure that Larsen was let go as of October 16, because the night supervisor, Orelia Williams, was then named acting Assistant Head Nurse as Armstead took over Larsen's position. On November 16, upon receiving her first monthly check in her new position, Williams wrote Dr. Kenney to complain that she had assumed all along she would get a raise, but the check was for the same amount she had always received. Thus, Williams had started in the Assistant position exactly a month earlier, on October 16. Orelia Williams to Kenney, 16 November 1916, RRMP/LC.

82. *Quicksand*, p. 19.

83. "Mrs. E. P. Roberts," née Ruth Logan, the daughter of Acting Principal Warren Logan, had grown up next door to the Washingtons at Tuskegee and had been an instructor while Larsen was there. Emmett Scott's daughter Clarissa Mae Scott, who was valedictorian in the spring of 1916, would be an oft-remarked presence at Harlem social events

and a published poet before her early death in the late Twenties. She married Hubert Delaney, a good friend of Larsen's husband. Larsen also socialized occasionally with Emmett Scott, Jr.

1. Warranty Deed conveyed from Peter and Mary Larson to Minnie Weidenaar, dated 1 July 1916, document no. 5904161; and Warranty Deed conveyed from Minnie Weidenaar and Hessel Weidenaar to Peter and Mary Larson, dated 26 June 1916, document no. 5904162, in the Office of the Recorder of Deeds, Cook County, Illinois. Mary and Peter are identified "as joint tenants but not as tenants in common" for the property on Maryland Avenue—an arrangement whereby each owned a half share, so to speak, in the house. This was very unusual for married couples. That George and Anna Gardner moved in next door is evident from the *Lakeside Annual Directory of the City of Chicago* (Chicago: Chicago Directory Co., 1917).

2. Thomas Lee Philpott, *The Slum and the Ghetto: Immigrants, Blacks, and Reformers in Chicago, 1880–1930* (Belmont, Calif.: Wadsworth, 1991), pp. 147, 152; "Citizens Oppose Negro Neighbors," *Chicago Tribune*, 22 August 1909, sect. 1, p. 2; "Lawyer in Radical Stand to Oust Negro Residents," *Chicago Tribune*, 23 August 1909, p. 2.

3. Nella Larsen Imes, Application for Admission to the Library School of the New York Public Library, NYPL LS; Committee for the Study of Nursing Education, *Nursing and Nursing Education in the United States* (New York: Macmillan, 1923), p. 390; Committee on Education of the National League of Nursing Education, *Standard Curriculum for Schools of Nursing* (New York: National League of Nursing Education, 1919). The latter two reports are based on studies of what was actually being taught in American nursing schools in the late 1910s and early 1920s.

4. There was an abbreviated version of the same study by Lavinia Dock and Isabel M. Stewart, *A Short History of Nursing.*

5. Adelaide Nutting and Lavinia L. Dock, *A History of Nursing,* 2 vols. (New York: G. P. Putnam's Sons, 1907), vol. 1, p. 143.

6. Ibid., pp. 146–147.

7. Ibid., pp. 147–150, quotation from p. 150.

8. Ibid., p. 499.

9. Ibid., p. 501.

10. *Standard Curriculum,* 125–126.

11. See Adelaide M. Nutting, "Skilled Nurses Available for War," *New York Times,* 26 May 1918, sect. 4, p. 2; "25,000 War Nurses Needed This Year," *New York Times,* 12 May 1918, sect. 2, p. 3.

12. "Red Cross Parade Brikbatz," *Bronx Home News,* 19 May 1918, pp. 1, 10.

13. "American Red Cross Officially Enrolls First Colored Nurse; Red Cross Meeting in Harlem," *New York Age,* 20 July 1918, p. 1.

14. James Weldon Johnson, "The Colored Nurses," *New York Age,* 20 July 1918, p. 4.

15. "American Red Cross," p. 1.

16. "Assign Colored Nurses to Base Hospitals 'Over There,'" *New York Age,* 28 July 1918, p. 1.

17. Ethel Johns, "A Study of the Present Status of the Negro Woman in Nursing," 1925 (typescript), pp. 29 and 14–15, Exhibits A (New York) and B (Chicago), and Appendix I,

in Laura Spelman Rockefeller Memorial Archives, Rockefeller Archive Center, Tarrytown, New York.

Davis' assertion that Larsen "visited the sick, mainly low-income blacks, in their often cramped living spaces in the Columbus Hill or Harlem districts, where African-American nurses were assigned" seems to be based upon the fact that black nurses for the Henry Street service worked in these sections of the city; see Thadious M. Davis, *Nella Larsen, Novelist of the Harlem Renaissance: A Woman's Life Unveiled* (Baton Rouge: Louisiana State University Press, 1994), p. 126. The purported segregation, according to Davis, bred discontentment with her job, and Larsen "began to drop in at the 137th Street Branch of the YWCA, where on April 5, 1918, the NACGN headquarters and registry had opened" (ibid.). The NACGN registry was for low-level jobs in private nursing, not for the kind of high-level positions Larsen held. Larsen's dissatisfaction grew, we are told, because "African-American nurses seemed destined to function in 'colored-only' clinics, hospitals, or homes located primarily in Harlem or Columbus Hill, and they were to do so under the direction or supervision of whites who were often younger and less experienced" (ibid., p. 139).

The records, of which Davis was apparently unaware, contradict the claim. Nurses were assigned to districts irrespective of race, and the records of nurses' pay in the civil list, which Davis did not consult, reveal that all nurses in Larsen's department received pay increases in the same progression based on seniority. All the supervising public health nurses in the Health Department had at least eleven years' experience, and no black nurses had taken the civil service examination for a supervisory position during Larsen's period of service. When one did, and passed, she was assigned a supervisory position. (See Minutes of the Board of Health of New York City, 1918–1921, Municipal Archives of New York; "Society," New York *Amsterdam News*, 18 January 1928, p. 6.) This was about the time Larsen might have been able to move to a supervisory job, had she chosen to stay with nursing rather than move into librarianship and writing.

The above facts should not, however, be taken to suggest that black nurses faced no discrimination; racism was surely pervasive in New York, and the higher authorities were very worried about appointing black nurses to supervisory posts.

18. See Adelaide M. Nutting, "Skilled Nurses Available for War," *New York Times*, 26 May 1918, sect. 4, p. 2; "25,000 War Nurses Needed This Year," *New York Times*, 12 May 1918, sect. 2, p. 3; Annie M. Brainard, *The Evolution of Public Health Nursing* (Philadelphia: W. B. Saunders, 1922), pp. 346–348; "Public Health Nurses in Demand," *Health News* (n.s.), 13.8 (August 1918): 233; Helen F. Boyd, *A Study of the Nursing Situation in New York as of July and August 1917* (New York: Mayor's Committee of Woman on National Defense, 1917), p. 10.

19. "The Health Crisis in New York," *Survey* 40 (4 May 1918): 129; see also "The Service and Plight of the New York Health Department," *Survey* 40 (20 April 1918): 64; "Endangering the Health of New Yorkers," *Outlook* 119 (8 May 1918): 56–57; and articles in *Survey* cited above; *City Record*, 6 July 1918, p. 3473; and "Municipal Service Commission: Eligible Lists Promulgated May 29, 1918," *City Record*, 6 June 1918, p. 2944.

20. *The Lincoln Hospital and Home: 78th Annual Report* (New York, 1917), n.p.; Minutes of 11 June 1918, Board of Health of New York City minutes, Municipal Archives, New York; and *City Record*, 6 June 1918, p. 2944; the name of Larsen's friend is spelled "Stickland" in the City Record, but in documents from Lincoln it is spelled "Strickland." See also

"Supplement: Officials and Employees of the City of New York from January 1, 1918, to June 30, 1918, Inclusive," *City Record,* 31 July 1918, p. 345.

21. Information on the house and neighborhood comes from *Atlas of the Borough of the Bronx* (Philadelphia: G. W. Bromley, 1921), in Bronx County Historical Society, with special thanks to Gary Hermalyn, Director of the Society, who spent part of an afternoon helping me out and telling me what he knew of the area's character in 1918–1920. See also Fourteenth Census of the United States, 1920: Population Schedules, Enumeration Districts 64–68. Of a Bronx population totaling 732,000, Negroes made up 4,800, or 0.7 percent. Fourteenth Census of the United States, 1920, vol. 3: Population, 1920 (Washington, D.C.: Government Printing Office, 1922), p. 684.

22. Lloyd Ultan, *The Beautiful Bronx, 1920–1950* (New Rochelle, N.Y.: Arlington House, 1979), pp. 31–32.

23. On benefits and expectations, see *Rules for Employees of the Bureau of Preventable Diseases* (New York: Department of Health, 1915), pp. 5–8, 20–22.

24. Susan L. Smith, *Sick and Tired of Being Sick and Tired: Black Women's Health Activism in America, 1890–1950* (Philadelphia: University of Pennsylvania Press, 1995), pp. 61–63, 71.

25. *Nursing and Nursing Education in the United States,* p. 50; Brainard, pp. 289–291.

26. *Nursing and Nursing Education in the United States,* pp. 10–11. Other very helpful sources on public health nursing at the time, particularly in New York, are *Manual for Public Health Nurses* (Albany: New York State Department of Health, 1920), a book that Larsen probably owned; the *Monthly Bulletin* of the New York City Department of Health, which she automatically received; the *Rules for Employees of the Bureau of Preventable Diseases* (1915), which she was required to carry with her on the job; Bessie Amerman Haasis, "What a Public Health Nurse Can Do for a Community," *Health News* (n.s.), 13.8 (August 1918): 217; Brainard, *Evolution;* Ysabella Waters, "The Rise, Progress and Extent of Visiting Nursing in the United States," *Charities and the Commons* 16.1 (7 April 1906): 16–19; and *Annual Report of the Department of Health of the City of New York* (New York: Department of Health, 1917–1921).

27. Brainard, pp. 199–290, 316–338; E.J. [Ethel Johns], "Negro Women in Nursing: Present Status," in Mary Adelaide Nutting Collection, Fiche 2535, Teachers College, Columbia University. The typescript, marked "Confidential," is undated, but "E.J." is clearly Ethel Johns, who wrote an extensive report on black nursing education and nursing conditions for the Rockefeller Foundation in 1925.

28. Johns, Exhibit A, p. 16. This was in 1924–1925, three or four years after Larsen's period of service, but it suggests something of the uniqueness of her professional relationships.

29. Ibid.

30. Ibid., p. 17.

31. Ibid., p. 32.

32. See also Darlene Clark Hine, "The Ethel Johns Report: Black Women in the Nursing Profession, 1925," *Journal of Negro History* 67 (1982): 218. I am indebted to Hine's article for bringing the Johns Report to my attention. Hine's article, covering the report's conclusions on the situation of black nurses across the country, does not paint a rosy picture of the situation in New York, but Johns certainly found that situation—particularly in Larsen's bureau—vastly better than what could be found everywhere else. See also Stanley Rayfield, comp., "A Study of Negro Public Health Nursing" (1930), in Darlene Clark Hine, ed., *Black Women in the Nursing Profession* (New York: Gar-

land, 1985). Another useful study of the rise of black public health nursing is Marie Oleatha Pitts Mosley, "A History of Black Leaders in Nursing: The Influence of Four Black Community Health Nurses on the Establishment, Growth, and Practice of Public Health Nursing in New York City, 1900–1930," Ed.D. dissertation, Teachers College, Columbia University, 1992 (Ann Arbor, Mich.: UMI Dissertation Services, 1997).

33. Darlene Clark Hine, *Black Women in White: Racial Conflict and Cooperation in the Nursing Profession, 1890–1950* (Bloomington: Indiana University Press, 1989), pp. 98–102; Rayfield, pp. 66–67.

34. Clinic locations from *Rules for Employees*. In the lists of nurses recorded in the minutes of the Board of Health, names appear clustered by district "team," with the supervising nurse apparently listed first. From this list we can see that in December 1918, for example, Larsen was one of twenty-one nurses assigned to her subdistrict, headed by Martha J. Peltier. Minutes of December 31, 1918, Board of Health, New York City Municipal Archives. Occupations of African Americans in Larsen's neighborhood from the Fourteenth Census of the United States, 1920: Population Schedules, Bronx County, Enumeration Districts 64–68, 124–125. For general information on the black population in the Bronx before the 1930s, see also John McNamara, *McNamara's Old Bronx* (Bronx: Bronx County Historical Society, 1989), pp. 58, 79; Sandor Evan Schick, *Neighborhood Change in the Bronx, 1905–1960* (Ph.D. dissertation, Harvard University, 1982), pp. 60–62; Lloyd Ultan, "Blacks in the Bronx," *Bronx Press Review,* 3 February 1994, p. 14; and Adrienne Breeden et al., "A History of Black People in the Bronx," *Bronx County Historical Society Journal* 13.2 (Fall 1976): 80–88.

35. *Rules for Employees,* pp. 60, 48, 59. Information on activities of Larsen and her colleagues also comes from *Manual for Public Health Nurses,* which, though published by the state rather than city Health Department, discusses the duties and routines of municipal public health nurses in New York State.

36. *Rules for Employees,* p. 59.

37. Ibid., p. 48.

38. At the time of her hiring, an elementary school teacher in the city made $900 per year, city hospital nurses $660, and beginning hospital physicians $1,200. Domestics in the hospitals made up to $300 per year, and stenographers for the Department of Health $720. See salary listings in Supplement to *City Record,* January 1919.

39. Elizabeth Gregg, "Public Health Nursing in Relation to Infectious Diseases," *Public Health Nurse Quarterly* 9 (October 1917): 398–401; and Elizabeth Gregg, "Nursing Service of the Department of Health," *Monthly Bulletin of the Department of Health* 9.9 (September 1919): 211–215. Both of these articles are based on the practices of nurses for the New York City Department of Health between 1917 and 1919.

40. Gregg, "Public Health Nursing," pp. 399–400; and Elizabeth Gregg, "The Tuberculosis Nurse under Municipal Direction," *Public Health Nurse Quarterly* 5.4 (October 1913): 21.

41. *Rules for Employees,* p. 46.

42. *Manual,* pp. 100–101, 105.

43. For a general history of the pandemic, see especially Alfred W. Crosby, Jr., *Epidemic and Peace, 1918* (Westport, Conn.: Greenwood Press, 1976). On the arrival and spread of the disease in New York, see, for example, "Negligent Doctors Arouse Copeland," *New York Times,* 27 October 1918, sect. 1, p. 14; "Revise Timetable in Influenza Fight," *New York*

Times, 6 October 1918, p. 1, col. 2; "Summary of Vital Statistics for the Month of January, 1919," *Monthly Bulletin of the Department of Health* 9.2 (February 1919): 58; "Statistics of the Epidemic of Influenza in New York City," *Monthly Bulletin of the Department of Health* 8.12 (December 1918): 269–277.

44. W. H. Guilfoy, "Vital Statistics of the City of New York for the Year 1918," *Monthly Bulletin of the Department of Health* 9.3 (March 1919): 71–72; "How to Know and Avoid Influenza," *Staff News* 6.11 (November 1, 1918): 7–8, quotations from p. 7.

45. Lillian Wald, "The Work of the Nurses' Emergency Council," *Public Health News* 10 (1918): pp. 306–307; Permelia Murnan Doty, "A Retrospect of the Influenza Epidemic," *Public Health Nurse* 11 (December 1919): pp. 950–951; "Fight Stiffens Here against Influenza," *New York Times,* 12 October 1918, p. 13, col. 1.

46. New York City Health Department, *Annual Report, 1918,* p. 53. Doty, "A Retrospect of the Influenza Epidemic," pp. 954–956; "Copeland Asks Aid in Influenza Fight," *New York Times,* 16 October 1918, p. 24, col. 1. See also "Bureau of Preventable Diseases," *Staff News* 6.11 (November 1, 1918): 7; *Annual Report, 1918,* p. 53; and Wald, "The Work of the Nurses' Emergency Council," p. 309. Wald's report is perhaps the best source for a general overview of nurses' responses to the epidemic in New York (pp. 305–313).

47. Elizabeth Gregg, "Emergency Nursing Service during the Epidemic," *Monthly Bulletin of the Department of Health* 8.12 (December 1918): 289.

48. Ibid., p. 289.

49. Wald, "The Work of the Nurses' Emergency Council," p. 311.

50. "Copeland Asks Aid in Influenza Fight," *New York Times,* 16 October 1918, p. 24; "1,000 Cases of Influenza and 148 Deaths Reported in Bronx," *Bronx Home News,* 22 October 1918, p. 1. "Over 170 Deaths Are Reported in the Bronx," *Bronx Home News,* 10 October 1918, p. 1.

51. "Over 170 Deaths," p. 1; "Physicians Profiteer Because of Spanish Influenza Epidemic," *Bronx Home News,* 17 October 1918, p. 1.

52. "Druggists Profiteering as Result of Influenza Epidemic," *Bronx Home News,* 24 October 1918, p. 1.

53. "Druggists," p. 1; "617 Cases of Spanish Influenza Reported in Bronx Co. Yesterday," *Bronx Home News,* 27 October 1918, p. 14.

54. Doty, p. 957.

55. "Bronx Celebration of the Victory Announcement Wildly Enthusiastic," *Bronx Home News,* 12 November 1918, p. 1. The minutes of the Health Department report all of Larsen's days of leave; she had none in 1918.

56. Crosby, pp. 60–61; "Work of Taking Care of Families of Bronx Influenza Victims Started," *Bronx Home News,* 17 November 1918, p. 10; Doty, p. 957.

57. Board of Health Minutes, 25 February 1919. Since the epidemic was in a period of resurgence at this time, it seems very unlikely that Larsen got four days of vacation, suggesting that the paid leave was for illness.

58. Gregg, "The Emergency Nursing Service," p. 290.

59. See, e.g., "Teaching the People How to Keep Well," *New York Times,* 26 January 1919, sect. 7, p. 10.

60. "Copeland Satisfied by Influenza Tour," *New York Times,* 30 October 1918, p. 10, col. 8; "Start Public Health Drive," *New York Times,* 23 February 1919, p. 6, col. 2.

61. For comments on Imes's personality, derived from people who knew him in his early years, see Ann Allen Shockley, *Afro-American Women Writers, 1746–1933: An Anthology and Critical Guide* (Boston: G. K. Hall, 1988), p. 437; and Davis, pp. 120–121.

62. Davis writes that "Imes especially liked Larsen's interest in books and was intrigued by her habit of reading during his courtship visits to the apartment she shared with other nurses at 984 Morris Avenue, Bronx" (Davis, p. 121). Apparently, her interviewee, Frankie Lee Houchins, who worked for Elmer and Nella in Nashville years later, mentioned the anecdote about Larsen's reading habits. Davis, however, was not aware of the 161st Street address where Larsen lived with Strickland.

63. Elmer S. Imes to Thomas E. Jones, 7 June 1929, Box 34, Folder 15, Thomas E. Jones Papers, Special Collections, Fisk University.

64. See Davis, p. 117.

65. W. F. G. Swann, "Elmer Samuel Imes," *Science* (n.s.), 94 (26 December 1941): 600–601.

66. William Lloyd Imes, *The Black Pastures: An American Pilgrimage in Two Centuries* (Nashville: Hemphill Press, 1957), p. 1.

67. William Lloyd Imes, "The Black Pastures in Retrospect," in Paul F. Swarthout et al., *The Hills beyond the Hills* (Lakemont, N.Y.: North Country Books, 1971), pp. 115–117.

68. Information on Imes's education and family background comes from "Report of the Demonstrators [exhibit personnel] in Connection with the Fisk University Exhibit," James E. Merrill Papers, Folder 15, Special Collections, Fisk University Library; *Catalogue of Fisk University* for 1913–1914, p. 6; 1914–1915, p. 6; 1915–1916, p. 7; James G. Merrill correspondence with Elmer S. Imes, James G. Merrill Papers, Folders 14–15, Special Collections, Fisk University Library; Thomas E. Jones to Elmer S. Imes, 7 June 1929, Box 34, Folder 15, Thomas E. Jones Papers, Special Collections, Fisk University Library; W. F. G. Swann, obituary for Elmer S. Imes.

69. Quotation from Wallace Thurman, *Negro Life in New York's Harlem: A Lively Picture of a Popular and Interesting Section* (Girard, Kansas: Haldeman-Julius, 1928), p. 55. Thomas E. Jones to Elmer S. Imes, 7 June 1929. This letter asks Imes for his curriculum vitae, which Imes filled out on the letter and returned. It includes his fraternal and church affiliations. On his invitation to the Social Workers Club event, see "Social Workers Club Entertains," *New York Age,* 31 May 1919, n.p. (society page). On St. Philip's church, see also Seth M. Scheiner, *Negro Mecca: A History of the Negro in New York City, 1865–1920* (New York: New York University Press, 1965), p. 88.

70. Quotation from Thurman, p. 53. See also Arthur Gary, "An Account of the Nail and Parker Business Enterprises," 25 July 1939, in Works Progress Administration, *Negroes of New York* (New York: New York Public Library, 1939, microfilm edition).

71. Elmer S. Imes, "Measurements on the Near Infra-Red Absorption of Some Diatomic Gases," *Astrophysical Journal* 50 (1919): 251–276; Elmer S. Imes and H. M. Randall, "The Fine-Structure of the Near Infra-Red Absorption Bands of the Gases HC1, HBr, and HF 1/4," *Physical Review* 15.2 (1920): 152–155; Notes from lecture by Dr. Earle Plyler at Fisk Infrared Institute's 25th Anniversary Silver Jubilee Celebration, August 1974, in Biographical File of Elmer S. Imes, Special Collections, Fisk University Library.

72. W. F. G. Swann, "Elmer Samuel Imes," *Science* (n.s.), 94 (December 26, 1941): 600–601, quotation from p. 601.

73. Affidavit for License to Marry, and Marriage License no. 1325, Bronx County, New York City Municipal Archives.

74. "Marriage Licenses," Bronx *Home News,* 17 April 1919, p. 3. Larsen took a leave for March 13–21, which suggests she may have moved then. Board of Health of New York City Minutes, 29 April 1919.

75. See lists of Health Department employees, *City Record,* July 1918 and January 1919 supplements, pp. 345 and 353, respectively; and "Board of Health," *City Record,* 6 June 1918, p. 2944. Thomas moved to another address in the Bronx, suggesting that, like Larsen, she worked in this borough.

76. Whereas the marriage license application shows Elmer S. Imes living at Belmont Place on Staten Island and Nella at 984 Morris Avenue, the 1920 New York City directory lists Elmer at 984 Morris Avenue. Since Larsen was already living here at the time of the application, it seems clear that he moved in with her; the civil service list also shows Larsen living here in July 1919. The city directory had no listing for Larsen in 1920, since she was married. See *Trow General Directory of New York City* (Manhattan and Bronx), vol. 132 (New York: R. L. Polk, 1920).

77. Davis, p. 122. Elmer S. Imes and Nella M. Larsen, Marriage Certificate, 3 May 1919, Bronx County, New York City Municipal Archives.

78. Report from the Director of the Bureau of Preventable Diseases for name changes by marriage, in Minutes of 17 December 1919, New York City Department of Health Minutes, Municipal Archives, New York. In some Health Department documents, the initial *M.* would remain, before "Imes" or "Larsen Imes." Thus, the *City Record* lists her as "Nella M. Imes" on the civil list of July 1921; and the Health Board minutes of 31 December 1919 list her as "Nellie M. Larsen Imes." Prior to marriage, she is almost always listed as "Nella M. Larsen."

79. *Atlas of the Borough of the Bronx* (Philadelphia: G. W. Bromley, 1921).

80. Fourteenth Census of the United States, 1920: Population, Bronx County, Enumeration Districts 124–125. These blocks were enumerated in January 1920. Nella and Elmer had apparently moved out by then, for the civil list shows Nella living at 785 Fingerboard Road, Staten Island, in January and July 1920 (see *City Record* supplements of January and July 1920, pp. 299, 274, respectively). Yet neither the Imeses nor the address 785 Fingerboard Road appears in the 1920 census for Staten Island (Richmond County). They must have been out when the census worker came by.

81. "Call Militia in Chicago Race Riots as 13 Die and 200 Fall in Battle Between Whites and Negroes," *Bronx Home News,* 29 July 1919, p. 1.

82. Board of Health of New York City Minutes, meeting of 20 August 1919.

83. *Annual Report of the Department of Health of the City of New York for the Calendar Year 1919* (New York: Department of Health, 1920), p. 76. On the diphtheria drive in the Bronx, see also "Commissioner Copeland Tells Bronx Parents That Diphtheria Taken in Time Is Easily Preventable," Bronx *Home News,* 6 April 1919, p. 7. See also W. L. Somerset and W. Godfinger, "Diphtheria, Scarlet Fever, and Measles under Sanitary Control in the City of New York," *Monthly Bulletin of the Department of Health* 9.11 (November 1919): 260.

84. "Urgent Call for Nurses to Fight Flu Epidemic; Lack of Whiskey a Handicap," Bronx *Home News,* 27 January 1920, pp. 1, 2.

85. "Influenza Epidemic Near End; Bronx Health Board Prepares to Stamp Out Minor Diseases," Bronx *Home News,* 15 February 1920, p. 11; "781 New Influenza Cases in the Bronx," Bronx *Home News,* 29 January 1920, pp. 1, 11; "Rats Fatten on Garbage While

Officials Explain; New Epidemic Feared as 'Flu' Drops," Bronx *Home News,* 8 February 1920, p. 13.

86. "So Many Bronx Families Are Being Evicted, Health of Borough Is Menaced," Bronx *Home News,* 5 October 1919, p. 1; "Says Crowding in Flats Causes Big Increase in Tuberculosis in Bronx," Bronx *Home News,* 4 December 1919, p. 2. Tenants at 280 166th Street showed up in force for a hearing on rent problems in their area.

87. Supplement to New York *City Record,* July 1920, p. 299; *Atlas of the City of New York, Borough of Richmond,* vol. 2 (Philadelphia: G. W. Bromley, 1917), plate 7, in Division of Maps, NYPL. The Imeses would live here for about a year before moving up to 129th Street in Harlem by July 1921, and the house was soon torn down. The lot where it had stood would remain vacant as late as 1937, according to insurance atlases. Nella's name appears in the *City Record* as "Nella McInness" due to a typographical error (for "Nella M. Imes"—the name given for her in later listings, along with "Nella M. Larsen Imes"), but there can be no mistake that this is Larsen, for the name appears in the proper alphabetical order for "Imes," not "McInness," within the list, and no "Nella Imes" or "Nella Larsen" shows up in this particular supplement. The July 1920 Supplement (p. 274) lists her as "Nella M. Imes" at the same address, 785 Fingerboard Road. The civil list appears to be more reliable than the New York city directory, which for 1920–1921 lists Elmer S. Imes as still living at 984 Morris Avenue; the directory was printed in 1920, apparently based on information collected just before the Imeses moved. Nella took a leave of absence with pay for October 17–26, 1919, according to the Health Department minutes for 17 December 1919; perhaps this is when she and Elmer moved. These minutes also record her official change of name (for payroll purposes) to "Nella Larsen Imes."

88. Fourteenth Census of the United States, 1920: Population, Richmond County, New York, Enumeration District 1594; issues of the *Staten Islander* for 1920–1921. In 1924–1925 there would be a series of fearful racist responses several miles away when a black professional couple moved into a previously all-white suburban district. See "Staten Island Grand Jury Indicts Big Realtor and Five Others on Vandalism Charge; Wanted to Make Negroes Move," *New York Age,* 29 August 1925, p. 1; and files on "Samuel A. Browne Residential Segregation Case," in Papers of the NAACP, Part 5, Reel 2, Library of Congress.

9. SOJOURNER IN HARLEM

1. Dianne Johnson-Feelings, "Afterword," *The Best of the Brownies' Book,* ed. Johnson-Feelings (New York: Oxford University Press, 1996), p. 335.

2. Quoted in Johnson-Feelings, "Afterword," p. 335. On *The Brownies' Book,* see also David Levering Lewis, *W. E. B. Du Bois: The Fight for Equality and The American Century, 1919–1963* (New York: Holt, 2000), pp. 32–34; Carolyn Wedin Sylvander, *Jessie Redmon Fauset: Black American Writer* (Troy, N.Y.: Whitston, 1981), pp. 115–116; and Elinor Sinnette, "The Brownies' Book: A Pioneer Publication for Children," *Freedomways* (Winter 1965): 133–142.

3. Quoted in Johnson-Feelings, "Afterword," pp. 346, 344.

4. Nella Larsen Imes, "Three Scandinavian Games," *The Brownies' Book,* June 1920, p. 191.

5. Nella Larsen Imes, "Danish Fun," *The Brownies' Book,* July 1920, p. 219. The games are

entitled "The Fox Game," "Hide the Shoe," and "The King Is Here." "The Fox Game" is a version of what Evald Tang Kristensen collected as "Ræven og Gåsen" [Foxes and Geese] in *Danske Børnerim, Remser og Lege* [Danish Children's Rhymes, Jingles, and Games] (Aarhus: Jacob Zeuners Bogtrykkeri, 1896), entry 2036, p. 247.

6. *City Record,* Supplement, January 1921, p. 287; "Hostesses: Letters Sent to the Following," records of the Negro Arts Exhibit of 1921, Box 1, Folder 11, SCR.

7. *Atlas of the Borough of Manhattan: Desk and Library Edition* (Philadelphia: G. W. Bromley, 1921); and personal observation of the restoration of the building.

8. Fourteenth Census of the United States, 1920: Population, Manhattan, Enumeration District 1334, Sheet 4A. Residents of the Imeses' building at the time of the census, January 1920, included an artist, a weaver, a sailor, a proofreader for a publishing house, a fireman, a jewelry salesman, a teacher, and several art school students. At the time of the census, no blacks lived on West 129th Street, or on 128th or 130th in that section of Harlem; west of Lenox Avenue, the area from 128th Street south to Central Park was inhabited by whites only. Between Lenox and Fifth Avenue, the edge of black Harlem began at West 131st.

9. Information on Lillian Alexander comes from "Sidelights on Society," *Amsterdam News,* 18 January 1928, p. 6; "Among Those Helping in the Annual Budget Campaign of the Y.W.C.A.," *New York Age,* 10 November 1928, p. 3; "Lillian A. Alexander," *Crisis* 40 (December 1933): 286; and Langston Hughes, *The Big Sea,* p. 94. In the late 1920s, the Alexanders lived on "Strivers' Row," 139th Street; but city directories of the early Twenties through 1925 list them at 34 West 129th, the Imeses' address in 1921.

10. See, e.g., Etnah R. Boutté to Grace Nail Johnson, 27 August 1919, in GNJ/JWJ, Box 27, Folder 39. According to Thadious Davis, Nella had met Elmer Imes "through a service organization of visiting nurses formed by Thoms to work for the Circle for Negro War Relief. Larsen became professionally active in the organization and personally acquainted with its board of directors, which included among its influential members Du Bois, Moton, Grace Nail Johnson, and Arthur B. Spingarn. The work provided Larsen with an access to social functions with some of the city's leading citizens." Thadious M. Davis, *Nella Larsen, Novelist of the Harlem Renaissance: A Woman's Life Unveiled* (Baton Rouge: Louisiana State University Press, 1994), p. 117.

11. Claude McKay, *A Long Way from Home* (1937; rpt. New York: Harcourt, Brace and World, 1970), pp. 153–154. See also James Weldon Johnson, *Along This Way* (1933; rpt. New York: Viking, 1967), p. 376.

12. Rev. Richard Manuel Bolden, "An Interview with Dr. Louis T. Wright, Stormy Petrel of Harlem Hospital," *New York Age,* 11 February 1933, p. 7.

13. Langston Hughes, "Walter White: A White Negro," in "Our Negro Writers," draft essay by Hughes for a Russian magazine, in WWPC, Reel 16; the article is filed with a letter to Amy and Joel Spingarn of 3 August 1933. See also Edward Waldron, *Walter White and the Harlem Renaissance* (Port Washington, N.Y.: Kennikat Press, 1978), pp. 3, 11. A fine biography published after this chapter was written is Kenneth Robert Janken, *White: The Biography of Walter White, Mr. NAACP* (New York: New Press, 2003).

14. Stanley High, quoted in Waldron, p. 15.

15. Walter White, *A Man Called White: The Autobiography of Walter White* (New York: Viking Press, 1948), p. 39.

16. Ibid., p. 65.

17. Fauset quoted in Marion L. Starkey, "Jessie Fauset," *Southern Workman* 61 (May 1932): 219.
18. Hughes, "Walter White," n.p.
19. Celeste Tibbets, "Ernestine Rose and the Origins of the Schomburg Center," *Schomburg Center Occasional Papers Series,* no. 2 (1989); and Betty L. Jenkins, "A White Librarian in Black Harlem," *Library Quarterly* 60.3 (1990): 216–218. Celeste Tibbets' article, though neglected by Harlem Renaissance scholars, is an invaluable source on Rose and the 135th Street Branch during the 1920s and 1930s.
20. Ernestine Rose, *Bridging the Gulf: Work with the Russian Jews and Other Newcomers* (New York: Immigrant Publication Society, 1917), p. 10.
21. Ibid., p. 21.
22. Jenkins, p. 218; and Tibbets, pp. 16–17.
23. Ernestine Rose, "Serving New York's Black City," *Library Journal,* 46 (15 March 1921): 251.
24. Ibid., p. 258.
25. Ernestine Rose, "Books and the Color Line," *Survey* 48 (15 April 1922): 75–76. For further expression of her philosophy along these lines, see Rose, "Where White and Black Meet," *Southern Workman* 51 (October 1922): 467–471.
26. Rose, "Serving," p. 256.
27. Rose, "A Librarian in Harlem," *Opportunity* 1 (July 1923): 220.
28. "Reminiscences of Pura Belpre White," Oral History Research Office, Columbia University, 1976, pp. 7–8.
29. Ibid., Appendix.
30. C. C. Williamson, "Edward C. Williams, 1871–1929," *Negro Library Conference: Fisk University,* Papers Presented 20–23 November 1931, pp. 7–12. Williams also wrote several unpublished plays and the serialized epistolary novel *Letters of Davy Carr: A True Story of Colored Vanity Fair,* which has recently been published in book form for the first time under the title *When Washington Was in Vogue,* ed. Adam McKible (New York: Amistad, 2003).
31. Nella L. Imes to Mrs. [Ruth] Whitehurst, [May] 1921; and A. A. Schomburg to Mrs. Nella L. Imes, 17 August 1921, both in Box 1, Folder 11, SCR. E. C. Williams to members of the Ladies Sub-Committee, Negro Arts Exhibit, 2 July 1921, Box 1, Folder 11, SCR. E. C. Williams, form letter dated 15 July 1921, Box 1, Folder 11, SCR. List of women and the churches they are to contact, on letterhead of "Negro Arts Exhibit," 1921, Box 1, Folder 11, SCR.
32. Maude Cuney-Hare, *Negro Musicians and Their Music* (Washington, D.C.: Associated Publishers, 1936), pp. 275–276, 328.
33. "Negro Arts Exhibit Showing at 135th St. Public Library," *New York Age,* 6 August 1921, p. 8.
34. Ibid., p. 8.
35. James A. Porter, *Modern Negro Art* (New York: Arno, 1969; orig. pub. 1943), p. 94.
36. Department of Health Minutes, 8 September 1921.
37. "Negro Arts Exhibition Draws Large Number of Sightseers," *New York Age,* 20 August 1921, p. 2.
38. Ibid., p. 2.
39. Note for "Mrs. Nella Larsen Imes," 1 September 1921, Box 1, Folder 11, SCR.

40. Health Department Minutes, 20 October 1921.

41. Substitute Record for Nella L. Imes, Personnel Office, New York Public Library. For standard salaries, see *Brief Outline of Scheme of Service in the Circulation Department* (New York: NYPL, 1923), p. 3; and "Salary Statistics," *Bulletin of the American Library Association* 16 (1922): A14.

42. New York Public Library, *Brief Outline of Scheme of Service in the Circulation Department* (New York: NYPL, 1923), p. 3; and "Report of the Library for 1922," *Bulletin of the New York Public Library* 27.5 (May 1923): 377.

43. Thadious Davis interprets Larsen's career move as once again betraying Larsen's racial self-hatred and craving for genteel status, claiming that Larsen henceforth avoided mentioning her nursing career and was ashamed of having been trained in and having worked in an "all-black" environment. "Nursing became a topic she avoided; if she found it necessary to address her nursing career, she would either state or suggest that she trained at Columbia University. . . . Not only was Columbia a more prestigious educational environment, but it was also outside the usual and expected all-black environment, which Larsen Imes associated with inferiority" (Davis, p. 139). Assuming that the Health Department was segregated, Davis did not realize that when Larsen shifted to librarianship she moved from an almost all-white environment to a primarily black one. The other charges do not hold up either. People who knew Larsen were perfectly aware of her nursing background. The biographical statement she wrote for Knopf's publicity department spoke of her nurse training and work at Tuskegee, as would other documents throughout her life. In numerous instances she mentioned or listed her training at Lincoln. Moreover, Larsen never claimed to have gone to nursing school at Columbia. A nomination form for a Harmon Foundation Award, the basis of Davis' charge against her, lists as types of "Special Training or Study," "(1) Nursing (2) Library Science" and then on the one line available for "school," "Columbia University"—which is where the NYPL Library School had moved by that time. On her Guggenheim Fellowship application a year later, Larsen listed, under "Special Study," "Lincoln Hospital Training School for Nurses 1912–15," and under "Accomplishments" she listed positions at Tuskegee, Lincoln Hospital, the Department of Health, and the New York Public Library, all accurately.

44. See "Brief Outline of Scheme of Service in the Circulation Department," dated April 1923 (four-page pamphlet), in NYPL Archives, Record Group 8.

45. One historian has credited Sadie M. Peterson (later Delaney) with completing a one-year program in the NYPL Library School before beginning as an assistant at the 135th Street Branch in 1920 (Stephanie J. Shaw, *What a Woman Ought To Be and To Do: Black Professional Women Workers during the Jim Crow Era* [Chicago: University of Chicago Press, 1996], p. 153). Peterson did receive her training at the NYPL, but she did not attend the school, a crucial professional distinction (Sadie Peterson Delaney Papers, Schomburg).

    A. P. Marshall, in a directory of black librarians, wrote that E. C. Williams was the only black library school graduate until 1926. He missed Larsen's graduation in 1923 because his source was the Columbia Civic Library Association's *Directory of Negro Graduates of Accredited Library Schools, 1900–1936* (Washington, D.C.: Columbia Civic Library Association, 1937), which included only graduates of library schools still in existence at the time of publication. By this time, the NYPL Library School had folded into the school at Columbia University. A. P. Marshall, "The Black Librarian's Stride toward Equality," in *The Black Librarian in the Southeast,* ed. Annette L. Phinazee (Durham: North Carolina Central University, 1980).

46. "Faculty Meeting, Jan. 26, 1922," memorandum in folder entitled "Faculty Meetings, 1921–22," Box 12, NYPL LS.

47. Rose, "Books and the Color Line," p. 26.

48. Rose, "Serving New York's Black City," p. 257.

49. "Library Aids Negroes," *New York Times,* 17 April 1921, sect. 2, p. 9.

50. Rose, "Serving New York's Black City," p. 257.

51. "Report of the Library for 1921," *Bulletin of the New York Public Library* 26.4 (April 1922): 291.

52. "'Work with Negroes' Round Table," *Bulletin of the American Library Association* 16 (1922): 360–366, quotation from p. 363. See also "American Librarians Confer on Work among Negroes," *New York Age,* 15 July 1922, p. 8. One other library was planning to have a black student in 1922–1923, the Carnegie Library in Pittsburgh, where Rose had worked a few years earlier. A clarification is in order here: a very few black librarians may have received formal library school training, but if so they did not work in public libraries.

53. "Admission of Students," NYPL LS, Box 11.

54. Application for Admission to Library School of New York Public Library, "Imes, Mrs. Nella Larsen," Box 30, NYPL LS.

55. Williamson, "Edward C. Williams, 1871–1929," quotation from p. 7.

56. Nella Larsen Imes Application File, Box 30, NYPL LS.

57. "Procedures with Regard to Admission to the Library School of the New York Public Library," Box 11, NYPL LS.

58. Student record in folder for "Imes, Mrs. Nella Larsen," Box 30, NYPL LS.

59. Ernestine Rose, "A Librarian in Harlem," *Opportunity* 1 (July 1923): 206–207. The article is a reprint of her paper delivered at the 1923 American Library Association Conference in Hot Springs, Arkansas.

60. "News of Greater New York," *New York Age,* 18 March 1922, p. 8.

61. "135th Street Library," *New York Age,* 12 August 1922, p. 8.

62. "News of Greater New York," *New York Age,* 15 April 1922, p. 8.

63. Ibid., 29 April 1922, p. 8.

64. Ibid., 29 April 1922, p. 8.

65. Ibid., 4 March 1922, p. 3.

66. A. B. Thoms to Ernestine Rose, 28 April 1922, Box 1, Folder 13, SCR. In this letter Thoms agrees to serve—but eventually Louise Latimer, for some reason, replaced her.

67. See, e.g., George E. Haynes to Mrs. Nella L. Imes, 27 March 1922; Stella Hawkins to Mrs. Nella Larsen Imes, 30 March 1922; Elizabeth Davis to Mrs. Nella Larsen Imes, 30 March 1922. All are in Box 1, Folder 13, SCR.

68. Jessie Fauset to Ernestine Rose, [1922], Box 1, Folder 13, SCR. The letter dates from spring or summer 1922.

69. Rose may have wooed Fauset back into helping on the terms she demanded; a later newspaper report credited Fauset with putting together musical and literary programs. This attribution, however, may have derived from programs printed prior to Fauset's

resignation. "Original Paintings at Negro Art Exhibit," *New York Age*, 19 August 1922, p. 8.

70. Art Exhibit Committee meeting, minutes, 25 May 1922, Box 1, Folder 13, SCR.

71. Warranty Deed conveyed from Peter and Mary Larson to David S. Lafler and James J. Flanagan dated 1 May 1922, and attestations of notary publics, all in document no. 7503005, Office of the Cook County Recorder of Deeds. Mildred Phillips informed Charles R. Larson that the Gardner family slightly preceded Peter and Mary Larsen in moving to California. It seems they continued to live next door to each other in a double, and Mary largely raised Anna's son, since Anna suffered from multiple sclerosis. See Charles R. Larson, *Invisible Darkness: Jean Toomer and Nella Larsen* (Iowa City: University of Iowa Press, 1983), pp. 117–119.

72. *Catalog of Exhibition by Negro Artists*, 1 August to 1 October 1922, in SCR; and "Second Annual Art Exhibit at 135th Street Library," *New York Age*, 12 August 1922, p. 8.

73. "Negro Portraits," *Survey Graphic* 69.5 (1 December 1922): 326–327. Two of the portrait artists were students in the National Academy of Design, and one in the school at the Boston Museum of Fine Arts.

74. "Negro Artists' Exhibition Opened in Harlem Library," *New York Age*, 5 August 1922, p. 8.

75. "National Certification and Training," *Library Journal* 46 (1 November 1921): 886–888; Sarah K. Vann, *Training for Librarianship before 1923* (Chicago: American Library Association, 1961), p. 163. On the feminization of librarianship and its connection with compensation, see Anita R. Schiller, "Women in Librarianship," rpt. in Dathleen Weibel and Kathleen M. Heim, eds., *The Role of Women in Librarianship, 1876–1976: The Entry, Advancement, and Struggle for Equalization in One Profession* (Phoenix: Oryx Press, 1979), pp. 233–243; M. S. R. James, "Women and Their Future in Library Work" (1899), in Weibel and Heim, pp. 32–33; and Dee Garrison, "The Tender Technicians: The Feminization of Public Librarianship, 1876–1905," *Journal of Social History* 6 (1972): 131–159, reprinted in Weibel and Heim, pp. 201–221.

76. "National Certification and Training," pp. 886–888.

77. "Training for Library Service," *Library Journal* 48 (1 September 1923): 712. For a general history of the development of library education, see Carl M. White, *The Origins of the American Library School* (New York: Scarecrow Press, 1961).

78. "Annual Report, 1922–1923," Box 1, NYPL LS.

79. "Our Origins," *Library School Notes* 10 (February 1923): 6–7. See also "Training Librarians," *New York Times*, 16 October 1921, sect. 2, p. 2.

80. Information on guest lecturers, calendar, and fees comes from Library School of the New York Public Library, *Circular of Information, 1922–23* (New York: New York Public Library, 1923), pp. 4–14.

81. The actual typed schedules for all courses in the 1922–1923 school year can be found in Box 13, "Folder of Schedules, 1922–23," NYPL LS. These provide an hour-by-hour, daily account of what was taught.

82. Library School of the New York Public Library, "Junior Book Selection, 1922–23" (schedule of coursework), Box 13, NYPL LS; and *Circular of Information*, pp. 17–19.

83. "Library School of the New York Public Library: Student Record" for "Mrs. Nella Larson [sic] Imes," Box 30, NYPL LS. The grade-book (bound in black) that gives an

exact record of all Larsen's and other students' grades, by individual quiz, test, and exercise, can be found in Box 18 of this collection. In this way one can compare students' performances in detail for the entire academic year.

84. Davis, p. 126.
85. "Biographical Sketch of William Lloyd Imes," in Biographical File for William Lloyd Imes, Special Collections, Fisk University Library.
86. "Description of Junior Field Work" (1922–1923), NYPL LS.
87. Augusta Markowitz, "Student Report Sheet" for Mrs. Nella L. Imes, in folder for "Imes, Mrs. Nella Larsen," Box 30, NYPL LS.
88. Alice Keats O'Connor, "Student Report Sheet" for Mrs. Nella L. Imes, ibid.
89. Student record, ibid.
90. "Folder of Schedules, 1922–23."
91. "Annual Inspection Trip: Albany, Boston, Providence," 23–29 March 1923 (printed program), in "Spring Inspection Trip" folder, NYPL LS.
92. "135th St. Library Notes," *Amsterdam News,* 24 January 1923, p. 8.
93. "Bust of Dr. Du Bois to Adorn Library," *Amsterdam News,* 10 January 1923, p. 12; "Present Du Bois Bust to Branch Library," *Amsterdam News,* 17 January 1923, p. 1. "135th St. Library Notes," *Amsterdam News,* 24 January 1923, p. 8.
94. *The Nation* 116 (10 January 1923): 33–36. For the response of black intellectuals, see, for example, Jessie Fauset to Alain Locke, 10 January 1923: "Like you I am quite carried away with Clement Wood's article in The Nation. If he had just written 'Nigger' with half as much abandon and assurance his book would, I am sure, have been a great success." Alain Locke Papers, Moorland-Spingarn Research Center, Howard University.
95. "Noted Author Talks at 135th Street Library," *Amsterdam News,* 21 February 1923, p. 12; see also "Items of Social Interest," *Amsterdam News,* 14 February 1923, p. 8.
96. "135th St. Library Notes," *Amsterdam News,* 21 February 1923, p. 12.
97. "Birth Control Advocate Speaks to Large Audience at Public Library," *Amsterdam News,* 7 March 1923, p. 1.
98. "Life and Arts of Ancient Egypt," *Amsterdam News,* 25 April 1923, p. 7.
99. "Colored Artists in Serious Drama on Broadway," *Amsterdam News,* 2 May 1923, p. 5. For the *Amsterdam News*'s coverage of the Ethiopian Art Theatre, see ibid.; "'Salome' Scores at Lafayette," 25 April 1923; "How Colored Players in Serious Drama Are Received on B'way," 16 May 1923, p. 5; "Colored Dramatists Present 'Comedy of Errors,'" 16 May 1923, p. 5; "Colored Group Presenting 'Salome' to Make International Tour Soon," 25 April 1923, p. 6.
100. A. H. Lawrence, *Duke Ellington and His World: A Biography* (New York: Routledge, 2001), p. 26.
101. Ibid., pp. 35–36.
102. Ernestine Rose, quoted in "Interest Increases in Negro Literature," *Amsterdam News,* 2 May 1923, p. 7.
103. Rose, "A Librarian in Harlem," p. 207.
104. Ibid.
105. See "Course Outlines from the Library School of the New York Public Library" (typescript), p. 4; and Class Schedule, Library School of the New York Public Library, Junior Program, Week of 30 April 1923. Both in NYPL LS.

106. "'Work with Negroes' Round Table," *American Library Association Bulletin* 17 (1923): 275.

107. Ibid., pp. 278–279, quotation from p. 278.

108. Student Record, for "Imes, Mrs. Nella Larson"; Black-bound grade-book, Box 18, NYPL LS.

109. "Annual Report, 1922–23," Box 1, NYPL LS.

110. "15 Decisive Books: Who Will Name Them?" *New York Times*, 9 June 1923, p. 13.

111. Ibid. The full text of the speech was printed as a pamphlet and is now in the folder of commencement addresses, Box 19, NYPL LS.

112. James I. Wyer, "The Soul of the Library" (New York: NYPL, 1923), p. 8. In commencement addresses folder, Box 19, NYPL LS.

10. Rooms Full of Children

1. Memorandum dated 9 June 1923, in folder labeled "Faculty Meetings: 1922–23," Box 12, NYPL LS.

2. Personnel card for Nella L. Imes, NYPL Personnel Office.

3. See *Staff News* 13.39 (27 September 1923): 115–116.

4. Personnel card for Nella L. Imes. Thadious Davis made a number of errors in reading Larsen's personnel card, concluding that Larsen spent almost all her time at the 135th Street Branch, whereas she actually worked at Seward Park from 1 November 1923 to October 1924, before transferring to 135th Street to take over the Children's Room there. This reading of the personnel card is confirmed by the alumni register of the library school, *Library School of the New York Public Library: Register 1911–1926* (New York: NYPL, 1929), listing for "Imes, Mrs. Nella Larsen," in NYPL LS. Her Guggenheim Fellowship application specifies that she worked as an assistant in the Children's Room.

5. Personnel card for Nella L. Imes; and "Brief Outline of Scheme of Service in the Circulation Department," April 1923, NYPL Archives, Research Group 8, p. 3. Thadious Davis' notions of Larsen's mistreatment seem to be based on erroneous earlier accounts of the experiences of a different black assistant at the branch, Regina Anderson (later Andrews), whom I discuss later. Anderson's experience aside, the record of Larsen's pay and promotion history judged in relation to library salary policy (never heretofore consulted) is unambiguous. Larsen did well.

6. "Reminiscences of Pura Belpre White," Oral History Research Office, Columbia University, 1976, p. 8. Prior to World War I, O'Connor had worked under Anne (always known as "Annie") Carroll Moore, the mother of modern librarianship for children and its indefatigable champion. Just after the war, O'Connor took a leave of absence to work for the American Committee for Devastated France, which used libraries to help restore French village life; she was one of the chief children's librarians engaged in this effort. Frances Clarke Sayers, *Anne Carroll Moore: A Biography* (New York: Atheneum, 1972), p. 131.

7. Margaret Munger Stokes, "Library Experiences among the Children of the Russian Jews," *Scribner's* 73 (May 1923): 609–612. Stokes worked briefly as a substitute assistant at the Seward Park Branch during the very season Larsen had done her fieldwork for library school there, in early 1923.

8. Ibid., p. 609.

9. Konrad Bercovici, *Around the World in New York* (New York: Century Co., 1924), p. 86.

10. Ibid., pp. 78, 87.

11. Ibid., p. 85.

12. "Library Notes," *Amsterdam News,* 7 November 1923, p. 8.

13. Description drawn from Esther Johnston, "A Square Mile of New York," *Bulletin of the New York Public Library* 70 (1966): 427. Johnston worked in the Children's Room at Seward Park in 1921.

14. Stokes, p. 610.

15. Johnston, p. 426.

16. Ibid., p. 435; Jenna Weissman Joselit, "Reading, Writing, and a Library Card: New York Jews and the New York Public Library," *Biblion* 5 (1996): 105.

17. Kay E. Vandergrift, "Female Advocacy and Harmonious Voices: A History of Public Library Services and Publishing for Children in the United States," *Library Trends* 44 (Spring 1996): 686.

18. Alice Keats O'Connor, "Annual Report for Mr. Hopper, 1923," dated 15 January 1924, Seward Park Branch Archives, Research Group 8, NYPL.

19. Seward Park's Children's Room had a yearly circulation of nearly 180,000 for slightly fewer than 9,000 volumes—about half the number of books the library needed to properly serve the population "with fairness to the children as well as to the Staff," according to the annual reports of 1923 and 1924. "Report of the Library for 1923," *Bulletin of the New York Public Library* 28.4 (April 1924): 315; and "Report of the Library for 1924," *Bulletin of the New York Public Library* 29.4 (April 1925): 191–290, quotation from p. 231.

20. "Report of the New York Public Library for 1925," *Bulletin of the New York Public Library* 30.5 (May 1926): 275–401, quotation from p. 334.

21. Stokes, p. 610; also Johnston, p. 429.

22. Ibid.

23. Children's librarian from Seward Park, quoted in Joselit, p. 101.

24. Johnston, pp. 429–430.

25. "Report of the Library for 1924," p. 231.

26. O'Connor, "Annual Report for Mr. Hopper, 1923."

27. Johnston, pp. 431, 434.

28. Stokes, p. 611.

29. Joselit, p. 105.

30. Stokes, p. 611.

31. Ibid., p. 612.

32. Phyllis Dain, *The New York Public Library: A History of Its Founding and Early Years* (New York: NYPL, Astor, Lenox and Tilden Foundations, 1972), p. 304.

33. Stokes, p. 609.

34. Quoted in Joselit, p. 102.

35. Seward Park Mothers' Club to Mrs. Gladys Leslie, 28 March 1925, Archives of the Seward Park Branch Library, Seward Park Library, New York.

36. Anne Lundin, "The Pedagogical Context of Women in Children's Services and Literature Scholarship," *Library Trends* 44.4 (Spring 1996): 840–850, quotation from 844.

37. Vandergrift, p. 694; Dain, p. 303.

38. Sayers, pp. 80, 81.

39. Vandergrift, p. 694.
40. Dain, p. 303.
41. Sayers, pp. 211–212. In fact, Moore's columns resulted from solicitations by Eugene Saxton, later an important editor at Harper's who sought out African American authors ranging from Countee Cullen through Richard Wright.
42. John Tebbel, "For Children, with Love and Profit: Two Decades of Book Publishing for Children," in Sybille A. Jagusch, ed., *Stepping Away from Tradition: Children's Books of the Twenties and Thirties* (Washington, D.C.: Library of Congress, 1988), p. 13.
43. Ibid., p. 15.
44. Ibid., p. 17; "The John Newbery Medal," *Library Journal* 47 (May 1922): 399.
45. Bertha E. Mahony and Elinor Whitney, "Introduction," *Five Years of Children's Books* (New York: Doubleday Doran, 1936), p. 7.
46. Tebbel, p. 22.
47. Moore, "Opening the New Children's Books," *Bookman* 58.2 (October 1923): 185–193.
48. Anne MacLeod, "Literary and Social Aspects of Children's Books of the Twenties and Thirties," in Jagusch, ed., *Stepping Away from Tradition*, p. 54.
49. Ibid., pp. 54–55.
50. Charles S. Johnson to E. Franklin Frazier, 20 November 1924, Box 131-11, Folder 9, Special Collections, Fisk University Library.
51. Langston Hughes, *The Big Sea* (1940; rpt. New York: Hill and Wang, 1963), p. 252.
52. Helen M. Boardman, "Jerome B. Peterson: A Negro Friend," typescript dated 1943, in JWJ Files, Box N–P.
53. Information on Jerome Peterson comes from Helen M. Boardman, "Jerome B. Peterson: A Negro Friend," typescript dated 1943 in JWJ Files, Box N–P; anonymous typescript (probably by Dorothy Peterson), "Jerome Bowers Peterson, 1859–1943," in Dorothy Peterson box, CVV/JWJ; F. H. French, "Biographical Sketch of Mr. Jerome Peterson," in files for "Negroes of New York," Federal Writers Project of New York, Schomburg; and Sydney H. French, "Biographical Sketch of Mr. Jerome Peterson," in files for "Negroes of New York."
54. Dorothy Peterson to Grace Nail Johnson, 30 July 1923, Box 15, Folder 373, JWJ/JWJ.
55. Dorothy Peterson to Thomas Rutherford, 22 August [no year, but probably of the early 1930s], Box 2, Folder 44, DPP.
56. Anita Thompson Dickinson Reynolds, "American Cocktail," unpublished manuscript, first version, p. 58, in Box 129-4, Folder 1, Anita Thompson Dickinson Reynolds Papers, Moorland-Spingarn Research Center, Howard University.
57. Reynolds, "American Cocktail," p. 94 of the second version, manuscript dated January 1979.
58. Reynolds, first version, p. 63.
59. Ibid., pp. 64–65.
60. Davis has identified Audrey Denney with the beautiful Harlem socialite and reputed "kept woman" Blanche Dunn, apparently because of Dunn's legendary sex appeal; but Dunn was brown-skinned, "fresh from the West Indies" in 1926 (with an accent that limited her stage opportunities), and lived in Harlem. See Bruce Nugent, "On Blanche Dunn," and Abram Hill, "Blanche Dunn," both in "Sketches of Colorful Harlem Characters," Federal Writers Project of New York City, "Negroes of New York," Reel 1, Schomburg.

61. Reynolds, second version, p. 91.

62. Reynolds, first version, p. 76.

63. Reynolds, second version, p. 99. The fact that Thompson went with black men to the Cotton Club is one of many pieces of evidence that the famous club was not, as legend has it, always whites-only; its policies actually shifted through time, about which more later.

64. Claude McKay, *A Long Way from Home* (1937; rpt. New York: Harcourt, Brace and World, 1970), pp. 153–154; see also James Weldon Johnson, *Along This Way* (1933; rpt. New York: Viking, 1967), p. 376.

65. Walter White, *A Man Called White* (New York: Arno Press, 1969), p. 43.

66. The Whites lived at 90 Edgecombe until they went to France in 1927; it was not until their return that they moved into 409 Edgecombe and the apartment more commonly described in anecdotes of the era. See, for example, Walter White to Blanche Knopf, 8 December 1925, WWPC.

67. See, for example, the report of Fauset's large birthday party for her sister Helen Lanning, "Society," *Amsterdam News,* 25 January 1928, p. 6.

68. "Jessie Fauset Honored at Tea," *Amsterdam News,* 20 February 1929, p. 4. This article lists all members of the Saturday Night Club, which included Lillian Alexander, Ruth Logan Roberts (daughter of Warren Logan), Helen Lanning, Bertha Randolph, and Helen Hagan—all good friends of Fauset's.

69. Hughes, p. 94.

70. On the back of one of Fauset's letters to Hughes in the mid-1920s, he wrote, in anticipation of her response to his first book of poems, "There will probably be uproar enough that one of their leading (?) poets, and a public representative of the Race allows such a 'delightfully fantastic career' to be exposed to the world. They would have me a 'nice boy' and a college graduate. In other words—a good example. Middle-class colored people are very conventional." Fauset to Hughes, n.d., leaf 71 in Hughes-Fauset Correspondence, LHP.

71. McKay, p. 112.

72. Transcripts of interviews with Mae Sullivan and Wilhelmina Adams in David L. Lewis / Voices from the Renaissance Collection, Schomburg.

73. Jessie Fauset to Joel Spingarn, 25 January 1922, quoted in Lewis, p. 123.

74. Ethel Ray Nance, oral history interview by Ann Allen Shockley, 18 November and 23 December 1970, Fisk University Library.

75. Hughes, p. 244.

76. Nella Larsen, *Quicksand,* in *Quicksand and Passing,* ed. Deborah E. McDowell (New Brunswick, N.J.: Rutgers University Press, 1986), pp. 51–52.

77. Ethel Ray Nance to Charles R. Larson, n.d. (ca. early 1980s). Many thanks to Professor Larson for sharing this correspondence with me.

78. David Levering Lewis, taped interview with Regina Andrews, David L. Lewis / Voices from the Renaissance Collection, Schomburg.

79. Countee Cullen addressbook, Folder 2 of Box 10, Countee Cullen Papers, Amistad Research Center, Tulane University.

80. Florence Smith Vincent, "There Are 20,000 Persons 'Passing,' Says Noted Author," *Pittsburgh Courier,* 11 May 1929, illustrated feature section, p. 1.

81. Nance, interviews by Ann Allen Shockley.

82. See Arnold Rampersad, "Racial Doubt and Racial Shame in the Harlem Renaissance," in Geneviève Fabre and Michel Fleiss, eds., *Temples for Tomorrow: Looking Back at the Harlem Renaissance* (Bloomington: Indiana University Press, 2002), pp. 31–44.

83. Barbara Johnson, "The Quicksands of the Self: Nella Larsen and Heinz Kohut," in Elizabeth Abel, Barbara Christian, and Helene Moglen, eds., *Female Subjects in Black and White: Race, Psychoanalysis, Feminism* (Berkeley: University of California Press, 1997), pp. 252–265.

84. "Society News," *Amsterdam News,* 19 September 1923, p. 8.

85. In a letter to Alain Locke of 4 March 1924, Charles S. Johnson lists the members of the Writers Guild as Eric Walrond, Countee Cullen, Langston Hughes, Gwendolyn Bennett, Jessie Fauset, Eloise Bibb Thompson, Regina Anderson, Harold Jackman, and himself (Alain Locke Papers, Moorland-Spingarn Research Center, Howard University). Members were evidently nominated and elected by the members, to judge from a letter Gwendolyn Bennett wrote Jackman: "You're [sic] recounting of the Writers Guild Meeting was so interesting. . . . So Zora Neale Hurston and Eunice Hunton are now members, eh? I didn't vote on them!!!!" Gwendolyn Bennett to Harold Jackman, 27 October 1925, in JWJ Files.

86. See, for example, "Side Lights on Society," *Amsterdam News,* 1926–1927, while Larsen was living in Harlem.

87. David Levering Lewis, transcript of interview with G. James Fleming, David L. Lewis / Voices from the Renaissance Collection, Schomburg.

88. Edward Waldron, *Walter White and the Harlem Renaissance* (Port Washington, N.Y.: Kennikat Press, 1978), pp. 65, 66.

89. Charles S. Johnson to Alain Locke, 29 February 1924 and 7 March 1924 (quotation from the latter), Alain Locke Papers, Moorland-Spingarn Research Center, Howard University.

90. For more extensive explanation of this point, see George Hutchinson, *The Harlem Renaissance in Black and White* (Cambridge, Mass.: Harvard University Press, 1995), pp. 42–60, 170–208.

91. Adah B. Thoms, *Pathfinders* (1929; rpt. New York: Garland, 1985), p. 114.

92. "Ballanta-Taylor Addressed Forum at Library on Negro Music of America and Africa," *New York Age,* 22 March 1924, p. 7. "Dr. Locke to Address Booklover's Evening at 135th St. Library," *New York Age,* 29 March 1924, p. 8. On Goldenweiser and Boas: "135th St. Public Library," *New York Age,* 15 March 1924, p. 8. On Broun: "135th Street Library," *New York Age,* 5 April 1924, p. 8. The black press not infrequently quoted Broun's columns; see "Heywood Broun Comments on Race Segregation in Theatres," *New York Age,* 20 May 1922, p. 6; and Bob Slater, "Florence Mills Is Now a Star of First Magnitude," *New York Age,* 15 November 1924, p. 6. On the National Ethiopian Art Theatre School: "The Ethiopian Art School, Anne Wolter Director, Now Open," *New York Age,* 22 March 1924, p. 6; "National Ethiopian Art Theatre School Was Opened in New York City March 17," *New York Age,* 5 April 1924, pp. 1, 6.

93. Walter White to James Weldon Johnson, 23 August 1924, WWPC.

94. Carl Van Vechten daybook for 1924, entry for Tuesday, 26 August 1924; in Box 111, CVV/NYPL.

95. Van Vechten daybook for 1924, entries for 27 September, 5 October, 14 October, 16 October, 25 October, CVV daybooks.

96. Employment card for Nella L. Imes. The salary was standard for persons with her responsibilities.
97. "Statistics of Work with Children Circulation Department, 1925," in "Report of the NYPL for 1925," *Bulletin of the New York Public Library* 30.5 (May 1926): 366.
98. Ibid.
99. "Plan Systematic Courses for Reading and Study at 135th Street Library," *New York Age,* 18 October 1924, p. 10.
100. "135th Street Library," *New York Age,* February 1925, p. 10.
101. "Series of Art Exhibits by Individual Artists at 135th St. Library," *New York Age,* 25 October 1924, p. 10.
102. "Book Evenings at the 135th St. Branch Library," *New York Age,* 15 November 1924, p. 10.
103. "Classes in English Are Offered at the 135th St. Library by Board of Ed'n," *New York Age,* 29 November 1924, p. 9.
104. Sayers, p. 207.
105. Ibid., pp. 110, 126. *New York Public Library Staff News* 13 (4 October 1923): 119.
106. Sayers, p. 129. Such reports and essays, which went directly to Moore, were required of all the children's librarians.
107. Ibid., pp. 201, 203.
108. Alice I. Hazeltine, "The Children's Librarian as a Book Buyer," *Library Journal* 48 (June 1, 1923): 505–509.
109. "List of Meetings Held at the Branch Libraries," in "Report of the NYPL for 1924," *Bulletin of the New York Public Library* 29 (1925): 278.
110. "Tuskegee Association Tenders Reception to Ex-Treasurer Warren Logan," *New York Age,* 4 October 1924, p. 10.
111. "Book Evenings at the 135th St. Branch Library," *New York Age,* 15 November 1924, p. 10; "135th Street Library," *New York Age,* 22 November 1924, p. 10.
112. "135th Street Library," *New York Age,* 7 February 1925, p. 10.
113. "Poets' Evening," unidentified clipping, Gwendolyn Bennett Papers, Schomburg Center for Research in Black Culture. This event can be dated by the fact that, according to the article, one of Bennett's poems had won the poetry prize in a class at the Brooklyn branch of City College.
114. "Staff Association," *Staff News* 14 (11 December 1924 and 25 December 1924): 132. The *Staff News* of 23 July 1925 shows that the 135th Street Branch had 100 percent membership in the Staff Association (p. 96).
115. Ernestine Rose, "Books and the Negro," *Library Journal* 52 (1927): 1012–14.
116. "Library's West 135th Street Branch Will Mark 25th Anniversary Tuesday," *Amsterdam News,* 9 July 1930, p. 3.
117. Rose, "Books and the Negro," pp. 1012–14.
118. A. C. Sterling, "Those Were the Fabulous Days!" *Courier Magazine Section,* n.d., clipping in Countee Cullen / Harold Jackman Collection, Box 17, Folder 9, Woodruff Library, Atlanta University.
119. Personnel card for Regina Andrews, Records Office, Department of Human Resources, NYPL. See also "Biographical Material: Personal," "Biographical Data" (late 1960s résumé), and Curriculum Vitae, September 1979, all in Regina Andrews Papers, Schomburg. Some of Andrews' statements about precisely when she worked at the 135th Street Branch are extremely vague or evasive, which makes the personnel card the most reli-

able source. But even her résumés conflict with the usual accounts of her role at the branch. Andrews did aid, as a volunteer, with some dramatic activities at the 135th Street Branch—but so did many others, such as Dorothy Peterson.

120. Depending on letters by W. E. B. Du Bois, David Levering Lewis calls Andrews Ernestine Rose's "first assistant" and charges that she, "like her somewhat older colleague Catherine Latimer, though filling the duties of first assistant librarian, was denied the position's title and pay, as well as the opportunity for a lateral move outside Harlem that would have positioned her for advancement. Nor was there much prospect that the 135th Street head librarian might apply for a transfer, as Miss Rose confronted her own professional barrier—the public library's unofficial quota on Jewish head librarians" (Lewis, p. 240). Rose was not Jewish, and Regina Anderson (later Andrews) never functioned as her "first assistant"—nor did she claim to have done so, although she did mislead later interviewers on some points in ways that encouraged them to exaggerate her role. Certainly Rose had no desire to transfer out of Harlem, since she deeply believed in the work she was doing there. Andrews did not work at the branch after 1925, and did not attend library school until 1926–1929; therefore, during her early years of employment she was paid at a standard rate for subprofessional assistants in the system, rather than at the rate of those who had library school certificates and "professional" standing. In an autobiographical sketch, she attests to the fact that her low initial salary was due to her lack of a certificate. W. E. B. Du Bois was an old friend of her prestigious father and, unaware of this situation, made a vituperative attack on the library administrators, including Ernestine Rose. When Andrews completed library school, she immediately received a transfer and promotion; she thereafter advanced at a fairly standard rate, moving among several different branches, mostly in nonblack neighborhoods—Rivington Street, Woodstock, 135th Street, 115th Street, and Washington Heights. Accounts of Andrews' experience have depended almost exclusively on Du Bois's correspondence and make no reference to library records, including Andrews' own résumés. See "Biographical Material: Personal," "Biographical Data" (late 1960s résumé), and Curriculum Vitae, September 1979, all in Regina Andrews Papers; and Jean Blackwell Hudson interview with Regina Andrews (videotape), Schomburg Center for Research in Black Culture.

121. See "Biographical Material: Personal," "Biographical Data" (late 1960s résumé), and Curriculum Vitae, September 1979, all in Regina Anderson Papers; and Jean Blackwell Hudson interview with Regina Anderson (videotape), Schomburg.

122. Jean Blackwell Hutson to Louise Fox, 1 August 1969, Nella Larsen file, Schomburg.

11. HIGH BOHEMIA

1. Her hours officially changed on 16 February 1925. Nella Larsen Imes personnel card, New York Public Library human resources office.

2. Entry for 8 February 1925, CVV daybooks; Dorothy Peterson to Carl Van Vechten, 10 February 1953, in Van Vechten Papers, James Weldon Johnson Collection, Beinecke. Van Vechten ran out of space in his daybook to list everyone he'd met that evening, and so he doesn't mention Nella Imes, but he would always remember this as the date of their first meeting. In later years, there would be many notes on this date between the parties involved.

3. Bruce Kellner, *Carl Van Vechten and the Irreverent Decades* (Norman: University of Oklahoma Press, 1968), pp. 115, 130.

4. After Van Vechten met White and Johnson, his first big introduction to the fold of New Negroes had been at the NAACP benefit dance at Happy Rhone's Orchestra Club in the fall of 1924, when he met many people Nella and Elmer knew—but he did not meet Nella there.

5. Harold Jackman to Carl Van Vechten, 14 February 1925, CVV/JWJ.

6. "N.A.A.C.P. Dance at Manhattan Casino One of the Season's Biggest Successes," *Amsterdam News,* 1 April 1925, p. 5; Wallace Thurman, *Negro Life in New York's Harlem: A Lively Picture of a Popular and Interesting Section* (Girard, Kansas: Haldeman-Julius, 1928), pp. 32–33; "Society News," *Amsterdam News,* 4 March 1925, p. 7; Mrs. H. Binga Dismond, "La Mode Ultra To Be Displayed at Spring Dance," *Amsterdam News,* 18 March 1925, p. 7; Entry for 27 March 1925, CVV daybooks.

7. "N.A.A.C.P. Benefit at Happy Rhone's Club," *New York Age,* 8 November 1924, p. 6. On the importance of Louis Armstrong's one-year stint with Fletcher Henderson's Orchestra, see, for example, Gunther Schuller, *Early Jazz: Its Roots and Musical Development* (New York: Oxford University Press, 1968), pp. 90–97, 258–262; Geoffrey C. Ward, *Jazz: A History of America's Music* (New York: Alfred A. Knopf, 2000), pp. 108–115; Samuel Charters and Leonard Kunstad, *Jazz: A History of the New York Scene* (New York: Doubleday, 1962), p. 179.

8. Lewis A. Erenberg, *Steppin' Out: New York Nightlife and the Transformation of American Culture, 1890–1930* (Westport, Conn.: Greenwood Press, 1981), p. 77.

9. "Fisk Students in Strike, Desert Class and Chapel," *New York Age,* 14 February 1925, p. 2.

10. E. Elliott Rawlins, "Will the Women of To-Day Make as Good Wives As the Wives of Yesterday?" *Amsterdam News,* 25 March 1925, p. 12.

11. E. Elliott Rawlins, "Jazz: A Drug," *Amsterdam News,* 1 April 1925, p. 16.

12. "A Quaternity of K's," *Amsterdam News,* 4 February 1925, p. 16.

13. Paul Kellogg, "The Gist of It," *Survey Graphic* 6 (1925): 627.

14. Alain Locke, "Harlem," *Survey Graphic* 6 (1925): 630.

15. James Weldon Johnson, "The Making of Harlem," *Survey Graphic* 6 (1925): 637.

16. "Move to Preserve Negro Literature," *New York Times,* 15 March 1925, sect. 2, p. 16, quoting Ernestine Rose.

17. Ibid.

18. Announcement in *Staff News* 15.15 (9 April 1925): 48.

19. Jeffrey C. Stewart, *To Color America* (Washington, D.C.: National Portrait Gallery, 1989), p. 50.

20. Elise McDougald to Alain Locke, n.d., in *Survey Graphic* correspondence files, Alain Locke Papers, Moorland-Spingarn Research Center.

21. Ibid.

22. Alain Locke, "To Certain of Our Philistines," *Opportunity* 3 (1925): 155. Locke considered the pictures exhibited at the library "deliberately conceived and executed as a pathbreaker in the inevitable direction of a racially representative type of art."

23. The portraits that didn't remain in Reiss's family, unsold, he mostly ended up giving away to Fisk University after Charles S. Johnson had moved there. Stewart, p. 62.

24. George Bornstein pointed this out in a hard-hitting paper at the April 2000 meeting of the Society for Textual Scholarship, New York University.

25. "Reception to Jean Toomer," *New York Age*, 2 May 1925, p. 2; "Library Notes," *Amsterdam News*, 15 April 1925, p. 7; "135th Street Library News," *Amsterdam News*, 29 April 1925, p. 14.

26. Jean Toomer's talk was the basis of, or a version of, his unpublished essay "The Negro Emergent." A number of handwritten sheets from spring 1925 deal with the same theme as the typescript—in particular, a handwritten manuscript fragment filed with "The Negro Emergent," JTP. This manuscript can be dated to spring 1925 with confidence, since it refers to the Harlem issue of *Survey Graphic* and not to *The New Negro*, which came out the following fall. Toomer spent the fall, winter, and spring of 1924–1925 in New York, and then left in the summer.

27. Toomer, "The Negro Emergent," in *Jean Toomer: Selected Essays and Literary Criticism*, ed. Robert B. Jones (Knoxville: University of Tennessee Press, 1996), pp. 48, 47.

28. Ibid., pp. 51–52.

29. Ibid., p. 54.

30. Ibid.

31. John Farrar, "The Gossip Shop," *Bookman* 61 (1925): 624.

32. Recently Jon Woodson has tried to correct the record, recognizing that Hughes, who had almost nothing to do with the "Work," is an unreliable source. Woodson, however, overestimates Larsen's commitment to the cult. See Jon Woodson, *To Make a New Race: Gurdjieff, Toomer, and the Harlem Renaissance* (Jackson: University of Mississippi Press, 1999). A source closely focused on Toomer's interest in Gurdjieff's theories and its effect on his writing is Rudolph P. Byrd, *Jean Toomer's Years with Gurdjieff: Portrait of an Artist, 1923–1936* (Athens: University of Georgia Press, 1990).

33. Nella Larsen Imes to Carl Van Vechten, 29 June 1927, CVV/JWJ.

34. Tape-recorded interview with Marjorie Content Toomer, 24 October 1970, Oral History Collection, Fisk University Library.

35. See letters from Aaron Douglas to Alta Sawyer (later Douglas), 1924–1926. Douglas Papers, Schomburg.

36. Members of the group are named in Pearle M. Fisher, "This Harlem," Baltimore *Afro-American*, 19 February 1927, clipping in Carl Van Vechten scrapbook for 1927, CVV/NYPL; in Toomer's notes, "A New Group, 1926," JTP; Langston Hughes, *The Big Sea* (New York: Hill and Wang, 1940), p. 241. Scattered references to individuals involved can be found in the correspondence of Nella Larsen and Aaron Douglas. Hughes's whimsical discussion of Toomer's meetings, which he did not attend, became the basis of a host of misrepresentations that unfortunately continue to circulate in the scholarly literature.

37. Aaron Douglas to Alta Sawyer, n.d., Box 1, Folder 3, Douglas Papers, Schomburg. The letter, one of several that discusses Douglas' interest in the Gurdjieff system, evidently dates from spring 1925, because that is when some of the events mentioned in the correspondence took place.

38. Manuscript notes and fragments, Box 48, Folder 1010, JTP.

39. Louise Welch, *Orage with Gurdjieff in America* (Boston: Routledge and Kegan Paul, 1982), p. 57. At one point in the late Twenties, Orage even gave each member of his group the project of writing and publishing some sustained work on a subject they knew well, and "a spate of articles and books soon followed"—at about the same time Nella Larsen's novels appeared (Welch, p. 59). The writings included Muriel Draper's

Music before Midnight (1929), a memoir of her years as a legendary salon hostess in Paris and Florence, Isa Glenn's novel *Transport,* architect Hugh Ferriss' visionary *Metropolis of Tomorrow,* Samuel Hoffenstein's comical *Poems in Praise of Practically Nothing,* and an avant-garde story collection by the mathematician John Riordan. Many of the participants began selling sketches and articles as a result of Orage's workshops (Welch, pp. 57, 60). Toomer held similar workshops in Chicago after he left New York.

40. Gorham Munson, *The Awakening Twenties: A Memoir-History of a Literary Period* (Baton Rouge: Louisiana State University Press, 1985), p. 260; Welch, pp. 50, 40; on Draper's poverty, see also Virgil Thomson, *Virgil Thomson* (New York: Alfred A. Knopf, 1966), p. 140. Amy H. Kirschke, *Aaron Douglas: Art, Race, and the Harlem Renaissance* (Jackson: University of Mississippi Press, 1995).

41. Cynthia Kerman and Richard Eldridge, *The Lives of Jean Toomer: A Hunger for Wholeness* (Baton Rouge: Louisiana State University Press, 1987), pp. 143–145; letters of Dorothy Peterson to Jean Toomer, JTP. Munson, p. 260. By 1926, Orage was holding his weekly meetings at Muriel Draper's; Munson identifies Douglas as a regular participant.

42. T. S. Matthews, *Name and Address* (New York: Simon and Schuster, 1960), p. 206.

43. Jean Toomer, "On Being an American," typescript, pp. 50–52, JTP (quotation from p. 52).

44. Ethel Ray Nance, "The New York Arts Renaissance, 1924–1926," *Negro History Bulletin* 31.4 (April 1968): 19; Carl Van Vechten to Fania Marinoff, 3 May 1925, Box 36, Folder 10, CVV/NYPL. See also Van Vechten's 1925 daybook, entry for 1 May, which lists the Imeses among many others he saw at the dinner.

45. Casper Holstein, quoted in Nance, "The New York Arts Renaissance," p. 21.

46. Van Vechten to Marinoff, 3 May 1925; and Aaron Douglas to Alta Sawyer, n.d., in folder for correspondence of 1924–1926, Douglas Papers, Schomburg.

47. "Folk Songs Sung by Robeson and Brown at Greenwich Village Theatre," *Amsterdam News,* 6 May 1925, p. 6. See also the discussion in Paul Allen Anderson, *Deep River: Music and Memory in Harlem Renaissance Thought* (Durham: Duke University Press, 2001), pp. 93–99.

48. Carl Van Vechten to Fania Marinoff, 6 May 1925, Box 36, Folder 10, CVV/NYPL.

49. Entry for Sunday, 3 May 1925, CVV daybooks.

50. Bruce Kellner, ed., *The Harlem Renaissance: A Historical Dictionary for the Era* (Westport, Conn.: Greenwood Press, 1984), p. 172.

51. On Ray's marriages, "Nora Ray Returns from Paris," *Pittsburgh Courier,* 5 March 1927, sect. 1, p. 1; quotation from Van Vechten to Fania Marinoff, CVV/NYPL, 29 June 1925.

52. Carl Van Vechten to H. L. Mencken, ca. 1925, in *Letters of Carl Van Vechten,* ed. Bruce Kellner (New Haven: Yale University Press, 1987), p. 87.

53. "Ray Divorce Case Reaches Higher Court as Husband's 'Wealth' Fades," *Pittsburgh Courier,* 20 November 1926, pp. 1–2. Thanks to Bruce Kellner for identifying the lawyer for me.

54. "Negro Literature to Be Preserved in New Department Opened in N.Y. Library," *New York Age,* 16 May 1925, p. 2. See also "Programme of the Opening of the Department of Negro Literature and History and Exhibition of W. E. Braxton's paintings," 7 May 1925, in Programs and Playbills Collection, Schomburg; "Historical Society Is Launched at Library," *Amsterdam News* 13 May 1925, p. 9.

55. Walter White to Claude McKay, 20 May 1925, WWPC.

56. "A Negro Renaissance," New York *Herald Tribune,* 7 May 1925; reprinted in *New York Age,* 23 May 1925, p. 4.

57. Carl Van Vechten to Fania Marinoff, 6 May 1925, CVV/NYPL; and entry for 8 May 1925, CVV Daybooks.

58. Entry for 9 May 1925, CVV daybooks.

59. Entry for 16 May 1925, CVV daybooks; Carl Van Vechten to Fania Marinoff, 17 May 1925, CVV/NYPL; "The Reminiscences of Carl Van Vechten," Oral History Research Office, Columbia University, 1960, p. 211.

60. Entry for 2 July 1925, CVV daybooks.

61. Entries for 24 and 27 July 1925, and for 1 August 1925, CVV daybooks.

62. Entry for 7 August 1925, CVV daybooks.

63. Entry for 8 August 1925, CVV daybooks.

64. Eric Walrond, "The Stone Rebounds," *Opportunity* (September 1923): 277–278.

65. George Schuyler, "Views and Reviews," *Pittsburgh Courier,* 24 December 1927, sect. 2, p. 8.

66. *Quicksand,* p. 60–61.

67. Ibid., pp. 61–62.

68. Schuyler, p. 8.

69. Anita Thompson Dickinson Reynolds, "American Cocktail," unpublished manuscript, p. 68, in Box 129-4, Folder 1, Anita Thompson Dickinson Reynolds Papers, Moorland-Spingarn Research Center, Howard University.

70. Kellner, *Carl Van Vechten and the Irreverent Decades,* p. 22; and Carl Van Vechten, *The Splendid Drunken Twenties: Selections from the Daybooks,* ed. Bruce Kellner, p. 307, n. 3.

71. Van Vechten to H. L. Mencken, 29 May 1925, in *The Letters of Carl Van Vechten,* p. 78.

72. Kellner, *Carl Van Vechten and the Irreverent Decades,* p. 65, quoting from Mabel Dodge Luhan, *Movers and Shakers.*

73. Thomas Wirth, "Introduction," in *Gay Rebel of the Harlem Renaissance: Selections from the Work of Richard Bruce Nugent,* ed. Thomas Wirth (Durham: Duke University Press, 2002), pp. 43–44, quoting from Carl Van Vechten, *The Blind Bow-Boy* (New York: Knopf, 1922), p. 160.

74. Emily Bernard, "What He Did for the Race: Carl Van Vechten and the Harlem Renaissance," *Soundings* 80 (1997): 531.

75. Nella Imes to Carl Van Vechten, "Wednesday Seventeenth" (July 1925), CVV/JWJ.

76. "More Liberal Appropriations Asked for Maintenance of N.Y. Public Library," *Amsterdam News,* 12 August 1925, p. 16; "Public Library Workers Appeal for Larger Wage," *New York Age,* 22 August 1925, p. 10; "Says City Is Stingy toward Library," *New York Library,* 2 August 1925, sect. 2, p. 1; "Better Pay for Librarians," *New York Times,* 6 August 1925, p. 18. (Reports and editorials on the issue continued appearing through September.) Personnel record for Nella L. Imes.

12. THE NEW NEGRO

1. E. Franklin Frazier, *The Negro Family in Chicago* (Chicago: University of Chicago Press, 1932), pp. 198–199.

2. Allen Semi [Nella Larsen], "The Wrong Man," *Young's Realistic Stories Magazine*, 50, no. 5 (January 1926): 244.
3. Ibid., p. 244.
4. Ibid.
5. Ibid., p. 245.
6. Ibid., p. 246.
7. Allen Semi [Nella Larsen], "Freedom," *Young's Realistic Stories Magazine*, 51, no. 2 (April 1926): p. 242.
8. Ibid., p. 243.
9. Carl Van Vechten, entry for 19 March 1926, CVV daybooks.
10. Entry for 20 March 1926, CVV daybooks. The Harrises were not just moving into the Village; they had been at 61 Grove Street.
11. James Weldon Johnson, *Black Manhattan* (1930; New York: Arno Press, 1968), pp. 205–206; Hubert Harrison, "The Significance of 'Lulu Belle,'" *Opportunity* (July 1926): 228–229.
12. Entry for 28 May 1926, CVV daybooks.
13. A. C. Sterling, "Those Were the Fabulous Days!" *Courier Magazine Section*, p. 9 (clipping, without date, but clearly from the 1950s). Countee Cullen Harold Jackman Memorial Collection, Box 17, Folder 9, Woodruff Library, Morehouse College, Atlanta, Georgia.
14. Samuel Charters, *Jazz: A History of the New York Scene* (Garden City, N.Y.: Doubleday, 1962), p. 187; Wallace Thurman, *Negro Life in New York's Harlem: A Lively Picture of a Popular and Interesting Section* (Girard, Kansas: Haldeman-Julius, 1928), p. 31; Smith and Hoefer, p. 137; and anonymous, "Savoy Ballroom," in "Negroes of New York" files, Federal Writers Project of New York, Schomburg. The prices and so forth I use are those of the first year of operation.
15. Bronislaw Malinowski, "Memorandum for the Rockefeller Foundation Written for Mr. Embree in March 1926," typescript, Malinowski Papers, Archives Division, British Library of Political and Economic Science, London School of Economics, quotation from p. 5.
16. Eslanda Goode Robeson to Bronislaw Malinowski, 8 March [1926], in folder labeled "To Be Left in London / Mixed Pickles," Malinowski Papers, London School of Economics. (For the timing of Malinowski's movements, see also his train schedule in "American Sociological Documents" file, Malinowski Papers.) The anthropologist probably was not swayed. In 1931, he would argue for forcible removal of all whites from Kenya, the "danger spot of the whole world's racial situation." Clippings from *The Spectator* (London) of 15 August, 11 July, and 25 July 1931; in Malinowski Papers.
17. Bronislaw Malinowski to Elsie Masson Malinowski, 1 June 1926 and 4 June 1926, in *The Story of a Marriage: The Letters of Bronislaw Malinowski and Elsie Masson*, ed. Helena Wayne (New York: Routledge, 1995), vol. 2, pp. 71, 72.
18. Participants are mentioned in "A New Group. / 1926," JTP; Aaron Douglas to Alta Sawyer, n.d., Box 1, Folder 3, Aaron Douglas Papers, Schomburg (one of these letters can be dated to May 1926, because Douglas mentions attending the *Opportunity* dinner at the Fifth Avenue Restaurant, which took place 1 May 1926); and Pearle M. Fisher, "This Harlem," Baltimore *Afro-American*, 19 February 1927, in which Fisher remembers "constantly hearing" about Toomer's group the preceding spring. Douglas specifies loca-

tions of some of the meetings, which seem to have taken place mainly at the Harrises', Charles S. Johnson's (in Brooklyn), or Dorothy Peterson's.

19. John Macy, "The Kingdom of Art," *Opportunity* (June 1926): 185. See also "'Opportunity' Magazine Awards 22 Literature Prizes at 5th Ave. Dinner," *Amsterdam News,* 5 May 1926, p. 1.

20. Entries for 1 May and 5 May 1926, CVV daybooks.

21. Entry for 11 June 1926, CVV daybooks.

22. Nella Larsen Imes to Carl Van Vechten, 30 June 1926, CVV/JWJ.

23. Nella Larsen Imes to Carl Van Vechten, Wednesday, 14 July 1926, CVV/JWJ.

24. Entry for 17 July 1926 in CVV daybooks. On the Nest at this time, see Charters, pp. 196, 203; Willie the Lion Smith with George Hoefer, *Music on My Mind: The Memoirs of an American Pianist* (1964; rpt. New York: Da Capo, 1975), p. 172; and "The Nest Club," *New York Age,* 8 November 1924, p. 6.

25. Nella Larsen Imes to Carl Van Vechten, Wednesday, 21 July 1926, CVV/JWJ. Like other black sophisticates of the time, Elmer and Nella frequently used the phrase "your people" with each other as an ironic reference to African Americans as a group.

26. Entries for 16 May, 11 June, and 13 June 1926, in CVV daybooks.

27. Nella Larsen Imes to Carl Van Vechten, Wednesday, 30 June 1926.

28. Ibid.

29. Ibid.

30. Nella Larsen Imes to Carl Van Vechten, Wednesday, 21 July 1926, CVV/JWJ.

31. Walter White to Charles S. Johnson, 6 July 1926, WWPC.

32. Walter White to Charles S. Johnson, 28 July 1926, WWPC; quotation from Charles S. Johnson to Walter White, 5 August 1926, WWPC.

33. Nella Imes to Walter White, "Tues., Twelfth," August 1926, WWPC. Tuesday was actually August 10. Larsen got the date wrong.

34. Frank Horne, review of *Flight,* in *Opportunity* (July 1926): 227.

35. Nella Imes, "Correspondence," *Opportunity* (September 1926): 295. Larsen is referring to the heroine of John Galsworthy's novel *The Forsyte Saga* (1922) and the title character of Jens Peter Jacobsen's *Marie Grubbe* (1876; English translation 1917), a novel that Georg Brandes termed "one of the greatest *tours de force* of modern Danish Literature," as quoted in Hanna Astrup Larsen's introduction to the 1917 American edition, the only English translation, which Nella Larsen must have known. (Hanna Astrup Larsen, "Introduction," in Jens Peter Jacobsen, *Marie Grubbe, A Lady of the Seventeenth Century,* trans. Hanna Astrup Larsen [New York: American-Scandinavian Foundation, 1917], p. xiv.) The first Danish novel to treat a woman as a sexual being, *Marie Grubbe* was based on a seventeenth-century noblewoman's social descent from royalty to poor ferryman's wife, driven by her desire for a satisfying and autonomous erotic life. The preceding allusions, from Horne's review, concern the title character of the French-Canadian classic by Louis Hémon, *Maria Chapdelaine* (1913), a tale of survival focusing on the heroine's choice between three contrasting suitors on the Quebec frontier; the servant girl Mattie Silver, who wins the heart of the title character in Edith Wharton's bleakly tragic *Ethan Frome* (1911); and the title character of Flaubert's sensual, exotic fantasy of ancient Carthage published in 1862. All of these novels feature powerful women characters in challenging circumstances.

36. Niels Lyhne Jensen, *Jens Peter Jacobsen* (Boston: Twayne, 1980), pp. 146–147.

37. Allen L. Semi [Nella Larsen] to Charles S. Johnson, n.d., WWPC. Anderson's novel, often criticized today for its primitivist depiction of blacks, came out in 1925; as did Van Vechten's *Firecrackers*, about Manhattan's sophisticates. Joseph Hergesheimer's *Tubal Cain*, concerning a self-made iron magnate, dated to 1918. (Larsen misspells the title as *Tubal Cane*.)

38. Ibid.

39. Walter White to Nella Imes, 16 August 1926, WWPC.

40. Nella Imes to Carl Van Vechten, Friday, 6 August 1926, CVV/JWJ.

41. Note by Kellner in Carl Van Vechten, *The Splendid, Drunken Twenties: Selections from the Daybooks,* ed. Bruce Kellner (Urbana Champaign: University of Illinois Press, 2003), p. 73, n. 4.

42. Carl Van Vechten, *Nigger Heaven* (New York: Alfred A. Knopf, 1926), p. 42.

43. Ibid., p. 43.

44. Nella Imes to Carl Van Vechten, Wednesday, 11 August 1926, CVV/NYPL. Lasca Sartoris is a flamboyant black femme fatale who gets what she wants, whatever it takes. Byron Kasson falls prey to her allure after professional disappointments and out of frustration with Mary Love's high-mindedness.

45. Ibid.

46. Lally (Lillian A.) Alexander to Elmer S. Imes, 23 October 1926, Box 20, Folder 4, CVV/NYPL.

47. Sadie Delaney Tandy to Carl Van Vechten, 2 September 1926, CVV/NYPL.

48. Eden Bliss [Pearle Fisher], "This Harlem," Baltimore *Afro-American*, 16 October 1926, p. 14.

49. Alain Locke to Carl Van Vechten, 2 September 1926, CVV/NYPL; and Alain Locke to Langston Hughes, 2 September 1926, LHP.

50. Gwendolyn B. Bennett, "The Ebony Flute," *Opportunity* (April 1928): 122.

51. Nora Holt to Carl Van Vechten, 22 September 1926, Box 20, Folder 5, CVV/NYPL.

52. Nella Imes to Carl Van Vechten, Monday, 6 September, and Wednesday, 7 September 1926, CVV/NYPL.

53. Carl Van Vechten, "Memoirs of Fania Marinoff," pamphlet (Bruce Kellner, 1987), Berg Collection, NYPL.

54. The biography of Marinoff here comes chiefly from Bruce Kellner, *Carl Van Vechten and the Irreverent Decades* (Norman: University of Oklahoma Press, 1968), pp. 59–63; and from her memoirs, supplemented by comments Kellner kindly made on my manuscript.

55. Lawrence Langner, *The Magic Curtain: The Story of a Life in Two Fields, Theatre and Invention, by the Founder of the Theatre Guild* (New York: Dutton, 1951), p. 196.

56. Taylor Gordon, quoted in Kellner, p. 205.

57. Carl Van Vechten, *Fragments from an Unwritten Autobiography*, vol. 2 (New Haven: Yale University Library, 1955), p. 62.

58. Nella Imes to Carl Van Vechten, "Monday 6th" and "Wednesday" [6 and 7 September 1926], CVV/NYPL. I date this letter to the sixth and seventh based on the events to which it refers and the calendar that year.

59. Harry Stillwell Edwards, *Eneas Africanus* (New York: Grosset and Dunlap, 1940; orig. pub. 1920), p. xvii.

60. Nella Imes to Carl Van Vechten, [6 and 7 September 1926], CVV/NYPL.

61. Hubert Harrison, "Homo Africanus Harlemi," *Amsterdam News,* 1 September 1926, p. 20.
62. Ibid.
63. James Weldon Johnson to Carl Van Vechten, 10 [September] 1926, CVV/NYPL. Concerning Harrison's earlier attacks on Johnson and others, see Claude McKay to Hubert Harrison, 7 January 1922 (copy), and Claude McKay to James Weldon Johnson, 3 February 1922 (copy), in WWPC.
64. Nella Imes to Carl Van Vechten, Friday, 24 September 1926, CVV/NYPL.
65. Nella Imes to Carl Van Vechten, 6 October 1926, CVV/NYPL.
66. Nella Imes to Carl Van Vechten, Friday, 24 September 1926, CVV/NYPL.
67. Entry for 28 September 1926, CVV daybooks; G. C. Booth and W. W. Scott to Walter White, 4 September 1926; and Francis E. Rivers and George C. Booth to Walter White, 10 March 1926, WWPC.
68. Biographical file for Elmer S. Imes; and Curriculum Vitae for Elmer S. Imes in Thomas E. Jones Papers. Fisk University Special Collections. When Imes moved to Fisk in 1930, for a salary of $5,000, he mentioned to the university president that Nella was not very happy about his taking a 25 percent cut in salary from his previous position.
69. Nella Imes to Carl Van Vechten, 29 September 1926, CVV/JWJ.
70. Ibid.
71. Walter White to Nella L. Imes, 1 October 1926, WWPC.
72. Ibid.
73. Ibid.
74. Nella Imes to Carl Van Vechten, 6 October 1926, CVV/JWJ.
75. Walter White to Nella L. Imes, 1 October 1926, WWPC.
76. Frank Horne, "Correspondence," *Opportunity* (October 1926): 326.
77. Walter White to Charles S. Johnson, 9 October 1926, WWPC.
78. Entry for 16 October 1926, CVV daybooks.
79. Floyd Calvin, "Calvin's Weekly Diary of the New York Show World," *Pittsburgh Courier,* 16 October 1926, sect. 2, p. 10; "'Deep River': Native American Opera," *New York Age,* 9 October 1926, p. 7.
80. Entry for Sunday, 24 October 1926, CVV daybooks.
81. Ernestine Rose to Carl Van Vechten, 20 October 1926, Box 20, Folder 4, CVV/NYPL.
82. "Harlem Condemns Van Vechten's Book," *Pittsburgh Courier,* 6 November 1926, sect. 1, p. 1.
83. Nella Larsen Imes to Carl Van Vechten, 6 October 1926, CVV/JWJ.
84. Entry for 4 November 1926, CVV daybooks.
85. Quoted from Leon Coleman, *Carl Van Vechten and the Harlem Renaissance: A Critical Assessment* (New York: Garland, 1998), p. 100.
86. Nella Imes to Carl Van Vechten, 12 November 1926, CVV/JWJ.
87. James M. Hutchisson, *Du Bose Heyward: A Charleston Gentleman and the World of Porgy and Bess* (Jackson: University Press of Mississippi, 2000), pp. 176–179.
88. Nella Imes to Carl Van Vechten, 12 November 1926.
89. Floyd Calvin, "Calvin's Weekly Diary of the New York Show World," *Pittsburgh Courier,* 6 November 1926, sect. 2, p. 3.
90. Nella Imes to Carl Van Vechten, 12 November 1926, CVV/JWJ.
91. W. E. B. Du Bois, "Books," *Crisis* (December 1926): 81.

92. Walter White to W. E. B. Du Bois, 26 November 1926, WWPC.

93. Du Bois, p. 82. Bernard discusses Du Bois's attitudes to Van Vechten in her introduction to *Remember Me to Harlem: The Letters of Langston Hughes and Carl Van Vechten, 1925–1964,* ed. Emily Bernard (New York: Alfred A. Knopf, 2001); and in Emily Bernard, "What He Did for the Race: Carl Van Vechten and the Harlem Renaissance," *Soundings* 80 (1997): 531–542.

94. "The Slumming Hostess," *New York Age,* 6 November 1926, p. 4; Dorothy Peterson to Carl Van Vechten, November 1926, CVV/JWJ.

95. For an excellent discussion of this and other aspects of the ways in which *Nigger Heaven* served different black authors symbolically to define their critical positions, see Bernard, "What He Did for the Race."

96. Kellner, p. 225.

97. Nella Imes to Walter White, Monday [November 15, 1926], WWPC.

98. Walter White to Nella Imes, 16 November 1926, WWPC.

99. File for Nella Larsen, Alfred A. Knopf Papers, HRHRC.

100. Entry for 4 December 1926, CVV daybooks.

101. Nella Larsen Imes to Carl Van Vechten, 7 December 1926, CVV/JWJ.

102. Ibid.

13. *QUICKSAND*

1. Werner Sollors makes this point about James Weldon Johnson's *Autobiography of an Ex-Colored Man* and Abraham Cahan's *The Rise of David Levinsky;* see Sollors, *Beyond Ethnicity: Consent and Descent in American Culture* (New York: Oxford University Press, 1986), p. 171.

2. In her column for *Opportunity* written in January or February, Gwendolyn Bennett reported: "We understand . . . that Nella Imes is lengthening a rather good novel for *Knopf*." Gwendolyn Bennett, "The Ebony Flute," *Opportunity* 5 (March 1927): 90. Since Larsen did not take the revised manuscript to Knopf until mid-March, the "lengthening" must have occurred after an earlier submission, doubtless in December 1926, after Van Vechten received the manuscript typed by White's secretary.

3. Nella Larsen, *Quicksand,* in *Quicksand and Passing,* ed. Deborah E. McDowell (New Brunswick, N.J.: Rutgers University Press, 1986), xlii. Subsequent references to *Quicksand* will appear in parentheses in the text. Portions of this chapter initially appeared in George Hutchinson, "Subject to Disappearance: Interracial Identity in Nella Larsen's *Quicksand,*" in Geneviève Fabre and Michel Fleiss, eds., *Temples for Tomorrow: Looking Back at the Harlem Renaissance* (Bloomington: Indiana University Press, 2001), pp. 177–192. Readers interested in how the discussion relates to other scholarship on Larsen should consult that essay.

4. Allen L. Semi [Nella Larsen] to Charles S. Johnson, n.d., WWPC.

5. *Oxford Classical Dictionary,* ed. M. Cary et al. (Oxford: Clarendon, 1949), pp. 88, 898.

6. Ovid, *The Metamorphoses,* trans. Mary M. Innes (London: Penguin, 1955), p. 183.

7. Nora Holt to Carl Van Vechten, correspondence of fall 1926, especially 22 October 1926, Nora Holt Papers, JWJ. See also "Nora Ray Returns from Paris," *Pittsburgh Courier,* 5 March 1927, sect. 1, p. 1.

8. Werner Sollors points out that in much American interracial literature, escape to a Eu-

ropean country allows "a happy alternative to a tragic America." Sollors, *Neither Black nor White, Yet Both: Thematic Explorations of Interracial Literature* (New York: Oxford University Press, 1997), p. 3.

9. Edward Wasserman, "A Young American's Friendship with Anatole France," *Bookman* 61 (April 1925): 200. Wasserman was so close to France that when France finally got married late in life, Wasserman picked him up in his own car, drove him to the wedding, and then brought him back to the private wedding breakfast, which Wasserman attended as one of the guests.

10. Anatole France, "The Procurator of Judaea," *Golden Tales of Anatole France* (New York: Dodd, Mead, 1926), pp. 23–24. Larsen's quotations of the tale derive from this translation.

14. IN THE MECCA

1. J. A. Rogers, "Rogers Calls Langston Hughes' Book of Poems 'Trash,'" *Pittsburgh Courier,* 12 February 1927, sect. 1, p. 4.
2. Floyd J. Calvin, "Langston Hughes Answers Critics," *Pittsburgh Courier,* 26 February 1927, sect. 1, p. 3.
3. Langston Hughes, "These Bad New Negroes: A Critique on Critics," *Pittsburgh Courier,* 9 April 1927, sect. 2, p. 1.
4. Nella Imes to Carl Van Vechten, "Monday, 7" (March 1927), CVV/JWJ.
5. Ibid.
6. Entry for 22 February 1927, CVV daybooks.
7. Nella Imes to Carl Van Vechten, "Monday, 7" (March 1927).
8. Entry for 16 March 1927, CVV daybooks.
9. Lawrence Langner, *The Magic Curtain: The Story of a Life in Two Fields, Theatre and Invention, by the Founder of the Theatre Guild* (New York: Dutton, 1951), p. 196.
10. Ibid.
11. Elmer Imes to Carl Van Vechten, 18 March 1927, CVV/JWJ.
12. Entry for 20 March 1927, CVV daybooks.
13. Geraldyn Dismond, "New York Society," *Pittsburgh Courier,* 9 April 1927, sect. 1, p. 6.
14. Entry for Tuesday, 29 March 1927, CVV daybooks.
15. Paul Morand, *Black Magic,* trans. Hamish Miles (New York: Viking, 1929), p. 75.
16. Ibid., p. 190.
17. Ibid., p. 168.
18. Paul Morand, *New York,* trans. Hamish Miles (New York: Holt, 1930), p. 268.
19. Ibid., pp. 268–269.
20. Ibid., pp. 274–275.
21. See, for example, Maxwell Bodenheim, *Ninth Avenue* (New York: Boni and Liveright, 1926), pp. 201, 204.
22. Sterling Brown, quoted in Genevieve Ekaete, "Sterling Brown: A Living Legend," *New Directions: The Howard University Magazine* 1 (Winter 1974): 9. Emily Bernard has suggested that much of the animosity toward Van Vechten in Harlem Renaissance historiography is colored by homophobia. See her introduction to *Remember Me to Harlem: The Correspondence of Langston Hughes and Carl Van Vechten, 1925–1964,* ed. Emily Bernard (New York: Alfred A. Knopf, 2001).

23. Arthur Huff Fauset, "Homage to Sterling Brown," in *Sterling Brown: A UMUM Tribute,* ed. Black History Museum Committee (Philadelphia: Black History Museum UMUM Publishers, 1976), p. 2.

24. People who met through Van Vechten included Langston Hughes and Zora Neale Hurston, Hurston and Ethel Waters, Larsen and Waters, Hughes and A'Lelia Walker, and probably Larsen and Hurston. No doubt there were others. Larsen came to know Hughes mainly by way of Van Vechten. On Hughes and Hurston, Hurston and Waters, and Hughes and Walker, see Leon Coleman, *Carl Van Vechten and the Harlem Renaissance: A Critical Assessment* (New York: Garland, 1998), p. 100.

25. On Crystal Bird: "To Establish Many Recreation Centers for Colored Girls," *New York Age,* 2 November 1918, p. 1; "A. H. Fauset Takes Bride," *Amsterdam News,* 22 July 1931, p. 4; "News of Greater New York," *New York Age,* 14 April 1923, p. 8.

26. On the Booths: Geraldyn Dismond, "Social Snapshots," *Inter-State Tattler,* 19 July 1929, p. 5.

27. On Alonzo Smith: Geraldyn Dismond, "Through the Lorgnette," *Pittsburgh Courier,* 11 June 1927, sect. 2, p. 1; "Harlem Nurse School Makes Proud Record," *New York Age,* 29 May 1926, pp. 1, 3; "Bride To Become a New Yorker," *Amsterdam News,* 20 June 1928, p. 4.

28. Dorothy Peterson to Carl Van Vechten, 27 September 1940, CVV/JWJ.

29. Bruce Nugent, quoted in Thadious M. Davis, *Nella Larsen, Novelist of the Harlem Renaissance: A Woman's Life Unveiled* (Baton Rouge: Louisiana State University Press, 1994), p. 142.

30. Nella Larsen, *Quicksand,* in *Quicksand and Passing,* ed. Deborah E. McDowell (New Brunswick, N.J.: Rutgers University Press, 1986), p. 34.

31. Nella Imes to Carl Van Vechten, Monday, 14 March 1927, CVV/JWJ.

32. Nella Larsen to Carl Van Vechten, "Wednesday," 6 April 1927, CVV/JWJ.

33. Thelma E. Berlack, "New Author Unearthed Right Here in Harlem," *Amsterdam News,* 23 May 1928, editorial page.

34. Larsen to Van Vechten, "Wednesday," 6 April 1927.

35. Geraldyn Dismond, "New York Society," *Pittsburgh Courier,* 9 April 1927, sect. 1, p. 6.

36. Geraldyn Dismond, "New York Society," *Pittsburgh Courier,* 16 April 1927, sect. 1, p. 6. Van Vechten also noted the ball in his daybook (entry for 6 April 1927).

37. "The Fort Valley Spectacle," *New York News,* 23 April 1927; clipping in scrapbook for 1927, CVV/NYPL.

38. "Renaissance," *Chicago Whip,* 23 April 1927; clipping in scrapbook for 1927, CVV/NYPL.

39. Geraldyn Dismond, "The Ballet Mécanique as Heard in America," *Pittsburgh Courier,* 23 April 1927, sect. 2, p. 3. On the personnel, see advertisement, "Ballet Mechanique: All-Antheil Concert," *New York Times,* 10 April 1927, p. X14.

40. Dismond, "Ballet Mécanique," p. 3.

41. Carl Van Vechten to Fania Marinoff, 12 April 1927, CVV/NYPL.

42. Entry for 11 April 1927, CVV daybooks.

43. Entry for 13 April 1927, CVV daybooks.

44. Entry for 25 April 1927, CVV daybooks.

45. Entry for 26 April 1927, CVV daybooks.

46. Carl Van Vechten to Gertrude Stein, 28 May 1927, in *The Letters of Gertrude Stein and*

Carl Van Vechten, 1913–1946, ed. Edward Burns (New York: Columbia University Press, 1986), vol. 1, pp. 146–147.

47. Gertrude Stein to Carl Van Vechten, 26 December 1926, ibid., p. 139.

48. Geraldyn Dismond, "New York Society," *Pittsburgh Courier,* 14 May 1927, sect. 1, p. 6.

49. Dorothy Peterson to Carl Van Vechten, n.d., "Dorothy Peterson" box, CVV/JWJ; entry for 7 May 1927, CVV daybooks; and Van Vechten to Dorothy Peterson, 2 May 1927, DPP.

50. Carl Van Vechten to Langston Hughes, 11 May 1927, in *Letters of Carl Van Vechten,* ed. Bruce Kellner (New Haven: Yale University Press, 1987), p. 95; and Eugene Gordon, "The Opportunity Dinner: An Impression," *Opportunity* (July 1927): 208.

51. Gordon, p. 208.

52. "Prizes Awarded in 'Opportunity' Literary and Musical Contests at Dinner at 5th Avenue Restaurant," *New York Age,* 14 May 1927, p. 3.

53. Entry for 7 May 1927, CVV daybooks.

54. Entries for 11, 13, and 15 May 1927 CVV daybooks.

55. Entry for 19 May 1927, CVV daybooks.

56. Hubert Harrison, "Cabaret School of Negro Writers Does Not Represent One-Tenth of Race," *Pittsburgh Courier,* 28 May 1927, sect. 1, p. 3.

57. Entry for 29 May 1927, CVV daybooks.

58. Harrison, p. 3.

59. Nella Larsen Imes to Carl Van Vechten, 2 June 1927, CVV/JWJ.

60. Entry for 10 June 1927, CVV daybooks.

61. Nella Larsen Imes to Carl Van Vechten, 29 June 1927, CVV/JWJ.

62. Van Vechten daybook for 1927.

63. Ethel Waters with Charles Samuels, *His Eye Is on the Sparrow: An Autobiography* (Garden City, N.Y.: Doubleday, 1951), p. 196.

64. Ibid., pp. 195, 196.

65. Entry for 23 June 1927, CVV daybooks.

66. Nella Larsen Imes to Carl Van Vechten, 29 June 1927, CVV/JWJ.

67. Randall Cherry, "Ethel Waters: The Voice of an Era," in Geneviève Fabre and Michel Feith, eds., *Temples for Tomorrow: Looking Back at the Harlem Renaissance* (Bloomington: Indiana University Press, 2001), p. 100.

68. James Weldon Johnson, *Black Manhattan* (1930; New York: Arno Press, 1968), p. 210.

69. Nella Larsen Imes to Carl Van Vechten, 29 June 1927, CVV/JWJ.

70. Waters, pp. 195, 196.

71. Ibid., p. 196.

72. Nella Larsen Imes to Carl Van Vechten, 29 June 1927, CVV/JWJ.

73. Ibid.

74. "An Old-Fashioned Negro," *Light and Heebie Jeebies,* 25 June 1927, clipping in scrapbook for 1927, CVV/NYPL. Larsen was almost certainly Van Vechten's source for this clipping, since she clipped items out of black newspapers for him as well as for herself. They were not so available downtown.

75. Walter White to George N. White, 20 June 1927, WWPC. White misspells "insistence" as "insistance" in the original letter.

76. Walter White to Carl Roberts, 9 July 1927; and "Affidavit," 8 July 1927, WWPC.

77. Nella Larsen Imes to Dorothy Peterson, "Thursday 21st" (July 1927), DPP.

78. Nella Larsen Imes to Carl Van Vechten, 29 June 1927, CVV/JWJ. Nella misspells "pseudo" as "psuedo" in the original letter.
79. Nella Larsen Imes to Dorothy Peterson, 12 July 1927, DPP.
80. Nella Larsen Imes to Dorothy Peterson, "Tuesday 19th" [July 1927], DPP.
81. A. R. Orage, "Talks with Katherine Mansfield," quoted in James Webb, *The Harmonious Circle* (New York: G. P. Putnam's Sons, 1980), p. 252.
82. Ibid.
83. Ibid., p. 253.
84. John Middleton Murry, quoted ibid.
85. Dorothy Peterson, 11 August 1927, CVV/JWJ.
86. Nella Larsen Imes to Dorothy Peterson, 12 July 1927; Tuesday 19th (July 1927); "Thursday 21st" (July 1927). All in DPP.
87. Nella Larsen Imes to Dorothy Peterson, 12 July 1927, DPP.
88. Nella Larsen Imes to Dorothy Peterson, "Thursday 21st" (July 1927), DPP.
89. Entry for 3 July 1927, CVV daybooks.
90. Nella Larsen Imes to Dorothy Peterson, 12 July 1927, DPP.
91. Ibid.; Viola Woodlyn James, "New York Society," *Pittsburgh Courier*, 16 July 1927, sect. 1, p. 6.
92. Nella Larsen Imes to Dorothy Peterson, 12 July 1927, DPP. See also entry for 10 July 1927, CVV daybooks. Larsen lists Witter Bynner rather than Colin McPhee as one of those who came for dinner, but Van Vechten indicates that McPhee was there for dinner and Bynner came afterward.
93. On Isa Glenn and her husband, see John Chamberlain, "Books of the Times," *New York Times*, 12 October 1933, p. 23; "Our Attaché a Contrast," *New York Times*, 19 September 1907, p. 3; and Percy A. Hutchison, "Moral Degeneration in the Tropics," *New York Times Book Review*, 16 January 1927, p. 9.
94. "Prominent Harlemites at 'Africana' Premiere," *New York Age*, 16 July 1927, p. 6.
95. Walter Winchell, "Opening Nights," *New York Graphic*, 12 July 1927, clipping in CVV/NYPL.
96. "Ethel Waters and 'Africana' Pleases at 63rd St. Theatre," *New York Age*, 16 July 1927, p. 6. "Threatened with Suit for Impersonation of Josephine Baker," *New York Age*, 30 July 1927, p. 6.
97. Nella Larsen Imes to Dorothy Peterson, 12 July 1927, DPP.
98. Entry for 11 June 1927, CVV daybooks.
99. Waters, p. 189.
100. "Prominent New Yorkers Congratulate Ethel Waters on 'Africana' Success," *Pittsburgh Courier*, 30 July 1927, clipping in scrapbook for 1927, CVV/NYPL; and Nella Larsen Imes to Dorothy Peterson, "Tuesday 2nd" (August 1927), DPP.
101. Larsen's emphasis, with triple-underscoring on the word "author." Nella Larsen Imes to Dorothy Peterson, "Tuesday 2nd" (August 1927), DPP.
102. Nella Larsen Imes to Dorothy Peterson, 19 July 1927, DPP.
103. "Persons to Whom It Will Be Advantageous to Send Copy of 'Copper Sun,'" WWPC.
104. Nella Larsen Imes to Dorothy Peterson, "Tuesday 19th" (July 1927), DPP.
105. Nella Larsen Imes to Dorothy Peterson, "Thursday 21st" (July 1927), DPP.
106. Ibid.
107. "Nordic Invasion of Harlem," *New York Age*, 6 August 1927, p. 4.

108. Nella Larsen to Dorothy Peterson, "Tuesday 19th" (July 1927).

109. Nella Larsen Imes to Dorothy Peterson, "Tuesday 2nd" (August 1927), DPP.

110. Ibid.

111. Nella Larsen Imes to Dorothy Peterson, "Tuesday 19th" (July 1927).

112. Dorothy Peterson to Carl Van Vechten, 11 August 1927, CVV/JWJ.

113. Nella Larsen Imes to Dorothy Peterson, "Tuesday 2nd" (August 1927), DPP.

114. Nella Larsen Imes to Dorothy Peterson, "Tuesday 19th" (July 1927).

115. Ibid.

116. Nella Larsen Imes to Dorothy Peterson, "Thursday 21st" (July 1927).

117. Alice R. Carper, taped interview with Charles R. Larson, 11 June 1986, in possession of the author. An extensive search in the land records of that section of Connecticut (primarily Fairfield County) and nearby parts of New York has turned up no title in the name of Nella or Elmer Imes or Nella Larsen. Harlan Jessup to George Hutchinson, August 2003. Where Nella may have owned a house remains an open question.

118. Entry for 14 August 1927, CVV daybooks; "One of Four," *Pittsburgh Courier*, 21 May 1927, sect. 1, p. 4; Geraldyn Dismond, "New York Society," *Pittsburgh Courier*, 16 April 1927, sect. 1, p. 6.

119. Nella Larsen Imes to Dorothy Peterson, "Thursday 21st" (July 1927). Larsen mentioned that the bout would be at the Polo Grounds, but she was mistaken.

120. On the Dempsey-Sharkey fight: W. O. McGeehan, "Dempsey Whips Sharkey by 7th Round Knockout; 85,000 Cheer Fighters On," *New York Herald Tribune*, 22 July 1927, pp. 1, 20; Grantland Rice, "Huge Crowd in Uproar as Bostonian Is Dropped When He Seems to Have Even Chance of Victory," *New York Herald Tribune*, 22 July 1927, pp. 1, 19; Isabel Ross, "Women Thrilled By 'Come-Back' of Ex-Champion," *New York Herald Tribune*, 22 July 1927, pp. 1, 19; John Durant, *The Heavyweight Champions* (6th rev. ed.; New York: Hastings House, 1976), pp. 77–83; John D. McCallum, *The World Heavyweight Boxing Championship: A History* (Radner, Penn.: Chilton, 1974), pp. 150–152; "Jack Dempsey Will Defy Tradition in Attempted Comeback against Jack Sharkey Thursday," *New York Herald Tribune*, 17 July 1927, sect. 2, p. 5.

121. Nella Larsen Imes to Dorothy Peterson, "Tuesday 2nd" (August 1927), DPP. Larsen spells Langner's name "Langer."

122. Johnson, *Black Manhattan* (New York: Alfred A. Knopf, 1930), p. 208.

123. Entry for 20 August 1927, CVV daybooks.

124. Entry for 21 August 1927, CVV daybooks.

125. Entry for 6 September 1927, CVV daybooks.

126. Entry for 29 September 1927, CVV daybooks.

127. Nella and Fania exchanged dresses on 29 September; on 16 October they were working on a dress together, and by 1 November Mary Mackinnon was painting her portrait of Fania in Nella's Paul Poiret dress, the Golden Forest. Daybook of Carl Van Vechten for 1927, entries for 29 September, 16 October, and 1 November. Thanks to Bruce Kellner for his help, and for a copy of the portrait.

128. Entry for 5 October 1927, CVV daybooks.

129. Viola Woodlyn James, "New York Society," *Pittsburgh Courier*, 15 October 1927, sect. 1, p. 6.

130. "'Flo' Mills Is Guest of Club Ebony," *Pittsburgh Courier*, 8 October 1927, sect. 2, p. 3; "Manhattan Personals," *New York Age*, 1 October 1927, p. 10.

131. Lester A. Walton, "Art and Business Join Their Hands in Harlem," *New York Age*, 29 October 1927, p. 6.

132. Viola Woodlyn James, "New York Society," p. 6.

133. Geraldyn Dismond, "Rapid Rise of the Cabaret Seen as Social Marvel," *Pittsburgh Courier*, 29 October 1927, sect. 2, p. 2.

134. "Harlem Bids for Control of Own Night Life," *Pittsburgh Courier*, 15 October 1927, sect. 2, p. 3.

135. Gwendolyn B. Bennett, "The Ebony Flute," *Opportunity* (November 1927): 340.

136. "Harlem Bids," p. 3.

137. "Harlem Resents Emphasis on Its Vice," *Pittsburgh Courier*, 10 September 1927, clipping in Van Vechten scrapbook for 1927, CVV/NYPL.

138. Terence Williams, "Writer Scores Best Girls Who Entertain 'Nordics,'" *Pittsburgh Courier*, 1 October 1927, sect. 2, p. 1.

139. Ibid., p. 1.

140. "Lyle Warns 'Flo' against Carl Van Vechten," *Pittsburgh Courier*, 8 October 1927, sect. 1, p. 1.

141. Robert Garland, "Well—What of It?" *New York Telegraph*, 21 October 1927, clipping in scrapbook for 1927, CVV/NYPL.

142. Viola Woodlyn James, "New York Society," *Pittsburgh Courier*, 22 October 1927, sect. 1, p. 6. Harold Jackman once named a number of those in the short list of people who "didn't need an invitation"—including himself, Van Vechten, Langston Hughes, Countee Cullen, Bruce Nugent, and others—but he didn't mention Nella Imes, who was a good friend of his. (A. C. Sterling, "Those Were the Fabulous Days!" *Courier Magazine Section*, n.d., p. 9, in Box 17, Folder 9, Countee Cullen / Harold Jackman Collection, Robert W. Woodruff Library, Atlanta University Center.) At the parties Van Vechten attended at A'Lelia Walker's two homes—her townhouse in Harlem and Villa Lewaro on the Hudson—Nella was never with him, according to his diaries. If she had been present he would have listed her, so it seems clear that Walker did not invite her.

143. Professor Davis charges that Walker, though fabulously rich, "was not one of the 'higher' social class that Larsen courted. Had she been the white daughter of a washerwoman, turned businesswoman and self-made millionaire, she would have been more greatly admired by Larsen, who did not discriminate class position as distinct from wealth so keenly among the whites she met. Larsen was becoming even more of a snob" (p. 227). Ethel Waters and Edna Thomas both came from far lowlier backgrounds than A'Lelia Walker, and Thomas became one of Larsen's most intimate friends in the 1930s.

144. Bruce Nugent, "On the Dark Tower," p. 1, in files for "Negroes of New York," Federal Writers Project, New York, Schomburg.

145. Ibid., p. 4. Other information on the Dark Tower comes from Viola Woodlyn James's column, *Pittsburgh Courier*, 22 October 1927, sect. 1, p. 6; Sterling, p. 9; "Royalty and Blue-Blooded Gentry Entertained by A'Lelia Walker at Lewaro and Town House," *Amsterdam News*, 26 August 1931, pp. 11, 19; William Pickens, "The Dark Tower," *Amsterdam News*, 25 January 1928, "magazine" page.

146. Geraldyn Dismond, "Social Snapshots," *Inter-State Tattler*, 25 October 1929, p. 5; "Manhattan Personals," *New York Age*, 19 October 1929, p. 2.

147. Entry for 15 October 1927, CVV daybooks.

148. See, e.g., "Race Cast Given Credit for Success of 'Porgy,'" *Pittsburgh Courier*, 12 November 1927, sect. 2, p. 2; "Famous Drama Critic Says 'Porgy' Is Best Negro Play in Years," *New York Age*, 15 October 1927, p. 6; review in *Amsterdam News*, 19 October 1927, p. 8.

149. James Weldon Johnson, *Black Manhattan* (1930; rpt. New York: Arno Press, 1968), p. 212.

150. Ibid., p. 211.

151. Playbill for *Porgy*, Theatre Guild Production, p. 6, in Manuscripts and Archives, Schomburg.

152. Bruce Kellner to the author, 14 November 2002; Van Vechten identifies the dress as Nella's in his *Fragments from an Unwritten Autobiography* (New Haven: Yale University Library, 1955), vol. 2, p. 62.

153. Entry for 16 October 1927, CVV daybooks.

154. "World Weeps as Florence Goes to Rest," *Amsterdam News*, 9 November 1927, p. 1.

155. Description based on "150,000 Throng Harlem to Pay Last Tribute and Honor to Dainty Star, Florence Mills," *New York Age*, 12 November 1927, pp. 1, 2.

156. "Florence Mills," *New York Age*, 12 November 1927, p. 4.

157. "Paul Robeson and Lawrence Brown Have 'Immense Success' in First Singing of Spirituals in Paris," *New York Age*, 3 December 1927, p. 7.

15. YEAR OF ARRIVAL

1. James M. Hutchisson, *DuBose Heyward: A Charleston Gentleman and the World of Porgy and Bess* (Jackson: University Press of Mississippi, 2000), p. 78.

2. Entry for 3 February 1928, CVV daybooks.

3. "Nella" to Carl Van Vechten, 8 February 1928, CVV/JWJ.

4. "Nella" to Carl Van Vechten, 18 February 1928, CVV/JWJ.

5. Quoted by Carl Van Vechten in letter to James Weldon Johnson, 19 May 1928, Box 21, Folder 498, JWJ/JWJ.

6. "'Meek Mose' in Its Premier in Broadway House," *New York Age*, 11 February 1928, p. 6.

7. Summary digested from "'Meek Mose' in Its Premier," p. 6; and Percy Hammond, "The Theatres," *New York Herald Tribune*, 7 February 1928, p. 18.

8. Lucien H. White, "Spirituals Sung by Company in 'Meek Mose' Most Striking Element in Presentation of Weak Production," *New York Age*, 18 February 1928, p. 7.

9. Rollo Wilson, "Meek Mose Is a Show Built for White Audiences: Preaches Submission to Judgment of Whites," *Pittsburgh Courier*, 11 February 1928, sect. 2, p. 2.

10. Hammond, p. 18.

11. "Nella" to Carl Van Vechten, "Wednesday," 8 February 1928, CVV/JWJ.

12. Ibid.

13. Entry for 10 February 1928, CVV daybooks. In a later letter, Nella mentions Eddie's "grand birthday party" as the last time she saw him; his birthday was February 11. Nella Larsen to Eddie Wasserman, "Thursday" (April 5) 1928. Nella Larsen Correspondence, Schomburg. This letter has been marked, erroneously, April 3; but April 3 was not a Thursday; the postmark on the envelope was April 5.

14. "Women's Auxiliary, N.A.A.C.P., Secures Dabney and Orchestra for Dance," *New York Age*, 28 January 1928, p. 6.

15. Entry for 6 March 1928, CVV daybooks.
16. Bruce Kellner, *Carl Van Vechten and the Irreverent Decades* (Norman: University of Oklahoma Press, 1968), p. 232.
17. "Nella" to Carl Van Vechten, 18 February 1928, CVV/JWJ.
18. Ibid.
19. Carl Van Vechten to Fania Marinoff, 22 February 1928, CVV/NYPL. On Holt as hostess at the Apex Club, see "Nora Holt Opens Chicago's Finest Night Club; Hundreds Attend Debut," *Pittsburgh Courier,* 9 July 1927, sect. 1, p. 1.
20. Elmer Imes to Carl Van Vechten, 3 March 1928, CVV/JWJ.
21. Ibid.
22. Claude McKay, *Home to Harlem* (Boston: Northeastern University Press, 1987; orig. pub. 1928), p. 228. On the connection between McKay's cultural nationalism and primitivism, see especially Tracy McCabe, "The Multifaceted Politics of Primitivism in Harlem Renaissance Writing," *Soundings* 80 (1997): 475–497.
23. McKay's primitivism, as Tracy McCabe has pointed out, is politically radical but "inflected by traditional class and gender hierarchies" (McCabe, p. 492). For a critique of McKay's sexism and classism, see also Hazel V. Carby, "Policing the Black Woman's Body in an Urban Context," *Critical Inquiry* 18 (Summer 1992): 738–755.
24. "Elmer" to Carl Van Vechten, 3 March 1928, CVV/JWJ.
25. "Nella" to Carl Van Vechten, "Thursday," postmarked 19 March 1928, CVV/JWJ. The letter had been sent to California and then reposted from there, since Carl got back to New York on the seventeenth. The nineteenth was a Monday, so clearly Nella had written the letter on the fifteenth, the preceding Thursday.
26. Ibid.
27. Ibid.
28. David Levering Lewis, *W. E. B. Du Bois: The Fight for Equality and The American Century, 1919–1963* (New York: Henry Holt, 2000), pp. 188, 220–223.
29. Presentation copy of *Quicksand* to Carl Van Vechten and Fania Marinoff, Yale Collection of American Literature, Beinecke; Item 332 in auction catalogue by Peter B. Howard, *Catalogue 43;* and presentation copy to Dorothy Peterson, cited in Abebooks online bookstore, Spring 2005 (for sale by Between the Covers Rare Books).
30. "Nella" to Carl Van Vechten, Tuesday, April [10] 1928, CVV/JWJ.
31. "Nella" to Langston Hughes, "May 1st" (1928), LHP.
32. From copy in the Yale Collection of American Literature, Beinecke.
33. Carl Van Vechten to Fania Marinoff, 3 April 1928, CVV/NYPL.
34. Entry for 4 April 1928, CVV daybooks.
35. "Nella" to Carl Van Vechten, Tuesday, April [10] 1928, CVV/JWJ.
36. "A Mulatto Girl," *New York Times Book Review,* 8 April 1928, p. 16.
37. Ibid., p. 17.
38. Nella Larsen Imes to Eddie Wasserman, 5 April 1928, Nella Larsen Correspondence, Schomburg. See note 13 on the proper dating of this letter.
39. Nella Larsen Imes to Eddie Wasserman, 15 April 1928, Nella Larsen Correspondence, Schomburg.
40. "Miss Du Bois Weds Countee Cullen," *Amsterdam News,* 11 April 1928, pp. 1, 6. David Levering Lewis gives a vivid description of the planning for the wedding, and of Du

Bois's view of its significance, in *W. E. B. Du Bois*, pp. 220–223. A detailed description of the event itself is Edward G. Perry, "Yolande Du Bois Becomes Bride of Countee Cullen," *Pittsburgh Courier*, 14 April 1928, sect. 1, p. 6.

41. "Photographic Exhibit at 135th St. Library," *New York Age*, 14 April 1928, p. 10; "Photographer's Art Exhibited at Library," *Amsterdam News*, 16 May 1928, p. 2.

42. George Schuyler, "Views and Review," *Pittsburgh Courier*, 14 April 1928, sect. 2, p. 8.

43. Nella Larsen Imes to Langston Hughes, "May 1st" (1928), LHP.

44. "Nella" to Carl Van Vechten, 1 May 1928, CVV/JWJ.

45. Gwendolyn B. Bennett, "The Ebony Flute," *Opportunity* (May 1928): 153.

46. Rent and down-payment information from Walter White to James Weldon Johnson, 1 January 1928, WWPC; and advertisements in *Dunbar News*, Schomburg.

47. "How Rockefeller's Harlem Apartments Will Look," and "Rockefeller Apartments for Harlem Planned after Similar Project on Mott Ave. for 166 White Families—Rents Low," *New York Age*, 19 February 1929, pp. 1, 2.

48. Robert A. M. Stern et al., *New York 1930: Architecture and Urbanism between the Two World Wars* (1987; rpt. New York: Rizzoli, 1994), p. 479.

49. Ibid., p. 481.

50. "Poor Layout of Rooms and Added Costs May Check the Movement to Apartments Built by Rockefeller," *New York Age*, 8 October 1927, p. 3; floor plan in Stern et al., p. 420.

51. "Rockefeller Millions To Be Used in Harlem for Erecting of Model Apartments for Negro," *New York Age*, 15 May 1926, p. 1. On the philanthropic philosophy of the plan, see Elmer A. Carter, "The New Philanthropy," *Opportunity* 7.1 (January 1929): 5; "Rockefeller and Harlem," *Pittsburgh Courier*, 6 November 1926, sect. 2, p. 8.

52. Roscoe Conkling Bruce to Walter White, 12 December 1930, WWPC.

53. Lewis, pp. 189, 212.

54. "Garden Apts. House Intellectuals," *Amsterdam News*, 15 February 1928, p. 5.

55. See issues of the *Dunbar News*, Schomburg.

56. Entry for 10 May 1928, CVV daybooks.

57. "The Bookshelf," *Chicago Defender*, 12 May 1928, part 2, p. 1.

58. Thelma E. Berlack, "New Author Unearthed Right Here in Harlem," *Amsterdam News*, 23 May 1928, p. 16.

59. "Nella Larsen, Author of 'Quicksand,' Honor Guest at N.A.A.C.P. Tea," *Amsterdam News*, 23 May 1928, p. 5; and entry for 20 May 1928, CVV daybooks.

60. Entry for 20 May 1928, CVV daybooks.

61. Jerome Peterson, recommendation for Nella Larsen Imes, 17 September 1928, Harmon Foundation Award files, Library of Congress.

62. Alice Beals Parsons, "Three Novels," *Nation* 126 (9 May 1928): 540.

63. Roark Bradford, "Mixed Blood," *New York Herald Tribune Books*, 13 May 1928, p. 522.

64. "Book a Week," Baltimore *Afro-American*, 5 May 1928, p. 6.

65. See, e.g., "Miscegenation? Bah!" *Amsterdam News*, 16 May 1923, p. 16. "The New Books," *Saturday Review of Literature*, 19 May 1928, p. 896. Another review worth mentioning is by Jean Toomer's future wife, Margery Latimer: "Nella Larsen's 'Quicksand,'" *New York World*, 22 July 1928. Generally quite positive, it begins, "This book makes you want to read everything that Nella Larsen will ever write," not because it is "distinguished" or even "excellent," but because it "wakes you up." That is, "it makes you aware that there

are other races besides the white race." Latimer, unfortunately, reduces Helga Crane's conflict to the popular mythos of "warring blood." Clipping in DPP, correspondence with Nella Larsen Imes.

66. Ruth L. Yates, review of *Quicksand, Pittsburgh Courier*, 26 May 1928, sect. 2, p. 8.
67. Ibid.
68. Ibid.
69. See, e.g., T. S. Mathews, "What Gods! What Gongs!" *The New Republic* 55 (30 May 1928): 50–51; Raymond Mortimer, "New Novels," *Nation and Atheneum* 43 (23 June 1928): 396–397.
70. H.W.R., "Quicksand," *Boston Evening Transcript*, 20 June 1928, part 3, p. 2.
71. W. E. B. Du Bois, "Two Novels," *The Crisis* 35 (June 1928): 202.
72. Eda Lou Walton, review of *Quicksand, Opportunity* 6.7 (July 1928): 212.
73. Ibid.
74. Ibid.
75. Ibid., p. 213.
76. Mary White Ovington, "Book Chat," news release dated 3 August 1928, in Schomburg clipping file. I have not been able to establish whether this particular review was ever published, but it does appear that a copy was sent to Nella Larsen.
77. Other contemporary reviews include Barefield Gordon, "The Quest of Life," *Chicago Defender*, 25 August 1928, Part 2, p. 1; Katharine Shepard Hayden, review of *Quicksand, Annals* (American Academy of Political and Social Science) 140 (November 1928): 345; and E. Merrill Root, "Ebony Hour-Hand, Pointing to Midnight," *Christian Century*, 45 (18 October 1928): 1261–62. Root's essay was much more admiring than most, and unique in its focus on the spiritual pessimism of the novel, which Root took as symptomatic of the malady of the modern soul.
78. James Weldon Johnson, *Black Manhattan* (1930; rpt. New York: Arno Press, 1968), p. 214.
79. Carl Van Vechten to Fania Marinoff, 9 June 1928, CVV/NYPL. Also entry for 13 June 1928, CVV daybooks; Nella Larsen Imes to Carl Van Vechten, 3 September 1928, CVV/JWJ.
80. Presentation copy to Elizabeth Shaffer, in Lilly Library, Indiana University, Bloomington.
81. Entries for 15 and 17 August 1928, CVV daybooks.
82. Entry for 27 August 1928, CVV daybooks.
83. Elmer S. Imes to Thomas Elsa Jones, 25 September 1928, Box 34, Folder 15, Thomas Elsa Jones Papers, Fisk.
84. "Nella" to Carl Van Vechten, "Saturday" (n.d.), in CVV/JWJ.
85. Nella Larsen Imes to Dr. George E. Haynes, 25 August 1928, Harmon Foundation Award files, Library of Congress. On the letter's date line, someone at the foundation crossed out "August" as written by Larsen and wrote in "July," apparently unaware that the deadline had already been extended.
86. "Candidates for Harmon Awards Have More Time," *New York Age*, 25 August 1928, p. 10.
87. "Nella" to Carl Van Vechten, "Saturday," CVV/JWJ. McKay's name is misspelled "MacKay" in the letter.
88. Entry for 28 August in 1928 Daybook, CVV/NYPL.

89. Nella Larsen Imes to Carl Van Vechten, 3 September 1928, CVV/JWJ.

90. Kellner, *Carl Van Vechten and the Irreverent Decades*, p. 237. Langston Hughes also describes the party in *The Big Sea* (1940; rpt. New York: Hill and Wang, 1963), p. 254.

91. Nella Larsen Imes to Carl Van Vechten, 15 October 1928, CVV/JWJ.

92. Dorothy Peterson to Carl Van Vechten, 22 October 1928, CVV/JWJ.

93. Nella Larsen Imes to Carl Van Vechten, 15 October 1928.

94. Ibid.

95. Hughes, *The Big Sea*, p. 247–248.

96. Nella Larsen Imes to Carl Van Vechten, 15 October 1928.

97. Walter White to Samuel Craig, 25 September 1928, WWPC.

98. Ibid.

99. Elmer S. Imes to Thomas Elsa Jones, 25 September 1928, Box 34, Folder 15, Thomas Elsa Jones Papers, Fisk.

100. David Roderick to Walter White, 18 October 1928, WWPC.

101. Walter White to Nella Larsen Imes, 19 October 1928, WWPC.

102. Elmer S. Imes to Thomas Elsa Jones, 12 February 1929, Thomas Elsa Jones Papers, Fisk.

103. Nella Larsen Imes to Carl Van Vechten, 15 October 1928, CVV/JWJ.

104. Ibid.

105. Dorothy Peterson to Carl Van Vechten, 22 October 1928, CVV/JWJ.

106. Scholley Pace Alexander to Dorothy Peterson, 13 October 1928, DPP.

107. Bruce Nugent to Dorothy Peterson, 8 November 1928 and 4 December 1928, DPP.

108. Wallace Thurman, "High, Low, Past and Present," *Harlem: A Forum of Negro Life* 1 (November 1928): 32.

109. Nella Larsen Imes to Carl Van Vechten, 15 October 1928, CVV/JWJ.

110. Bruce Nugent to Dorothy Peterson, postmarked 22 November 1928, DPP.

111. "Intimate Talk on Theatre Tuesday," *New York Times,* 6 December 1928, p. 35.

112. "Plays and Novels Misleading," *New York Age,* 17 November 1928, p. 4.

16. *PASSING*

1. Mae Gwendolyn Henderson, "Critical Foreword" to Nella Larsen, *Passing* (1929; rpt. New York: Modern Library, 2002), p. xvi. For other valuable comments on the "doubling" between Clare and Irene, see Cheryl A. Wall, *Women of the Harlem Renaissance* (Bloomington: Indiana University Press, 1995), p. 130; Ann DuCille, *The Coupling Convention: Sex, Text, and Tradition in Black Women's Fiction* (New York: Oxford University Press, 1993), p. 105; and Jacquelyn Y. McLendon, *The Politics of Color in the Fiction of Jessie Fauset and Nella Larsen* (Charlottesville: University Press of Virginia, 1995), p. 98.

2. Nella Larsen, *Passing* (New York: Alfred A. Knopf, 1929), p. 18. Subsequent references to this work will appear in parentheses in the text.

3. Judith R. Berzon, *Neither White nor Black: The Mulatto Character in American Fiction* (New York: New York University Press, 1978), p. 159.

4. Ibid.

5. Hazel Carby, *Reconstructing Womanhood: The Emergence of the Afro-American Woman Novelist* (New York: Oxford University Press, 1987), p. 90.

6. Mary Condé, "Passing in the Fiction of Jessie Redmon Fauset and Nella Larsen," *Yearbook of English Studies* 24 (1994): 103.

7. Wall, p. 138.
8. Nathan Irvin Huggins, *Harlem Renaissance* (London: Oxford University Press, 1971), p. 236. Huggins nevertheless considered Larsen's fiction among the best of the renaissance for its realism and psychological complexity.
9. bell hooks, *Black Looks: Race and Representation* (Boston: South End Press, 1992), pp. 165–178.
10. An excellent discussion of Larsen's use of "irritation" in *Quicksand*—and the irritation her fiction causes because of its peculiar treatment of racial feeling and "incorrect" response to racism, is Sianne Ngai, *Ugly Feelings* (Cambridge, Mass.: Harvard University Press, 2005), pp. 174–208.
11. Carl Van Vechten, *The Tiger in the House* (New York: Alfred A. Knopf, 1921), p. 3.
12. Ibid., p. 4.
13. Ibid., p. 1.
14. Ibid., p. 304.
15. Ibid., p. 302.
16. Carl Van Vechten, *Peter Whiffle; His Life and Works* (New York: Alfred A. Knopf, 1922), p. 245. Bruce Kellner, Van Vechten's literary executor, informs me that Van Vechten copied this statement almost verbatim from Mabel Dodge's response to his "cat book," *The Tiger in the House.*
17. Samira Kawash, *Dislocating the Color Line: Identity, Hybridity, and Singularity in African-American Literature* (Stanford: Stanford University Press, 1997), p. 157.
18. Ibid., p. 159.
19. Ann DuCille's compelling interpretation of the novel has influenced mine in important respects. DuCille sees Clare as a kind of "alter libido" to Irene, who is bent on denying her in order to preserve her secure middle-class existence. DuCille cites Lauren Berlant's insight that Irene wants to wear Clare's way of wearing her body, "like a prosthesis, or a fetish." See DuCille, pp. 104–105; and Lauren Berlant, "National Brands / National Body: *Imitation of Life,*" in Hortense Spillers, ed., *Comparative American Identities: Race, Sex, and Nationality in the Modern Text* (New York: Routledge, 1991), p. 111.
20. Judith Butler, *Bodies That Matter: On the Discursive Limits of "Sex"* (New York: Routledge, 1993), p. 173. My own approach to the concepts of abjection, transgression, and fetishization, as applied here to *Passing*, derive chiefly from Butler, and also from Julia Kristeva, *Powers of Horror: An Essay on Abjection* (New York: Columbia University Press, 1982); Laura Mulvey, *Fetishism and Curiosity* (Bloomington: Indiana University Press, 1996); and Peter Stallybrass and Allon White, *The Politics and Poetics of Transgression* (Ithaca: Cornell University Press, 1986). Also very suggestive is Freud's essay "The Uncanny." Helena Michie suggests that Larsen creates an "erotics of passing"; see Michie, *Sororophobia: Differences among Women in Literature and Culture* (New York: Oxford University Press, 1992). Merrill Horton, "Blackness, Betrayal, and Childhood: Race and Identity in Nella Larsen's *Passing,*" *CLA Journal* 38 (1994): 31–45, builds on this view to argue that Irene secretly desires to pass, accounting for an erotics that Freud identified with the adult's desire to feel the joy of childhood play.
21. Kawash, too, has emphasized this symmetrical relationship between Irene and Jack in their response to Clare.
22. Deborah E. McDowell, "Introduction" to Nella Larsen, *Quicksand and Passing* (New Brunswick, N.J.: Rutgers University Press, 1986), pp. xxiii–xxx. See also, in particu-

lar, Judith Butler, "Passing, Queering: Nella Larsen's Psychoanalytic Challenge," in Butler, *Bodies That Matter;* and David L. Blackmore, "'That Unreasonable Restless Feeling': The Homosexual Subtexts of Nella Larsen's *Passing*," *African American Review* 26 (1992): 475–484.

23. Kathleen Pfeiffer gives a number of compelling reasons for resisting the all-too-simplistic identification of Wentworth with Van Vechten. I nonetheless feel he is a composite including some Van Vechtenesque features, particularly in his solicitude for Irene and concern about her marital fears. See Pfeiffer, *Race Passing and American Individualism* (Amherst: University of Massachusetts Press, 2003), pp. 128–146.

24. Henderson points to this parallelism as well, pp. lxiii–lxv.

25. It is not clear that Larsen was aware of the extent of racism and color hierarchy in the "actual" Brazil—something Brazilians themselves for a long time disavowed.

26. Nella Larsen Imes to Carl Van Vechten, 3 September 1928, CVV/JWJ.

27. Mark J. Madigan, "'Then Everything Was Dark'? The Two Endings of Nella Larsen's *Passing*," *Papers of the Bibliographical Society of America* 83 (1989): 521–523.

17. A STAR IN HARLEM

1. "Our Book Shelf," *Opportunity* 7 (February 1929): 58.

2. *Staff News* 19.4 (24 January 1929): 10. Rare Books and Manuscripts Room, NYPL.

3. George E. Haynes to Mrs. Nella Larsen Imes, 31 December 1928, in Harmon Foundation Collection, Library of Congress.

4. Alain Locke, "1928: A Retrospective Review," *Opportunity* 7 (1929): 8–11, quotation from p. 9.

5. Nella Larsen, review of *Black Sadie*, by T. Bowyer Campbell, *Opportunity* 7 (1929): 24.

6. George E. Haynes to James Melvin Lee, 14 June 1928, Box 26, Harmon Foundation Collection, Library of Congress.

7. Claude McKay to Langston Hughes, 22 September 1924, LHP.

8. William Stanley Braithwaite to George E. Haynes, 26 December 1928, in Box 27, Harmon Foundation Collection, Library of Congress.

9. See "Ranking of Dr. J. Melvin Lee: Literature" (filled-out form); James Melvin Lee to George E. Haynes, 5 December and 22 December 1928; Dorothy Scarborough to George E. Haynes, 12 December and 27 December 1928; John Farrar to George E. Haynes, 29 October and 22 December 1928; and W. D. Howe to George E. Haynes, 24 December 1928. All in Box 27, Harmon Foundation Collection, Library of Congress.

10. "Improving," *Amsterdam News,* 6 February 1929, p. 4.

11. Bruce Nugent to Dorothy Peterson, postmarked 13 February 1929, Box 2, Folder 35, DPP.

12. Nella Larsen Imes to Gertrude Stein, postmarked 1 February 1929, Gertrude Stein Correspondence, Beinecke.

13. Gertrude Stein to Carl Van Vechten, 18 February 1929, in *The Letters of Gertrude Stein and Carl Van Vechten, 1913–1946,* ed. Edward Burns (New York: Columbia University Press, 1986), vol. 1, p. 192.

14. Gertrude Stein to Carl Van Vechten, postmarked 29 January 1931, ibid., pp. 234–235.

15. "Twelve Negroes Honored for Achievements," *New York Times,* 13 February 1929, p. 13, from scrapbook of 1928 Harmon Awards, Box 144, Harmon Foundation Collection, Li-

brary of Congress. Apparently this article was carried simultaneously by most of the New York papers.

16. "Fisk Graduates Receive Awards," *Nashville Tennessean,* 6 January 1929, from scrapbook of 1928 Harmon Awards, ibid.

17. Mary Mackay to Walter White, 12 February 1929; Walter White to Mary Mackay, 13 February 1929. Both in WWPC, quotation from the latter.

18. Entry for 13 February 1929, CVV daybooks.

19. Entry for 28 February 1929, CVV daybooks.

20. Harold Jackman to Countee Cullen, 31 January 1929, Countee Cullen Papers, Amistad Research Center, Tulane University.

21. "A Novel with a Moral," *New York Age,* 4 September 1926, p. 4.

22. This and other inverse relationships between the novels have been noted in Kathleen Pfeiffer, *Race Passing and American Individualism* (Amherst, Mass.: University of Massachusetts Press, 2003), pp. 128–130.

23. On Larsen's and Fauset's contrasting uses of fictional romance conventions, see Hazel Carby, *Reconstructing Womanhood: The Emergence of the Afro-American Woman Novelist* (New York: Oxford University Press, 1987).

24. "Jessie Fauset Is Honor Guest at Club Caroline," *New York Age,* 23 February 1929, p. 10.

25. Entry of 15 March 1929, CVV daybooks.

26. "Theatrical Stars Lend Unique Note to N.A.A.C.P. Dance," *Amsterdam News,* 20 March 1929, p. 4; Geraldyn Dismond, "Social Snapshots," *Inter-State Tattler,* 22 March 1929, p. 5; "Bill Robinson to Preside at Midnite Benefit," *New York Age,* 9 March 1929, p. 6; and "NAACP Dance Promises To Be Gala Affair," *New York Age,* 16 March 1929, p. 2.

27. Substitute Record for Nella L. Imes, Personnel Office, Human Resources Division of New York Public Library.

28. "Report of the New York Public Library for 1929," *Bulletin of the New York Public Library,* 34 (June 1930): 359–480; Bessye J. Bearden, "Tid-Bits of New York Society," *Chicago Defender,* 9 March 1929, Part 1, p. 11.

29. "Experimental Theatre Tryouts on February 27 at 135th Street Library," *New York Age,* 23 February 1929, p. 6.

30. Elmer S. Imes to Thomas Elsa Jones, 12 February 1929, Thomas Elsa Jones Papers, Fisk.

31. Thomas Elsa Jones to Elmer S. Imes, 27 February 1929, ibid.

32. Elmer S. Imes to Thomas Elsa Jones, 4 May 1929, ibid.

33. Thomas Elsa Jones to Elmer S. Imes, 4 May 1929, ibid.

34. Substitute Record for Nella L. Imes.

35. Bessye J. Bearden, "Tid-Bits of New York Society," *Chicago Defender,* 13 April 1929, Part 1, p. 11; Hallie Queen-Jackson, "Harris-Fauset Wedding," *New York Age,* 13 April 1929, p. 2; Geraldyn Dismond, "Social Snapshots," *Inter-State Tattler,* 5 April 1929, p. 5.

36. The back flap pointed out that *Quicksand* had won the Harmon Foundation's second prize and quoted flattering statements from the reviews in the *New York World* and the *New York Times Book Review.* The back of the jacket carried a brief synopsis: "The heroine of this novel is a beautiful colored girl who crosses the color-line into the white world. Her life as a white woman brings her superior advantages of almost every kind, and yet after a time there comes an inexplicable longing to go back to her own people. A chance meeting with a Negro schoolmate — and she renews her old racial contacts, although she is aware of the accompanying danger and senses the tragedy that will un-

doubtedly overtake the double life she attempts to lead." All quotations from jacket are from the copy of the book given to Carl Van Vechten, now in Beinecke.

37. Copy of *Passing* in American Literature Collection, Beinecke.

38. Entry for 3 April 1929, CVV daybooks.

39. Entry for 4 April 1929, CVV daybooks.

40. Blanche Knopf to Walter White, 4 April 1929, WWPC.

41. Abe Lerner, "Designing Children's Books: A Look at the Twenties and Thirties," in Sybille A. Jagusch, ed., *Stepping Away from Tradition* (Washington, D.C.: Library of Congress, 1988), p. 45; and Robert A. M. Stern, Gregory Gilmartin, and Thomas Mellins, *New York 1930: Architecture and Urbanism between the Two World Wars* (1987; rpt. New York: Rizzoli, 1994), pp. 141, 362, 590.

42. Entry for 10 April 1929, CVV daybooks.

43. Copy in American Literature Collection, Beinecke.

44. Advertisement in *Publishers Weekly* 65 (13 April 1929): 1780.

45. James Weldon Johnson to Blanche Knopf, stamped 13 April 1929, Alfred A. Knopf Collection, HRHRC.

46. Clipping, Nella Larsen file, Alfred A. Knopf Collection, HRHRC.

47. Nella Larsen Imes to Carl Van Vechten, 15 April 1929, CVV/JWJ.

48. Mary Rennals, "Behind the Backs of Books and Authors," *New York Telegram*, 13 April 1929, sect. 2, p. 2.

49. Marion L. Starkey, "Negro Writers Come into Their Own," unpublished ms., in Alfred A. Knopf Collection, HRHRC.

50. Ibid. Starkey misspells Larsen's name as "Larson" throughout.

51. "What Is Going on This Week," *New York Times*, 14 April 1929, p. N5; "Brooklyn News and Social Briefs," *Amsterdam News*, 24 April 1929, p. 10.

52. Geraldyn Dismond, "Social Snapshots," *Inter-State Tattler*, 26 April 1929, p. 5; Carl Van Vechten, entry for 17 April 1929, CVV daybooks.

53. On the Sherry-Netherland at this time, see Stern, Gilmartin, and Mellins, p. 217. The hotel was built in 1926; still a classically luxurious New York hostelry, it retains many of its original features inside as well as out.

54. Invitation in Carl Van Vechten Papers, Beinecke. Entry for 25 April 1929, CVV daybooks.

55. Quoted in Peter B. Howard, Catalogue 43, Item 332. Thanks to Charles R. Larson for sharing a typescript page of this catalogue with me.

56. Lewis A. Erenberg, *Steppin' Out: New York Nightlife and the Transformation of American Culture* (Westport, Conn.: Greenwood, 1981), p. 79.

57. Wilbur Young, "Gladys Bentley," in "Sketches of Colorful Harlem Characters," in "Negroes of New York" files, Federal Writers Project of New York, Schomburg.

58. "Nella" to "Mr. and Mrs. Carl Van Vechten," 9:17 A.M., 10 May 1929, CVV/JWJ.

59. Entry for 10 May 1929, CVV daybooks.

60. Geraldyn Dismond, "Social Snapshots," *Inter-State Tattler*, 17 May 1929, p. 5; "Women's Committee Fetes Walter White," *Amsterdam News*, 15 May 1929, p. 5.

61. Alfred A. Knopf to Carl Van Vechten, 28 May 1929, CVV/NYPL.

62. *Opportunity* magazine periodically listed the books most in demand at the library.

63. "Beyond the Color Line," *New York Times Book Review*, 28 April 1929, p. 14.

64. "The Color Line," *New York Herald Tribune Books*, 28 April 1929, p. 6.

65. "The Dilemma of Mixed Race: Another Study of the Color-Line in New York," New York *Sun*, 1 May 1929, p. 33.

66. Aubrey Bowser, "Long Live King Voodoo!" *Amsterdam News*, 20 March 1929, p. 16 (editorial page).

67. W. B. Seabrook, "Touch of the Tar-brush," *Saturday Review of Literature*, 18 May 1929, pp. 1017–18.

68. Nella Larsen Imes to Carl Van Vechten, 14 June 1929, CVV/JWJ.

69. Aubrey Bowser, "The Cat Came Back," *Amsterdam News*, 5 June 1929, p. 20.

70. Esther Hyman, review of *Passing*, *Bookman* 69 (June 1929): 428.

71. W. E. B. Du Bois, "The Browsing Reader," *Crisis* 36 (July 1929): 234, 248–249.

72. Nella Larsen Imes to Carl Van Vechten, 14 June 1929, CVV/JWJ. The plays included *Man's Estate,* starring Armina Marshall herself, in which a young man sacrifices his ambitions for a pregnant bride and a small cottage. *Caprice,* by the Viennese playwright Sil-Vara, was the hit of the season, a comedy in which a rich man's mistress seduces his teenage son. Eugene O'Neill's *Strange Interlude* filled in when his unremarkable *Dynamo* ran down early. And Czech playwright Frantisek Langer's light comedy *The Camel through the Needle's Eye* ended the season. Theatre Guild advertisement, New York *Herald Tribune*, 17 May 1929, p. 18; and Roy S. Waldau, *Vintage Years of the Theatre Guild, 1928–1939* (Cleveland: Press of Case Western Reserve University, 1972), pp. 44–51.

73. Nella Larsen Imes to Carl Van Vechten, 14 June 1929, CVV/JWJ.

74. Ibid.

75. Ibid. "Fays" is short for "ofays," meaning white people. "Quaint" is an uncertain reading; the word is difficult to decipher.

76. Ibid.

77. On Hackforth-Jones, see Federico García Lorca, *Epistolario completo,* ed. Andrew A. Anderson and Christopher Maurer (Madrid: Catedra, 1997), p. 637n.; and Andrew A. Anderson, "Una amistad inglesa de García Lorca," *Insula* (Madrid) 40, no. 462 (May 1985): 3–4.

78. Nella Larsen Imes to Carl Van Vechten, 14 June 1929, CVV/JWJ.

79. Nella Larsen Imes to Carl Van Vechten, "Sunday," postmarked 28 July 1929, CVV/JWJ.

80. Ibid.

81. García Lorca to his family, 28 June 1929, in *Epistolario completo,* p. 617.

82. Nella Larsen Imes to Carl Van Vechten, "Sunday," postmarked 28 July 1929, CVV/JWJ.

83. Federico García Lorca to his family, Sunday, 14 July 1929, *Epistolario completo,* pp. 625–626. Thanks to Diana Dunkelberger for help with the translation.

84. Ian Gibson, *Federico García Lorca,* 2nd ed. (Barcelona: Ediciones Grijalbo, 1987), vol. 2, p. 29.

85. Gil Benumeya, "La vuelta de Nueva York: Estampa de García Lorca," *La Gaceta Literaria,* 15 January 1931; reprinted in Federico García Lorca, *Manuscritos Neoyorquinos: Poeta en Nueva York y otras hojas y poemas,* ed. Mario Hernández (Madrid: Taba Press, 1990), pp. 239–240; L. Méndez Dominguez, "Poema de Nueva York en el Cerebro de García Lorca," *Blanco y Negro,* 5 March 1933, reprinted in García Lorca, *Manuscritos Neoyorquinos,* pp. 241–242.

86. Dominguez, p. 241. Thanks to Diana Dunkelberger for the translation. The Spanish reads: "En Nueva York se dan cita las razas de toda la tierra; pero chinos, armenios,

rusos, alemanes siguen siendo extranjeros. Todos menos los negros. Es indudable que ellos ejercen enorme influencia en Norteamérica, y pese a quien pese, son lo más espiritual y lo más delicado de aquel mundo."

87. Nella Larsen Imes to Carl Van Vechten, "Sunday," postmarked 28 July 1929, CVV/JWJ.

88. Geraldyn Dismond, "Social Snapshots," *Inter-State Tattler,* 2 August 1929, p. 5. Van Vechten's daybook for 1929 shows that in February Sidney had come to ask him what he thought of "miscegenation." See entry for 18 February 1929, CVV daybooks.

89. "Wave of Intermarriage Strikes Nordic Purists," *Amsterdam News,* 24 July 1929, pp. 1–2.

90. Geraldyn Dismond, "Social Snapshots," *Inter-State Tattler,* 2 August 1929, p. 5.

91. Nella Larsen Imes to Carl Van Vechten, postmarked 28 July 1929, CVV/JWJ.

92. "Summer Crowds of Harlemites Throng Rockaway," *New York Age,* 3 August 1929, p. 10.

93. Nella Larsen Imes to Carl Van Vechten, "Sunday," postmarked 28 July 1929, CVV/JWJ.

94. "Tanned Nordics Insulted in Hotel," *Amsterdam News,* 15 May 1929, p. 3; "Fad for Dark Skins," *New York Age,* 2 March 1929, p. 4.

95. Nella Larsen Imes to Carl Van Vechten, "Sunday," postmarked 28 July 1929, CVV/JWJ.

96. Ibid.

97. "From 'Blackbird' Chorine to 'Talkie' Star," *Pittsburgh Courier,* 8 June 1929, sect. 2, p. 1.

98. W. E. B. Du Bois to George E. Haynes, 10 August 1927, in 1929 Harmon Award files, Harmon Foundation Collection, Library of Congress.

99. Carl Van Vechten, recommendation for Nella Larsen Imes, ibid.

100. Dorothy R. Peterson, recommendation for Nella Larsen Imes, ibid.

101. Autograph books, vol. 2, CVV/JWJ.

102. Entries for 21, 23, and 24 August 1929, CVV daybooks.

103. "A Director's Dilemma," *New York Age,* 4 January 1930, p. 4.

104. Wesley Cartwright, "Motion Pictures of Negroes," p. 2, in "Negroes of New York" files, Federal Writers Project.

105. Elmer S. Imes to Thomas Elsa Jones, 15 August 1929, Jones Papers, Fisk.

106. Thomas E. Jones to Elmer S. Imes, 21 August 1929, Jones Papers.

107. "Salary Payments: Arts and Sciences," Box 47, Folder 23, Jones Papers.

108. Entry for 5 September 1929, CVV daybooks.

109. Nella Larsen Imes to Carl Van Vechten, "Sunday," postmarked 28 July 1929, CVV/JWJ.

110. Ethel Bedient Gilbert to Walter White, 10 October 1929, WWPC.

111. Ethel B. Gilbert, "Dept. of Publicity and Finance," dated December 1930, in Thomas E. Jones Correspondence with Administrative Officers—Director of Publicity, 1928–1933, Fisk.

112. Elmer and Nella went to Van Vechten's for cocktails on October 10 (CVV daybooks).

113. Entry for 16 October 1929, CVV daybooks.

114. Entry for 20 October 1929, CVV daybooks. Description from Willie the Lion Smith with George Hoefer, *Music on My Mind: Memoirs of an American Pianist* (1964; rpt. New York: Da Capo, 1975), p. 166, see also pp. 167, 172; and A. H. Lawrence, *Duke Ellington and His World* (New York: Routledge, 2001), pp. 102–103.

115. Entry for 20 October 1929, CVV daybooks.

116. Entry for 21 October 1929, CVV daybooks.

117. See, e.g., Gene Mathews, "Harlem Night Life," *Inter-State Tattler,* 10 May 1929, p. 11, and other nightlife columns in the *Tattler,* which had an almost exclusively black readership and reported on the Cotton Club favorably. In contrast, two years earlier, its most pop-

ular columnist, Geraldyn Dismond, had been turned away as part of a mixed party and threatened to sue (Viola Woodlyn James, "New York Society," *Pittsburgh Courier,* 23 July 1927, sect. 1, p. 6; and "Cotton Club, Harlem, Bars Colored Couple Accompanied by White Friends Giving Police Orders as the Reason," *New York Age,* 9 July 1927, p. 6). In 1925, during a flap over a police crackdown on "black and tans," the *Age* complained that the police clamped down only on black-managed clubs for catering to both blacks and whites, while it allowed the Cotton Club and Connie's Inn to continue ("Black and Tan," *New York Age,* 30 May 1925, p. 4). According to Bruce Kellner, Ethel Waters would perform at the Cotton Club only when it admitted black patrons.

118. Entry for 2 November 1929, CVV daybooks.
119. Nella Larsen Imes to Carl Van Vechten, "Tuesday," 11 November 1929 (postmarked 12 November), CVV/JWJ.
120. Ibid.
121. Ibid.
122. "Actor's Death Laid to Speakeasy Fight," *New York Times,* 10 November 1929, sect. 1, p. 22; "Actor, Injured on Head in Cafe Quarrel, Dies," *New York Herald Tribune,* 10 November 1929, sect. 1, p. 18; "Held in Actor's Death," *New York Times,* 11 November 1929, p. 16.
123. Nella Larsen Imes, fellowship application for 1930–1931, John Simon Guggenheim Memorial Foundation, New York.
124. Entry for 28 November 1929, CVV daybooks; Nella Larsen Imes to Carl Van Vechten, Friday, 29 November 1929, CVV/JWJ.
125. "Memorandum for Mr. White," 14 October 1929; Walter White to James Weldon Johnson, telegram dated 4 December 1929, both in Special Correspondence — Walter White, NAACP Papers, Part 1, Reel 25; "Broadway Headliners Volunteer for N.A.A.C.P. Benefit Show," *Amsterdam News,* 20 November 1929, p. 5.
126. Forrest Theatre All-Star Benefit program, December 8, 1929, p. 10, in Programs and Playbills Collection, Schomburg Center for Research in Black Culture.
127. Carl Van Vechten, "Keep A-Inchin' Along," Forrest Theatre All-Star Benefit program, p. 8.
128. Walter White, "What I Think of the N.A.A.C.P.," Forrest Theatre All-Star Benefit program, p. 8.
129. "N.A.A.C.P. Sponsors First Sunday Night Benefit at Downtown Theatre," *Amsterdam News,* 11 December 1929, p. 5.
130. "Broadway Headliners Volunteer," p. 5; and "N.A.A.C.P. Sponsors First Sunday Night Benefit," p. 5.
131. Geraldyn Dismond, "Social Snapshots," *Inter-State Tattler,* 13 December 1929, in Carl Van Vechten scrapbook for 1928–1930, CVV/NYPL.

18. TROUBLE IN MIND

1. "Important Events of the Year 1929," *Amsterdam News,* 1 January 1930, p. 10. The article uses the name "Larsen," not "Imes."
2. "Leach, Henry Goddard," *National Cyclopaedia of American Biography,* vol. 56 (Clifton, N.J.: James T. White, 1975), pp. 559–560; Henry Goddard Leach, *My Last Seventy Years* (New York: Bookman Associates, 1956), pp. 177–187.

3. Charles R. Larson, *Invisible Darkness: Jean Toomer and Nella Larsen* (Iowa City: University of Iowa Press, 1993), p. 95.

4. Nella Larsen, "Sanctuary," *Forum* 83 (January 1930): 18.

5. Entry for 18 January 1930, CVV daybooks.

6. Dorothy Peterson to Carl Van Vechten, 6 November 1941, CVV/JWJ.

7. Harold Jackman to Countee Cullen, 27 January 1930, Countee Cullen Correspondence, Amistad Research Center, Tulane University.

8. Harold Jackman to Countee Cullen, 10 February 1930, ibid.

9. Harold Jackman to Countee Cullen, 13 March 1930, ibid.

10. "The Author's Explanation," *Forum*, suppl. 4, 83 (April 1930): xli–xlii.

11. Ibid., p. xlii.

12. Alain Locke alone had given her his vote for the gold, while John Farrar, Lewis Mumford, and Joel Spingarn had voted to award her the second place and Dorothy Scarborough third. White had the first-place votes of Scarborough, Farrar, and Mumford, although Mumford had qualified his vote by writing that "it would be fairer to those who have reached a high standard before to give a second prize rather than a first one this year." He and Spingarn both believed that none of the candidates merited a gold medal. Locke, unenthusiastic about "propaganda" literature, had voted White third. None of the other candidates were seriously in the running. Since two judges felt that no gold should be given and White had clearly outdistanced Larsen in first-place votes, and since Larsen was ineligible for the bronze, the committee decided to give White a bronze. George E. Haynes to judges in Literature, 10 December 1929; and J. E. Spingarn to George E. Haynes, 13 December 1929, Harmon Foundation Award files, Harmon Foundation Collection, Library of Congress.

13. Joel Spingarn to Walter White, 9 January 1919, WWPC.

14. Elmer Imes to Carl Van Vechten, 11 February 1930, CVV/JWJ.

15. On "attachment problems" deriving from threats to a child's relationship with a primary attachment figure (usually a mother), see especially John Bowlby, *Attachment and Loss*, vol. 1, *Attachment* (New York: Basic Books, 1969), pp. 303–309; vol. 3, *Loss: Sadness and Depression* (New York: Basic Books, 1980), pp. 217–218.

16. Entries for 10 January, 2 February, and 15 February 1930, CVV daybooks; and Carl Van Vechten to Fania Marinoff, 11 January 1930, 15 January 1930, CVV/NYPL.

17. Entries for 2 and 15 February 1930, CVV daybooks.

18. Entry for 24 February 1930, CVV daybooks.

19. On dress rehearsal, clipping from *Inter-State Tattler*, 7 March 1930, in Carl Van Vechten scrapbook for 1930–1931, CVV/NYPL.

20. Dorothy Peterson to Carl Van Vechten, 31 December 1929, CVV/JWJ; Harold Jackman to Countee Cullen, 27 January 1930, Countee Cullen Correspondence.

21. Lucien H. White, "'The Green Pastures,' Given by an All-Negro Cast of 100, Is Biggest Sensation New York Has Had in Age," *New York Age*, 8 March 1930, p. 7.

22. For other contemporary responses that correspond to Larsen's, see James Weldon Johnson, *Black Manhattan* (1930; rpt. New York: Arno Press, 1968), p. 218; J. Brooks Atkinson, "The Green Pastures," *New York Times*, 9 March 1930, p. 1X; and Harold Jackman to Countee Cullen, 13 March 1930, Countee Cullen Correspondence.

23. Harold Jackman to Countee Cullen, 28 February 1930, Countee Cullen Correspondence.

24. Quotation from "Nina Mae McKinney Is Big Hit at Lafayette," *Pittsburgh Courier,* 8 February 1930, p. 16. See also "Gets Long Movie Contract," *Pittsburgh Courier,* 11 January 1930, p. 7. McKinney's other credits include films entitled *Taking It Big* and *They Learned about Woman,* then in production.

25. Carl Van Vechten to Fania Marinoff, 28 February 1930, reprinted in *Letters of Carl Van Vechten,* ed. Bruce Kellner (New Haven: Yale University Press, 1987), pp. 112–113; and entry for 27 February 1930, CVV daybooks.

26. Nella Larsen to Carl Van Vechten, "Tuesday" [4 March 1930], postmarked 5 March 1930, CVV/JWJ.

27. Ibid.; and entry for 5 March 1930, CVV daybooks.

28. David Killingray and Willie Henderson, "Bata Kindai Amgoza Ibn Lo Bagola and the Making of *an African Savage's Own Story,* in Bernth Lindfors, ed., *Africans on Stage: Studies in Ethnological Show Business* (Bloomington: Indiana University Press, 1999), pp. 228–265.

29. Ibid., pp. 229, 249–250.

30. Entry for 15 March 1930, CVV daybooks.

31. Walter White (1927), Countee Cullen (1928), and Eric Walrond (1928) had preceded her. Later Guggenheim Fellows in the 1930s included the composer William Grant Still (1934), Langston Hughes (1935), Zora Neale Hurston (1936), Sterling Brown (1937), and Richard Wright (1939).

32. Harold Jackman to Countee Cullen, 17 March 1930, Countee Cullen Correspondence. When the Four-to-Seven Club, a group of "literarians," gave a tea and symposium at Dorothy West's apartment on West Sixty-Sixth Street in honor of Richard B. Harrison and Daniel L. Haynes, Nella was not among the guests, who included Harold Jackman, Walter White, Langston Hughes, Alta Douglas, Fannie Hurst, and Louise Thompson. The club members were West herself, Roberta Bosley of the library, Glenn Carrington, Bernard Reines, Helene Johnson, and Leo Black. "Literarians Honor Two Members of the 'Green Pastures' Cast with Tea," *Amsterdam News,* 2 April 1930, p. 5.

33. Thomas E. Jones to Elmer S. Imes, 3 April 1930; and Elmer S. Imes to Thomas E. Jones, 18 April 1930, Thomas Elsa Jones Papers, Fisk.

34. Entry for 11 April 1930, CVV daybooks.

35. Nella Larsen Imes to Carl Van Vechten and Fania Marinoff, "Monday" [14 April 1930], CVV/JWJ. In the correspondence files, this letter is dated the fourth of April. This date was added years after it was written, probably by Van Vechten himself, and is clearly erroneous, for Carl and Fania bought the gift on the eleventh, the same day that Carl took Nella to the theater, and her birthday was the thirteenth.

36. Entry for 18 April 1930, CVV daybooks; and Geraldyn Dismond, column in *Inter-State Tattler,* 25 April 1930, clipping in Van Vechten Scrapbook, CVV/NYPL.

37. Entry for 20 April 1930, CVV daybooks.

38. Entry for 29 April 1930, CVV daybooks. The film opened that night at the Central Theatre on Broadway and 47th Street, according to the announcement in the *Herald Tribune,* 27 April 1930, sect. 8, p. 3.

39. Kenneth Robert Janken, *White: The Biography of Walter White, Mr. NAACP* (New York: New Press, 2003), pp. 137–138, 141–144; "Opponents on Parker Mass for Protest," *New York Times,* 5 April 1930, p. 3; "Fight over Parker Laid before House," *New York Times,* 12 April 1930, p. 3; "Negroes Hail Senate Vote," *New York Times,* 8 May 1930, p. 2.

40. Nella Larsen Imes, "Sunday," postmarked 11 May 1930, CVV/JWJ.

41. See *Fisk University Bulletin* for 1907–1908 and 1930–1931. Among the faculty remaining from 1907–1908: English professor Dora Scribner, who had been a core faculty member since 1892 and one of the main "protectors" of the girls in Jubilee Hall in 1907–1908; Mary Elizabeth Spence, a retired professor of Greek and former disciplinarian for social infractions, who remained on campus; Belle Ruth Parmenter, professor of Education and Methods; Thomas Talley of the Chemistry Department; Mary Elizabeth Chamberlin; and Minnie Lou Crosthwaite, the head of the Normal Department during Nella's youth. On Scribner, see "Professor Dora A. Scribner," *Fisk News* 6.9 (May 1933): 3.

42. "A Letter from Mrs. Imes," *Fisk News* 4.2 (November 1930): 6–8; "A Jubilee Message from Mrs. Mabel Lewis Imes," *Fisk News* 5.2 (December 1931): 5–6.

43. "Faculty Salary Schedule" for 1930–1931, in Jones Papers.

44. Joe M. Richardson, *A History of Fisk University, 1865–1946* (Tuscaloosa: University of Alabama Press, 1980), pp. 113–114.

45. "Society," *Amsterdam News*, 29 October 1930, p. 6.

46. Nella Larsen Imes to Carl Van Vechten, "Thursday" [22 May 1930], CVV/JWJ.

47. Entry for 3 June 1930, CVV daybooks.

48. Percy Hammond, "The Theatres," *New York Herald Tribune*, 5 June 1930, p. 16.

49. Nella Larsen Imes to Carl Van Vechten, "Monday" [9 June 1930], CVV/JWJ.

50. "Van Vechten's Wife Here; Still Miss Maranoff [*sic*]," *Los Angeles Examiner*, 12 June 1930, in Van Vechten scrapbook for 1930, CVV/NYPL.

51. Nella Larsen Imes to Carl Van Vechten, "Monday" [9 June 1930].

52. Carl Van Vechten, *Parties: Scenes from Contemporary New York Life* (New York: Alfred A. Knopf, 1930).

53. Nella Larsen Imes to Carl Van Vechten, "Sunday 13th" [July 1930], CVV/JWJ.

54. Nella Imes to James Weldon Johnson, "Tuesday July 22nd" [1930], JWJ/JWJ.

55. Nella Larsen Imes to Carl Van Vechten, "Sunday 13th" [July 1930], CVV/JWJ.

56. James Weldon Johnson, Preface to *Saint Peter Relates an Incident of the Resurrection Day* (New York: Viking, 1930).

57. "Asks Refusal of Gold Star Trips," *Amsterdam News*, 7 May 1930, p. 4; "Harlem Leaders Hit U.S. Jim Crow," *Amsterdam News*, 16 July 1930, p. 3.

58. Nella Larsen Imes to Carl Van Vechten, "Sunday 13th" (July 1930), CVV/JWJ.

59. "Harlem Leaders Hit U.S. Jim Crow," p. 3.

60. Nella Larsen Imes to Carl Van Vechten, "Sunday 13th."

61. Nella Larsen Imes to Carl Van Vechten, 21 July 1930, CVV/JWJ.

62. Nella Imes to Langston Hughes, "Tuesday 22nd" (July 1930), LHP.

63. Quoted in Hugh Gloster, *Negro Voices in American Fiction* (1948; rpt. New York: Russell and Russell, 1965), p. 185.

64. Langston Hughes, *Not without Laughter* (1930; rpt. New York: Simon and Schuster, 1995), p. 298.

65. Theophilus Lewis, "The Harlem Sketch Book," *Amsterdam News*, 16 July 1930, p. 9.

66. Ibid., 23 July 1930, p. 9.

67. Aubrey Bowser, "Invincible Laughter," *Amsterdam News*, 23 July 1930, p. 20.

68. Nella Larsen Imes to Carl Van Vechten, 21 July 1930, CVV/JWJ.

69. Elmer S. Imes to Thomas E. Jones, 14 August 1930, Jones Papers, Fisk.

70. Nella Larsen Imes to Carl Van Vechten, 16 August 1930, CVV/JWJ.
71. Elmer Imes to Carl Van Vechten, 18 September 1930, CVV/JWJ. Elmer says here that she told him "about three weeks ago" of her knowledge of the affair, which dates the confrontation to the last week of August.
72. Elmer S. Imes to Thomas E. Jones, 26 August 1930, Jones Papers, Fisk.
73. Nella Larsen Imes to Carl Van Vechten, "Monday 25th" (August 1930), CVV/NYPL.
74. Nella Larsen Imes to Carl Van Vechten, 16 August 1930 and "Monday 25th."
75. Nella Larsen Imes to Carl Van Vechten, "Monday 25th" (August 1930), CVV/NYPL.
76. Ibid.
77. Ibid.
78. Nella Larsen Imes to Carl Van Vechten, 16 August 1930.
79. Entry for 18 September 1930, CVV daybooks.
80. Elmer S. Imes to Carl Van Vechten, dated "Wednesday night [September 17]," postmarked 18 September 1930, CVV/JWJ.

19. A NOVELIST ON HER OWN

1. "Outgoing Passenger and Mail Ships," *New York Herald Tribune,* 14 September 1930, sect. 13, p. 8; "Shipping News—Marine Reports," *New York Herald Tribune,* 19 September 1930, p. 39; "Shipping News," *New York Herald Tribune,* 21 September 1930, sect. 13, p. 8, and 28 September 1930, sect. 8, p. 8.
2. Elmer S. Imes to Carl Van Vechten, "Wednesday night" [September 17], postmarked 18 September 1930, CVV/JWJ.
3. Carl Van Vechten to Dorothy Peterson, 30 October 1941, CVV/JWJ.
4. "Outgoing Passenger and Mail Ships," *New York Herald Tribune,* 14 September 1930, sect. 13, p. 8; "Shipping News—Marine Reports," *New York Herald Tribune,* 19 September 1930, p. 39; "Shipping News," *New York Herald Tribune,* 21 September 1930, sect. 13, p. 8, and 28 September 1930, sect. 8, p. 8.
5. Nella Larsen Imes to Carl Van Vechten, "Wednesday 1st" [October 1930], CVV/JWJ.
6. Nella Larsen Imes to "Mr. and Mrs. Carl Van Vechten," postmarked 19 September 1930, CVV/JWJ.
7. Nella Larsen Imes to Carl Van Vechten, "Wednesday 1st" [October 1930].
8. Ibid.
9. Ibid.
10. Ibid.
11. Ibid.
12. Description based on J. Escalas, *Mallorca: Illustrated Guide* (Palma: Galerias Costa, 1933), pp. 32–33; E. Allison Peers, *Spain: A Companion to Spanish Travel* (New York: Farrar and Rinehart, 1930), pp. 286–290.
13. See the reminiscence by Paul Morand in Escalas, p. iv.
14. Lawrence Dundas, *Behind the Spanish Mask* (London: Robert Hale, 1943), p. 69; Matias Mut Oliver, *Breve historia del fomento del turismo da Mallorca, 1905–1980* (Palma: Sa Nostra, 1980), p. 14.
15. Figures from Escalas, p. 19.
16. Elmer S. Imes to Carl Van Vechten, 18 October 1930, CVV/JWJ.
17. *Come to Palma* (Palma: n.p., n.d. [ca. 1930–1933]); Lluis Fabregas, *Estampas de "El*

Terreno" (Palma: Ediciones Cort, 1974), pp. 159–160; Rafael Alcover, "Evolución del turismo en Mallorca desde el siglo XVIII," in J. Mascaro Pesarius, ed., *Historia de Mallorca,* vol. 3 (Palma: Graficas Miramar, 1970), p. 644.

18. Nella Larsen Imes to Henry Allen Moe, "Monday 20th" (October 1930), Nella Larsen Imes files, John Simon Guggenheim Foundation, New York.

19. Nella Larsen Imes to Carl Van Vechten, "Wednesday 12th" (November 1930), CVV/JWJ.

20. "Terreno, El," in *Gran encyclopèdia de Mallorca* (Palma: Promomallorca Ediciones, n.d.), vol. 17, p. 168; Luis Sainz M. de Bujanda and Manuel Alvarez de Sotomayor, *Mallorca turística, 1967* (Palma: Jorvich, 1967), pp. 40–42.

21. Escalas, pp. 96–97.

22. Nella Larsen Imes to Carl Van Vechten, [12 November 1930?]. The description of the Valldemossa trip seems to be an extended addendum to the letter dated "Wednesday 12th" and mailed in the same envelope.

23. Nella Larsen Imes to Carl Van Vechten, "Wednesday 12th" (November 1930), CVV/JWJ.

24. Information on the house and environs from personal observation and conversation with Diane Kerrigan, who lives in Stein's former home, Mirabel; photographs and post-cards in the collection at the Biblioteca de Lluís Alemany, Consell Insular de Mallorca, Palma; and Carlos Garrido, "Un paraíso perdido," *Mediterranean Magazine* 21 (October–November 1990): 26–30. Many thanks to Sr. Juan Carlos Llop at the Biblioteca de Lluís Alemany for his help in identifying houses and streets in the photograph collection. Larsen's home is now a double, 28 and 30 Josep Villalonga, and a more recent structure housing a small press next door now carries the address 32 Josep Villalonga.

25. Nella Larsen Imes to Carl Van Vechten, "Thursday 12th" (November 1930), CVV/JWJ. The date on this letter is wrong by a day. The twelfth of November was Wednesday, and the next "twelfth" that is a Thursday is in February, by which time Larsen had been living in her house for some three months. If she took the house for five months, she would have moved into it on the first of December.

26. Nella Larsen Imes to Carl Van Vechten, "Thursday 12th" (November 1930).

27. Nora Holt to Carl Van Vechten, 3 December 1930, CVV/JWJ.

28. Nora Holt to Carl Van Vechten, 9 December 1930, CVV/JWJ.

29. Elmer S. Imes to Carl Van Vechten, 3 December 1930, CVV/JWJ.

30. Dorothy Peterson to Carl Van Vechten, 16 December 1930, CVV/JWJ.

31. Elmer S. Imes to Carl Van Vechten, December 8, 1930.

32. Nella Larsen Imes to Henry Allen Moe, 11 January 1931, John Simon Guggenheim Foundation.

33. Nella Larsen Imes to Henry Allen Moe, 11 January 1931; Nella Larsen Imes to Carl Van Vechten, 25 January 1931, CVV/JWJ (quotation is from the latter). On O'Flaherty, see James H. O'Brian, *Liam O'Flaherty* (Lewisburg, Penn.: Bucknell University Press, 1973); and *The Letters of Liam O'Flaherty,* ed. A. A. Kelly (Dublin: Wolfhound, 1996).

34. Nella Larsen Imes to Carl Van Vechten, 25 January 1931. On the Riding-Graves ménage, see T. S. Matthews, *Jacks or Better* (New York: Harper and Row, 1977), pp. 125–157.

35. Nella Larsen Imes to Carl Van Vechten, 25 January 1931.

36. See *The Collected Poems of Norman Cameron* (London: Hogarth Press, 1957), and Robert Graves's Introduction to that volume, which erroneously gives early 1932 as the date Cameron moved to Deyá; Miranda Seymore, *Life on the Edge* (New York: Henry Holt, 1995), pp. 164, 200; Richard Percival Graves, *Robert Graves: The Years with Laura, 1926–*

1940 (London: Weidenfeld and Nicolson, 1990), pp. 155, 350n.108; Martin Seymour-Smith, *Robert Graves: His Life and Work* (London: Hutchinson, 1982), p. 216; Jonathan Barker, "Norman Cameron: An Introduction," *Poetry Review* (London) 76 (1986): 93–94; and Norman Cameron, *Collected Poems and Selected Translations*, ed. Warren Hope and Jonathan Barker (London: Anvil Press, 1990), which includes a biographical sketch by Hope.

37. Nella Larsen Imes to Carl Van Vechten, 25 January 1931.

38. Ibid.

39. Ibid.

40. Ibid.

41. "Mallorca y Norte América," *La Ultima Hora,* 24 January 1931, p. 9.

42. Nella Larsen Imes to Gertrude Stein, 26 January 1931, Gertrude Stein Correspondence, Beinecke Rare Book and Manuscript Library, Yale University.

43. Nella Larsen Imes to Gertrude Stein, "February Twenty-Sixth" (1931), Gertrude Stein Correspondence.

44. Dorothy Peterson to Carl Van Vechten, 12 February 1954, CVV/JWJ.

45. Nella Larsen Imes to Carl Van Vechten, 3 March 1931, CVV/JWJ.

46. Ibid.

47. Ibid.

48. George S. Schuyler, *Black No More* (Boston: Northeastern University Press, 1989; orig. pub. 1931), pp. 101–102.

49. Schuyler, pp. 90, 92, 95–96.

50. Nella Larsen Imes to Carl Van Vechten, 3 March 1931, CVV/JWJ.

51. Nella Larsen Imes to Langston Hughes, n.d., LHP. The letter mentions that Larsen will be leaving in early April for the South of France, so it was probably written in February or early to mid-March 1931.

52. Nella Larsen Imes to Carl Van Vechten, 22 March 1931, CVV/JWJ.

53. Ibid.

54. Nella Larsen Imes to Henry Allen Moe, 31 March 1931, John Simon Guggenheim Foundation.

55. Nella Larsen Imes to Carl Van Vechten, 31 March 1931, CVV/JWJ.

56. Frank L. Kluckhohn, "Foes Demand Alfonso Quit or Face Republic by Force; Spanish Cabinet to Resign," *New York Times,* 14 April 1931, pp. 1, 2.

57. Walter White to Dorothy Peterson, 13 March 1931, WWPC.

58. Nella Larsen Imes to Carl Van Vechten, 7 April 1931, CVV/JWJ.

59. Reader's Report on "Mirage," dated 31 August 1931, Alfred A. Knopf Papers, NYPL.

60. Nella Larsen Imes to Carl Van Vechten, 7 April 1931, CVV/JWJ.

61. Ibid.

62. Alin Laubreaux, *Mulatto Johnny,* trans. Coley Taylor (New York: E. P. Dutton, 1931), p. 238.

63. Frank L. Kluckhohn, "Republicans Sweep Polls in Most of Spanish Cities; New Perils Loom for King," *New York Times,* 13 April 1931, pp. 1, 11; "Liberal Autonomy for Catalans," *New York Times,* 18 April 1931, p. 8; "Foes Demand Alfonso Quit or Face Republic by Force; Spanish Cabinet to Resign," *New York Times,* 14 April 1931, pp. 1, 2; "Navy Strikes Royal Colors," *New York Times,* 16 April 1931, p. 4; Pere Gabriel, Josep Massot i Muntaner, and Damià Ferrà-Ponç, "Cronolica de Mallorca, 1930–1939," *Randa* 4 (1976):

244–246; "Los primeros pasos de la República: La situación en Palma," *El Día* (Palma), 16 April 1931, p. 2; J. Mascaró Pasarius, "La Segunda Republica Española," in *Historia de Mallorca,* ed. J. Mascaró Pasarius (Palma: Graficas Miralles, 1978), vol. 4, pp. 349–354.

64. Nella Larsen Imes to Carl Van Vechten, 11 May 1931, CVV/JWJ.

65. Nella Larsen Imes to Henry Allen Moe, 21 April 1931, John Simon Guggenheim Foundation.

66. The boat to Marseilles left weekly on Tuesdays, arriving in Marseilles at 7:00 the next morning.

67. "Nora Holt Opens Chicago's Finest Night Club; Hundreds Attend Debut," *Pittsburgh Courier,* 9 July 1927, sect. 1, p. 1; Nora Holt to Carl Van Vechten, 27 February 1929, CVV/JWJ; and Geraldyn Dismond, "Social Snapshots," *Inter-State Tattler,* 22 March 1929, p. 5.

68. Entry for 15 January 1929, CVV daybooks.

69. John Houseman, who worked with Jack Carter on the "Voodoo Macbeth" in the 1930s, believed that Carter's mother was one of the "original Florodora Girls"—that is, a member of the Florodora Sextette that was such a sensation around the turn of the century and in some ways precursors to the floor show chorus-lines of the 1920s. All of these women were apparently white, however, and none bore the name "Margaret."

70. Nella Larsen Imes to Carl Van Vechten, 3 May 1931, CVV/JWJ.

71. "Society in Nice Is Seen at Parties, Many Receptions," *New York Herald Tribune,* Paris Edition, 22 April 1931, p. 8.

72. Nella Larsen Imes to Carl Van Vechten, 3 May 1931, CVV/JWJ.

73. Nella Larsen Imes to Carl Van Vechten, 27 April 1931, CVV/JWJ.

74. *Paris: Kleine Ausgabe* (Berlin: Grieben Verlag, 1932), p. 27.

75. Ghislaine Wood, "The Exotic," in Charlotte Benton, Tim Benton, and Ghislaine Wood, eds., *Art Deco, 1910–1939* (London: Victoria and Albert Museum, 2003), p. 127.

76. Carl Van Vechten to Gertrude Stein, 4 May 1931, in *The Letters of Gertrude Stein and Carl Van Vechten, 1913–1946,* ed. Edward Burns (New York: Columbia University Press, 1986), vol. 1, p. 241.

77. Anita Thompson to Walter White, 2 April 1931, in WWPC. In her unpublished autobiography, Thompson (later Reynolds) wrote that she left Paris before April 14, but this letter is clearly dated and written from the rue Jacques Mawas, Paris.

78. Anita Thompson Dickinson Reynolds, "American Cocktail," unpublished manuscript, p. 78, in Box 129-4, Folder 1, Anita T. Reynolds Papers, Moorland-Spingarn Research Center, Howard University. This statement is at odds with some of the claims made in Tyler Stovall's *Paris Noir* (Boston: Houghton Mifflin, 1996), which stresses the existence of an African American community centered in Montmartre. It is certainly true that Montmartre had a black community, mainly of French colonial subjects, and it was well known for its "black" nightclubs. But except for Langston Hughes, none of Larsen's black friends who spent time in Paris lived in Montmartre or spent most of their time there; they more often lived, worked, and amused themselves on the Left Bank. "American Cocktail," Anita Thompson Dickinson Reynolds' unpublished autobiography, contains fascinating observations about Paris at the time. So far as I know, it has never before been consulted by scholars.

79. Nella Larsen Imes to Carl Van Vechten, postmarked 11 May 1931, CVV/JWJ.

80. Phyllis Rose, *Jazz Cleopatra: Josephine Baker in Her Time* (New York: Doubleday, 1989), p. 146.

81. Ibid., p. 148.
82. Nella Larsen Imes to Carl Van Vechten, postmarked 11 May 1931, CVV/JWJ. The play is mentioned, disparagingly, by Genêt (Janet Flanner) in her "Paris Letter," *New Yorker*, 18 April 1931, pp. 55–57. The "Guitrys," as Larsen called them, had performed in New York to enormous acclaim in the winter of 1926–1927. Even their Paris performances were regularly covered by New York papers in the 1920s.
83. Nella Larsen Imes to Carl Van Vechten, postmarked 11 May 1931; "Roland Hayes Wins Acclaim in Varied Fare of Songs," *New York Herald Tribune*, Paris edition, 9 May 1931, p. 3.
84. Stovall, p. 45.
85. Nella Larsen Imes to Carl Van Vechten, postmarked 11 May 1931.
86. William Seabrook, *No Hiding Place: An Autobiography* (Philadelphia: Lippincott, 1942), p. 315.
87. Aubrey Bowser, "Long Live King Voodoo!" *Amsterdam News*, 20 March 1929, Editorial Page.
88. Nancy Cunard, "Meeting Mr. and Mrs. Seabrook (Autumn 1929, Café Select, Montparnasse, Paris)" in WWPC.
89. Man Ray, *Self-Portrait* (Boston: Little, Brown, 1963), p. 191.
90. Advertisement in *New Yorker*, 11 April 1931, p. 101.
91. Ray, p. 191.
92. William Seabrook, *Jungle Ways* (New York: Harcourt, Brace, 1931), pp. 161, 163.
93. Seabrook, *No Hiding Place*, p. 306.
94. Seabrook, *Jungle Ways*, p. 308.
95. Ray, p. 192.
96. Nella Larsen to Carl Van Vechten, 11 May 1931, CVV/JWJ.
97. Ibid., p. 267.
98. Reynolds, p. 92.
99. Ray, pp. 267–270; and Neil Baldwin, *Man Ray: American Artist* (New York: Clarkson N. Potter, 1988), pp. 134–135.
100. Reynolds, p. 161.
101. Ibid., p. 92.
102. Ibid., pp. 94–95.
103. Nella Larsen Imes to Carl Van Vechten, postmarked 11 May 1931, CVV/JWJ. Misspellings in the original.
104. Man Ray to Carl Van Vechten, 8 November 1930, 24 November 1930, and 2 February 1931, Carl Van Vechten Papers, Yale Collection of American Literature, Beinecke.
105. What makes the existence of the photo unlikely is the fact that it does not show up in Carl Van Vechten's collections. On the other hand, Man Ray was interested in black subjects at this time, and it would have been very easy for him to arrange a sitting for Carlo's good friend.
106. Nella Larsen Imes to Carl Van Vechten, postmarked 11 May 1931, CVV/JWJ.
107. See especially Stovall, pp. 79–80.
108. Nella Larsen Imes to Carl Van Vechten, postmarked 11 May 1931, CVV/JWJ.
109. Carl Van Vechten to Gertrude Stein, 6 June 1931, in *Letters of Gertrude Stein and Carl Van Vechten*, vol. 1, pp. 243 and 244n.1.
110. Nella Larsen Imes to Carl Van Vechten, 4 June 1931, CVV/JWJ; and Edward Wasserman

to Carl Van Vechten, 6 July 1931, Carl Van Vechten Papers, Yale Collection of American Literature, Beinecke.

111. Information on Hotel Paris-Dinard from hotel letterhead, Nella Larsen Imes to Henry Allen Moe, 25 May 1931; and classified advertisement in the *New York Herald Tribune*, Paris edition, 30 July 1931, p. 11.

112. Bill Klüver and Julie Martin, "Man Ray, Paris," in Merry Foresta et al., *Perpetual Motif: The Art of Man Ray* (New York: Abbeville, 1988), p. 123.

113. "2,000 See 'Mt. Vernon' Opened by Edge and Pershing," *New York Herald Tribune*, Paris edition, 27 May 1931, p. 1.

114. "French Colonial Exposition Opens at Vincennes May 6," *New York Herald Tribune*, Paris edition, 25 April 1931, p. 1; Genêt, "Paris Letter," *New Yorker*, 30 May 1931, pp. 43–45; Rose, pp. 144–145.

115. Nella Larsen Imes to Carl Van Vechten, 4 June 1931, CVV/JWJ.

116. "Ne visitez pas l'Exposition Coloniale," manifesto enclosed with letter from Nancy Cunard to Walter White of 16 June 1931, WWPC.

117. Rose, p. 146.

118. Gouverneur Général Olivier, "Les Origines et les buts de l'Exposition Coloniale," *Revue des Deux Mondes*, 101st year, vol. 3 (1 May 1931), p. 55, my translation.

119. Nella Larsen Imes to Carl Van Vechten, 4 June 1931, CVV/JWJ; "Texas Guinan Sails to Give Whoopee Display in Paris," *New York Herald Tribune*, Paris edition, 23 May 1931, p. 1; "Two Guinan 'Kids' Missing in Havre on Eve of Sailing," *New York Herald Tribune*, Paris edition, 3 June 1931, pp. 1, 3; Genêt, "Paris Letter," *New Yorker*, 27 June 1931, pp. 58–60.

120. Nella Larsen Imes to Carl Van Vechten, 4 June 1931, CVV/JWJ.

121. Ibid.

122. Nella Imes to Mr. and Mrs. James Weldon Johnson, postmarked 18 June 1931, JWJ/JWJ.

123. Klüver and Martin, p. 123; see also Morrill Cody with Hugh Ford, *The Women of Montparnasse* (New York: Cornwall Books, 1984), p. 9.

124. Ray, p. 149.

125. Nora Holt to Carl Van Vechten, 22 October 1926, CVV/JWJ; Michel Fabre and John A. Williams, *A Street Guide to African Americans in Paris* (Paris: Cercle d'Etudes Afro-Américaines, 1996), p. 139.

126. Fabre and Williams, p. 139; "Hale Woodruff Returns after Study in France," *Amsterdam News*, 9 September 1931, p. 7.

127. Ray, p. 149; see also Cody, p. 121.

128. Cody, p. 114.

129. Fabre and Williams, p. 139.

130. Edward Wasserman to Carl Van Vechten, 6 July 1931, CVV/JWJ.

131. Dorothy Peterson to Carl Van Vechten, 19 July 1931, CVV/JWJ.

132. Seabrook, *No Hiding Place*, p. 119.

133. Ibid., pp. 149–151.

134. At one party attended by Man Ray, Van Vechten, Marinoff, and Nora Holt, among others, both Nora and Fania performed in the nude. Entry of 7 July 1929, CVV daybooks.

135. The postmark is from a station at the Square d'Orléans, south of Montmartre.

136. Dorothy Peterson to Carl Van Vechten, 19 July 1931, CVV/JWJ.

137. "Society," *Amsterdam News*, 15 July 1931, p. 5. There was no "Susan Gilbert" on the staff

at Fisk; and Ethel Gilbert spent the summer abroad, according to a letter from Thomas E. Jones to Paul D. Cravath, 21 September 1931, Jones Papers, Fisk. Years later, Dorothy Peterson informed Van Vechten that she had first met Gilbert in Paris (Peterson to Van Vechten, 22 September 1941, CVV/JWJ). There can be little doubt that "Susan Gilbert" is Ethel.

138. Carl Van Vechten to Grace Nail Johnson, 11 July 1931, GNJ/JWJ.

139. Elmer S. Imes to Carl Van Vechten, 25 August 1931, CVV/JWJ.

140. Harold Jackman to Carl Van Vechten, 13 August 1931, CVV/JWJ.

141. Nella Larsen Imes to Carl Van Vechten, postmarked 11 May 1931, CVV/JWJ; Edward Wasserman to Carl Van Vechten, 6 July 1931, Carl Van Vechten Papers, Yale Collection of American Literature, Beinecke; Seabrook, *No Hiding Place*, pp. 191, 323.

142. "Now Special Guest of French Princess," *Amsterdam News*, 5 August 1931, p. 4.

143. Nella Larsen Imes to Carl Van Vechten, postmarked 30 August 1931, CVV/JWJ.

144. "To Study in Paris," *Amsterdam News*, 9 September 1931, p. 7.

145. "In the Latin Quarter," *New York Herald Tribune*, Paris edition, 16 September 1931, p. 2; "In the Latin Quarter," *New York Herald Tribune*, Paris edition, 25 September 1931, p. 2; "In Europe with J. A. Rogers," *Amsterdam News*, 2 September 1931, p. 10.

146. "In Europe with J. A. Rogers," p. 10.

147. Nella Larsen Imes to Carl Van Vechten, postmarked 30 August 1931, CVV/JWJ.

148. J. A. Rogers, "In Europe with J. A. Rogers," p. 10; and "Rambling Ruminations," *Amsterdam News*, 19 August 1931, p. 8.

149. Nella Larsen Imes to Henry Allen Moe, 26 September 1931, John Simon Guggenheim Foundation.

150. Reader's Report on "Mirage," dated 31 August 1931, Alfred A. Knopf Papers, NYPL.

151. Elmer S. Imes to Thomas E. Jones, 8 September 1931, Jones Papers, Fisk.

152. Ibid.

153. Nella Larsen Imes to Henry Allen Moe, 26 September 1931, John Simon Guggenheim Foundation.

154. Nella Larsen Imes to Carl Van Vechten, postmarked 27 September 1931, CVV/JWJ. The card pictured a Javanese mask from the British Museum and bore a Gare d'Austerlitz postmark—the Austerlitz station being near the Jardin des Plantes.

155. Dorothy Peterson to Carl Van Vechten, 12 February 1954, CVV/JWJ; and Dorothy Peterson to Jean Toomer, 22 December 1931, JTP.

156. E. Allison Peers, *Spain: A Companion to Spanish Travel* (New York: Farrar and Rinehart, 1930), p. 133.

157. Dorothy Peterson to Carl Van Vechten, 11 December 1931, CVV/JWJ; and Dorothy Peterson to Jean Toomer, 22 December 1931, JTP.

158. Dorothy Peterson to Carl Van Vechten, 5 February 1963, CVV/JWJ.

159. Nella Larsen Imes to Carl Van Vechten, n.d. [October or November 1931], CVV/JWJ. Though posted from Málaga, Larsen probably picked the card up in Gibraltar or Paris, for it credited the British Museum.

160. Nella Larsen Imes to Mr. and Mrs. Carl Van Vechten, from Gibraltar, 26 November 1931, CVV/JWJ.

161. Reynolds, pp. 158–167.

162. Ibid., p. 173.

163. Nella Larsen Imes to Carl Van Vechten, postmarked 1 December 1931, CVV/JWJ.

164. Dorothy Peterson to Carl Van Vechten, 11 December 1931.
165. Ibid.
166. Nella Imes and Dorothy Peterson to Mr. and Mrs. James Weldon Johnson, JWJ/JWJ. The postcard, from Granada, shows a woman in local dress, identified as a gypsy dancer. Another card was sent to Carl and Fania at the same time, showing the Sala de las Dos Hermanas of the Alhambra.
167. Dorothy Peterson to Jean Toomer, 22 December 1931, JTP.
168. Ibid. Dorothy mentions that she is leaving "next week," giving no indication that Nella is sailing with her, although Nella certainly left at nearly the same time, and stayed at the Petersons' in Brooklyn upon arrival in the States. By the end of January, both women had been in New York at least a few days, to judge from correspondence of Van Vechten and his niece Elizabeth Hull. Dorothy, at least, must have taken the *S.S. Augustus,* which departed Gibraltar on January 3 and arrived at the 57th Street Pier on January 9. It was the first ship to leave after the time Dorothy said she would be in Gibraltar, and no other ships left until at least a week after that. The phrasing of each woman's last cards or letters home suggests they did not travel together, although the evidence is inconclusive—e.g., a postcard from Larsen only to Van Vechten, undated: "I am getting ready to get back home" (CVV/JWJ); and Peterson to Toomer, 22 December 1931: "I'm going to Gibraltar next week and then I sail back to New York from there." Postcard from Peterson and Larsen, n.d. (from Granada): "I'm coming home soon. Love Dorothy / Me too Nella" (JWJ/JWJ).

20. THE CRACK-UP

1. T. R. Poston, "Every Day Is Dog Day in Harlem," *Dunbar News,* 30 December 1931, p. 6.
2. Elizabeth Hull to Grace Nail Johnson, 2 February 1932, GNJ/JWJ.
3. Carl Van Vechten to James Weldon Johnson, 31 January (1932), JWJ/JWJ.
4. Dorothy Peterson to Grace Nail Johnson, 7 March 1932, GNJ/JWJ.
5. Elizabeth Hull to Carl Van Vechten, 9 February 1932, CVV/NYPL.
6. Dorothy Peterson to Grace Nail Johnson, 7 March 1932, GNJ/JWJ.
7. Ibid. See also "Society," *Amsterdam News,* 9 March 1932, p. 4.
8. Dorothy Peterson to Grace Nail Johnson, 7 March 1932; "Paul Robeson Begins Farewells," *New York Times,* 7 March 1932, p. 20.
9. Dorothy Peterson to Grace Nail Johnson, 15 April 1932, GNJ/JWJ.
10. Nella Larsen Imes to Carl Van Vechten, "Saturday—2nd" (April 1932), CVV/NYPL.
11. Nella Larsen Imes to Carl Van Vechten, "Sunday" (postmarked 11 April 1932), CVV/JWJ.
12. Nella Larsen Imes to Carl Van Vechten and Fania Marinoff, "Wednesday" (postmarked 20 April 1932), CVV/JWJ.
13. Ibid.
14. Ibid.
15. Nella Larsen Imes to Carl Van Vechten, "Friday" (14 May 1932), CVV/JWJ.
16. Ibid.
17. Ibid.
18. Elizabeth Hull to Grace Johnson, 26 May 1932, GNJ/JWJ.
19. Nella Larsen Imes to Carl Van Vechten, "Friday" (14 May 1932), CVV/JWJ.
20. Thadious M. Davis, *Nella Larsen, Novelist of the Harlem Renaissance: A Woman's Life*

Unveiled (Baton Rouge: Louisiana State University Press, 1994), p. 395, based on interview with Youra Qualls.

21. Thomas E. Jones to Paul D. Cravath, 13 April 1932, Jones Papers, Fisk.
22. Ethel B. Gilbert to Thomas E. Jones, 25 March 1932, Jones Papers.
23. Ibid.
24. Elmer S. Imes to Carl Van Vechten, telegram of 19 May 1932, CVV/JWJ.
25. Elmer S. Imes to Carl Van Vechten, 21 June 1932, CVV/JWJ.
26. Francis G. Knight to Arnold A. Levin, 20 May 1964, in Nella Larsen Imes estate files, Municipal Archives of New York City.
27. Elizabeth Hull to Carl Van Vechten, 19 August 1932, CVV/NYPL.
28. Nella Larsen Imes to Carl Van Vechten, "Sunday 11th" (September 1932), CVV/JWJ.
29. Thomas E. Jones to Paul Cravath, 12 September 1932, Jones Papers.
30. Davis, p. 399.
31. Ibid., p. 400.
32. Edward Donahoe to Grace Nail Johnson, 21 October 1932, GNJ/JWJ.
33. Andrew Meyer, letter of January 1982, quoted in Davis, p. 424. The trip had to have taken place at this time, because Larsen would not return to New York until after her divorce, and she never returned to Nashville after that. As we know, on her earlier trip to Nashville, she took a train and flew alone. Mabry's connection with Fisk began in early 1932, so the trip could not have taken place before then. Finally, we know that Mabry was in New York in the fall of 1932 and returned to Nashville about the same time as Larsen, because he was offered a job by President Jones soon after.
34. Edward Donahoe to Langston Hughes, n.d. [1927, while Hughes was at Lincoln University], LHP.
35. Carl Van Vechten, *The Splendid, Drunken Twenties: Selections from the Daybooks,* ed. Bruce Kellner (Urbana Champaign: University of Illinois Press, 2003), n.p., following p. 188.
36. Tom Mabry to Muriel Draper, 7 February 1932, Muriel Draper Papers, Beinecke.
37. Allen Tate to Tom Mabry, 20 January 1932, copy in WWPC.
38. Tom Mabry to Allen Tate, 22 January 1932, copy in WWPC.
39. Allen Tate to Tom Mabry, 25 January 1932, in WWPC.
40. Thomas Dabney Mabry to Walter White, 30 August 1932, WWPC. Edward Donahoe, who co-hosted the party and invited Langston Hughes, indicates that Thomas E. Jones came to the party; Donahoe to Grace Johnson, 21 October 1932, GNJ/JWJ.
41. Thomas Dabney Mabry to Walter White, 30 August 1932, WWPC.
42. Walter White to James Weldon Johnson, 8 September 1932, JWJ/JWJ.
43. James Weldon Johnson to Walter White, 7 September 1930, WWPC.
44. Esther B. Jones to Grace N. Johnson, postmarked 20 October 1932, GNJ/JWJ.
45. Ethel Gilbert to Grace N. Johnson, 18 October 1932, GNJ/JWJ.
46. "Love Triangle behind Fisk Divorce," Baltimore *Afro-American,* 21 October 1933.
47. Esther B. Jones to Grace Nail Johnson, 21 October 1932, GNJ/JWJ.
48. Ibid.
49. Esther B. Jones to Grace Nail Johnson, 15 November 1932, GNJ/JWJ.
50. Davis, pp. 372, 400–401, 407.
51. Ibid., p. 399.
52. Ibid., p. 400.

53. Nella Larsen Imes to Grace Nail Johnson, "Thursday" (1932), in GNJ/JWJ.

54. Walter White Office Diary for 1934, WWPC.

55. Edward Donahoe wrote Nella in August 1933, "I know you miss the Johnsons. When *are* they coming back?" (Quoted by Larsen in letter to Grace Nail Johnson, "Thursday" [August 1933], GNJ/JWJ.) Larsen kept the Johnsons' pet for them when they were gone in the summer of 1933, and she sent birthday greetings to Jim every year through at least 1935.

56. Davis, p. 406, quoting Pearl Creswell, a 1932 Fisk graduate and wife of an administrator.

57. See, e.g., Edward L. Donahoe to Walter White, 17 April 1925, WWPC; Donahoe to Grace Nail Johnson, 24 December 1965, GNJ/JWJ; Donahoe to Langston Hughes, 17 January 1932, LHP; Donahoe to Langston Hughes, 28 April 1927 (on Knopf letterhead), LHP. An undated letter written probably later in 1927 (when Hughes was at Lincoln University) refers to the fact that Donahoe and Hughes had eaten and drunk together in the past in New York, and asks Hughes to send some blues records to Donahoe in Europe (LHP).

58. Edward Donahoe to Grace Nail Johnson, 21 October 1932, GNJ/JWJ.

59. Carl Van Vechten, description of Edward Donahoe, in Donahoe file of Carl Van Vechten Papers, Yale Collection of American Literature, Beinecke.

60. Thomas E. Jones to James Weldon Johnson, 5 December 1932, JWJ/JWJ.

61. Ethel B. Gilbert to Thomas E. Jones, Sunday, 15 December (1932), Jones Papers.

62. Thomas Elsa Jones to Paul D. Cravath, 2 February 1933, Jones Papers.

63. Carl Van Vechten to Grace Nail Johnson, 11 February 1933, GNJ/JWJ.

64. Nella Larsen Imes to Carl Van Vechten, telegram, 12 May 1933, CVV/JWJ.

65. Nella Larsen Imes to Carl Van Vechten, telegram, 9 June 1933, in file entitled "CVV's 53rd Birthday—June 12, 1933," CVV/NYPL.

66. Edward Donahoe to Langston Hughes, 27 August 1934, LHP.

67. Davis, p. 425.

68. Ibid., pp. 400, 401.

69. Nella Larsen Imes to Dorothy Peterson, "Saturday" (postmarked 29 July 1933), DPP.

70. Davis, p. 400.

71. Elmer S. Imes to Thomas E. Jones, 22 July 1933, Jones Papers.

72. Quoted by Davis, p. 401.

73. Ibid.

74. Ibid., p. 407. These are Davis' words.

75. "Fisk Professor Is Divorced by N.Y. Novelist," Baltimore *Afro-American*, 7 October 1933, p. 1.

76. Davis, p. 407.

77. Thomas E. Jones to Paul Cravath, 26 June 1933, Jones Papers.

78. Nella Larsen Imes to Carl Van Vechten and Fania Marinoff, "Wednesday" (postmarked 27 June 1933), CVV/JWJ.

79. Nella Larsen Imes to Dorothy Peterson, "Saturday," 29 July 1933, DPP.

80. Edward Donahoe to Grace N. Johnson, 12 August 1933, GNJ/JWJ; Thomas E. Jones to James Weldon Johnson, 26 August 1933, Jones Papers.

81. The correspondence seems to be irrecoverable, but Larsen refers to it in a letter to Grace Johnson of 19 August 1933.

82. Nella Larsen Imes to Dorothy Peterson, "Saturday," 29 July 1933, DPP.

83. Ibid.

84. Davis, p. 405.
85. Elmer S. Imes to Thomas E. Jones, 22 July 1933, Jones Papers.
86. Ibid.
87. Nella Larsen Imes to Dorothy Peterson, "Saturday," 29 July 1933, DPP.
88. Davis suggests that Elmer felt the "gentlemanly" thing to do was to let the woman divorce the man, not vice versa; but Nella had made sure that he wouldn't have a legal leg to stand on.
89. Esther B. Jones to Grace Nail Johnson, 19 August 1933, GNJ/JWJ.
90. Nella Larsen Imes to Grace Nail Johnson, "Thursday" (August 1932), GNJ/JWJ.
91. *Nella Larsen Imes vs. Elmer S. Imes,* Final Decree, granted 30 August 1933, Minute Book 76, p. 207, First Circuit Court for Davidson County, Tennessee.

<h2 style="text-align:center">21. Letting Go</h2>

1. Nella Larsen Imes to Grace and Jim Johnson, 6 September 1933, JWJ/JWJ.
2. Nella Larsen Imes to Dorothy Peterson, 6 September 1933, DPP. Thadious Davis writes that Donahoe joined Larsen in Chicago, but this seems unlikely, since she wrote Grace Nail Johnson that he was "still in Oklahoma but may be in New York before you leave." Nella Larsen Imes to Grace Nail and James Weldon Johnson, 6 September 1933, JWJ/JWJ.
3. Nella Larsen Imes to Dorothy Peterson, 6 September 1933; and Nella Larsen Imes to Grace Nail Johnson and James Weldon Johnson, 6 September 1933.
4. Nella Larsen Imes to Dorothy Peterson, 6 September 1933.
5. Ibid.
6. Ibid. The municipal records of Wellington, Ohio, contain no evidence of the supposed wedding, and later official papers concerning Elmer, including his death certificate, suggest that it did not take place. Ethel Gilbert had no children in later life, and there is no mention of a child in Elmer's will.
7. A letter from James Weldon Johnson of October 8 and addressed to Dorothy Peterson at 320 Second Avenue begins, "Dear Dorothy and Nella" (JWJ/JWJ).
8. Listing for "Larsen, Nella" in "Persons invited to join Independent Writers' Committee against Lynching," by Walter White, dated 2 December 1933, shows her at Bordentown (JWJ/JWJ). *Trow's General Directory of the Boroughs of Manhattan and Bronx* for 1933–1934 lists "Mrs. Nella L. Imes at 2388 Seventh Avenue," but this was long outdated. Walter White's 1934 "office diary" listing letters he had written indicates that Larsen lived at 320 Second Avenue (WWPC).
9. Dorothy Peterson to Jean Toomer, 18 January and 23 February 1934, JTP.
10. "Nella" and "Dorothy" to James Weldon Johnson, Western Union telegram, 4 October 1933, in JWJ/JWJ.
11. James Weldon Johnson to "Dorothy and Nella," 8 October 1933, JWJ/JWJ. The envelope is addressed to Dorothy alone at 320 Second Avenue.
12. "New York Novelist Divorces Fisk Professor," Baltimore *Afro-American,* 7 October 1933, p. 1.
13. "Love Triangle behind Fisk Divorce," Baltimore *Afro-American,* 21 October 1933, p. 1.
14. Ibid., p. 2.
15. Ibid.

16. Carl Van Vechten to James Weldon Johnson, 27 October 1933, JWJ/JWJ.

17. Elizabeth Hull to Grace Nail Johnson, 22 November 1933, GNJ/JWJ.

18. "Writers Appeal to Roosevelt," *New York Times,* 5 December 1933, p. 3. See also Walter White to James Weldon Johnson, 2 December 1933, in JWJ/JWJ.

19. Walter White, *A Man Called White* (New York: Viking, 1948), p. 167.

20. Gwendolyn Bennett, "The Plight of the Negro Is Tragic," *Better Times,* 12 March 1934, p. 27. In Gwendolyn Bennett Papers, Schomburg.

21. Carl Van Vechten to James Weldon Johnson, 11 February 1934, JWJ/JWJ.

22. Brooks Atkinson, "The Play," *New York Times,* 2 October 1933, p. 22.

23. Anthony Tommasini, *Virgil Thomson: Composer on the Aisle* (New York: Norton, 1997), p. 223; John Houseman, *Run-Through: A Memoir* (New York: Simon and Schuster, 1972), p. 100.

24. Tommasini, *Virgil Thomson,* p. 226; Houseman, p. 105.

25. "Behind Studio Scenes," *New York Times,* 28 January 1934, p. X11; "Today on the Radio," *New York Times,* 8 February 1934, p. 22.

26. Carl Van Vechten to James Weldon Johnson, 11 February 1934.

27. "In the Drama Editor's Mail," *New York Times,* 18 February 1934, p. X2.

28. Walter White to W. E. B. Du Bois, 8 February 1934, in Walter White Special Correspondence, NAACP Papers, Library of Congress.

29. Vera E. Johns, "In the Name of Art," *New York Age,* 3 March 1934, p. 6.

30. Virgil Thomson, quoted in "Four Saints in Three Acts," *New York Times,* 31 January 1934; Tommasini, p. 211.

31. Playbill for *Stevedore,* Programs and Playbills Collection, Schomburg.

32. Carl Van Vechten to James Weldon Johnson, 25 February 1934, JWJ/JWJ.

33. Mary McCarthy, *Intellectual Memoirs: New York, 1936–1938* (New York: Harcourt Brace Jovanovich, 1992), p. 27. Despite the dates specified in her book's subtitle, McCarthy says she moved to Beekman Place in October 1933; moreover, she and Harold Johnsrud were married from 1933 to 1936. Thus, McCarthy's memories of Larsen date from this period.

34. Ibid.

35. Walter White to Dorothy Peterson, 27 December 1933; and Walter White to Tom Mabry, 27 December 1933, WWPC. See also Edward Donahoe to Langston Hughes, 29 March 1934 and 27 August 1934, LHP; and Tom Mabry to Ettie Stettheimer, 12 April 1934, Florine and Ettie Stettheimer Collection, Beinecke.

36. Dorothy Peterson to Jean Toomer, 23 February 1934, JTP.

37. Tom Mabry to Ettie Stettheimer, postmarked 23 February 1934, Florine and Ettie Stettheimer Collection, Beinecke.

38. Edward Donahoe to Langston Hughes, 29 March 1934 (from Ponca City, Oklahoma), LHP.

39. Nella Larsen Imes to Carl Van Vechten and Fania Marinoff, "Wednesday" (postmarked 18 April 1934), CVV/JWJ.

40. Grace Nail Johnson to "Mrs. Nellie Larsen Imes," 22 June 1934, GNJ/JWJ.

41. Quoted in Thadious M. Davis, *Nella Larsen, Novelist of the Harlem Renaissance: A Woman's Life Unveiled* (Baton Rouge: Louisiana State University Press, 1994), p. 425, from a letter to Davis by Becker of 14 July 1982.

42. Edward Donahoe to Langston Hughes, 27 August 1934, LHP.

43. Ibid.

44. "Art Post for T. D. Mabry, Jr.," *New York Times,* 13 March 1935, p. 17.

45. "Nella and Dorothy" to Fania Marinoff, 12 September 1934, Western Union telegram, in CVV/JWJ.

46. Percy Hammond, "The Theaters," *New York Herald Tribune,* 13 September 1934, p. 16; Brooks Atkinson, "The Play," *New York Times,* 13 September 1934, p. 26.

47. Alice B. Toklas, *What Is Remembered* (New York: Holt, Rinehart and Winston, 1963), p. 146.

48. Dorothy Peterson to Carl Van Vechten, 10 November 1934, CVV/JWJ.

49. Carl Van Vechten to Gertrude Stein, 10 November 1934, in *The Letters of Gertrude Stein and Carl Van Vechten, 1913–1946,* ed. Edward Burns (New York: Columbia University Press, 1986), vol. 1, p. 342.

50. Gertrude Stein to Carl Van Vechten, 15 November 1934, ibid., p. 343.

51. Gertrude Stein to Carl Van Vechten, 26 November 1934, ibid., pp. 345–347.

52. Portraits of 23 November 1934, by Carl Van Vechten, in Van Vechten photograph collection, Beinecke.

53. "Writers Score Lynching," *New York Times,* 13 January 1935, p. 33. Letterhead for the organization, which switched directors about the beginning of the year, continued to list "Nella Larsen" as assistant secretary, one of the chief officers. See correspondence from Writers League against Lynching to Jean Toomer, JTP.

54. Margaret Rose Venryes, "Hanging on Their Walls: *An Art Commentary on Lynching,* the Forgotten 1935 Art Exhibition," in Judith Jackson Fossett and Jeffrey A. Tucker, eds., *Race Consciousness: African-American Studies for a New Century* (New York: New York University Press, 1997), pp. 153–176.

55. "Nella" and "Dorothy" to Mr. and Mrs. James Weldon Johnson, Western Union telegram, 27 February 1935, JWJ/JWJ.

56. Dorothy Peterson to Lawrence Harrison, 12 May 1935, JWJ Manuscripts 10, Box 1, Folder 16, James Weldon Johnson Memorial Collection, Beinecke.

57. Edward Donahoe to Langston Hughes, 28 July 1936, LHP. Donahoe writes Hughes that he is staying in Mabry's New York apartment while Tom is on vacation in Tennessee. On 13 March 1937, he wrote Hughes again: he and Tom were still the best of friends.

58. "Art Post for T. D. Mabry, Jr.," *New York Times,* 13 March 1935, p. 17. Susan Menees (Mabry's daughter), telephone conversation with the author, May 2003.

59. Edward Donahoe to Grace Nail Johnson, 17 July 1938, 21 July 1938, GNJ/JWJ.

60. Bruce Kellner to George Hutchinson, 15 December 2003.

61. Elizabeth Schaffer Hull to Carl Van Vechten, 19 August 1936, CVV/NYPL.

62. Some of this information comes from Davis, p. 421.

63. Ibid. Floyd G. Snelson, "Negro Actors Guild of America Incorporated," Federal Writers Project, New York, 1 March 1938, in *Negroes of New York* (Federal Writers Program, 1939), Schomburg.

64. "Freddie Steps Out," *Pittsburgh Courier,* 18 February 1927, sect. 2, p. 1.

65. Thin red address book of Countee Cullen, from the mid-1930s, in Countee Cullen Papers, Amistad Research Center, Tulane University. This address book lists Larsen as "Nella Larsen" at 320 Second Avenue, phone GR5-3868; it also has a crossed-out address and phone number for Dorothy Peterson: 320 Second Avenue, GR5-5822. There is no evidence that Larsen and Peterson lived together at 320 Second Avenue. When Larsen

moved to 320 Second Avenue, Peterson moved out to Brooklyn. The address for Lloyd and Edna Thomas at 1890 Seventh Avenue comports with Macpherson's reference to "1890" as the home of Edna and Olivia Wyndham. A slightly earlier address book belonging to Cullen, from the early 1930s, which contains no address for either Imes or Larsen, lists "Edna & Lloyd Thomas (Olivia)" at "450 W. 22nd." Countee Cullen Papers, Amistad Research Center.

66. George W. Henry, *Sex Variants: A Study of Homosexual Patterns,* 1-vol. edition (New York: Paul B. Hoeber, 1948; orig. pub. 2 vols., 1941), p. 564. Thanks to Thomas Wirth for alerting me to Henry's study and the fact that Edna Thomas and Olivia Wyndham were among his subjects. In the book, Thomas is identified as "Pearl M." and Wyndham as "Pamela D."

67. Ibid., p. 565.

68. Ibid., p. 566.

69. "Recital by Edna Thomas," *New York Times,* 25 April 1927, p. 16; "England," *New York Times,* 5 October 1924, p. X6; "Falstaff Closes London Season," *New York Times,* 11 July 1926, p. X5; and various advertisements in the *Times* throughout the mid-1920s.

70. Information on Edna Thomas' stage career comes from Bruce Kellner, *The Harlem Renaissance: A Historical Dictionary for the Era* (Westport, Conn.: Greenwood Press, 1984), p. 353; Wesley Cartwright, "Brief Outline of Negro Movie Actors in America," *Negroes of New York,* p. 5; "Leading Lady," *Pittsburgh Courier,* 5 May 1928, sect. 2, p. 3; "Colored Stars in Curtain Raiser to 'Emperor Jones,'" *Amsterdam News,* 18 February 1925, p. 6; "Experimental Group To Give Two Plays," *Amsterdam News,* 21 May 1930, p. 15; Mordaunt Hall, "The Screen," *New York Times,* 21 April 1930, p. 26; Playbill for *Run, Little Chillun!* p. 16, in Programs and Playbills Collection, Schomburg.

71. Henry, p. 567.

72. Ibid., p. 678.

73. Ibid., pp. 672, 674, 678.

74. Andrew Meyer, quoted in Davis, p. 422.

75. Davis, p. 421, drawing on interviews and correspondence with Andrew Meyer. Minedo is described by Kenneth Macpherson in a letter to Bryher, 23 May 1939, Bryher Papers, Beinecke. Some accounts have suggested that Wyndham owned it, but land records for the township indicate that the women owned the estate jointly from 1933 to 1957.

76. Davis, pp. 422–423.

77. Jervis Anderson, *This Was Harlem: A Cultural Portrait* (New York: Farrar Straus Giroux, 1982), p. 278.

78. Simon Callow, *Orson Welles* (New York: Viking, 1996), p. 241.

79. Kenneth Macpherson to Bryher, 23 May 1939, Bryher Papers, Beinecke.

80. Bryher to H.D., 7 December 1936, H.D. Papers, Beinecke.

81. Kenneth Macpherson, "A Negro Film Union—Why Not?" in Nancy Cunard, ed., *The Negro* (1934; rpt. New York: Frederick Ungar, 1970), pp. 205–207.

82. See, e.g., comments appended by Macpherson to a letter Bryher wrote H.D. on 10 January 1934: "Plumped forth last night and met Van Vechten at his very lovely apartment and he took some photos of the Big Dog [Macpherson]. Then we went out and spent all night 'doing' Harlem—which exceeds imagination just as the sun is always a million times brighter than you can picture it!" Bryher was considerably less enthusiastic on that visit, writing H.D. two weeks later about her discomfort in watching "Dog in ec-

static contemplation of a pack of wriggling monkeys. . . . Result—a terrific fight with Dog. . . . Harlem's full of whites trying to pass as blacks, and cavorting." In the clubs, "They did peculiar and porno dances which reduced me to feeling like an elderly anthropologist taking notes under a palm tree—in the best [Havelock] Ellis manner." Bryher to H.D., 24 January 1934, H.D. Papers.

83. Kenneth Macpherson to H.D., "Sunday" (probably winter 1934–1935), H.D. Papers.

84. Bryher to H.D., [31?] January 1934 (first page of letter missing), H.D. Papers. The couple attended dinner at Moore's on January 31.

85. Bryher to H.D., 13 December 1936, H.D. Papers.

86. Ibid.

87. Information on *The Hedgehog* from advertisements and from Perdita Schaffner's Introduction to the 1988 New Directions reprint.

88. Kenneth Macpherson to Bryher, 9 February 1937, Bryher Papers.

89. Ibid.

90. Kenneth Macpherson to Bryher, 25 February 1937, Bryher Papers.

91. According to Macpherson, Edna Thomas was appointed "second in command of the Negro Federal Theatre" in late March or April that year; two years later she was named the head of the operation. Macpherson to Bryher, April 1937 and 23 May 1939, Bryher Papers.

92. Kenneth Macpherson to Bryher, early March 1937, Bryher Papers.

93. Arna Bontemps to Countee Cullen, "Monday, the 4th" [January 1937], Countee Cullen Papers, Amistad Research Center. This is a "Happy New Year" letter.

94. Kenneth Macpherson to Bryher, 18 March 1937, Bryher Papers.

95. Elizabeth Hull to Grace and James Weldon Johnson, 22 April 1937, JWJ/JWJ.

96. Carl Van Vechten to Grace Nail Johnson, 28 April 1937, GNJ/JWJ.

97. Telegram from "Nella" to Carl Van Vechten, 17 June 1937, CVV/NYPL.

98. Dorothy Peterson to Carl Van Vechten, 26 July 1937, and 4 August 1937, CVV/JWJ. The first of these letters does not list Larsen among the invitees; the second goes into some detail about those who attended, but makes no mention of Nella. Since Carl was particularly concerned about Nella at this point, it seems unlikely that she was at the party.

99. Davis, p. 431.

100. Ibid., p. 432.

101. Alice Carper, telephone conversation with George Hutchinson, 19 August 1997.

102. Richard Wright, "Blueprint for Negro Writing," *New Challenge* 2 (Fall 1937), reprinted in Nathan Irvin Huggins, ed. *Voices from the Harlem Renaissance* (New York: Oxford University Press, 1976), p. 395.

103. Ibid.

104. Alain Locke, "Spiritual Truancy," *New Challenge* 2 (Fall 1937), reprinted ibid., p. 406.

22. THE RECLUSE ON SECOND AVENUE

1. See letters of Dorothy Peterson to Carl Van Vechten, 1938, in Carl Van Vechten correspondence, CVV/JWJ; and Arnold Rampersad, *The Life of Langston Hughes,* vol. 1 (New York: Oxford University Press, 1986), pp. 356–361, 363–365, 369, 371. Intended as a left-oriented crucible for black theatrical experimentation, the Harlem Suitcase Theatre

had one strong season and then gradually petered out as Hughes lost interest, leaving Dorothy and one or two friends to try to hold it together.

2. Edward Donahoe to Grace Nail Johnson, 13 November 1938, GNJ/JWJ, Box 28, Folder 50.

3. Dorothy Peterson to Carl Van Vechten, postmarked 2 January 1939, CVV/JWJ.

4. Dorothy Peterson to Carl Van Vechten, postmarked 4 January 1939, CVV/JWJ.

5. Dorothy Peterson to Carl Van Vechten, postmarked 16 January 1939, CVV/JWJ.

6. Elmer S. Imes to Carl Van Vechten, 10 April 1939, CVV/JWJ. See also "Program of the Tenth Festival of Music and Fine Arts," Fisk University, 21–23 April 1939, in Countee Cullen Papers, Amistad Research Center, Tulane University.

7. Carl Van Vechten to Dorothy Peterson, 2 January 1940, DPP.

8. Elmer S. Imes to Carl Van Vechten, 24 February 1940, CVV/JWJ.

9. Carl Van Vechten to Dorothy Peterson, postmarked 30 March 1940, DPP.

10. Guild's Committee for Federal Writers' Publications, *New York City Guide* (New York: Random House, 1939), p. 189.

11. Thadious M. Davis, *Nella Larsen, Novelist of the Harlem Renaissance: A Woman's Life Unveiled* (Baton Rouge: Louisiana State University Press, 1994), pp. 444–445, drawing on interview with Alice Carper. Also Charles R. Larsen, taped interview with Alice Carper, 11 June 1986.

12. Carl Van Vechten to Dorothy Peterson, 31 July 1940, Box 2, Folder 51, DPP.

13. See Ward Dorrance and Thomas Mabry, *The White Hound and Other Stories,* introd. by Caroline Gordon (Columbia: University of Missouri Press, 1959).

14. Dorothy Peterson to Carl Van Vechten, 27 September 1940, CVV/JWJ.

15. Elmer S. Imes to Carl Van Vechten, "Sunday," postmarked 9 June 1941, CVV/JWJ.

16. Dorothy Peterson to Carl Van Vechten, 3 November 1941, CVV/JWJ; and Carl Van Vechten to Dorothy Peterson, postmarked 4 November 1941, DPP.

17. Dorothy Peterson to Carl Van Vechten, 26 December 1941, CVV/JWJ.

18. Elmer S. Imes to Carl Van Vechten, Saturday, 14 June 1941, CVV/JWJ.

19. Elmer S. Imes to Carl Van Vechten and Fania Marinoff, 19 June 1941, CVV/JWJ.

20. Carl Van Vechten to Dorothy Peterson, 11 July 1941, DPP.

21. Elmer S. Imes to Carl Van Vechten, 19 July 1941, CVV/JWJ.

22. Carl Van Vechten to Dorothy Peterson, 18 August 1941, DPP.

23. Carl Van Vechten to Dorothy Peterson, 9 January 1942, DPP.

24. Dorothy Peterson to Carl Van Vechten, 22 September 1941, CVV/JWJ.

25. Carl Van Vechten to Dorothy Peterson, 24 September 1941, DPP.

26. Dorothy Peterson to Carl Van Vechten, 25 September 1941, CVV/JWJ.

27. Dorothy Peterson to Carl Van Vechten, 22 September 1941, CVV/JWJ.

28. Carl Van Vechten to Dorothy Peterson, 2 October 1941, DPP.

29. Carl Van Vechten to Dorothy Peterson, 30 October 1941, DPP.

30. Dorothy Peterson to Carl Van Vechten, postmarked 6 November 1941, CVV/JWJ.

31. Dorothy Peterson to Carl Van Vechten, 26 December 1941, CVV/JWJ.

32. Ibid.

33. Carl Van Vechten to Dorothy Peterson, 9 January 1942, DPP.

34. Carl Van Vechten to Dorothy Peterson, 30 October 1941, DPP.

35. Elmer S. Imes, Last Will and Testament, 6 July 1941; probated 1 October 1941, Davidson

County Circuit Court Clerk, Nashville, Tennessee. Thanks to Charles R. Larson for sharing his copy of the will with me. The bulk of the estate, after some cash disbursements to immediate family, went to "Mrs. Ethel B. Gilbert," whom Elmer termed "my friend and best beloved," indicating that they were not legally married.

36. Charles R. Larson, notes from interview with Carolyn Lane, 24 February 1985.
37. Lucile Miller file, in JWJ Files.
38. File entitled "James Weldon Johnson Birthday Celebration," JWJ/JWJ.
39. Harold Jackman to Carl Van Vechten, 18 June 1942, CVV/JWJ.
40. Ibid.
41. Harold Jackman to Carl Van Vechten, 20 June 1942, CVV/JWJ.
42. Carl Van Vechten to Dorothy Peterson, postmarked 29 June 1942, DPP.
43. Carl Van Vechten to Dorothy Peterson, card postmarked 11 July 1942, DPP.
44. Dorothy Peterson to Carl Van Vechten, 30 November 1942, CVV/JWJ.
45. Carl Van Vechten to Dorothy Peterson, 22 September 1922, DPP.
46. Dorothy Peterson to Carl Van Vechten, 29 October 1942, CVV/JWJ.
47. "Xmas Cheer show and Van Vechten Dinner Socially Tops," *Amsterdam Star-News,* 21 November 1942, p. 10.
48. "Notables Aplenty Attended the Carl Van Vechten Testimonial," *Amsterdam Star-News,* 28 November 1942, p. 10.
49. Dorothy Peterson to Carl Van Vechten, 21 June 1943, CVV/JWJ. The latest book by Vincent Sheean—his name is misspelled in Dorothy's letter—was *Between the Thunder and the Sun* (New York: Random House, 1943), a journalistic account of his experiences in the war. Sheean had earlier been known primarily for books on the Middle East, one of Larsen's perennial interests.
50. Dorothy Peterson to Carl Van Vechten, 21 June 1943, CVV/JWJ.
51. Dorothy Peterson to Carl Van Vechten, 22 February 1944, CVV/JWJ.
52. Carl Van Vechten to Dorothy Peterson, 23 February 1944, DPP.

23. NELLA LARSEN IMES, R.N.

1. *Statistical Abstract of the United States: 1964* (Washington, D.C.: U.S. Government Printing Office, 1964), pp. 56, 57; and *Statistical Abstract of the United States: 1930* (Washington, D.C.: U.S. Government Printing Office, 1930), p. 83.
2. Thadious M. Davis, *Nella Larsen, Novelist of the Harlem Renaissance: A Woman's Life Unveiled* (Baton Rouge: Louisiana State University Press, 1994), p. 461: "Larsen's story . . . is a sad one, because it reveals the complex tragedy of a more subtle racism that twists and undermines the individual's sense of who and what is valuable, all the while distorting the worth of the person into a sequence of material goods or public accolades."
3. Marta Fraenkel and Carl L. Erhardt, *Morbidity in the Municipal Hospitals of the City of New York* (New York: Russell Sage Foundation, 1955), pp. 39, 70.
4. "$65,000 Life Hoard Found Amid Refuse," *New York Times,* 26 October 1958, p. 31; "Elderly Pair Beaten," *New York Times,* 25 November 1959, p. 12.
5. Fraenkel and Erhardt, p. 70.
6. Ibid., p. 40. Overall, 35 percent of the patients in city hospitals were nonwhite.
7. Obituary for Dr. Siegfried Boxer, *New York Times,* 8 July 1949, p. 19.

8. Davis, p. 445; Alice Carper, telephone conversation with George Hutchinson, 19 August 1997.

9. See New York City Civil List, Gouverneur Hospital listings for 1944–1961, on microfilm in Municipal Archives, New York City. Other information on Carolyn Lane from Alice Carper, taped interview with Charles R. Larson, 11 June 1986; and from Davis, p. 446.

10. Carper, taped interview with Charles R. Larson, 11 June 1986.

11. Ibid.

12. Davis, p. 444.

13. Alice Carper, telephone conversation with George Hutchinson, 19 August 1997.

14. Carper, taped interview with Charles R. Larson, 11 June 1986.

15. Charles R. Larson, *Invisible Darkness: Jean Toomer and Nella Larsen* (Iowa City: University of Iowa Press, 1993), p. 117.

16. Alice Carper, telephone conversation with George Hutchinson, 19 August 1997.

17. Quoted in Davis, p. 444.

18. Ibid., p. 447.

19. Carper, taped interview with Charles R. Larson, 11 June 1986.

20. Charles R. Larson, notes from interview with Carolyn Lane, 19 May 1985.

21. Carper, telephone conversation with George Hutchinson, 19 August 1997.

22. Ibid.

23. Ibid. See also Davis, p. 447.

24. Davis, p. 446.

25. Carper, interview with Charles R. Larson, 11 June 1986.

26. Ibid.

27. Davis, p. 446.

28. Carper, taped interview with Charles R. Larson, 11 June 1986; Davis, p. 446.

29. Death Certificate for Peter "Larson," California Department of Public Health, dated 27 January 1945; and Petition for Letters of Administration and/or Assignment of Estate to Widow, Superior Court of the State of California, County of Los Angeles, case no. 240163.

30. Carper, taped interview with Charles R. Larson, 11 June 1986.

31. Davis, p. 446; Carper, telephone conversation with George Hutchinson, 19 August 1997; Carper, taped interview with Charles R. Larson, 11 June 1986.

32. Carper, taped interview with Charles R. Larson, 11 June 1986.

33. Ibid.

34. Davis, p. 447; Carper, taped interview with Charles R. Larson, 11 June 1986.

35. Davis, p. 446.

36. Carper, telephone conversation with George Hutchinson, 19 August 1997.

37. Davis, p. 446.

38. "Text of Mayor's Message to City Council Outlining Four-Year Plan," *New York Times*, 15 March 1950, p. 25; "Delay in Building Hospitals Asked," *New York Times*, 14 October 1960, p. 17; Paul Crowell, "Patterson Holds 15-Cent Fare Is Safe," *New York Times*, 17 November 1960, p. 39.

39. Death Certificate for Mary "Larson," File 13645, Registrar-Recorder of Los Angeles County, California.

40. Last Will and Testament of Anna Elizabeth Gardner, Superior Court of California for the County of Los Angeles.

41. Nella Larsen Imes, Application for Employment, dated 2 December 1961, Metropolitan Hospital.

42. Bruce Kellner to George Hutchinson, email, 14 November 2002.

43. Carl Van Vechten to Dorothy Peterson, 9 February 1954, DPP.

44. Dorothy Peterson to Carl Van Vechten, 12 February 1954, CVV/JWJ.

45. Nella Larsen Imes, application for Social Security Account Number, dated January 5, 1954. The number she was assigned was 062–30–0298. Davis suggests that the first three digits indicate an address in Connecticut, but officials I contacted said it merely indicates that a regional office for the Northeast, including New York, assigned the number.

46. Civil List for 1953–1954, listing for Gouverneur Hospital; Application for Employment (transfer to Metropolitan Hospital), dated 2 December 1961, obtained from Metropolitan Hospital; and Employees Record Card for Gouverneur Hospital, in employee file from Metropolitan Hospital.

47. Civil List for 1955–1956 and after; Application for Employment, dated 2 December 1961; and Nella Larsen Imes, Employees Record Card for Gouverneur Hospital, in employee file from Metropolitan Hospital.

48. Hurricane Carol was the worst to hit the Eastern Seaboard since the hurricane of 1938, and ravaged the coast. Several cities declared states of emergency. Fairfield County, where Danbury is located, was hit particularly hard. Numerous reports on the storm and its aftereffects appeared in newspapers throughout September and beyond. Concerning the lack of flood insurance at the time, see Thomas P. Swift, "Hurricane Losses Put at $100,000,000," *New York Times,* 9 September 1954, p. 33. Hurricane coverage, which was available, did not cover damage from flooding caused by ordinary storms.

49. Joseph C. Ingraham, "Our Changing City: Old Lower Manhattan Area," *New York Times,* 24 June 1955, p. 23.

50. Ibid., p. 23; "Hospital Facilities Urged," *New York Times,* 2 September 1954, p. 20.

51. Charles G. Bennett, "New City Hospitals Are Held Unneeded," *New York Times,* 12 September 1955, pp. 1, 2.

52. J. A. Bates and Carl Turchin, Board of Elections for the City of New York, to Arnold A. Levin, 15 May 1964, in Surrogate's Court files for Nella Larsen Imes, Hall of Records, New York City.

53. Alice Carper, taped interview with Charles R. Larson, 11 June 1986. Carper's technical date of retirement was 15 October 1959, according to the Civil List of 1959–1960, but city hospital nurses automatically got a pre-retirement vacation and leave of nearly a month, so Carper probably stopped working in September.

54. Carper, taped interview with Charles R. Larson, 11 June 1986.

55. Davis, p. 450. Carper specified that the money willed to her was from an account in one East Side bank; Larsen had accounts in two different banks—Union Square Savings Bank and Manufacturers Hanover Trust—so she apparently was not making Carper her sole beneficiary.

56. "Panel Urges City to Shut Hospital," *New York Times,* 17 February 1961, p. 18; "Support Hinted for Gouverneur," *New York Times,* 16 March 1961, p. 42.

57. Alice Carper, taped interview with Charles R. Larson, 11 June 1986; and Davis, p. 448.

58. Carolyn Lane quoted in Davis, p. 448.

59. Civil List of 1960–1961.

60. Paul Crowell, "Delay in Building Hospitals Asked," *New York Times,* 14 October 1960, p. 17.

61. "Gouverneur Hospital Picketed," *New York Times,* 22 November 1960, p. 19.

62. "Panel Urges City to Shut Hospital," *New York Times,* 17 February 1961, p. 18.

63. Morris Kaplan, "Gouverneur Hospital Is Closing, but Will Retain Some Services," *New York Times,* 18 March 1961, p. 25.

64. "Support Hinted for Gouverneur," *New York Times,* 16 March 1961, p. 42.

65. Kaplan, p. 25.

66. "Crucial Hospital Decisions," *New York Times,* 18 March 1961, p. 25.

67. *New York City's Municipal Hospitals: A Policy Review* (Washington, D.C.: Institute for Policy Studies, 1967), p. 127.

68. Ibid., p. 121.

69. Nella Larsen Imes, Application for Employment, City of New York Department of Hospitals, dated 2 December 1961.

70. Ibid.

71. Alice Carper, taped interview with Charles R. Larson, 11 June 1986; confirmed by the Civil List, which shows that several R.N.'s from Gouverneur started at Metropolitan when Larsen did.

72. Vera Joseph to Charles R. Larson, 6 December 1985, files of Charles R. Larson.

73. Dorothy Peterson to Carl Van Vechten, 11 May 1963, CVV/JWJ.

74. Vera Joseph to Charles R. Larson, 17 November 1985, files of Charles R. Larson.

75. Dorothy Peterson to Carl Van Vechten, 23 February 1962, CVV/JWJ.

76. Fraenkel and Erhardt, p. 38.

77. Based on photographs of staff and ceremonial functions at Metropolitan Hospital, ca. 1960, in the Municipal Archives.

78. Civil List for 1962–1963; Employment record for Nella Larsen Imes, Metropolitan Hospital.

79. Quotation from Alice Carper, taped interview with Charles R. Larson, 11 June 1986; see also Davis, p. 448. Carper told Larson that the trip to California took place a little more than a year before Larsen's death, meaning the winter of 1962–1963. Charles R. Larson, notes from telephone interview with Alice Carper, 22 February 1985.

80. Davis, p. 448. Charles R. Larson, notes from telephone interview with Alice Carper, 22 February 1985.

81. Mildred Phillips to Charles R. Larson, 11 February 1986.

82. Alice Carper, taped interview with Charles R. Larson, 11 June 1986.

83. "Request for Leave of Absence," 11 June 1963, employment file for Nella Larsen Imes, Metropolitan Hospital.

84. Davis, p. 450. Carper believed Larsen was becoming senile and did not want anyone to see her growing old, but since Larsen had not been speaking to her for months, Carper had little basis for this judgment.

85. Alice Carper, taped interview with Charles R. Larson, 11 June 1986. Davis writes that "near the end of March 1964, it became apparent that [Larsen] had not reported to work for one week." She had had "a long Easter week-end off from work," so no one questioned her absence; "but when she did not report the Monday after Easter, the hospital staff feared something had happened. Because she had become once again so pri-

vate a person, she did not have a close enough association with anyone at the hospital who might have immediately become alarmed. She lay dead for days before the land-lady, contacted by the hospital, discovered her body, notified the police, and called Alice Carper" (Davis, pp. 450–451). Davis bases this information on a telephone interview with Carper in 1982. It reveals that Carper had completely lost touch with Larsen by June 1963, comporting with Carolyn Lane's statement to Charles R. Larson that Nella did not speak to Carper for the last six months before she died. Larson, notes of inter-view with Carolyn Lane, 19 May 1985.

86. "Complaint Report," "Unidentified Person Report," and "Supplementary Complaint Report," all in file on the death of Nella Larsen Imes, New York City Police Department. Records acquired through the Freedom of Information Act. Because of privacy con-cerns, the names of individuals contacted have been heavily crossed out in the copies I received, but portions of the addresses can be made out. See also Certificate of Death for Nella Larsen Imes, Department of Health of New York City, Office of Records, New York.

87. Carper, taped interview with Charles R. Larson, 11 June 1986.

88. Ibid.

89. Quoted in Davis, pp. 452–453.

90. "Imes—Nella Larsen," under "Deaths," *New York Times,* 7 April 1964, p. 35. The name "Gardner" is misspelled. But Larsen, whose spelling was often inexact, had spelled the name "Gardener" on her application for employment at Metropolitan Hospital.

91. Jean Blackwell Hutson to Louise Fox, 1 August 1989, Nella Larsen file, Schomburg.

Epilogue

1. Schedule A, Appraisal of the Estate of Nella Larsen Imes, for Surrogate's Court, Hall of Records, New York City.

2. Alice Carper, taped interview with Charles R. Larson, 11 June 1986.

3. Thadious M. Davis, *Nella Larsen, Novelist of the Harlem Renaissance: A Woman's Life Unveiled* (Baton Rouge: Louisiana State University Press, 1994), p. 453.

4. Mildred Phillips to Charles R. Larson, 11 February 1986.

5. Surrogate's Court papers regarding the estate of Nella Larsen Imes, Hall of Records, New York.

6. Ibid.

7. Carper, taped interview with Charles R. Larson, 11 June 1986.

8. Surrogate's Court papers regarding the estate of Nella Larsen Imes.

9. Dorothy Peterson to Carl Van Vechten, postmarked 25 September 1964, CVV/JWJ. "Publicly" is misspelled as "publically."

10. Ibid.

11. Hoyt Fuller, "Introduction," in Nella Larsen, *Passing* (New York: Collier/Macmillan, 1971), p. 12, n. 1.

12. Hoyt Fuller, "Introduction," in Nella Larsen, *Passing* (New York: Collier Books, 1971), p. 14.

13. Ibid., pp. 18, 19.

14. Ibid., p. 24.

15. Adelaide Cromwell Hill, "Introduction," in Nella Larsen, *Quicksand* (New York: Collier Books, 1971), p. 12.
16. Ibid., pp. 13, 17.
17. Ibid., p. 17.
18. Amritjit Singh, *Novels of the Harlem Renaissance* (University Park: Pennsylvania State University Press, 1976), p. 25, quoted in Deborah E. McDowell, Introduction to *Quicksand and Passing* (New Brunswick, N.J.: Rutgers University Press, 1986), p. xv.
19. McDowell, p. xxx.
20. Ibid., pp. xxx–xxxi.

ACKNOWLEDGMENTS

H AD it not been for the two previous biographies of Nella Larsen, by Charles R. Larson and Thadious M. Davis, I would never have undertaken this project. I owe them a lot. After I published an essay highly critical of their books in 1997, Professor Larson invited me to his home in Maryland, where he set me up in his dining room with all his files on Larsen, and then took me to Kinko's to copy some of them—which was only the beginning. He has very generously aided me time and again, most notably by supplying photographs I could not otherwise have obtained. Professor Davis' book stimulated my thinking, provided important leads, and saved me time and again from error. She has been rightly honored for first attempting a full-scale reclamation of Larsen.

My initial footsteps on this journey took me to Denmark, where Vibeke Filipsen of the Landsarkiv for Sjaelland first located evidence of Larsen's residence in that country. She and everyone else I spoke to on visits to Denmark furthered my project with generosity and passion. To these also thanks: Bent Blüdnikow of the Rigsarkiv; Henrik Vedel-Smith of the Erhvervsarkiv; Linda Klitmøller of the Vejen local history archive; Arne Knudsen; and Carl Pedersen and Martyn Bone of the University of Copenhagen. In the United States, Jenny Hansen was a great help on matters of Danish genealogy. I also had the generous help of archivists and librarians at the Danish Folkmuseum in Brede, the City Museum of Copenhagen, the Tivoli Museum, and the Copenhagen Public Library.

In St. Croix, the St. Croix Landmarks Society at Estate Whim houses extraordinary genealogical resources for the former Danish West Indies, which I enjoyed poring over with the aid of archivist Carol Wakefield while my sons snorkeled near Frederiksted. Gary Horlacher, a genealogist and graduate student in history at Brigham Young University, was a fount of knowledge concerning the Danish West Indies and pointed me to Whim; David Knight was also a big help concerning the Walkers of St. Croix. Subsequently, Svend Holsoe took an interest in the project and gave me advice concerning people named Walker in the Danish West Indies.

Early and often in the course of my research I relied on the genealogical resources of the Church of Christ of Latter-Day Saints and the advice of staff members at Knoxville's Family History Center, especially Nikki Russler. In Chicago, staff members of the Chicago Historical Society, the Newberry Library, the University of Illinois at Chicago, the University of Chicago Library, the Harold Washington Library (Chicago Public Library), the Recorder of Deeds, and the Student Records office of Chicago Public Schools were all extremely helpful.

In New York, I would like to acknowledge the help of the Human Resources Department of the New York Public Library, especially Ms. Winsome Holler; the NYPL Manuscripts and Archives division; the NYPL Maps division; the NYPL Business and Technology Library; the Seward Park Branch Archives; the Schomburg Center for Research in Black Culture; the Central Library's Robert Sink, who knows so much of its history; the Laura Spelman Rockefeller Foundation Archives in Tarrytown; the Guggenheim Foundation Archives; the human resources departments of Beth Israel Medical Center and Metropolitan Hospital; the New York City Municipal Archives; the office of Cypress Hills Cemetery in Brooklyn (especially Valerie Swan Young), and the Hall of Records of the Surrogates' Court of New York. At the Bronx Historical Society, Gary Hermalyn took time out to spend part of an afternoon with me. Thanks to Harlan Jessup for looking up land records in Connecticut and Westchester County for me.

By far the most important sources for this book are housed at the Beinecke Rare Book and Manuscript Library, Yale University, and I benefited frequently from the help of its staff, including Patricia Willis, Nancy Kuhl, Stephen Jones, Leigh Golden, and Clifford Johnson. Joellen ElBashir of Howard University's Moorland-Spingarn Research Center has been extremely helpful on a number of occasions, and Beth Howse of Special Collections at the John Hope and Alexander Heard Library, Fisk University, has patiently and very kindly responded to my repeated visits and calls over the years. Cynthia Wilson of the Tuskegee University Archives was very gracious when I visited there and has responded quickly to subsequent requests. At the Library of Congress, the efficient staff of the busy Manuscripts Division has been especially helpful. Thanks as well to the Archives Department at the Atlanta University Center Woodruff Library; the Amistad Research Center, Tulane University; the Harry Ransom Humanities Research Center at the University of Texas, Austin; and to Cliff Farrington at the University of Texas. Bernard Horrocks of the National Portrait Gallery, London, was extremely patient and generous in helping me locate the heirs of Ben Pinchot, whose beautiful portrait of Larsen graces the book's front. To Sue Pinchot, thanks for the permission.

In Palma, Mallorca, at the Biblioteca de Lluis Alemany of the Consell Insular de Mallorca, Juan Carlos Llop was very helpful. I learned much from the local history resources at the Library of the Fundación Bartolomé March, the Central Library at Plaça Cort, and the bookshelves of the Librería Ripoll, whose owners allowed me to browse freely through the books they were trying to sell and referred me to Mr. Llop. Diane Kerrigan allowed me a pleasant chat about the neighborhood where Nella Larsen lived for several months. In Paris, Michel Fabre took the trouble to find out for me what collections there might hold copies of Paris-based American periodicals long defunct, and staff at the Pompidou Center checked the collection of Man Ray photographs (in vain) for portraits of Nella Larsen. Thanks to Geneviève Fabre for inviting me to the conference on the Harlem Renaissance that she and Michel Feith hosted, which gave me an excuse to spend several days in Paris seeking out Nella Larsen's haunts.

Before I had any intention of writing a biography of Larsen, at a point when I actually considered it impossible, I spoke at Princeton about Larsen and problems with the extant biographies; since then, Arnold Rampersad's support and advice have meant more to me than he probably imagines. Many of my friends and colleagues have listened to me carry on about the joys and surprises of this project, from well before it was a project: Allen Dunn, Rob Stillman, Kenny Mostern, Stan Garner, Mary Papke, and LaVinia Jennings at the University of Tennessee; Phil Melling, Jon Roper, and their students at the University of Wales, Swansea; Laura Yow, Margo Crawford, Paul John Eakin and the Life Writing Seminar, Shane Vogel, Susan Gubar, Judith Brown, Ed Comentale and the Modernist Exchange at Indiana University.

Several dear friends read the manuscript in an earlier, somewhat longer form and gave me invaluable advice, especially Christoph Irmscher at the University of Maryland, Baltimore County, and Emily Bernard at the University of Vermont. It was from Professor Bernard, some years ago, that I first learned about Carl Van Vechten's daybooks, and *In Search of Nella Larsen* has benefited enormously from her perspective on Van Vechten. Judith Brown also read the entire manuscript and provided valuable insights. Another new colleague, Shane Vogel, read a number of chapters from the middle of the book and had wonderful insights into the nature of the subject matter and the peculiarities of my method. Christa Schwarz, an independent scholar in Berlin, read portions of the manuscript and was very encouraging; she also gave me great leads concerning the sexual networks of the Harlem Renaissance. Susan Menees of Allenville, Kentucky, the daughter of Tom Mabry, read a couple of chapters in which he figures, and made useful comments. Mark Whalan at the University of Exeter, who has been doing exciting work on Jean Toomer, read portions of the manuscript and gave me useful encouragement and advice. Thomas Wirth is another aficionado of Harlem Renaissance arcana, an independent scholar and collector whose conversation never failed to turn up a new thought or line of research, especially with regard to the sexual subculture of the renaissance. Bruce Kellner, executor of the Van Vechten Trust, read portions of the manuscript with a keen eye for detail and greatly improved the chapters he saw, in addition to telling me things I didn't know to ask about, sending me copies of photographs, and answering innumerable queries cheerfully and with lightning speed. Of course, the blame for any errors that remain is entirely my own.

Thanks to Ana Owusu-Tyo, Clark Barwick, Kara Kendall, Kate Goldstein, and Jim Berkey for their meticulous work on citations and quotations in the manuscript. Very early in the research process, Sara Ford worked as my graduate assistant at the University of Tennessee and was a big help.

The research for this book would not have been possible without the generous support of the John C. Hodges Better English Fund at the University of Tennessee and the Booth Tarkington Chair Endowment at Indiana University, Bloomington. Thanks to my department chairs: Allen Carroll at Tennessee, and Kenneth Johnston and Stephen Watt at Indiana.

Sincerest thanks to Lindsay Waters at Harvard University Press for his help, hard-nosed judgment, patience, and support; to Thomas Wheatland; to the anonymous readers for the Press, and especially to Maria Ascher for helping get it all together with such panache.

To my wife, Portia Spencer Hutchinson, and my sons, Spencer and Geoffrey, I'd like to express my thanks for the affection that persists despite my many faults. With them I have learned a lot about the central issues in this book. My regard for Larsen's nursing career admittedly owes much to being married to a Nurse Practitioner. I have spoken often of this project with her mother, Barbara Anne Rather, and her sister, the art historian and librarian Deirdre Spencer (University of Michigan), whose love and support I cherish. The Hutchinsons and Friedmans have been wonderful interlocutors at our holiday meetings when someone asks, "What's up with the book?" and I am challenged to make the story interesting to quick, smart, questioning nonspecialists. It is always an education. My final and deepest thanks, and the book's dedication, are to my mother and father, simply the best.

INDEX